Dewey Decimal Classification and Relative Index

Dewey Decimal Classification and Relative Index

Devised by Melvil Dewey

EDITION 21

Edited by

Joan S. Mitchell, Editor

Julianne Beall, Assistant Editor

Winton E. Matthews, Jr., Assistant Editor

Gregory R. New, Assistant Editor

VOLUME 1

Introduction ■ Tables

FOREST PRESS

A Division of
OCLC Online Computer Library Center, Inc.
ALBANY, NEW YORK
1996

Library of Congress Cataloging-in-Publication Data
Dewey, Melvil, 1851-1931.
    Dewey decimal classification and relative index / devised by
Melvil Dewey. -- Ed. 21 / edited by Joan S. Mitchell, Julianne Beall,
Winton E. Matthews, Jr., Gregory R. New.
    p.   cm.
    Contents: v. 1. Introduction. Tables --v. 2-3. Schedules --v. 4. Relative
index. Manual.
ISBN 0-910608-50-4 (set : alk. paper)
    1. Classification, Dewey decimal. I. Mitchell, Joan S. II. Beall,
Julianne, 1946-   . III. Matthews, Winton, E. IV. New, Gregory R. V.
Forest Press. VI. Title.
Z696.D52   1996   96-7393
025.4'31--dc20   CIP

The paper used in this publication meets the requirements of ANSI/NISO Z39.48-1992 (Permanence of Paper).

ISBN: (set) 0-910608-50-4; v. 1 0-910608-51-2; v. 2 0-910608-52-0;
v. 3 0-910608-53-9; v. 4 0-910608-54-7

 Recycled paper

Dedicated

to

Benjamin A. Custer

Editor
Dewey Decimal Classification
1956-1980

Reaching out to library organizations
and users throughout the world,
he turned the development of the
Dewey Decimal Classification
into a worldwide cooperative
venture.

Contents

Volume 1

Contents

Publisher's Foreword

The seven years since the publication of Edition 20 of the Dewey Decimal Classification have been filled with important accomplishments and activities for OCLC Forest Press. These include publication of the first electronic version of the Dewey Decimal Classification; the development of twelve new products for the Forest Press catalog, mostly aids to understanding and using the DDC; an expanded education and training program, with over twenty-one work-shops given in six years; a vigorous translation program, with eight translations of DDC 20, Abridged 12, and DDC 21 either published or in progress; and the initiation of research efforts to facilitate the use of the Classification as an information retrieval tool in online environments.

With the publication of DDC 21, an edition of the Dewey Decimal Classification is appearing in two formats for the very first time: in print and on the Dewey for Windows CD-ROM. With the increased use of faceting in this edition, the twenty-first edition of the Classification will truly be a tool for the 21st century.

To help users, a second and revised edition of the textbook *Dewey Decimal Classification: A Practical Guide* is being published at the same time as Edition 21. Similarly, a workbook for the abridged edition will be published in 1997, when Abridged Edition 13 appears.

Our commitment to helping users is also reflected in our education and training program, a carefully planned series of conferences and workshops to be held around the country and abroad upon the release of this edition.

Our translation program has been vigorously pursued, with a view to finding long-term partners in other regions or countries, to developing electronic databases of foreign language editions, and to making translations available more quickly. At present, there are translations of Editions 20 and 12 (in print or in process) in Italian, French, Spanish, Arabic, Turkish, Greek, Hebrew, and Persian. For the first time ever, a Russian edition of Dewey will be published in 1997, under the aegis of the Russian National Public Library for Science and Technology in Moscow.

For all of these activities, we are grateful to many organizations and individuals for their help and support.

Since Forest Press became a division of OCLC Online Computer Library Center in 1988, the staff and management of OCLC have provided a wide range of skills and resources to enable the Press to carry out its expanded programs. Thanks particularly to Dr. K. Wayne Smith, President and CEO; to Don Muccino, Executive Vice-President; and to Vice-Presidents Phyllis Bova Spies and Gary Houk for their continuing encouragement and support. In addition, we have received much help from the OCLC Office of Research, under the direction first of Martin Dillon and later Terry Noreault.

An equally important role in our work is played by the Library of Congress, where editorial work on the Classification is performed under contract between OCLC Forest Press and the Library of Congress.

The American Library Association and the (British) Library Association have been most generous in appointing committees to advise us on specific problems, such as developing priorities in the application of Dewey numbers or reviewing Dewey classes undergoing revision or expansion.

I acknowledge with pleasure the debt of the Dewey world to Joan S. Mitchell, who was appointed editor of the Dewey Decimal Classification in 1993, filling the gap left by the death of John Comaromi, who served as editor from 1980 to 1991. Ms. Mitchell has brought wit, wisdom, patience, vision, and seemingly boundless energy to the task of maintaining high quality and meeting publishing deadlines. We are also grateful to the Dewey Decimal Classification Chief David A. Smith, and Assistant Editors Julianne Beall, Winton E. Matthews, Jr., and Gregory R. New, who carried forward the work on Edition 21 while the position of editor was vacant between 1991 and 1993.

I thank Forest Press staff: Judith Kramer-Greene, Judith Pisarski, and Elizabeth Hansen for their dedication, skill, and enthusiasm under the widest variety of circumstances.

Lastly, I acknowledge with gratitude the permission given by Margaret Cockshutt to use her words on the dedication page of this book.

Peter J. Paulson
Executive Director
Forest Press

30 January 1996

DECIMAL CLASSIFICATION, ADDITIONS, NOTES AND DECISIONS

To keep users of Dewey Decimal Classification Edition 21 up to date on developments regarding the Classification, *Dewey Decimal Classification, Additions, Notes and Decisions*, popularly known as *DC&*, is published annually. All purchasers of Edition 21 are entitled to subscribe to *DC&* and may be placed on the mailing list for this publication by either returning the enclosed card or by writing to OCLC Forest Press, 85 Watervliet Avenue, Albany, New York, 12206-2082, U.S.A.

Preface by the Decimal Classification Editorial Policy Committee

Edition 21 of the *Dewey Decimal Classification* (DDC), begun in 1988, brings to fruition the work of the editors, the Decimal Classification Editorial Policy Committee (EPC), and the many advisors representing various fields who contributed time and expertise.

Issuing a relevant and useful edition of the Classification that is reflective of current thought underlies all committee decisions. Edition 21 continues the major reevaluation of areas of the Classification that need further consideration, areas that were identified and prioritized during work on Edition 20. The Classification is the product of an evolutionary process encompassing thoughtful analysis, measured deliberation, and commitment to the needs of the user.

Subject Development

Because a classification must develop continually in order to maintain its vigor and usefulness, schedules and tables are reviewed and evaluated by EPC for each edition. The degree of change varies depending on the priorities identified, the direction of the publishing world, and the need to correct errors or to improve classification structure.

The completely revised schedules in this edition are 350–354 Public administration and 560–590 Life sciences. The extensive changes in these disciplines demanded altering their fundamental classification structure. The new structure in the life sciences and in public administration is vital, relevant, and ultimately more useful in both a print and online environment. 370 Education was extensively revised to accommodate current thinking and to correct an outdated structure.

The expansions in 004–006 Computer science exemplify the need to accommodate a rapidly growing and complex discipline. The thorough analysis of 368 Insurance was undertaken in order to make necessary modifications and adjustments to ensure currency. The increase in interdisciplinary works also requires that certain areas of the schedules and tables be scrutinized regularly and that timely adjustments be made.

The committee is always mindful of the stress of implementation of a new edition. Proposed changes are debated with the needs of the user firmly in mind and anticipated benefits must be apparent before approval.

International Needs

Care and concern for international users and those collections which contain non-Christian and nonwestern materials are an ongoing priority. Sensitivity to cultural and social issues outside of the United States increases the international usefulness of the Classification.

The reevaluation of the standard subdivisions for Christianity and for religion in general, as well as the revisions of 296 Judaism and 297 Islam, exemplify this concern. Change in the language used to describe persons, the expansions of Table 2 to reflect the needs of particular countries, and the regular review of the U.S. perspective throughout the compilation of Edition 21 further carry out this intent.

The appointment of the first member from Australia, who joins members from the United Kingdom and Canada, strengthened the international perspective of the committee.

Technical Development and Electronic Communication

This edition reaffirms faceting as a direction for future revisions and as a means of strengthening the subject retrieval capabilities of the Classification, especially in an online environment. In particular, the revisions in public administration and the life sciences take full advantage of this structural evolution in the Classification.

Where possible, the EPC also approved regular use of standard subdivisions, taking into consideration the effect on existing collections. The refinement and enhancement of the index to the Classification is another continuing advancement in structural usefulness.

The compilation of the edition was enhanced by the ability to search databases electronically and to use literary warrant data to analyze specific parts of the Classification. During the review process, EPC began to utilize the Internet for continuing communication between meetings. This facilitated and accelerated consideration of classification details and editorial refinements.

Consultation and Advisory Process

Edition 21 reflects greatly increased consultation with outside reviewers and experts in specific disciplines. In particular, the changes in Judaism and Islam benefited from analysis by persons intimately involved in the study of these religions.

The various subcommittees of the Subject Analysis Committee (Cataloging and Classification Section, Association for Library Collections & Technical Services, American Library Association), as well as those of the Dewey Decimal Classification Committee of the Library Association (United Kingdom), contributed enormously to the wide-ranging and thorough review of proposed changes, expansions, and revisions.

Of special note is the work of Ross Trotter (British Library) on the life sciences, which added an important new dimension to the consultative review process. EPC wishes to express its appreciation for his extraordinary effort.

Decimal Classification Editorial Policy Committee Membership

The Decimal Classification Editorial Policy Committee was established in 1937 to provide advice in determining the direction and policy of the Dewey Decimal Classification. It was reconstituted as a joint committee of the Lake Placid Education Foundation and the American Library Association in 1955. Although the connection with the Lake Placid Education Foundation was dissolved in 1988 with the sale of Forest Press to OCLC Online Computer Library Center, Inc., the Decimal Classification Editorial Policy Committee continues in its advisory role at the request of OCLC Forest Press. The committee works with the editors of DDC to facilitate changes, innovations, and the general development of the Classification.

Many persons served on the Decimal Classification Editorial Policy Committee during the drafting of Edition 21, each bringing his or her particular perspective to the undertaking. The present committee is composed of ten persons from public, special, and academic libraries as well as from library education. The members represent the American Library Association, the Library of Congress, OCLC Forest Press (publisher of the DDC), and the Library Association (United Kingdom). Additionally, the committee includes members from Canada and Australia.

These individuals are listed together with the positions they held or now hold as members: Joanne S. Anderson, Collection Development Supervisor, San Diego Public Library (Chair, April 1993–1995); Henriette D. Avram, Associate Librarian for Collections Services, Library of Congress; David Balatti, Director, Bibliographic Services, National Library of Canada; Lizbeth J. Bishoff, Manager, Cataloging and Database Services, OCLC; Barbara Branson, Principal Cataloger, Perkins Library, Duke University; Pamela P. Brown, Information Technology Services Director, Suburban Library System; Lois Mai Chan, Professor, School of Library and Information Science, University of Kentucky (Chair, 1986–1991); Giles Martin, Auchmuty Library, University of Newcastle, New South Wales, Australia; Joan S. Mitchell, Director, Educational Technology, Carnegie Mellon University (Chair, 1992–March 1993); Peter J. Paulson, Executive Director, OCLC Forest Press; Andrea L. Stamm, Head, Catalog Department, Northwestern University Library; Elaine Svenonius, Graduate School of Library and Information Science, University of California, Los Angeles; Russell Sweeney, Head of Department, Library and Information Studies, Leeds Polytechnic University, England; Winston Tabb, Associate Librarian for Library Services, Library of Congress; Sarah Thomas, Director for Cataloging, Library of Congress; Patricia M. Thomas, Head Cataloger, Stockton-San Joaquin County Public Library; Helena M. Van Deroef, Technical Cataloger/Database Administrator, Library and Information Services Network, Bellcore; Arnold S. Wajenberg, Principal Cataloguer, University of Illinois at Urbana-Champaign; Beacher Wiggins, Acting Director for Cataloging, Library of Congress; Susi Woodhouse, Library Association (United Kingdom).

The Future

The Decimal Classification Editorial Policy Committee commends to you Edition 21 of the *Dewey Decimal Classification*. Each edition marks the progress of the Classification at a particular point in time and is a distillation of the best thinking and analysis to date. In order for the next edition of the Classification to grow and develop, the suggestions and comments of its users are welcomed by the committee. Communications may be addressed to the chair, the editor of DDC, or via e–mail <dewey@loc.gov>.

Joanne S. Anderson
Chair, April 1993–1995

Lois Mai Chan
Chair, 1986–1991
Decimal Classification
Editorial Policy Committee

15 June 1995

Acknowledgments

The birth of an edition of the Dewey Decimal Classification is a complex process that involves the efforts of many individuals. I extend my gratitude and thanks to all of them.

I joined the active work on Edition 21 halfway in its development cycle. From the beginning, the three assistant editors of the Classification, Julianne Beall, Winton E. Matthews, Jr., and Gregory R. New, were patient and generous in guiding me through the editorial process. They undertook an ambitious and unforgiving work plan to produce the edition on time. I greatly admire their scholarly work, dedication, and commitment.

The assistant editors did the bulk of revision of the schedules and tables. Some highlights of their contributions follow. Ms. Beall developed the revision and expansion of 297 Islam, prepared numerous expansions in Table 6, and updated 004–006 Computer science. Mr. Matthews revised the area numbers for countries of the former Soviet Union, and worked with several national libraries to develop other expansions in Table 2. Mr. New led development efforts on the three major revisions in Edition 21: 350–354 Public administration, 370 Education, and 560–590 Life sciences. I am tempted to call Edition 21 the "New" edition in recognition of Mr. New's contribution.

Edition 21 has stayed on course through the support and encouragement of Peter J. Paulson, executive director of OCLC Forest Press. I am also grateful to the Forest Press staff: Elizabeth Hansen, Judith Kramer-Greene, and Judith Pisarski.

The advice and critical review offered by the members of the Decimal Classification Editorial Policy Committee have enabled us to respond to the needs of our users throughout the world and to move the Classification forward with knowledge. I value their wise counsel.

David A. Smith, chief of the Library of Congress Decimal Classification Division, is a constant source of guidance and colleagueship. He and the Decimal Classification Division staff have continuously supported the editorial efforts by offering an expert view of emerging topics and areas requiring revision. In addition to the three assistant editors, present and past staff members who have contributed to the development of Edition 21 include: Darlene Banks, Victoria Behrens, Frances A. Bold, Michael B. Cantlon, Carletta Cartledge, Rosalee Connor, Eve M. Dickey, Adrian Gore, Keith Harrison, William S. Hwang, Jeannette Jackson, Sterlin S. Johnson, Shirley D. Jones, Sarah Keller, Walter McClughan, Nobuko Ohashi, Letitia J. Reigle, Virginia A. Schoepf, Emily Spears, Cosmo Tassone, Dorothy A. Watson, and Susanne Welsh. The contributions of several staff members deserve special mention. Mr. Cantlon led revision efforts for 296 Judaism, and religion and philosophy in general. Ms. Schoepf revised 368 Insurance. Ms. Behrens proposed several important additions and expansions for 004–006 Computer science. Ms. Dickey provided much helpful advice on the revision of 370 Education. Ms. Ohashi prepared the Table 6 expansion for Polynesian languages.

Ross Trotter, British Library, joined the editorial team as a guest editor for the revision of 560–590 Life sciences. Mr. Trotter worked closely with Mr. New to shape the final version of this major revision. We are fortunate to have such a knowledgeable and dedicated colleague at the British Library.

Many other groups and individuals have made significant contributions to Edition 21. Special committees appointed by the (British) Library Association Dewey Decimal Committee and by the Subject Analysis Committee of the American Library Association (ALA) offered advice on the priorities for Edition 21 and reviewed each of its major revisions. Subcommittees of the ALA Committee on Cataloging: Asian and African Materials reviewed 296 Judaism; 297 Islam, Babism, Bahai Faith; and the expansion for African languages in Table 6. The Cataloging Committee of the Africana Librarians Council, African Studies Association, also provided advice on the revision of 297 and African languages. Colleagues in other divisions at the Library of Congress shared their subject expertise, notably Henry Lefkowitz, Dennis McGovern, and Ruta Penkiunas. Frances Corcoran, Consolidated School District #62, Des Plaines, Illinois (retired), suggested a development of elementary reading and language arts for inclusion in 370 Education. Esther Bierbaum, University of Iowa, reviewed taxonomic names of plants and animals. Barbara J. Bell, College of Wooster, provided a selected list of current national bibliographies using Dewey numbers.

The OCLC Office of Research, particularly Diane Vizine-Goetz, Mark Bendig, and other members of the cataloging productivity tools team, spearheaded efforts to enable electronic distribution of the Dewey Decimal Classification through the development of Electronic Dewey and Dewey for Windows. We look forward to continuing to work closely with the Office of Research to develop classifier productivity tools and to explore new uses for the Classification.

I will close by acknowledging the legacy of my predecessor, John P. Comaromi. His unwavering commitment to making the Dewey Decimal Classification easier to use is reflected in the pages of this edition.

Joan S. Mitchell
Editor
Dewey Decimal Classification
OCLC Forest Press

New Features in Edition 21

Overview

The Dewey Decimal Classification system is continuously revised to keep pace with knowledge. This means accommodating new topics, as well as revising existing schedules to reflect new views of the field or to reduce bias. Edition 21 includes major revisions of three schedules: 350–354 Public administration, 370 Education, and 560–590 Life sciences. Each has been underway for over a decade (the life sciences for over two decades) in response to user requests and to changes in the nature of the literature.

In religion, the standard subdivisions of Christianity in 201–209 have been relocated to 230–270 as part of a multi-edition plan to reduce Christian bias. Both 296 Judaism and 297 Islam have been revised and expanded.

There are numerous adjustments to reflect political and social changes, such as the major revision of Table 2—47 for the countries of the former Soviet Union and a new number for the administration of Nelson Mandela. Many new topics that have gained literary warrant since the publication of Edition 20 are now mentioned in the Classification, e.g., rap music, in-line skating, snowboarding. Terminology throughout the Classification has been updated to achieve currency, ensure sensitivity, and reflect international usage. Since the Classification is used by diverse libraries throughout the world, Edition 21 includes several changes to address international or special needs.

Edition 21 is the first edition prepared with online access to the OCLC Online Union Catalog for guidance on literary warrant. The OCLC database provides information on Dewey application to a wide range of materials by different types of libraries in the U.S. and other countries.

Some of the special features of Edition 21 are highlighted below.

User Convenience

The aim of Edition 20 was user convenience. How is user convenience furthered in Edition 21? Edition 21 includes more information located strategically to guide the classifier in decision making.

Numerous captions have been rewritten to eliminate vague headings or headings composed solely of adjectival or prepositional phrases. The note structure in the schedules has been simplified by replacing "example" and "contains" notes with an existing note type, the "including" note. Many notes have been added to provide guidance on which concepts in a multiple term heading may have standard subdivisions applied to them.

The Relative Index has more entries than the index to Edition 20, including entries for selected built numbers, terms to provide entry vocabulary for international users, and index terms for Manual notes. More interdisciplinary numbers are identified in the schedules and Relative Index.

Edition 21 has an expanded Manual. Each Manual note is located at the preferred or "if-in-doubt" number. Sample titles with corresponding DDC numbers accompany Manual notes in 004–006, 350–354, 560–590, and 780. A comprehensive Manual note on the treatment of directories, buyers guides, yellow pages, trade catalogs, and consumer reports has been added at 338 vs. 060, 381, 382, 670.294, 910, T1—025, T1—0294, T1—0296.

Regularization

Regularization, the replacement of special developments for standard subdivision concepts with regular use of Table 1, has continued in Edition 21. For example, in the extensive revision of 370, the enumerated irregular development of standard subdivision concepts at 370.7 has been replaced by regular use of Table 1—07 Education, research, related topics. Regularization makes the Classification easier to apply and promotes the effectiveness of subject retrieval by using uniform notation to represent standard subdivision concepts throughout the Classification.

Faceting

Facet indicators and notational synthesis are basic to the design of the two complete revisions in Edition 21: 350–354 Public administration and 560–590 Life sciences. The Decimal Classification Editorial Policy Committee, the editorial board that advises OCLC Forest Press on the development of the Classification, has endorsed the general trend toward more faceting in the Classification. Why are facet indicators and notational synthesis important? The use of facet indicators to identify meaningful components in a number and the use of uniform notation to express recurring aspects of topics within a schedule expand retrieval possibilities by providing access to information represented by parts of a number.

Terminology

Terminology for persons in the schedules and tables has been updated to reflect currency, sensitivity, and international usage. Terminology for persons with disabilities has been changed to reflect a "person first, disability second" viewpoint. For example, "persons with physical disabilities" replaces "physically handicapped persons."

International Needs and Cooperative Development

Special attention has been given to reduction of U.S. bias and Christian bias in the Classification. For example, the U.S. bias in structure and wording of the new public administration development has been greatly reduced. In addition to the aforementioned changes in religion, Edition 21 includes a new optional arrangement for the books of the Old Testament (Tanakh) in the order found in Jewish Bibles.

The area tables for Brazil, Greece, New Zealand, and Norway have been revised and expanded in cooperation with the national libraries and library associations in those countries. Many historical and literary periods of different countries have been revised and expanded.

Table 6 features expansions for several languages. Numbers for several peoples in Table 5 (many of which are built using numbers in Table 6) have also been expanded.

Changes in the Database

Underlying the print version of Edition 21 is a database with additional information in each classification record. The DDC database includes natural language index terms and index terms from other thesauri that cannot appear in the print index due to space constraints. These terms are included as additional entry vocabulary in the index to the electronic edition of the DDC,

Dewey for Windows. The history of many expanded, relocated, and discontinued numbers has been documented in the DDC database using the 685 history note field provided by the *USMARC Format for Classification Data*. This information could be used in online systems to guide users to relevant information split between former and current numbers.

Joan S. Mitchell
Editor
Dewey Decimal Classification
OCLC Forest Press

Selected List of Changes in Edition 21

Volume 1 of Edition 21 contains tables of relocations, reductions, and reused numbers; and comparative and equivalence tables for the major revisions: T2—47 Eastern Europe Russia, 350–354 Public Administration, 370 Education, and 560–590 Life sciences. Listed below are summaries of the major revisions in Edition 21 and selected other revisions in the tables and schedules.

MAJOR REVISIONS IN EDITION 21

T2—47   Eastern Europe   Russia
Completely revised

T2—499   Bulgaria
Relocated from—4977; completely revised. This number was previously used for the Aegean Islands (which were relocated to—495 in *DC&* 5:3)

296   Judaism
Revised and expanded. An optional arrangement for the books of Tanakh in the order found in Jewish Bibles is provided in the Manual note for 221. A similar option with the same arrangement is included at 296.11

297   Islam, Babism, Bahai faith
Revised and expanded

350–354   Public administration
Completely revised. Public administration still occupies 351–354, but the subdivisions and citation order have been changed. Citation order reversed from jurisdiction/topic to topic/jurisdiction, and U.S. bias in wording and structure reduced. The schedule features significant use of facet indicators and notational synthesis

368   Insurance
Revised and expanded

370   Education
Extensively revised. The main outline has remained basically the same, but some subdivisions have been reworked, and expansions provided for new topics. The most visible change is the relocation of 376 Education of women and 377 Schools and religion to subdivisions of 371. Other changes include the relocation of home schools from 649.68 to 371.042; relocation of educational sociology from 370.19 to 306.43; regularization of 370.7 Education, research, related topics; and updating and internationalization of terminology. The schedule includes a new development for reading and language arts in elementary education

560–590	Life sciences

570 (Biology in general) and 583 (Dicotyledons) completely revised; the rest extensively revised. Features of the revision include reversal of citation order from organism/process to process/organism for internal biological processes in 571–575; collocation of microorganisms, fungi, and algae in 579; regularization of use of notation 1 for general topics in the taxonomic schedules in 579–590; and more specific and shorter numbers for fishes and mammals. The Edition 20 number for biology (574) was left vacant in the revision to aid library implementation of the new schedule, since samples of library holdings in the OCLC Online Union Catalog indicated that 70% of holdings among Dewey libraries on internal biological processes were in 574

Selected Revisions in the Tables

TABLE 1. STANDARD SUBDIVISIONS

—024	The subject for persons in specific occupations

Limited to works for persons in specific occupations. Works for other kinds of persons relocated to—08

—0284	Apparatus, equipment, materials
—0286	Waste technology

New numbers

—071	Education

Broadened from "Schools and courses" to include education and teaching

—0727	Statistical methods
—0728	Presentation of statistical data

New numbers

—0785	Computer-assisted instruction

New number

—08	History and description with respect to kinds of persons

New table of modified standard subdivisions that can be used with—08

—08341	Boys six to eleven
—08342	Girls six to eleven

New numbers

—0835	Young people twelve to twenty

Comprehensive works on young adults relocated to—0842

—0842	Young adults

Comprehensive works on young adults (formerly—0835)

—08421	Young men
—08422	Young women
	New numbers
—0869	Persons with special social status
	New subdivisions for various kinds of persons
—09005	Serial publications [of Historical, geographic, persons treatment]
	New number
—0923	Collected persons treatment of members of specific racial, ethnic, national groups
	New number
—0929	Persons treatment of nonhumans
	New number for forms such as biographies of animals

TABLE 2. GEOGRAPHIC AREAS, HISTORICAL PERIODS, PERSONS

—481–484	Norway
	Expanded with minor revisions (*DC&* 5:4)
—495	Greece
	Extensively revised (*DC&* 5:3)
—5693	Cyprus
	Relocated from —5645 (*DC&* 5:3)
—5695	Jordan
	Revised and expanded
—669	Nigeria
	Revised and expanded (*DC&* 5:4)
—7294	Haiti
	Revised and expanded
—81	Brazil
	Revised (*DC&* 5:5)
—93	New Zealand
	Revised and expanded to use all subdivisions of —93 (*DC&* 5:4)

TABLE 3–C. NOTATION TO BE ADDED WHERE INSTRUCTED IN TABLE 3–B, 700.4, 791.4, 808–809

—1	Arts and literature displaying specific qualities of style, mood, viewpoint
—3	Arts and literature dealing with specific themes and subjects
	Expanded and modified for use at 700.4 Special topics in the arts

TABLE 5. RACIAL, ETHNIC, NATIONAL GROUPS

—9157   Tajik
             Relocated from—9159

—9159   Other Iranian peoples
             New subdivisions for Kurds and Baluchi

—9594   Miao (Hmong) and Yao peoples
             New number

TABLE 6. LANGUAGES

—391   Yiddish
             Relocated from—37. Specific Old Low Germanic languages relocated
             to —392–394

—943   Turkic languages
—963   Niger-Congo languages
—97   North American native languages
—983   Quechan (Kechuan), Aymaran, Tucanoan, Tupí, Arawakan languages
—994   Polynesian languages
—999   Caucasian (Caucasic) languages
             Expansions for languages

Selected Revisions in the Schedules

004–006   Data processing   Computer science
             Revised and expanded. New special provisions for processing modes,
             operating systems, and user interfaces

004.678   Internet
             New number

006.32   Neural nets (Neural networks)
             New number

006.33   Knowledge-based systems
             Expanded

006.7   Multimedia systems
             New number; relocated from 006.6

133.5   Astrology
             Expanded

200.1–.9	Standard subdivisions of religion
	The standard subdivisions of comparative religion relocated from 291.01–291.09, with the exception of philosophy and theory of comparative religion and language of comparative religion, which have been relocated from 291.01 to 210
[201–209]	Standard subdivisions of Christianity.
	Vacated in Edition 21 as part of the move to reduce Christian bias. Standard subdivisions of Christianity have been relocated to appropriate subdivisions of 230–270
210	Philosophy and theory of religion
	Heading formerly "Natural religion." Philosophy and theory of religion relocated from 200.1; philosophy and theory of comparative religion and language of comparative religion relocated from 291.01
230	Christianity Christian theology
	Comprehensive works on Christianity relocated from 200. The development for Christianity is now in one continuous span, 230–280 (with the Bible remaining in 220)
230.071	Education in Christianity, in Christian theology
	Education in Christianity (formerly 207.1) and education in Christian theology. Regular subdivisions used for seminaries and divinity schools (relocated from subdivisions of 207)
259	Pastoral care of families, of specific kinds of persons
	Expanded
263.041	Pilgrimages
	Relocated from 248.463
280.042	Relations between [Christian] denominations
	Ecumenical movement relocated from 270.82
291.61	[Religious] Leaders and their work
	Leaders with supernatural powers, divinely inspired persons, and interpreters of religion relocated from 291.62–291.64
304.6	Population
	Population size and composition of communities relocated from 307.2
305.569	The poor
	Consolidation of "the poor" (formerly 305.56) and "the impoverished" (former heading)
306.43	[Sociology of] Education
	Relocated from 370.19

324.24–.29   Parties in specific countries in modern world
    New notation 01 and subdivisions of 08 in add table provide additional
    concepts to be added for parties in specific countries

326.8   Emancipation
    Number reinstated in Edition 21 after elimination in Edition 15

327.174   Disarmament and arms control
    Expanded to provide for limitation by type of weapon

332.042   International finance
    International capital transactions relocated from 382.173; international
    currency movements relocated from 382.174

333.95   Biological resources
    Revised and expanded to provide notation for many specific kinds of
    animals and plants. Comprehensive number for mammals relocated from
    333.959 to 333.954, the general number for animals

342–349   Branches of law; laws (statutes), regulations, cases; law of specific juris-
    dictions, areas, socioeconomic regions
    Heading expanded to reflect content of subdivisions. Number-building
    instructions moved here from 340 Law

355.07   Military research and development
    Military research relocated from 355.0072

355.6   Military administration
    Revised and expanded to provide for aspects of administration available
    for nonmilitary agencies in 351–354. Provisions for supply and pro-
    curement simplified

362–363   Specific social problems and services
    Expanded add table (*DC&* 5:3)

362.196–.198   [Services to patients with] Specific conditions
    New add table for specific services

394.261–.267   [Specific holidays]
    Specific holidays relocated from 394.268 to provide a better arrange-
    ment and shorter numbers (*DC&* 5:4)

398.2093–   Treatment of [Folk literature] by specific continents, countries, localities
.2099   Tales and lore by place relocated from 398.21–.27, with new add table
    for topics (*DC&* 5:5)

420–490   Specific languages
    Special provision for adding from Table 4 for language families with
    high literary warrant (e.g., Slavic languages at 491.804)

508.2	Seasons New number
511.52	Trees
514.742	Fractals New numbers
515	Analysis Numerical analysis added to class-here note; applied numerical analysis remains in 519.4
530.1423	Supergravity New number
535.35	Luminescence Expanded
539.736	Supercolliders New number
551.524	Atmosphere interactions with earth's surface Broadened and expanded
551.87	Faults and folds Expanded
553.87	Semiprecious stones Expanded. Jet relocated from 553.22 and amber from 553.29
613.2	Dietetics Expanded. Applied nutrition relocated from 641.1, and beverages from 613.3
616.079	Immunity Revised and expanded
616.7	Diseases of musculoskeletal system Nonsurgical aspects of and comprehensive works on orthopedics relocated from 617.3
617.47	[Surgery of the] Musculoskeletal system Orthopedic surgery of the system relocated from 617.3
620.5	Nanotechnology
621.35	Superconductivity
621.3694	Nonlinear optics
621.3821	Communications networks New numbers

631.5233   Agricultural genetics
632.9517   Insecticides
           New numbers

633.3   Legumes, forage crops other than grasses and legumes
           Comprehensive works on legumes in agriculture relocated from 635.65

635.952   Groupings [of plants] by climatic factors
           Expanded

636   Animal husbandry
           Interdisciplinary works on species of domestic mammals relocated
           from 599

636.083   Care, maintenance, training [of livestock]
636.084   Feeding [livestock]
           Expanded

636.085–.086 Feeds and applied nutrition; Field-crop feeds
           Revised to eliminate dual provision and to provide numbers for specific
           components in applied nutrition, e.g., proteins 636.08522

636.5   Poultry   Chickens
           Interdisciplinary works on species of domestic birds relocated from 598

636.72–.75 Specific breeds and groups of dogs
           Expansion for several specific breeds

636.9   Other mammals
           Revised to parallel revisions in 599. Animals raised for fur relocated
           from 636.08844 to 636.97

639   Hunting, fishing, conservation, related technologies
           Several subdivisions revised to parallel revisions in 590, notably
           639.37 and 639.5–.6

641.568   Cooking for special occasions
           Cooking for Christmas relocated from 641.566 to remove dual provision

641.815   Breads and bread-like foods
           Comprehensive number for baked goods

700.4   Special topics in the arts
           New provisions for adding from expanded Table 3–C for iconography
           of the arts

746.1–.9   [Textile] Products and processes
           Preference order changed so that process is usually preferred (*DC&* 5:5)

778.59	Video production (Television photography) Expanded
781.64	Western popular music New subdivisions added for ragtime, reggae, and rap
792.78	Theatrical dancing Relocated from 792.8
796.04	General kinds of sports and games New development. Intramural sports relocated from 371.89 (*DC&* 5:5)
796.22	Skateboarding (*DC&* 5:4)
796.4257	Triathalon
796.63	Mountain biking
796.964	Curling (*DC&* 5:2)
797.1224	Kayaking (*DC&* 5:4)
798.83	Sled dog racing New numbers for sports
799.2	Hunting Comprehensive works on commercial and sports hunting relocated from 639.1
799.24	[Hunting] birds Subdivisions revised to match literary warrant and new development for birds in 598
810–890	Literature of specific languages and language families Literary periods updated and expanded
919.904	Travel on extraterrestrial worlds Projected accounts of manned space flight relocated from 629.4501
940–990	General history of modern world, of extraterrestrial worlds New add table for wars. History of individual countries updated to include changes in administrations and forms of governments, e.g., Czech Republic and Slovakia 943.7; Heisei period in Japan 952.049
947.5–.9	Countries of former Soviet Union other than Russia; Caucasus area of Russia Revised

Introduction to the Dewey Decimal Classification

About the Introduction

1.1   This Introduction explains the basic principles and structure of the Dewey Decimal Classification.

1.2   The Introduction is meant to be used in conjunction with the Glossary and the Manual. The Glossary defines terms used in the Introduction and elsewhere in the Classification. The Manual contains additional and more detailed information about specific areas of the Classification, offers advice on classifying in difficult areas, and explains how to choose between related numbers.

Classification: What It Is and What It Does

2.1   *Classification* provides a system for organizing knowledge. Classification may be used to organize knowledge represented in any form, e.g., books, documents, electronic records.

2.2   *Notation* is the system of symbols used to represent the classes in a classification system. In the Dewey Decimal Classification system (DDC), the notation is expressed in Arabic numerals. The notation gives at once both the unique meaning of the class and its relation to other classes. No matter how words describing subjects may differ, the notation provides a universal language to identify the class within which the subject belongs and related classes.

2.3   Libraries usually arrange their collections according to the systematic structure of a library classification. Each item is assigned a *call number (shelf mark)*. The call number consists of the Dewey notation for its class, accompanied by a book number or some other device to subarrange the items of a class. The call number provides a unique identifying code that is used as an "address" on the shelf, and as a tag for library recordkeeping in circulation and inventory control.

History and Current Use of the Dewey Decimal Classification

3.1   The DDC was conceived by Melvil Dewey in 1873 and first published in 1876. The Dewey Decimal Classification is the most widely used library classification system in the world. It is used in more than 135 countries, and has been translated into over 30 languages. In the United States, 95% of all public and school libraries, 25% of all college and university libraries, and 20% of special libraries use the DDC.

3.2   The DDC is developed, maintained, and applied in the Decimal Classification Division of the Library of Congress (LC), where annually over 110,000 DDC numbers are assigned to works cataloged by the Library. DDC numbers are incorporated into machine-readable cataloging (MARC) bibliographic records, and distributed to libraries by way of computer media, Cataloging-in-Publication (CIP) data, and LC cards. DDC numbers appear in MARC records issued by countries throughout the world and are used in the national bibliographies of Australia, Botswana, Brazil, Canada, Iceland, India, Indonesia, Italy, Namibia, New Zealand, Norway, Pakistan, Papua New Guinea, the Philippines, South Africa, Turkey, the United Kingdom, Venezuela, Zimbabwe, and other countries. Various bibliographic utilities and services in the United States and elsewhere make DDC numbers available to libraries through online access, publications, and production of catalog cards.

Overview of the Dewey Decimal Classification

CONCEPTUAL FRAMEWORK

4.1   In the DDC, basic classes are organized by disciplines or fields of study. No principle is more basic to the DDC than this: the parts of the Classification are arranged by *discipline*, not by *subject*.

4.2   The consequence of this principle is that there is likely to be no single place for a given subject. A subject may appear in any discipline. For example, "clothing" has aspects that fall under several disciplines. The psychological influence of clothing belongs in 155.95 as part of the discipline of psychology; customs associated with clothing belong in 391 as part of the discipline of customs; and clothing in the sense of fashion design belongs in 746.92 as part of the discipline of the arts. The Relative Index assembles the disciplinary aspects of the subject of clothing in one place:

Clothing	391
armed forces	355.81
costume	355.14
arts	746.92
commercial manufacturing	687
fur	685.24
instruments	681.767 7
leather	685.22
customs	391
health	613.482
home economics	646.3
home sewing	646.4
product safety	363.19
law	344.042 35
see also Product safety	
psychological influence	155.95
social welfare	361.05
see Manual at 391 vs. 646.3, 746.92	

NOTATION

4.3   At the broadest level, the DDC is divided into ten *main classes*, which together cover the entire world of knowledge. These classes are further divided into ten *divisions* and each division into ten *sections*, although not all the numbers for the divisions and sections have been used. (The word *class* may be used to indicate main classes, divisions, sections, and any other notational level in the hierarchy.)

4.4   The ten main classes are:

000	Generalities
100	Philosophy, paranormal phenomena, psychology
200	Religion
300	Social sciences
400	Language
500	Natural sciences and mathematics
600	Technology (Applied sciences)
700	The arts Fine and decorative arts
800	Literature (Belles-lettres) and rhetoric
900	Geography, history, and auxiliary disciplines

4.5   Main class 000 is the most general class, and is used for works not limited to any one specific discipline, e.g., encyclopedias, newspapers, general periodicals. This class is also used for certain specialized disciplines that deal with knowledge and information, e.g., computer science, library and information science, journalism. Main classes 100–900 each consist of a major discipline or group of related disciplines.

4.6   The first digit in the numbers listed above indicates the main class. Zeros are used to fill out the notation to the minimum required length of three digits.

4.7   Each main class consists of ten divisions, also numbered 0 through 9. The number of significant digits here is two, the second digit indicating the division. For example, 500 is used for general works on the sciences, 510 for mathematics, 520 for astronomy, 530 for physics.

4.8   Each division has ten sections, again numbered 0 through 9. The third digit in each three-digit number indicates the section. Thus, 530 is used for general works on physics, 531 for classical mechanics, 532 for fluid mechanics, 533 for gas mechanics.

4.9   A *decimal point* follows the third digit, after which division by ten continues to the specific degree of classification needed.

PRINCIPLE OF HIERARCHY

4.10   *Hierarchy* in the DDC is expressed through structure and notation.

4.11   *Structural hierarchy* means that all topics (aside from the ten main classes) are subordinate to and part of all the broader topics above it. The corollary is also true: whatever is true of the whole is true of the parts. This important concept is sometimes called *hierarchical force*. Any note regarding the nature of a class holds true for all the subordinate classes, including logically subordinate topics classed at coordinate numbers. (For a discussion of notes with hierarchical force, see paragraphs 7.8–7.15 and 7.19–7.21.)

Because of the principle of hierarchical force, hierarchical notes are usually given only once—at the highest level of application. For example, the scope note at 700 applies to 730, to 736, and to 736.4. The words "Description, critical appraisal . . ." found in the scope note at 700 also govern the critical appraisal of wood carving in 736.4 Wood [carving]. In order to understand the structural hierarchy, the classifier must read up and down the schedules (and remember to turn the page).

4.12   *Notational hierarchy* is expressed by length of notation. As the following example shows, numbers at any given level are usually *subordinate* to a class whose notation is one digit shorter; *coordinate* with a class whose notation has the same number of significant digits; and *superordinate* to a class with numbers one or more digits longer. The underlined digits in the example below demonstrate this notational hierarchy:

<u>6</u>00	Technology (Applied sciences)	
<u>63</u>0	Agriculture and related technologies	
<u>636</u>	Animal husbandry	
<u>636.7</u>	Dogs	
<u>636.8</u>	Cats	

4.13   "Dogs" and "Cats" are more specific than (subordinate to) "Animal husbandry"; they are equally specific as (coordinate with) each other; and "Animal husbandry" is less specific than (superordinate to) "Dogs" and "Cats."

4.14   Sometimes, other devices must be used to express the hierarchy when it is not possible or desirable to do so through the notation. Relationships among topics that violate notational hierarchy are indicated by special headings, notes, and entries. A dual heading is used when a subordinate topic is the major part of the subject; the subject as a whole and the subordinate topic as a whole share the same number (e.g., 610 Medical sciences   Medicine). A see reference leads the classifier to subdivisions of a subject located outside the notational hierarchy. A centered entry (so called because its numbers, heading, and notes appear in the center of the page) constitutes a major departure from notational hierarchy. A centered entry is used to indicate and relate structurally a span of numbers that together form a single concept for which there is no specific hierarchical notation available. In the DDC, centered entries are always flagged typographically by the symbol > in the number column.

Classifying with the DDC

5.1   Classifying a work with the DDC requires determination of the subject, the disciplinary focus, and, if applicable, the approach or form. (For advice on determining the subject and discipline of a work, see paragraphs 5.2–5.9; for a discussion of approach or form, see paragraph 8.3.)

Please note that works of the imagination are generally classified by literary form rather than by subject in the DDC.

DETERMINING THE SUBJECT OF A WORK

5.2   Classifying a work properly depends first upon determining the subject of the work in hand.

(A)   The title is often a clue to the subject, but should never be the sole source of analysis. For example, *The Greening of America* is a book about social conditions and social change, not a work on ecology.

(B)   The table of contents may list the main topics discussed. Chapter headings may substitute for the absence of a table of contents. Chapter subheadings often prove useful.

(C)   The preface or introduction usually states the author's purpose. If a foreword is provided, it often indicates the subject of the work and suggests the place of the work in the development of thought on the subject. The book jacket or accompanying material may include a summary of the subject content.

(D)   A scan of the text itself may provide further guidance or confirm preliminary subject analysis.

(E)   Bibliographical references and index entries are sources of subject information.

(F)   Cataloging copy from centralized cataloging services is often helpful by providing subject headings, classification numbers, and notes. Such copy appears on the verso of the title page of many U.S., Australian, British, and Canadian books as part of Cataloging-in-Publication (CIP) data. Data from these sources should be verified with the book in hand, since cataloging-in-publication is based on prepublication information.

(G)   Occasionally, consultation of outside sources such as reviews, reference works, and subject experts may be required to determine the subject of the work.

DETERMINING THE DISCIPLINE OF A WORK

5.3   After determining the subject, the classifier must then select the proper discipline, or field of study, of the work.

5.4   The guiding principle of the DDC is that a work is classed in the discipline for which it is intended, rather than the discipline from which the work derives. This enables works that are used together to be found together. For example, a general work by a zoologist on agricultural pest control should be classed in agriculture, not zoology, along with other works on agricultural pest control.

5.5   Once the subject has been determined, and information on the discipline has been found, the experienced classifier will turn to the schedules. The summaries are a good means of mental navigation for beginners. The headings and notes in the schedules themselves and the Manual provide much guidance. The Relative Index may help by suggesting the disciplines in which a subject is normally treated. (For a discussion of the summaries, see paragraph 7.1; for a discussion of the Manual, see paragraphs 10.1–10.6; for a discussion of the Relative Index, see paragraphs 11.1–11.15.)

5.6   If the Relative Index is used, the classifier must still rely on the structure of the Classification and various aids throughout to arrive at the proper place to classify a work. Even the most promising Relative Index citations must be verified in the schedules; the schedules are the only place where all the information about coverage and use of the numbers may be found.

More Than One Subject in the Same Discipline

5.7   A work may include multiple aspects of one subject, or more than one subject, from the viewpoint of a single discipline. Use the following guidelines in determining the best placement for the work:

(A)   Class a work dealing with interrelated subjects with the subject that is being acted upon. This is called the *rule of application*, and takes precedence over any other rule. For instance, class an analytical work dealing with Shakespeare's influence on Keats with Keats.

(B)   Class a work on two subjects with the subject receiving fuller treatment.

(C)   If two subjects receive equal treatment, and are not used to introduce or explain one another, class the work with the subject whose number comes first in the DDC schedules. This is called the *first-of-two rule*. For example, a history dealing equally with the United States and Japan, in which the United States is discussed first and is given first in the title, is classed with the history of Japan because 952 Japan precedes 973 United States.

Often, specific instructions are given to use numbers that do not come first in the schedules. These instructions may be in the form of a note or table on preference order, an add note with instructions on citation order in number building, or a note identifying the comprehensive number for the subject. For example, at 598, the note "class comprehensive works on warm-blooded vertebrates in 599" tells the classifier to ignore the first-of-two rule and class a work on birds (598) and mammals (599) in 599, which is the comprehensive number for warm-blooded vertebrates.

Also disregard the first-of-two rule when the two topics are the two major subdivisions of a subject. For example, water supply (628.1) and waste technology (628.4) taken together constitute most of 628 Sanitary and municipal engineering; works covering both of these topics are classed in 628 (not 628.1).

(For a discussion of number building, including the addition of standard subdivisions, see paragraphs 8.1–8.20; for a discussion of citation and preference order, see paragraphs 9.1–9.5; for a discussion of the first-of-two rule versus preference order, see paragraph 9.6; for a discussion of comprehensive numbers, see paragraphs 7.15 and 7.19–7.20.)

(D)   Class a work on three or more subjects that are all subdivisions of a broader subject in the first higher number that includes them all (unless one subject is treated more fully than the others). This is called the *rule of three*. For example, a history of Portugal (946.9), Sweden (948.5), and Greece (949.5) is classed with the history of Europe (940).

(E) Subdivisions beginning with zero should be avoided if there is a choice between 0 and 1–9 at the same point in the hierarchy of the notation. Similarly, subdivisions beginning with 00 should be avoided when there is a choice between 00 and 0. This is called the *rule of zero*. For example, a biography of an American Methodist missionary in China belongs in 266 Missions. The content of the work can be expressed in three different numbers:

266.0092	biography of a missionary
266.02373051	foreign missions of the United States in China
266.76092	biography of a United Methodist Church missionary

The last number is used since it has no zero at the fourth position.

MORE THAN ONE DISCIPLINE

5.8   Treating a subject from the point of view of more than one discipline is different from treating several subjects in one discipline. Use the following guidelines in determining the best placement for the work:

(A) Use the *interdisciplinary number* provided in the schedules or Relative Index if one is given. An important consideration in using such an interdisciplinary number is that the work must contain significant material on the discipline in which the interdisciplinary number is found. For example, 305.231 (a sociology number) is provided for interdisciplinary works on child development. However, if a work that is interdisciplinary with respect to child development gives little emphasis to social development and a great deal of emphasis to the psychological and physical development of the child (155.4 and 612.65, respectively), class it in 155.4 (the first number in the schedules of the next two obvious choices). In short, interdisciplinary numbers are not absolute; they are to be used only when applicable. (For a discussion of interdisciplinary numbers, see paragraphs 7.15, 7.19–7.20, and 11.8–11.9.)

(B) Class works not given an interdisciplinary number in the discipline given the fullest treatment in the work. For example, a work dealing with both the scientific and the engineering principles of electrodynamics is classed in 537.6 if the engineering aspects are introduced primarily for illustrative purposes, but in 621.31 if the basic scientific theories are only preliminary to the author's exposition of engineering principles and practices.

(C) When classifying interdisciplinary works, do not overlook the possibilities of main class 000 Generalities, e.g., 080 for a collection of interviews of famous people from various disciplines.

Any other situation is treated in the same fashion as those found in the instructions at More Than One Subject in the Same Discipline (paragraph 5.7).

TABLE OF LAST RESORT

5.9   When several numbers have been found for the work in hand, and each seems as good as the next, the following table of last resort (in order of preference) may be used as a guideline in the absence of any other rule:

Table of last resort

(1)	Kinds of things
(2)	Parts of things
(3)	Materials from which things, kinds, or parts are made
(4)	Properties of things, kinds, parts, or materials
(5)	Processes within things, kinds, parts, or materials
(6)	Operations upon things, kinds, parts, or materials
(7)	Instrumentalities for performing such operations

For example, surveillance by border patrols could be classed in either 363.285 Border patrols, or 363.232 Patrol and surveillance. Choose 363.285 since border patrols are a kind of police service, while patrol and surveillance are processes performed by police services.

Do not apply this table or any other guideline if it appears to disregard the author's intention and emphasis.

How DDC 21 Is Arranged

6.1   DDC 21 is composed of nine major parts in four volumes as follows:

Volume 1

(A)   New Features in Edition 21: A brief explanation of the special features and changes in DDC 21

(B)   Introduction: A description of the DDC and how to use it

(C)   Glossary: Short definitions of terms used in the DDC

(D)   Index to the Introduction and Glossary

(E)   Tables: Seven numbered tables of notation that can be added to class numbers to provide greater specificity

(F)   Lists that compare Editions 20 and 21: Relocations and Reductions; Comparative and Equivalence Tables for the former Soviet Union, Public administration, Education, and Life sciences; Reused Numbers

Volumes 2 and 3

(G)   Schedules: The organization of knowledge from 000–999

Volume 4

(H)   Relative Index: An alphabetical list of subjects with the disciplines in which they are treated subarranged alphabetically under each entry

(I)   Manual: A guide to classifying in difficult areas, information on new schedules, and an explanation of the policies and practices of the Decimal Classification Division at the Library of Congress. Information in the Manual is arranged by the numbers in the tables and schedules

Key Features of the Schedules and Tables

SUMMARIES

7.1   *Summaries* provide an overview of the structure of classes. Three types of summaries appear in the DDC:

     (A)   The summaries of the schedules as a whole are found at the front of the schedules.

     (B)   Two-level summaries are provided for each main class and division of the schedules and main numbers of Table 2 that have subdivisions extending over more than forty pages. See the summaries at the beginning of Table 2 —4 Europe   Western Europe and 370 Education for examples of two-level summaries.

     (C)   Single-level summaries in the schedules and tables provide an overview of classes that have subdivisions covering between four and forty pages. For example, 382 International commerce (Foreign trade) has the following summary:

SUMMARY

382.01–.09	**Standard subdivisions**
.1	**Generalities of international commerce**
.3	**Commercial policy**
.4	**International commerce by product and service**
.5	**Import trade**
.6	**Export trade**
.7	**Tariff policy**
.9	**Trade agreements**

ENTRIES

7.2   Entries in the schedules and tables are composed of a DDC number in the number column (the column at the left margin), a heading describing the class that the number represents, and often one or more notes. DDC numbers are printed in groups of three digits for ease of reading and copying. All entries (numbers, headings, and notes) should be read in the context of the hierarchy. (For a discussion of the principle of hierarchy, see paragraphs 4.10–4.14.)

7.3   The first three digits of schedule numbers (main classes, divisions, sections) appear only once in the number column, when first used. They are repeated at the top of each page where their subdivisions continue. Subordinate numbers appear in the number column, beginning with a decimal point, with the initial three digits understood.

7.4 Table numbers are given in full in the number column of the tables, and are never used alone. There are seven numbered tables in DDC 21:

T1 Standard Subdivisions
T2 Geographic Areas, Historical Periods, Persons
T3 Subdivisions for the Arts, for Individual Literatures, for Specific Literary Forms
  T3-A Subdivisions for Works by or about Individual Authors
  T3-B Subdivisions for Works by or about More than One Author
  T3-C Notation to Be Added Where Instructed in Table 3-B, 700.4, 791.4, 808–809
T4 Subdivisions of Individual Languages and Language Families
T5 Racial, Ethnic, National Groups
T6 Languages
T7 Groups of Persons

Except for notation from Table 1 (which may be added to any number unless there is an instruction in the schedules or tables to the contrary), table notation may be added only as instructed in the schedules and tables. (For a detailed discussion of the use of the seven tables, see paragraphs 8.3–8.15.)

7.5 When a subordinate topic is a major part of a number, it is sometimes given as a part of a dual heading. For example:

—72 Middle America   Mexico
610 Medical sciences   Medicine

7.6 Some numbers in the schedules and tables are enclosed in parentheses or square brackets. Numbers and notes in parentheses provide options to standard practice. Numbers in square brackets represent topics that have been relocated or discontinued, or are unassigned. Square brackets are also used for standard subdivision concepts that are represented in another location. Bracketed numbers should never be used. (For a discussion of options, see paragraphs 12.1–12.7; for a discussion of bracketed standard subdivisions, see paragraph 7.25.)

7.7 Standard subdivisions are also bracketed under a *hook number*, that is, a number that has no meaning in itself, but is used to introduce specific examples of a topic. The headings for hook numbers often include terms such as "miscellaneous," "other," "special," or "specific." For example:

652.302   Specific levels of skill

[.302 01–.302 09]   Standard subdivisions

Do not use; class in 652.3001–652.3009

Some numbers with headings using the aforementioned terms are not hook numbers, and works may be classed in the number. For example:

004.165   Specific digital microcomputers

Arrange alphabetically by name of microcomputer or microprocessor, e.g., Macintosh®

NOTES

7.8   Notes are important because they supply information that is not obvious in the notational hierarchy or in the heading with regard to order, structure, subordination, and other matters. The notes described below (A) define what is found in the class and its subdivisions; (B) identify topics in *standing room*, i.e., topics with insufficient literature to have their own number; (C) describe what is found in other classes; and (D) explain changes in the schedules and tables. Other notes are described in the sections on number building (paragraphs 8.1–8.20), citation and preference order (paragraphs 9.1–9.6), the Manual (paragraphs 10.1–10.6), and options (paragraphs 12.1–12.5).

7.9   Notes in categories (A) and (C) have hierarchical force (i.e., are applicable to all the subdivisions of a particular number). Those in category (B) do not have hierarchical force.

(A)   Notes That Describe What Is Found in a Class

7.10   *Definition notes* indicate the meaning of the class. For example:

> 004.7   Peripherals
>
> > Input, output, storage devices that work with a computer but are not part of its central processing unit or internal storage

7.11   *Scope notes* indicate whether the meaning of the number is narrower or broader than is apparent from the heading. For example:

> 700   The arts   Fine and decorative arts
>
> > Description, critical appraisal, techniques, procedures, apparatus, equipment, materials of the fine, decorative, literary, performing, recreational arts

7.12   *Former-heading notes* are given only when a heading has been altered to such a degree that the new heading bears little or no resemblance to the old. There is usually no change in the meaning of the number. For example:

> —983 2   Quechuan (Kechuan) and Aymaran languages
>
> Former heading: Andean languages

7.13   *Variant-name notes* are used for synonyms or near synonyms. For example:

> 332.32   Savings and loan association
>
> > Variant names: building and loan associations, home loan associations, mortgage institutions

7.14   *Class-here notes* list major topics in a class. These topics may be broader or narrower than the heading, overlap it, or define another way of looking at essentially the same material. Topics in class-here notes are considered to *approximate the whole* of the class. For example:

371.192   Parent-school relations

Class here parent participation in schools; comprehensive works on teacher-parent relations

Standard subdivisions may be added for any topic in a class-here note. (For a detailed discussion of the use of standard subdivisions for concepts that approximate the whole of a class, see paragraphs 8.3–8.5, the beginning of Table 1, and sections 4 and 5 of the Table 1 note in the Manual.)

7.15   Class-here notes are also used to indicate where interdisciplinary and comprehensive works are classed. In the DDC, *interdisciplinary works* treat a subject from the perspective of more than one discipline. For example:

391   Costume and personal appearance

Class here interdisciplinary works on costume, clothing, fashion

Comprehensive works treat a subject from various points of view within a single discipline. Comprehensive works may be stated or implied in a class-here note. For example:

641.815   Breads and bread-like foods

Class here comprehensive works on baked goods   *(stated)*

—411 5   Highland Region

Class here Scottish Highlands   *(implied)*

(B) Including Notes (Notes That Identify Topics in Standing Room)

7.16   *Including notes* identify topics that have "standing room" in the number where the note is found. Standing room numbers provide a location for topics with relatively few works written about them, but whose literature may grow in the future, at which time they may be assigned their own number. For example:

374.22   Groups in adult education

Including discussion, reading, self-help, special-interest, study groups

Standard subdivisions cannot be added for topics in standing room, nor are other number-building techniques allowed.

7.17   Including notes are also used for the kinds of information previously found in contains, examples, and common name notes.

7.18   Entries in the taxonomic schedules in 579–590 may have two including notes. The first including note contains the scientific taxonomic names above the level of family. The second one contains common and genus names. For example:

593.55   Hydrozoa

Including Chondrophora, Hydroida, Milleporina, Pteromedusae, Siphonophora, Stylasterina, Trachylina

Including hydras, Portuguese man-of-war

(C) Notes on What Is Found in Other Classes

7.19   *Class-elsewhere notes* lead the classifier to interrelated topics, or distinguish among numbers in the same notational hierarchy. They are used to show preference order, to lead to the comprehensive or interdisciplinary number, to override the first-of-two rule, or to lead to broader or narrower topics in the same hierarchical array that might otherwise be overlooked. They may point to a specific number, or to a concept scattered throughout the schedules. All notes that begin with the word "class" are class-elsewhere notes, except when they begin with "class here."

791.43   Motion pictures

Class photographic aspects of motion pictures in 778.53; class made-for-TV movies, videotapes of motion pictures in 791.45

370.15   Educational psychology

Class interdisciplinary works on psychology in 150. Class psychology of a specific topic in education with the topic, plus notation 019 from Table 1, e.g., psychology of adult education 374.0019

155.4   Child psychology

Class interdisciplinary works on child development in 305.231

7.20   *See references* lead from a stated or implied comprehensive number for a concept to the component (subordinate) parts of that concept. See references also lead from the interdisciplinary number for a concept to treatment of the concept in other disciplines. A see reference may point to a specific number, or to a concept scattered throughout the schedules. Each see reference begins with the word "For" and appears in italics. For example:

577.7   Marine ecology

Class here saltwater ecology

For salt lake ecology, see 577.639; for saltwater wetland and seashore ecology, see 577.69

305.4   Women

Class here interdisciplinary works on women, on females

For a specific aspect of women not provided for here, see the aspect, e.g., women's suffrage 324.623, legal status of women 346.0134

7.21   *See-also references* lead the classifier to related topics. They are reminders that minor differences in wording and context can imply differences in classification. Each see-also reference appears in italics. For example:

> 584.3   Liliidae
>
> Class here Liliales, lilies
>
> *For Orchidales, see 584.4*
>
> *See also 583.29 for water lilies*

(D) Notes Explaining Changes or Irregularities in the Schedules and Tables

7.22   *Revision notes* warn users that there have been changes in the subdivisions of a class since the previous edition. A *complete* or *extensive revision* is always introduced by a revision note that appears first under the heading of the class affected. (For an example of a complete revision note, see 570 Life sciences   Biology; for an example of an extensive revision note, see 370 Education.)

7.23   *Discontinued notes* indicate that all or part of the contents of a number have been moved to a more general number in the same hierarchy, or have been dropped entirely. For example:

> [516.363]   Local and intrinsic differential geometry
>
> Number discontinued; class in 516.36
>
> 636.826   Abyssinian cat
>
> Use of this number for other shorthair cats discontinued; class in 636.42

7.24   *Relocation notes* state that all or part of the contents of a number have been moved to a different number. For example:

> [370.19]   Sociology of education
>
> Sociology of education relocated to 306.43
>
> 307.2   Movement of people to, from, within communities
>
> Population size and composition relocated to 304.6

The former number is usually given at the new number, either in the heading or in the appropriate note. For example:

> 306.43   Education [*formerly* 370.19]
>
> 304.6   Population
>
> Class here population size and composition [*both formerly also* 307.2] . . .

7.25   *Do-not-use notes* instruct the classifier not to use all or part of the regular standard subdivision notation or an add table provision in favor of a special provision, or standard subdivisions at a broader number. When the whole standard subdivision should not be used, the note appears under a bracketed standard subdivision; when only part of the standard subdivision is *displaced*, the part displaced is specified. For example:

[374.809]	Historical, geographic, persons treatment
	Do not use; class in 374.9
351.09	Historical and persons treatment
	Do not use for treatment by areas, regions, places in general; class in 351.1. Do not use for treatment by specific continents, countries, localities; class in 351.3–351.9

Number Building

8.1   The classifier will often find that to arrive at a precise number for a work it is necessary to build or synthesize a number that is not specifically printed in the schedules. Such *built numbers* allow for greater depth of content analysis. They are used only when instructions in the schedules make them possible (except for standard subdivisions, which are discussed in paragraphs 8.3–8.5). Number building begins with a base number (always stated in the instruction note) to which another number is added.

8.2   There are four sources of notation from which to build numbers: (A) Table 1 Standard Subdivisions; (B) Tables 2–7; (C) other parts of the schedules; and (D) add tables in the schedules.

(A) Adding Standard Subdivisions from Table 1

8.3   Notation from Table 1 Standard Subdivisions may be added to any number in the schedules unless there is a specific instruction to the contrary. A *standard subdivision* represents a recurring physical form (such as a dictionary, periodical, or index) or approach (such as history or research) and thus is applicable to any subject or discipline. Here are a few examples with the standard subdivision concept underlined:

150.5	Periodical on psychology
230.003	Dictionary of Christianity
340.02573	Directory of lawyers in the U.S.
401	Philosophy of language
507.8	Use of apparatus and equipment in the study and teaching of science, e.g., science fair projects
624.0285	Computer applications in civil engineering
796.912092	Biography of a figure skater
808.0071	Teaching of rhetoric

The classifier should never use more than one zero in applying a standard subdivision unless instructed to do so. If more than one zero is needed, the number of zeros is always indicated in the schedules. When using standard subdivisions with numbers built by adding from Tables 2–7 or other parts of the schedules, be sure to check the table or schedule used for the segment preceding the standard subdivision for special instructions on the number of zeros.

8.4 *Standard-subdivisions-are-added notes* indicate which topics in a multiterm heading may have standard subdivisions added for them because the designated topics are considered to *approximate the whole* of the subject. For example:

> 639.2 Commercial fishing, whaling, sealing
>
> > Standard subdivisions are added for commercial fishing, whaling, sealing together; for commercial fishing alone

Standard-subdivisions-are-added notes do not have hierarchical force.

8.5 *The most important caveat with respect to standard subdivisions is that they are added only for works that cover or approximate the whole of the subject of the number.* For example, a work on black widow spiders of California should be classed in the number for spiders 595.44 (not 595.4409794, the number for spiders in California). The classifier should not attempt to specify California because black widow spiders do not approximate the whole universe of spiders in California. (For further instructions on using Table 1, see the beginning of Table 1 and the Table 1 note in the Manual.)

(B) Adding from Tables 2–7

8.6 The classifier may be instructed to add notation from Tables 2–7 to a base number from the schedules or to a number from a table. A summary of the use of each table follows. Further instructions on using Tables 2–7 are found at the beginning of each table. See also the Manual notes for Tables 2–6.

8.7 *Table 2 Geographic Areas, Historical Periods, Persons.* Notation from Table 2 is added through the use of one of several standard subdivisions from Table 1 (09, 025, 074, etc.), e.g., reading instruction in the primary schools of Australia is 372.40994 (372.4 reading instruction in primary schools + 09 Historical, geographic, persons treatment from Table 1 + 94 Australia from Table 2).

8.8 Area notation is sometimes added directly to schedule numbers, but only when specified in a note. For example:

> 373.3–373.9 Secondary education in specific continents, countries, localities
>
> > Add to base number 373 notation 3–9 from Table 2, e.g., secondary schools of Australia 373.94

8.9 *Table 3 Subdivisions for the Arts, for Individual Literatures, for Specific Literary Forms.* These subdivisions are used in class 800 as instructed, usually following numbers for specific languages in 810–890. Table 3-C subdivisions may be added as instructed to Table 3-B, 700.4, 791.4, and 808–809.

8.10 *Table 4 Subdivisions of Individual Languages and Language Families.* These subdivisions are used as instructed in class 400, following numbers for designated specific languages or language families in 420–490.

8.11　*Table 5 Racial, Ethnic, National Groups.* Notation from Table 5 is added through the use of standard subdivision 089 from Table 1, e.g., Ceramic arts of Chinese artists throughout the world is 738.089951 (738 Ceramic arts + 089 Racial, ethnic, national groups from Table 1 + 951 Chinese from Table 5).

8.12　Table 5 notation may also be added directly to schedule numbers, but only when specified in a note. For example:

> 155.84　Specific racial and ethnic groups
>
> > Add to base number 155.84 notation 03–99 from Table 5, e.g., ethnopsychology of African Americans 155.8496073

8.13　*Table 6 Languages.* The major uses of Table 6 notation are to provide the basis for building a specific language number in 490 (to which notation from Table 4 is sometimes added) and to provide the basis for building a specific literature number in 890 (to which notation from Table 3 is sometimes added). Table 6 notation is also used in Table 2 under —175 Regions where specific languages predominate, and at various points in the schedules.

8.14　*Table 7 Groups of Persons.* Table 7 notation is used to show groups of persons through specific instructions in several places in the tables and schedules. Table 7 notation is added to standard subdivision 024 from Table 1 to show treatment of a subject for persons in specific occupations. For example, Arithmetic for carpenters is 513.024694 (513 Arithmetic + 024 The subject for persons in specific occupations from Table 1 + 694 carpenters from Table 7).

Table 7 notation is also added to standard subdivision 088 from Table 1 to show a subject with respect to a specific occupational or religious group, e.g., economists in Canadian history 971.088339 (971 Canadian history + 088 Occupational and religious groups from Table 1 + 339 economists from Table 7).

8.15　In a few places in the schedules, Table 7 notation is added directly to the schedule number to show persons by religious or occupational group. For example:

> 305.909　Persons by occupation
>
> > Add to base number 305.9 notation 09–99 from Table 7, e.g., persons occupied with religion 305.92, postal workers 305.9383

Elsewhere in the Classification, kinds of persons may be shown through use of notation 08 in Table 1.

(C) Adding from Other Parts of the Schedules

8.16　There are many instructions to make a direct addition to a number from another part of the schedules. For example:

> 809.935　Literature emphasizing subjects
>
> > Add to base number 809.935 notation 001–999, e.g., religious works as literature 809.9352, biography and autobiography as literature 809.93592

In this example, the 2 in 809.9352 comes from 200 Religion, the 92 in 809.93592 from 920 Biography, genealogy, insignia.

8.17   In many cases, part of a number may be added to another number upon instruction. For example:

> 372.011   Elementary education for specific objectives
>
> > Add to base number 372.011 the numbers following 370.11 in 370.111–370.119, e.g., character education 372.0114

In this example, 4 comes from 370.114 Moral, ethical, character education. Sometimes numbers are taken from more than one place in the schedules; in such cases the procedure for the second addition is the same as for the first.

(D) Adding from Tables Found in the Schedules

8.18   Add tables in the schedules provide numbers to be added to designated schedule numbers (identified by an asterisk and accompanying footnoted instruction); these tables must be used only as instructed. For example:

> 616.51   *Papular eruptions
>
> > Including urticaria (hives)
> >
> > Class here dermatitis

The asterisk in the entry above leads to the following footnote: "Add as instructed under 616.1–616.9." The add table at 616.1–616.9 is used only for diseases tagged with an asterisk or for diseases in class-here notes under headings tagged with an asterisk. Notation from the add table, such as 061 Drug therapy, may be used for 616.51 Papular eruptions (tagged with an asterisk) and for dermatitis (in the class-here note); but not for urticaria (hives), because this topic appears in an including note.

8.19   *Subdivisions-are-added notes* indicate which terms in a multiterm heading may have subdivisions applied to them. For example:

> 616.5   *Diseases of integument, hair, nails
>
> > Subdivisions are added for diseases of integument, hair, nails together; for diseases of integument alone

8.20   *Number-built notes* identify and explain the source of built numbers included in the schedules and tables. Built numbers are occasionally included in the schedules or tables to provide additional information or to indicate exceptions to regular add instructions. For example:

> 353.132 63 Foreign service
>
> > Number built according to instructions under 352–354
> >
> > Class here consular and diplomatic services

Citation and Preference Order

9.1   Citation and preference order must be considered when multiple aspects or characteristics of a subject (such as age, area, gender, historical periods, national origin) are provided for in the Classification, and a single work treats more than one of them.

CITATION ORDER

9.2   Citation order allows the classifier to build or synthesize a number using two or more characteristics *(facets)* as specified in instruction notes. Success in building a DDC number requires determining which characteristics apply to a specific work, and then determining from the instructions in the schedule the sequence in which the facets will be ordered.

9.3   Citation order is always carefully detailed in number-building instructions. For example:

> 909.04   History with respect to racial, ethnic, national groups
>
> > Add to base number 909.04 notation 03–99 from Table 5, e.g., world history of Jews 909.04924; then add 0 and to the result add the numbers following 909 in 909.1–909.8, e.g., world history of Jews in 18th century 909.0492407

For a work on the world history of the Jews in the 18th century, this note stipulates the following citation order for the individual facets of the full subject: world history + specific racial, ethnic, national group + historical period. The historical period is introduced by the *facet indicator* 0.

PREFERENCE ORDER

9.4   If there is no provision to show more than one of the aspects or characteristics, it is a matter of preference (because a choice must be made among several characteristics). Preference notes supply either an instruction or table establishing the order in which to make the choice. An example of a preference instruction is found at 305.9:

> 305.9   Occupational and miscellaneous groups
>
> > Unless otherwise instructed, class complex subjects with aspects in two or more subdivisions of 305.9 in the number coming last, e.g., unemployed bibliographers 305.9091 (*not* 305.906941)

In this case, the base subject is a group of persons; the two characteristics are employment status and occupational status. The occupation of bibliographer (305.9091) comes after unemployed status (305.906941) in the classification hierarchy; following the instructions in the preference note, the characteristic that must be chosen is bibliographer (305.9091). (For an example of a preference instruction using a class-elsewhere note, see paragraph 7.19.)

9.5 An example of a table indicating preference order is found at 305:

305 Social groups

Unless other instructions are given, observe the following table of preference, e.g., black Roman Catholic middle-class male youths 305.235 (*not* 305.31, 305.55, 305.62, or 305.896):

Persons by physical and mental characteristics	305.908
Age groups	305.2
Groups by sex	305.3 –.4
Social classes	305.5
Religious groups	305.6
Racial, ethnic, national groups	305.8
Language groups	305.7
Occupational and miscellaneous groups (except 305.908)	305.9

9.6 Classifiers often must distinguish between preference order instructions and the first-of-two rule in the same schedule. If the work treats two subjects, apply the first-of-two rule. If the work treats two aspects of the same subject, apply the preference order instructions. Sometimes, the first-of-two rule and the preference order instructions may lead the classifier in separate directions. For example, a bibliography of newspapers and pamphlets giving equal treatment to each would be classed according to the first-of-two rule in 011.33 (bibliography of pamphlets) rather than 011.35 (bibliographies of newspapers). A bibliography of microform newspapers (i.e., newspapers in microform form) would be classed according to the preference note at 011.1–011.7: "Unless other instructions are given, class a subject with aspects in two or more subdivisions of 011.1–011.7 in the number coming last. . ."; thus, the bibliography of microform newspapers would be classed in 011.36 (bibliographies of microforms) rather than 011.35 (bibliographies of newspapers). (For a discussion of the first-of-two rule, see paragraph 5.7.)

The Manual

10.1 The Manual gives advice on classifying in difficult areas, provides in-depth information on major revisions, and explains the policies and practices of the Decimal Classification Division at the Library of Congress.

10.2 *See-Manual references* in the schedules and tables refer the classifier to the Manual for additional information about a certain number, range of numbers, or choice among numbers. In some cases, the see-Manual reference refers only to a portion of a longer Manual note, or topic narrower than the numbers in the heading, e.g., "See Manual at 573.44 vs. 571.74: Hormones." The see-Manual reference is repeated in the entries for each of the numbers or number spans covered in the Manual note. For example, "See Manual at 657 vs. 658.1511, 658.1512" is listed in the entries for 657, 658.1511, and 658.1512.

10.3 Brief Manual-like notes are sometimes given directly in the schedule or table entry. For example:

631.583 Controlled-environment agriculture

Most works on use of artificial light in agriculture will be classed in 635.0483 and 635.9826

ARRANGEMENT AND FORMAT OF THE MANUAL

10.4   The Manual is arranged by table and schedule numbers, with the broadest span coming before entries for narrower spans or individual numbers. Manual notes are entered under the preferred or "if-in-doubt" number. After the entry number, schedule numbers are listed before table numbers in each part of the heading.

10.5   The terms in the Manual note headings match the terms associated with the same number(s) in the tables and schedules. Additional terms are added in square brackets to provide context. For example:

    782.1 vs. 792.5

        [Musical aspects of] Dramatic vocal forms   Operas vs. [Staging]
        Dramatic vocal forms   Operas

10.6   If the Manual note is very long, or focuses on a topic narrower than the heading, subheadings may be provided. For example:

    004.6 vs. 621.382, 621.3981

        Interfacing and communications [in computer science] vs. Communications engineering vs. [Computer] Interfacing and communications devices

                Digital communications   *(subheading)*

The Relative Index

11.1   The Relative Index is so named because it relates subjects to disciplines. In the schedules, subjects are distributed among disciplines; in the Relative Index subjects are arranged alphabetically, with terms identifying the disciplines in which they are treated subarranged alphabetically under them. For example:

Hospitals	362.11
accounting	657.832 2
animal husbandry	636.083 2
architecture	725.51
armed forces	355.72
Civil War (United States)	973.776
construction	690.551
institutional housekeeping	647.965 1
landscape architecture	712.7
law	344.032 11
liability law	346.031
pastoral theology	291.61
Christianity	259.411
social theology	291.178 321 1
Christianity	261.832 11
social welfare	362.1
United States Revolutionary War	973.376
World War I	940.476
World War II	940.547 6
see also Health services	

In some cases the term implies rather than states the discipline. In the example above, the discipline of architecture is listed, but the discipline of military science is implied by "armed forces."

11.2   The Relative Index is primarily an index to the DDC as a system. It includes most terms found in the schedules and tables, and terms with literary warrant for concepts represented by the schedules and tables. The Relative Index is not exhaustive. If the term sought is not found, the classifier should try a broader term, or consult the schedules and tables directly. The schedules and tables should always be consulted before a number found in the Relative Index is applied.

ARRANGEMENT AND FORMAT OF THE RELATIVE INDEX

11.3   Index entries are arranged alphabetically word by word, e.g., Birth order precedes Birthday. Entries with the same word or phrase but with different marks of punctuation are arranged in the following order:

> Term
> Term. Subheading
> Term (Parenthetical qualifier)
> Term, inverted term qualifier
> Term as part of phrase

Initialisms and acronyms are entered without punctuation and are filed as if spelled as one word. Hyphens are ignored and treated as a space. Terms indented below the main headings are alphabetized in one group even though they may be a mixture of disciplines, topical subheadings, and, to a limited extent, words that form phrases or inverted phrases when combined with the main heading.

11.4   Class numbers are printed in groups of three digits for ease of reading and copying. The spaces are not part of the numbers and do not represent convenient places to abridge the number.

11.5   See-also references are used for synonyms and for references to broader terms (but only when three or more new numbers will be found at the synonym or broader term), and for references to related terms (which may provide only one or two new numbers).

11.6   See-Manual references lead the classifier to relevant discussions in the Manual.

11.7   Numbers drawn from Tables 1–7 are prefixed by T1 through T7. (For a complete listing of table names and abbreviations, see paragraph 7.4.)

INTERDISCIPLINARY NUMBERS

11.8   The first class number displayed in an index entry (the unindented term) is the number for interdisciplinary works. If the term also appears in the tables, the table numbers are listed next, followed by other aspects of the term. The discipline of the interdisciplinary number may be repeated as a subentry if the discipline is not clear. For example:

Adult education	374
	T1—071 5
law	344.074
public administrative support	353.84
public support	379.114
law	344.076 85
university extension	378.175

11.9   Interdisciplinary numbers are not provided for all topics in the Relative Index. They are omitted when the index entry is ambiguous, does not have a disciplinary focus, or lacks literary warrant. In such cases, a blank appears opposite the unindented entry. For example:

Coagulation	
blood	573.159
human physiology	612.115
see also Cardiovascular system	
water supply treatment	628.162 2

(For more information on interdisciplinary numbers, see paragraphs 5.8–5.12, 7.15, 7.19–7.20.)

TERMS INCLUDED IN THE RELATIVE INDEX

11.10   The Relative Index contains most terms found in the headings and notes of the schedules and tables, and synonyms and terms with literary warrant for concepts represented by the schedules and tables. The Relative Index also contains terms for the broad concepts covered in Manual notes.

Inverted phrases are avoided, except for personal and geographic names (see paragraphs 11.12–11.13). Qualifiers are used for homonyms, ambiguous terms, and most initialisms and abbreviations. The most common use of the term may not be qualified. Disciplinary qualifiers are avoided.

11.11   The following types of names from Table 2 Geographic Areas are included in the Index: (A) names of countries; (B) names of the states and provinces of most countries; (C) names of the counties of the United States; (D) names of capital cities and other important municipalities; and (E) names of certain important geographic features.

11.12   Also included in the Relative Index are the personal names of the following groups of persons: heads of state used to identify historical periods, e.g., Louis XIV; founders or revealers of religions, e.g., Muhammad; initiators of schools of thought when used to identify the school, e.g., Smith, Adam.

11.13   Place names and other proper names are generally given in the form specified by the second edition, revised, of the *Anglo-American Cataloguing Rules (AACR2R)*, based on the names established in the Library of Congress authority files. If the AACR2R form is not the common English name, an entry is also included under the familiar form of the name.

Plants and animals are indexed under their scientific and common names.

11.14   The choice of singular form versus plural form follows BS 3700: 1988, *British Standard Recommendations for Preparing Indexes to Books, Periodicals and Other Documents*. Count nouns are generally in the plural; noncount nouns and abstract concepts are generally in the singular. Parts of the body are in the plural only when more than one occurs in a fully formed organism (e.g., ears, hands, nose). Plants and animals follow scientific convention in choice of singular form versus plural form, with the decision based on whether the taxonomic class has more than one member (e.g., Horses, Lion, Lipizzaner horse). Where usage varies across disciplines, the index entry reflects the form preferred in the discipline where interdisciplinary works are classified.

TERMS NOT INCLUDED IN THE RELATIVE INDEX

11.15   Terms usually not included in the Relative Index are:

(A)   Phrases beginning with the adjectival form of countries, languages, nationalities, religions, e.g., English poetry, French cooking, Italian architecture, Hindu prayer books.

(B)   Phrases that contain general concepts represented by standard subdivisions such as education, statistics, laboratories, and management, e.g., Art education, Educational statistics, Medical laboratories, Bank management.

When there is strong literary warrant for such a phrase heading as a sought term, it may be included in the Relative Index, e.g., English literature. When the phrase heading is a proper name or provides the only form of access to the topic, it may also be included, e.g., English Channel, French horns, Amharic literature.

Options

12.1   Some devices are required to enable the Classification to serve needs beyond those represented in the standard English-language edition. At a number of places in the schedules and tables, *options* are provided to give emphasis to an aspect in a library's collection not given preferred treatment in the standard notation. In some cases, options are also suggested to provide shorter notation for the aspect.

12.2   Options are provided throughout the Classification to emphasize jurisdiction; racial, ethnic, national group; language; topic; or other characteristic.

12.3   Options described in notes appear in parentheses and begin with "Option:". Options that apply to the full entry appear at the end of the entry; options to a specific instruction in the entry are indented under the appropriate note. For example, the following option appears at the end of the entry for 420–490:

> (Option B: To give local emphasis and a shorter number to a specific language, place it first by use of a letter or other symbol, e.g., Arabic language 4A0 [preceding 420], for which the base number is 4A. Option A is described under 410)

12.4   Some *optional numbers* are enumerated in the schedules and tables and appear in parentheses in the number column. A special optional arrangement (222)–(224) for books of the Bible as arranged in Tanakh appears as a subsection of the Manual note for 221.

12.5   *Arrange-alphabetically* and *arrange-chronologically notes* are not placed in parentheses, but are also options. They represent suggestions only; the material need not be arranged alphabetically or chronologically. An example of an arrange-alphabetically note is found at 005.133 Specific programming languages: "Arrange alphabetically by name of programming language, e.g., C++."

12.6   Some national libraries and central cataloging authorities assign a few optional numbers, e.g., the National Library of Canada uses C810 for Canadian literature in English and C840 for Canadian literature in French. Optional numbers assigned by the Library of Congress are described in the appendix to the Manual in volume 4.

12.7   Most of the time, however, the responsibility for implementing an option rests with the local library. If options are needed, the library should prefer those described in the Classification rather than attempting local developments.

Close and Broad Classification

13.1   The Dewey Decimal Classification provides the basic option of close versus broad classification. *Close classification* means that the content of a work is specified by notation to the fullest extent possible. *Broad classification* means that the work is placed in a broad class by use of notation that has been logically abridged. For example, a work on French cooking is classed closely at 641.5944 (641.59 Cooking by place + 44 France from Table 2), or broadly at 641.5 (Cooking).

13.2   A library should base its decision on close versus broad classification on the size of its collection and the needs of its users. For example, a work on the sociology of sibling relationships in Canadian society would be most usefully classed in 306.8750971 (306.875 Sibling relationships + 09 Geographic treatment from Table 1 + 71 Canada from Table 2) in a research library or large public library. A small school library might prefer to class the same work in the broader number (306.875) without including the geographic facet in the notation. An engineering library might prefer close classification for works in engineering, but broad classification for disciplines outside science and technology.

13.3   The classifier should never reduce the notation to less than the most specific three-digit number (no matter how small the library's collection). A number also must never be reduced so that it ends in a 0 anywhere to the right of the decimal point.

13.4   One aid to logical abridgment of DDC numbers is the segmentation device provided by the Decimal Classification Division of the Library of Congress and some other centralized cataloging services. A more detailed description of this device is provided in the appendix to the Manual in volume 4.

13.5   The abridged edition of the Dewey Decimal Classification is another source for broad classification. It is intended for libraries with collections of 20,000 volumes or less.

Selected Bibliography

14.1   Classifiers desiring a more in-depth introduction to the Dewey Decimal Classification may consult *Dewey Decimal Classification: A Practical Guide*, 2nd ed., by Lois Mai Chan, John P. Comaromi, Joan S. Mitchell, and Mohinder P. Satija (Albany, N.Y.: OCLC Forest Press, 1996). OCLC Forest Press also issues training materials to accompany each new edition of the DDC.

14.2   For the history of the DDC through Edition 18, see John P. Comaromi's *The Eighteen Editions of the Dewey Decimal Classification* (Albany, N.Y.: Forest Press, 1976).

14.3   For a list of book numbers, consult *Cutter-Sanborn Three-Figure Author Table*, Swanson-Swift revision, 1969 (distributed by Libraries Unlimited, Littleton, Colo.). For descriptive works on book numbers, see John P. Comaromi's *Book Numbers: A Historical Study and Practical Guide to Their Use* (Littleton, Colo.: Libraries Unlimited, 1981) and Donald J. Lehnus's *Book Numbers: History, Principles, and Applications* (Chicago: American Library Association, 1980).

Glossary

The Glossary defines terms used in the Introduction and throughout the schedules and tables. Fuller explanations and examples for many terms may be found in the relevant section of the Introduction. An index to the Introduction and Glossary follows the Glossary.

Add note. A note instructing the classifier to append digits found elsewhere in the Classification to a given base number. *See also* **Base number.**

Add table. *See* **Table (2).**

Application. *See* **Rule of application.**

Approximate the whole. When the topic of a work is nearly coextensive with the topic of a DDC heading, the work is said to "approximate the whole." The term is also used to characterize works that cover more than half the content of the heading, and works that cover representative examples from three or more subdivisions of a class. When a work approximates the whole of a subject, standard subdivisions may be added. Topics that do not approximate the whole are said to be in "standing room" in the number. *See also* **Class-here note; Standard-subdivisions-are-added note; Standing room; Unitary term.**

Arrange-alphabetically note. A note suggesting the option of alphabetical subarrangement where identification by specific name or other identifying characteristic is desired. *See also* **Option.**

Arrange-chronologically note. A note suggesting the option of chronological subarrangement where identification by date is desired. *See also* **Option.**

Artificial digit. A letter or other symbol used optionally as a substitute for digits 0–9 to provide a more prominent location or shorter notation for a jurisdiction; language; literature; religion; racial, ethnic, national group; or other characteristic. *See also* **Option.**

Aspect. An approach to a subject, or a characteristic (facet) of a subject. *See also* **Discipline; Facet; Subject.**

Attraction. *See* **Classification by attraction.**

Author number. *See* **Book number.**

Base number. A number to which other numbers are appended. *See also* **Add note.**

Bibliographic classification. A fully developed classification system that specifies categories down to the finest gradations; it provides the means to relate the categories and to specify in the notation all of the aspects or facets of a work. *See also* **Aspect; Facet.**

Bibliothecal classification. *See* **Library classification.**

Book number. The part of a call number that distinguishes a specific item from other items within the same class number. A library using the Cutter-Sanborn system can have D548d indicate David Copperfield by Dickens (where D stands for the D of Dickens, 548 for "ickens," and d for David Copperfield). *See also* **Call number; Cutter number; Work mark.**

Broad classification. The classification of works in broad categories by logical abridgment, even when more specific numbers are available, e.g., classing a cookbook of Mexican recipes in 641.5 Cooking (instead of in 641.5972 Mexican cooking).

Built number.   A number constructed according to add instructions stated or implied in the schedules and tables.   *See also* **Number building.**

Call number.   A set of letters, numerals, or other symbols (in combination or alone) used by a library to identify a specific copy of a work. A call number may consist of the class number; book number; and other data such as date, volume number, copy number, and location symbol.   *See also* **Book number; Class number.**

Centered entry.   An entry representing a subject covered by a span of numbers, e.g., 372–374 Specific levels of education. The entry is called "centered" because the span of numbers is printed in the center of the page rather than in the number column on the left side of the page. Centered entries are identified by the symbol > in the number column.

Characteristic of division.   *See* **Facet.**

Citation order.   The order in which two or more characteristics (facets) of a class are to be combined in number building. When number building is not permitted or possible, instructions on preference order with respect to the choice of facets are provided.   *See also* **Facet; Number Building; Preference order.**

Class.   (Noun) (1) A group of objects exhibiting one or more common characteristics, identified by a specific notation. (2) One of the ten major groups of the DDC numbered 0–9. *See also* **Main class.** (3) A subdivision of the DDC of any degree of specificity. (Verb) To assign a class number to an individual work.   *See also* **Classify.**

Class-elsewhere note.   A note instructing the classifier on the location of interrelated topics. The note may show preference order, lead to the interdisciplinary or comprehensive number, override the first-of-two rule, or lead to broader or narrower numbers in the same hierarchical array that might otherwise be overlooked.   *See also* **Comprehensive number; Interdisciplinary number; Preference order.**

Class-here note.   An instruction identifying topics that are to be classed in the given number and in its subdivisions. Topics identified in class-here notes, even if broader or narrower than the heading, are said to "approximate the whole" of the number; therefore, standard subdivisions may be added for topics in class-here notes. Class-here notes also may identify the comprehensive or interdisciplinary number for a subject.   *See also* **Approximate the whole; Comprehensive number; Interdisciplinary number.**

Class number.   Notation that designates the class to which a given item belongs.   *See also* **Call number.**

Classification.   A logical system for the arrangement of knowledge.

Classification by attraction.   The classification of a specific aspect of a subject in an inappropriate discipline, usually because the subject is named in the inappropriate discipline but not mentioned explicitly in the appropriate discipline.

Classified catalog.   A catalog arranged according to the notational order of a classification system.

Classify.   (1) To arrange a collection of items according to a classification system. (2) To assign a class number to an individual work.

Close classification.   The classification of works to the fullest extent permitted by the notation.

Coextensive.   Describes a topic equal in scope to the concept represented by the number.

Cognate number.   A number related to another number by virtue of having been built with the same notation to represent a common aspect. For example, 616.241075 Diagnosis of pneumonia and 616.3623075 Diagnosis of hepatitis are cognate numbers of 616.075 because they are built by addition of notation 075 from 616.075, the general number in medicine for diagnosis of diseases.

Comparative table.   A table for a complete or extensive revision that lists in alphabetical order selected topics accompanied by their previous number and their number in the current edition.   *See also* **Equivalence table; Revision.**

Complete revision.   *See* **Revision** *(Complete revision).*

Complex subject.   A complex subject is a subject that has more than one characteristic. For example, "unemployed bibliographers" is a complex subject because it has more than one characteristic (employment status and occupation).   *See also* **Preference order.**

Comprehensive number.   A number (often identified by a "Class here comprehensive works" note) that covers all the components of the subject treated within that discipline. The components may be in a span of consecutive numbers or distributed in the Classification.   *See also* **Interdisciplinary number.**

Coordinate.   Describes a number or topic at a level equal to another number or topic in the same hierarchy.

Cross classification.   Placing works on the same subject in two different class numbers. This tends to occur when works deal with two or more characteristics of a subject in the same class. Notes on preference order should prevent cross classification.   *See also* **Preference order.**

Cross reference.   *See* **Class-elsewhere note; See-also reference; See reference.**

Cutter number.   The notation in a book number derived from the Cutter-Sanborn tables. *See also* **Book number.**

DDC.   Dewey Decimal Classification.

Decimal point.   The dot that follows the third digit in a DDC number. In strict usage the word "decimal" is not accurate; however, common usage is followed in this edition's explanatory material.

Definition note.   A note indicating the meaning of a term in the heading.

Discipline.   An organized field of study or branch of knowledge, e.g., 200 Religion, 530 Physics, 364 Criminology. In the DDC, subjects are arranged by disciplines.   *See also* **Subject.**

Discontinued number. A number from the previous edition that is no longer used because the concept represented by the number has been moved to a more general number in the same hierarchy, or has been dropped entirely. Numbers are discontinued because they identify a concept with negligible current literature or represent a distinction no longer valid in the literature or common perception of the field. Discontinued numbers appear in square brackets. *See also* **Schedule reduction.**

Displaced standard subdivision. A standard subdivision concept given special notation in the schedule in place of its regular notation from Table 1. A do-not-use note is always provided at the regular location of the standard subdivision concept. *See also* **Do-not-use note; Standard subdivisions.**

Division. The second level of subdivision in the Classification, represented by the first two digits in the notation, e.g., 62 in 620 Engineering and allied operations. *See also* **Main class; Section.**

Do-not-use note. A note instructing the classifier not to use all or part of a regular standard subdivision notation or an add table provision in favor of a special provision, or standard subdivisions at a broader number. *See also* **Displaced standard subdivision.**

Dual heading. A heading with two separate terms, the first of which is the main topic and the second of which is a major subordinate topic, e.g., 570 Life sciences   Biology. A dual heading is used when the subject as a whole and the subordinate topic as a whole share the same number. Standard subdivisions may be added for either or both topics in a dual heading.

Dual provision. The inadvertent provision of more than one place for the same aspect of a subject in the Classification.

Entry. (1) In the schedules and tables, a self-contained unit consisting of a number or span of numbers, a heading, and often one or more notes.   (2) In the Relative Index, a term or phrase usually followed by a DDC number.

Equivalence table. A table for a complete or extensive revision that lists in numerical order the classes of the current edition with their equivalent numbers in the previous edition (and vice versa). *See also* **Comparative table; Revision.**

Expansion. The development of a class in the schedules or tables to provide further subdivisions. *See also* **Revision.**

Extensive revision. *See* **Revision** *(Extensive revision).*

Facet. Any of the various categories into which a given class may be divided, e.g., division of the class "people" by the categories race, age, education, and language spoken. Each category contains terms based on a single characteristic of division, e.g., children, adolescents, and adults are characteristics of division of the "ages" category. *See also* **Citation order.**

Facet indicator. A digit used to introduce notation representing a characteristic of the subject. For example, "0" is often used as a facet indicator to introduce standard subdivision concepts.

First-of-two rule. The rule instructing that works dealing equally with two subjects not used to introduce or explain one another are classed in the number coming first in the schedules or tables.

Former-heading note. A note listing the heading associated with the class number in the previous edition. The note is used when the heading has changed so much that it bears little or no resemblance to the previous heading, even though the meaning of the number has remained substantially the same.

Heading. The word or phrase used as the caption of a given class.

Hierarchical force. The principle that the attributes of a class as defined in the heading and in certain basic notes apply to all the subdivisions of the class, and to all other classes to which reference is made.

Hierarchy. The arrangement of a classification system from general to specific. In the Dewey Decimal Classification, the degree of specificity of a class is usually indicated by the length of the notation and the corresponding depth of indention of the heading. Hierarchy may also be indicated by special headings, notes, and centered entries.

Hook number. A number in the Classification without meaning in itself, but used as a "hook" to introduce examples of the topic. Headings for hook numbers may include the words "other," "specific," "special," or "miscellaneous." Standard subdivisions are always bracketed under hook numbers.

Including note. A note enumerating topics that are logically part of the class but are less extensive in scope than the concept represented by the class number. These topics do not have enough literature to warrant their own number. Standard subdivisions may not be added to the numbers for these topics. *See also* **Literary warrant; Standing room.**

Interdisciplinary number. A number (often identified by a "Class here interdisciplinary works" note) to be used for works covering a subject from the perspective of more than one discipline, including the discipline where the interdisciplinary number is located, e.g., the interdisciplinary number for marriage is 306.81 in Sociology. *See also* **Comprehensive number.**

Library classification. A classification designed to arrange the physical items of a library collection. Also called bibliothecal classification.

Literary warrant. Justification for the development of a class or naming of a topic in the schedules, tables, or Relative Index, based on the existence of a body of published literature on the topic.

Main class. One of the ten major subdivisions of the Dewey Decimal Classification, represented by the first digit in the notation, e.g., the 3 in 300. *See also* **Division; Section.**

Manual. A guide to the use of the DDC that is made up primarily of extended discussions of problem areas in the application of the Classification. In the schedules and tables, see-Manual references indicate where relevant discussions are located in the Manual.

Notation. Numerals, letters, and/or other symbols used to represent the main and subordinate divisions of a classification scheme. In the DDC, Arabic numerals are used to represent the classes, e.g., notation 07 from Table 1 and 511.3 from the schedules.

Notational synthesis. *See* **Number building.**

Number building. The process of constructing a number by adding notation from the tables or other parts of the schedules to a base number. *See also* **Base number; Citation order.**

Number column. The column of numbers printed in the left margin of the schedules and tables, and to the right of the alphabetical entries in the Relative Index.

Option. An alternative to standard notation provided in the schedules and tables to give emphasis to an aspect in a library's collection not given preferred treatment in the standard notation. In some cases, an option may provide shorter notation for the aspect. *See also* **Optional number.**

Optional number. (1) A number listed in parentheses in the schedules or tables that is an alternative to the standard notation. (2) A number constructed by following an option. *See also* **Option.**

Order of preference. *See* **Preference order.**

Phoenix schedule. *See* **Revision** *(Complete revision).*

Preference order. The order indicating which one of two or more numbers is to be chosen when different characteristics of a subject cannot be shown in full by number building. A note (sometimes containing a table of preference) indicates which characteristic is to be selected for works covering more than one characteristic. When the notation can be synthesized to show two or more characteristics, it is a matter of citation order. *See also* **Citation order.**

Preference table. *See* **Preference order.**

Reduction of schedules. *See* **Schedule reduction.**

Regularization. The replacement of special developments for standard subdivision concepts by use of the regular standard subdivisions found in Table 1.

Relative Index. The index to the DDC, called "Relative" because it relates subjects to disciplines. In the schedules, subjects are arranged by disciplines. In the Relative Index, subjects are listed alphabetically; indented under each subject is an alphabetical list of the disciplines in which the subject is found.

Relocation. The shifting of a topic in a new edition of the DDC from one number to another number which differs from the old number in respects other than length.

Reused number. A number with a total change in meaning from one edition to another. Usually numbers are reused only in complete revisions or when the reused number has been vacant for two consecutive editions.

Revision. The result of editorial work that alters the text of any class of the DDC. There are three degrees of revision: *Routine revision* is limited to updating terminology, clarifying notes, and providing modest expansions. *Extensive revision* involves a major reworking of subdivisions but leaves the main outline of the schedule intact. *Complete revision* (formerly called a phoenix) is a new development; the base number remains as in the previous edition, but virtually all subdivisions are changed. Changes for complete and extensive revisions are shown through comparative and equivalence tables rather than through relocation notes in the schedule or table affected. *See also* **Comparative table; Equivalence table.**

Routine revision. *See* **Revision** *(Routine revision).*

Rule of application. The rule instructing that works about the application of one subject to a second subject are classified with the second subject.

Rule of three. The rule instructing that works that give equal treatment to three or more subjects that are all subdivisions of a broader subject are classified in the first higher number that includes all of them.

Rule of zero. The rule instructing that subdivisions beginning with zero should be avoided if there is a choice between 0 and subdivisions beginning with 1–9 in the same position in the notation. Similarly, subdivisions beginning with 00 should be avoided when there is a choice between 00 and 0.

Scatter note. A class-elsewhere, see-reference, or relocation note that leads to multiple locations in the Classification.

Schedule reduction. The elimination of certain provisions of a previous edition, often resulting in discontinued numbers. *See also* **Discontinued number.**

Schedules. The series of DDC numbers 000–999, their headings, and notes.

Scope note. A note indicating that the use of a class number is broader or narrower than is apparent from the heading.

Section. The third level of subdivision in the Classification, represented by the first three digits in the notation, e.g., 625 in 625 Engineering of railroads and roads. *See also* **Division; Main class.**

See-also reference. (1) In the schedules and tables, a note leading to classes that are tangentially related to the topic and therefore might be confused with it. (2) In the Relative Index, a note leading to a synonym, broader term, or related term.

See-Manual reference. A note leading to additional information about the number in the Manual.

See reference. A note (introduced by the word "for") that leads from the stated or implied comprehensive or interdisciplinary number for a concept to component parts of the subject located elsewhere. *See also* **Class-elsewhere note.**

Segmentation.   The indication of logical breaks in a number by a typographical device, e.g., slash marks or prime marks. Segmentation marks indicate the end of an abridged number or the beginning of a standard subdivision.

Separates.   Extensive segments of the DDC that are published between editions.

Shelf mark.   *See* **Call number.**

Standard subdivisions.   Subdivisions found in Table 1 that represent frequently recurring physical forms (dictionaries, periodicals) or approaches (history, research) applicable to any subject or discipline. They may be used with any number in the schedules and tables for concepts that approximate the whole of the number unless there are instructions to the contrary.

Standard-subdivisions-are-added note.   A note indicating which topics in a multiterm heading may have standard subdivisions applied to them. The designated topics are considered to approximate the whole of the number.   *See also* **Approximate the whole.**

Standing room.   A term characterizing a topic without sufficient literature to have its own number, and considerably narrower in scope than the class number in which it is included. Standard subdivisions cannot be added to a topic in standing room, nor are other number-building techniques allowed. Topics listed in including notes have standing room in the class number, as do minor unnamed topics that logically fall in the same place in the Classification. To have standing room is the opposite of approximating the whole.   *See also* **Approximate the whole.**

Subdivisions-are-added note.   A note used where subdivisions are provided by add instructions indicating which topics in a multiterm heading may have subdivisions applied to them. The designated topics are considered to approximate the whole of the number. *See also* **Approximate the whole.**

Subject.   An object of study. Also called topic. It may be a person or a group of persons, thing, place, process, activity, abstraction, or any combination of these. In the DDC, subjects are arranged by disciplines. A subject is often studied in more than one discipline, e.g., marriage is studied in several disciplines such as ethics, religion, sociology, and law. *See also* **Discipline.**

Subject catalog.   An index to the contents of a library's collection. If access is provided alphabetically by words, it is called an alphabetical subject catalog. If access is provided by the notation of a library classification system, it is called a classified catalog.   *See also* **Classified catalog.**

Subordinate.   Describes a number or topic at a lower (narrower) level than another number or topic in the same hierarchy.   *See also* **Superordinate.**

Summary.   A listing of the chief subdivisions of a class that provides an overview of its structure. Summaries are also provided for the main classes, divisions, and sections of the Classification as a whole.

Superordinate.   Describes a number or topic at a higher (broader) level than another number or topic in the same hierarchy.   *See also* **Subordinate.**

Synthesis of notation. *See* **Number building.**

Table. In the DDC, a table of numbers that may be added to other numbers to make a class number appropriately specific to the work being classified. The numbers found in a table are never used alone. There are two kinds: (1) The seven numbered tables (Tables 1–7) representing standard subdivisions, geographic areas, languages, ethnic groups, etc. (2) Lists of special notation found in add notes under specific numbers throughout the schedules and occasionally in Tables 1–7. These lists are called add tables.

Table of preference. *See* **Preference order.**

Topic. *See* **Subject.**

Unitary term. A heading or term in a note containing two or more words joined by "and" that have such overlapping meanings that the literature on them is unlikely to be clearly separated. In the DDC, unitary terms are treated as single subjects. Unitary terms that appear in headings or class-here notes may have standard subdivisions added for the whole term or for either of its parts; that is, each part of a unitary term is regarded as approximating the whole. Unitary terms in headings are accompanied by standard-subdivisions-are-added or subdivisions-are-added notes.

> The following are examples of unitary terms:
> Religious congregations and orders
> Economic development and growth
> Colleges and universities
> Disputes and conflicts between states
> Educational tests and measurements

> The following are not considered unitary terms:
> Culture and institutions
> Marriage and family
> Interest and discount

> *See also* **Approximate the whole.**

Variant-name note. A note listing synonyms or near synonyms for a topic when they might not be immediately recognized.

Work mark. The part of a book number that consists of a letter appended to the author (or biographee) designation to show the first letter of the title (or first letter of the surname of the biographer). *See also* **Book number.**

Index to the Introduction and Glossary

References to the Introduction are identified by paragraph numbers. References to the alphabetically arranged Glossary are identified by G.

Publishing History of the Dewey Decimal Classification

EDITION	DATE	PAGES	COPIES	EDITOR
1	1876	44	1,000	Melvil Dewey
2	1885	314	500	Melvil Dewey
3	1888	416	500	Melvil Dewey
4	1891	466	1,000	Evelyn May Seymour
5	1894	467	2,000	Evelyn May Seymour
6	1899	511	7,600	Evelyn May Seymour
7	1911	792	2,000	Evelyn May Seymour
8	1913	850	2,000	Evelyn May Seymour
9	1915	856	3,000	Evelyn May Seymour
10	1919	940	4,000	Evelyn May Seymour
11	1922	988	5,000	Jennie Dorkas Fellows
12	1927	1,243	9,340	Jennie Dorkas Fellows
13	1932	1,647	9,750	Jennie Dorkas Fellows
14	1942	1,927	15,632	Constantin Mazney
15	1951	716	11,200	Milton J. Ferguson
15 rev	1952	927	11,045	Godfrey Dewey
16	1958	2,439	31,011	Benjamin A. Custer
17	1965	2,153	38,677	Benjamin A. Custer
18	1971	2,718	52,892	Benjamin A. Custer
19	1979	3,385	51,129	Benjamin A. Custer
20	1989	3,388	34,706*	John P. Comaromi
21	1996			Joan S. Mitchell

* As of December 1995

Tables

Use of the Tables

Full instructions on the use of the tables are found in paragraphs 8.3–8.15 of the Introduction to the Dewey Decimal Classification in this volume. Instructions for the use of each table precede the table. Important supplemental general instructions for Tables 1, 3, and 5 are found in the Manual in volume 4.

These are auxiliary tables, and are to be used only in conjunction with the schedules. In some instances, numbers from one table may be added to those of another table; but in all cases, numbers from one table or a combination of tables are to be used only with appropriate numbers from the schedules.

The dash preceding each number indicates that the number never stands alone. The dash is omitted when the table number is added to a schedule number to make a complete class number.

Numbers in square brackets [ ] are not used. Numbers in parentheses ( ) are options to standard usage.

Table 1. Standard Subdivisions

The following notation is never used alone, but may be used as required with any regular schedule number, e.g., workbooks (—076 in this table) in arithmetic (513): 513.076. When adding to a number from the schedules, always insert a decimal point between the third and fourth digits of the complete number

Standard subdivisions should be added only when the work in hand covers the whole, or approximately the whole, subject of the number in the schedules. (*See sections 4 and 5 of Manual at Table 1*)

When standard subdivision notation from Table 1 is printed in the schedules, all of its subdivisions as given in this table may be used. In addition, other Table 1 notation that is not printed in the schedules may be used. For example, the fact that 610.9 is printed does not exclude the use of 610.92 or 610.8. (*See section 1 of Manual at Table 1*)

Full notation from Table 1 (beginning with 0) is never added to normal standard subdivisions except where specially provided for in this table. Numbers in the schedules that look as though they were built with notation from this table but have headings with a broader or different meanings are not considered "standard" subdivisions. Hence notation from Table 1 may be added to such schedule numbers

If the 0 subdivisions of a number in a schedule are used for special purposes, use 001–009 for standard subdivisions; if the 00 subdivisions also are used for special purposes, use 0001–0009 for standard subdivisions

(continued)

Table 1. Standard Subdivisions (continued)

Unless other instructions are given, observe the following table of preference, e.g., language and communication in education and research —07 (*not* —014):

Special topics	—04
Persons	—092
Auxiliary techniques and procedures; apparatus, equipment, materials	—028
(*except* —0288)	
Drafting illustrations	—0221
Education, research, related topics	—07
(*except* —074, —075, —076, —077)	
Management	—068
Philosophy and theory	—01
(*except* —0112, —014)	
The subject as a profession, occupation, hobby	—023
The subject for persons in specific occupations	—024
Directories of persons and organizations	—025
Patents and identification marks	—027
Commercial miscellany	—029
Standards	—0218
Formulas and specifications	—0212
Organizations	—0601–0609
Organizations (without subdivision)	—06
History and description with respect to kinds of persons	—08
Treatment by specific continents, countries, localities; extraterrestrial	
worlds	—093–099
Treatment by areas, regions, places in general	—091
Maintenance and repair	—0288
Historical periods	—0901–0905
Forecasting and forecasts	—0112
Museums, collections, exhibits	—074
Museum activities and services Collecting	—075
Review and exercise	—076
Programmed texts	—077
Illustrations, models, miniatures	—022
(*except* —0221)	
Tabulated and related materials	—021
(*except* —0212, —0218)	
Synopses and outlines	—0202
Humorous treatment	—0207
Audiovisual treatment	—0208
Language and communication	—014
Dictionaries, encyclopedias, concordances	—03
Historical and geographic treatment (without subdivision)	—09
Serial publications	—05

See Manual at Table 1

SUMMARY

—01	**Philosophy and theory**
—02	**Miscellany**
—03	**Dictionaries, encyclopedias, concordances**
—04	**Special topics**
—05	**Serial publications**
—06	**Organizations and management**
—07	**Education, research, related topics**
—08	**History and description with respect to kinds of persons**
—09	**Historical, geographic, persons treatment**

—01 Philosophy and theory

Class here methodology, schools of thought

Class interdisciplinary works on philosophy in 100

See Manual at T1—01

—011 Systems

Class here models (simulation), operations research

Add to base number —011 the numbers following 003 in 003.1–003.8, e.g., computer modeling and simulation —0113, forecasting and forecasts —0112; however, for short term forecasts (ten years or less) in a specific historical period, see —0901–0905, plus notation 01 from table under —0901–0905, e.g., forecasts for 1996–1999 —0904901; for forecasts in a specific continent, country, locality, see —093–099, plus notation 01 from table under —093–099, e.g., forecasts for United States —097301

Class models (simulations) in study and teaching in —078

See Manual at T1—0285 vs. T1—0113; also at 510, T1—0151 vs. 003, T1—011

—012 Classification

Class classification of bibliographic material in 025.42; class classification of bibliographic material on a specific subject in 025.46; class interdisciplinary works on classification in 001.012

—013 Value

Class interdisciplinary works on values in 121.8

—014   **Language and communication**

> Including content analysis, semiotic analysis
>
> Class here terminology
>
> Class subject headings and thesauri in information retrieval in 025.49001–025.49999; class interdisciplinary works on communication in 302.2; class interdisciplinary works on language in 400; class interdisciplinary works on terminology in 401.4
>
> > *For dictionaries, see —03*
> >
> > *See Manual at T1—014 vs. T1—03; also at T1—014 vs. T4—864*

—014 2   **Etymology**

—014 8   **Abbreviations and symbols**

> Symbols classed here are limited to conventional or standard signs such as those used in mathematics, chemistry, flow charts, circuit diagrams, maps, road signs
>
> Class interdisciplinary works on abbreviations in 411; class interdisciplinary dictionaries of abbreviations in 413.1; class interdisciplinary works on symbols in 302.2223

—015   **Scientific principles**

> Use of science to analyze and describe the subject, to support or attack its validity, to carry out operations in the subject, to provide information needed in a subject
>
> Add to base number —015 the numbers following 5 in 510–590, e.g., mathematical techniques —0151, meteorology —015515
>
> Class scientific method in —072; class statistical methods in —0727; class interdisciplinary works on natural sciences and mathematics in 500
>
> > *For psychological principles, see —019*
> >
> > *See Manual at T1—015 vs. T1—0245–0246; also at 510, T1—0151 vs. 003, T1—011; also at 510, T1—0151 vs. 004–006, T1—0285; also at 519.5, T1—015195 vs. 001.422, T1—0727*

—(016)   **Bibliographies, catalogs, indexes**

> (Optional number: prefer 016)

—019   Psychological principles

> Use for applications of individual psychology only, not for applications of
> social psychology
>
> Including psychology of learning specific subjects [*formerly also* —071,
> 370.156]
>
> Class social psychology in 302; class psychology of learning a specific
> subject at elementary level in 372.3–372.8; class interdisciplinary works on
> psychology in 150
>
> > *See Manual at T1—019: Counseling; also at 302–307 vs. 150, T1—019*

—02   **Miscellany**

SUMMARY

—020 2–020 8	**[Synopses and outlines, humorous treatment, audiovisual treatment]**
—021	**Tabulated and related materials**
—022	**Illustrations, models, miniatures**
—023	**The subject as a profession, occupation, hobby**
—024	**The subject for persons in specific occupations**
—025	**Directories of persons and organizations**
—027	**Patents and identification marks**
—028	**Auxiliary techniques and procedures; apparatus, equipment, materials**
—029	**Commercial miscellany**

—020 2   Synopses and outlines

> Including chronologies
>
> Class works called synopses and outlines that are regular treatises or
> introductions to a subject in 001–999 without use of notation 0202 from
> Table 1; class interdisciplinary chronologies in 902.02

—020 7   Humorous treatment

> > *See Manual at T1—0207 vs. T3B—7, T3A—8 + 02, T3B—802,*
> > *T3B—8 + 02, T3A—8 + 07, T3B—807, T3B—8 + 07*

—020 8   Audiovisual treatment

—021   Tabulated and related materials

> Including statistics, statistical graphs
>
> Class interdisciplinary collections of statistics in 310
>
> > *See also —0727 for analysis of statistical data, —0728 for methods of*
> > *presenting statistical data*

—021 2   Formulas and specifications

> Class here formulas and specifications in specific times and places
> [*formerly* —09], tables of values for use in formulas and specifications
>
> Use of this number for comprehensive works on tables discontinued;
> class in —021

—021 6   Lists, inventories, catalogs

Not provided for elsewhere

Class directories of persons and organizations in —025; class lists and catalogs of products and services offered for sale, lease, or free distribution in —029; class catalogs of collections and exhibits in —074; class price trends for collectors in —075; class bibliographic catalogs on specific subjects in 016; class directories of databases on specific subjects in 016.02506

—021 8   Standards

Add to base number —0218 notation 1–9 from Table 2, e.g., standards in Israel —02185694; however, for persons treatment, see —092

Class interdisciplinary works on standardization in 389.6; class interdisciplinary collections of standards in 602.18

For specifications, see —0212

—022   Illustrations, models, miniatures

Including graphs

Class statistical graphs in —021; class interdisciplinary works on illustrations in 760

—022 1   Drafting illustrations

Class interdisciplinary works on drafting illustrations in 604.2

See also —0728 for techniques of presenting statistical data

—022 2   Pictures and related illustrations

Class here cartoons, drawings, pictorial charts and designs, sketches

Class interdisciplinary works on cartoons in 741.5

For humorous cartoons, see —0207

See Manual at T1—0222 vs. T1—0223

—022 3   Maps, plans, diagrams

Class comprehensive works on historical maps and atlases in 911; class interdisciplinary works on maps, plans, diagrams; on maps, plans, diagrams of geography and travel in general and in specific areas in 912

See Manual at T1—0222 vs. T1—0223; also at 912 vs. T1—0223

—022 8   Models and miniatures

Class simulation models in —011; class model and miniature educational exhibits in —074; class interdisciplinary works in 688.1

—023   The subject as a profession, occupation, hobby

     Class here vocational guidance, choice of vocation, career opportunities, occupational specialties, professional relationships; the subject as a profession, occupation, hobby for specific kinds of persons

     Add to base number —023 notation 1–9 from Table 2, e.g., the subject as a profession in Great Britain —02341; however, for persons treatment, see —092

     Class interdisciplinary works on professional relationships in 331.7; class interdisciplinary works on vocational guidance, choice of vocation, career opportunities, occupational specialties in 331.702; class interdisciplinary works on hobbies in 790.13

—024   The subject for persons in specific occupations

     Former heading: Works for specific types of users

     Class here the subject for persons in specific occupations in specific times and places [*formerly* —09]

     See Manual at T1—024; also at T1—088 vs. T1—024

—[024 03–024 08]   The subject for persons with various nonoccupational characteristics

     Relocated to —08

—024 09–024 9   Specific occupations

     Add to base number —024 notation 09–9 from Table 7, e.g., the subject for engineers —02462

     See Manual at T1—024; also at T1—015 vs. T1—0245–0246

—025   Directories of persons and organizations

     Class here directories of public officials and employees; membership lists containing directory information, e.g., employment and education

     Add to base number —025 notation 1–9 from Table 2, e.g., directories of Ohio —025771; however, for persons treatment, see —092

     Class directories giving biographical information in —0922

     See also —029 for directories of products and services, 016.02506 for directories of databases on specific subjects

     See Manual at T1—025 vs. T1—0601–0609; also at 338 vs. 060, 381, 382, 670.0294, 910, T1—025, T1—0294, T1—0296

—(026)   **Law**

                 (Optional number; prefer 341–347)

                 Add to base number —026 notation 1–9 from Table 2, e.g., law of Australia —02694; however, for persons treatment, see —092

                 A special development of —026 covering treaties and cases in international law is given in centered entry at 341.2–341.7 for use with subdivisions in 341.2–341.7; another special development of —026 covering laws, regulations, cases, procedures, courts in the rest of law is given in centered entry at 342–347 for use with subdivisions in 342–347

—027   **Patents and identification marks**

—027 2   **Patents**

                 Add to base number —0272 notation 1–9 from Table 2, e.g., patents of Japan —027252; however, for persons treatment, see —092

                 Class interdisciplinary works on patents in 346.0486; class interdisciplinary collections of patents in 608

>   —027 5–027 8   **Identification marks**

            Class comprehensive works in —027

—027 5   **Trademarks and service marks**

                 Class comprehensive works on trademarks generally found on products rather than identifying services in 602.75; class interdisciplinary works on trademarks and service marks in 929.95

—027 7   **Ownership marks**

—027 8   **Artists' and craftsmen's marks**

                 Class interdisciplinary works in 700.278

—028   **Auxiliary techniques and procedures; apparatus, equipment, materials**

                 See Manual at T1—028

—028 4   **Apparatus, equipment, materials**

                 Limited to apparatus, equipment, materials used in a subject

                 Class here instruments, instrumentation

                 Class apparatus, equipment, materials used in a specific auxiliary technique or procedure in —0285–0289; class collectibles, memorabilia in —075; class products of a subject in 001–999 without adding notation 0284 from Table 1

>   **—028 5–028 9   Auxiliary techniques and procedures**

     Class laboratory manuals in —078; class comprehensive works in —028

     For drafting illustrations, see —0221; for research techniques, statistical methods, see —072

—028 5   Data processing   Computer applications

     Class here data processing in research

     Unless it is redundant, add to base number —0285 the numbers following 00 in 004–006, e.g., digital microcomputers —0285416, but digital computers —0285 (*not* —02854)

     Class computer modeling and simulation in —0113; class interdisciplinary works on data processing in 004

     See Manual at T1—0285; also at T1—0285 vs. T1—0113; also at T1—0285 vs. T1—068; also at 510, T1—0151 vs. 004–006, T1—0285

—028 6   Waste technology

     Class here environmental engineering, pollution control technology

     Class interdisciplinary works on waste technology in 628.4; class interdisciplinary works on pollution control technology in 628.5

—028 7   Testing and measurement

     Class here laboratory manuals for testing, mensuration

     Class technology of testing and measuring instruments in 681.2; class interdisciplinary works on measurement and mensuration in 530.8

     For educational testing, see —076

—028 8   Maintenance and repair

     Use this subdivision only with numbers denoting fabrication, manufacture, construction, installation, not with numbers denoting use, operation, or application when these are different, e.g., maintenance and repair of textile manufacturing machinery 681.76770288 (*not* 677.02850288), of tools 621.900288

     Class here conservation, preservation, restoration

     Maintenance and repair in areas, regions, places in general relocated to —091, plus notation 028 from table under —093–099; maintenance and repair in specific continents, countries, localities relocated to —093–099, plus notation 028 from table under —093–099

     Class conservation in the sense of environmental engineering and waste technology in —0286; class interdisciplinary works on maintenance and repair in 620.0046; class interdisciplinary works on artistic conservation, preservation, restoration in 702.88

     See also —0682 for management of maintenance

—028 9   Safety measures

Use only for personal safety and safety engineering

Class interdisciplinary works on safety in 363.1; class interdisciplinary works on personal safety in 613.6; class interdisciplinary works on safety engineering in 620.86

See Manual at 363.1

—029   Commercial miscellany

Class here listings of products and services offered for sale, lease, or free distribution

Class house organs in —05; class interdisciplinary commercial miscellany in 380.1029

See also —074 for listings of noncommercial collections and exhibits

—029 4   Trade catalogs and directories

Listing of products and services without independent evaluations or comparisons

Including commercial circulars and advertisements

Class here product directories, price lists, listings of free products and services, prospectuses of products for sale or lease

Add to base number —0294 notation 4–9 from Table 2 for the area in which the products are sold, e.g., directories of products sold in Mexico —029472

Class noncurrent offers for sale used primarily to illustrate civilization and customs of an earlier period in 900

For catalogs of bibliographic materials on specific subjects, see 016

See also —0296 for listings of products and services with independent evaluations or comparisons

See Manual at T1—074 vs. T1—0294; also at 338 vs. 060, 381, 382, 670.0294, 910, T1—025, T1—0294, T1—0296

—029 6   Buyers' guides and consumer reports

Listings of products and services with independent evaluations or comparisons

Including evaluations of single products

Add to base number —0296 notation 4–9 from Table 2 for the area in which products are sold, e.g., buyers' guides for Canadian market —029671

Class evaluation and purchasing manuals in —0297

See also —0294 for listings of products and services without independent evaluations or comparisons

See Manual at 338 vs. 060, 381, 382, 670.0294, 910, T1—025, T1—0294, T1—0296

—029 7   Evaluation and purchasing manuals

Manuals that explain how to evaluate and purchase products and services but do not contain listings of what is available

Class here price trends

Class listings of products and services with independent evaluations and comparisons in —0296; class interdisciplinary evaluation and purchasing manuals in 381.33

For price trends for collectors, see —075

See also —0294 for listings of products and services without independent evaluations or comparisons, —0687 for management of procurement

—029 9   Estimates of labor, time, materials

Class here quantity surveying

Class interdisciplinary works on quantity surveying in 692.5

—03   **Dictionaries, encyclopedias, concordances**

Class interdisciplinary encyclopedias in 030; class interdisciplinary dictionaries in 413

See Manual at T1—014 vs. T1—03

—04   **Special topics**

Use this subdivision only when it is specifically set forth in the schedules. Add other standard subdivisions —01–09 to it and its subdivisions as required, e.g., participatory democracy in France 323.0420944

—05   **Serial publications**

Regardless of frequency

Class here house organs, magazines, newspapers, yearbooks

Class monographic series in 001–999 without adding notation 05 from Table 1; class interdisciplinary serial publications in 050; class interdisciplinary newspapers in 071–079

For a special kind of serial publication, see the kind, e.g., directories in serial form —025, administrative reports of organizations —06

—06   **Organizations and management**

>   **—060 1–060 9   Organizations**

Class here Greek-letter societies [*formerly* 371.854], student organizations [*formerly* 371.84]; history, charters, regulations, membership lists, administrative reports

Class directories of organizations, membership lists with directory information in —025; class organizations engaged in education, research, related topics in —07; class business enterprises in 338.7; class government administrative and military organizations in 350; class nonadministrative proceedings and reports in 001–999 without adding notation 06 from Table 1; class comprehensive works on organizations active in a subject in —06; class interdisciplinary works on organizations in 060

See Manual at T1—0601–0609; also at T1—025 vs. T1—0601–0609; also at T1—072 vs. T1—0601–0609

—060 1   International organizations

Class guides to national organizations of the world in —06

—060 3–060 9   National, state, provincial, local organizations

Add to base number —060 notation 3–9 from Table 2, e.g., national organizations in France —06044

—068   Management

The science and art of conducting organized enterprises and projects

Class management in the sense of carrying out ordinary activities of a subject in 001–999 without adding notation 068 from Table 1, e.g., management of patients 616 (*not* 616.0068); class interdisciplinary works in 658

See Manual at 658 and T1—068; also at T1—0285 vs. T1—068; also at T1—068 vs. 353–354; also at 302.35 vs. 658, T1—068

(Option: Class management of specific enterprises in 658.9)

—068 1 **Organization and financial management**

Including fund raising, initiation of business enterprises

For internal organization, see —0684

See also —079 for fundraising for competitions, festivals, awards, financial support

See Manual at 658.15 and T1—0681; also at 338.09 vs. 332.67309, 338.6042, 346.07, 658.11, T1—0681, 658.21, T1—0682

—068 2 **Plant management**

Including equipment and utilities; maintenance

Class here comprehensive works on energy management

For a specific aspect of energy management, see the aspect, e.g., energy conservation in production management —0685

See also —0288 for technology of maintenance

See Manual at 658.2 and T1—0682; also at 338.09 vs. 332.67309, 338.6042, 346.07, 658.11, T1—0681, 658.21, T1—0682; also at 647 vs. 647.068, 658.2, T1—0682

—068 3 **Personnel management (Human resource management)**

Including management of fringe benefits, of in-service training and residency, of wages and salaries

Class comprehensive works on in-service training and residency in —07155; class interdisciplinary works on labor relations in 331.88

For management of executive personnel, see —0684

See also 331.21 for wages, see also 331.255 for fringe benefits

See Manual at 658.3 and T1—0683; also at 331 vs. 658.3

—068 4 **Executive management**

Including internal organization, safety management

For a specific aspect of safety management, see the aspect, e.g., personnel safety —0683

See Manual at 658.4 and T1—0684

—068 5 **Management of production**

Class factory operations engineering in 670.42

See Manual at 658.5 and T1—0685

—068 7 **Management of materials**

Including physical distribution, procurement of office equipment

See also —0297 for evaluation and purchasing manuals

See Manual at 658.7 and T1—0687

—068 8   Management of distribution (Marketing)

> Including market research, personal selling

> Class financial aspects of marketing management in —0681; class results of market research in 380.1–382

>> *For physical distribution, see —0687; for advertising, see 659.1*

>> *See Manual at 658.8 and T1—0688; also at 380.1 vs. 658.8; also at 658.8, T1—0688 vs. 659*

—07   Education, research, related topics

> Class here subject-oriented study programs; comprehensive works on education and research, on resources for education and research

> Psychology of learning specific subjects relocated to —019

>> *For a specific resource not provided for here, see the resource, e.g., directories —025, bibliographies 016, libraries 026*

>> *See Manual at 016 vs. 026, T1—07*

SUMMARY

—070 1–070 9	**Geographic treatment**	
—071	**Education**	
—072	**Research; statistical methods**	
—074	**Museums, collections, exhibits**	
—075	**Museum activities and services**	**Collecting**
—076	**Review and exercise**	
—077	**Programmed texts**	
—078	**Use of apparatus and equipment in study and teaching**	
—079	**Competitions, festivals, awards, financial support**	

—070 1–070 9   Geographic treatment

> Add to base number —070 notation 1–9 from Table 2, e.g., education and research in France —07044

—071   Education

Class here curricula directed toward specific subject objectives [*formerly* 375.008], curricula in specific subjects [*formerly* 375.01–375.9], study (education), teaching, vocational education

Class student organizations in —0601–0609; class religious education to inculcate religious faith and values in 291.75 (*not* 200.71); class religious education to inculcate Christian faith and values in 268 (*not* 230.0071); class textbooks, school activities in a subject in 001–999 without adding notation 071 from Table 1; class comprehensive works on education and research in —07; class interdisciplinary works on education in 370; class interdisciplinary works on teaching in 371.102

For review and exercise, see —076; for use of apparatus and equipment in education, see —078; for competitions, festivals, awards, financial support in education, see —079; for special education in specific subjects, see 371.9

See Manual at 407.1, T1—071 vs. 401.93, 410.71, 418.0071, T4—80071

—071 01–071 09   Geographic treatment

Class here treatment of any two levels of education, e.g., secondary and higher education

Add to base number —0710 notation 1–9 from Table 2, e.g., education in Argentina —071082

\>   —071 1–071 5   Specific levels of education

Class comprehensive works in —071

For education in specific subjects at elementary level, see 372.3–372.8

—071 1   Higher education

Class here curricula directed toward specific subject objectives in higher education [*formerly* 378.1992–378.1998], professional education

Add to base number —0711 notation 1–9 from Table 2, e.g., universities in Japan —071152; however, for persons treatment, see —092

For extension departments and services, see —0715

—071 2   Secondary education

Class here curricula directed toward specific subject objectives in secondary education [*formerly* 373.192–373.198]

Add to base number —0712 notation 1–9 from Table 2, e.g., secondary schools in rural regions —07121734; however, for persons treatment, see —092

—071 5   Adult education and on-the-job training

Class here continuing, further, lifelong, permanent, recurrent education; correspondence schools and courses, distance education; extension departments and services; institutes and workshops; occupational and vocational training; radio and television classes

—[071 52–071 54]   Institutes and workshops, radio and television classes, correspondence courses

Numbers discontinued; class in —0715

—071 55   On-the-job training

Class here apprenticeship, in-service training, residency

Class management of on-the-job training by employers in —0683; class interdisciplinary works in 331.2592

—072   Research; statistical methods

Class here laboratory manuals used in research, research techniques not provided for elsewhere in Table 1, comprehensive works on scientific method

Class operations research in —011; class financial support of research in —079; class results of research in 001–999 without adding notation 072 from Table 1; class interdisciplinary works on research in 001.4

For scientific method used in systems analysis, see —011. For a specific research technique provided for elsewhere in Table 1, see the technique, e.g., mathematical techniques —0151, data processing —0285, testing —0287

See Manual at T1—072 vs. T1—0601–0609

—072 01–072 09   Geographic treatment of research and statistical methods together, of research alone

Add to base number —0720 notation 1–9 from Table 2, e.g., research in England —072042

See Manual at T1—07201–07209 vs. T1—0722–0724

>   —072 2–072 4   Specific kinds of research

Avoid notation for a specific kind of research when it is redundant, e.g., historical research in history 907.2 (*not* 907.22)

Statistical methods used in specific kinds of research relocated to —0727

Class comprehensive works in —072

See Manual at T1—07201–07209 vs. T1—0722–0724

—072 2   Historical research

Including use of case studies

Class here historiography

It is redundant to use the final digit of —0722 in history (900); stop at —072, e.g., historical research in European history 940.072

Class interdisciplinary works on historical research in 001.432; class interdisciplinary works on historiography in 907.2

—072 3   Descriptive research

Including sampling techniques

Class here data collection, surveys and survey methodology

Class management of information collection in —0684; class collection of operational data in 001–999 without adding notation 0723 from Table 1; class interdisciplinary works on data collection in research in 001.433

For analysis of statistical data, see —0727; for presentation of statistical data, see —0728

See also —075 for collection of objects

—072 4   Experimental research

Class models (simulation) in —011

—072 7   Statistical methods

Class here statistical methods used in specific kinds of research [*formerly* —0722–0724]

Class statistical methods used in systems analysis in —011; class interdisciplinary works on statistical methods in 001.422

For data collection, see —0723; for presentation of statistical data, see —0728

See also —021 for works containing the statistics themselves

See Manual at 519.5, T1—015195 vs. 001.422, T1—0727

—072 8   Presentation of statistical data

Class here graphic presentation

Class the statistics themselves (no matter how presented) in —021

—074   **Museums, collections, exhibits**

Class here catalogs, lists regardless of whether or not articles are offered for sale; guidebooks, history and description

To show area in which museums, collections, exhibits are found, add to base number —074 notation 1–9 from Table 2, e.g., museums in Pennsylvania —074748

Class comprehensive works on museology of a subject in —075; class interdisciplinary works in 069

> *For collections of books and related informational materials in specific subjects, see 016. For collections representing a specific time period, see the period in —0901–0905, plus notation 074 from table under —0901–0905, e.g., collections from 19th century —09034074; for collections representing a specific kind of area, region, place, see the kind of area, region, place in —091, plus notation 074 from table under —093–099, e.g., collections from Mediterranean region —091822074; for treatment by area represented in the collections, see the area in —093–099, plus notation 074 from table under —093–099, e.g., collections of Brazilian objects —0981074, collections of Brazilian objects in Pennsylvania —0981074748*

> *See Manual at T1—074 vs. T1—0294*

—075   **Museum activities and services   Collecting**

Class here museology, collectibles, memorabilia, price trends for collectors

Class interdisciplinary works on museum activities and services in 069; class interdisciplinary works on museum collecting in 069.4; class interdisciplinary works on recreational collecting in 790.132

> *For specific museological techniques not provided for here, see —028, e.g., maintenance and repair of collected objects —0288; for activities and services of or relating to specific museums, collections, exhibits, see —074*

—075 3   **Organizing and preparing collections and exhibits**

Including prevention of theft; recording, registration, storage, transportation

—075 5   **Service to patrons**

Including regulation of patrons

—076   Review and exercise

Including workbooks with problems, questions, answers; civil service examinations; testing, test construction and evaluation

Class programmed texts with problems, questions, answers in —077; class interdisciplinary works on civil service examinations in 351.076; class interdisciplinary works on examinations and tests in 371.26

For review and exercise using apparatus and equipment, see —078

(Option: Class civil service examinations in specific subjects in 351.076)

—077   Programmed texts

Class here programming of texts and their use

—078   Use of apparatus and equipment in study and teaching

Class here laboratory manuals, student projects and experiments

For laboratory manuals used in testing, see —0287; for laboratory manuals used in research, see —072

—078 5   Computer-assisted instruction

Class here teaching machines

Unless it is redundant, add to base number —0785 the numbers following 00 in 004–006, e.g., use of digital microcomputers —0785416, but digital computers —0785 (*not* —07854); interactive video —078567

—079   Competitions, festivals, awards, financial support

Including fund raising to support such activities; judging competitions

Class here bursaries, fellowships and scholarships, grants-in-aid, honorary titles, prizes

Add to base number —079 notation 4–9 from Table 2, e.g., competitions in California —079794
Subdivisions are added for any or all topics in heading

Class description of works that are entered into competitions and festivals, that receive awards, or that are the results of financial support in 001–999 without adding notation 079 from Table 1; class interdisciplinary works on awards in 929.81

See also —0681 for fund raising

—08   **History and description with respect to kinds of persons**

Class here the subject for persons with various nonoccupational characteristics [*formerly also* —02403–02408], minorities

Add to each subdivision identified by * as follows:

01	Forecasting and forecasts
02	Statistics and illustrations
021	Statistics
022	Illustrations
05	Serial publications
07	Museums and collecting
074	Museums, collections, exhibits

     Add to base number 074 notation 4–9 from Table 2, e.g., collections in Pennsylvania 074748

075	Collecting objects
09	Historical and geographic treatment

     Add to 09 notation 01–9 from Table 2, e.g., the kind of person in Japan 0952

Unless other instructions are given, class a subject with aspects in two or more subdivisions of —08 in the number coming last, e.g., children with disabilities —087 (*not* —083)

Class racial, ethnic, national minorities in —089; class treatment of specific kinds of persons as individuals in —092, e.g., collected biography of specific racial, ethnic, national groups —0923

See Manual at T1—08

SUMMARY

—080 1–080 9	**Forecasting, statistics, illustrations, serials, museums and collecting, historical and geographic treatment**
—081	**Men**
—082	**Women**
—083	**Young people**
—084	**Persons in specific stages of adulthood**
—085	**Relatives** **Parents**
—086	**Persons by miscellaneous social characteristics**
—087	**Persons with disabilities and illnesses, gifted persons**
—088	**Occupational and religious groups**
—089	**Racial, ethnic, national groups**

—080 1–080 9   Forecasting, statistics, illustrations, serials, museums and collecting, historical and geographic treatment

     Add to base number —080 the numbers following 0 in notation 01–09 from table under —08, e.g., statistics —08021

—081   *****Men**

     Class here males

     See Manual at T1—081 and T1—082, T1—08351, T1—08352, T1—08421, T1—08422

*Add as instructed under —08

22

—082	*Women

Class here females; feminist views of a subject, e.g., feminist Christian theology 230.082

> *For women with characteristics of another group, see the group, e.g., unmarried mothers —086947*

> *See Manual at T1—081 and T1—082, T1—08351, T1—08352, T1—08421, T1—08422*

—083	*Young people

Class here children

> *For young people with characteristics of another group, see the group, e.g., abandoned children, abused children, children born out of wedlock, orphans —086945*

—083 2	*Infants

Children from birth through age two

—083 3	*Children three to five

Class here preschool children

—083 4	*Children six to eleven

Class here school children

> *For school children over eleven, see —0835*

—083 41	*Boys six to eleven
—083 42	*Girls six to eleven
—083 5	*Young people twelve to twenty

Variant names: adolescents, teenagers, young adults, youth

Comprehensive works on young adults relocated to —0842

Class youth twenty-one and over in —0842

—083 51	*Males twelve to twenty

> *See Manual at T1—081 and T1—082, T1—08351, T1—08352, T1—08421, T1—08422*

—083 52	*Females twelve to twenty

> *See Manual at T1—081 and T1—082, T1—08351, T1—08352, T1—08421, T1—08422*

—084	Persons in specific stages of adulthood

Class comprehensive works on adults in 001–999 without adding notation 084 from Table 1

---

*Add as instructed under —08

—084 2   *Young adults

         Aged twenty-one and above

         Class here comprehensive works on young adults [*formerly* —0835]

         For young adults under twenty-one, see —0835

—084 21   *Young men

            See Manual at T1—081 and T1—082, T1—08351, T1—08352, T1—08421, T1—08422

—084 22   *Young women

            See Manual at T1—081 and T1—082, T1—08351, T1—08352, T1—08421, T1—08422

—084 4   *Persons in middle adulthood

—084 6   *Persons in late adulthood

—085   *Relatives   Parents

         Class here adoptive and foster parents, stepparents

—085 1   *Fathers

—085 2   *Mothers

         For unmarried mothers, see —086947

—085 3   *Grandparents

         Including great-grandparents of any degree (ancestors)

—085 4   *Progeny

         Class here children considered in relation to parents

—085 5   *Siblings

         Brothers and sisters by blood, adoption, foster care, remarriage of parents

—086   *Persons by miscellaneous social characteristics

         Not provided for elsewhere

—086 2   *Persons by social and economic levels

         Class here social classes

         Class groups with special social status in —0869

—086 21   *Upper classes

         Including nobility, royalty, wealthy

         Class here elites

         For reigning monarchs and their regents, see —088351

*Add as instructed under —08

—086 22	*Middle classes (Bourgeoisie)
	Including entrepreneurs, managers, professionals
	Class here moderately well-to-do persons
	For lower middle classes, see —08623
—086 23	*Lower middle classes
	Class here moderate-income persons, the working class in developed areas, blue collar workers
—086 24	*Lower classes
	Including migrant workers, unskilled workers
	Class blue collar workers in —08623; class peasants, sharecroppers in —08863
	For slaves, serfs, peons, see —08625; for the poor, see —086942
—086 25	*Slaves, serfs, peons
—086 3	*Persons by level of cultural development
—086 31	*Persons of high cultural development
	Class here intellectuals
—086 32	*Persons of medium cultural development
—086 33	*Persons of low cultural development
	Including nonliterate persons
	Class here culturally disadvantaged persons
—086 5	*Persons by marriage status
	Including unmarried couples
—086 52	*Single persons
	For separated and divorced persons, see —08653; for widowed persons, see —08654
—086 523	*Engaged persons
—086 53	*Separated and divorced persons
	Subdivisions are added for either or both topics in heading
—086 54	*Widowed persons
—086 55	*Married persons
	Including persons married in common law
	For polygamous persons, see —08659
—086 59	*Polygamous persons

*Add as instructed under —08

—086 6   *Persons by sexual orientation

       Including persons with no sexual orientation, transsexuals

—086 62   *Heterosexuals

—086 63   *Bisexuals

—086 64   *Gays

—086 642   *Gay men

—086 643   *Lesbians

—086 9   *Persons with special social status

—086 91   *Persons with status defined by changes in residence

       Including aliens, exiles, foreigners, immigrants, nomads, refugees

       Class migrant workers in —08624; class runaway children in —086923; class vagrants in —086942; class aliens, foreigners, immigrants of a specific racial, ethnic, national group in —089

—086 92   *Antisocial and asocial persons

       Subdivisions are added for either or both topics in heading

       Vagrants relocated to —086942

—086 923   *Juvenile delinquents and predelinquents

       Subdivisions are added for either or both terms in heading

—086 927   *Offenders

       Class here convicts, criminals

       Class juvenile delinquents in —086923

—086 93   *Nondominant groups

       Comprehensive works on nondominant religious groups relocated to —0882; comprehensive works on nondominant racial, ethnic, national groups relocated to —089

       Class a specific nondominant group with the group, e.g., serfs —08625

—086 94   *Socially disadvantaged persons

       Class here alienated and excluded classes

       Class a specific kind of persons socially disadvantaged for a reason not provided for here with the kind, e.g., addicts in recovery —0874

—086 941   *Unemployed persons

       Class poverty-stricken and destitute unemployed persons in —086942

*Add as instructed under —08

—086 942	*The poor
	Including vagrants [*formerly* —08692], homeless persons
—086 945	*Abandoned children, abused children, children born out of wedlock, orphans
	See also —086923 for runaway children
—086 947	*Unmarried mothers
—086 949	*Victims of war and crime
—086 96	*Retired persons
—086 97	*Veterans of military service
—087	*Persons with disabilities and illnesses, gifted persons
	Including persons with learning disabilities
	Class here persons with physical disabilities
—087 1	*Persons with blindness and visual impairments
	Class here blind-deaf persons
	Subdivisions are added for either or both topics in heading
—087 2	*Persons with hearing impairments
	Class here deaf persons
	Class persons who are deaf and blind in —0871
—087 3	*Persons with mobility impairments
	Class persons with mobility impairments resulting from developmental disabilities in —0875
—087 4	*Persons with mental illness and disabilities
	Including addicts, addicts in recovery, alcoholics
—087 5	*Persons with developmental disabilities
	Class persons with congenital visual disabilities in —0871; class persons with congenital hearing disabilities in —0872
	For persons with mental developmental disabilities, see —0874
—087 7	*Shut-in (Housebound) persons
	Class here persons with physical illnesses not provided for elsewhere, comprehensive works on persons with physical illnesses
	Class a specific kind of shut-in persons with the kind, e.g., shut-in persons with developmental disabilities —0875
	For persons with mental illnesses, see —0874

*Add as instructed under —08

—087 9   *Gifted persons

—088   Occupational and religious groups

See Manual at T1—088 vs. T1—024

—088 001–088 009   Forecasting, statistics, illustrations, serials, museums and collecting, historical and geographic treatment

Add to base number —08800 the numbers following 0 in notation 01–09 from table under —08, e.g., statistics —0880021

—088 09–088 9   Specific occupational and religious groups

Add to base number —088 notation 09–9 from Table 7, e.g., comprehensive works on nondominant religious groups —0882 [*formerly* —08693], Catholic teachings on socioeconomic problems 261.808822

Class works on the subject for persons in specific occupations in —024

See Manual at T1—0882 and 200; also at T1—0882 vs. T1—09

—089   Racial, ethnic, national groups

Class here comprehensive works on nondominant racial, ethnic, national groups [*formerly* —08693]; racial, ethnic, national minorities

Class treatment with respect to miscellaneous specific kinds of persons of a specific racial, ethnic, national group in —081–088, e.g., Chinese children —083; class persons treatment (e.g., biography) of members of a specific racial, ethnic, national group in —0923; class treatment with respect to specific racial, ethnic, national groups in places where they predominate in —091–099

See Manual at T1—09 vs. T1—089

—089 001–089 009   Forecasting, statistics, illustrations, serials, museology, historical and geographic treatment

Add to base number —08900 the numbers following 0 in notation 01–09 from table under —08, e.g., statistics —0890021

—089 03–089 9   Specific racial, ethnic, national groups

Add to base number —089 notation 03–9 from Table 5, e.g., the subject with respect to Chinese —089951, with respect to Chinese in United States —089951073

*Add as instructed under —08

—09   **Historical, geographic, persons treatment**

Formulas and specifications in specific times and places relocated to —0212; the subject for persons in specific occupations in specific times and places relocated to —024

Class historiography in —0722; class historical and geographic treatment of museums, collections, exhibits representing the whole subject in —074; class historical and geographic treatment of museum activities and services representing the whole subject in —075

> *See Manual at T1—09; also at T1—0601–0609; also at T1—0882 vs. T1—09; also at T1—09 vs. T1—089*

SUMMARY

—090 05	**Serial publications**
—090 1–090 5	**Historical periods**
—091	**Treatment by areas, regions, places in general**
—092	**Persons**
—093–099	**Treatment by specific continents, countries, localities; extraterrestrial worlds**

—090 05   Serial publications

>   **—090 1–090 5**   Historical periods

Add to each subdivision identified by * as follows:

01	Short term forecasts
	Ten years or less
	Class long term forecasts (more than ten years) in —0112
02	Statistics and illustrations
021	Statistics
022	Illustrations
03	Dictionaries, encyclopedias, concordances
05	Serial publications
07	Museums, collections, exhibits; collecting objects
074	Museums, collections, exhibits
	Add to base number 074 notation 4–9 from Table 2, e.g., collections in Pennsylvania 074748, collections of ancient objects in Pennsylvania —0901074748
075	Collecting objects

Class historical periods in specific areas, regions, places in general in —091; class historical periods in specific continents, countries, localities in —093–099; class comprehensive works in —09

See Manual at T1—0901–0905

—090 1   *To 499 A.D.

The ancient period when the coverage is not limited to areas provided for in —093

---

*Add as instructed under —0901–0905

—090 12	*To 4000 B.C.
—090 13	*3999–1000 B.C.
—090 14	*999–1 B.C.
—090 15	*1st–5th centuries, 1–499
—090 2	*6th–15th centuries, 500–1499

Class here Middle Ages (Medieval period)

See Manual at T1—0940902 vs. T1—0902

—090 21	*6th–12th centuries, 500–1199
—090 22	*13th century, 1200–1299
—090 23	*14th century, 1300–1399
—090 24	*15th century, 1400–1499
—090 3	*Modern period, 1500–

For 20th century, see —0904; for 21st century, see —0905

—090 31	*16th century, 1500–1599
—090 32	*17th century, 1600–1699
—090 33	*18th century, 1700–1799
—090 34	*19th century, 1800–1899
—090 4	*20th century, 1900–1999
—090 41	*1900–1919

Class here early 20th century

For 1920–1929, see —09042; for 1930–1939, see —09043; for 1940–1949, see —09044

—090 42	*1920–1929
—090 43	*1930–1939
—090 44	*1940–1949

Class here period of World War II

For 1939, see —09043

—090 45	*1950–1959

Class here late 20th century, post World War II period

For 1945–1949, see —09044; for 1960–1969, see —09046; for 1970–1979, see —09047; for 1980–1989, see —09048; for 1990–1999, see —09049

—090 46	*1960–1969

*Add as instructed under —0901–0905

—090 47	*1970–1979
—090 48	*1980–1989
—090 49	*1990–1999
—090 5	*21st century, 2000–2099
—090 51	*2000–2019
—090 511	*2000–2009

—091   Treatment by areas, regions, places in general

> History and description
>
> Add to base number —091 the numbers following —1 in notation 11–19 from Table 2, e.g., Torrid Zone —0913; then add further as instructed under —093–099, e.g., conservation and preservation in tropical areas —0913028 [*formerly* —0288]
>
> Class history and description with respect to kinds of persons in —08; class persons regardless of area, region, place in —092; class treatment by specific continents, countries, localities in —093–099

—092   Persons

> Biography, autobiography, description and critical appraisal of work, diaries, reminiscences, correspondence of persons regardless of area, region, or place who are part of the subject or who study the subject, e.g., biographers, collectors, leaders and followers, practitioners and clients, scholars
>
> Class here treatment of individuals
>
> Class treatment with respect to kinds of persons in —08; class biography not clearly related to any specific subject in 920; class belletristic diaries, reminiscences, correspondence in 800
>
> Observe instructions not to use —092 (or 92 or 2 when the standard subdivision has been displaced) that apply to 180–190, 748.29, 748.59, 749.2, 759, 809, 810–890. (The instructions for 810–890 are found under notation 09 from Table 3–B)
>
> Do not use —092 for a person whose name is used in a schedule heading, e.g., class Muḥammad the Prophet in 297.63 (*not* 297.63092)
>
> > *See Manual at T1—092; also at 913–919: Add table: 04: Biography; also at 930–990: Wars: Personal narratives; also at 930–990: Biography*
>
> (Option A: Class biography in 920.1–928.9
>
> (Option B: Class individual biography in 92, or B
>
> (Option C: Class individual biography of men in 920.71, of women in 920.72)

---

*Add as instructed under —0901–0905

—092 2   **Collected persons treatment**

         Add to base number —0922 notation 3–9 from Table 2, e.g., collected biography of a subject in Italy —092245

         Collected persons treatment of members of specific racial, ethnic, national groups relocated to —0923

         Class collectibles and memorabilia related to more than one person in —075; class collected treatment of persons of specific areas when not limited to a specific subject in 920.03–920.09

         See Manual at T1—0922; also at T1—0922 vs. T1—093–099

         (Option: Class collected biography in 92, or 920 without subdivision)

—092 3   **Collected persons treatment of members of specific racial, ethnic, national groups** [*formerly* —0922]

         Add to base number —0923 notation 03–9 from Table 5, e.g., biography of Irish-Americans —09239162073

         Class collected persons treatment of members of specific racial, ethnic, national groups in areas where they predominate in —0922, e.g., biography of Irish in Ireland —0922415

—092 9   **Persons treatment of nonhumans**

         Use this number for animals and plants treated as individuals, e.g., a biography of Secretariat 798.400929

—093–099   **Treatment by specific continents, countries, localities; extraterrestrial worlds**

         History and description by place, by specific instance of the subject

         Add to base number —09 notation 3–9 from Table 2, e.g., the subject in North America —097, United States —0973, in Brazil —0981; then add further as follows:

         01   Forecasts

         02   Statistics, illustrations; conservation, preservation, restoration

         021   Statistics

         022   Illustrations

                     See Manual at 912 vs. T1—0223

         028   Conservation, preservation, restoration

                     Class here maintenance and repair [*formerly* —0288]; conservation, preservation, restoration projects

         03   Dictionaries, encyclopedias, concordances

         05   Serial publications

         07   Museums, collections, exhibits; collecting objects

         074   Museums, collections, exhibits

                     Add to base number 074 notation 4–9 from Table 2, e.g., collections in Pennsylvania 074748, collections of Brazilian objects in Pennsylvania —0981074748

         075   Collecting objects

                                                 (continued)

—093–099   Treatment by specific continents, countries, localities; extraterrestrial worlds (continued)

      09   Historical and geographic treatment
            Add to 09 the numbers following —09 in notation 090–099 from Table 1, e.g., 20th century 0904, rural regions 091734
            Use 093–099 to add notation for a specific continent, country, locality when first area notation is used to specify area of origin, while second one identifies area in which subject is found or practiced, e.g., Polish political refugees 325.2109438, Polish political refugees in Canada 325.21094380971

In table above, observe preference as given at beginning of Table 1, e.g., a periodical of statistics 021 (*not* 05); however, class museums, collections, exhibits of the subject in an area in 074 regardless of historical period, e.g., collections of twentieth century Brazilian art 709.81074 (*not* 709.810904)

(Option: Add historical period numbers that appear in subdivisions of 930–990, using one 0 in all cases except 00 for North America and South America, e.g., United States during Reconstruction —097308, Brazil during Empire —098104, North America in 20th century —097005. If option is used, do not use notation 090 from table above. An extra zero is used for the balance of notation from table above, e.g., statistics of Brazil —09810021)

Class history and description with respect to kinds of persons regardless of continent, country, locality in —08; class treatment by areas, regions, places not limited by continent, country, locality in —091; class persons treatment regardless of continent, country, locality in —092

See Manual at T1—0922 vs. T1—093–099; also at T1—093–099 and T2—3–9; also at T1—0940902 vs. T1—0902

Table 2. Geographic Areas, Historical Periods, Persons

The following numbers are never used alone, but may be used as required (either directly when so noted or through the interposition of notation 09 from Table 1) with any number from the schedules, e.g., wages (331.29) in Japan (—52 in this table): 331.2952; railroad transportation (385) in Brazil (—81 in this table): 385.0981. They may also be used when so noted with numbers from other tables, e.g., notation 025 from Table 1. When adding to a number from the schedules, always insert a decimal point between the third and fourth digits of the complete number

SUMMARY

—001–009	**Standard subdivisions**
—01–05	**Historical periods**
—1	**Areas, regions, places in general**
—11	**Frigid zones**
—12	**Temperate zones (Middle latitude zones)**
—13	**Torrid zone (Tropics)**
—14	**Land and landforms**
—15	**Regions by type of vegetation**
—16	**Air and water**
—17	**Socioeconomic regions**
—18	**Other kinds of terrestrial regions**
—19	**Space**
—2	**Persons**
—22	**Collected treatment**
—3	**The ancient world**
—31	**China**
—32	**Egypt**
—33	**Palestine**
—34	**India**
—35	**Mesopotamia and Iranian Plateau**
—36	**Europe north and west of Italian Peninsula**
—37	**Italian Peninsula and adjacent territories**
—38	**Greece**
—39	**Other parts of ancient world**

—4   **Europe   Western Europe**
—41   **British Isles**
—42   **England and Wales**
—43   **Central Europe   Germany**
—44   **France and Monaco**
—45   **Italian Peninsula and adjacent islands   Italy**
—46   **Iberian Peninsula and adjacent islands   Spain**
—47   **Eastern Europe   Russia**
—48   **Scandinavia**
—49   **Other parts of Europe**

—5   **Asia   Orient   Far East**
—51   **China and adjacent areas**
—52   **Japan**
—53   **Arabian Peninsula and adjacent areas**
—54   **South Asia   India**
—55   **Iran**
—56   **Middle East (Near East)**
—57   **Siberia (Asiatic Russia)**
—58   **Central Asia**
—59   **Southeast Asia**

—6   **Africa**
—61   **Tunisia and Libya**
—62   **Egypt and Sudan**
—63   **Ethiopia and Eritrea**
—64   **Northwest African coast and offshore islands   Morocco**
—65   **Algeria**
—66   **West Africa and offshore islands**
—67   **Central Africa and offshore islands**
—68   **Southern Africa   Republic of South Africa**
—69   **South Indian Ocean islands**

—7   **North America**
—71   **Canada**
—72   **Middle America   Mexico**
—73   **United States**
—74   **Northeastern United States (New England and Middle Atlantic states)**
—75   **Southeastern United States (South Atlantic states)**
—76   **South central United States   Gulf Coast states**
—77   **North central United States   Lake states**
—78   **Western United States**
—79   **Great Basin and Pacific Slope region of United States   Pacific Coast states**

—8   **South America**
—81   **Brazil**
—82   **Argentina**
—83   **Chile**
—84   **Bolivia**
—85   **Peru**
—86   **Colombia and Ecuador**
—87   **Venezuela**
—88   **Guiana**
—89   **Paraguay and Uruguay**

—9	**Other parts of world and extraterrestrial worlds**		**Pacific Ocean islands**
—93	**New Zealand**		
—94	**Australia**		
—95	**Melanesia**	**New Guinea**	
—96	**Other parts of Pacific Ocean**	**Polynesia**	
—97	**Atlantic Ocean islands**		
—98	**Arctic islands and Antarctica**		
—99	**Extraterrestrial worlds**		

—001–008   Standard subdivisions

—009   Historical treatment

> If "historical" appears in the heading for the number to which notation 009 could be added, this notation is redundant and should not be used

—[009 01–009 9]   Historical periods, geographic and persons treatment

> Do not use; class in —01–9

—01–05   Historical periods

> Add to base number —0 the numbers following —090 in notation 0901–0905 from Table 1, e.g., 20th century —04

—1   Areas, regions, places in general

Not limited by continent, country, locality

Unless other instructions are given, class an area with aspects in two or more subdivisions of —1 in the number coming last in the table, e.g., forested plateaus in north temperate zone —152 (*not* —123 or —143)

Class persons regardless of area, region, place in —2; class specific continents, countries, localities in —3–9

See Manual at T2—1

(Option: Add to each number in —1 as follows:
     03–09   Treatment by continent, country, locality
                 Add to 0 notation 3–9 from Table 2, e.g., Asia 05, Torrid Zone of Asia —1305, rivers of Asia —169305, cities of Asia —173205

Prefer —3–9)

SUMMARY

—11	**Frigid zones**
—12	**Temperate zones (Middle latitude zones)**
—13	**Torrid zone (Tropics)**
—14	**Land and landforms**
—15	**Regions by type of vegetation**
—16	**Air and water**
—17	**Socioeconomic regions**
—18	**Other kinds of terrestrial regions**
—19	**Space**

—11   Frigid zones

Class here polar regions

—113   North frigid zone

—116   South frigid zone

—12   **Temperate zones (Middle latitude zones)**

—123   North temperate zone

—126   South temperate zone

—13   **Torrid zone (Tropics)**

—14   **Land and landforms**

—141   Continents

         Including continental shelves

—142   Islands

         Including atolls, coral reefs

—143   Elevations

         Including mountains, plateaus, hills, slopes

—144   Depressions and openings

         Including canyons, chasms, gorges, gulches, ravines, valleys; caves, karsts

—145   Plane regions

         Including pampas, plains, prairies, steppes, tundras

—146   Coastal regions and shorelines

         Including beaches, deltas

—148   Soil

—15   **Regions by type of vegetation**

—152   Forests

—153   Grasslands

—154   Deserts

—16   **Air and water**

SUMMARY

—161	Atmosphere
—162	Oceans and seas
—163	Atlantic Ocean
—164	Pacific Ocean
—165	Indian Ocean
—167	Antarctic waters
—168	Special oceanographic forms and inland seas
—169	Fresh and brackish waters

—161	Atmosphere
—161 2	Troposphere
—161 3	Stratosphere
—161 4	Ionosphere
—162	Oceans and seas

> For Atlantic Ocean, see —163; for Pacific Ocean, see —164; for Indian Ocean, see —165; for Antarctic waters, see —167; for special oceanographic forms and inland seas, see —168
>
> See also —182 for ocean and sea basins
>
> See Manual at T2—162

—163	Atlantic Ocean

> See Manual at T2—162; also at T2—163 and T2—164, T2—165; also at T2—163, T2—164, T2—165 vs. T2—182

—163 1	North Atlantic Ocean

> For Arctic Ocean, see —1632; for northeast Atlantic Ocean, see —1633; for northwest Atlantic Ocean, see —1634
>
> See Manual at T2—1631 and T2—1635

—163 2	Arctic Ocean (North Polar Sea)
—163 24	European sector

Including Denmark Strait; Barents, Greenland, Norwegian, White Seas

—163 25	Asian sector

Including Chukchi, East Siberian, Kara, Laptev Seas

> For Bering Strait, see —16451

—163 27	American sector

Including Beaufort and Lincoln Seas, seas of Canadian Arctic Archipelago, Baffin and Hudson Bays

> For Bering Strait, see —16451

—163 3	Northeast Atlantic Ocean
—163 34	Baltic Sea

Including Gulfs of Bothnia, Finland, Riga; Great and Little Belts; Kattegat, Oresund

—163 36	North Sea and English Channel

Including Firth of Forth, Skagerrak, Strait of Dover

—163 37	Western waters of British Isles
	Including Firth of Clyde, Irish Sea, North and Saint George's Channels, Solway Firth
—163 38	French and Spanish coastal waters to Strait of Gibraltar
	Including Bay of Biscay
	For Strait of Gibraltar, see —16381
—163 4	**Northwest Atlantic Ocean**
—163 42	Davis Strait
—163 43	Labrador Sea
—163 44	Gulf of Saint Lawrence and coastal waters of Newfoundland and eastern Nova Scotia
—163 45	North American coastal waters from Bay of Fundy to Massachusetts Bay
	Including Cape Cod Bay
—163 46	United States coastal waters from Cape Cod to Cape Charles
	Including Long Island, Nantucket, Rhode Island, Sounds; Buzzards, Delaware, Narragansett, New York Bays
—163 47	Chesapeake Bay
—163 48	United States coastal waters from Cape Henry to Straits of Florida
	Including Albemarle, Pamlico Sounds; Biscayne Bay; Biscayne National Park
	For Straits of Florida, see —16363
—163 5	**South Atlantic Ocean**
	For southwest Atlantic Ocean, see —1636; for southeast Atlantic Ocean, see —1637; for Atlantic sector of Antarctic waters, see —1673
	See Manual at T2—1631 and T2—1635
—163 6	**Southwest Atlantic Ocean**
	Class here west Atlantic Ocean
	For northwest Atlantic Ocean, see —1634
—163 62	Sargasso Sea
—163 63	Bahama waters
	Including Straits of Florida
—163 64	Gulf of Mexico
	Including Yucatán Channel
	For Straits of Florida, see —16363

—163 65   Caribbean Sea

           Including Gulfs of Darien, Honduras, Venezuela

           For Yucatán Channel, see —16364

—163 66   South American coastal waters from Gulf of Paria to Cape São Roque

—163 67   Brazilian coastal waters southward from Cape São Roque

—163 68   Uruguayan and Argentine coastal waters

           Including Bahía Blanca Estuary, Rio de la Plata

—163 7   Southeast Atlantic Ocean

           Class here east Atlantic Ocean

           For northeast Atlantic Ocean, see —1633; for Mediterranean Sea, see —1638

—163 72   African coastal waters from Cape of Good Hope to Congo River

—163 73   Gulf of Guinea

           African coastal waters from Congo River to Cape Palmas

—163 75   West African coastal waters from Cape Palmas to Strait of Gibraltar

           For Strait of Gibraltar, see —16381

—163 8   Mediterranean Sea

—163 81   Western Mediterranean

           Strait of Gibraltar to Strait of Sicily

           For waters between Spain and Sardinia-Corsica, see —16382; for Tyrrhenian Sea, see —16383

—163 82   Waters between Spain and Sardinia-Corsica

           Including Balearic and Ligurian Seas, Gulf of Lions

—163 83   Tyrrhenian Sea

           For Strait of Messina, see —16386

—163 84   Eastern Mediterranean

           East of Strait of Sicily

           For Adriatic Sea, see —16385; for Ionian Sea, see —16386; for Mediterranean east of Crete, see —16387; for Sea of Crete and Aegean Sea, see —16388; for Black Sea, see —16389

—163 85   Adriatic Sea

           Including Gulf of Venice

—163 86   Ionian Sea

               Including Strait of Messina, Gulf of Taranto

               For Strait of Otranto, see —16385

—163 87   Mediterranean east of Crete

               For Suez Canal, see —16533

—163 88   Sea of Crete and Aegean Sea

               For Dardanelles, see —16389

—163 89   Black Sea

               Including Bosporus, Dardanelles, Seas of Azov and Marmara

—164   Pacific Ocean

               See Manual at T2—162; also at T2—163 and T2—164, T2—165; also at T2—163, T2—164, T2—165 vs. T2—182

—164 1   Southeast Pacific Ocean

               American coastal waters from Strait of Magellan to Mexico-United States boundary

               Including Gulfs of California, Guayaquil, Panama, Tehuantepec

               Panama Canal relocated to —72875

               For Strait of Magellan, see —1674

—164 2   East Pacific Ocean

               For southeast Pacific Ocean, see —1641; for northeast Pacific Ocean, see —1643

—164 3   Northeast Pacific Ocean

               North American coastal waters from California to tip of Alaska

—164 32   United States waters

               Including Monterey and San Francisco Bays, Puget Sound, Strait of Juan de Fuca

               For Alaskan waters, see —16434

—164 33   Canadian waters

               Including Dixon Entrance, Hecate and Queen Charlotte Straits, Queen Charlotte Sound, Strait of Georgia

               For Strait of Juan de Fuca, see —16432

—164 34   Alaskan waters

               Including Bristol Bay, Cook Inlet, Gulf of Alaska, Norton Sound, Shelikof Strait

               For Dixon Entrance, see —16433

—164 4   North Pacific Ocean

         For northeast Pacific Ocean, see —1643; for northwest Pacific Ocean, see —1645

         See Manual at T2—1644 and T2—1648, T2—1649

—164 5   Northwest Pacific Ocean

—164 51   Bering Sea

         Including Bering Strait

—164 52   Coastal waters of southeast Kamchatka

—164 53   Sea of Okhotsk

         Including La Perouse Strait

—164 54   Sea of Japan

         Including Korea, Tatar, Tsugaru Straits

         For La Perouse Strait, see —16453

—164 55   Eastern coastal waters and inner seas of Japan

         Including Inland Sea (Seto-naikai)

—164 56   Yellow Sea

—164 57   East China Sea

         Including Formosa Strait

         For Korea Strait, see —16454

—164 58   Philippine Sea

         Including Luzon Strait

—164 6   West Pacific Ocean

         For northwest Pacific Ocean, see —1645; for southwest Pacific Ocean, see —1647

—164 7   Southwest Pacific Ocean

—164 71   Inner seas of Philippines

         For Sulu Sea, see —16473

—164 72   South China Sea

         Including Gulf of Thailand, Singapore Strait

         For Formosa Strait, see —16457; for Luzon Strait, see —16458

—164 73   Inner seas of Malay Archipelago

         Including Celebes, Ceram, Molucca, Sulu Seas; Makasar Strait

         For seas adjoining southern Sunda Islands, see —16474

—164 74	Seas adjoining Sunda Islands
	Including Bali, Banda, Flores, Java, Savu Seas
	For Karimata Strait, see —16472
—164 75	Arafura Sea
	For Torres Strait, see —16476
—164 76	Coral Sea and seas adjoining Melanesia
	Including Bismarck and Solomon Seas, Torres Strait; eastern Queensland coastal waters
—164 77	Fiji Sea
—164 78	Tasman Sea
	Including New South Wales coastal waters, Cook Strait
	For Tasmanian coastal waters, see —16576
—164 79	Eastern coastal waters of New Zealand
—164 8	South Pacific Ocean
	For southeast Pacific Ocean, see —1641; for southwest Pacific Ocean, see —1647; for Pacific sector of Antarctic waters, see —1674
	See Manual at T2—1644 and T2—1648, T2—1649
—164 9	Central Pacific Ocean
	Including coastal waters of Hawaii
	See Manual at T2—1644 and T2—1648, T2—1649
—165	Indian Ocean
	For Indian Ocean sector of Antarctic waters, see —1675
	See Manual at T2—162; also at T2—163 and T2—164, T2—165; also at T2—163, T2—164, T2—165 vs. T2—182
—165 2	Southwest Indian Ocean
	Class here west Indian Ocean
	For northwest Indian Ocean, see —1653
—165 23	Eastern coastal waters of Madagascar
—165 24	Coastal waters of south and southeast Africa
	From Cape of Good Hope to and including Delagoa Bay
—165 25	Mozambique Channel
—165 26	Coastal waters of east Africa
	From Cape Delgado to Cape Guardafui (tip of the "Horn")

—165 3   Northwest Indian Ocean

—165 32   Gulf of Aden

                Including 'Bab el Mandeb

—165 33   Red Sea

                Including Gulfs of Aqaba and Suez, Suez Canal

                For 'Bab el Mandeb, see —16532

—165 35   Persian Gulf

                Including Strait of Hormuz

—165 36   Gulf of Oman

                For Strait of Hormuz, see —16535

—165 37   Arabian Sea

                Including Laccadive Sea

—165 6   Northeast Indian Ocean

—165 64   Bay of Bengal

—165 65   Andaman Sea

                Including Gulf of Martaban, Strait of Malacca

                For Singapore Strait, see —16472

—165 67   Coastal waters of southern Sumatra, Java, Lesser Sunda Islands

                For Timor Sea, see —16574

—165 7   Southeast Indian Ocean

                Class here east Indian Ocean

                *For Arafura Sea, see —16475; for northeast Indian Ocean, see
                —1656*

—165 74   Northwest Australian coastal waters

                From Melville Island to Northwest Cape

                Including Timor Sea

—165 75   West Australian coastal waters

                From Northwest Cape to Cape Leeuwin

—165 76   South Australian coastal waters

                From Cape Leeuwin to Cape Howe

                Including Bass Strait, Great Australian Bight, Tasmanian coastal
                waters

—167   Antarctic waters

                See Manual at T2—162; also at T2—163 and T2—164, T2—165

—167 3   Atlantic sector

         Including Drake Passage, Scotia and Weddell Seas

         For Strait of Magellan, see —1674

—167 4   Pacific sector

         Including Amundsen, Bellingshausen, Ross Seas; Strait of Magellan

—167 5   Indian Ocean sector

—168   Special oceanographic forms and inland seas

         Including coastal pools, saltwater lagoons

         Class specific inland seas in —4–9

         See Manual at T2—162

—169   Fresh and brackish waters

\>   —169 2–169 4   Surface waters

         Class comprehensive works in —169

—169 2   Lakes, ponds, freshwater lagoons

—169 3   Rivers and streams

—169 4   Waterfalls

—169 8   Groundwaters (Subsurface waters)

—17   **Socioeconomic regions**

—171   Socioeconomic regions by political orientation

—171 2   Noncontiguous empires and political unions

         Add to base number —1712 notation 3–9 from Table 2 for "mother country", e.g., French Community —171244

         Class Roman Empire in —37

—171 3   Western bloc

—171 6   Unaligned blocs

—171 65   Afro-Asian bloc

—171 7   Communist bloc

—171 8   Wartime groupings

—171 82   Belligerents

—171 83   Nonbelligerents and neutrals

—171 9   Non-self-governing territories

—172	Socioeconomic regions by degree of economic development
—172 2	Developed regions
—[172 3]	Medium degree of development
	Number discontinued; class in —172
—172 4	Developing regions
—173	Socioeconomic regions by concentration of population
—173 2	Urban regions
—173 3	Suburban regions
—173 4	Rural regions
	Including rural villages
—174	Regions where specific racial, ethnic, national groups predominate
	Add to base number —174 notation 03–99 from Table 5, e.g., regions where Arabs predominate —174927
—175	Regions where specific languages predominate
	Add to base number —175 notation 1–9 from Table 6, e.g., regions where Spanish language predominates —17561
—176	Regions where specific religions predominate
—176 1	Christianity
—176 12	Catholicism
—176 14	Protestantism
—176 2–176 9	Other religions
	Add to base number —176 the numbers following —29 in notation 292–299 from Table 7, e.g., regions where Islam predominates —17671
—177	Nations belonging to specific international organizations
	Including nations belonging to Organization of Petroleum Exporting Countries
	Arrange alphabetically by name of organization
—18	**Other kinds of terrestrial regions**
—181	Hemispheres
	Class zonal, physiographic, socioeconomic regions in a specific hemisphere in —11–17
—181 1	Eastern Hemisphere

—181 2   Western Hemisphere

> Class works emphasizing North and South America in —7; class geography of Western Hemisphere in 917; class history of Western Hemisphere in 970

> *See Manual at T2—7 vs. T2—1812*

—181 3   Northern Hemisphere

—181 4   Southern Hemisphere

—182   Ocean and sea basins

> The totality of continents facing and islands in specific major bodies of water

> Class ocean and sea waters in —162; class zonal, physiographic, socioeconomic regions in a specific ocean or sea basin in —11–17

> *See Manual at T2—163, T2—164, T2—165 vs. T2—182*

—182 1   Atlantic region   Occident

> Class here western world

> *See also —729 for Caribbean Area*

—182 2   Mediterranean region

—182 3   Pacific region

—182 4   Indian Ocean region

—19   **Space**

> Class extraterrestrial worlds in —99

> *See Manual at T2—99 vs. T2—19*

—2   **Persons**

> Regardless of area, region, place

> Class here description and critical appraisal of work, biography, autobiography, diaries, reminiscences, correspondence of persons associated with the subject, e.g., elementary educators 372.92

> All schedule and Manual notes for notation 092 and its subdivision from Table 1 are applicable here

—22   **Collected treatment**

> Add to base number —22 notation 3–9 from Table 2, e.g., collected biography of persons from Italy —2245

> ## —3–9 Specific continents, countries, localities; extraterrestrial worlds

Class here specific instances of the subject

An area is classed in its present number even if it had a different affiliation at the time under consideration, e.g., Arizona under Mexican sovereignty —791 (*not* —72)

Class areas, regions, places not limited by continent, country, locality in —1; class parts of oceans and non-inland seas limited by country or locality in —163–168; class persons regardless of area, region, place in —2; class comprehensive works in 001–999, without adding notation from Table 2

> *See Manual at T1—093–099 and T2—3–9; also at T2—162; also at T2—3 vs. T2—4–9*

(Option: Class areas and regions limited by continent, country, locality in —1)

—3 The ancient world

Class a specific part of ancient world not provided for here in —4–9

See Manual at T2—3 vs. T2—4–9

(Option: Class specific parts in —4–9 as detailed below)

SUMMARY

—31	China
—32	Egypt
—33	Palestine
—34	India
—35	Mesopotamia and Iranian Plateau
—36	Europe north and west of Italian Peninsula
—37	Italian Peninsula and adjacent territories
—38	Greece
—39	Other parts of ancient world

—31 China

(Option: Class in —51)

—32 Egypt

Including Alexandria, Giza, Memphis, Abydos, Karnak, Luxor, Thebes

(Option: Class Egypt in —62; Alexandria in —621; Giza, Memphis in —622; Abydos, Karnak, Luxor, Thebes in —623)

—33 Palestine

Including Israel, Judah; Galilee, Judaea, Samaria; Jerusalem

(Option: Class Palestine, Israel in —5694; Jerusalem in —569442; Galilee in —56945; Judah, Judaea in —56949; Samaria in —56953)

—34   **India**

      (Option: Class in —54)

—35   **Mesopotamia and Iranian Plateau**

      Including Media, Elam, Persia, Assyria, Babylonia, Sumer; Ecbatana, Susa, Pasargadae, Persepolis, Ashur, Nineveh, Babylon, Ur

      Class here Seleucid Empire

      Class central Asia in —396

      (Option: Class Iranian Plateau in —55; Media, Ecbatana in —555; Elam, Susa in —556; Persia, Pasargadae, Persepolis in —5572; Mesopotamia, Seleucid Empire in —567; Assyria, Ashur, Nineveh in —5674; Babylonia, Sumer, Babylon, Ur in —5675)

—36   **Europe north and west of Italian Peninsula**

      Class here comprehensive works on Europe

        For a specific part of Europe not provided for here, see the part, e.g., Greece —38

      (Option: Class in —4)

—361   British Isles   Northern Britain and Ireland

      Add to base number —361 the numbers following —41 in notation 411–419 of this table, e.g., ancient Border Country —36137

        For southern Britain, see —362

      (Option: Class British Isles in —41, northern Britain in —411, Ireland in —415)

—362   Southern Britain   England

      Add to base number —362 the numbers following —42 in notation 421–429 of this table, e.g., ancient Chester —362714

      Class comprehensive works on British Isles in —361

      (Option: Class in —42)

—363   Germanic regions

      Including Vindelicia, Noricum, Raetia

        For British Isles, see —361

      (Option: Class Germanic regions in —43; Vindelicia in —433; Noricum in —436; Raetia in —4364)

—364   Celtic regions

Including Germania Superior, Lugdunensis, Aquitania, Narbonensis, Germania Inferior, Belgica

Class here Gaul (Gallia Transalpina)

For British Isles, see —361

See also —372 for Gallia Cisalpina

(Option: Class Celtic regions, Gaul [Gallia Transalpina] in —44; Germania Superior in —4438; Lugdunensis in —445; Aquitania in —447; Narbonensis in —449; Germania Inferior in —492; Belgica in —493)

—366   Iberian Peninsula and adjacent islands

Including Tarraconensis, Baetica, Lusitania

(Option: Class Iberian Peninsula and adjacent islands, Tarraconensis in —46; Baetica in —468; Lusitania in —469)

—37   Italian Peninsula and adjacent territories

Class here Roman Empire

For a specific part of Roman Empire not provided for here, see the part, e.g., Britain —361

(Option: Class in —45)

—371   Liguria

(Option: Class in —4518)

—372   Gallia Cisalpina

(Option: Class in —451)

—373   Venetia and Istria

(Option: Class Venetia in —453; Istria in —4972)

—374   Region northeast of Rome

Including Umbria, Picenum; Volsinii (Orvieto)

(Option: Class Umbria in —4565; Volsinii [Orvieto] in —45652; Picenum in —4567)

—375   Etruria

(Option: Class in —455)

—376   Latium

Including Volsinii Novi (Bolsena), Ostia, Veii

Class here Rome

(Option: Class Latium in —4562; Volsinii Novi [Bolsena] in —45625; Ostia, Veii in —4563; Rome in —45632)

—377   Southern Italy

Including Samnium, Campania, Apulia, Calabria, Lucania, Bruttium

Including Naples, Herculaneum, Pompeii, Stabiae, Brundusium

(Option: Class Southern Italy in —457; Samnium in —4571; Campania in —4572; Naples, Herculaneum, Pompeii, Stabiae in —4573; Apulia, Calabria, Brundusium in —4575; Lucania in —4577; Bruttium in —4578)

—378   Sicily and Malta

Including Syracuse

(Option: Class Sicily in —458; Syracuse in —45814; Malta in —4585)

—379   Sardinia and Corsica

(Option: Class Corsica in —44945; Sardinia in —459)

—38   Greece

Class here comprehensive works on Greece and the Roman Empire; the Hellenistic World; southern Europe

For the Roman Empire, see —37. For a specific part of Greece, Hellenistic World, southern Europe not provided for here, see the part, e.g., Aegean Islands —391, Ptolemaic Egypt —32

(Option: Class Greece in —495; southern Europe in —4)

—381   Macedonia

(Option: Class in —4956)

—382   Thessaly, Epirus, adjacent Ionian Islands

Class here comprehensive works on Ionian Islands

For Ithaca Island, see —383; for southern Ionian Islands, see —386

(Option: Class Epirus in —4953; Thessaly in —4954; Ionian Islands, northern Ionian Islands in —4955)

—383   Aetolia, Acarnania, Doris, Locris, Malis, Phocis; Ithaca Island

Including Amphissa, Delphi

(Option: Class Doris, Locris, Malis, Phocis, Amphissa, Delphi in —49515; Aetolia, Acarnania in —49518; Ithaca Island in —4955)

—384   Boeotia, Megaris; Euboea Island

Including Chalcis, Thebes

(Option: Class Boeotia, Euboea Island, Chalcis, Thebes in —49515; Megaris in —49522)

—385   Attica

     Including Marathon

     Class here Athens

     (Option: Class Attica, Athens, Marathon in —49512)

—386   Peloponnesus and adjacent Ionian Islands

     For divisions of Peloponnesus, see —387–389

     (Option: Class Peloponnesus in —4952; southern Ionian Islands in —4955)

>   —387–389   Divisions of Peloponnesus

     Class comprehensive works in —386

—387   Achaea and Corinth

     (Option: Class Corinth in —49522, Achaea in —49527)

—388   Arcadia, Argolis, Elis

     Including Mycenae, Olympia, Phigalia, Tiryns

     (Option: Class Arcadia, Argolis, Mycenae, Tiryns in —49522; Elis, Olympia, Phigalia in —49527)

—389   Laconia and Messenia

     Class here Sparta

     (Option: Class in —49522)

—39   **Other parts of ancient world**

SUMMARY

—391	**Aegean Islands**
—392	**Western Asia Minor**
—393	**Eastern Asia Minor and Cyprus**
—394	**Middle East**
—395	**Black Sea and Caucasus regions**
—396	**Central Asia**
—397	**North Africa**
—398	**Southeastern Europe**

—391   Aegean Islands

     Class here Sporades

     (Option: Class comprehensive works in —4958)

—391 1   Northern Aegean Islands

> Including Northern Sporades (including Skyros Island), Thasos Island, Samothrace Island, Lemnos Island; Imbros, Tenedos islands
>
> (Option: Class Skyros Island in —49515; Northern Sporades in —4954; Samothrace Island, Thasos Island in —4957; Lemnos Island in —49582; Imbros, Tenedos islands in —562)

—391 2   Lesbos

> (Option: Class in —49582)

—391 3   Chios

> (Option: Class in —49582)

—391 4   Samos

> (Option: Class in —49582)

—391 5   Southwestern Aegean Islands

> Class here Cyclades
>
> (Option: Class in —49585)

—391 6   Southern Sporades

> Including Dodecanese, Rhodes
>
> *For Karpathos, see —3917*
>
> (Option: Class in —49587)

—391 7   Karpathos

> (Option: Class in —49587)

—391 8   Crete

> Including Knossos
>
> (Option: Class in —4959)

—392   Western Asia Minor

> Class here comprehensive works on Asia Minor
>
> *For eastern Asia Minor, see —393*
>
> (Option: Class in —561)

—392 1   Mysia and Troas

> Including Pergamum, Troy
>
> (Option: Class in —562)

—392 2   Lydia

> Including Sardis
>
> (Option: Class in —562)

—392 3   Ionia

    Including Ephesus, Magnesia ad Maeandrum, Miletus, Smyrna

    For Aegean Islands, see —391

    (Option: Class in —562)

—392 4   Caria

    Including Halicarnassus

    (Option: Class in —562)

—392 5   Bithynia

    (Option: Class in —563)

—392 6   Phrygia

    (Option: Class in —562)

—392 7   Pisidia

    (Option: Class in —564)

—392 8   Lycia

    (Option: Class in —564)

—392 9   Pamphylia

    (Option: Class in —564)

—393   Eastern Asia Minor and Cyprus

    (Option: Class eastern Asia Minor in —561)

\>   —393 1–393 6   Eastern Asia Minor

    Class comprehensive works in —393

—393 1   Paphlagonia

    (Option: Class in —563)

—393 2   Galatia

    (Option: Class in —563)

—393 3   Pontus

    (Option: Class in —565)

—393 4   Cappadocia

    (Option: Class in —564)

—393 5   Cilicia

    (Option: Class in —564)

—393 6   Commagene

                   (Option: Class in —564)

—393 7   Cyprus

                   (Option: Class in —5693)

—394   Middle East

                   For a specific part of Middle East not provided for here, see the part, e.g., Egypt —32, Palestine —33

                   (Option: Class in —56)

—394 3   Syria

                   Including Antioch, Palmyra, Ebla, Ugarit, Damascus

                   For Phoenicia, see —3944

                   (Option: Class Antioch in —564; Syria in —5691; Palmyra in —56912; Ebla, Ugarit in —56913; Damascus in —569144)

—394 4   Phoenicia

                   Including Coelesyria; Baalbek, Byblos, Sidon, Tyre

                   (Option: Class in —5692)

—394 6   Edom and Moab

                   (Option: Class Edom in —56949; Moab in —56956)

—394 7   Arabia Deserta

                   (Option: Class in —567)

—394 8   Arabia Petraea

                   Including Sinai Peninsula; Petra

                   (Option: Class Arabia Petraea in —53; Sinai Peninsula in —531; Petra in —56957)

—394 9   Arabia Felix

                   Class here comprehensive works on Arabia

                   For Arabia Deserta, see —3947; for Arabia Petraea, see —3948

                   (Option: Class Arabia Felix, Arabia in —53)

—395   Black Sea and Caucasus regions

                   Including Albania, Colchis, Iberia, Sarmatia

                   (Option: Class Caucasus in —475; Albania in —4754; Colchis, Iberia in —4758; Black Sea region, Sarmatia in —477)

—395 1   Scythia

                   (Option: Class in —4983)

—395 5   Armenia

(Option: Class in —5662)

—396   Central Asia

Including Hyrcania, Ariana, Bactria, Margiana, Sogdiana; Parthia

(Option: Class Hyrcania in —5523; Central Asia in —58; Ariana, Bactria, Parthia in —581; Margiana in —585; Sogdiana in —587)

—397   North Africa

For Egypt, see —32

(Option: Class in —61)

—397 1   Mauretania

Including Mauretania Caesariensis, Mauretania Tingitana

(Option: Class Mauretania Tingitana in —64; Mauretania Caesariensis, comprehensive works on Mauretania in —65)

—397 2   Numidia

(Option: Class in —655)

—397 3   Carthage

(Option: Class in —611)

—397 4   Tripolis

Including Leptis Magna, Oea, Sabrata

(Option: Class in —612)

—397 5   Cyrenaica

(Option: Class in —612)

—397 6   Marmarica

(Option: Class in —612)

—397 7   Gaetulia

(Option: Class in —657)

—397 8   Ethiopia

Class here Cush, Nubia

(Option: Class in —625)

—398   Southeastern Europe

Including Pannonia, Thrace, Illyria, Dacia, Moesia; Constantinople

For Greece, see —38; for Black Sea region, see —395

(Option: Class Pannonia in —439; Thrace in —4957; southeastern Europe in —496; Constantinople in —49618; Illyria in —497; Dacia in —498; Moesia in —499)

> ## —4–9   The modern world; extraterrestrial worlds

Class comprehensive works on specific jurisdictions, regions, or features extending over more than one country, state, county, or other unit and identified by * with the unit where noted in this table, e.g., Rocky Mountain National Park —78869, Lake Huron —774, Appalachian Mountains —74. For works on a part of such a jurisdiction, region, or feature, see the specific unit where the part is located, e.g., Rocky Mountain National Park in Larimer County —78868, Lake Huron waters and shores in Ontario —7132, Cumberland Mountains —7691, Cumberland Mountains in Bell County, Kentucky —769123

Class comprehensive works in 001–999, without adding notation from Table 2

See Manual at T2—4–9; also at T2—3 vs. T2—4–9

(Option: Class here specific parts of the ancient world; prefer —3)

(Option: To give local emphasis and a shorter number to a specific country, place it first under its own continent or major region by use of a letter or other symbol, e.g., Pakistan —5P [preceding —51]; then subarrange each such number like the corresponding number in this table, e.g., Peshawar —5P23. Apply like any other area notation, e.g., geology of Peshawar 555.P23, history of Pakistan since 1971 95P.05, history of medical sciences in Pakistan 610.95P)

—4   Europe   Western Europe

Class here nations belonging to the Council of Europe, southern Europe

Class Eurasia in —5

(Option: Class here ancient Europe, western Europe, southern Europe; prefer —36 for ancient Europe, western Europe, —38 for ancient southern Europe)

SUMMARY

—41	**British Isles**
—411	Scotland
—412	Northeastern Scotland
—413	Southeastern Scotland
—414	Southwestern Scotland
—415	Ireland
—416	Ulster Northern Ireland
—417	Republic of Ireland (Eire)
—418	Leinster
—419	Munster
—42	**England and Wales**
—421	Greater London
—422	Southeastern England
—423	Southwestern England and Channel Islands
—424	Midlands of England
—425	East Midlands of England
—426	Eastern England East Anglia
—427	Northwestern England and Isle of Man
—428	Northeastern England
—429	Wales
—43	**Central Europe Germany**
—431	Northeastern Germany
—432	Saxony and Thuringia
—433	Bavaria (Bayern)
—434	Southwestern Germany
—435	Northwestern Germany
—436	Austria and Liechtenstein
—437	Czech Republic and Slovakia
—438	Poland
—439	Hungary
—44	**France and Monaco**
—441	Northwestern France Brittany (Bretagne) region
—442	Northern France Normandy (Normandie) region
—443	Northeastern France Champagne region
—444	Eastern France Burgundy (Bourgogne) region
—445	Central France Centre region
—446	Western France Poitou region
—447	Southwestern France Guyenne (Aquitaine) region
—448	Southern France Languedoc region
—449	Southeastern France and Monaco Provence region
—45	**Italian Peninsula and adjacent islands Italy**
—451	Northwestern Italy Piedmont (Piemonte) region
—452	Lombardy (Lombardia) region
—453	Northeastern Italy Veneto region
—454	Emilia-Romagna region and San Marino
—455	Tuscany (Toscana) region
—456	Central Italy and Vatican City
—457	Southern Italy
—458	Sicily and adjacent islands
—459	Sardinia

—46	Iberian Peninsula and adjacent islands Spain
—461	Northwestern Spain Galicia autonomous community
—462	Western Spain León region
—463	Castile
—464	New Castile region Castilla-La Mancha autonomous community
—465	Northeastern Spain
—466	País Vasco autonomous community
—467	Eastern Spain and Andorra Cataluña autonomous community
—468	Andalusia autonomous community and Gibraltar
—469	Portugal
—47	Eastern Europe Russia
—471	Northern area of European Russia
—472	Western area of Russia
—473	West central area of Russia
—474	Eastern area of European Russia
—475	Caucasus
—476	Moldova
—477	Ukraine
—478	Belarus
—479	Lithuania, Latvia, Estonia
—48	Scandinavia
—481	Norway
—482	Southeastern Norway (Østlandet)
—483	Southwestern Norway (Sørlandet and Vestlandet)
—484	Central and northern Norway (Trøndelag and Nord-Norge)
—485	Sweden
—486	Southern Sweden (Götaland)
—487	Central Sweden (Svealand)
—488	Northern Sweden (Norrland)
—489	Denmark and Finland
—49	Other parts of Europe
—491	Northwestern islands
—492	Netherlands (Holland)
—493	Southern Low Countries Belgium
—494	Switzerland
—495	Greece
—496	Balkan Peninsula
—497	Yugoslavia, Croatia, Slovenia, Bosnia and Hercegovina, Macedonia
—498	Romania
—499	Bulgaria

—41 British Isles

Class here Great Britain, United Kingdom

For England and Wales, see —42

See Manual at T2—41 and T2—42

(Option: Class here ancient British Isles; prefer —361)

SUMMARY

—411	Scotland
—412	Northeastern Scotland
—413	Southeastern Scotland
—414	Southwestern Scotland
—415	Ireland
—416	Ulster Northern Ireland
—417	Republic of Ireland (Eire)
—418	Leinster
—419	Munster

—411   Scotland

> *For northeastern Scotland, see —412; for southeastern Scotland, see —413; for southwestern Scotland, see —414*

(Option: Class here ancient northern Britain; prefer —361)

—411 1   Northern Scotland

> *For divisions of northern Scotland, see —4112–4119*

> —411 2–411 9   Divisions of northern Scotland

Class comprehensive works in —4111

—411 2   Islands authorities

> *For Orkney and Shetland, see —4113; for Western Isles, see —4114*

—411 3   Orkney and Shetland Islands authorities

—411 32   Orkney Islands Authority

—411 35   Shetland Islands Authority

—411 4   Western Isles (Outer Hebrides) Islands Authority

Class here comprehensive works on Hebrides

> *For Inner Hebrides, see —4118*

—411 5   Highland Region

Class here *Scottish Highlands

> *For districts of Highland Region, see —4116–4119*

> —411 6–411 9   Districts of Highland Region

Class comprehensive works in —4115

—411 6   Northern districts of Highland Region

---

*For a specific part of this jurisdiction, region, or feature, see the part and follow instructions under —4–9

—411 62	Caithness District
—411 65	Sutherland District
—411 7	Central districts of Highland Region
—411 72	Ross and Cromarty District
—411 75	Inverness District
	Class here *Great Glen
—411 8	Western districts of Highland Region
	Class here *Inner Hebrides
—411 82	Skye and Lochalsh District
—411 85	Lochaber District
—411 9	Eastern districts of Highland Region
—411 92	Badenoch and Strathspey District
	Class here *Spey River
—411 95	Nairn District
—412	Northeastern Scotland
—412 1	Grampian Region
	Class here *Grampian Mountains
	For districts of Grampian, see —4122–4124

>	—412 2–412 4	Districts of Grampian

Class comprehensive works in —4121

—412 2	Northern districts of Grampian
—412 23	Moray District
—412 25	Banff and Buchan District
	Class here *Deveron River
—412 3	Central districts of Grampian
—412 32	Gordon District
	Class here former *Aberdeenshire; *Don River
—412 35	City of Aberdeen
	Class here Aberdeen
—412 4	Kincardine and Deeside District
	Class here *Cairngorm Mountains; *Dee River

*For a specific part of this jurisdiction, region, or feature, see the part and follow instructions under —4–9

—412 5	Tayside Region
	Class here *Strathmore
	For districts of Tayside, see —4126–4128

>	—412 6–412 8 Districts of Tayside
	Class comprehensive works in —4125
—412 6	Angus District
—412 7	City of Dundee
	Class here Dundee
—412 8	Perth and Kinross District
	Class here *Ochil Hills; *Tay River
—412 9	Fife Region
—412 92	North East Fife District
—412 95	Kirkcaldy District
—412 98	Dunfermline District
—413	Southeastern Scotland
	Class here *Central Lowlands
—413 1	Central Region
	Class here *Forth River
	See also —16336 for Firth of Forth
—413 12	Stirling District
	Class here *Lennox Hills
—413 15	Clackmannan District
—413 18	Falkirk District
—413 2	Lothian Region
	For districts of Lothian, see —4133–4136

>	—413 3–413 6 Districts of Lothian
	Class comprehensive works in —4132
—413 3	West Lothian District

*For a specific part of this jurisdiction, region, or feature, see the part and follow instructions under —4–9

—413 4	City of Edinburgh
	Class here Edinburgh
—413 5	Midlothian District
	Class here *Pentland Hills
—413 6	East Lothian District
	Class here *Lammermuir Hills
—413 7	Borders Region
	Class here *Border Country, *Southern Uplands; *Tweed River
	For districts of Borders Region, see —4138–4139

>	—413 8–413 9 Districts of Borders Region
	Class comprehensive works in —4137
—413 8	Western districts of Borders Region
—413 82	Tweeddale District
	Former name: Peeblesshire
—413 85	Ettrick and Lauderdale District
	Including former Selkirkshire
—413 9	Eastern districts of Borders Region
—413 92	Roxburgh District
—413 95	Berwickshire District
—414	Southwestern Scotland
—414 1	Strathclyde Region
	Class here *Clyde River
	For districts of Strathclyde, see —4142–4146
	See also —16337 for Firth of Clyde

>	—414 2–414 6 Districts of Strathclyde
	Class comprehensive works in —4141
—414 2	Northwestern districts of Strathclyde
—414 23	Argyll and Bute District
—414 25	Dumbarton District
	Class here former *Dunbartonshire; *Loch Lomond

*For a specific part of this jurisdiction, region, or feature, see the part and follow instructions under —4–9

—414 28	Inverclyde District
—414 3	North central districts of Strathclyde
—414 32	Clydebank District
—414 34	Bearsden and Milngavie District
—414 36	Strathkelvin District
—414 38	Cumbernauld and Kilsyth District
—414 4	Central districts of Strathclyde
—414 41	Renfrew District
—414 43	City of Glasgow

Class here Glasgow

—414 46	Monklands District
—414 49	Motherwell District
—414 5	South central districts of Strathclyde
—414 51	Eastwood District
—414 54	East Kilbride District
—414 57	Hamilton District
—414 6	Southern districts of Strathclyde

Class here former Ayrshire

—414 61	Cunninghame District
—414 63	Kilmarnock and Loudoun District
—414 64	Kyle and Carrick District
—414 67	Cumnock and Doon Valley District
—414 69	Clydesdale District

Former name: Lanark District

—414 7	Dumfries and Galloway Region

For districts of Dumfries and Galloway, see —4148–4149

See also —16337 for Solway Firth

>	**—414 8–414 9 Districts of Dumfries and Galloway**

Class comprehensive works in —4147

—414 8	Eastern districts of Dumfries and Galloway

Class here former Dumfriesshire

—414 83	Annandale and Eskdale District
—414 86	Nithsdale District
	Class here *Nith River
—414 9	**Western districts of Dumfries and Galloway**
	Class here former *Galloway
—414 92	Stewartry District
	Class here former *Kirkcudbrightshire
—414 95	Wigtown District
—415	Ireland

For divisions of Ireland, see —416–419

(Option: Class here ancient Ireland; prefer —361)

>   **—416–419   Divisions of Ireland**

Class comprehensive works in —415

—416	Ulster	Northern Ireland

Class here *Bann River, *Lough Neagh

>   **—416 1–416 7   Northern Ireland**

Class comprehensive works in —416

—416 1	Northeast area
	Class here former *Antrim county
—416 12	Antrim Borough
—416 13	Ballymena Borough
—416 14	Ballymoney Borough
—416 15	Moyle District
—416 16	Larne Borough
—416 17	Carrickfergus Borough
—416 18	Newtownabbey Borough
—416 19	Lisburn Borough

>   **—416 2–416 4   Western area**

Class comprehensive works in —4162

*For a specific part of this jurisdiction, region, or feature, see the part and follow instructions under —4–9

—416 2	**Western area**

Class here former Londonderry (Derry) county; *Sperrin Mountains

For Fermanagh District, see —4163; for West central area, see —4164

—416 21	City of Derry

Class here Derry (Londonderry)

—416 25	Limavady District
—416 27	Coleraine Borough
—416 29	Magherafelt District
—416 3	**Fermanagh District**
—416 4	**West central area**

Class here former Tyrone county

—416 41	Strabane District
—416 43	Cookstown District
—416 45	Dungannon District
—416 47	Omagh District
—416 5	**Southeast area**

Class here former Down county

—416 51	Castlereagh Borough
—416 53	North Down Borough
—416 54	Ards Borough

Class here *Strangford Lough

—416 56	Down District
—416 57	Banbridge District
—416 58	Newry and Mourne District

Class here *Mourne Mountains

—416 6	**Southern area**

Class here former *Armagh county

—416 61	Armagh District
—416 64	' Craigavon Borough
—416 7	**City of Belfast**

Class here Belfast, *Greater Belfast

*For a specific part of this jurisdiction, region, or feature, see the part and follow instructions under —4–9

—416 9   Counties of Republic of Ireland in Ulster

—416 93   Donegal County

—416 97   Monaghan County

—416 98   Cavan County

—417   Republic of Ireland (Eire)

                Class here *Shannon River

                    For counties in Ulster, see —4169; for Leinster, see —418; for Munster,
                    see —419

—417 1   Connacht

                    For divisions of Connacht, see —4172–4176

>   —417 2–417 6   Divisions of Connacht

                Class comprehensive works in —4171

—417 2   Sligo County

—417 25   Sligo

—417 3   Mayo County

—417 4   Galway County

—417 45   Galway

—417 48   Aran Islands

—417 5   Roscommon County

—417 6   Leitrim County

—418   Leinster

                Class here *Barrow River

—418 1   Northwest Leinster

—418 12   Longford County

—418 15   Westmeath County

—418 2   Northeast Leinster

—418 22   Meath County

                    Class here *Boyne River

—418 25   Louth County

—418 256   Drogheda

---

*For a specific part of this jurisdiction, region, or feature, see the part and follow instructions
    under —4–9

—418 3	Dublin County
	Class here *Liffey River
—418 35	Dublin
—418 38	Dún Laoghaire
—418 4	Wicklow County
—418 5	Kildare County
	Class here *Bog of Allen
—418 6	Offaly County
—418 7	Laois County
—418 8	Southeast Leinster
—418 82	Carlow County
—418 85	Wexford County
—418 856	Wexford
—418 9	Kilkenny County
	Class here *Nore River
—419	Munster
—419 1	Waterford County
	Class here *Suir River
—419 15	Waterford
—419 2	Tipperary County
—419 25	Clonmel
—419 3	Clare County
—419 4	Limerick County
—419 45	Limerick
—419 5	Cork County
	Class here *Blackwater River
—419 56	Cork
—419 6	Kerry County
—419 65	Killarney

*For a specific part of this jurisdiction, region, or feature, see the part and follow instructions under —4–9

—42   **England and Wales**

See Manual at T2—41 and T2—42

(Option: Class here ancient southern Britain, England; prefer —362)

SUMMARY

—421	**Greater London**
—422	**Southeastern England**
—423	**Southwestern England and Channel Islands**
—424	**Midlands of England**
—425	**East Midlands of England**
—426	**Eastern England East Anglia**
—427	**Northwestern England and Isle of Man**
—428	**Northeastern England**
—429	**Wales**

>   —421–428   England

Class comprehensive works in —42

—421   Greater London

—421 2   City of London

—421 3   West London

—421 32   City of Westminster

—421 33   Hammersmith and Fulham London Borough

—421 34   Kensington and Chelsea Royal Borough

—421 4   North London

—421 42   Camden London Borough

—421 43   Islington London Borough

—421 44   Hackney London Borough

—421 5   Tower Hamlets London Borough

—421 6   South London

—421 62   Greenwich London Borough

—421 63   Lewisham London Borough

—421 64   Southwark London Borough

—421 65   Lambeth London Borough

—421 66   Wandsworth London Borough

—421 7   Outer London

For boroughs created from Middlesex, see —4218; for boroughs created from Surrey, see —4219

>	—421 72–421 76 Boroughs created from Essex
	Class comprehensive works in —4217
—421 72	Waltham Forest London Borough
—421 73	Redbridge London Borough
—421 74	Havering London Borough
—421 75	Barking and Dagenham London Borough
—421 76	Newham London Borough

>	—421 77–421 78 Boroughs created from Kent
	Class comprehensive works in —4217
—421 77	Bexley London Borough
—421 78	Bromley London Borough
—421 8	**Boroughs created from Middlesex**
	Class here former Middlesex
—421 82	Hounslow London Borough
—421 83	Hillingdon London Borough
—421 84	Ealing London Borough
—421 85	Brent London Borough
—421 86	Harrow London Borough
—421 87	Barnet London Borough
—421 88	Haringey London Borough
—421 89	Enfield London Borough
—421 9	**Boroughs created from Surrey**
—421 91	Croydon London Borough
—421 92	Sutton London Borough
—421 93	Merton London Borough
—421 94	Kingston upon Thames London Borough
—421 95	Richmond upon Thames London Borough
—422	**Southeastern England**
	Class here *Home Counties; *Thames River
	For Greater London, see —421

*For a specific part of this jurisdiction, region, or feature, see the part and follow instructions under —4–9

—422 1	Surrey
	Class London boroughs created from Surrey in —4219
—422 11	Runnymede Borough
—422 12	Spelthorne Borough
—422 13	Surrey Heath Borough
—422 14	Woking and Elmbridge Boroughs
—422 142	Woking Borough
	Class here Woking
—422 145	Elmbridge Borough
—422 15	Epsom and Ewell Borough
—422 16	Guildford Borough and Mole Valley District
—422 162	Guildford Borough
—422 165	Mole Valley District
—422 17	Reigate and Banstead Borough
—422 18	Tandridge District
—422 19	Waverley Borough
—422 3	Kent
	Class here *North Downs
	Class London boroughs created from Kent in —42177–42178
—422 31	Dartford and Gravesham Boroughs
—422 312	Dartford Borough
—422 315	Gravesham Borough
—422 32	City of Rochester upon Medway and Gillingham Borough
—422 323	City of Rochester upon Medway
—422 325	Gillingham Borough
	Class here Gillingham
—422 33	Swale Borough
—422 34	City of Canterbury
—422 35	Dover and Thanet Districts
—422 352	Dover District
	Class here *Cinque Ports

*For a specific part of this jurisdiction, region, or feature, see the part and follow instructions under —4–9

—422 357	Thanet District
—422 36	Sevenoaks District
—422 37	Tonbridge and Malling, and Maidstone Boroughs
—422 372	Tonbridge and Malling Borough
—422 375	Maidstone Borough
—422 38	Tunbridge Wells Borough
—422 39	Ashford Borough and Shepway District
—422 392	Ashford Borough
—422 395	Shepway District
—422 5	East Sussex

Class here former Sussex; the *Weald

For West Sussex, see —4226

—422 51	Wealden District
—422 52	Rother District
—422 54	Hove Borough

Class here Hove

—422 56	Brighton Borough

Class here Brighton

—422 57	Lewes District
—422 58	Eastbourne Borough

Class here Eastbourne

—422 59	Hastings Borough

Class here Hastings

—422 6	West Sussex

Class here *South Downs

—422 61	Crawley Borough

Class here Crawley

—422 62	Chichester District
—422 64	Horsham District
—422 65	Mid Sussex District
—422 67	Arun District

*For a specific part of this jurisdiction, region, or feature, see the part and follow instructions under —4–9

—422 68	Worthing Borough
	Class here Worthing
—422 69	Adur District
—422 7	**Hampshire**
—422 71	Basingstoke and Deane Borough
—422 72	Hart District and Rushmoor Borough
—422 723	Hart District
—422 725	Rushmoor Borough
—422 73	Test Valley Borough and City of Winchester
—422 732	Test Valley Borough
	Class here *Test River
—422 735	City of Winchester
—422 74	East Hampshire District
—422 75	New Forest District
—422 76	City of Southampton
	Class here Southampton
—422 77	Eastleigh and Fareham Boroughs
—422 772	Eastleigh Borough
—422 775	Fareham Borough
	Class here Fareham
—422 78	Gosport Borough
	Class here Gosport
—422 79	City of Portsmouth and Havant Borough
—422 792	City of Portsmouth
	Class here Portsmouth
—422 795	Havant Borough
—422 8	**Isle of Wight**
—422 82	Medina Borough
—422 85	South Wight Borough
—422 9	**Berkshire**
—422 91	Newbury District

*For a specific part of this jurisdiction, region, or feature, see the part and follow instructions under —4–9

—422 93	Reading Borough
	Class here Reading
—422 94	Wokingham District
—422 96	Windsor and Maidenhead Royal Borough
—422 97	Slough Borough
	Class here Slough
—422 98	Bracknell Forest Borough
—423	Southwestern England and Channel Islands
—423 1	Wiltshire
—423 12	North Wiltshire District
—423 13	Thamesdown Borough
—423 15	West Wiltshire District
—423 17	Kennet District
—423 19	Salisbury District
	Class here *Salisbury Plain; *East Avon River
—423 3	Dorset
	Class here *Stour River
—423 31	West Dorset District
—423 32	North Dorset District
—423 34	East Dorset District
—423 35	Weymouth and Portland Borough
—423 36	Purbeck District
—423 37	Poole Borough
	Class here Poole
—423 38	Bournemouth Borough
	Class here Bournemouth
—423 39	Christchurch Borough
—423 4	Channel Islands
—423 41	Jersey
	For Minquiers, see —42348; for Dirouilles, Ecrehous, Paternosters, see —42349

*For a specific part of this jurisdiction, region, or feature, see the part and follow instructions under —4–9

—423 42	Guernsey
	For Jethou, see —42347; for Lihou, Lihoumel, see —42349
—423 43	Alderney
	For Burhou, see —42347; for Casquets, see —42348
—423 45	Sark
	For Brecqhou, see —42347
—423 46	Herm
—423 47	Brecqhou, Burhou, Jethou
—423 48	Casquets, Chausey Islands, Minquiers
—423 49	Other islands
	Including Barnouic, Dirouilles, Ecrehous, Lihou, Lihoumel, Paternosters, Roches Douvres
—423 5	Devon
	Class here *Exe River, *Tamar River
—423 51	Torridge District
—423 52	North Devon District
—423 53	West Devon Borough
	Class here *Dartmoor
—423 54	Mid Devon District
—423 55	Teignbridge District
—423 56	City of Exeter
	Class here Exeter
—423 57	East Devon District
—423 58	City of Plymouth
	Class here Plymouth
—423 59	South Hams District and Torbay Borough
—423 592	South Hams District
	Class here *Dart River
—423 595	Torbay Borough
	Class here Torbay
—423 7	Cornwall and Scilly Isles

*For a specific part of this jurisdiction, region, or feature, see the part and follow instructions under —4–9

>		—423 71–423 78 Cornwall
		Class comprehensive works in —4237
—423 71		North Cornwall District
—423 72		Restormel Borough
—423 74		Caradon District
—423 75		Penwith District
—423 76		Kerrier District
—423 78		Carrick District
		Class here *Fal River
—423 79		Scilly Isles
—423 8	Somerset	
—423 81		Sedgemoor District
—423 83		Mendip District
		Class here *Mendip Hills
—423 85		West Somerset District
		Class here *Exmoor, *Quantock Hills
—423 87		Taunton Deane District
		Class here *Blackdown Hills
—423 89		South Somerset District
—423 9	Avon	
		Class here *Lower (Bristol) Avon River
—423 91		Northavon District
—423 93		City of Bristol
		Class here Bristol
—423 94		Kingswood Borough
—423 96		Woodspring District
—423 97		Wansdyke District
—423 98		City of Bath
		Class here Bath

*For a specific part of this jurisdiction, region, or feature, see the part and follow instructions under —4–9

—424	Midlands of England

Class here *Welsh Marches; *Severn River

For East Midlands, see —425

—424 1	Gloucestershire
—424 12	Tewkesbury Borough
—424 13	Forest of Dean District
—424 14	City of Gloucester

Class here Gloucester

—424 16	Cheltenham Borough

Class here Cheltenham

—424 17	Cotswold District

Class here *Cotswolds

—424 19	Stroud District
—424 4	Hereford and Worcester

Class here *Upper (Warwickshire) Avon River

—424 41	Wyre Forest District
—424 42	Bromsgrove District
—424 43	Redditch Borough

Class here Redditch

—424 44	Leominster District
—424 45	South Herefordshire District
—424 46	City of Hereford

Class here Hereford

—424 47	Malvern Hills District
—424 48	City of Worcester

Class here Worcester

—424 49	Wychavon District
—424 5	Shropshire
—424 51	Oswestry Borough
—424 53	North Shropshire District
—424 54	Shrewsbury and Atcham Borough

*For a specific part of this jurisdiction, region, or feature, see the part and follow instructions under —4–9

—424 56	The Wrekin District
—424 57	South Shropshire District
—424 59	Bridgnorth District
—424 6	**Staffordshire**
—424 61	Staffordshire Moorlands District
—424 62	Newcastle-under-Lyme Borough
—424 63	City of Stoke-on-Trent
	Class here Stoke-on-Trent
—424 64	Stafford Borough
—424 65	East Staffordshire Borough
—424 66	South Staffordshire District
—424 67	Cannock Chase District
—424 68	Lichfield District
—424 69	Tamworth Borough
	Class here Tamworth
—424 8	**Warwickshire**
—424 81	North Warwickshire Borough
—424 83	Nuneaton and Bedworth Borough
—424 85	Rugby Borough
—424 87	Warwick District
—424 89	Stratford-on-Avon District
—424 9	**West Midlands Metropolitan County** **Black Country**
—424 91	Wolverhampton Metropolitan Borough
	Class here Wolverhampton
—424 92	Walsall Metropolitan Borough
	Class here Walsall
—424 93	Dudley Metropolitan Borough
—424 94	Sandwell Metropolitan Borough
—424 96	City of Birmingham
	Class here Birmingham
—424 97	Solihull Metropolitan Borough
—424 98	City of Coventry
	Class here Coventry

—425   East Midlands of England

         Class here *Chilterns; *Trent River

SUMMARY

—425 1	Derbyshire
—425 2	Nottinghamshire
—425 3	Lincolnshire
—425 4	Leicestershire
—425 5	Northamptonshire
—425 6	Bedfordshire
—425 7	Oxfordshire
—425 8	Hertfordshire
—425 9	Buckinghamshire

—425 1   Derbyshire

         Class here *Derwent River of Derbyshire

—425 11   High Peak Borough

         Class here *Peak District

—425 12   Chesterfield Borough

—425 13   Derbyshire Dales District

         Class here *Dove River

—425 14   North East Derbyshire District

—425 15   Bolsover District

—425 16   Amber Valley Borough

—425 17   City of Derby

         Class here Derby

—425 18   Erewash Borough

—425 19   South Derbyshire District

—425 2   Nottinghamshire

—425 21   Bassetlaw District

—425 23   Mansfield District

—425 24   Newark and Sherwood District

         Class here *Sherwood Forest

—425 25   Ashfield District

—425 26   Broxtowe Borough

—425 27   City of Nottingham

         Class here Nottingham

*For a specific part of this jurisdiction, region, or feature, see the part and follow instructions under —4–9

—425 28	Gedling Borough
—425 29	Rushcliffe Borough
—425 3	Lincolnshire

Class here *Lincoln Heath; *the Wash; *Witham River

—425 31	West Lindsey District

Class here former *Parts of Lindsey

—425 32	East Lindsey District

Class here *Lincoln Wolds

—425 34	City of Lincoln

Class here Lincoln

—425 35	North Kesteven District

Class here former Parts of Kesteven

For South Kesteven, see —42538

—425 37	Boston Borough
—425 38	South Kesteven District
—425 39	South Holland District

Class here former Parts of Holland; *Welland River

For Boston Borough, see —42537

—425 4	Leicestershire
—425 41	Blaby District
—425 42	City of Leicester

Class here Leicester

—425 43	Oadby and Wigston Borough
—425 44	Harborough District
—425 45	Rutland District
—425 46	Melton Borough
—425 47	Charnwood Borough
—425 48	North West Leicestershire District
—425 49	Hinckley and Bosworth Borough
—425 5	Northamptonshire

Class here *Nene River

*For a specific part of this jurisdiction, region, or feature, see the part and follow instructions under —4–9

—425 51	Corby Borough
—425 52	Kettering Borough
—425 54	East Northamptonshire District
—425 56	Daventry District
	Class here *Northampton Uplands
—425 57	Northampton Borough
	Class here Northampton
—425 58	Wellingborough Borough
—425 59	South Northamptonshire District
—425 6	Bedfordshire
—425 61	Bedford Borough
	Former name: North Bedfordshire Borough
—425 63	Mid Bedfordshire District
—425 65	South Bedfordshire District
—425 67	Luton Borough
	Class here Luton
—425 7	Oxfordshire
—425 71	West Oxfordshire District
—425 73	Cherwell District
—425 74	City of Oxford
	Class here Oxford
—425 76	Vale of White Horse District
—425 79	South Oxfordshire District
—425 8	Hertfordshire
—425 81	North Hertfordshire District
—425 82	Stevenage Borough
	Class here Stevenage
—425 83	East Hertfordshire District
—425 84	Dacorum District
—425 85	City of Saint Albans
—425 86	Welwyn Hatfield District

*For a specific part of this jurisdiction, region, or feature, see the part and follow instructions under —4–9

—425 87	Broxbourne Borough
—425 88	Three Rivers District
—425 89	Watford and Hertsmere Boroughs
—425 892	Watford Borough
	Class here Watford
—425 895	Hertsmere Borough
—425 9	**Buckinghamshire**
—425 91	Milton Keynes Borough
	Class here Milton Keynes
—425 93	Aylesbury Vale District
—425 95	Wycombe District
—425 97	Chiltern District
—425 98	South Bucks District
—426	**Eastern England East Anglia**
	Class here *The Fens; *Great Ouse River

>	**—426 1–426 5 East Anglia**
	Class comprehensive works in —426
—426 1	**Norfolk**
	Class here *Yare River
—426 12	North Norfolk District
—426 13	King's Lynn and West Norfolk Borough
—426 14	Breckland District
—426 15	City of Norwich
	Class here Norwich
—426 17	Broadland District
	Class here *Norfolk Broads
—426 18	Great Yarmouth Borough
—426 19	South Norfolk District
	Class here *Waveney River
—426 4	**Suffolk**

*For a specific part of this jurisdiction, region, or feature, see the part and follow instructions under —4–9

—426 41	Waveney District
—426 43	Forest Heath District
—426 44	Saint Edmundsbury Borough
	Class here former *West Suffolk
—426 45	Mid Suffolk District
—426 46	Suffolk Coastal District
	Class here former *East Suffolk
—426 48	Babergh District
—426 49	Ipswich Borough
	Class here Ipswich
—426 5	Cambridgeshire
—426 51	City of Peterborough
—426 53	Fenland District
	Class here former Isle of Ely
	See also —42656 for Ely
—426 54	Huntingdonshire District
—426 56	East Cambridgeshire District
—426 57	South Cambridgeshire District
—426 59	City of Cambridge
	Class here Cambridge
—426 7	Essex
	Class London boroughs created from Essex in —42172–42176
—426 71	Uttlesford and Braintree Districts
—426 712	Uttlesford District
—426 715	Braintree District
—426 72	Colchester Borough and Tendring District
—426 723	Colchester Borough
—426 725	Tendring District
—426 73	Harlow District
	Class here Harlow
—426 74	Epping Forest District

*For a specific part of this jurisdiction, region, or feature, see the part and follow instructions under —4–9

—426 75	Chelmsford Borough and Maldon District
—426 752	Chelmsford Borough
—426 756	Maldon District
—426 76	Brentwood Borough
—426 77	Basildon and Rochford Districts
—426 772	Basildon District
	Class here Basildon
—426 775	Rochford District
—426 78	Thurrock Borough
	Class here Thurrock
—426 79	Castle Point District and Southend-on-Sea Borough
—426 792	Castle Point District
—426 795	Southend-on-Sea Borough
	Class here Southend-on-Sea

—427 Northwestern England and Isle of Man

Class here comprehensive works on northern England

For northeastern England, see —428

—427 1	**Cheshire**
—427 12	Crewe and Nantwich Borough
—427 13	Congleton Borough
—427 14	City of Chester
—427 15	Vale Royal Borough
—427 16	Macclesfield Borough
—427 17	Ellesmere Port and Neston Borough
—427 18	Halton Borough
—427 19	Warrington Borough
—427 3	**Greater Manchester Metropolitan County**
—427 31	Trafford Metropolitan Borough
—427 32	City of Salford
—427 33	City of Manchester
	Class here Manchester
—427 34	Stockport Metropolitan Borough

—427 35	Tameside Metropolitan Borough
—427 36	Wigan Metropolitan Borough
—427 37	Bolton Metropolitan Borough
—427 38	Bury Metropolitan Borough
—427 39	Rochdale and Oldham Metropolitan Boroughs
—427 392	Rochdale Metropolitan Borough
—427 393	Oldham Metropolitan Borough
—427 5	**Merseyside Metropolitan County**
	Class here *Mersey River
—427 51	Wirral Metropolitan Borough
—427 53	City of Liverpool
	Class here Liverpool
—427 54	Knowsley Metropolitan Borough
—427 57	Saint Helens Metropolitan Borough
—427 59	Sefton Metropolitan Borough
—427 6	Lancashire
—427 61	West Lancashire District and Chorley Borough
—427 612	West Lancashire District
—427 615	Chorley Borough
—427 62	Blackburn and Hyndburn Boroughs
—427 623	Blackburn Borough
—427 625	Hyndburn Borough
—427 63	Rossendale Borough
—427 64	Burnley and Pendle Boroughs
—427 642	Burnley Borough
—427 645	Pendle Borough
—427 65	Blackpool Borough
	Class here Blackpool
—427 66	Fylde and Preston Boroughs
—427 662	Fylde Borough
	Class here *The Fylde

*For a specific part of this jurisdiction, region, or feature, see the part and follow instructions under —4–9

—427 665	Preston Borough
—427 67	South Ribble Borough
—427 68	Wyre and Ribble Valley Boroughs
—427 682	Wyre Borough
—427 685	Ribble Valley Borough

Class here *Forest of Bowland; *Ribble River

—427 69	City of Lancaster
—427 8	**Cumbria**

Class here former Cumberland, former Westmorland; Lake District; Cumbrian Mountains

—427 81	Barrow-in-Furness Borough
—427 83	South Lakeland District
—427 84	Copeland Borough
—427 86	Eden District

Class here *Eden River

—427 87	Allerdale District

See also — *16337 for Solway Firth*

—427 89	City of Carlisle
—427 9	**Isle of Man**
—428	**Northeastern England**

Class here the *Pennines

—428 1	**West Yorkshire Metropolitan County**

Class here former *Yorkshire, former *West Riding of Yorkshire

—428 12	Calderdale Metropolitan Borough
—428 13	Kirklees Metropolitan Borough
—428 15	City of Wakefield

Class here *Aire River

—428 17	City of Bradford
—428 19	City of Leeds
—428 2	**South Yorkshire Metropolitan County**
—428 21	City of Sheffield
—428 23	Rotherham Metropolitan Borough

*For a specific part of this jurisdiction, region, or feature, see the part and follow instructions under —4–9

—428 25	Barnsley Metropolitan Borough
—428 27	Doncaster Metropolitan Borough
—428 3	Humberside

         Class here former *East Riding of Yorkshire; *Yorkshire Wolds; *Humber River

—428 31	Scunthorpe Borough

         Class here Scunthorpe

—428 32	Glanford Borough
—428 33	Cleethorpes Borough
—428 34	Great Grimsby Borough

         Class here Grimsby

—428 35	Boothferry Borough
—428 36	Beverley Borough
—428 37	City of Kingston upon Hull

         Class here Hull

—428 38	Holderness Borough
—428 39	East Yorkshire Borough
—428 4	North Yorkshire

         Class here former *North Riding of Yorkshire; *Yorkshire Dales; *Derwent River of Yorkshire, *Ouse River

—428 41	Craven District
—428 42	Harrogate Borough
—428 43	City of York

         Class here York

—428 45	Selby District
—428 46	Ryedale District

         Class here *North Yorkshire Moors

—428 47	Scarborough Borough
—428 48	Richmondshire District

         Class here *Swale River, *Ure River

—428 49	Hambleton District

         Class here *Cleveland Hills

*For a specific part of this jurisdiction, region, or feature, see the part and follow instructions under —4–9

—428 5	Cleveland
	Including former Teesside
	Class here *Tees River
—428 51	Stockton-on-Tees Borough
—428 53	Middlesbrough Borough
—428 54	Langbaurgh-on-Tees Borough
—428 57	Hartlepool Borough
	Class here Hartlepool
—428 6	Durham
	Class here *Wear River
—428 61	Teesdale District
—428 62	Sedgefield District
—428 63	Darlington Borough
—428 64	Wear Valley District
—428 65	City of Durham
—428 67	Easington District
—428 68	Derwentside District
—428 69	Chester-le-Street District
—428 7	Tyne and Wear Metropolitan County
	Class here *Tyne River
—428 71	Sunderland Metropolitan Borough
—428 73	Gateshead Metropolitan Borough
—428 75	South Tyneside Metropolitan Borough
—428 76	City of Newcastle upon Tyne
	Class here Newcastle upon Tyne
—428 79	North Tyneside Metropolitan Borough
—428 8	Northumberland
	Class here *Cheviot Hills
—428 81	Tynedale District
	Class here *Hadrian's Wall
—428 83	Castle Morpeth Borough

*For a specific part of this jurisdiction, region, or feature, see the part and follow instructions under —4–9

—428 84	Blyth Valley Borough
—428 86	Wansbeck District
—428 87	Alnwick District
	Class here *Coquet River
—428 89	Berwick-upon-Tweed Borough
—429	Wales
	Class here *Cambrian Mountains
—429 1	North Wales

> For Gwynedd, see —4292; for Clwyd, see —4293; for Montgomery, see —42951

—429 2	Gwynedd
	Class here former Caernarvonshire
—429 21	Ynys Môn Borough (Isle of Anglesey)
—429 23	Dwyfor District
—429 25	Arfon Borough
	Class here *Snowdonia
—429 27	Aberconwy Borough
—429 29	Meirionnydd District
	Class here former *Merioneth
—429 3	Clwyd
	Class here former *Denbighshire
—429 31	Colwyn Borough
—429 32	Rhuddlan Borough
—429 33	Delyn Borough
	Class here former *Flintshire
—429 36	Alyn and Deeside District
—429 37	Glyndŵr District
—429 39	Wrexham Maelor District
—429 4	South Wales

> For Powys, see —4295; for Dyfed, see —4296; for Mid Glamorgan, see —4297; for West and South Glamorgan, see —4298; for Gwent, see —4299

*For a specific part of this jurisdiction, region, or feature, see the part and follow instructions under —4–9

—429 5	Powys
	Class here *mid Wales; *Wye River
—429 51	Montgomery District
	Class here *Severn River in Wales
—429 54	Radnor District
—429 56	Brecknock Borough
	Class here former *Breconshire
—429 6	Dyfed
—429 61	Ceredigion District
	Former name: Cardiganshire
—429 62	Preseli District
	Class here former *Pembrokeshire
—429 63	South Pembrokeshire District
—429 65	Carmarthen District
—429 67	Llanelli Borough
—429 68	Dinefwr Borough
—429 7	Mid Glamorgan
	Class here former Glamorgan
	For West and South Glamorgan, see —4298
—429 71	Ogwr Borough
—429 72	Rhondda Borough
	Class here Rhondda
—429 73	Cynon Valley Borough
—429 75	Merthyr Tydfil Borough
	Class here Merthyr Tydfil
—429 76	Rhymney Valley District
—429 78	Taff-Ely Borough
—429 8	West and South Glamorgan
—429 81	West Glamorgan
	For City of Swansea, see —42982; for Lliw Valley Borough, see —42983; for Neath Borough, see —42984; for Afan Borough, see —42985

*For a specific part of this jurisdiction, region, or feature, see the part and follow instructions under —4–9

—429 82	City of Swansea
—429 83	Lliw Valley Borough
—429 84	Neath Borough
—429 85	Afan Borough
—429 86	South Glamorgan

> *For City of Cardiff, see —42987; for Vale of Glamorgan Borough, see —42989*

—429 87	City of Cardiff

                  Class here Cardiff

—429 89	Vale of Glamorgan Borough
—429 9	Gwent

                  Class here former *Monmouthshire

—429 91	Newport Borough
—429 93	Islwyn Borough
—429 95	Blaenau Gwent Borough
—429 97	Torfaen Borough
—429 98	Monmouth District
—43	**Central Europe Germany**

                  Class here Federal Republic of Germany, *Holy Roman Empire

                  For Switzerland, see —494

                  (Option: Class here ancient Germanic regions; prefer —363)

SUMMARY

—431	**Northeastern Germany**
—432	**Saxony and Thuringia**
—433	**Bavaria (Bayern)**
—434	**Southwestern Germany**
—435	**Northwestern Germany**
—436	**Austria and Liechtenstein**
—437	**Czech Republic and Slovakia**
—438	**Poland**
—439	**Hungary**

>	—431–435 Germany

                  Class comprehensive works in —43

---

*For a specific part of this jurisdiction, region, or feature, see the part and follow instructions under —4–9

>   —431–432 Eastern Germany

      Class comprehensive works in —431

—431   Northeastern Germany

      Class here former German Democratic Republic (East Germany)

      For Saxony and Thuringia, see —432

—431 5   Brandenburg and Berlin

>   —431 51–431 53 Brandenburg

      Class comprehensive works in —4315

      For Potsdam district, see —43157

—431 51   Cottbus district (Bezirk)

—431 53   Frankfurt district (Bezirk)

—431 532   Frankfurt an der Oder

—431 55   Berlin

—431 552   East Berlin

—431 554   West Berlin

—431 57   Potsdam district (Bezirk)

—431 572   Potsdam

—431 7   Mecklenburg-Vorpommern

      Including German Pomerania

—431 72   Neubrandenburg district (Bezirk)

—431 74   Rostock district (Bezirk)

—431 76   Schwerin district (Bezirk)

—431 8   Saxony-Anhalt (Sachsen-Anhalt)

      Including Prussian Saxony

—431 82   Magdeburg district (Bezirk)

      Class here *Harz Mountains

—431 822   Magdeburg

—431 84   Halle district (Bezirk)

—432   Saxony and Thuringia

*For a specific part of this jurisdiction, region, or feature, see the part and follow instructions under —4–9

—432 1	Saxony (Sachsen)
—432 12	Leipzig district (Bezirk)
—432 122	Leipzig
—432 14	Dresden district (Bezirk)
—432 142	Dresden
—432 16	Karl-Marx-Stadt district (Bezirk)
—432 162	Karl-Marx-Stadt (Chemnitz)
—432 2	Thuringia (Thüringen)
	Including *Thuringian Forest
—432 22	Gera district (Bezirk)
—432 24	Erfurt district (Bezirk)
—432 26	Suhl district (Bezirk)

>   —433–435   Western Germany

Class here Federal Republic of Germany (West Germany, 1947–1990)

Class comprehensive works in —43

For West Berlin, see —431554

—433	Bavaria (Bayern)
	Class here *Franconian Jura; *Danube River in Germany
	(Option: Class here ancient Vindelicia; prefer —363)
—433 1	Upper Franconia district (Oberfranken Regierungsbezirk)
—433 11	Coburg
—433 15	Bayreuth
—433 18	Bamberg
—433 2	Middle Franconia district (Mittelfranken Regierungsbezirk)
—433 22	Erlangen
—433 24	Nuremberg (Nürnberg)
—433 3	Lower Franconia district (Unterfranken Regierungsbezirk)
—433 31	Aschaffenburg
—433 36	Schweinfurt
—433 39	Würzburg

*For a specific part of this jurisdiction, region, or feature, see the part and follow instructions under —4–9

—433 4	Upper Palatinate district (Oberpfalz Regierungsbezirk)
—433 47	Regensburg
—433 5	Lower Bavaria district (Niederbayern Regierungsbezirk)
	Class here *Bavarian Forest
—433 55	Passau
—433 58	Landshut
—433 6	Upper Bavaria district (Oberbayern Regierungsbezirk)
—433 62	Ingolstadt
—433 64	Munich (München)
—433 7	Swabia district (Schwaben Regierungsbezirk)
—433 75	Augsburg
—434	Southwestern Germany
	Class here *Main, *Rhine Rivers
—434 1	Hessen (Hesse)
—434 12	Kassel district (Regierungsbezirk)
—434 124	Kassel
—434 14	Giessen district (Regierungsbezirk)
	Class here *Lahn River
—434 16	Darmstadt district (Regierungsbezirk)
	Including *Taunus Mountains
—434 163	Offenbach am Main
—434 164	Frankfurt am Main
—434 165	Wiesbaden
—434 167	Darmstadt
—434 2	Saarland
	Class here *Saar River
—434 21	Saarbrücken
—434 3	Rhineland-Palatinate (Rheinland-Pfalz)
	Class here Rhine Province (Rhenish Prussia); *Moselle River
	For Saarland, see —4342; for North Rhine-Westphalia, see —4355
—434 31	Trier district (Regierungsbezirk)

*For a specific part of this jurisdiction, region, or feature, see the part and follow instructions under —4–9

—434 313	Trier
—434 32	Koblenz district (Regierungsbezirk)
—434 323	Koblenz
—434 35	Rheinhessen-Pfalz district (Regierungsbezirk)
	Class here Palatinate
	For Upper Palatinate, see —4334
—434 351	Mainz
—434 352	Worms
—434 353	Ludwigshafen am Rhein
—434 6	Baden-Württemberg
	Class here *Black Forest
	For Stuttgart and Tübingen districts, see —4347
—434 62	Freiburg district (Regierungsbezirk)
	Including *Lake Constance
—434 626	Freiburg im Breisgau
—434 64	Karlsruhe district (Regierungsbezirk)
	Class here former *Baden
—434 643	Karlsruhe
—434 645	Heidelberg
—434 646	Mannheim
—434 7	Stuttgart and Tübingen districts (Regierungsbezirke)
	Class here former *Württemberg
—434 71	Stuttgart district (Regierungsbezirk)
—434 715	Stuttgart
—434 73	Tübingen district (Regierungsbezirk)
	Including former Hohenzollern
	Class here *Swabian Jura
—435	Northwestern Germany
—435 1	Northernmost states
—435 12	Schleswig-Holstein
	Including North Friesland; *North Frisian Islands

*For a specific part of this jurisdiction, region, or feature, see the part and follow instructions under —4–9

—435 15	Hamburg
—435 2	**Bremen**
—435 21	Bremerhaven
—435 5	**North Rhine-Westphalia (Nordrhein-Westfalen)**

Class here *Ruhr River

For Münster, Arnsberg, Detmold districts, see —4356

—435 51	Cologne district (Köln Regierungsbezirk)
—435 511	Aachen
—435 514	Cologne (Köln)
—435 518	Bonn
—435 53	Düsseldorf district (Regierungsbezirk)
—435 532	Wuppertal
—435 534	Düsseldorf
—435 536	Duisburg
—435 538	Essen
—435 6	**Münster, Arnsberg, Detmold districts (Regierungsbezirke)**

Class here Westphalia; *Lippe River

—435 61	Münster district (Regierungsbezirk)
—435 614	Münster
—435 618	Gelsenkirchen
—435 63	Arnsberg district (Regierungsbezirk)
—435 632	Bochum
—435 633	Dortmund
—435 65	Detmold district (Regierungsbezirk)

Including *Teutoburg Forest

—435 655	Bielefeld
—435 9	**Lower Saxony (Niedersachsen)**
—435 91	Weser-Ems district (Regierungsbezirk)
—435 911	Osnabrück
—435 914	Oldenburg

*For a specific part of this jurisdiction, region, or feature, see the part and follow instructions under —4–9

—435 917	East Friesland region
	Including Aurich, Friesland, Leer, Wittmund Kreise; Emden, Wilhelmshaven cities
	Class here *East Frisian Islands
—435 93	Lüneburg district (Regierungsbezirk)
—435 95	Hannover district (Regierungsbezirk)
—435 954	Hannover
—435 958	Hildesheim
—435 97	Braunschweig district (Regierungsbezirk)
—435 976	Braunschweig

—436   Austria and Liechtenstein

Class here *Austrian Empire, *Dual Monarchy of Austria-Hungary

(Option: Class here ancient Noricum; prefer —363)

—436 1	Northeastern Austria
—436 12	Lower Austria province (Niederösterreich Land)
—436 13	Vienna province (Wien Land)
	Class here Vienna
—436 15	Burgenland province (Land)

—436 2   Upper Austria province (Oberösterreich Land)

—436 3   Salzburg province (Land)

—436 4   Western Austria, and Liechtenstein

(Option: Class here ancient Raetia; prefer —363)

—436 42	Tyrol province (Land)
—436 45	Vorarlberg province (Land)
—436 48	Liechtenstein
	Independent principality

—436 5   Styria province (Steiermark Land)

—436 6   Carinthia province (Kärnten Land)

—437   Czech Republic and Slovakia

Class here Czechoslovakia

---

*For a specific part of this jurisdiction, region, or feature, see the part and follow instructions under —4–9

—437 1　　　　　Czech Republic

　　　　　　　　Including Jihočeský, Severočeský, Středočeský, Východočeský, Západočeský regions (krajs)

　　　　　　　　Including Sudetenland

　　　　　　　　Class here Bohemia

　　　　　　　　　For Moravia, see —4372

—437 12　　　　Prague (Praha)

—437 2　　　　　Moravia

　　　　　　　　Including Jihomoravský and Severomoravský regions (krajs); Czech Silesia

—437 3　　　　　Slovakia

　　　　　　　　Including Bratislava, Středoslovenský, Východoslovenský, Západoslovenský regions (krajs)

—438　　　　　Poland

—438 1　　　　　Northwestern Poland　　　Polish Pomerania

　　　　　　　　Including Gorzów Wielkopolski, Koszalin, Słupsk, Szczecin, Zielona Góra provinces (voivodeships)

　　　　　　　　Class here Pomerania

　　　　　　　　　For German Pomerania, see —4317

—438 2　　　　　North central Poland

　　　　　　　　Including Bydgoszcz, Elbląg, Gdańsk (Danzig), Toruń, Włocławek provinces (voivodeships)

　　　　　　　　Including Pomerelia, West Prussia

—438 3　　　　　Northeastern Poland

　　　　　　　　Including Białystok, Łomża, Olsztyn, Suwałki provinces (voivodeships); comprehensive works on East Prussia

　　　　　　　　　For Kaliningrad province (oblast) of Russia, see —4724

—438 4　　　　　Central Poland

　　　　　　　　Including Biała Podlaska, Chełm, Ciechanów, Kalisz, Kielce, Konin, Leszno, Łódź, Lublin, Ostrołęka, Piła, Piotrków Trybunalski, Płock, Poznań, Radom, Siedlce, Sieradz, Skierniewice, Tarnobrzeg, Warsaw, Zamość provinces (voivodeships)

—438 5   Southwestern Poland

Including Częstochowa, Jelenia Góra, Katowice, Legnica, Opole, Wałbrzych, Wrocław provinces (voivodeships)

Class here Silesia

For Czech Silesia, see —4372

—438 6   Southeastern Poland   Polish Galicia

Including Bielsko (Bielsko-Biała), Kraków, Krosno, Nowy Sącz, Przemyśl, Rzeszów, Tarnów provinces (voivodeships)

Class here Galicia

For East Galicia, see —4779

—439   Hungary

(Option: Class here ancient Pannonia; prefer —398)

—439 1   Pest county (Megye) and Budapest

—439 12   Budapest

—439 7   Hungary west of Danube

Including Baranya, Fejér, Győr-Sopron, Komárom, Somogy, Tolna, Vas, Veszprém, Zala counties (megyek)

For Pest county, see —4391

—439 8   Hungary east of Danube

Including Bács-Kiskun, Csongrád, Heves, Nógrád, Szolnok counties (megyek)

For Pest county, see —4391; for easternmost Hungary, see —4399

—439 9   Easternmost Hungary

Including Békés, Borsod-Abaúj-Zemplén, Hajdú-Bihar, Szabolcs-Szatmár counties (megyek)

—44   **France and Monaco**

For a specific overseas department of France, see the department, e.g., Martinique —72982

(Option: Class here ancient Celtic regions, Gaul [Gallia Transalpina]; prefer —364)

SUMMARY

—441	Northwestern France	Brittany (Bretagne) region
—442	Northern France	Normandy (Normandie) region
—443	Northeastern France	Champagne region
—444	Eastern France	Burgundy (Bourgogne) region
—445	Central France	Centre region
—446	Western France	Poitou region
—447	Southwestern France	Guyenne (Aquitaine) region
—448	Southern France	Languedoc region
—449	Southeastern France and Monaco	Provence region

—441   Northwestern France   Brittany (Bretagne) region

> —441 1–441 5   Brittany region

Class comprehensive works in —441

—441 1   Finistère department

—441 2   Côtes-d'Armor department

Former name: Côtes-du-Nord department

—441 3   Morbihan department

—441 4   Loire-Atlantique department

Former name: Loire-Inférieure

—441 5   Ille-et-Vilaine department

—441 6   Mayenne department

Class here former region of *Maine, modern region of *Pays de la Loire

—441 7   Sarthe department

—441 8   Maine-et-Loire department

Class here former region of *Anjou

—442   Northern France   Normandy (Normandie) region

> —442 1–442 5   Former region of Normandy   Modern region of Basse-Normandie

Class comprehensive works on Normandy, on Basse-Normandie in —442

—442 1   Manche department

—442 2   Calvados department

—442 3   Orne department

---

*For a specific part of this jurisdiction, region, or feature, see the part and follow instructions under —4–9

—442 4   Eure department

         Class here modern region of Haute-Normandie

         For Seine-Maritime department, see —4425

—442 5   Seine-Maritime department

         Former name: Seine-Inférieure

         Class here Rouen

—442 6   Somme department

         Class here *Picardy (Picardie) region

—442 7   Pas-de-Calais department

         Including former region of Artois

         Class here modern region of Nord-Pas-de-Calais

         For Nord department, see —4428

—442 8   Nord department (Former region of French Flanders)

—443   Northeastern France   Champagne region

         Class here *Marne River

>   —443 1–443 3   Modern region of Champagne-Ardenne

       Class here former region of *Champagne

       Class comprehensive works on Champagne, on Champagne-Ardenne in —443

—443 1   Ardennes department

—443 2   Marne department

—443 3   Aube and Haute-Marne departments

—443 31   Aube department

—443 32   Haute-Marne department

—443 4   Former region of *Ile-de-France

         Class here *Seine River

—443 45   Aisne department

—443 5   Oise department

---

*For a specific part of this jurisdiction, region, or feature, see the part and follow instructions under —4–9

—443 6	Paris metropolitan area

> Including former Seine department, former Seine-et-Oise department
>
> Class here modern Région parisienne
>
> *For Seine-et-Marne department, see —4437*

—443 61	Paris department
—443 62	Seine-Saint-Denis department
—443 63	Val-de-Marne department
—443 64	Hauts-de-Seine department
—443 65	Essonne department
—443 66	Yvelines department
—443 67	Val-d'Oise department
—443 7	Seine-et-Marne department
—443 8	Lorraine and Alsace regions

> Class here *Argonne; *Vosges Mountains
>
> (Option: Class here ancient Germania Superior; prefer —364)

>	—443 81–443 82 *Lorraine region

Class comprehensive works in —4438

—443 81	Meuse department
—443 82	Meurthe-et-Moselle and Moselle departments
—443 823	Meurthe-et-Moselle department
—443 825	Moselle department
—443 83	Alsace region

> *For territory of Belfort, see —44455*

—443 833	Haut-Rhin department
—443 835	Bas-Rhin department
—443 835 3	Strasbourg
—443 9	Vosges department
—444	Eastern France Burgundy (Bourgogne) region

> Class here *Saône River

*For a specific part of this jurisdiction, region, or feature, see the part and follow instructions under —4–9

> —444 1–444 4 *Burgundy region

Class comprehensive works in —444

—444 1   Yonne department

—444 2   Côte-d'Or department

—444 3   Saône-et-Loire department

—444 4   Ain department

Including former regions of Bugey and Dombes

—444 5   *Franche-Comté region and Territory of Belfort

Class here *Jura Mountains in France

—444 53   Haute-Saône department

—444 55   Territory of Belfort

—444 6   Doubs department

—444 7   Jura department

—444 8   Savoie department

Class here former region of Savoy

For Haute-Savoie department, see —4449

—444 9   Haute-Savoie department

—445   Central France   Centre region

Class here *Loire River

(Option: Class here ancient Lugdunensis; prefer —364)

> —445 1–445 5 Modern region of Centre   Former region of *Orléanais

Class comprehensive works on modern Centre, on former Orléanais in —445

—445 1   Eure-et-Loir department

—445 2   Loiret department

—445 3   Loir-et-Cher department

—445 4   Indre-et-Loire department

Class here former region of Touraine

For Indre department, see —44551; for Cher department, see —44552

*For a specific part of this jurisdiction, region, or feature, see the part and follow instructions under —4–9

—445 45	Tours
—445 5	Former region of Berry

> *For Creuse department, see —4468*

—445 51	Indre department
—445 52	Cher department
—445 6	Nièvre department (Former region of Nivernais)
—445 7	Allier department

> Class here former region of *Bourbonnais

—445 8	Former region of Lyonnais

> Class here modern region of *Rhône-Alpes; *Rhône River

—445 81	Loire department
—445 82	Rhône department
—445 823	Lyon
—445 9	Auvergne region

> Class here *Massif Central

>> *For Allier department, see —4457; for Haute-Loire department, see —44813*

—445 91	Puy-de-Dôme department
—445 92	Cantal department
—446	Western France Poitou region
—446 1	Vendée department

>	—446 2–446 5 Modern region of Poitou-Charentes

> Class here former region of Poitou

> Class Vendée department in —4461; class comprehensive works on modern Poitou-Charentes, on former Poitou in —446

—446 2	Deux-Sèvres department
—446 3	Vienne department
—446 4	Charente-Maritime department

> Former name: Charente-Inférieure

> Including former region of Aunis

> Class here former region of *Saintonge

---

*For a specific part of this jurisdiction, region, or feature, see the part and follow instructions under —4–9

—446 5	Charente department
	Class here former region of *Angoumois; *Charente River
—446 6	Haute-Vienne department
	Class here *Limousin region
—446 7	Corrèze department
—446 8	Creuse department
	Class here former region of Marche
	For Haute-Vienne department, see —4466
—447	Southwestern France Guyenne (Aquitaine) region
	Class here *Garonne River
	(Option: Class here ancient Aquitania; prefer —364)

>	—447 1–447 6 Former region of Guyenne (Aquitaine)
	Class here modern region of *Aquitaine
	Class comprehensive works on former Guyenne, on modern Aquitaine in —447
—447 1	Gironde department
—447 14	Bordeaux
—447 2	Dordogne department
—447 3	Lot department
—447 4	Aveyron department
	Including former region of Rouergue
—447 5	Tarn-et-Garonne department
—447 6	Lot-et-Garonne department
—447 7	Former region of *Gascony (Gascogne)
—447 71	Gers department
—447 72	Landes department
—447 8	Hautes-Pyrénées department
—447 9	Pyrénées-Atlantiques department
	Former name: Basses-Pyrénées
	Including former region of Béarn

*For a specific part of this jurisdiction, region, or feature, see the part and follow instructions under —4–9

—448 Southern France   Languedoc region

Class here *Cévennes Mountains

See also —16382 for Gulf of Lions

\> —448 1–448 8 Former region of Languedoc

Class here modern region of Languedoc-Roussillon

Class comprehensive works on former Languedoc, on modern Languedoc-Roussillon in —448

For Tarn-et-Garonne department, see —4475; for Pyrénées-Orientales department, see —4489

—448 1 Haute-Loire and Lozère departments

—448 13 Haute-Loire department

—448 15 Lozère department

—448 2 Ardèche department

—448 3 Gard department

—448 4 Hérault department

—448 5 Tarn department

—448 6 Haute-Garonne department

Class here modern region of *Midi-Pyrénées

—448 62 Toulouse

—448 7 Aude department

—448 8 Ariège department

Including former region of Foix

—448 9 Pyrénées-Orientales department (Former region of Roussillon)

Class here *Pyrenees Mountains in France

—449 Southeastern France and Monaco   Provence region

Class here *Alps in France, *Riviera

For Italian Riviera, see —4518

(Option: Class here ancient Narbonensis; prefer —364)

---

*For a specific part of this jurisdiction, region, or feature, see the part and follow instructions under —4–9

>	—449 1–449 3　Former region of *Provence

> Class here modern region of *Provence-Alpes-Côte d'Azur (Provence-Côte d'Azur)
>
> Class comprehensive works in —449

—449 1	Bouches-du-Rhône department
—449 12	Marseilles
—449 2	Vaucluse department

> Including Valréas enclave

—449 22	Avignon
—449 3	Var department
—449 4	Alpes-Maritimes, Corsica, Monaco
—449 41	Alpes-Maritimes department

> Including former region of Nice

—449 414	Nice
—449 45	Corsica (Corse)

> (Option: Class here ancient Corsica; prefer —379)

—449 452	Corse-de-Sud department
—449 456	Haute-Corse department
—449 49	Monaco

> Independent principality, enclave in Alpes-Maritimes

—449 5	Alpes de Haute-Provence department

> Former name: Basses-Alpes

—449 6	Former region of *Dauphiné
—449 7	Hautes-Alpes department
—449 8	Drôme department

> *For Valréas enclave of Vaucluse department, see —4492*

—449 9	Isère department
—45	**Italian Peninsula and adjacent islands　　Italy**

> Class here *Apennines
>
> (Option: Class here ancient Italian Peninsula and adjacent territories, Roman Empire; prefer —37)

---

*For a specific part of this jurisdiction, region, or feature, see the part and follow instructions under —4–9

SUMMARY

—451	Northwestern Italy Piedmont (Piemonte) region
—452	Lombardy (Lombardia) region
—453	Northeastern Italy Veneto region
—454	Emilia-Romagna region and San Marino
—455	Tuscany (Toscana) region
—456	Central Italy and Vatican City
—457	Southern Italy
—458	Sicily and adjacent islands
—459	Sardinia

—451   Northwestern Italy   Piedmont (Piemonte) region

Class here *Alps in Italy

(Option: Class here ancient Gallia Cisalpina; prefer —372)

—451 1   Valle d'Aosta region

Class here Aosta

>   **—451 2–451 7 Piedmont (Piemonte) region**

Class comprehensive works in —451

—451 2   Turin (Torino) province

Class here Turin

—451 3   Cuneo province

—451 4   Alessandria province

—451 5   Asti province

—451 6   Novara province

Including *Lake Maggiore

—451 7   Vercelli province

—451 8   Liguria region

Class here *Italian Riviera

See also —16382 for Ligurian Sea

(Option: Class here ancient Liguria; prefer —371)

—451 82   Genoa (Genova) province

Class here Genoa

—451 83   La Spezia province

—451 84   Savona province

---

*For a specific part of this jurisdiction, region, or feature, see the part and follow instructions under —4–9

—451 87	Imperia province
—452	Lombardy (Lombardia) region
	Class here *Po River
—452 1	Milan (Milano) province
	Class here Milan
—452 2	Varese province
—452 3	Como province
	Class here Como
—452 4	Bergamo province
	Class here Bergamo
—452 5	Sondrio province
—452 6	Brescia province
	Including *Lake Garda
	Class here Brescia
—452 7	Cremona province
	Class here Cremona
—452 8	Mantua (Mantova) province
	Class here Mantua
—452 9	Pavia province
—453	Northeastern Italy Veneto region
	See also —16385 for Gulf of Venice
	(Option: Class here ancient Venetia; prefer —373)

>	—453 1–453 7 Veneto region
	Class comprehensive works in —453
—453 1	Venice (Venezia) province
	Class here Venice
—453 2	Padua (Padova) province
	Class here Padua
—453 3	Rovigo province (Polesine)

*For a specific part of this jurisdiction, region, or feature, see the part and follow instructions under —4–9

—453 4	Verona province
	Class here Verona
—453 5	Vicenza province
	Class here Vicenza
—453 6	Treviso province
	Class here Treviso
—453 7	Belluno province
—453 8	Trentino-Alto Adige region
—453 83	Bolzano province (Alto Adige)
	Class here South Tyrol
—453 85	Trento province
	Including Trento
—453 9	Friuli-Venezia Giulia region
—453 91	Udine province
—453 92	Gorizia province
—453 93	Trieste province
	Class here Trieste
—453 94	Pordenone province
—454	Emilia-Romagna region and San Marino
—454 1	Bologna province
	Class here Bologna
—454 2	Modena province
	Class here Modena
—454 3	Reggio Emilia (Reggio nell'Emilia) province
—454 4	Parma province
	Class here Parma
—454 5	Ferrara province
	Class here Ferrara
—454 6	Piacenza province
—454 7	Ravenna province
	Class here Ravenna

—454 8	Forlì province
—454 9	San Marino
	Independent state
—455	Tuscany (Toscana) region
	(Option: Class here ancient Etruria; prefer —375)
—455 1	Florence (Firenze) province
	Class here Florence
—455 2	Pistoia province
—455 3	Lucca province
—455 4	Massa-Carrara (Massa e Carrara) province
—455 5	Pisa province
	Class here Pisa
—455 6	Livorno province
	Including Elba island
—455 7	Grosseto province
	Class here *Maremma
—455 8	Siena province
	Class here Siena
—455 9	Arezzo province
—456	Central Italy and Vatican City
	Class here former *Papal States (States of the Church)
—456 2	Lazio (Latium) region
	For Rome province, see —4563
	(Option: Class here ancient Latium; prefer —376)
—456 22	Frosinone province
—456 23	Latina province
	Including Pontine Islands
	Class here Pontine Marshes
—456 24	Rieti province

*For a specific part of this jurisdiction, region, or feature, see the part and follow instructions under —4–9

—456 25	Viterbo province
	Class here Viterbo
	(Option: Class here ancient Volsinii Novi [Bolsena]; prefer —376)
—456 3	Rome (Roma) province and Vatican City
	(Option: Class here ancient Ostia, Veii; prefer —376)
—456 32	Rome
	(Option: Class here ancient Rome; prefer —376)
—456 34	Vatican City
	Independent papal state, enclave in Rome
—456 5	Umbria region
	(Option: Class here ancient Umbria; prefer —374)
—456 51	Perugia province
	Class here Perugia
—456 52	Terni province
	(Option: Class here ancient Volsinii [Orvieto]; prefer —374)
—456 7	Marches (Marche) region
	(Option: Class here ancient Picenum; prefer —374)
—456 71	Ancona province
	Including Ancona
—456 73	Macerata province
—456 75	Ascoli Piceno province
—456 77	Pesaro e Urbino province
—457	Southern Italy
	For Sicily, see —458
	(Option: Class here ancient southern Italy; prefer —377)
—457 1	Abruzzi and Molise regions
	(Option: Class here ancient Samnium; prefer —377)

>	—457 11–457 17 **Abruzzi region**
	Class comprehensive works in —4571
—457 11	Aquila (L'Aquila) province
	Including L'Aquila

—457 13	Chieti province
—457 15	Teramo province
—457 17	Pescara province
—457 19	Molise region
—457 192	Campobasso province
	Including Campobasso
—457 194	Isernia province
—457 2	Campania region

For Naples province, see —4573; for Salerno province, see —4574

(Option: Class here ancient Campania; prefer —377)

—457 21	Avellino province
—457 23	Benevento province
—457 25	Caserta province
—457 3	Naples (Napoli) province

Including Capri, Ischia Islands

Class here Naples

(Option: Class here ancient Naples, Herculaneum, Pompeii, Stabiae; prefer —377)

—457 4	Salerno province

Class here Salerno

—457 5	Puglia (Apulia) region

See also —16386 for Gulf of Taranto

(Option: Class here ancient Apulia, Calabria, Brundusium; prefer —377)

—457 51	Bari province

Class here Bari

—457 53	Lecce province
—457 54	Brindisi province

Class here Brindisi

—457 55	Taranto province
—457 57	Foggia province
—457 7	Basilicata (Lucania) region

See also —16386 for Gulf of Taranto

(Option: Class here ancient Lucania; prefer —377)

—457 71	Potenza province
—457 72	Matera province
—457 8	Calabria region

        See also —16386 for Gulf of Taranto, Strait of Messina

        (Option: Class here ancient Bruttium; prefer —377)

—457 81	Catanzaro province
—457 83	Reggio di Calabria province

        Class here Reggio di Calabria

—457 85	Cosenza province
—458	Sicily and adjacent islands

        (Option: Class here ancient Sicily; prefer —378)

>	—458 1–458 2 Sicily region

        Class comprehensive works in —458

—458 1	Eastern Sicily
—458 11	Messina province

        Including Lipari Islands

        Class here Messina

        See also —16386 for Strait of Messina

—458 12	Enna province
—458 13	Catania province

        Including Mount Etna

        Class here Catania

—458 14	Syracuse (Siracusa) province

        Class here Syracuse

        (Option: Class here ancient Syracuse; prefer —378)

—458 15	Ragusa province
—458 2	Western Sicily
—458 21	Caltanissetta province
—458 22	Agrigento province

        Including Pelagian Islands

        Class here Agrigento

—458 23　　　　　　Palermo province

　　　　　　　　　　Class here Palermo

—458 24　　　　　　Trapani province

　　　　　　　　　　Including Egadi Islands

—458 5　　　　Malta

　　　　　　　　　　Independent state

　　　　　　　　　　(Option: Class here ancient Malta; prefer —378)

—459　　　　Sardinia

　　　　　　　　　　(Option: Class here ancient Sardinia; prefer —379)

—459 1　　　　Cagliari province

　　　　　　　　　　Class here Cagliari

—459 2　　　　Nuoro province

—459 3　　　　Sassari province

—459 4　　　　Oristano province

—46　　　**Iberian Peninsula and adjacent islands　　　Spain**

　　　　　　　　　　(Option: Class here ancient Iberian Peninsula and adjacent islands,
　　　　　　　　　　Tarraconensis; prefer —366)

SUMMARY

—461	**Northwestern Spain　　Galicia autonomous community**
—462	**Western Spain　　León region**
—463	**Castile**
—464	**New Castile region　　Castilla-La Mancha autonomous community**
—465	**Northeastern Spain**
—466	**País Vasco autonomous community**
—467	**Eastern Spain and Andorra　　Cataluña autonomous community**
—468	**Andalusia autonomous community and Gibraltar**
—469	**Portugal**

>　　　　—461–468　Spain

　　　　　　　　Class comprehensive works in —46

　　　　　　　　For Canary Islands, see —649

—461　　　　Northwestern Spain　　　Galicia autonomous community

>　　　　—461 1–461 7　Galicia autonomous community

　　　　　　　　Class comprehensive works in —461

—461 1   La Coruña province

        Including Santiago de Compostela

—461 3   Lugo province

—461 5   Orense province

—461 7   Pontevedra province

—461 9   Asturias autonomous community (Asturias province)

        Former name for Asturias province: Oviedo province

        Class here Oviedo

—462   Western Spain   León region

        Class here Castilla-León autonomous community; *Cantabrian Mountains

        For Burgos province, see —46353; for Soria province, see —46355; for Segovia province, see —46357; for Avila province, see —46359

\>   —462 1–462 5   León region

        Class comprehensive works in —462

—462 1   León province

—462 2   Palencia province

—462 3   Valladolid province

        Class here Valladolid

—462 4   Zamora province

—462 5   Salamanca province

—462 6   Extremadura autonomous community

        For Badajoz province, see —4627; for Cáceres province, see —4628

—462 7   Badajoz province

        Including Mérida

—462 8   Cáceres province

        Class here *Tagus River in Spain

—463   Castile

        For New Castile region, see —464

—463 5   Old Castile region

        For Palencia province, see —4622; for Valladolid province, see —4623

---

*For a specific part of this jurisdiction, region, or feature, see the part and follow instructions under —4–9

—463 51	Cantabria autonomous community (Cantabria province)
	Former name for Cantabria province: Santander province
	Including Santander
—463 53	Burgos province
	For Treviño, see —4667
—463 54	La Rioja autonomous community (La Rioja province)
	Former name of La Rioja province: Logroño province
	Including Logroño
—463 55	Soria province
—463 57	Segovia province
	Class here Segovia
—463 59	Avila province
—464	New Castile region Castilla-La Mancha autonomous community
	Class here La Mancha
—464 1	Madrid autonomous community (Madrid province)
	Class here Madrid

>	—464 3–464 8 Castilla-La Mancha autonomous community
	Class comprehensive works in —464
—464 3	Toledo province
	Class here Toledo
—464 5	Ciudad Real province
—464 6	Albacete province
—464 7	Cuenca province
—464 9	Guadalajara province
—465	Northeastern Spain
	Class here *Pyrenees Mountains, *Ebro River
	For Cataluña autonomous community, see —467
—465 2	Navarra autonomous community (Navarra province)
	Including Pamplona
—465 5	Aragon autonomous community

*For a specific part of this jurisdiction, region, or feature, see the part and follow instructions
under —4–9

—465 51	Teruel province
—465 53	Zaragoza (Saragossa) province
	Class here Zaragoza
—465 55	Huesca province
—466	País Vasco autonomous community

Former names: Basque Provinces, Vascongadas

Class here territory of the Basque people

> *For Pyrénées-Atlantiques department of France, see —4479; for Navarra autonomous community, see —4652*

—466 1	Guipúzcoa

Class here San Sebastián

—466 3	Vizcaya (Biscay)

Class here Bilbao

> *For Orduña, see —4669*

—466 5	Alava

Including Vitoria

—466 7	Treviño

Enclave of Burgos province in Alava province

—466 9	Orduña

Enclave of Vizcaya province between Alava and Burgos provinces

—467	Eastern Spain and Andorra Cataluña autonomous community

>	—467 1–467 4 Cataluña autonomous community

Former name: Catalonia region

Class comprehensive works in —467

—467 1	Gerona province
—467 2	Barcelona province
	Class here Barcelona
—467 3	Tarragona province
—467 4	Lérida province
—467 5	Baleares autonomous community (Balearic Islands)
—467 52	Minorca (Menorca)

—467 54	Majorca (Mallorca)
—467 542	Palma
—467 56	Formentera and Ibiza
—467 6	Valencia autonomous community
—467 61	Castellón province
—467 63	Valencia province
	Class here Valencia
—467 65	Alicante province
—467 7	Murcia autonomous community (Murcia province)
	Including Cartagena
	Class here former Murcia region
	For Albacete province, see —4646
—467 9	Andorra
	Independent state
—468	Andalusia autonomous community and Gibraltar
	Class here *Guadalquivir River
	(Option: Class here ancient Baetica; prefer —366)

>	—468 1–468 8 Andalusia autonomous community
	Class comprehensive works in —468
—468 1	Almería province
—468 2	Granada province
	Class here Granada
—468 3	Jaén province
—468 4	Córdoba province
	Class here Córdoba
—468 5	Málaga province
	Class here Málaga
	For Melilla, see —642
—468 6	Seville province
	Class here Seville

*For a specific part of this jurisdiction, region, or feature, see the part and follow instructions under —4–9

—468 7	Huelva province
—468 8	Cádiz province

        For Ceuta, see —642

—468 9	Gibraltar

        British crown colony

—469	Portugal

        (Option: Class here ancient Lusitania; prefer —366)

—469 1	Historic province of Entre Douro e Minho
—469 12	Modern province of Minho

        Including Braga and Viana do Castelo districts

—469 15	Modern province of Douro Litoral

        Including Porto district

        For Viseu district, see —46931; for Aveiro district, see —46935

—469 2	Historic province of Trás-os-Montes Modern province of Trás-os-Montes e Alto Douro

        Including Bragança and Vila Real districts

        For Guarda and Viseu districts, see —46931

—469 3	Historic province of Beira

        For modern province of Douro Litoral, see —46915; for modern province of Trás-os-Montes e Alto Douro, see —4692

—469 31	Modern province of Beira Alta

        Including Guarda and Viseu districts

        For Coimbra district, see —46935

—469 33	Modern province of Beira Baixa

        Including Castelo Branco district

        For Coimbra district, see —46935; for Santarém district, see —46945

—469 35	Modern province of Beira Litoral

        Including Aveiro and Coimbra districts

        For Leiria district, see —46942; for Santarém district, see —46945

—469 4	Historic province of Estremadura

        For modern province of Beira Litoral, see —46935; for modern province of Baixo Alentejo, see —46955

—469 42	Modern province of Estremadura
	Including Leiria and Setúbal districts
—469 425	Lisbon (Lisboa) district
	Class here Lisbon
—469 45	Modern province of Ribatejo
	Including Santarém district
	Class here *Tagus River

> *For Lisbon district, see —469425; for Portalegre district, see —46952*

—469 5	Historic province of Alentejo
—469 52	Modern province of Alto Alentejo
	Including Evora and Portalegre districts
—469 55	Modern province of Baixo Alentejo
	Including Beja district

> *For Setúbal district, see —46942*

—469 6	Algarve province (Faro district)
—469 8	Madeira (Funchal district)
	Islands in Atlantic Ocean
—469 9	Azores
	Islands in Atlantic Ocean
	Including Angra do Heroísmo, Horta, Ponta Delgada districts
—47	**Eastern Europe Russia**

This schedule is new and has been prepared with little or no reference to previous editions. Most numbers have been reused with new meanings

A comparative table giving both old and new numbers for a substantial list of topics and equivalence tables showing the numbers in the old and new schedules appear in volume 4 in this edition

Class here Commonwealth of Independent States, former Union of Soviet Socialist Republics (Soviet Union)

> *For Balkan Peninsula, see —496; for Commonwealth of Independent States in Asia, see —58*

---

*For a specific part of this jurisdiction, region, or feature, see the part and follow instructions under —4–9

SUMMARY

—471	**Northern area of European Russia**
—472	**Western area of Russia**
—473	**West central area of Russia**
—474	**Eastern area of European Russia**
—475	**Caucasus**
—476	**Moldova**
—477	**Ukraine**
—478	**Belarus**
—479	**Lithuania, Latvia, Estonia**

> **—471–474 Russia**

Class comprehensive works in —47

For Caucasus area of Russia, see —4752; for Siberia (Asiatic Russia), see —57

—471 Northern area of European Russia

For Komi republic, see —4743

See also —16324 for White Sea

—471 1 Nenets National District

—471 3 Murmansk province (oblast)

Including Kola Peninsula

—471 5 Karelia republic

Including Lakes *Ladoga and *Onega

—471 7 Arkhangel´sk province (oblast)

For Franz Josef Land, see —985; for Novaya Zemlya, see —986

—471 9 Vologda province (oblast)

—472 Western area of Russia

—472 1 Leningrad province (oblast)

Class here Saint Petersburg (Leningrad); Baltic Sea area of Russia

For Novgorod province (oblast), see —4722; for Pskov province (oblast), see —4723; for Kaliningrad province (oblast), see —4724

See also —16334 for Baltic Sea

—472 2 Novgorod province (oblast)

—472 3 Pskov province (oblast)

*For a specific part of this jurisdiction, region, or feature, see the part and follow instructions under —4–9

—472 4	Kaliningrad province (oblast)
—472 5	Bryansk province (oblast)
—472 6	Kaluga province (oblast)
—472 7	Smolensk province (oblast)
—472 8	Tver´ province (oblast)

                    Variant name: Kalinin province (oblast)

—473	West central area of Russia
—473 1	Moscow province (oblast)

                    Class here Moscow

—473 2	Yaroslavl´ province (oblast)
—473 3	Ivanovo, Kostroma, Ryazan, Vladimir provinces (oblasts)
—473 4	Tula province (oblast)
—473 5	Central Black Earth Region

                    Including Belgorod, Kursk, Lipetsk, Orel, Tambov, Voronezh provinces (oblasts)

—474	Eastern area of European Russia

                    Class here *Volga River

                    See also —57 for Asiatic Russia (eastern half of Russia)

—474 1	Nizhegorod (Nizhniy Novgorod) province (oblast)

                    Former name: Gor´ki province (oblast)

—474 2	Kirov province (oblast)
—474 3	Ural Mountains region

                    Including Chelyabinsk, Orenburg, Perm´, Sverdlovsk provinces (oblasts); Bashkortostan (Baskir) and Komi republics; Komi-Permiãk autonomous area (avtonomnyĭ okrug)

                    Class here *Ural Mountains

—474 4	Samara province (oblast)

                    Former name: Kuĭbyshev province (oblast)

—474 5	Tatarstan republic
—474 6	Penza, Saratov, Ul´yanovsk provinces (oblasts); Chuvashia, Mari El, Mordvinia, Udmurtia republics
—474 7	Volgograd province (oblast)

*For a specific part of this jurisdiction, region, or feature, see the part and follow instructions under —4–9

—474 8   Astrakhan province (oblast), Kalmykia republic

—474 9   Rostov province (oblast)

        Class here *Don River

—475   Caucasus

        Class here *Caspian Sea

        (Option: Class here ancient Caucasus; prefer —395)

—475 2   Caucasus area of Russia

        Including Krasnodar and Stavropol´ territories (krays); Adygea,
        Chechnya, Dagestan, Ingushetia, Kabardino-Balkaria,
        Karachay-Cherkessia, North Ossetia republics

        See also — 16389 for Sea of Azov

\>   —475 4–475 8   Transcaucasus

        Class comprehensive works in —475

—475 4   Azerbaijan

        Including Nagorno-Karabakh autonomous region, Nakhichevan
        autonomous republic

        Class comprehensive works on Azerbaijan region in —553

        (Option: Class here ancient Albania; prefer —395)

—475 6   Armenia

        Class comprehensive works on Armenia region in —5662

—475 8   Georgia

        Including Abkhaz and Adzhar autonomous republics, South Osset
        autonomous province (oblast)

        (Option: Class here ancient Colchis, Iberia; prefer —395)

—476   Moldova

        Class here *Bessarabia

        Class comprehensive works on Moldavia in —4981

—477   Ukraine

        Including *Dnieper River

        Class here *Black Sea area of Commonwealth of Independent States

        See also — 16389 for Black Sea

        (Option: Class here ancient Black Sea region, Sarmatia; prefer —395)

---

*For a specific part of this jurisdiction, region, or feature, see the part and follow instructions
under —4–9

—477 1	Crimea province (oblast)
—477 2	Odessa province (oblast)
—477 3	Kherson, Mykolayiv (Nikolayev), Zaporizhzhya provinces (oblasts)

                       See also — 16389 for Sea of Azov

—477 4	*Donets Basin

                       Including Dnepropetrovsk, Donets´k, Luhans´k (Voroshylovhrad) provinces (oblasts)

                       Class here *Donets River

—477 5	Kharkiv province (oblast)
—477 6	Cherkasy, Chernihiv, Kirovohrad, Poltava, Sumy provinces (oblasts)
—477 7	Kiev province (oblast)
—477 8	Khmel´nyts´kyy, Vinnytsa, Zhytomyr provinces (oblasts)
—477 9	Western Ukraine

                       Including Chernivtsy, Ivano-Frankivs´k, L´viv, Rivne, Ternopil´, Volyn, Zakarpats´ka (Transcarpathia) provinces (oblasts); North Bukovina

                       Class here East Galicia; *Carpathian Mountains, *Dniester River

—478	Belarus

                       Variant names: Belorussia, Byelarus

                       Including *Pripet Marshes

—478 1	Homel´ (Gomel´) province (voblasts)
—478 2	Mahilîoŭ (Mogilev) province (voblasts)
—478 4	Vitebsk province (voblasts)
—478 6	Mensk (Minsk) province (voblasts)
—478 8	Hrodzen (Grodno) province (voblasts)
—478 9	Brėst province (voblasts)
—479	Lithuania, Latvia, Estonia

                       Class here Baltic States

                       See also — 16334 for Baltic Sea

—479 3	Lithuania
—479 6	Latvia

                       Including Courland

---

*For a specific part of this jurisdiction, region, or feature, see the part and follow instructions under —4–9

—479 8   Estonia

         Class here Livonia

         For Latvia, see —4796

         See also —16334 for Gulf of Finland

—48   **Scandinavia**

         Class here northern Europe

         For northwestern islands, see —491

SUMMARY

—481	**Norway**
—482	**Southeastern Norway (Østlandet)**
—483	**Southwestern Norway (Sørlandet and Vestlandet)**
—484	**Central and northern Norway (Trøndelag and Nord-Norge)**
—485	**Sweden**
—486	**Southern Sweden (Götaland)**
—487	**Central Sweden (Svealand)**
—488	**Northern Sweden (Norrland)**
—489	**Denmark and Finland**

—481   Norway

         For divisions of Norway, see —482–484; for Svalbard, see —981; for Jan Mayen Island, see —983

>   —482–484   Divisions of Norway

         Class comprehensive works in —481

—482   Southeastern Norway (Østlandet)

         Aust-Agder county (fylke) relocated to —4831; Vest-Agder county (fylke) relocated to —4832

         See also —16336 for Skagerrak

—482 1   Oslo county (fylke) [*formerly* —4823]

         Class here Oslo

—482 2   Akershus county (fylke)

—482 3   Østfold county (fylke)

         Oslo county (fylke) relocated to —4821

—482 4   Hedmark county (fylke)

—482 5   Oppland county (fylke)

—482 6   Buskerud county (fylke)

—482 7	Vestfold county (fylke)
—482 8	Telemark county (fylke)
—483	Southwestern Norway (Sørlandet and Vestlandet)
—483 1	Aust-Agder county (fylke) [*formerly* —482]

Class here Sørlandet

For Vest-Agder county, see —4832

See also —16336 for Skagerrak

—483 2	Vest-Agder county (fylke) [*formerly* —482]
—483 3	Vestlandet

For counties of Vestlandet, see —4834–4839

>	—483 4–483 9 Counties of Vestlandet

Class comprehensive works in —4833

—483 4	Rogaland county (fylke)
—483 6	Hordaland county (fylke)
—483 8	Sogn og Fjordane county (fylke)
—483 9	Møre og Romsdal county (fylke)
—484	Central and northern Norway (Trøndelag and Nord-Norge)
—484 1	Sør-Trøndelag county (fylke)

Class here Trøndelag

For Nord-Trøndelag county, see —4842

—484 2	Nord-Trøndelag county (fylke)
—484 3	Northern Norway (Nord-Norge) [*formerly* —4845]

For counties of northern Norway (Nord-Norge), see —4844–4846

>	—484 4–484 6 Counties of northern Norway (Nord-Norge)

Class comprehensive works in —4843

—484 4	Nordland county (fylke) [*formerly* —4845]

Including Lofoten, Vesterålen islands

—484 5	Troms county (fylke)

Comprehensive works on northern Norway (Nord-Norge) relocated to —4843; Nordland county (fylke) relocated to —4844; Finnmark county (fylke) relocated to —4846

—484 6   Finnmark county (fylke) [*formerly* —4845]

—485   Sweden

> *For divisions of Sweden, see —486–488*

>   —486–488   Divisions of Sweden

> Class comprehensive works in —485

—486   Southern Sweden (Götaland)

> Including Älvsborg, Blekinge, Göteborg och Bohus, Gotland, Halland, Jönköping, Kalmar, Kristianstad, Kronoberg, Malmöhus, Östergötland, Skaraborg counties (länet)

> Including Öland Island

> *See also —16334 for Baltic Sea, Kattegat*

—487   Central Sweden (Svealand)

> Including Gävleborg, Kopparberg, Örebro, Södermanland, Uppsala, Värmland, Västmanland counties (länet)

—487 3   Stockholm county (Stockholms län)

> Class here Stockholm

—488   Northern Sweden (Norrland)

> Including Jämtland, Norrbotten, Västerbotten, Västernorrland counties (länet)

> *See also —16334 for Gulf of Bothnia*

—489   Denmark and Finland

>   —489 1–489 5   Denmark

> Class comprehensive works in —489

> *For Greenland, see —982*

—489 1   Zealand (Sjælland) island

> Including Frederiksborg, Roskilde, Storstrøms, Vestsjælland counties (amts)

> *For Falster and Lolland islands portion of Storstrøms county, see —4893*

> *See also —16334 for Great Belt, Oresund*

—489 13   Copenhagen

> Including Frederiksberg

> Copenhagen county (Københavns amt) relocated to —48914

—489 14	Copenhagen county (Københavns amt) [*formerly* —48913]
—489 2	Bornholm island
	Class here Bornholms county (amt)
—489 3	Falster and Lolland islands
	Class here former Maribo county (amt)
	Class comprehensive works on Storstrøms county in —4891
—489 4	Fyn and Langeland islands
	Class here Fyns county (amt)
	See also —16334 for Great and Little Belts
—489 5	Jutland peninsula
	Including Århus, Nordjylland, Ribe, Ringkøbing, Sonderjylland, Vejle, Viborg counties (amts)
	See also —16336 for Skagerrak
—489 7	Finland
	See also —16334 for Gulf of Finland
—489 71	Southern Finland
	Including Kymi, Uusimaa provinces (läänit)
	Including Helsinki
—489 73	Southwestern Finland
	Including Ahvenanmaa, Häme, Keski-Suomi, Turku ja Pori, Vaasa provinces (läänit)
	Including Åland Islands
—489 75	Southeastern Finland
	Including Kuopio, Mikkeli, Pohjois-Karjala provinces (läänit)
—489 76	Oulu province (lääni)
—489 77	Lappi province (lääni)
	Class here Lapland
	For Murmansk province of Russia, see —4713; for northern Norway, see —4843; for northern Sweden, see —488
—49	**Other parts of Europe**

SUMMARY

—491	Northwestern islands
—492	Netherlands (Holland)
—493	Southern Low Countries Belgium
—494	Switzerland
—495	Greece
—496	Balkan Peninsula
—497	Yugoslavia, Croatia, Slovenia, Bosnia and Hercegovina, Macedonia
—498	Romania
—499	Bulgaria

—491	Northwestern islands
—491 2	Iceland
—491 5	Faeroes
—492	Netherlands (Holland)

Class here comprehensive works on Low Countries, on Benelux countries

For southern Low Countries, see —493; for Netherlands Antilles, see —72986

(Option: Class here ancient Germania Inferior; prefer —363)

—492 1	Northeastern provinces
—492 12	Groningen
—492 13	Friesland

Including *West Frisian Islands

—492 15	Drenthe
—492 16	Overijssel

Including North East Polder

—492 18	Gelderland

Including Arnhem, Nijmegen

Class here *IJssel River

—492 2	Flevoland (Zuidelijke IJsselmeerpolders) and Markerwaard

Including Almere, Dronten, Lelystad, Zeewolde

Class here *IJssel Lake (Zuider Zee)

—492 3	Northwestern provinces
—492 32	Utrecht

Class here Utrecht

---

*For a specific part of this jurisdiction, region, or feature, see the part and follow instructions under —4–9

—492 35	North Holland (Noord-Holland)
	Including Haarlem; Wieringermeer
—492 352	Amsterdam
—492 38	South Holland (Zuid-Holland)
	Including Delft, Leiden
—492 382	The Hague
—492 385	Rotterdam

—492 4   Southern provinces

Class here *Meuse (Maas) River

—492 42	Zeeland
—492 45	North Brabant (Noord-Brabant)
	Including Eindhoven
—492 48	Limburg
	Including Maastricht

—493   Southern Low Countries   Belgium

(Option: Class here ancient Belgica; prefer —364)

>   —493 1–493 4   Belgium

Class comprehensive works in —493

—493 1   Northwestern provinces of Belgium

Class here Flanders

For French Flanders region, see —4428

—493 12	West Flanders
—493 122	Bruges (Brugge)
—493 14	East Flanders
—493 142	Ghent (Gent)

—493 2   Northern provinces of Belgium

—493 22	Antwerp
—493 222	Antwerp (Anvers)
—493 24	Limburg

—493 3   Brabant province

---

*For a specific part of this jurisdiction, region, or feature, see the part and follow instructions under —4–9

—493 32	Brussels
—493 4	Southern provinces of Belgium (Wallonia)
—493 42	Hainaut
—493 44	Namur
—493 46	Liège

         Class here *Meuse (Maas) River in Belgium

—493 48	Luxembourg

         Class here *Ardennes

—493 5	Luxembourg

         Grand duchy

—494	Switzerland
—494 3	Jura region cantons

         Class here *Jura Mountains

—494 32	Basel-Stadt (Bâle-Ville)

         Class here former Basel canton

         For Baselland, see —49433

—494 33	Baselland
—494 35	Solothurn
—494 36	Jura
—494 38	Neuchâtel
—494 5	Swiss Plateau (Mittelland) cantons
—494 51	Geneva

         Class here Geneva

—494 52	Vaud

         Class here *Lake Geneva

—494 53	Fribourg (Freiburg)
—494 54	Bern

         Class here *Bernese Alps

—494 542	Bern
—494 55	Luzern

         Class here *Lake Lucerne

---

*For a specific part of this jurisdiction, region, or feature, see the part and follow instructions under —4–9

—494 56	Aargau
—494 57	Zurich
	Class here Zurich
—494 58	Schaffhausen (Schaffhouse)
—494 59	Thurgau
	Class here *Lake of Constance in Switzerland
—494 7	Alpine region cantons
	Class here *Alps
—494 71	Appenzell
—494 712	Appenzell Ausser-Rhoden
—494 714	Appenzell Inner-Rhoden
—494 72	Saint Gall
—494 73	Graubünden (Grisons)
	Including Graubünden National Park
—494 74	Glarus
—494 75	Schwyz and Zug
—494 752	Schwyz
—494 756	Zug
—494 76	Nidwalden and Obwalden
	Class here former Unterwalden canton
—494 762	Nidwalden
—494 764	Obwalden
—494 77	Uri
—494 78	Ticino
—494 79	Valais (Wallis)
—495	Greece
	See also —16388 for Aegean Sea
	(Option: Class here ancient Greece; prefer —38)
—495 1	**Attica (Attikē) and Central Greece (Sterea Hellada) regions (periphereias) and Aetolia and Acarnania (Aitōlia kai Akarnania) nome**

---

*For a specific part of this jurisdiction, region, or feature, see the part and follow instructions under —4–9

—495 12   Attica region (Attikē periphereia)

        Class here Athens

For Kythēra Island, Peloponnesus portion of Attica region, see —4952

(Option: Class here ancient Attica, Athens, Marathon; prefer —385)

—495 15   Central Greece region (Sterea Hellada periphereia)

Including Boeotia (Voiōtia), Euboea (Euvoia), Eurytania, Phocis (Phōkis), Phthiōtis nomes

Including Skyros Island [*formerly also* —499], Euboea Island

(Option: Class here ancient Doris, Locris, Malis, Phocis, Amphissa, Delphi, Boeotia, Euboea Island, Chalcis, Thebes, Skyros Island; prefer —383 for Doris, Locris, Malis, Phocis, Amphissa, Delphi; —384 for Boeotia, Euboea Island, Chalcis, Thebes; —3911 for Skyros Island)

—495 18   Aetolia and Acarnania (Aitōlia kai Akarnania) nome

(Option: Class here ancient Aetolia, Acarnania; prefer —383)

—495 2   Peloponnesus and Isthmus of Corinth

Including Kythēra Island, Peloponnesus portion of Attica region

See also —16386 for Gulf of Corinth

(Option: Class here ancient Peloponnesus; prefer —386)

—495 22   Peloponnesus region (Peloponnēsos periphereia)

Including Arcadia (Arkadia), Argolis, Corinth (Korinthia), Laconia (Lakōnia), Messēnia nomes; Isthmus of Corinth

(Option: Class here ancient Megaris, Corinth, Arcadia, Argolis, Mycenae, Tiryns, Laconia, Messenia, Sparta; prefer —384 for Megaris, —387 for Corinth, —388 for Arcadia, Argolis, Mycenae, Tiryns, —389 for Laconia, Messenia, Sparta)

—495 27   Western Greece region (Dytikē Hellada periphereia)

Including Achaea (Achaia), Elis (Ēleia) nomes

For Aetolia and Acarnania (Aitōlia kai Akarnania) nome, see —49518

(Option: Class here ancient Achaea, Elis, Olympia, Phigalia; prefer —387 for Achaea, —388 for Elis, Olympia, Phigalia)

—495 3   Epirus region (Ēpeiros periphereia)

Including Arta, Iōannina, Preveza, Thesprōtia nomes

Class here comprehensive works on Epirus; *Pindus Mountains

For Albanian Epirus, see —4965

(Option: Class here ancient Epirus; prefer —382)

—495 4   Thessaly region (Thessalia periphereia)

Including Karditsa, Larisa, Magnēsia, Trikala nomes

Including Northern Sporades [*formerly* —499]

For Skyros Island, see —49515

(Option: Class here ancient Thessaly, Northern Sporades; prefer —382 for Thessaly, —3911 for Northern Sporades)

—495 5   Ionian Islands region (Ionioi Nēsoi periphereia)

Including Cefalonia (Kephallēnia), Corfu (Kerkyra), Leukas, Zante (Zakynthos) nomes; Ithaca Island

Class here Ionian Islands

(Option: Class here ancient Ionian Islands; prefer —382 for northern Ionian Islands, comprehensive works on Ionian Islands, —383 for Ithaca Island, —386 for southern Ionian Islands)

—495 6   Former Macedonia region (Makedonia periphereia)

Class here comprehensive works on Macedonia region

Drama, Kavala nomes relocated to —4957

For country of Macedonia, see —4976; for Macedonia in Bulgaria, see —4998

(Option: Class here comprehensive works on ancient Macedonia; prefer —381)

—495 62   Western Macedonia region (Dytikē Makedonia periphereia)

Including Flórina (Phlorina), Grevena, Kastoria, Kozanē nomes

—495 65   Central Macedonia region (Kentrikē Makedonia periphereia)

Including Chalkidikē, Hematheia (Ēmathia), Kilkis, Pella, Pieria, Serrai, Thessalonikē nomes; Mount Athos

---

*For a specific part of this jurisdiction, region, or feature, see the part and follow instructions under —4–9

—495 7   Eastern Macedonia and Thrace region (Anatolikē Makedonia kai Thrakē periphereia)

Including Drama, Kavala nomes [*formerly* —4956]; Samothrace Island, Thasos Island [*formerly* —499]; Evros, Rodopē (Rhodope), Xanthē nomes

Class here comprehensive works on Thrace

For Turkish Thrace, see —4961; for Bulgarian Thrace, see —4995

(Option: Class here ancient Samothrace Island, Thasos Island, Thracia; prefer —3911 for Samothrace Island, Thasos Island, —398 for Thracia)

—495 8   Former Aegean Islands region (Aigaio Nēsoi periphereia)

Class here comprehensive works on *Aegean Islands [*formerly* —499]; *Sporades

See also —16388 for Aegean Sea

(Option: Class here ancient Aegean Islands, Sporades; prefer —391)

—495 82   Northern Aegean region (Voreio Aigaio periphereia)

Including Chios, Lesvos (Lesbos), Samos nomes

(Option: Class here ancient Lemnos Island, Lesbos, Chios, Samos; prefer —3911 for Lemnos Island, —3912 for Lesbos, —3913 for Chios, —3914 for Samos)

—495 85   Cyclades (Kyklades) nome

Class here Southern Aegean region (Notio Aigaio periphereia)

For Dodecanese nome, see —49587

(Option: Class here ancient Cyclades; prefer —3915)

—495 87   Dodecanese (Dōdekanēsos) nome

Class here Southern Sporades

(Option: Class here ancient Southern Sporades, Dodecanese, Rhodes, Karpathos; prefer —3916 for Southern Sporades, Dodecanese, Rhodes, —3917 for Karpathos)

—495 9   Crete region (Krētē periphereia) [*formerly* —4998]

Including Chania (Canea), Hērakleion, Lasithi, Rethymnē nomes

(Option: Class here ancient Crete; prefer —3918)

—496   *Balkan Peninsula

Class here *Danube River

See also —56 for Ottoman Empire

(Option: Class here ancient southeastern Europe; prefer —398)

---

*For a specific part of this jurisdiction, region, or feature, see the part and follow instructions under —4–9

—496 1	Turkey in Europe (Turkish Thrace)

Including Edirne (Adrianople), Kirklareli, Tekirdağ provinces (illeri); European portion of Çanakkale Province (İli)

See also —16389 for Dardanelles, Sea of Marmara

—496 18	İstanbul Province (İli)

Class here Istanbul (Constantinople)

For Asian portion of İstanbul Province, see —563

See also —16389 for Bosporus

(Option: Class here ancient Constantinople; prefer —398)

—496 5	Albania
—497	Yugoslavia, Croatia, Slovenia, Bosnia and Hercegovina, Macedonia

Class here Yugoslavia (1918–1991)

Class Yugoslavia (1991–) in —4971

(Option: Class here ancient Illyria; prefer —398)

—497 1	Serbia

Including Belgrade, Kosovo i Metohija, Voivodina, Yugoslav Banat

Class here Yugoslavia (1991–)

For Montenegro, see —49745

—497 2	Croatia

Including Dalmatia, Istria, Slavonia

(Option: Class here ancient Istria; prefer —373)

—497 3	Slovenia
—497 4	Bosnia and Hercegovina, Montenegro
—497 42	Bosnia and Hercegovina

Including Sarajevo

—497 45	Montenegro
—497 6	Macedonia

Class here Vardar River

Class comprehensive works on Macedonia region in —4956

—[497 7]	Bulgaria

Relocated to —499

—498	Romania

(Option: Class here ancient Dacia; prefer —398)

—498 1   Northeast Romania

Including Bacău, Botoşani, Brăila, Galaţi, Iaşi, Neamţ, Suceava, Vaslui, Vrancea districts (judeţe)

Class here *Moldavia

—498 2   Walachia (Southeast Romania)

Including Argeş, Bucureşti, Buzău, Călăraşi, Dîmboviţa, Giurgiu, Ialomiţa, Olt, Prahova, Teleorman, Vîlcea districts (judeţe)

Including Ploieşti

For Black Sea area, see —4983

—498 3   Black Sea area

Including Constanţa, Tulcea districts (judeţe)

Class here *Dobruja

For South Dobruja, see —4994

See also —16389 for Black Sea

(Option: Class here ancient Scythia; prefer —3951)

—498 4   Central and west Romania

Including Alba, Arad, Bihor, Bistriţa-Năsăud, Braşov, Caraş-Severin, Cluj, Covasna, Dolj, Gorj, Harghita, Hunedoara, Maramureş, Mehedinţi, Mureş, Sălaj, Satu Mare, Sibiu, Timiş districts (judeţe)

Including Oltenia, Transylvania

Class here *Bukovina, comprehensive works on *Banat

For North Bukovina, see —4779; for Yugoslav Banat, see —4971

—499   Bulgaria [*formerly* —4977]

Class here *Balkan Mountains

Skyros Island relocated to —49515; Northern Sporades relocated to —4954; Samothrace Island, Thasos Island relocated to —4957; comprehensive works on Aegean Islands relocated to —4958

(Option: Class here ancient Moesia; prefer —398)

—499 1   Montana region (oblast)

Former name: Mikhaylovgrad region (Mikhaĭlovgradska oblast)

Including former Mikhaylovgrad, Vidin, Vratsa provinces (okrŭzi)

—499 2   Lovech region (Loveshka oblast)

Including former Gabrovo, Lovech, Pleven, Veliko Tŭrnovo provinces (okrŭzi)

*For a specific part of this jurisdiction, region, or feature, see the part and follow instructions under —4–9

—499 3   Ruse region (Rusenska oblast)

> Former name: Razgrad region (Razgradska oblast)

> Including former Razgrad, Ruse, Silistra, Tŭrgovishte provinces (okrŭzi)

—499 4   Varna region (Varnenska oblast)

> Including former Shumen, Tolbukhin, Varna provinces (okrŭzi); South Dobruja

—499 5   Burgas region (Burgaska oblast)

> Including former Burgas, Sliven, Yambol provinces (okrŭzi); Bulgarian Thrace

—499 6   Khaskovo region (Khaskovska oblast)

> Including former Khaskovo, Kŭrdzhali, Stara Zagora provinces (okrŭzi)

—499 7   Plovdiv region (Plovdivska oblast)

> Including former Pazardzhik, Plovdiv, Smolyan provinces (okrŭzi)

> Class here *Rhodope Mountains

—499 8   Sofia region (Sofiĭska oblast)

> Including former Blagoevgrad, Kyustendil, Pernik, Sofia provinces (okrŭzi); Bulgarian Macedonia

> Crete region (Krētē periphereia) relocated to —4959

—499 9   Sofia city

> Class here comprehensive works on historic region of Sofia

>> *For parts of historic region of Sofia in Sofia region (Sofiĭska oblast), see —4998*

—5   Asia   Orient   Far East

> Class here Eurasia

>> *For Europe, see —4*

SUMMARY

—51	**China and adjacent areas**
—52	**Japan**
—53	**Arabian Peninsula and adjacent areas**
—54	**South Asia India**
—55	**Iran**
—56	**Middle East (Near East)**
—57	**Siberia (Asiatic Russia)**
—58	**Central Asia**
—59	**Southeast Asia**

---

*For a specific part of this jurisdiction, region, or feature, see the part and follow instructions under —4–9

—51 **China and adjacent areas**

Class here People's Republic of China

(Option: Class here ancient China; prefer —31)

—511 Northeastern China

Class here Northern Region; *Yellow River (Hwang Ho)

For Inner Mongolia Autonomous Region, see —5177; for Manchuria, see —518

See also —16456 for Yellow Sea

—511 3 Shanghai Municipality and Kiangsu Province

—511 32 Shanghai Municipality (Shanghai Shih)

—511 36 Kiangsu Province (Jiangsu Sheng)

Including Nanking (Nanjing)

—511 4 Shantung Province (Shandong Sheng)

—511 5 Hopeh Province and Tientsin and Peking municipalities

—511 52 Hopeh Province (Hebei Sheng)

—511 54 Tientsin Municipality (Tianjin Shih)

—511 56 Peking Municipality (Beijing Shih)

—511 7 Shansi Province (Shanxi Sheng)

—511 8 Honan Province (Henan Sheng)

—512 Southeastern China and adjacent areas

Class here Eastern and Central-Southern Regions; *Yangtze River

For Shanghai Municipality, see —51132; for Kiangsu Province, see —51136; for Shantung Province, see —5114; for Honan Province, see —5118

—512 1 Hupeh and Hunan provinces

—512 12 Hupeh Province (Hubei Sheng)

—512 15 Hunan Province (Hunan Sheng)

—512 2 Kiangsi and Anhwei provinces

—512 22 Kiangsi Province (Jiangxi Sheng)

—512 25 Anhwei Province (Anhui Sheng)

—512 4 East China Sea area

See also —16457 for East China Sea

---

*For a specific part of this jurisdiction, region, or feature, see the part and follow instructions under —4–9

—512 42	Chekiang Province (Zhejiang Sheng)
—512 45	Fukien Province (Fujian Sheng)

>   *See also —16457 for Formosa Strait*

—512 49	Taiwan (Formosa) and adjacent islands
	Republic of China (Nationalist China)

>   *See also —16457 for Formosa Strait*

—512 5	Hong Kong
	British crown colony
—512 6	Macao
	Overseas territory of Portugal
—512 7	Kwangtung Province (Guangdong Sheng)
	Hainan Province (Hainan Sheng), formerly part of Kwangtung Province, relocated to —5129
—512 75	Canton
—512 8	Kwangsi Chuang Autonomous Region (Guangxi Zhuangzu Zizhiqu)

>   *See also —16472 for Gulf of Tonkin*

—512 9	Hainan Province (Hainan Sheng) [*formerly* —5127]
—513	Southwestern China (South-Western Region)

>   *For Tibet, see —515*

—513 4	Kweichow Province (Guizhou Sheng)
—513 5	Yunnan Province (Yunnan Sheng)
—513 8	Szechwan Province (Sichuan Sheng)
	Including Chungking (Chongqing)
—514	Northwestern China (North-Western Region)

>   *For Sinkiang Uighur Autonomous Region, see —516; for Ningsia Hui Autonomous Region, see —5175*

—514 3	Shensi Province (Shaanxi Sheng)
—514 5	Kansu Province (Gansu Sheng)
—514 7	Tsinghai Province (Qinghai Sheng)
—515	Tibet Autonomous Region (Xizang Zizhiqu)
—516	Sinkiang Uighur Autonomous Region (Xinjiang Weiwuer Zizhiqu)
	Including *Tien Shan

*For a specific part of this jurisdiction, region, or feature, see the part and follow instructions under —4–9

—517	Mongolia
—517 3	Outer Mongolia (Mongolian People's Republic)
	Independent state
	Including *Gobi Desert; *Altai Mountains
—517 5	Ningsia Hui Autonomous Region (Ningxia Huizu Zizhiqu)
—517 7	Inner Mongolia Autonomous Region (Nei Monggol Zizhiqu)
—518	Manchuria
	Class here North-Eastern Region
—518 2	Liaoning Province (Liaoning Sheng)
—518 4	Heilungkiang Province (Heilongjiang Sheng)
—518 8	Kirin Province (Jilin Sheng)
—519	Korea
	See also —16456 for Yellow Sea
—519 3	North Korea (People's Democratic Republic of Korea)
—519 5	South Korea (Republic of Korea)
—52	**Japan**
—521	Honshū (Honsyū)
—521 1	Tōhoku region (chihō)
	See also —16454 for Tsugaru Strait
—521 12	Aomori prefecture (ken)
	Including *Towada Lake
—521 13	Akita prefecture (ken)
—521 14	Iwate prefecture (ken)
—521 15	Miyagi prefecture (ken)
—521 16	Yamagata prefecture (ken)
—521 17	Fukusima prefecture (ken)
—521 3	Kantō region (chihō)
	Including *Tone River
—521 31	Ibaraki prefecture (ken)
—521 32	Tochigi prefecture (ken)
—521 33	Gumma prefecture (ken)

*For a specific part of this jurisdiction, region, or feature, see the part and follow instructions under —4–9

—521 34   Saitama prefecture (ken)

—521 35   Tōkyō prefecture (to)

                Class here Tokyo

                    For Bonin (Ogasawara) Islands, see —528

—521 36   Kanagawa prefecture (ken)

—521 364   Yokohama

—521 37   Chiba prefecture (ken)

—521 5   Hokuriku region (chihō)

—521 52   Niigata prefecture (ken)

                Class here *Shinano River

—521 53   Toyama prefecture (ken)

—521 54   Ishikawa prefecture (ken)

—521 55   Fukui prefecture (ken)

—521 6   Chūbu region (chihō)

                Including *Akaishi Mountains

                    For Hokuriku region, see —5215

—521 62   Gifu prefecture (ken)

—521 63   Nagano prefecture (ken)

—521 64   Yamanashi prefecture (ken)

—521 65   Shizuoka prefecture (ken)

                    For Mount Fuji, see —52166

—521 66   Mount Fuji (Fuji-san, Fujiyama)

—521 67   Aichi prefecture (ken)

—521 674   Nagoya

—521 8   Kinki region (chihō)

—521 81   Mie prefecture (ken)

—521 82   Wakayama prefecture (ken)

—521 83   Ōsaka prefecture (fu)

                Class here *Yodo River

—521 834   Ōsaka

—521 84   Nara prefecture (ken)

*For a specific part of this jurisdiction, region, or feature, see the part and follow instructions under —4–9

—521 85	Shiga prefecture (ken)
—521 86	Kyōto prefecture (fu)
—521 864	Kyōto
—521 87	Hyōgo prefecture (ken)
—521 874	Kōbe
—521 9	Chūgoku region (chihō)

                 See also — 16455 for Inland Sea (Seto-naikai)

—521 93	Tottori prefecture (ken)
—521 94	Okayama prefecture (ken)
—521 95	Hiroshima prefecture (ken)
—521 954	Hiroshima
—521 96	Shimane prefecture (ken)
—521 97	Yamaguchi prefecture (ken)
—522	Kyusyu region (Kyūshū chihō)

>	—522 2–522 8 Kyusyu (Kyūshū) island

              Class comprehensive works in —522

—522 2	Fukuoka prefecture (ken)
—522 3	Saga prefecture (ken)
—522 4	Nagasaki prefecture (ken)
—522 44	Nagasaki
—522 5	Kumamoto prefecture (ken)
—522 6	Kagoshima prefecture (ken)
—522 7	Miyazaki prefecture (ken)
—522 8	Ōita prefecture (ken)
—522 9	Okinawa prefecture (ken)

              Class here Ryukyu Islands

—522 94	Okinawa island
—523	Shikoku
—523 2	Ehime prefecture (ken)
—523 3	Kōchi prefecture (ken)

—523 4	Tokushima prefecture (ken)
—523 5	Kagawa prefecture (ken)
—524	Hokkaidō

         Including Etorofu, Kunashiri (islands claimed by both Japan and Russia)

         See also —16453 for La Perouse Strait, —16454 for Tsugaru Strait

—528	Bonin (Ogasawara) Islands
—53	**Arabian Peninsula and adjacent areas**

         See also —16533 for Red Sea, —16535 for Persian Gulf

         (Option: Class here ancient Arabia, Arabia Felix, Arabia Petraea; prefer —3949 for ancient Arabia, Arabia Felix, —3948 for Arabia Petraea)

—531	Sinai Peninsula

         Including Janūb Sīnā', Shamāl Sīnā' provinces; Gaza Strip

         (Option: Class here ancient Sinai Peninsula; prefer —3948)

—533	Yemen

         Class here Republic of Yemen

—533 2	Northern Yemen

         Class here Yemen Arab Republic

—533 5	Southern Yemen

         Class here Federation of South Arabia, People's Democratic Republic of Yemen

—535	Oman and United Arab Emirates
—535 3	Oman

         See also —16536 for Gulf of Oman

—535 7	United Arab Emirates

         Including Abu Dhabi, 'Ajmān, Dubai, Fujairah, Ras al Khaimah, Shārjah, Umm al-Qaiwain

—536	Persian Gulf States

         For Oman and United Arab Emirates, see —535

—536 3	Qatar
—536 5	Bahrain
—536 7	Kuwait

—538   Saudi Arabia

Including Hejaz, Nejd; Mecca; *Rub'al-Khali, Syrian Desert in Saudi
Arabia

—54   South Asia   India

For southeast Asia, see —59

(Option: Class here ancient India; prefer —34)

SUMMARY

—541	**Northeastern India**
—542	**Uttar Pradesh**
—543	**Madhya Pradesh**
—544	**Rajasthan**
—545	**Punjab region of India**
—546	**Jammu and Kashmir**
—547	**Western India**
—548	**Southern India**
—549	**Other jurisdictions**

>   —541–548   India

Class comprehensive works in —54

—541   Northeastern India

Including *Ganges River

—541 2   Bihar

—541 3   Orissa

—541 4   West Bengal

Class here former province of Bengal

For former East Bengal, see —5492

—541 47   Calcutta

—541 5   Tripura

—541 6   Far northeast

Class here *Brahmaputra River in India

For Manipur, see —5417

—541 62   Assam

—541 63   Arunāchal Pradesh

—541 64   Meghalaya

---

*For a specific part of this jurisdiction, region, or feature, see the part and follow instructions
under —4–9

—541 65	Nāgāland
—541 66	Mizoram
—541 67	Sikkim
—541 7	Manipur
—542	Uttar Pradesh
—543	Madhya Pradesh
	Including Bhopal
—544	Rajasthan
	Class here *Thar (Great Indian) Desert
—545	Punjab region of India
	Class here former province of Punjab
	For Punjab Province of Pakistan, see —54914
—545 2	Himachal Pradesh
—545 5	Punjab and Haryana
	Class here former Punjab state
—545 52	Punjab
	Including Chandīgarh
—545 58	Haryana
—545 6	Delhi
	Class here Delhi, New Delhi
—546	Jammu and Kashmir
	Kashmir is claimed by both India and Pakistan
	Including *Karakoram Range
—547	Western India
—547 5	Gujarat
—547 9	Maharashtra and adjacent territories
—547 92	Maharashtra
—547 923	Bombay
—547 96	Dādra and Nagar Haveli
—547 99	Goa, Daman and Diu

*For a specific part of this jurisdiction, region, or feature, see the part and follow instructions under —4–9

—548	Southern India
	Class here *Deccan
—548 1	Lakshadweep
	Former name: Laccadive, Minicoy, and Amindivi Islands
—548 2	Tamil Nadu
	Former name: Madras
	Including Madras
—548 3	Kerala
—548 4	Andhra Pradesh
	Including Hyderabad
	Class here former state of Hyderabad
	For Maharashtra, see —54792; for Karnataka, see —5487
—548 6	Pondicherry
—548 7	Karnataka
	Former name: Mysore
—548 8	Andaman and Nicobar Islands
—549	Other jurisdictions
	Class here Pakistan (West and East, 1947–1971)
—549 1	Pakistan
	Former name: West Pakistan
	Class here *Indus River
—549 12	North-West Frontier
—549 122	Districts and agencies north of Peshawar
	Including Chitrāl, Dīr, Kalam, Swat
—549 123	Peshawar District
	Class here Peshawar
—549 124	Districts south of Peshawar
	Including Dera Ismāīl Khān District
—549 13	Kashmir
	Claimed by both Pakistan and India

*For a specific part of this jurisdiction, region, or feature, see the part and follow instructions under —4–9

—549 14	Punjab Province
	Including Multān, Sargodha Districts
	For Bahāwalpur District, see —54916
—549 142	Rāwalpindi District
	Including Islāmābād
—549 143	Lahore District
	Class here Lahore
—549 15	Baluchistan Province
	Class here comprehensive works on Baluchistan
	For Iranian Baluchistan, see —5583
—549 152	Quetta District
—549 153	Kalāt District
—549 16	Bahāwalpur District
—549 17	Khairpūr District
—549 18	Sind Province
	For Khairpūr District, see —54917
—549 182	Hyderabad District
	Class here Hyderabad
—549 183	Karachi District
	Class here Karachi
—549 2	Bangladesh
	Former names: East Bengal, East Pakistan
	Class here comprehensive works on Brahmaputra River
	For Brahmaputra River in India, see —5416
—549 22	Dhaka (Dacca) Division
	Class here Dacca
—549 23	Chittagong Division
	Class here Chittagong
—549 24	Rājshāhi Division
—549 25	Khulna Division
—549 3	Sri Lanka
	Former name: Ceylon
	Including Colombo

—549 5	Maldives
—549 6	Nepal

Class here *Himalaya Mountains

—549 8	Bhutan
—55	**Iran**

Former name: Persia

(Option: Class here ancient Iranian Plateau; prefer —35)

—551	Gīlān and Zanjān provinces
—552	Māzandarān, Semnān, Tehran, Markazī provinces
—552 3	Māzandarān and Semnān (Samnan) provinces

(Option: Class here ancient Hyrcania; prefer —396)

—552 5	Tehran province

Class here Tehran

Current Markazī province, part of former Markazī province, relocated to —5527

—552 7	Markazī province [*formerly* —5525]

Class comprehensive works on former Markazī province (which included Tehran) in —5525

—553	East Azerbaijan (Āzarbāyjān-i Khāvarī) province

Class here Azerbaijan region

For country of Azerbaijan, see —4754; for West Azerbaijan of Iran, see —554

—554	West Azerbaijan (Āzarbāyjān-i Bākhtarī) province
—555	Hamadān, Īlām, Kermānshāhān, Kordestān provinces

(Option: Class here ancient Media, Ecbatana; prefer —35)

—555 2	Hamadān, Īlām, Kermānshāhān provinces
—555 4	Kordestān province

Class comprehensive works on Kurdistan in —5667

—556	Boyer Ahmadī-ye Sardīr va Kohkīlūyeh, Khūzestān, Lorestān (Luristān) provinces

(Option: Class here ancient Elam [Susiana], Susa; prefer —35)

—557	Būshehr, Fārs, Persian Gulf (Hormozgān) provinces

---

*For a specific part of this jurisdiction, region, or feature, see the part and follow instructions under —4–9

—557 2   Fārs province

                      (Option: Class here ancient Persia, Pasargadae, Persepolis; prefer —35)

—557 5   Būshehr and Persian Gulf (Hormozgān) provinces

—558   Kirmān, Sīstān and Balūchestān provinces

—558 2   Kirmān (Kerman) province

—558 3   Sīstān and Balūchestān (Balūchistān va Sīstān) province

                      Class comprehensive works on Baluchistan in —54915

—559   Khorāsān, Bakhtīarī va Chahār Mahāll, Eṣfahān, Yazd provinces

—559 2   Khorāsān (Khurasan) province

—559 5   Bakhtīarī va Chahār Mahāll, Eṣfahān (Iṣfahān), Yazd provinces

—56   ***Middle East (Near East)**

             Class here *Ottoman Empire

             (Option: Class here ancient Middle East; prefer —394)

SUMMARY

—561	**Turkey**
—562	**Western Turkey**
—563	**North central Turkey**
—564	**South central Turkey**
—565	**East central Turkey**
—566	**Eastern Turkey**
—567	**Iraq**
—569	**Syria, Lebanon, Cyprus, Israel, Jordan**

—561   Turkey

                  Class here Asia Minor

                  For divisions of Turkey, see —562–566

                  (Option: Class here ancient Asia Minor, western Asia Minor, eastern Asia Minor; prefer —392 for Asia Minor, western Asia Minor, —393 for eastern Asia Minor)

>   —562–566 Divisions of Turkey

                  Class comprehensive works in —561

                  For Turkey in Europe, see —4961

*For a specific part of this jurisdiction, region, or feature, see the part and follow instructions under —4–9

—562 Western Turkey

Including Afyon, Aydin, Balikesir, Burdur, Çanakkale, Denizli, İzmir, Kütahya, Manisa, Muğla, Uşak provinces (illeri)

Including Bozca (Tenedos) and İmroz (Imbros) islands

For European portion of Çanakkale Province, see —4961

See also —16389 for Dardanelles

(Option: Class here ancient Imbros and Tenedos islands, Mysia, Troas, Lydia, Ionia, Caria, Phrygia; prefer —3911 for Imbros and Tenedos islands, —3921 for Mysia and Troas, —3922 for Lydia, —3923 for Ionia, —3924 for Caria, —3926 for Phrygia)

—563 North central Turkey

Including Amasya, Ankara, Bilecik, Bolu, Bursa, Çankiri, Çorum, Eskişehir, Kastamonu, Kocaeli, Sakarya, Samsun, Sinop, Yozgat, Zonguldak provinces (illeri); Asian portion of İstanbul Province (İli)

See also —16389 for Bosporus, Sea of Marmara

(Option: Class here ancient Bithynia, Paphlagonia, Galatia; prefer —3925 for Bithynia, —3931 for Paphlagonia, —3932 for Galatia)

—564 South central Turkey

Including Adana, Antalya, Gaziantep, Hatay, İçel, Isparta, Kayseri, Kirşehir, Konya, Nevşehir, Niğde provinces (illeri); Taurus Mountains

(Option: Class here ancient Pisidia, Lycia, Pamphylia, Cappadocia, Cilicia, Commagene, Antioch; prefer —3927 for Pisidia, —3928 for Lycia, —3929 for Pamphylia, —3934 for Cappadocia, —3935 for Cilicia, —3936 for Commagene, —3943 for Antioch)

—[564 5] Cyprus

Relocated to —5693

—565 East central Turkey

Including Adiyaman, Giresun, Gümüşhane, Kahraman Maraş, Malatya, Ordu, Şanliurfa (Urfa), Sivas, Tokat, Trabzon provinces (illeri)

(Option: Class here ancient Pontus; prefer —3933)

—566 Eastern Turkey

—566 2 Northeastern Turkey

Including Ağri, Artvin, Erzurum, Hakkâri, Kars, Rize, Van provinces (illeri)

Class here comprehensive works on Armenia region

For country of Armenia, see —4756

(Option: Class here ancient Armenia; prefer —3955)

—566 7   Southeast central Turkey

Including Bingöl, Bitlis, Diyarbakir, Elaziğ, Erzincan, Mardin, Muş, Siirt, Tunceli provinces (illeri)

Class here comprehensive works on Kurdistan

For Iranian Kurdistan, see —5554; for Iraqi Kurdistan, see —5672

—567   Iraq

Class here Mesopotamia

(Option: Class here ancient Mesopotamia, Seleucid Empire, Arabia Deserta; prefer —35 for Mesopotamia, Seleucid Empire; —3947 for Arabia Deserta)

—567 2   Kurdish Autonomous Region

Including Dahūk, Irbīl, Sulaymānīyah provinces

Class comprehensive works on Kurdistan in —5667

—567 4   Upper Mesopotamia

Including Anbār, Diyālá, Nīnawá (Nineveh), Ṣalāḥ ad-Dīn, Ta'mim provinces; Mosul; Syrian Desert in Iraq

(Option: Class here ancient Assyria, Ashur, Nineveh; prefer —35)

—567 47   Baghdād Province

Class here Baghdad

—567 5   Lower Mesopotamia

Including Bābil, Baṣrah, Dhī Qār, Karbalā', Maysān, Muthanná, Najaf, Qādisīyah, Wāsiṭ (Kūt) provinces

(Option: Class here ancient Babylonia, Sumer, Babylon, Ur; prefer —35)

—569   Syria, Lebanon, Cyprus, Israel, Jordan

Class here *Syrian Desert

—569 1   Syria

(Option: Class here ancient Syria; prefer —3943)

—569 12   Desert provinces

Including Dayr al-Zawr, Ḥasakah, Ḥimṣ, Raqqah

Class here Syrian Desert in Syria

(Option: Class here ancient Palmyra; prefer —3943)

—569 13   Northwest provinces

Including Aleppo (Ḥalab), Ḥamāh, Idlib, Latakia, Ṭarṭūs

(Option: Class here ancient Ebla, Ugarit; prefer —3943)

*For a specific part of this jurisdiction, region, or feature, see the part and follow instructions under —4–9

—569 14   Southwest provinces and city of Damascus

                 Including Damascus (Dimashq), Darʻā, Qunayṭirah, Suwaydāʼ provinces

                 Including *Anti-Lebanon

—569 144   City of Damascus

                 (Option: Class here ancient Damascus; prefer —3943)

—569 2   Lebanon

                 (Option: Class here ancient Phoenicia, Coelesyria, Baalbek, Byblos, Sidon, Tyre; prefer —3944)

—569 25   Beirut

—569 3   Cyprus [*formerly* —5645]

                 (Option: Class here ancient Cyprus; prefer —3937)

—569 4   Palestine   Israel

                 Palestine: area covering Israel, Gaza Strip, and West Bank of Jordan

                 Including *Jordan River; *Dead Sea

                 For Gaza Strip, see —531; for West Bank, see —56951–56953

                 (Option: Class here ancient Palestine, Israel; prefer —33)

—569 44   Jerusalem district

—569 442   Jerusalem

                   (Option: Class here ancient Jerusalem; prefer —33)

—569 45   Tsafon district

                 Class here Galilee

                 (Option: Class here ancient Galilee; prefer —33)

—569 46   Haifa district

—569 47   Merkaz district

—569 48   Tel Aviv district

                 Class here Tel Aviv

—569 49   Darom district

                 Class here Negev

                 (Option: Class here ancient Judah, Judaea, Edom; prefer —33 for Judah, Judaea, —3946 for Edom)

—569 5   West Bank and Jordan

                 (Option: Class here the Jordanian part of ancient Palestine; prefer —33)

---

*For a specific part of this jurisdiction, region, or feature, see the part and follow instructions under —4–9

>,   —569 51–569 53   West Bank

Class comprehensive works in —56953

—569 51   Hebron district

—569 52   Jerusalem district

Class city of Jerusalem in —569442

—569 53   Nablus district

Class here comprehensive works on West Bank

For Hebron district, see —56951; for Jerusalem district, see —56952

(Option: Class here ancient Samaria; prefer —33)

>   —569 54–569 59   Jordan

Class comprehensive works in —5695

—569 54   Irbid Province

Eastern part of former Irbid district, Syrian Desert in Jordan relocated to —56959

—569 55   Balqā' Province

—569 56   Karak and Ṭafīlah provinces

Former heading: Karak district

Eastern part of former Karak district relocated to —56957

(Option: Class here ancient Moab; prefer —3946)

—569 563   Karak Province

—569 567   Ṭafīlah Province

—569 57   Ma'ān Province

Including eastern part of former Karak district [*formerly* —56956]

(Option: Class here ancient Petra; prefer —3948)

—569 58   Amman ('Āṣimah) Province

Class here Amman

Northeastern part of former Amman district relocated to —56959

—569 59   Zarqā' and Mafraq provinces

Class here eastern part of former Irbid district, *Syrian Desert in Jordan [*both formerly* —56954], northeastern part of former Amman district [*formerly* —56958]

*For a specific part of this jurisdiction, region, or feature, see the part and follow instructions under —4–9

—569 593   Zarqā' Province

—569 597   Mafraq Province

—57   **Siberia (Asiatic Russia)**

—573   Western Siberia

Including Kemerovo, Kurgan, Novosibirsk, Omsk, Tomsk, Tyumen provinces (oblasts); Altay territory (kray); Gorno-Altay republic; Khantia-Mansia and Yamal-Nenets autonomous districts (okrugs)

For Chelyabinsk and Sverdlovsk provinces, see —4743

—575   Eastern Siberia

Including Chita and Irkutsk provinces (oblasts); Krasnoyarsk territory (kray); Buryatia, Khakass, Tuva, Yakutia republics; Agin Burîât, Evenki, Taĭmyr, Ust-Orda Burîât autonomous districts (okrugs); *Sayan Mountains

For Far Eastern Siberia, see —577; for Severnaya Zemlya, see —987; for New Siberian Islands, see —988

—577   Far Eastern Siberia

Including Amur, Kamchatka, Magadan, Sakhalin provinces (oblasts); Khabarovsk and Maritime (Primor´ye) territories (krays); Jewish autonomous region (Yevrey avtonomnaîâ oblast); Chukchi and Korîâk autonomous districts (okrugs); Kuril and Komandorski Islands, Wrangel Island; *Amur River

See also —16451 for Bering Strait, —16453 for Sea of Okhotsk, —16454 for Tatar Strait

—58   **Central Asia**

(Option: Class here ancient Central Asia; prefer —396)

—581   Afghanistan

Class here *Hindu Kush

(Option: Class here ancient Ariana, Bactria, Parthia; prefer —396)

—584   Turkestan

Class Sinkiang in —516

For Turkmenistan, see —585; for Tajikistan, see —586; for Uzbekistan, see —587

—584 3   Kyrgyzstan

Including *Tien Shan

—584 5   Kazakhstan

—585   Turkmenistan

(Option: Class here ancient Margiana; prefer —396)

*For a specific part of this jurisdiction, region, or feature, see the part and follow instructions under —4–9

—586   Tajikistan

         Including Gorno-Badakhshan autonomous province (oblast)

         Class here *Pamir

—587   Uzbekistan

         Including Karakalpak autonomous republic; *Aral Sea

         (Option: Class here ancient Sogdiana; prefer —396)

—59   **Southeast Asia**

         Class here *Indochina (southeast peninsula of Asia)

         Class works about "Indochina" when used to equate with French Indochina in —597

—591   Myanmar (Burma)

—593   Thailand

         Former name: Siam

           See also —16472 for Gulf of Thailand

—594   Laos

—595   Commonwealth of Nations territories   Malaysia

—595 1   Peninsular Malaysia (Malaya, West Malaysia)

         Including states of Johore, Kedah, Kelantan, Malacca (Melaka), Negeri Sembilan, Pahang, Perak, Perlis, Pinang (Penang), Selangor, Terengganu (Trengganu); Kuala Lumpur

         Class here Malay Peninsula

           For Myanmar (Burma), see —591; for Thailand, see —593

—595 3   Sabah

         State of Malaysia

         Including Labuan

         Class here northern Borneo, East Malaysia

           For Sarawak, see —5954; for Brunei, see —5955

—595 4   Sarawak

         State of Malaysia

—595 5   Brunei

---

*For a specific part of this jurisdiction, region, or feature, see the part and follow instructions under —4–9

—595 7   Singapore

            Independent republic

            See also —16472 for Singapore Strait

—596   Cambodia (Khmer Republic, Kampuchea)

—597   Vietnam

            Including *Mekong River

            Class here *French Indochina (Indochina)

            Class works about "Indochina" when used to equate with the southeast peninsula of Asia in —59

—598   Indonesia

            Class here Malay Archipelago, Sunda Islands

            For Philippines, see —599; for Irian Jaya, see —951

            See also —16473 for inner sea of Malay Archipelago, —16474 for seas adjoining Sunda Islands

—598 1   Sumatra

—598 2   Java and Madura

—598 22   Jakarta (Djakarta)

—598 3   Kalimantan

            Class here Borneo

            For northern Borneo, see —5953

—598 4   Celebes (Sulawesi)

—598 5   Maluku (Moluccas)

—598 6   Lesser Sunda Islands (Nusa Tenggara)

            Including Bali, Flores, Lombok, Sumba, Sumbawa, Timor; former Portuguese Timor

—599   Philippines

            See also —16471 for inner seas of Philippines

---

*For a specific part of this jurisdiction, region, or feature, see the part and follow instructions under —4–9

—599 1   Luzon and adjacent islands

> Including Abra, Albay, Bataan, Batanes, Batangas, Benguet, Bulacan, Cagayan, Camarines Norte, Camarines Sur, Catanduanes, Cavite, Ifugao, Ilocos Norte, Ilocos Sur, Isabela, Kalinga-Apayao, La Union, Laguna, Marinduque, Mountain, Nueva Ecija, Nueva Vizcaya, Pampanga, Pangasinan, Quezon, Rizal, Sorsogon, Tarlac, Zambales provinces

> *See also — 16458 for Luzon Strait*

—599 16   Manila

—599 3   Mindoro and adjacent islands

> Including Occidental Mindoro, Oriental Mindoro provinces

—599 4   Palawan and adjacent islands (Palawan province)

—599 5   Visayan Islands

> Including Aklan, Antique, Bohol, Capiz, Cebu, Eastern Samar, Iloilo, Leyte, Masbate, Negros Occidental, Negros Oriental, Northern Samar, Romblon, Southern Leyte, Western Samar provinces

> Including Cebu, Leyte, Negros, Panay, Samar Islands

—599 7   Mindanao and adjacent islands

> Including Agusan del Norte, Agusan del Sur, Basilan, Bukidnon, Camiguin, Davao del Norte, Davao del Sur, Davao Oriental, Lanao del Norte, Lanao del Sur, Maguindanao, Misamis Occidental, Misamis Oriental, North Cotabato, South Cotabato, Sultan Kudarat, Surigao del Norte, Surigao del Sur, Zamboanga del Norte, Zamboanga del Sur provinces

> Including Basilan, Dinagat Islands

—599 9   Sulu Archipelago

> Including Sulu and Tawitawi provinces

> *See also — 16473 for Sulu Sea*

—6   Africa

SUMMARY

—61	Tunisia and Libya
—62	Egypt and Sudan
—63	Ethiopia and Eritrea
—64	Northwest African coast and offshore islands Morocco
—65	Algeria
—66	West Africa and offshore islands
—67	Central Africa and offshore islands
—68	Southern Africa Republic of South Africa
—69	South Indian Ocean islands

—61   **Tunisia and Libya**

Class here *Barbary States, *North Africa

(Option: Class here ancient North Africa; prefer —397)

—611   **Tunisia**

Including Bizerte, Tunis

(Option: Class here ancient Carthage; prefer —3973)

—612   **Libya**

Including Banghāzī, Tripoli; *Libyan Desert

(Option: Class here ancient Tripolis, Leptis Magna, Oea, Sabrata, Cyrenaica, Marmarica; prefer —3974 for Tripolis, Leptis Magna, Oea, Sabrata, —3975 for Cyrenaica, —3976 for Marmarica)

—62   **Egypt and Sudan**

Class here Federation of Arab Republics, *Nile River

For Syria, see —5691; for Libya, see —612

(Option: Class here ancient Egypt; prefer —32)

———————————

\>   **—621–623   Egypt**

Class comprehensive works in —62

For Sinai, see —531

—621   **Lower Egypt**

Including Alexandria, Buḥayrah (Beheira), Damietta (Dumyāṭ), Daqahlīyah, Gharbīyah, Kafr al-Shaykh (Kafr el Sheikh), Marsá Maṭrūḥ (Maṭrūḥ), Minūfīyah, Mudīrīyat al-Sharqīyah (Sharqīyah), Qalyūbīyah provinces

Class here Nile River Delta

(Option: Class here ancient Alexandria; prefer —32)

—621 5   **Isthmus of Suez**

Including Ismailia, Port Said (Būr Saʻīd), Suez (Suways) provinces

See also —16533 for Gulf of Suez, Suez Canal

—621 6   Cairo (Qāhirah) province

Class here Cairo

———————————

*For a specific part of this jurisdiction, region, or feature, see the part and follow instructions under —4–9

—622   Middle Egypt

> Including Asyūṭ, Banī Suwayf, Fayyūm, Jīzah, Minyā, New Valley (Wādī al-Jadīd) provinces; *Western Desert, *Qattara Depression
>
> (Option: Class here ancient Giza, Memphis; prefer —32)

—623   Upper Egypt

> Including Aswān, Qinā, Red Sea (Bahr al Ahmar), Sūhāj (Sohāg) provinces; *Eastern (Arabian) Desert; *Lake Nasser
>
> (Option: Class here ancient Abydos, Karnak, Luxor, Thebes; prefer —32)

—624   Sudan

> *For provinces of Sudan, see —625–629*

>   —625–629   Provinces of Sudan

> Class comprehensive works in —624

—625   Eastern and Northern regions of Sudan

> Including Kassalā, Nīl, Northern (Shamālīyah), Red Sea (Baḥr al-Aḥmar) provinces; Port Sudan
>
> *See also —16533 for Red Sea*
>
> (Option: Class here ancient Ethiopia, Cush, Nubia; prefer —3978)

—626   Khartoum province and Central region of Sudan

—626 2   Khartoum province

> Class here Khartoum

—626 4   Central region

> Including Blue Nile (Nīl al-Azraq), Gezira (Jazīrah), White Nile (Baḥr al-Abyaḍ, Nīl al-Abyaḍ) provinces
>
> Class here *Blue Nile River
>
> Class comprehensive works on White Nile River in —6293

—627   Darfur region of Sudan

> Including Northern Darfur (Dārfūr al-Shamālīyah) and Southern Darfur (Dārfūr al-Janūbīyah) provinces

—628   Kordofan region of Sudan

> Including Northern Kordofan (Kurdufān al-Shamālīyah) and Southern Kordofan (Kurdufān al Janūbīyah) provinces

—629   Southern regions of Sudan

---

*For a specific part of this jurisdiction, region, or feature, see the part and follow instructions under —4–9

—629 3   Upper Nile region

           Including Junqali (Jongley) and Upper Nile (A'ālī al-Nīl) provinces

           Class here *White Nile River

           See also —6264 for White Nile Province

—629 4   Baḥr al Ghazāl and Buḥayrāh regions

—629 5   Equatoria region

           Including Eastern Equatoria (Mudīrīyah al-Istiwā'īyah al-Sharqīyah) and Western Equatoria (Mudīrīyah al-Istiwā'īyah al-Gharbīyah) provinces

—63   **Ethiopia and Eritrea**

           Class here Horn of Africa

           For Djibouti and Somalia, see —677

>   —632–634   Ethiopia

           Class comprehensive works in —63

—632   Provinces (Kifle hāgeroch) east of Great Rift Valley

           Including Ārsī, Balē, Hārergē, Sīdamo

—633   Provinces (Kifle hāgeroch) west of Great Rift Valley

           Including Gamo Gofa, Gojam, Īlubabor, Kefa, Shewa (Shoa), Welega provinces; Addis Ababa

—634   Northern provinces (kifle hāgeroch)

           Including Gonder (Bagēmder), Tigray, Welo

—635   Eritrea

           Including Asmara (Āsmera)

—64   **Northwest African coast and offshore islands**   **Morocco**

           Class here *Atlas Mountains

           (Option: Class here ancient Mauretania Tingitana; prefer —3971)

>   —642–646   Morocco

           Class comprehensive works in —64

—642   Mediterranean region of Morocco

           Including Chaouen, Hoceïma, Nador, Tangier, Tétouan provinces; Spanish cities of Ceuta and Melilla

           Class here former Spanish Morocco; *Rif Mountains

---

*For a specific part of this jurisdiction, region, or feature, see the part and follow instructions under —4–9

—643   Northern region of Morocco

> Including Ben Slimane, Boulemane, Fès (Fez), Figuig, Ifrane, Jadīda, Kenitra, Khemisset, Khenifra, Khouribga, Meknès, Oujda, Settat, Sidi Kacem, Taounate, Taza provinces; Ain Chok-Hay Hassani, Ben Msik-Sidi Othmane, Casablanca-Anfa, Hay Mohamed-Ain Sebaa, Mohamedia-Znata, Rabat-Salé, Skhirate-Temara prefectures; Casablanca, Rabat

> *For Mediterranean region, see —642*

—644   Azilal and Beni Mellal provinces

—645   Rachidia province

—646   Southwestern provinces of Morocco

> Including Agadir, Essaouira, Guelmim, Kelaa des Srarhna, Marrakech, Ouarzazate, Safi, Tan-Tan, Taroudant, Tata, Tiznit

—648   Western Sahara

> Former names: Spanish West Africa, Spanish Sahara (Saguia el Hamra, Rio de Oro)

> Including Ad Dakhla, Boujdour, Es Semara (Smara), Laâyoune provinces

—649   Canary Islands

> Including Las Palmas and Santa Cruz de Tenerife provinces of Spain

—65   Algeria

> (Option: Class here ancient Mauretania Caesariensis, comprehensive works on Mauretania; prefer —3971)

—651   Northwestern provinces

> Including Aïn Temouchent, Mascara, Mostaganem, Oran, Relizane, Saïda, Sidi Bel Abbès, Tiaret, Tissemsilt, Tlemcen

—653   North central provinces

> Including Aïn Defla, Algiers (Jaza'ir), Blida (Boulaida), Bouira, Boumerdes, Cheliff (Chlef, El Asnam, Orléansville), Djelfa, Médéa, Tipaza, Tizi-Ouzou

—655   Northeastern provinces

> Including Annaba (Bône), Batna, Bejaïa (Bougie), Biskra, Bordj Bou Arréridj, Constantine (Qacentina), Guelma, Jījil (Jijel), Khenchela, Mila, M'Sila, Oum el Bouaghi, Sétif, Skikda, Souk Ahras, Tarf, Tébessa

> (Option: Class here ancient Numidia; prefer —3972)

—657   Sahara provinces

> Including Adrar, Bayadh, Béchar, Ghardaia, Illizi, Laghouat, Naâma, Ouargla, Oued, Tamanrasset, Tindouf

> (Option: Class here ancient Gaetulia; prefer —3977)

—66 **West Africa and offshore islands**

Class here *Sahara Desert, *Sahel

SUMMARY

—661	**Mauritania**
—662	**Mali, Burkina Faso, Niger**
—663	**Senegal**
—664	**Sierra Leone**
—665	**Gambia, Guinea, Guinea-Bissau, Cape Verde**
—666	**Liberia and Côte d'Ivoire**
—667	**Ghana**
—668	**Togo and Benin**
—669	**Nigeria**

—661 Mauritania

Including Nouakchott

—662 Mali, Burkina Faso, Niger

Class here *Niger River

—662 3 Mali

Former name: French Sudan

Including Bamako

—662 5 Burkina Faso

Former name: Upper Volta

Including Bobo-Dioulasso, Ouagadougou

—662 6 Niger

Including Niamey

—663 Senegal

Including Cap Vert, Casamance, Diourbel, Fleuve, Louga, Sénégal Oriental, Sine-Saloum, Thiès regions; Dakar, Saint-Louis

Class here Senegambia

For Gambia, see —6651

—664 Sierra Leone

Including Freetown

—665 Gambia, Guinea, Guinea-Bissau, Cape Verde

Class here *Upper Guinea area

---

*For a specific part of this jurisdiction, region, or feature, see the part and follow instructions under —4–9

—665 1	Gambia
	Including Banjul
	Class here *Gambia River
—665 2	Guinea
	Former name: French Guinea
	Including Conakry, Kankan
—665 7	Guinea-Bissau
	Former name: Portuguese Guinea
	Including Bissau
—665 8	Cape Verde
	Including Praia
	Class here Cape Verde Islands
—666	Liberia and Côte d'Ivoire
—666 2	Liberia
	Including Monrovia
—666 8	Côte d'Ivoire (Ivory Coast)
	Including Abidjan, Bouaké, Yamoussoukro
—667	Ghana
	Former name: Gold Coast
	Including Accra, Kumasi
	Class here *Volta River
—668	Togo and Benin
—668 1	Togo
	Including Lomé
—668 3	Benin
	Former name: Dahomey
	Including Cotonou, Porto-Novo
—669	Nigeria
—669 1	Lagos State
	Class here Lagos

*For a specific part of this jurisdiction, region, or feature, see the part and follow instructions under —4–9

—669 2	Western states
	Class here former *Western State, former *Western Region
—669 23	Ogun State
—669 25	Oyo State
	Including Ibadan
	Osun State, formerly part of Oyo State, relocated to —66926
—669 26	Osun State [*formerly* —66925]
—669 28	Ondo State
—669 3	Bendel states
	Former names: Bendel State, Benin State, Mid-Western State
—669 32	Edo State
	Including Benin City
—669 36	Delta State
—669 4	Eastern states
	Class here former Eastern Region
—669 42	Rivers State
	Including Port Harcourt
—669 43	Akwa Ibom State [*formerly* —66944]
—669 44	Cross River State
	Including Calabar
	Class here former South-Eastern State
	Akwa Ibom State, formerly part of Cross River State, relocated to —66943
—669 45	Abia State [*formerly* —66946]
—669 46	Imo State
	Class here former East-Central State
	Abia State, formerly part of Imo State, relocated to —66945
	For Anambra State, see —66948
—669 48	Anambra State
	Enugu State, formerly part of Anambra State, relocated to —66949
—669 49	Enugu State [*formerly* —66948]
	Including Enugu

*For a specific part of this jurisdiction, region, or feature, see the part and follow instructions under —4–9

—669 5   Plateau, Benue, Kwara states

          Class here former *Northern Region

—669 52   Plateau State

          Including Jos

          Class here former Benue-Plateau State

          For Benue State, see —66954

—669 54   Benue State

          Including Makurdi

          Western part of former Benue State relocated to —66956

—669 56   Kogi State

          Including eastern part of former Kwara State [*formerly* —66957], western part of former Benue State [*formerly* —66954]

—669 57   Kwara State

          Including Ilorin

          Eastern part of former Kwara State relocated to —66956

—669 6   Sokoto, Kebbi, Niger states and Federal Capital Territory

          Class here former North-Western State

—669 62   Sokoto State

          Including Sokoto

          Kebbi State, formerly part of Sokoto State, relocated to —66963

—669 63   Kebbi State [*formerly* —66962]

—669 65   Niger State

          Including Minna

—669 68   Federal Capital Territory

          Class here Abuja

—669 7   Kaduna, Katsina, Jigawa, Kano states

—669 73   Kaduna State

          Including Kaduna

          Class here former North Central State

          Katsina State, formerly part of Kaduna State, relocated to —66976

—669 76   Katsina State [*formerly* —66973]

—669 77   Jigawa State [*formerly* —66978]

---

*For a specific part of this jurisdiction, region, or feature, see the part and follow instructions under —4–9

—669 78	Kano State
	Including Kano
	Jigawa State, formerly part of Kano State, relocated to —66977
—669 8	Bauchi, Borno, Yobe, Adamawa, Taraba states
	Class here former North-Eastern State
—669 82	Bauchi State
—669 85	Borno State
	Including Maiduguri
	Yobe State, formerly part of Borno State, relocated to —66987
—669 87	Yobe State [*formerly* —66985]
—669 88	Adamawa State
	Former name of Adamawa and Taraba States: Gongola State
	Taraba State, formerly part of Gongola State, relocated to —66989
—669 89	Taraba State [*formerly* —66988]

—67 Central Africa and offshore islands

Class here *Black Africa, *Sub-Saharan Africa (Africa south of the Sahara)

SUMMARY

—671	**Cameroon, Sao Tome and Principe, Equatorial Guinea**
—672	**Gabon and Republic of the Congo**
—673	**Angola**
—674	**Central African Republic and Chad**
—675	**Zaire, Rwanda, Burundi**
—676	**Uganda and Kenya**
—677	**Djibouti and Somalia**
—678	**Tanzania**
—679	**Mozambique**

—671	Cameroon, Sao Tome and Principe, Equatorial Guinea
	Class here Islands of Gulf of Guinea, *Lower Guinea area
	See also —16373 for Gulf of Guinea
—671 1	Cameroon
	Including Douala, Yaoundé
—671 5	Sao Tome and Principe
	Including São Tomé
—671 8	Equatorial Guinea
	Former name: Spanish Guinea

*For a specific part of this jurisdiction, region, or feature, see the part and follow instructions under —4–9

—671 83	Río Muni
—671 86	Bioko (Fernando Po) and Pagalu (Annobón) islands
	Including Malabo
—672	Gabon and Republic of the Congo
—672 1	Gabon
	Including Libreville
—672 4	Republic of the Congo
	Former names: French Congo, Middle Congo
	Including Brazzaville
	See also —6751 for Democratic Republic of the Congo (Zaire)
—673	Angola
—673 1	Cabinda province
	Exclave of Angola
—673 2	Northern provinces
	Including Bengo, Cuanza Norte, Cuanza Sul, Luanda, Uíge, Zaire; Luanda (capital city)
	For Cabinda province, see —6731
—673 4	Central provinces
	Including Benguela, Bié, Huambo, Lunda Norte, Lunda Sul, Malanje, Moxico
—673 5	Southern provinces
	Including Cuando Cubango, Huíla, Kunene, Namibe
—674	Central African Republic and Chad
—674 1	Central African Republic
	Former names: Central African Empire, Ubangi-Shari
	Including Bangui
—674 3	Chad
	Including Djamena
—675	Zaire, Rwanda, Burundi
—675 1	Zaire
	Former names: Democratic Republic of the Congo, Belgian Congo
	Class here *Congo (Zaire) River
	See also —6724 for Republic of the Congo

*For a specific part of this jurisdiction, region, or feature, see the part and follow instructions under —4–9

—675 11	Bas-Zaïre and Bandundu regions and Kinshasa
—675 112	Kinshasa
	Former name: Leopoldville
—675 114	Bas-Zaïre region
—675 116	Bandundu region
—675 12	Kasai-Occidental and Kasai-Oriental regions
—675 123	Kasai-Occidental region
—675 126	Kasai-Oriental region
—675 13	Equateur region
—675 15	Haute-Zaire region
	Including Kisangani
—675 17	Kivu region
	Including Maniema, Nord-Kivu, Sud-Kivu; *Lake Kivu
—675 18	Shaba region
	Former name: Katanga province
	Including Lubumbashi; *Lake Mweru
—675 7	Rwanda and Burundi
	Class here former Ruanda-Urundi
—675 71	Rwanda
	Including Kigali
—675 72	Burundi
	Including Bujumbura
—676	Uganda and Kenya
	Class here *East Africa, *Great Rift Valley
—676 1	Uganda
	Including Kampala
—676 2	Kenya
—676 22	North-Eastern Province
—676 23	Coast Province
	Including Mombasa
—676 24	Eastern Province

*For a specific part of this jurisdiction, region, or feature, see the part and follow instructions under —4–9

—676 25	Nairobi
—676 26	Central Province
—676 27	Rift Valley Province
	Including *Lake Turkana (Rudolf)
—676 28	Western Province
—676 29	Nyanza Province
—677	Djibouti and Somalia
	Class here Somaliland
—677 1	Djibouti
	Including Djibouti (capital city)
—677 3	Somalia
	Including Mogadishu
—678	Tanzania
—678 1	Zanzibar and Pemba regions
	Including Pemba North, Pemba South, Zanzibar Central/South, Zanzibar North, Zanzibar Urban/West
—678 2	Tanganyika
—678 22	Tanga Region
—678 23	Coast and Dar es Salaam regions
—678 232	Dar es Salaam Region
	Class here Dar es Salaam
—678 24	Lindi and Mtwara regions
—678 25	South central regions
	Including Iringa, Morogoro, Ruvuma
—678 26	North central regions
	Including Arusha, Dodoma, Kilimanjaro, Singida; *Mount Kilimanjaro; Kilimanjaro National Park
—678 27	Regions adjacent to Lake Victoria
	Including Kagera (West Lake, Ziwa Magharibi), Mara, Mwanza; Serengeti National Park
	Class here *Lake Victoria

---

*For a specific part of this jurisdiction, region, or feature, see the part and follow instructions under —4–9

—678 28	Western regions

        Including Kigoma, Mbeya, Rukwa, Shinyanga, Tabora; *Lake Tanganyika

—679	Mozambique

        Including *Zambezi River

—679 1	Maputo province

        Class here Maputo; *Komati River; Pongola River (Rio Maputo) in Mozambique

—679 2	Gaza province

        Class here *Limpopo River

—679 3	Inhambane province
—679 4	Manica and Sofala provinces
—679 5	Tete province
—679 6	Zambézia province
—679 7	Nampula province
—679 8	Cabo Delgado province
—679 9	Niassa province
—68	**Southern Africa Republic of South Africa**

SUMMARY

—682	**Transvaal**
—684	**Natal**
—685	**Orange Free State**
—687	**Cape of Good Hope**
—688	**Namibia, Botswana, Lesotho, Swaziland**
—689	**Zimbabwe, Zambia, Malawi**

>	—682–687 Republic of South Africa

        Class comprehensive works on Republic of South Africa in —68; class comprehensive works on Orange River in —687

—682	Transvaal

        Province of Republic of South Africa

        Class here *Highveld regions of South Africa; *Vaal River

*For a specific part of this jurisdiction, region, or feature, see the part and follow instructions under —4–9

> —682 1–682 7   Magisterial districts of Transvaal

    Class comprehensive works in —682

—682 1   Southern districts

    Including Heidelberg, Vanderbijlpark, Vereeniging

    Class here *Southern Transvaal, *Vaal Triangle

    Class comprehensive works on Pretoria-Witwatersrand-Vereeniging area (PWV area) in —6822

—682 2   Witwatersrand

    Including Alberton, Benoni, Boksburg, Brakpan, Delmas, Germiston, Kempton Park, Krugersdorp, Nigel, Oberholzer, Randburg, Randfontein, Roodepoort, Springs, Westonaria

    Class here East Rand, West Rand, Far Western Rand; *Pretoria-Witwatersrand-Vereeniging area (PWV area)

    Class Vaal Triangle in —6821

—682 21   Johannesburg

    Including Soweto

    Class here Johannesburg

—682 3   Central districts

    Including Brits, Bronkhorstspruit, Cullinan, Groblersdal, Marico, Rustenburg, Soshanguve, Swartruggens, Warmbaths; Marico River

    Class Vaal Triangle in —6821; class Pretoria-Witwatersrand-Vereeniging area (PWV area) in —6822

—682 35   Pretoria and Wonderboom

    Class here Pretoria

—682 4   Western districts

    Including Bloemhof, Christiana, Coligny, Delareyville, Klerksdorp, Koster, Lichtenburg, Potchefstroom, Schweizer-Reneke, Ventersdorp, Wolmaransstad

    Class here *Western Transvaal

—682 5   Northern districts

    Including Ellisras, Messina, Pietersburg, Potgietersrus, Soutpansberg, Thabazimbi, Waterberg districts; Louis Trichardt, Naboomspruit

    Class here *Northern Transvaal; *Limpopo River in South Africa

    Class comprehensive works on Kruger National Park in —6826

---

*For a specific part of this jurisdiction, region, or feature, see the part and follow instructions under —4–9

—682 6   Eastern districts

Including Barberton, Letaba, Lydenburg, Nelspruit, Phalaborwa, Pilgrim's Rest, White River districts; Sabie; *Kruger National Park; *Komati River in South Africa

Class here *Eastern Transvaal; *Lowveld regions of South Africa

—682 7   Southeastern districts

Including Amersfoort, Balfour, Belfast, Bethal, Carolina, Ermelo, Hoëveldrif, Middelburg, Piet Retief, Standerton, Volksrust, Wakkerstroom, Waterval-Boven, Witbank

—682 9   Homelands (National states [South Africa])

Class here comprehensive works on South African homelands

For KwaZulu, see —68491; for Qwaqwa, see —68591; for Transkei, see —68791; for Ciskei, see —68792

—682 91   Venda

Including Dzanani, Sibasa, Mutale, Vuwani

—682 92   Gazankulu

Including Giyani, Malamulele, Mhala, Ritavi

—682 93   Lebowa

Including Bochum, Bolobedu, Mapulaneng, Mokerong, Namakgale, Naphuno, Nebo, Sekgosese, Sekhukhuneland, Seshego, Thabamoopo districts; Lebowa-Kgomo; Sekhukhuneberg Range

Class here *Mogalakwena River

—682 94   Bophuthatswana

Including Ditsobotla, Ganyesa, Lehurutshe, Madikwe, Mankwe, Molopo, Moretele, Odi, Selosesha, Taung, Thlaping Tlaro districts; Mafikeng, Mmabatho; Pilanesberg Game Reserve

—682 95   KwaNdebele

Including Mdutjana, Mkobola, Moutse districts

—682 96   KaNgwane

Including Eerstehoek, Kamhlushwa, Nsikazi

—684   Natal

Province of Republic of South Africa

Class here *Tugela River

---

*For a specific part of this jurisdiction, region, or feature, see the part and follow instructions under —4–9

> —684 1–684 7   Magisterial districts of Natal

Class comprehensive works in —684

—684 1   Northwestern districts

Including Dannhauser, Dundee, Glencoe, Newcastle, Utrecht

Class here *Blood River

—684 2   North central districts

Including Babanango, Ngotshe, Paulpietersburg, Vryheid; *Pongola River

For Pongola River (Rio Maputo) in Mozambique, see —6791

—684 3   Northeastern districts

Including Hlabisa, Lower Umfolozi, Mtonjaneni districts; Empangeni, Melmoth, Richards Bay; Saint Lucia Game Reserve

Class Maputaland, Tongaland, Ulundi, Zululand in —68491

—684 4   Northern coastal districts

Including Eshowe, Inanda, Lower Tugela, Mtunzini districts; Stanger, Tongaat, Tugela, Umhlanga

Class here *North Coast (area from north of Durban to Richard's Bay)

—684 5   Southern coastal districts

Including Chatsworth, Pinetown, Port Shepstone, Umzinto districts; Scottburgh; Oribi Gorge Nature Reserve

Class here *South Coast (area south of Durban to Port Edward)

—684 55   Durban

Including Amanzimtoti, Kingsburgh

Class here Durban; *Durban-Pinetown industrial area

—684 6   Southern interior districts

Including Alfred, Mount Currie districts; Kokstad

Class here Griqualand East

For Mzimvubu River, see —68791

---

*For a specific part of this jurisdiction, region, or feature, see the part and follow instructions under —4–9

—684 7   Natal Midlands districts

Including Bergville, Camperdown, Estcourt, Impendle, Ixopo, Klip River, Kranskop, Lion's River, Mooi River, New Hanover, Polela, Richmond, Umvoti, Underberg, Weenen

Including Greytown, Howick, Ladysmith; Royal Natal National Park; Giant's Castle Game Reserve; *Mgeni River

Class here *Drakensberg Mountains

—684 75   Pietermaritzburg

Including Albert Falls and Nature Reserve

—684 9   Homelands (National states [South Africa])

—684 91   KwaZulu

Including Embumbulu, Emnambithi, Empumalanga, Emzumbe, Enseleni, Ezingolweni, Hlanganani, Ingwavuma, Inkanyezi, KwaMapumulu, Madadeni, Mahlabatini, Msinga, Ndwedwe, Nkandla, Nongoma, Nqutu, Ntuzuma, Okhahlamba, Ongoye, Simdlangentsha, Ubombo, Umlazi, Vulamehlo, Vulindlela districts

Including Ulundi; Maputaland, Tongaland; Hluhluwe, Mkuze, Ndumu, Umfolozi Game Reserves

Class here Zululand

> *For a specific city or town in a district which is partly KwaZulu and partly Natal, see the city or town in —6841–6847, e.g., Eshowe —6844*

—685   Orange Free State

Province of Republic of South Africa

Class Bophuthatswana in —68294

>   —685 1–685 8 Magisterial districts of Orange Free State

Class comprehensive works in —685

—685 1   Northeastern districts

Including Bethlehem, Ficksburg, Fouriesburg, Frankfort, Harrismith, Lindley, Reitz, Senekal, Vrede; Golden Gate Highlands National Park

Class here *Northeastern Orange Free State

—685 2   Northern districts

Including Bothaville, Heilbron, Koppies, Kroonstad, Parys, Viljoenskroon, Verdefort

Class here *Northern Orange Free State

---

*For a specific part of this jurisdiction, region, or feature, see the part and follow instructions under —4–9

—685 25	Sasolburg
—685 3	North central districts

> Including Brandfort, Bultfontein, Hennenman, Hoopstad, Odendaalsrus, Theunissen, Ventersburg, Virginia, Wesselsbron, Winburg; Willem Pretorius Game Reserve

—685 35	Welkom
—685 4	Bloemfontein
—685 5	Eastern districts

> Including Clocolan, Excelsior, Ladybrand, Marquard

—685 6	Southeastern districts

> Including Botshabelo, Dewetsdorp, Reddersburg, Rouxville, Smithfield, Wepener, Zastron

> Class here *Caledon River

> *For Caledon River in Lesotho, see —6885*

—685 7	Southwestern districts

> Including Bethulie, Edenburg, Fauresmith, Jagersfontein, Petrusburg, Philippolis, Trompsburg

—685 8	Western districts

> Including Boshof, Jacobsdal, Koffiefontein

—685 9	Homelands (National states [South Africa])
—685 91	Qwaqwa

> Including Witsieshoek district, Phuthaditjhaba

—687	Cape of Good Hope

> Province of Republic of South Africa

> Class here *Orange River

> Class comprehensive works on Bophuthatswana in —68294

>	—687 1–687 6 Magisterial districts of Cape of Good Hope

> Class comprehensive works in —687

—687 1	Interior arid regions

---

*For a specific part of this jurisdiction, region, or feature, see the part and follow instructions under —4–9

—687 11   Northern districts

> Including Barkly West, Hartswater, Hay, Herbert, Kimberley, Kuruman, Postmasburg, Vryburg, Warrenton

> Class here *Northern Cape; *Kalahari Desert in South Africa

> Class comprehensive works on Kalahari Desert in —6883

> *For Gordonia, Kenhardt, Prieska, see —68712*

—687 12   Gordonia, Kenhardt, Prieska

> Including Aughrabies, Kalahari Gemsbok National Parks

—687 13   Eastern Upper Karoo districts

> Including Albert, Britstown, Colesberg, De Aar, Hanover, Hopetown, Noupoort, Philipstown, Richmond, Steynsburg, Venterstad districts; *P. K. le Roux Dam

> Class here *Upper Karoo

> *For western Upper Karoo districts, see —68717*

—687 14   Cape Midlands districts

> Including Cradock, Graaff-Reinet, Hofmeyr, Jansenville, Middelburg, Pearston, Somerset East, Steytlerville, Tarka; Mountain Zebra National Park

—687 15   Great Karoo districts

> Including Aberdeen, Beaufort West, Laingsburg, Murraysburg, Prince Albert, Willowmore; Karoo National Park

> Class here the *Karoo

—687 16   Little Karoo districts

> Including Calitzdorp, Ladismith, Oudtshoorn

—687 17   Western Upper Karoo districts

> Including Calvinia, Carnarvon, Fraserburg, Sutherland, Victoria West, Williston

—687 2   Northwestern districts

> Including Clanwilliam, Namaqualand, Vanrhynsdorp, Vredendal districts; Port Nolloth

> Class here *Northwestern Cape; *Cedarberg

---

*For a specific part of this jurisdiction, region, or feature, see the part and follow instructions under —4–9

—687 3   Western and southwestern districts

Including Bredasdorp, Caledon, Ceres, Heidelberg, Hermanus, Hopefield, Malmesbury, Montagu, Moorreesburg, Paarl, Piketberg, Riversdale, Robertson, Somerset West, Stellenbosch, Strand, Swellendam, Tulbagh, Vredenburg, Wellington, Worcester

Class here *Western Province; Boland, Overberg regions

—687 35   Cape Peninsula districts

Including Bellville, Goodwood, Kuils River, Simonstown, Wynberg districts; Crossroads; Cape of Good Hope; Robben Island

—687 355   Cape district

Including Kirstenbosch Botanic Gardens; Table Mountain

Class here Cape Town

—687 4   Southern districts

Including George, Hankey, Humansdorp, Joubertina, Knysna, Mossel Bay, Uniondale districts; Plettenberg Bay, Wilderness; Tsitsikamma Forest and Coastal National Park

Class here *Southern Cape; Garden Route

—687 5   Eastern districts

Including Adelaide, Albany, Alexandria, Bathurst, Bedford, Cathcart, Fort Beaufort, King William's Town, Kirkwood, Komga, Queenstown, Sterkstroom, Stutterheim, Uitenhage districts; Despatch, Grahamstown, Port Alfred; Addo Elephant National Park

Class here *Eastern Province; British Kaffraria

For Great Kei River, see —68791; for Keiskamma River, see —68792

—687 52   Port Elizabeth

Class here Port Elizabeth-Uitenhage-Despatch industrial area

—687 55   East London

—687 6   Northeastern districts

Including Aliwal North, Barkly East, Elliot, Indwe, Lady Grey, Maclear, Molteno, Wodehouse

Class here *Stormberg Range

—687 9   Homelands (National states [South Africa])

*For a specific part of this jurisdiction, region, or feature, see the part and follow instructions under —4–9

—687 91   Transkei

                 Including Butterworth, Cala, Cofimvaba, Elliotdale, Engcobo, Flagstaff, Herschel, Idutywa, Kentani, Lady Frere, Libode, Lusikisiki, Mount Ayliff, Mount Fletcher, Mount Frere, Mqanduli, Ngqeleni, Nqamakwe, Port St. Johns, Qumbu, Thabankulu, Tsolo, Tsomo, Umtata, Umzimkulu, Willowvale

                 Class here Pondoland

—687 92   Ciskei

                 Including Alice, Hewu, Keiskammahoek, Mdantsane, Middledrift, Peddie, Zwelitsha

—688   Namibia, Botswana, Lesotho, Swaziland

—688 1   Namibia

                 Former name: South-West Africa

                 Including Windhoek

—688 3   Botswana

                 Former name: Bechuanaland

                 Including Gaborone

                 Class here *Kalahari Desert

—688 5   Lesotho

                 Former name: Basutoland

                 Including Maseru

—688 7   Swaziland

                 Including Mbabane

—689   Zimbabwe, Zambia, Malawi

                 Former name: Rhodesia and Nyasaland

—689 1   Zimbabwe

                 Former names: Southern Rhodesia, Zimbabwe Rhodesia

                 Including Manicaland, Mashonaland Central, Mashonaland East, Mashonaland West, Masvingo, Matabeleland North, Matabeleland South, Midlands provinces; Bulawayo, Harare; Victoria Falls

                 For Victoria Falls in Zambia, see —6894

—689 4   Zambia

                 Former name: Northern Rhodesia

                 Including Central, Copperbelt, Eastern, Luapala, Lusaka, North-Western, Northern, Southern, Western provinces; Lusaka

---

*For a specific part of this jurisdiction, region, or feature, see the part and follow instructions under —4–9

—689 7   Malawi

       Former name: Nyasaland

       Including Blantyre, Lilongwe

       Class here *Lake Nyasa (Lake Malawi)

—69   **South Indian Ocean islands**

—691   Madagascar

       Former name: Malagasy Republic

       Including Antananarivo, Antsiranana, Fianarantsoa, Mahajanga, Toamasina, Toliara provinces; Antananarivo (capital city)

—694   Comoro Islands

—694 1   Comoros (Federal and Islamic Republic of the Comoros)

       Including Moroni

—694 5   Mayotte

—696   Seychelles

       Including Victoria; Aldabra, Mahé islands

—697   Chagos Islands

—698   Réunion and Mauritius

       Class here Mascarene Islands

—698 1   Réunion

       Overseas department of France

       Including Saint-Denis

—698 2   Mauritius

       Including Port Louis; Cargados Carajos Shoals, Rodrigues Island

—699   Isolated islands

       Including Amsterdam, Cocos (Keeling), Crozet, Kerguelen, Prince Edward, Saint Paul

—7   **North America**

       Class Western Hemisphere in —1812

       See Manual at T2—7 vs. T2—1812

---

*For a specific part of this jurisdiction, region, or feature, see the part and follow instructions under —4–9

SUMMARY

—71	Canada
—711	British Columbia
—712	Prairie Provinces
—713	Ontario
—714	Quebec
—715	Atlantic Provinces Maritime Provinces
—716	Nova Scotia
—717	Prince Edward Island
—718	Newfoundland and Labrador, Saint Pierre and Miquelon
—719	Northern territories
—72	Middle America Mexico
—721	Northern states of Mexico
—722	Lower California peninsula
—723	Central Pacific states of Mexico
—724	Central states of Mexico
—725	Valley of Mexico
—726	Southern Gulf states of Mexico
—727	Southern Pacific states of Mexico
—728	Central America
—729	West Indies (Antilles) and Bermuda
—73	United States
—74	Northeastern United States (New England and Middle Atlantic states)
—741	Maine
—742	New Hampshire
—743	Vermont
—744	Massachusetts
—745	Rhode Island
—746	Connecticut
—747	New York
—748	Pennsylvania
—749	New Jersey
—75	Southeastern United States (South Atlantic states)
—751	Delaware
—752	Maryland
—753	District of Columbia (Washington)
—754	West Virginia
—755	Virginia
—756	North Carolina
—757	South Carolina
—758	Georgia
—759	Florida
—76	South central United States Gulf Coast states
—761	Alabama
—762	Mississippi
—763	Louisiana
—764	Texas
—766	Oklahoma
—767	Arkansas
—768	Tennessee
—769	Kentucky

—77	**North central United States** **Lake states**
—771	Ohio
—772	Indiana
—773	Illinois
—774	Michigan
—775	Wisconsin
—776	Minnesota
—777	Iowa
—778	Missouri
—78	**Western United States**
—781	Kansas
—782	Nebraska
—783	South Dakota
—784	North Dakota
—786	Montana
—787	Wyoming
—788	Colorado
—789	New Mexico
—79	**Great Basin and Pacific Slope region of United States** **Pacific Coast states**
—791	Arizona
—792	Utah
—793	Nevada
—794	California
—795	Oregon
—796	Idaho
—797	Washington
—798	Alaska

—71   **Canada**

> *See Manual at T2—73 vs. T2—71*

SUMMARY

—711	British Columbia
—712	Prairie Provinces
—713	Ontario
—714	Quebec
—715	Atlantic Provinces Maritime Provinces
—716	Nova Scotia
—717	Prince Edward Island
—718	Newfoundland and Labrador, Saint Pierre and Miquelon
—719	Northern territories

—711   British Columbia

> Class here *Rocky Mountains in Canada; *Rocky Mountain Trench

---

*For a specific part of this jurisdiction, region, or feature, see the part and follow instructions under —4–9

—711 1   Northern coastal region

Coastal mainland and Coast Mountains from Alaska border to Powell River

Including Central Coast, Skeena-Queen Charlotte Regional Districts; mainland parts of Comox-Strathcona, Mount Waddington Regional Districts; Kitimat-Stikine Regional District south of 54°30′ N

Including Bella Coola, Kitimat, Ocean Falls, Prince Rupert; Cortes, Hardwicke, Maurelle, Read, East and West Redonda, Sonora, East and West Thurlow Islands; Bella Coola River

Class here comprehensive works on Kitimat-Stikine Regional District; *Pacific Coast in Canada; *Coast Mountains

> *For coasts of southwestern British Columbia, see —7113; for Kitimat-Stikine Regional District north of 54°30′ N, see —71185*

> *See also —16433 for Dixon Entrance, Hecate Strait, Inside Passage, Queen Charlotte Sound*

—711 12   Queen Charlotte Islands

—711 2   Vancouver Island

Including Alberni-Clayoquot, Nanaimo, Cowichan Valley Regional Districts; parts of Comox-Strathcona, Mount Waddington Regional Districts on Vancouver Island

Including Nanaimo; comprehensive works on Comox-Strathcona, Mount Waddington Regional Districts; Pacific Rim National Park; Denman, Hope, Hornby, Malcolm, Nigei, Quadra Islands; Koksilah River; Shawnigan Lake

> *For mainland parts of Comox-Strathcona, Mount Waddington Regional Districts, see —7111*

> *See also —16433 for Strait of Georgia, Queen Charlotte Strait*

—711 28   Victoria region

Including Capital Regional District (Vancouver Island south of San Juan and Koksilah Rivers and Shawnigan Lake)

Including Central Saanich, Esquimalt, Metchosin, North Saanich, Oak Bay, Port Renfrew, Saanich, Sidney, Sooke, Victoria; Saanich Peninsula; *Gulf Islands; San Juan River; Sooke Lake

> *See also —16432 for Strait of Juan de Fuca*

—711 3   Southwestern region

Class here *Fraser River, *Lillooet River

---

*For a specific part of this jurisdiction, region, or feature, see the part and follow instructions under —4–9

—711 31   Southern coastal region

Mainland coast from Powell River to Howe Sound

Including Powell River, Squamish-Lillooet, Sunshine Coast Regional Districts

Including Lillooet, Pemberton, Powell River, Squamish, Whistler; *Garibaldi Provincial Park; Desolation Sound Provincial Marine Park; Anvil, Gambier, Hernando, Keats, Lasqueti, Texada Islands; Malaspina Peninsula; Bridge River; Carpenter, Lillooet Lakes

—711 33   Greater Vancouver Regional District

Including Langley [*formerly* —71137], Burnaby, Coquitlam, Delta, Lions Bay, New Westminster, North Vancouver, Port Coquitlam, Port Moody, Richmond, Surrey, West Vancouver, White Rock; Bowen Island

Class here city of Vancouver

—711 37   Lower Fraser Valley

Including Central Fraser Valley, Dewdney-Alouette, Fraser-Cheam Regional Districts

Including Abbotsford, Chilliwack, Hope, Maple Ridge, Mission, Pitt Meadows; Golden Ears Provincial Park; Fraser Canyon; Coquihalla, Nahatlatch, *Pitt Rivers; Harrison Lake

Langley relocated to —71133

—711 5   Okanagan-Similkameen region

Including Central Okanagan, North Okanagan, Okanagan-Similkameen Regional Districts

Including Armstrong, Enderby, Kelowna, Osoyoos, Penticton, Princeton, Vernon; Manning Provincial Park; Shuswap, Tulameen Rivers; Okanagan Lake

Class here *Cascade Mountains in British Columbia

—711 6   Southeastern region

Class here *Columbia River in British Columbia

—711 62   West Kootenay region

Including Central Kootenay, Kootenay Boundary Regional Districts

Including Castlegar, Creston, Grand Forks, Greenwood, Nelson, Rossland, Trail; *Monashee Mountains; *Granby, *Kettle, *West Kettle Rivers; Upper and Lower Arrow, Slocan, Kootenay Lakes

---

*For a specific part of this jurisdiction, region, or feature, see the part and follow instructions under —4–9

—711 65   East Kootenay Regional District

> Approximately the area drained by the upper Columbia and Kootenay Rivers

> Including Cranbrook, Invermere, Kimberley; Kootenay National Park

> Class here *Purcell Mountains; *Kootenay River

—711 68   Columbia-Shuswap Regional District

> Including Golden, Revelstoke, Salmon Arm; Glacier, Mount Revelstoke, Yoho National Parks; Hamber Provincial Park; Illecillewaet, Seymour, Spillimacheen Rivers; *Kinbasket (McNaughton), Shuswap Lakes

> Class here *Selkirk Mountains

—711 7   Central interior region

> Class here *Cariboo Mountains

—711 72   Thompson-Nicola Regional District

> Approximately the area drained by the Thompson and Nicola Rivers

> Including Cache Creek, Chase, Clinton, Kamloops, Lytton, Merritt; Wells Gray Provincial Park; Bonaparte, Clearwater, Coldwater, Nicola, North and South Thompson, Thompson Rivers; Adams Lake

—711 75   Cariboo Regional District

> Approximately the central Fraser Valley and the area drained by the Chilcotin, Nazko, and Quesnel Rivers

> Including Anahim Lake, Barkerville, 100 Mile House, Quesnel, Wells, Williams Lake; Bowron Lake Provincial Park; Adams, Chilcotin, Chilko, Horsefly, Nazko, Quesnel, Taseko, West Road Rivers; Quesnel Lake

> Class here *Fraser Plateau

—711 8   Northern region

—711 82   North central region

> Approximately the corridor formed by the Bulkley, Nechako, and upper Fraser valleys

> Including Bulkley-Nechako, Fraser-Fort George Regional Districts

> Including Mackenzie, McBride, Prince George, Smithers, Valemount, Vanderhoof; Mount Robson, *Tweedsmuir Provincial Parks; *Bulkley, Chilako, McGregor, Morice, Nation, *Omineca, Parsnip Rivers; Morice, Takla Lakes; Nechako Reservoir

> Class here *Nechako Plateau; Nechako River

---

*For a specific part of this jurisdiction, region, or feature, see the part and follow instructions under —4–9

—711 85   Northwestern region

            Including Stikine Regional District; parts of Kitimat-Stikine Regional District north of 54°30′ N

            Including Hazelton, Stewart, Terrace; *Hazelton, *Omineca Mountains; Gataga, Kechika, Nass, Osilinka, Skeena, Spatsizi, *Stikine, Sustut Rivers

            Class here *Cassiar, *Skeena Mountains

—711 87   Northeastern region

            Former heading: Peace River-Liard Regional District

            Including Fort Nelson-Liard, Peace River Regional Districts

            Including Dawson Creek, Fort Nelson, Fort St. John, Tumbler Ridge; Finlay, Fort Nelson, Ingenika, Mesilinka, Murray, Pine, Sukunka Rivers; *Williston Lake

            Class here Peace River in British Columbia, *Liard River

—712   Prairie Provinces

        Class here *western Canada

—712 3   Alberta

—712 31   Northwestern region

            Area north of 55° N, and west of 114° W

            Including Grande Prairie, Peace River; Lesser Slave Lake

            Class here *northern Alberta; *Peace River

—712 32   Northeastern region

            Area north of 55° N, and east of 114° W

            Including Fort McMurray

            Class here *Wood Buffalo National Park; *Athabaska River

—712 33   Central region

            Area between 55° N and 51° N

            Including Drumheller, Red Deer; Elk Island National Park; Lac La Biche

            Class here *Rocky Mountains in Alberta; *Bow, *North Saskatchewan, *Red Deer Rivers

*For a specific part of this jurisdiction, region, or feature, see the part and follow instructions under —4–9

—712 332   Rocky Mountain parks region

                                   Including Banff; Banff, Jasper National Parks; Peter Lougheed Provincial Park; Willmore Wilderness Provincial Park; Kananaskis Country

                                   See also —71234 for Waterton Lakes National Park

—712 334   Edmonton

—712 338   Calgary

—712 34   Southern region

                                     Area south of 51° N to international boundary

                                     Including Crowsnest Pass, Fort Macleod, Medicine Hat; Waterton Lakes National Park

—712 345   Lethbridge

—712 4   Saskatchewan

—712 41   Northern region

                                     Area north of 55° N

                                     Class here *Lake Athabasca

—712 42   Central region

                                     Area between 55° N and 51° N

                                     Including Battlefords, Lloydminster, Prince Albert, Yorkton; *Lake Diefenbaker

                                     Class here *Saskatchewan, *South Saskatchewan Rivers

                                     For parts of Lloydminster in Alberta, see —71233

—712 425   Saskatoon

—712 43   Southwestern region

                                     Area south of 51° N, and west of 106° W

                                     Including Swift Current; *Cypress Hills

—712 44   Southeastern region

                                     Area south of 51° N, and east of 106° W

                                     Including Fort Qu'Appelle, Melville, Moose Jaw

—712 445   Regina

—712 7   Manitoba

---

*For a specific part of this jurisdiction, region, or feature, see the part and follow instructions under —4–9

—712 71	Northern region
	Area north of 55° N
	Including Churchill, Port Nelson, Thompson
	Class here *Churchill, *Nelson Rivers
—712 72	Central region
	Area between 55° N and 50°30′ N
	Including Dauphin, Flin Flon, The Pas; Interlake region; Lakes *Manitoba, Winnipegosis, *Winnipeg
	Class here *Canadian Shield in Manitoba
—712 73	Southwestern region
	Area south of 50°30′ N, and west of 98° W
	Including Brandon, Minnedosa, Portage la Prairie
	Class here *Assiniboine River
—712 74	Southeastern region
	Area south of 50°30′ N, and east of 98° W
	Including Selkirk; Whiteshell Provincial Park
	Class here *Red River of the North in Manitoba
—712 743	Winnipeg
—713	**Ontario**
	Including *Niagara Escarpment
	Class here *eastern Canada; *Great Lakes in Canada
—713 1	Northern Ontario and Georgian Bay regions
	Including Patricia portion of Kenora District
	Class here Canadian Shield in Ontario, northern Ontario
	See also —16327 for Hudson, James Bays

>	—713 11–713 14 Northern Ontario region
	Class comprehensive works in —7131
—713 11	Northwestern Ontario
	Including *Lake of the Woods in Canada
	For Thunder Bay District, see —71312

*For a specific part of this jurisdiction, region, or feature, see the part and follow instructions under —4–9

—713 112	Kenora District
	For Patricia portion of Kenora District, see —7131
—713 117	Rainy River District
—713 12	Thunder Bay District
	Class here *Lake Superior in Ontario
—713 13	Northeastern Ontario
	For clay belt, see —71314; for Parry Sound District, see —71315; for District Municipality of Muskoka, see —71316
—713 132	Algoma District
	Including *North Channel
—713 133	Sudbury District
	Including Regional Municipality of Sudbury
—713 135	Manitoulin District
—713 14	Clay belt
—713 142	Cochrane District
	Including *Lake Abitibi
—713 144	Timiskaming District
—713 147	Nipissing District
	Including Algonquin Provincial Park; *Lake Nipissing

> —713 15–713 18 Georgian Bay region

Class comprehensive works in —7131

—713 15	Parry Sound District
	Class here *Georgian Bay
—713 16	District Municipality of Muskoka
—713 17	Simcoe County
—713 18	Grey County

> —713 2–713 8 Southern Ontario

Class comprehensive works in —713

For Simcoe County, see —71317; for Grey County, see —71318

—713 2	Lake Huron region
	Class here *southwestern Ontario; *Lake Huron in Ontario

*For a specific part of this jurisdiction, region, or feature, see the part and follow instructions under —4–9

—713 21	Bruce County
—713 22	Huron County
—713 23	Perth County
—713 25	Middlesex County
	For London, see —71326
—713 26	London
—713 27	Lambton County
	Including *Saint Clair River in Ontario

—713 3	Lake Erie region
	Class here *Lake Erie in Ontario
—713 31	Essex County
	Including *Lake Saint Clair in Ontario
	For Windsor, see —71332
—713 32	Windsor
—713 33	Kent County
—713 34	Elgin County
	Including St. Thomas [formerly —71335]
—[713 35]	St. Thomas
	Relocated to —71334
—713 36	Regional Municipality of Haldimand-Norfolk
	Class here former Haldimand County [formerly —71337], former Norfolk County
—[713 37]	Former Haldimand County
	Relocated to —71336
—713 38	Regional Municipality of Niagara
	Including Niagara Falls (city); *Niagara River; Welland Canal
	Class here former Lincoln County [formerly —71351], former Welland County; *Niagara Peninsula
	Class Niagara Falls (physiographic feature) in —71339
	For Niagara River in New York, see —74798
—713 39	Niagara Falls
	Physiographic feature
	For Niagara Falls in New York, see —74799

*For a specific part of this jurisdiction, region, or feature, see the part and follow instructions under —4–9

—713 4	West central region
—713 41	Dufferin County
—713 42	Wellington County
	For Guelph, see —71343
—713 43	Guelph
—713 44	Regional Municipality of Waterloo
	Waterloo (city) relocated to —71345
	For Kitchener, see —71345
—713 45	Kitchener-Waterloo
	Including Waterloo (city) [*formerly* —71344]
	Class here Kitchener
—713 46	Oxford County
—713 47	Brant County
	Including Brantford [*formerly* —71348]
—[713 48]	Brantford
	Relocated to —71347
—713 5	Lake Ontario region
	Class here *Lake Ontario in Ontario
—[713 51]	Former Lincoln County
	Relocated to —71338
—713 52	Regional Municipality of Hamilton-Wentworth
	Class here former Wentworth County; Hamilton
—713 53	Halton and Peel Regional Municipalities
—713 533	Regional Municipality of Halton
—713 535	Regional Municipality of Peel
—713 54	Metropolitan Toronto and Regional Municipality of York
	Class here former York County
—713 541	Metropolitan Toronto
	Including cities of Etobicoke, North York, Scarborough, Toronto, York; borough of East York
—713 547	Regional Municipality of York

*For a specific part of this jurisdiction, region, or feature, see the part and follow instructions under —4–9

—[713 55]	Former Ontario County
	Relocated to —71356
—713 56	Regional Municipality of Durham
	Class here former *Ontario County [*formerly* —71355], former *Durham County
—713 57	Northumberland County
	Including *Rice Lake
—713 58	Hastings and Prince Edward Counties
—713 585	Hastings County
—713 587	Prince Edward County
—713 59	Lennox and Addington County
—713 6	East central region
—713 61	Haliburton County
—713 64	Victoria County
—713 67	Peterborough County
	Including Peterborough [*formerly* —71368]
—[713 68]	Peterborough
	Relocated to —71367
—713 7	Saint Lawrence River region
	Class here *eastern Ontario; *Thousand Islands in Ontario; *Saint Lawrence River in Ontario; *Saint Lawrence Seaway in Ontario
—713 71	Frontenac County
	For Kingston, see —71372
—713 72	Kingston
—713 73	United Counties of Leeds and Grenville
	Class here former Grenville County [*formerly* —71374], former Leeds County
—[713 74]	Former Grenville County
	Relocated to —71373
—713 75	United Counties of Stormont, Dundas and Glengarry
	Class here former Glengarry County [*formerly* —71377], former Stormont County [*formerly* —71376], former Dundas County

*For a specific part of this jurisdiction, region, or feature, see the part and follow instructions under —4–9

—[713 76]	Former Stormont County
	Relocated to —71375
—[713 77]	Former Glengarry County
	Relocated to —71375
—713 8	Ottawa River region
	Class here *Ottawa River
—713 81	Renfrew County
—713 82	Lanark County
—713 83	Regional Municipality of Ottawa-Carleton

Class here former Carleton County; comprehensive works on National Capital Region

For Ottawa, see —71384; for National Capital Region in Quebec province, Outaouais Regional Community, see —714221

—713 84	Ottawa
—713 85	United Counties of Prescott and Russell

Class here former Prescott County [*formerly* —71386], former Russell County

—[713 86]	Former Prescott County
	Relocated to —71385
—714	Quebec

Class here *Canadian Shield; *Saint Lawrence River; comprehensive works on *Saint Lawrence Seaway

See also —16344 for Gulf of Saint Lawrence

—714 1	Northern region
—714 11	New Quebec (Nouveau-Québec)

See also —7182 for Labrador

—714 111	Extreme northern region (Grand-nord québécois, Administration régionale Kativik)

Area north of 55° N

Including Hudson Bay and Ungava Bay regions

Class here Kativik Regional Administration

See also —16327 for Hudson, Ungava Bays

---

*For a specific part of this jurisdiction, region, or feature, see the part and follow instructions under —4–9

—714 115   Mid-northern region (Moyen-nord québécois)

> Including former Abitibi Territory, former Mistassini Territory; Caniapiscau (Regional County Municipality); James Bay region; Chibougamau, Gagnon, Lebel-sur-Quévillon, Matagami, Schefferville
>
> Class here *Nouveau-Québec Administrative Region

—714 13   Abitibi-Témiscamingue region

> Including former Abitibi, Témiscamingue Counties; Abitibi, Abitibi-Ouest, *Vallée-de-l'Or, Rouyn-Noranda, Témiscamingue Regional County Municipalities
>
> Class here *Abitibi-Témiscamingue Administrative Region

—714 14   Lac-Saint-Jean region

> Including former Lac-Saint-Jean-Est, Lac-Saint-Jean-Ouest Counties; *Le Domaine-du-Roy, *Lac-Saint-Jean-Est, *Maria-Chapdelaine Regional County Municipalities; Chibougamau Wildlife Reserve
>
> Class here *Saguenay-Lac-Saint-Jean Administrative Region

—714 16   Chicoutimi region

> Former name: Chicoutimi County
>
> Including Le Fjord-du-Saguenay Regional County Municipality; *Saguenay River

—714 17   Côte-Nord region

> Former name: Saguenay County
>
> Including Le Haute-Côte-Nord, Manicouagan, Minganie, Sept-Rivières Regional County Municipalities; Anticosti Island
>
> Class here *Côte-Nord Administrative Region
>
> *See also —7182 for Labrador*

—714 2   Western counties (Ottawa Valley counties)

> Class here *Ottawa River in the province of Quebec

—714 21   Pontiac region

> Former name: Pontiac County
>
> Including La Vérendrye Provincial Park
>
> Class here Pontiac Regional County Municipality

—714 22   Outaouais region

> Class here *Outaouais Administrative Region

---

*For a specific part of this jurisdiction, region, or feature, see the part and follow instructions under —4–9

—714 221   Gatineau-Hull region

Including former Gatineau, Hull Counties; Aylmer, Gatineau, Hull; National Capital Region in the province of Quebec; Gatineau Park

Class here *La Vallée-de-la-Gatineau Regional County Municipality, *Outaouais Regional Community (Communauté régionale de l'Outaouais); *Gatineau River

Class comprehensive works on National Capital Region in —71383

For Gatineau Park in Pontiac region, see —71421

—714 225   Labelle region

Former name: Labelle County

Class here *Antoine-Labelle Regional County Municipality

—714 227   Papineau region

Former name: Papineau County

Class here Papineau Regional County Municipality

—714 23   Argenteuil region

Former name: Argenteuil County

Including Argenteuil Regional County Municipality

—714 24   Terrebonne region

Former name: Terrebonne County

Class here lower Laurentians region

Including *Les Laurentides, *Les Moulins, *Les Pays-d'en-Haut, *La Rivière-du-Nord, *Thérèse-de-Blainville Regional County Municipalities

—714 25   Deux-Montagnes region

Former name: Deux-Montagnes County

Including Deux-Montagnes, Mirabel Regional County Municipalities

—714 26   Vaudreuil-Soulanges region

Including former Vaudreuil, Soulanges Counties

Class here Vaudreuil-Soulanges Regional County Municipality

—714 27   *Montreal Administrative Region

Including former Île-de-Montréal, Île-Jésus Counties

For Montreal Urban Community, see —71428

---

*For a specific part of this jurisdiction, region, or feature, see the part and follow instructions under —4–9

—714 271	Laval (Jésus island)
—714 28	Montreal Urban Community (Communauté urbaine de Montréal)
	Including Bizard, Dorval islands
	Class here Montréal island
—714 3	Southwestern region
	Area south of Saint Lawrence River, and west of Richelieu River
	Including *Richelieu River
—714 31	Huntingdon region
	Former name: Huntingdon County
	Class here *Le Haut-Saint-Laurent Regional County Municipality
—714 32	Beauharnois region
	Former name: Beauharnois County
	Class here *Beauharnois-Salaberry Regional County Municipality
—714 33	Châteauguay region
	Former name: Châteauguay County
—714 34	Laprairie region
	Former name: Laprairie County
	Class here *Roussillon Regional County Municipality
—714 35	Napierville region
	Former name: Napierville County
	Class here *Les Jardins-de-Napierville Regional County Municipality
—714 36	Verchères region
	Former name: Verchères County
	Including *Lajemmerais, *La Vallée-du-Richelieu Regional County Municipalities
—714 37	Chambly region
	Former name: Chambly County
	Class here *Champlain Regional County Municipality
—714 38	Saint-Jean region
	Former name: Saint-Jean County

*For a specific part of this jurisdiction, region, or feature, see the part and follow instructions under —4–9

—714 4   North central region

Area north of Saint Lawrence River from Montreal to Saguenay River

Including *Mont-Tremblant, *Laurentides Provincial Parks

See also —71424 for lower Laurentians region

—714 41   Lanaudière region

Including *Matawini Regional County Municipality

—714 415   Montcalm region

Former name: Montcalm County

Class here *Montcalm Regional County Municipality

—714 416   L'Assomption region

Former name: L'Assomption County

Class here L'Assomption Regional County Municipality

—714 42   Joliette region

Former name: Joliette County

Including Joliette Regional County Municipality

—714 43   Berthier region

Former name: Berthier County

Class here *D'Autray Regional County Municipality

—714 44   Maskinongé region

Former name: Maskinongé County

Class here *Maskinongé Regional County Municipality

—714 45   Mauricie region

Including *Le-Haut-Saint-Maurice, *Mékinac Regional County Municipalities; La Mauricie National Park

Class here *Trois-Rivières Administrative Region

—714 451   Saint-Maurice region

Former name: Saint-Maurice County

Including *Le Centre-de-la-Mauricie, *Francheville Regional County Municipalities; Trois-Rivières

—714 455   Champlain region

Former name: Champlain County

Including Cap-de-la-Madeleine

---

*For a specific part of this jurisdiction, region, or feature, see the part and follow instructions under —4–9

—714 46   Portneuf region

                  Former name: Portneuf County

                  Including *Portneuf Wildlife Reserve

                  Class here *Portneuf Regional County Municipality

—714 47   Québec region and Jacques-Cartier River Valley

                  Former name: Québec County

                  Including *La Jacques-Cartier Regional County Municipality

                  Class here *Québec Administrative Region

—714 471   Quebec Urban Community (Communauté urbaine de Québec)

                  Including Ancienne-Lorette, Beauport, Cap-Rouge, Charlesbourg, Lac-Saint-Charles, Loretteville, Saint-Augustin-de-Desmaures, Saint-Foy, Saint-Emile, Sillery, Val-Bélair, Vanier

                  Class here Québec

—714 48   Montmorency region

                  Including former Montmorency no. 1 and no. 2 counties; La Côte-de-Beaupré, L'Île-d'Orléans Regional County Municipalities; Isle of Orléans (Île d'Orléans)

—714 49   Charlevoix region

                  Including former Charlevoix-Est, Charlevoix-Ouest Counties; Charlevoix, Charlevoix-Est Regional County Municipalities; Île aux Coudres

—714 5   **South central region**

                  Area south of Saint Lawrence River, and east of Richelieu River to Quebec

                  Class here *Saint-François River

                  For southern border area, see —7146

—714 51   Richelieu region

                  Former name: Richelieu County

                  Class here *Le Bas-Richelieu Regional County Municipality

—714 52   Saint-Hyacinthe and Bagot regions

—714 523   Saint-Hyacinthe region

                  Former name: Saint-Hyacinthe County

                  Class here *Les Maskoutains Regional County Municipality

*For a specific part of this jurisdiction, region, or feature, see the part and follow instructions under —4–9

—714 525   Bagot region

> Former name: Bagot County
>
> Class here *Acton Regional County Municipality

—714 53   Rouville region

> Former name: Rouville County
>
> Class here Rouville Regional County Municipality

—714 54   Yamaska region

> Former name: Yamaska County
>
> Class here *Nicolet-Yamaska Regional County Municipality

—714 55   Nicolet region

> Former name: Nicolet County
>
> Class here *Bécancour Regional County Municipality

—714 56   Drummond and Arthabaska regions

—714 563   Drummond region

> Former name: Drummond County
>
> Class here *Drummond Regional County Municipality

—714 565   Arthabaska region

> Former name: Arthabaska County
>
> Class here Bois-Francs region; *Arthabaska Regional County Municipality

—714 57   Wolfe and Mégantic regions

—714 573   Wolfe region

> Former name: Wolfe County
>
> Including *L'Amiante, *L'Or-Blanc Regional County Municipalities

—714 575   Mégantic region

> Former name: Mégantic County
>
> Class here *L'Érable Regional County Municipality

—714 58   Lotbinière region

> Former name: Lotbinière County
>
> Class here Lotbinière Regional County Municipality

---

*For a specific part of this jurisdiction, region, or feature, see the part and follow instructions under —4–9

—714 59   Lévis region

                      Former name: Lévis County

                      Including Les Chutes-de-la-Chaudière, Desjardins Regional County Municipalities

—714 6   Southern region

                      Southern border area east of Richelieu River

                      Class here *Eastern Townships, *Estrie

—714 61   Iberville region

                      Former name: Iberville County

                      Class here *Le Haut-Richelieu Regional County Municipality

—714 62   Missisquoi region

                      Former name: Missisquoi County

                      Class here *Brome-Missisquoi Regional County Municipality

—714 63   Shefford region

                      Former name: Shefford County

                      Class here *La Haute-Yamaska Regional County Municipality

—714 64   Brome region

                      Former name: Brome County

                      Including *Memphrémagog Regional County Municipality; *Lake Memphrémagog

—714 65   Richmond region

                      Former name: Richmond County

                      Class here *Le Val-Saint-François Regional County Municipality

—714 66   Sherbrooke region

                      Former name: Sherbrooke County

                      Class here *Sherbrooke Regional County Municipality

—714 67   Stanstead region

                      Former name: Stanstead County

                      Class here *Coaticook Regional County Municipality

—714 68   Compton region

                      Former name: Compton County

                      Class here *Le Haut-Saint-François Regional County Municipality

---

*For a specific part of this jurisdiction, region, or feature, see the part and follow instructions under —4–9

—714 69	Frontenac region
	Former name: Frontenac County
	Class here *Le Granit Regional County Municipality
—714 7	Southeastern region
	Area south of Saint Lawrence River from Quebec to Gulf of Saint Lawrence
	Class here eastern Quebec; *Notre Dame Mountains
—714 71	Beauce region
	Former name: Beauce County
	Including *Beauce-Sartigan, *La Nouvelle-Beauce, *Robert-Cliche Regional County Municipalities
	Class here *Chaudière River
—714 72	Dorchester region
	Former name: Dorchester County
	Class here *Les Etchemins Regional County Municipality
—714 73	Bellechasse and Montmagny regions
—714 733	Bellechasse region
	Former name: Bellechasse County
	Class here *Bellechasse Regional County Municipality
—714 735	Montmagny region
	Former name: Montmagny County
	Including Île aux Grues, Grosse Île
	Class here Montmagny Regional County Municipality
—714 74	L'Islet region
	Former name: L'Islet County
	Class here L'Islet Regional County Municipality
—714 75	Kamouraska region
	Former name: Kamouraska County
	Class here Kamouraska Regional County Municipality
—714 76	Témiscouata and Rivière-du-Loup regions
	Including former Rivière-du-Loup, Témiscouata counties; *Les Basques, Rivière-du-Loup, *Témiscouata Regional County Municipalities; Île Verte

*For a specific part of this jurisdiction, region, or feature, see the part and follow instructions under —4–9

—714 77	Gaspé Peninsula
	Class here Bas-Saint-Laurent-Gaspésie Administrative Region
	For Bonaventure region, see —71478; for Gaspé region, see —71479
—714 771	Rimouski region
	Former name: Rimouski County
	Including *La Mitis, Rimouski-Neigette Regional County Municipalities
—714 775	Matane and Matapédia regions
	Including former Matane, Matapédia counties; Matane, La Matapédia Regional County Municipalities
—714 78	Bonaventure region
	Former name: Bonaventure County
	Including Avignon, Bonaventure Regional County Municipalities
—714 79	Gaspé region
	Including former Gaspé-Est, Gaspé-Ouest counties; La Côte-de-Gaspé, Denis Riverin, Pabok Regional County Municipalities
—714 797	Magdalen Islands (Îles de la Madeleine)
	Class here Îles de la Madeleine Regional County Municipality
—715	Atlantic Provinces Maritime Provinces
	For Nova Scotia, see —716; for Prince Edward Island, see —717; for Newfoundland and Labrador, see —718
	See also —16344 for Gulf of Saint Lawrence, Northumberland Strait
—715 1	New Brunswick
	For eastern counties, see —7152; for southern counties, see —7153; for central counties, see —7154; for western counties, see —7155

>	—715 11–715 12 Northern counties
	Class comprehensive works in —7151
—715 11	Restigouche County
	Including *Restigouche River
—715 12	Gloucester County
	Including Bathurst

*For a specific part of this jurisdiction, region, or feature, see the part and follow instructions under —4–9

—715 2	Eastern counties
—715 21	Northumberland County
	Class here *Miramichi River
—715 22	Kent County
—715 23	Westmorland County
	Including Sackville
—715 235	Moncton
—715 3	Southern counties
	See also — 16345 for Bay of Fundy
—715 31	Albert County
—715 32	Saint John County
—715 33	Charlotte County
	Including Grand Manan Island; *Saint Croix River in New Brunswick
—715 4	Central counties
—715 41	Kings County
—715 42	Queens County
—715 43	Sunbury County
—715 5	Western counties
	Class here *Saint John River
—715 51	York County
—715 515	Fredericton
—715 52	Carleton County
—715 53	Victoria County
—715 54	Madawaska County
—716	Nova Scotia
—716 1	Northern counties
—716 11	Cumberland County
	Including Amherst
—716 12	Colchester County
	Including Truro

*For a specific part of this jurisdiction, region, or feature, see the part and follow instructions under —4–9

—716 13	Pictou County
	Including New Glasgow, Pictou
—716 14	Antigonish County
—716 2	**Southern counties**
—716 21	Guysborough County
—716 22	Halifax County
—716 225	Halifax-Dartmouth metropolitan area
	Class here Halifax
—716 23	Lunenburg County
—716 24	Queens County
	Including Liverpool
—716 25	Shelburne County
—716 3	**Bay of Fundy counties**
	See also —16345 for Bay of Fundy
—716 31	Yarmouth County
—716 32	Digby County
—716 33	Annapolis County
	Including Kejimkujik National Park
	For Kejimkujik National Park in Queens County, see —71624
—716 34	Kings County
	Including Wolfville
—716 35	Hants County
	Including Windsor
—716 9	**Cape Breton Island and Sable Island**
	Class here *Bras d'Or Lake

>	—716 91–716 98 Cape Breton Island
	Class comprehensive works in —7169
—716 91	Inverness County
	Including Cape Breton Highlands National Park
	For Cape Breton Highlands National Park in Victoria County, see —71693

*For a specific part of this jurisdiction, region, or feature, see the part and follow instructions under —4–9

—716 93	Victoria County
—716 95	Cape Breton County
—716 955	Louisbourg
	Class here Louisbourg National Historical Park
—716 98	Richmond County
—716 99	Sable Island
—717	Prince Edward Island
—717 1	Prince County
—717 4	Queens County

For Charlottetown, see —7175

—717 5	Charlottetown
—717 7	Kings County
—718	Newfoundland and Labrador, Saint Pierre and Miquelon

See also —16344 for Grand Banks of Newfoundland

—718 1	St. John's
—718 2	Labrador
—718 8	Saint Pierre and Miquelon
	Overseas territory of France
—719	Northern territories
	Class here *Canadian Arctic

See also —16327 for Beaufort Sea, Canadian Arctic waters, Northwest Passage

—719 1	Yukon Territory
	Including Dawson, Whitehorse
—719 2	Northwest Territories
	Class here Denendeh, Nunavut

For specific regions of Northwest Territories, see —7193–7197

>	—719 3–719 7 Specific regions of Northwest Territories

Class comprehensive works in —7192

See Manual at T2—7193–7197

---

*For a specific part of this jurisdiction, region, or feature, see the part and follow instructions under —4–9

—719 3   Fort Smith Region

> Including Fort Simpson, Fort Smith, Hay River, Pine Point, Rae, Rae Lakes, Snowdrift, Wrigley, Yellowknife; Nahanni National Park; *Mackenzie Mountains; *Slave River; *Great Bear, Great Slave Lakes

> Class here former *Mackenzie district

—719 4   Keewatin Region

> Including Baker Lake, Chesterfield Inlet, Coral Harbour, Rankin Inlet, Repulse Bay; Thelon Game Sanctuary; Coats, Southampton Islands; *Thelon River

> Class here former *Keewatin district

—719 5   Baffin Region

> Including Arctic Bay, Cape Dorset, Grise Fiord, Hall Beach, Igloolik, Iqaluit (Frobisher Bay), Pangnirtung, Pond Inlet, Resolute, Sanikiluaq; Auyuittuq National Park; Baffin, Bylot, Mansel, Nottingham, Salisbury, Somerset, Wales Islands; Melville Peninsula

> Class here former *Franklin district; *Canadian Arctic Archipelago

> *See also* —16327 for Hudson, James, Ungava Bays

—719 6   Inuvik region

> Including Aklavik, Fort Franklin, Fort Norman, Inuvik, Paulatuk, Sach Harbour, Tuktoyaktuk; Banks Island

> Class here *MacKenzie River

—719 7   Kitikmeot Region (Central Arctic Region)

> Including Bathurst Inlet, Cambridge Bay, Coppermine, Gjoa Haven, Holman, Pelly Bay, Spence Bay, Umingmaktok; King William, Prince of Wales, Victoria Islands; Boothia, Simpson Peninsulas; Contwoyto Lake

> *See also* —7193 for Great Bear Lake, —7194 for Repulse Bay

—72   Middle America   Mexico

SUMMARY

—721	**Northern states of Mexico**
—722	**Lower California peninsula**
—723	**Central Pacific states of Mexico**
—724	**Central states of Mexico**
—725	**Valley of Mexico**
—726	**Southern Gulf states of Mexico**
—727	**Southern Pacific states of Mexico**
—728	**Central America**
—729	**West Indies (Antilles) and Bermuda**

*For a specific part of this jurisdiction, region, or feature, see the part and follow instructions under —4–9

>   —721–727   Mexico

         Class comprehensive works in —72

—721   Northern states of Mexico

         Class here *Mexican-American Border Region

         For Lower California peninsula, see —722

—721 2   Tamaulipas

—721 3   Nuevo León

—721 4   Coahuila

—721 5   Durango

—721 6   Chihuahua

—721 7   Sonora

         See also —1641 for Gulf of California

—722   Lower California peninsula

         See also —1641 for Gulf of California

—722 3   Baja California Norte

—722 4   Baja California Sur

—723   Central Pacific states of Mexico

—723 2   Sinaloa

—723 4   Nayarit

—723 5   Jalisco

—723 6   Colima

—723 7   Michoacán

—724   Central states of Mexico

         For Valley of Mexico, see —725

—724 1   Guanajuato

—724 2   Aguascalientes

—724 3   Zacatecas

—724 4   San Luis Potosí

—724 5   Querétaro

*For a specific part of this jurisdiction, region, or feature, see the part and follow instructions under —4–9

—724 6	Hidalgo
—724 7	Tlaxcala
—724 8	Puebla
—724 9	Morelos
—725	*Valley of Mexico
—725 2	Mexico state
—725 3	Distrito Federal

> Class here Mexico City

—726	Southern Gulf states of Mexico
—726 2	Veracruz
—726 3	Tabasco
—726 4	Campeche
—726 5	Yucatán
—726 7	Quintana Roo
—727	Southern Pacific states of Mexico
—727 3	Guerrero
—727 4	Oaxaca
—727 5	Chiapas
—728	Central America

SUMMARY

—728 1	Guatemala
—728 2	Belize
—728 3	Honduras
—728 4	El Salvador
—728 5	Nicaragua
—728 6	Costa Rica
—728 7	Panama

—728 1	Guatemala
—728 11	Guatemala department

> Class here Guatemala City

—728 12	Petén department
—728 13	Izabal and Zacapa departments

*For a specific part of this jurisdiction, region, or feature, see the part and follow instructions under —4–9

—728 131	Izabal department
—728 132	Zacapa department
—728 14	Southeastern departments
—728 141	Chiquimula department
—728 142	Jalapa department
—728 143	Jutiapa department
—728 144	Santa Rosa department
—728 15	North central departments
—728 151	Alta Verapaz department
—728 152	Baja Verapaz department
—728 153	El Progreso department
—728 16	South central departments
—728 161	Chimaltenango department
—728 162	Sacatepéquez department
—728 163	Escuintla department
—728 164	Sololá department
—728 165	Suchitepéquez department
—728 17	Huehuetenango and Quiché departments
—728 171	Huehuetenango department
—728 172	Quiché department
—728 18	Southwestern departments
—728 181	Totonicapán department
—728 182	Quezaltenango department
—728 183	Retalhuleu department
—728 184	San Marcos department
—728 2	Belize
	Former name: British Honduras
—728 21	Corozal District
—728 22	Belize District
—728 23	Stann Creek District
—728 24	Toledo District
—728 25	Cayo District

—728 26	Orange Walk District
—728 3	Honduras
—728 31	Northern departments
—728 311	Cortés
—728 312	Atlántida
—728 313	Colón
—728 314	Yoro
—728 315	Islas de la Bahía
—728 32	Gracias a Dios department
—728 33	Olancho department
—728 34	El Paraíso department
—728 35	Southern departments
—728 351	Choluteca
—728 352	Valle
—728 36	La Paz department
—728 37	Central departments
—728 371	Francisco Morazán
	Class here Tegucigalpa
—728 372	Comayagua
—728 38	Western departments
—728 381	Intibucá
—728 382	Lempira
—728 383	Ocotepeque
—728 384	Copán
—728 385	Santa Bárbara
—728 4	El Salvador
—728 41	Western departments
—728 411	Ahuachapán
—728 412	Santa Ana
—728 413	Sonsonate
—728 42	Central departments
—728 421	Chalatenango

—728 422	La Libertad
—728 423	San Salvador
	Class here San Salvador
—728 424	Cuscatlán
—728 425	La Paz
—728 426	Cabañas
—728 427	San Vicente
—728 43	Eastern departments
—728 431	Usulután
—728 432	San Miguel
—728 433	Morazán
—728 434	La Unión
—728 5	Nicaragua
—728 51	Pacific departments
—728 511	Chinandega
—728 512	León
—728 513	Managua
	Class here Managua
—728 514	Masaya
—728 515	Granada
—728 516	Carazo
—728 517	Rivas
—728 52	Central departments
—728 521	Nueva Segovia
—728 522	Jinotega
—728 523	Madriz
—728 524	Estelí
—728 525	Matagalpa
—728 526	Boaco
—728 527	Chontales
—728 53	Atlantic region
—728 531	Río San Juan department

—728 532	Zelaya department
—728 6	Costa Rica
—728 61	Limón province
—728 62	Cartago province
—728 63	San José province
	Class here San José
—728 64	Heredia province
—728 65	Alajuela province
—728 66	Guanacaste province
—728 67	Puntarenas province
—728 7	Panama

See also —1641 for Gulf of Panama

—728 71	Western provinces
—728 711	Chiriquí
—728 712	Bocas del Toro
—728 72	Central provinces
—728 721	Coclé
—728 722	Veraguas
—728 723	Los Santos
—728 724	Herrera
—728 73	Metropolitan provinces
	Class Canal Area in —72875
—728 731	Panama
	Class here Panama City
—728 732	Colón
—728 74	Darien province
—728 75	Canal Area

Former names: Canal Zone, Panama Canal Zone

Class here Panama Canal [*formerly* —1641]

—729	West Indies (Antilles) and Bermuda

Class here *Caribbean Area

See also —16365 for Caribbean Sea

*For a specific part of this jurisdiction, region, or feature, see the part and follow instructions under —4–9

SUMMARY

—729 1	Cuba
—729 2	Jamaica and Cayman Islands
—729 3	Dominican Republic
—729 4	Haiti
—729 5	Puerto Rico
—729 6	Bahama Islands
—729 7	Leeward Islands
—729 8	Windward and other southern islands
—729 9	Bermuda

>   —729 1–729 5   Greater Antilles

Class comprehensive works in —729

—729 1   Cuba

—729 11   Pinar del Río province

—729 12   Ciudad da La Habana province (Havana), Havana province, Isla de la Juventud

—729 123   Ciudad da La Habana province (Havana)

—729 124   Havana province

—729 125   Isla de la Juventud

     Former name: Isle of Pines

—729 13   Matanzas province

—729 14   Villa Clara, Cienfuegos, Sancti Spíritus provinces

     Class here former Las Villas province

—729 142   Villa Clara province

—729 143   Cienfuegos province

—729 145   Sancti Spíritus province

—729 15   Ciego de Avila and Camagüey provinces

—729 153   Ciego de Avila province

—729 156   Camagüey province

—729 16   Eastern Cuba

     Class here former Oriente province

—729 162   Las Tunas province

—729 163   Granma province

—729 164   Holguín province

—729 165   Santiago de Cuba province

—729 167	Guantánamo province
—729 2	Jamaica and Cayman Islands
—729 21	Cayman Islands
—729 3	Dominican Republic

Class here comprehensive works on Hispaniola

For Haiti, see —7294

—729 32	Southwestern provinces
—729 323	Pedernales
—729 324	Barahona
—729 325	Independencia
—729 326	Bahoruco
—729 34	Western provinces
—729 342	San Juan
—729 343	La Estrelleta
—729 345	Dajabón
—729 35	Northwestern provinces
—729 352	Monte Cristi
—729 353	Santiago Rodríguez
—729 356	Santiago
—729 357	Valverde
—729 358	Puerto Plata
—729 36	North central provinces
—729 362	Espaillat
—729 363	Salcedo
—729 364	María Trinidad Sánchez
—729 365	Samaná
—729 367	Duarte
—729 368	Sánchez Ramírez
—729 369	Monseñor Nouel and La Vega provinces (Former La Vega province)
—729 369 3	Monseñor Nouel
—729 369 7	La Vega
—729 37	South central provinces

—729 372	Azua
—729 373	Peravia
—729 374	San Cristóbal

Monte Plata, formerly part of San Cristóbal, relocated to —729377

—729 375	Distrito Nacional

Class here Santo Domingo

—729 377	Monte Plata [*formerly* —729374]
—729 38	Eastern provinces
—729 381	Hato Mayor [*formerly* —729384]
—729 382	San Pedro de Macorís
—729 383	La Romana
—729 384	El Seibo

Hato Mayor, formerly part of El Seibo, relocated to —729381

—729 385	La Altagracia
—729 4	Haiti
—729 42	Nord-Ouest département

Including Ile de la Tortue

—729 43	Nord and Nord-Est départements

Class here former Nord département

Southeastern part of former Nord département relocated to —729442

—729 432	Nord département
—729 436	Nord-Est département
—729 44	Centre and Artibonite départements (Former Artibonite département)
—729 442	Centre département

Including northeastern part of former Ouest département [*formerly* —72945], southeastern part of former Nord département [*formerly* —72943]

—729 446	Artibonite département
—729 45	Ouest and Sud-Est départements (Former Ouest département)

Northeastern part of former Ouest département relocated to —729442

—729 452	Ouest département

Class here Port-au-Prince

—729 456   Sud-Est département

—729 46   Sud and Grand'Anse départements (Former Sud département)

—729 462   Sud département

—729 466   Grand'Anse département

—729 5   Puerto Rico

—729 51   San Juan district

                         Class here San Juan

—729 52   Bayamón district

—729 53   Arecibo district

—729 54   Aguadilla district

—729 56   Mayagüez district

—729 57   Ponce district

—729 58   Guayama district

—729 59   Humacao district

                         Including Vieques Island

—729 6   Bahama Islands

—729 61   Turks and Caicos Islands

>   —729 7–729 8   Lesser Antilles (Caribbees)

                         Class comprehensive works in —729

—729 7   Leeward Islands

                         For Dominica, see —729841

—729 72   Virgin Islands

—729 722   Virgin Islands of the United States

                                 Including Saint Croix, Saint John, Saint Thomas islands; Virgin
                                 Islands National Park

—729 725   British Virgin Islands

                                 Including Tortola, Virgin Gorda islands

—729 73   Anguilla and Saint Kitts-Nevis

                                 Former name: Saint Christopher-Nevis-Anguilla

                                 Class here West Indies Associated States

                                 For Antigua, see —72974; for Windward Islands, see —72984

—729 74   Antigua and Barbuda

—729 75	Montserrat
—729 76	Guadeloupe

Overseas department of France

Including islands of Désirade, Guadeloupe, Les Saintes, Marie Galante, Saint Barthélemy, part of Saint Martin

Class here French West Indies, comprehensive works on Saint Martin

> *For Netherlands part of Saint Martin, see —72977; for Martinique, see —72982*

—729 77	Leeward Netherlands islands

Including Saba, Saint Eustatius, part of Saint Martin

Class comprehensive works on Netherlands Antilles in —72986

—729 8	Windward and other southern islands

> *For Nueva Esparta, Venezuela, see —8754*

—729 81	Barbados
—729 82	Martinique

Overseas department of France

—729 83	Trinidad and Tobago
—729 84	Windward Islands
—729 841	Dominica
—729 843	Saint Lucia
—729 844	Saint Vincent and the Grenadines

> *For Carriacou, see —729845*

—729 845	Grenada and Carriacou
—729 86	Netherlands islands

Including Aruba, Bonaire, Curaçao

Class here Netherlands Antilles

> *For Leeward Netherlands islands, see —72977*

—729 9	Bermuda
—73	**United States**

> *For specific states, see —74–79*

> *See Manual at T2—73 vs. T2—71*

—(734–739)   Specific states

> (Optional numbers; prefer —74–79)

> Add to base number —73 the numbers following —7 in notation 74–79 of this table, e.g., Pennsylvania —7348

> ## —74–79 Specific states of United States

> Class comprehensive works in —73

> *For Hawaii, see —969*

> (Option: Class in —734–739)

—74   ## Northeastern United States (New England and Middle Atlantic states)

> Class here United States east of Allegheny Mountains, east of Mississippi River; *Appalachian Mountains; *Connecticut River

> *For southeastern United States, see —75; for south central United States, see —76; for north central United States, see —77*

SUMMARY

—741	Maine
—742	New Hampshire
—743	Vermont
—744	Massachusetts
—745	Rhode Island
—746	Connecticut
—747	New York
—748	Pennsylvania
—749	New Jersey

> —741–746 New England

> Class comprehensive works in —74

—741   Maine

—741 1   Aroostook County

—741 2   Northwestern counties

> Including Moosehead Lake

—741 22   Somerset County

> Class here *Kennebec River

—741 25   Piscataquis County

---

*For a specific part of this jurisdiction, region, or feature, see the part and follow instructions under —4–9

—741 3   Penobscot County

         Including Bangor

         Class here *Penobscot River

—741 4   Southeastern counties

—741 42   Washington County

             Class here *Saint Croix River

—741 45   Hancock County

             Including Mount Desert Island

             Class here Acadia National Park

                 For Acadia National Park in Knox County, see —74153

—741 5   South central counties

—741 52   Waldo County

—741 53   Knox County

—741 57   Lincoln County

—741 6   Kennebec County

         Including Augusta

—741 7   West central counties

         Class here *Rangeley Lakes

—741 72   Franklin County

—741 75   Oxford County

—741 8   Southwest central counties

         Class here *Androscoggin River

—741 82   Androscoggin County

—741 85   Sagadahoc County

—741 9   Southwestern counties

—741 91   Cumberland County

             Class here Portland

—741 95   York County

—742   New Hampshire

—742 1   Coos County

—742 2   *White Mountains

---

*For a specific part of this jurisdiction, region, or feature, see the part and follow instructions under —4–9

—742 3	Grafton County
—742 4	Counties bordering *Lake Winnipesaukee
—742 42	Carroll County
—742 45	Belknap County
—742 5	Strafford County
—742 6	Rockingham County
	Including Portsmouth
—742 7	West central counties
—742 72	Merrimack County
	Including Concord
	Class here *Merrimack River
—742 75	Sullivan County
—742 8	Hillsborough County
	Including Manchester
—742 9	Cheshire County
—743	Vermont
	Class here *Green Mountains
—743 1	Northwestern counties
	Class here *Lake Champlain in Vermont
—743 12	Grand Isle County
—743 13	Franklin County
—743 17	Chittenden County
	Including Burlington
	Class here *Winooski River
—743 2	Northeastern counties
—743 23	Orleans County
—743 25	Essex County
—743 3	North central counties
—743 34	Caledonia County
—743 35	Lamoille County

*For a specific part of this jurisdiction, region, or feature, see the part and follow instructions under —4–9

—743 4	Washington County
	Including Montpelier
—743 5	Addison County
—743 6	East central counties
—743 63	Orange County
—743 65	Windsor County
—743 7	Rutland County
—743 8	Bennington County
—743 9	Windham County
—744	Massachusetts
—744 1	Berkshire County
	Class here *Berkshire Hills
—744 2	Connecticut River counties
—744 22	Franklin County
—744 23	Hampshire County
—744 26	Hampden County
	Including Springfield
—744 3	Worcester County
—744 4	Middlesex County
	Including Cambridge, Lexington, Lowell; *Charles River
—744 5	Essex County
—744 6	Suffolk County
—744 61	Boston
—744 7	Norfolk County
—744 8	Southeastern counties
	For counties bordering Nantucket Sound, see —7449
	See also —16345 for Cape Cod Bay
—744 82	Plymouth County
—744 85	Bristol County
—744 9	Counties bordering Nantucket Sound
	See also —16346 for Nantucket Sound

*For a specific part of this jurisdiction, region, or feature, see the part and follow instructions under —4–9

—744 92	Barnstable County (Cape Cod)
	See also —16345 for Cape Cod Bay
—744 94	Dukes County
	Including Elizabeth Islands, Martha's Vineyard
—744 97	Nantucket County
	Class here Nantucket Island
—745	Rhode Island
	See also —16346 for Rhode Island Sound, Narragansett Bay
—745 1	Providence County
	For Providence, see —7452
—745 2	Providence
—745 4	Kent County
—745 5	Bristol County
—745 6	Newport County
	For Newport, see —7457
—745 7	Newport
—745 8	Block Island
—745 9	Washington County
	For Block Island, see —7458
—746	Connecticut
	See also —16346 for Long Island Sound
—746 1	Litchfield County
—746 2	Hartford County
	For Hartford, see —7463
—746 3	Hartford
—746 4	Northeastern counties
—746 43	Tolland County
—746 45	Windham County
—746 5	New London County
—746 6	Middlesex County
—746 7	New Haven County
	For New Haven, see —7468

—746 8	New Haven
—746 9	Fairfield County
	Including Stamford

>	—747–749 Middle Atlantic states
	Class comprehensive works in —74
—747	New York
—747 1	New York Borough of Manhattan (Manhattan Island, New York County)

> *For borough of Brooklyn, see —74723; for borough of Queens, see —747243; for borough of Richmond, see —74726; for borough of the Bronx, see —747275*
>
> *See also —16346 for New York Bay*

—747 2	Other parts of New York metropolitan area

> *For Fairfield County, Connecticut, see —7469; for New Jersey counties of metropolitan area, see —7493*

—747 21	Long Island

> *For specific parts of Long Island, see —74723–74725*
>
> *See also —16346 for Long Island Sound*

>	—747 23–747 25 Specific parts of Long Island
	Class comprehensive works in —74721
—747 23	Borough of Brooklyn (Kings County)
—747 24	Queens and Nassau Counties
—747 243	Borough of Queens (Queens County)
—747 245	Nassau County
—747 25	Suffolk County
—747 26	Staten Island (Borough of Richmond, Richmond County)
—747 27	Mainland east of Hudson River
—747 275	Borough of the Bronx (Bronx County)
—747 277	Westchester County
—747 28	Rockland County
—747 3	Other southeastern counties
	Class here *Hudson River

*For a specific part of this jurisdiction, region, or feature, see the part and follow instructions under —4–9

—747 31	Orange County
—747 32	Putnam County
—747 33	Dutchess County
—747 34	Ulster County
—747 35	Sullivan County
—747 36	Delaware County
—747 37	Greene County
—747 38	*Catskill Mountains
—747 39	Columbia County
—747 4	**Middle eastern counties**
—747 41	Rensselaer County
—747 42	Albany County
	For Albany, see —74743
—747 43	Albany
—747 44	Schenectady County
—747 45	Schoharie County
—747 46	Montgomery County
—747 47	Fulton County
—747 48	Saratoga County
—747 49	Washington County
—747 5	**Northern counties**
	Class here *Adirondack Mountains
—747 51	Warren County
	Including *Lake George
—747 52	Hamilton County
—747 53	Essex County
—747 54	Clinton County
	Class here *Lake Champlain
—747 55	Franklin County
—747 56	Saint Lawrence County
	Including *Saint Lawrence River in New York

*For a specific part of this jurisdiction, region, or feature, see the part and follow instructions under —4–9

—747 57	Jefferson County
—747 58	*Thousand Islands
—747 59	Lewis County
—747 6	**North central counties**
	Class here *Mohawk River
—747 61	Herkimer County
—747 62	Oneida County
	Including *Oneida Lake
—747 64	Madison County
—747 65	Onondaga County
	For Syracuse, see —74766
—747 66	Syracuse
—747 67	Oswego County
—747 68	Cayuga County
	Including *Cayuga Lake
—747 69	Seneca County
—747 7	**South central counties**
—747 71	Tompkins County
	Class here Ithaca
—747 72	Cortland County
—747 73	Chenango County
—747 74	Otsego County
—747 75	Broome County
—747 77	Tioga County
—747 78	Chemung County
—747 8	**West central counties**
	Class here *Finger Lakes
—747 81	Schuyler County
—747 82	Yates County
	Class here *Keuka Lake
—747 83	Steuben County

*For a specific part of this jurisdiction, region, or feature, see the part and follow instructions under —4–9

—747 84	Allegany County
—747 85	Livingston County
—747 86	Ontario County
—747 87	Wayne County
—747 88	Monroe County
	Class here *Genesee River
	For Rochester, see —74789
—747 89	Rochester
—747 9	Western counties
	Class here *Lake Ontario
—747 91	Orleans County
—747 92	Genesee County
—747 93	Wyoming County
—747 94	Cattaraugus County
—747 95	Chautauqua County
—747 96	Erie County
	For Buffalo, see —74797
—747 97	Buffalo
—747 98	Niagara County
	Including Niagara Falls (city)
	Class Niagara Falls (physiographic feature) in —74799
—747 99	Niagara Falls in New York
	Physiographic feature
—748	Pennsylvania
	Class here *Susquehanna River
—748 1	Southeastern counties
	Class here *Schuylkill River
—748 11	Philadelphia County (Philadelphia)
—748 12	Montgomery County
—748 13	Chester County
—748 14	Delaware County

*For a specific part of this jurisdiction, region, or feature, see the part and follow instructions under —4–9

—748 15	Lancaster County
—748 16	Berks County
—748 17	Schuylkill County
—748 18	Dauphin County
	Including Harrisburg
—748 19	Lebanon County
—748 2	**Eastern counties**
	Class here *Pocono Mountains
—748 21	Bucks County
—748 22	Northampton County
—748 23	Wayne County
	Including *Lake Wallenpaupack
—748 24	Pike County
—748 25	Monroe County
	Including *Delaware Water Gap
—748 26	Carbon County
—748 27	Lehigh County
—748 3	**Northeastern counties**
—748 31	Northumberland County
—748 32	Luzerne County
—748 34	Susquehanna County
—748 35	Wyoming County
—748 36	Lackawanna County
	For Scranton, see —74837
—748 37	Scranton
—748 38	Columbia County
—748 39	Montour County
—748 4	**Southeast central counties**
—748 41	York County
—748 42	Adams County
—748 43	Cumberland County

---

*For a specific part of this jurisdiction, region, or feature, see the part and follow instructions under —4–9

—748 44	Franklin County
—748 45	Perry County
	Class here *Juniata River
—748 46	Mifflin County
—748 47	Juniata County
—748 48	Union County
—748 49	Snyder County
—748 5	Northeast central counties
	Class here *West Branch of Susquehanna River
—748 51	Lycoming County
—748 53	Centre County
—748 54	Clinton County
—748 55	Potter County
—748 56	Tioga County
—748 57	Bradford County
—748 59	Sullivan County
—748 6	Northwest central counties
	Class here *Allegheny River
—748 61	Clearfield County
—748 62	Jefferson County
—748 63	McKean County
—748 65	Elk County
—748 66	Cameron County
—748 67	Warren County
—748 68	Forest County
—748 69	Clarion County
—748 7	Southwest central counties
	Class here *Allegheny Mountains
—748 71	Bedford County
—748 72	Fulton County
—748 73	Huntingdon County

*For a specific part of this jurisdiction, region, or feature, see the part and follow instructions under —4–9

—748 75	Blair County
—748 77	Cambria County
—748 79	Somerset County
—748 8	Southwestern counties

Class here *Monongahela River

—748 81	Westmoreland County
—748 82	Washington County
—748 83	Greene County
—748 84	Fayette County
—748 85	Allegheny County

For Pittsburgh, see —74886

—748 86	Pittsburgh
—748 88	Armstrong County
—748 89	Indiana County
—748 9	Northwestern counties
—748 91	Butler County
—748 92	Beaver County
—748 93	Lawrence County
—748 95	Mercer County
—748 96	Venango County
—748 97	Crawford County
—748 99	Erie County
—749	New Jersey

Class here *Delaware River

—749 2	Northeastern counties
—749 21	Bergen County

Class here *Hackensack River

—749 23	Passaic County
—749 26	Hudson County

For Jersey City, see —74927

—749 27	Jersey City

*For a specific part of this jurisdiction, region, or feature, see the part and follow instructions under —4–9

—749 3	*Counties of New York metropolitan area
	Class here *Passaic River
—749 31	Essex County
	For Newark, see —74932; for The Oranges, see —74933
—749 32	Newark
—749 33	The Oranges
	Including East Orange, Maplewood, Orange, South Orange, West Orange
—749 36	Union County
—749 4	East central counties
	See also —16346 for New York Bay
—749 41	Middlesex County
	For New Brunswick, see —74942
—749 42	New Brunswick
—749 44	Somerset County
	Class here *Raritan River
—749 46	Monmouth County
—749 48	Ocean County
—749 6	West central counties
—749 61	Burlington County
	Including *Mullica River
—749 65	Mercer County
	For Trenton, see —74966
—749 66	Trenton
—749 7	Northwestern counties
—749 71	Hunterdon County
—749 74	Morris County
—749 76	Sussex County
—749 78	Warren County
—749 8	South central counties
—749 81	Gloucester County

*For a specific part of this jurisdiction, region, or feature, see the part and follow instructions under —4–9

—749 84	Atlantic County
	For Atlantic City, see —74985
—749 85	Atlantic City
—749 87	Camden County
—749 9	Southern counties
	See also —16346 for Delaware Bay
—749 91	Salem County
—749 94	Cumberland County
—749 98	Cape May County

—75   **Southeastern United States (South Atlantic states)**

Class here southern states, *Piedmont, *Atlantic Coastal Plain

For south central United States, see —76

SUMMARY

—751	Delaware
—752	Maryland
—753	District of Columbia (Washington)
—754	West Virginia
—755	Virginia
—756	North Carolina
—757	South Carolina
—758	Georgia
—759	Florida

—751	Delaware
	See also —16346 for Delaware Bay
—751 1	New Castle County
	For Wilmington, see —7512
—751 2	Wilmington
—751 4	Kent County
	Including Dover
—751 7	Sussex County
—752	Maryland
	Class here *Potomac River
	See also —16347 for Chesapeake Bay

---

*For a specific part of this jurisdiction, region, or feature, see the part and follow instructions under —4–9

—752 1   Eastern Shore

        Class here *Delmarva Peninsula

        For southern counties of Eastern Shore, see —7522; for northern counties of Eastern Shore, see —7523

—752 2   Southern counties of Eastern Shore

—752 21   Worcester County

           Including *Assateague Island

—752 23   Somerset County

—752 25   Wicomico County

—752 27   Dorchester County

—752 3   Northern counties of Eastern Shore

—752 31   Caroline County

           Class here *Choptank River

—752 32   Talbot County

—752 34   Queen Annes County

           Class here *Chester River

—752 36   Kent County

—752 38   Cecil County

>   —752 4–752 9   Maryland west of Chesapeake Bay

        Class comprehensive works in —752

—752 4   Southern counties

           Class here *Patuxent River

—752 41   Saint Marys County

—752 44   Calvert County

—752 47   Charles County

—752 5   South central counties

—752 51   Prince George's County

—752 55   Anne Arundel County

           For Annapolis, see —75256

—752 56   Annapolis

---

*For a specific part of this jurisdiction, region, or feature, see the part and follow instructions under —4–9

—752 6	Independent city of Baltimore
—752 7	North central counties
	Class here *Piedmont in Maryland
—752 71	Baltimore County
—752 74	Harford County
	Including *Susquehanna River in Maryland
—752 77	Carroll County
—752 8	West central counties
—752 81	Howard County
—752 84	Montgomery County
—752 87	Frederick County
—752 9	Western counties
—752 91	Washington County
—752 94	Allegany County
—752 97	Garrett County
—753	District of Columbia (Washington)
—754	West Virginia
—754 1	Northern Panhandle counties
	Class here *Ohio River in West Virginia
—754 12	Hancock County
—754 13	Brooke County
—754 14	Ohio County
	Class here Wheeling
—754 16	Marshall County
—754 18	Wetzel County
—754 19	Tyler County
—754 2	Little Kanawha Valley counties
	Class here *Little Kanawha River
—754 21	Pleasants County
—754 22	Wood County
—754 24	Ritchie County

*For a specific part of this jurisdiction, region, or feature, see the part and follow instructions under —4–9

—754 26	Wirt County
—754 27·	Gilmer County
—754 29	Calhoun County
—754 3	**Kanawha Valley counties**
	Class here *Kanawha River
—754 31	Jackson County
—754 33	Mason County
—754 35	Putnam County
—754 36	Roane County
—754 37	Kanawha County
	Including Charleston
—754 39	Boone County
—754 4	**Southwestern border counties**
	Including *Tug Fork
	Class here *Guyandotte River
—754 42	Cabell County
—754 43	Lincoln County
—754 44	Logan County
—754 45	Wyoming County
—754 47	Wayne County
	Including *Big Sandy River
—754 48	Mingo County
—754 49	McDowell County
—754 5	**Monongahela Valley counties**
	Class here *Monongahela River in West Virginia
—754 52	Monongalia County
—754 54	Marion County
—754 55	Taylor County
—754 56	Doddridge County
—754 57	Harrison County
—754 59	Barbour County

*For a specific part of this jurisdiction, region, or feature, see the part and follow instructions under —4–9

—754 6	Central counties
—754 61	Lewis County
—754 62	Upshur County
—754 65	Webster County
—754 66	Braxton County
—754 67	Clay County
—754 69	Nicholas County
	Class here *Gauley River
—754 7	New River Valley counties
	Class here *New River
—754 71	Fayette County
—754 73	Raleigh County
—754 74	Mercer County
—754 76	Summers County
—754 78	Monroe County
—754 8	Allegheny Crest counties
	Class here *Allegheny Mountains in West Virginia; *Cheat River
—754 82	Preston County
—754 83	Tucker County
—754 85	Randolph County
—754 87	Pocahontas County
—754 88	Greenbrier County
	Class here *Greenbrier River
—754 9	Eastern Panhandle counties
	Class here *Potomac Valley of West Virginia
—754 91	Pendleton County
—754 92	Grant County
—754 93	Hardy County
—754 94	Mineral County
—754 95	Hampshire County
—754 96	Morgan County

*For a specific part of this jurisdiction, region, or feature, see the part and follow instructions under —4–9

—754 97	Berkeley County
—754 99	Jefferson County
—755	Virginia
	Class here *Blue Ridge
—755 1	Eastern Peninsula and Chesapeake Bay Region
	Class here *Tidewater Virginia
—755 15	Northampton County
—755 16	Accomack County
—755 18	*Chesapeake Bay Region
	See also —16347 for Chesapeake Bay
—755 2	Northern Neck
	Class here *Rappahannock River
—755 21	Northumberland County
—755 22	Lancaster County
—755 23	Richmond County
—755 24	Westmoreland County
—755 25	King George County
—755 26	Stafford County
—755 27	Prince William and Fauquier Counties and environs
—755 273	Prince William County, Manassas, Manassas Park
—755 273 2	Prince William County
—755 273 4	Independent city of Manassas
—755 273 6	Independent city of Manassas Park
—755 275	Fauquier County
—755 28	Loudoun County
—755 29	Washington metropolitan area of Virginia
—755 291	Fairfax County
—755 292	Independent city of Fairfax
—755 293	Independent city of Falls Church
—755 295	Arlington County
—755 296	Independent city of Alexandria

*For a specific part of this jurisdiction, region, or feature, see the part and follow instructions under —4–9

—755 3	Rappahannock-York region
—755 31	Mathews County
—755 32	Gloucester County
—755 33	Middlesex County
—755 34	Essex County
—755 35	King and Queen and King William Counties
—755 352	King and Queen County
—755 355	King William County
—755 36	Caroline and Spotsylvania Counties and environs
—755 362	Caroline County
—755 365	Spotsylvania County
—755 366	Independent city of Fredericksburg
—755 37	Orange and Greene Counties
—755 372	Orange County
—755 375	Greene County
—755 38	Madison County
—755 39	Culpeper and Rappahannock Counties
—755 392	Culpeper County
—755 395	Rappahannock County
—755 4	York-James region
	Class here *James River
—755 41	Southern end of peninsula
—755 412	Independent city of Hampton
—755 416	Independent city of Newport News
—755 42	York and James City Counties and environs
—755 422	Independent city of Poquoson
—755 423	York County
—755 425	James City County and Williamsburg
—755 425 1	James City County
—755 425 2	Independent city of Williamsburg
—755 43	New Kent County

*For a specific part of this jurisdiction, region, or feature, see the part and follow instructions under —4–9

—755 44	Charles City County
—755 45	Henrico and Goochland Counties and environs
—755 451	Independent city of Richmond
—755 453	Henrico County
—755 455	Goochland County
—755 46	Hanover and Louisa Counties
—755 462	Hanover County
—755 465	Louisa County
—755 47	Fluvanna County
—755 48	Albemarle County and environs
—755 481	Independent city of Charlottesville
—755 482	Albemarle County
—755 49	Nelson and Amherst Counties
—755 493	Nelson County
—755 496	Amherst County
—755 5	Southeastern region
—755 51	Independent city of Virginia Beach
—755 52	Independent cities of Norfolk, Portsmouth, Chesapeake
—755 521	Independent city of Norfolk
—755 522	Independent city of Portsmouth
—755 523	Independent city of Chesapeake
	Class here *Dismal Swamp
—755 53	Independent city of Suffolk
—755 54	Isle of Wight County
—755 55	Southampton County and environs
—755 552	Southampton County
—755 553	Independent city of Franklin
—755 56	Surry and Sussex Counties
—755 562	Surry County
—755 565	Sussex County
—755 57	Greensville and Brunswick Counties and environs

*For a specific part of this jurisdiction, region, or feature, see the part and follow instructions under —4–9

—755 572	Greensville County
—755 573	Independent city of Emporia
—755 575	Brunswick County
—755 58	Dinwiddie and Prince George Counties and environs
—755 581	Independent city of Petersburg
—755 582	Dinwiddie County
—755 585	Prince George County
—755 586	Independent city of Hopewell
—755 59	Chesterfield County and environs
—755 594	Chesterfield County
—755 595	Independent city of Colonial Heights
—755 6	South central region
	Class here *Piedmont in Virginia; *Roanoke River in Virginia
—755 61	Powhatan and Cumberland Counties
—755 612	Powhatan County
—755 615	Cumberland County
—755 62	Buckingham and Appomattox Counties
—755 623	Buckingham County
—755 625	Appomattox County
—755 63	Prince Edward, Amelia, Nottoway Counties
—755 632	Prince Edward County
—755 634	Amelia County
—755 637	Nottoway County
—755 64	Lunenburg and Mecklenburg Counties
—755 643	Lunenburg County
—755 645	Mecklenburg County
—755 65	Charlotte County
—755 66	Halifax and Pittsylvania Counties and environs
—755 661	Halifax County
—755 662	Independent city of South Boston
—755 665	Pittsylvania County

*For a specific part of this jurisdiction, region, or feature, see the part and follow instructions under —4–9

—755 666	Independent city of Danville
—755 67	Campbell and Bedford Counties and environs
—755 671	Independent city of Lynchburg
—755 672	Campbell County
—755 675	Bedford County
—755 676	Independent city of Bedford
—755 68	Franklin County
—755 69	Henry and Patrick Counties and environs
—755 692	Henry County
—755 693	Independent city of Martinsville
—755 695	Patrick County
—755 7	Southwestern region
—755 71	Floyd, Carroll, Grayson Counties and environs
—755 712	Floyd County
—755 714	Carroll County
—755 715	Independent city of Galax
—755 717	Grayson County
—755 72	Smyth and Washington Counties and environs
—755 723	Smyth County
—755 725	Washington County
—755 726	Independent city of Bristol
—755 73	Scott and Lee Counties
—755 732	Scott County
—755 735	Lee County
—755 74	Wise and Dickenson Counties and environs
—755 743	Wise County
—755 744	Independent city of Norton
—755 745	Dickenson County
—755 75	Buchanan and Russell Counties
—755 752	Buchanan County
—755 755	Russell County
—755 76	Tazewell and Bland Counties

—755 763	Tazewell County
—755 765	Bland County
—755 77	Wythe and Pulaski Counties
—755 773	Wythe County
—755 775	Pulaski County
—755 78	Giles and Montgomery Counties and environs
—755 782	Giles County
—755 785	Montgomery County
—755 786	Independent city of Radford
—755 79	Roanoke and Craig Counties and environs
—755 791	Independent city of Roanoke
—755 792	Roanoke County
—755 793	Independent city of Salem
—755 795	Craig County
—755 8	Central western region
—755 81	Alleghany County and environs
—755 811	Independent city of Clifton Forge
—755 812	Independent city of Covington
—755 816	Alleghany County
—755 83	Botetourt County
—755 85	Rockbridge County and environs
—755 851	Independent city of Buena Vista
—755 852	Rockbridge County
—755 853	Independent city of Lexington
—755 87	Bath County
—755 89	Highland County
—755 9	Northwestern region
	Class here *Shenandoah National Park; *Shenandoah Valley
—755 91	Augusta County and environs
—755 911	Independent city of Staunton
—755 912	Independent city of Waynesboro

*For a specific part of this jurisdiction, region, or feature, see the part and follow instructions under —4–9

—755 916	Augusta County
—755 92	Rockingham County and environs
—755 921	Independent city of Harrisonburg
—755 922	Rockingham County
—755 94	Page County
—755 95	Shenandoah County
—755 97	Warren County
—755 98	Clarke County
—755 99	Frederick County and environs
—755 991	Independent city of Winchester
—755 992	Frederick County
—756	North Carolina
—756 1	Northeast coastal plain counties

Class here *Coastal Plain in North Carolina; *Outer Banks

See also —16348 for Albemarle, Pamlico Sounds

—756 13	Currituck and Camden Counties
—756 132	Currituck County
—756 135	Camden County

Including *Dismal Swamp in North Carolina

—756 14	Pasquotank, Perquimans, Chowan Counties
—756 142	Pasquotank County
—756 144	Perquimans County
—756 147	Chowan County
—756 15	Gates and Hertford Counties

Class here *Chowan River

—756 153	Gates County
—756 155	Hertford County
—756 16	Bertie and Washington Counties

Class here *Roanoke River

—756 163	Bertie County
—756 165	Washington County

*For a specific part of this jurisdiction, region, or feature, see the part and follow instructions under —4–9

—756 17	Tyrrell and Dare Counties
—756 172	Tyrrell County
—756 175	Dare County
	Including Roanoke Island; Cape Hatteras
—756 18	Hyde and Beaufort Counties
—756 184	Hyde County
—756 186	Beaufort County
—756 19	Craven, Pamlico, Carteret Counties
	Class here *Neuse River
—756 192	Craven County
—756 194	Pamlico County
—756 197	Carteret County
—756 2	Southeast Coastal Plain counties
	Class here *Cape Fear River
—756 21	Jones County
—756 23	Onslow County
—756 25	Pender County
—756 27	New Hanover County
	Class here Wilmington
—756 29	Brunswick County
—756 3	Southwest Coastal Plain counties
—756 31	Columbus County
—756 32	Bladen County
—756 33	Robeson and Scotland Counties
—756 332	Robeson County
—756 335	Scotland County
—756 34	Richmond County
—756 35	Moore and Lee Counties
—756 352	Moore County
—756 355	Lee County
—756 36	Harnett and Hoke Counties

*For a specific part of this jurisdiction, region, or feature, see the part and follow instructions under —4–9

—756 362	Harnett County
—756 365	Hoke County
—756 37	Cumberland and Sampson Counties
—756 373	Cumberland County
—756 375	Sampson County
—756 38	Duplin and Lenoir Counties
—756 382	Duplin County
—756 385	Lenoir County
—756 39	Greene and Wayne Counties
—756 393	Greene County
—756 395	Wayne County
—756 4	Northwest Coastal Plain counties
—756 41	Johnston County
—756 43	Wilson County
—756 44	Pitt County
—756 45	Martin County
—756 46	Edgecombe County
—756 47	Nash County
—756 48	Halifax County
—756 49	Northampton County
—756 5	Northeast Piedmont counties
	Class here *Piedmont in North Carolina
—756 52	Warren County
—756 53	Vance and Granville Counties
—756 532	Vance County
—756 535	Granville County
—756 54	Franklin County
—756 55	Wake County
	Class here Raleigh
—756 56	Durham and Orange Counties
—756 563	Durham County

*For a specific part of this jurisdiction, region, or feature, see the part and follow instructions
  under —4–9

—756 565	Orange County
—756 57	Person and Caswell Counties
—756 573	Person County
—756 575	Caswell County
—756 58	Alamance County
—756 59	Chatham County
—756 6	Northwest Piedmont counties
—756 61	Randolph County
—756 62	Guilford County
—756 63	Rockingham County
—756 64	Stokes County
—756 65	Surry County
—756 66	Yadkin County
—756 67	Forsyth County
—756 68	Davidson County
	Class here *Yadkin River
—756 69	Davie County
—756 7	Southern Piedmont counties
—756 71	Rowan County
—756 72	Cabarrus County
—756 73	Stanly County
—756 74	Montgomery County
—756 75	Anson and Union Counties
—756 753	Anson County
—756 755	Union County
—756 76	Mecklenburg County
	Class here Charlotte
—756 77	Gaston and Cleveland Counties
—756 773	Gaston County
—756 775	Cleveland County
—756 78	Lincoln and Catawba Counties

*For a specific part of this jurisdiction, region, or feature, see the part and follow instructions under —4–9

—756 782	Lincoln County
—756 785	Catawba County
—756 79	Iredell and Alexander Counties
—756 793	Iredell County
—756 795	Alexander County
—756 8	**Northern Appalachian region counties**
	Class here *Blue Ridge in North Carolina, *Appalachian region in North Carolina
—756 82	Wilkes County
—756 83	Alleghany and Ashe Counties
—756 832	Alleghany County
—756 835	Ashe County
—756 84	Watauga and Caldwell Counties
—756 843	Watauga County
—756 845	Caldwell County
—756 85	Burke County
—756 86	Avery and Mitchell Counties
—756 862	Avery County
—756 865	Mitchell County
—756 87	Yancey and Madison Counties
—756 873	Yancey County
—756 875	Madison County
—756 88	Buncombe County
	Including Asheville
—756 89	McDowell County
—756 9	**Southern Appalachian region counties**
—756 91	Rutherford and Polk Counties
—756 913	Rutherford County
—756 915	Polk County
—756 92	Henderson County
—756 93	Transylvania County
—756 94	Haywood County

*For a specific part of this jurisdiction, region, or feature, see the part and follow instructions under —4–9

—756 95	Jackson County
—756 96	Swain County
	Class here *Great Smoky Mountains in North Carolina
—756 97	Graham County
—756 98	Macon and Clay Counties
—756 982	Macon County
—756 985	Clay County
—756 99	Cherokee County
—757	South Carolina
—757 2	Mountain counties
	Class here *Blue Ridge in South Carolina
—757 21	Oconee County
—757 23	Pickens County
—757 25	Anderson County
—757 27	Greenville County
—757 29	Spartanburg County
—757 3	Southwest Piedmont counties
	Class here *Piedmont in South Carolina
—757 31	Laurens County
—757 33	Greenwood County
—757 35	Abbeville County
—757 36	McCormick County
—757 37	Edgefield County
—757 38	Saluda County
—757 39	Newberry County
—757 4	Northeast Piedmont counties
	Class here *Broad River
—757 41	Union County
—757 42	Cherokee County
—757 43	York County
—757 45	Lancaster County
	Class here *Catawba River

*For a specific part of this jurisdiction, region, or feature, see the part and follow instructions under —4–9

—757 47	Chester County
—757 49	Fairfield County
—757 6	**Northeast counties of sand hills and upper pine belt**
	Class here *Coastal Plain in South Carolina
—757 61	Kershaw County
—757 63	Chesterfield County
—757 64	Marlboro County
—757 66	Darlington County
—757 67	Lee County
—757 69	Sumter County
—757 7	**Southwest counties of sand hills and upper pine belt**
—757 71	Richland County
	Class here Columbia
—757 72	Calhoun County
—757 73	Lexington County
—757 75	Aiken County
—757 76	Barnwell County
—757 77	Allendale County
—757 78	Bamberg County
—757 79	Orangeburg County
—757 8	**Northeast counties of lower pine belt**
	Including *Black, *Santee Rivers
	Class here *Pee Dee River
—757 81	Clarendon County
—757 83	Williamsburg County
—757 84	Florence County
—757 85	Dillon County
—757 86	Marion County
—757 87	Horry County
—757 89	Georgetown County
—757 9	**Southwest counties of lower pine belt**
	Including *Edisto River; *Savannah River in South Carolina

*For a specific part of this jurisdiction, region, or feature, see the part and follow instructions under —4–9

—757 91	Charleston County
—757 915	Charleston
—757 93	Berkeley County
—757 94	Dorchester County
—757 95	Colleton County
—757 97	Hampton County
—757 98	Jasper County
—757 99	Beaufort County
	Class here *Sea Islands
—758	**Georgia**
	Class here *Chattahoochee River
—758 1	**Northeastern counties**
	Class here *Savannah River
—758 12	Rabun and Habersham Counties
—758 123	Rabun County
—758 125	Habersham County
—758 13	Stephens and Franklin Counties
—758 132	Stephens County
—758 135	Franklin County
—758 14	Banks and Jackson Counties
—758 143	Banks County
—758 145	Jackson County
—758 15	Madison and Hart Counties
—758 152	Madison County
—758 155	Hart County
—758 16	Elbert and Lincoln Counties
—758 163	Elbert County
—758 165	Lincoln County
—758 17	Wilkes and Oglethorpe Counties
—758 172	Wilkes County
—758 175	Oglethorpe County

*For a specific part of this jurisdiction, region, or feature, see the part and follow instructions under —4–9

—758 18	Clarke County
	Class here Athens
—758 19	Oconee and Barrow Counties
—758 193	Oconee County
—758 195	Barrow County
—758 2	North central counties
	Class here *Blue Ridge in Georgia
—758 21	Walton and Rockdale Counties
—758 212	Walton County
—758 215	Rockdale County
—758 22	Gwinnett and De Kalb Counties
—758 223	Gwinnett County
—758 225	De Kalb County
—758 23	Fulton County
—758 231	Atlanta
—758 24	Douglas and Cobb Counties
—758 243	Douglas County
—758 245	Cobb County
—758 25	Cherokee and Pickens Counties
—758 253	Cherokee County
—758 255	Pickens County
—758 26	Dawson and Forsyth Counties
—758 263	Dawson County
—758 265	Forsyth County
—758 27	Hall, Lumpkin, White Counties
—758 272	Hall County
—758 273	Lumpkin County
—758 277	White County
—758 28	Towns and Union Counties
—758 282	Towns County
—758 285	Union County

*For a specific part of this jurisdiction, region, or feature, see the part and follow instructions under —4–9

—758 29	Fannin and Gilmer Counties
—758 293	Fannin County
—758 295	Gilmer County
—758 3	**Northwestern counties**
—758 31	Murray County
—758 32	Whitfield and Catoosa Counties
—758 324	Whitfield County
—758 326	Catoosa County
—758 33	Walker County
—758 34	Dade and Chattooga Counties
—758 342	Dade County
	Class here *Lookout Mountain in Georgia
—758 344	Chattooga County
—758 35	Floyd County
—758 36	Gordon and Bartow Counties
—758 362	Gordon County
—758 365	Bartow County
—758 37	Paulding and Polk Counties
—758 373	Paulding County
—758 375	Polk County
—758 38	Haralson County
—758 39	Carroll County
—758 4	**West central counties**
	Class here *Piedmont in Georgia
—758 42	Heard, Coweta, Fayette Counties
—758 422	Heard County
—758 423	Coweta County
—758 426	Fayette County
—758 43	Clayton and Henry Counties
—758 432	Clayton County
—758 435	Henry County

*For a specific part of this jurisdiction, region, or feature, see the part and follow instructions under —4–9

—758 44	Spalding and Lamar Counties
—758 443	Spalding County
—758 446	Lamar County
—758 45	Pike and Meriwether Counties
—758 453	Pike County
—758 455	Meriwether County
—758 46	Troup and Harris Counties
—758 463	Troup County
—758 466	Harris County
—758 47	Muscogee and Chattahoochee Counties
—758 473	Muscogee County
—758 476	Chattahoochee County
—758 48	Marion, Talbot, Upson Counties
—758 482	Marion County
—758 483	Talbot County
—758 486	Upson County
—758 49	Taylor and Schley Counties
—758 493	Taylor County
—758 495	Schley County
—758 5	Central counties
—758 51	Macon and Houston Counties
—758 513	Macon County
—758 515	Houston County
—758 52	Pulaski and Bleckley Counties
—758 523	Pulaski County
—758 525	Bleckley County
—758 53	Dodge and Laurens Counties
—758 532	Dodge County
—758 535	Laurens County
—758 54	Wilkinson and Twiggs Counties
—758 543	Wilkinson County
—758 545	Twiggs County

—758 55	Bibb and Peach Counties
—758 552	Bibb County
	Class here Macon
—758 556	Peach County
—758 56	Crawford, Monroe, Jones Counties
—758 562	Crawford County
—758 563	Monroe County
—758 567	Jones County
—758 57	Baldwin and Putnam Counties
—758 573	Baldwin County
—758 576	Putnam County
—758 58	Jasper and Butts Counties
—758 583	Jasper County
—758 585	Butts County
—758 59	Newton and Morgan Counties
—758 593	Newton County
—758 595	Morgan County
—758 6	East central counties
	Including *Oconee River
	Class here *Ogeechee River
—758 61	Greene and Taliaferro Counties
—758 612	Greene County
—758 616	Taliaferro County
—758 62	Hancock and Warren Counties
—758 623	Hancock County
—758 625	Warren County
—758 63	McDuffie and Columbia Counties
—758 632	McDuffie County
—758 635	Columbia County
—758 64	Richmond County
	Class here Augusta

*For a specific part of this jurisdiction, region, or feature, see the part and follow instructions under —4–9

—758 65	Burke County
—758 66	Jefferson and Glascock Counties
—758 663	Jefferson County
—758 666	Glascock County
—758 67	Washington and Johnson Counties
—758 672	Washington County
—758 676	Johnson County
—758 68	Treutlen and Emanuel Counties
—758 682	Treutlen County
—758 684	Emanuel County
—758 69	Jenkins and Screven Counties
—758 693	Jenkins County
—758 695	Screven County
—758 7	Southeastern counties
	Including *Sea Islands of Georgia
—758 72	Effingham and Chatham Counties
—758 722	Effingham County
—758 724	Chatham County
	Class here Savannah
—758 73	Bryan, Liberty, McIntosh Counties
—758 732	Bryan County
—758 733	Liberty County
—758 737	McIntosh County
—758 74	Glynn and Camden Counties
—758 742	Glynn County
—758 746	Camden County
—758 75	Charlton, Brantley, Wayne Counties
—758 752	Charlton County
	Class here *Okefenokee Swamp
—758 753	Brantley County
—758 756	Wayne County

*For a specific part of this jurisdiction, region, or feature, see the part and follow instructions under —4–9

—758 76	Long, Evans, Bulloch Counties
—758 762	Long County
—758 763	Evans County
—758 766	Bulloch County
—758 77	Candler and Tattnall Counties
—758 773	Candler County
—758 775	Tattnall County
—758 78	Toombs, Appling, Bacon Counties
—758 782	Toombs County
—758 784	Appling County
—758 787	Bacon County
—758 79	Pierce and Ware Counties
—758 792	Pierce County
—758 794	Ware County
—758 8	South central counties
—758 81	Clinch, Echols, Lanier Counties
—758 812	Clinch County
—758 814	Echols County
—758 817	Lanier County
—758 82	Atkinson, Coffee, Jeff Davis Counties
—758 822	Atkinson County
—758 823	Coffee County
—758 827	Jeff Davis County
—758 83	Montgomery and Wheeler Counties
—758 832	Montgomery County
—758 835	Wheeler County
—758 84	Telfair and Wilcox Counties
—758 843	Telfair County
—758 845	Wilcox County
—758 85	Ben Hill and Irwin Counties
—758 852	Ben Hill County
—758 855	Irwin County

—758 86	Berrien and Lowndes Counties
—758 862	Berrien County
—758 864	Lowndes County
—758 87	Brooks and Cook Counties
—758 874	Brooks County
—758 876	Cook County
—758 88	Tift and Turner Counties
—758 882	Tift County
—758 885	Turner County
—758 89	Crisp and Dooly Counties
—758 893	Crisp County
—758 895	Dooly County
—758 9	Southwestern counties
	Class here *Flint River
—758 91	Sumter and Webster Counties
—758 913	Sumter County
—758 916	Webster County
—758 92	Stewart, Quitman, Clay Counties
—758 922	Stewart County
—758 924	Quitman County
—758 927	Clay County
—758 93	Randolph and Terrell Counties
—758 932	Randolph County
—758 935	Terrell County
—758 94	Lee and Worth Counties
—758 943	Lee County
—758 945	Worth County
—758 95	Dougherty and Calhoun Counties
—758 953	Dougherty County
—758 956	Calhoun County
—758 96	Early, Miller, Baker Counties

*For a specific part of this jurisdiction, region, or feature, see the part and follow instructions under —4–9

—758 962	Early County
—758 964	Miller County
—758 967	Baker County
—758 97	Mitchell and Colquitt Counties
—758 973	Mitchell County
—758 975	Colquitt County
—758 98	Thomas and Grady Counties
—758 984	Thomas County
—758 986	Grady County
—758 99	Decatur and Seminole Counties
—758 993	Decatur County
—758 996	Seminole County

—759	Florida
—759 1	Northeastern counties

Class here *Saint Johns River

—759 11	Nassau County

Class here *Saint Marys River

—759 12	Duval County

Class here Jacksonville

—759 13	Baker County
—759 14	Union County
—759 15	Bradford County
—759 16	Clay County
—759 17	Putnam County
—759 18	Saint Johns County
—759 19	Flagler County
—759 2	East central counties
—759 21	Volusia County
—759 22	Lake County
—759 23	Seminole County
—759 24	Orange County

*For a specific part of this jurisdiction, region, or feature, see the part and follow instructions under —4–9

—759 25	Osceola County
—759 27	Brevard County
—759 28	Indian River County
—759 29	Saint Lucie County
—759 3	Southeastern counties
—759 31	Martin County
—759 32	Palm Beach County
—759 35	Broward County
	Including Fort Lauderdale
—759 38	Dade County
—759 381	Miami and Miami Beach
—759 39	*The Everglades and *Lake Okeechobee
	Class here *Everglades National Park
—759 4	Southwestern counties
—759 41	Monroe County
	Including Key West
	Class here *Florida Keys
—759 44	Collier County
	Including *Ten Thousand Islands
	Class here *Big Cypress Swamp
—759 46	Hendry County
—759 48	Lee County
	Class here *Caloosahatchee River
—759 49	Charlotte County
—759 5	South central counties
—759 51	Glades County
—759 53	Okeechobee County
	Class here *Kissimmee River
—759 55	Highlands County
—759 57	Hardee County
	Class here *Peace River

*For a specific part of this jurisdiction, region, or feature, see the part and follow instructions under —4–9

—759 59	De Soto County
—759 6	Southern west central counties
—759 61	Sarasota County
—759 62	Manatee County
—759 63	Pinellas County
—759 65	Hillsborough County
	Class here Tampa
—759 67	Polk County
—759 69	Pasco County
—759 7	Northern west central counties
	Class here *Withlacoochee River
—759 71	Hernando County
—759 72	Citrus County
—759 73	Sumter County
—759 75	Marion County
—759 77	Levy County
—759 78	Gilchrist County
—759 79	Alachua County
—759 8	North central counties
	Class here *Suwannee River
—759 81	Dixie and Lafayette Counties
—759 812	Dixie County
—759 816	Lafayette County
—759 82	Suwannee County
—759 83	Columbia County
—759 84	Hamilton County
—759 85	Madison County
—759 86	Taylor County
—759 87	Jefferson County
—759 88	Leon County
	Including Tallahassee

*For a specific part of this jurisdiction, region, or feature, see the part and follow instructions under —4–9

—759 89	Wakulla County
—759 9	Northwestern counties (Panhandle)
—759 91	Franklin County
—759 92	Liberty and Gadsden Counties
	Including *Apalachicola River
—759 923	Liberty County
—759 925	Gadsden County
—759 93	Jackson County
—759 94	Calhoun and Gulf Counties
—759 943	Calhoun County
—759 947	Gulf County
—759 95	Bay County
—759 96	Washington and Holmes Counties
—759 963	Washington County
—759 965	Holmes County
—759 97	Walton County
—759 98	Okaloosa and Santa Rosa Counties
—759 982	Okaloosa County
—759 985	Santa Rosa County
—759 99	Escambia County
	Including Pensacola

—76   **South central United States**   **Gulf Coast states**

Class here Old Southwest

SUMMARY

—761	**Alabama**
—762	**Mississippi**
—763	**Louisiana**
—764	**Texas**
—766	**Oklahoma**
—767	**Arkansas**
—768	**Tennessee**
—769	**Kentucky**

*For a specific part of this jurisdiction, region, or feature, see the part and follow instructions under —4–9

>   —761–764 Gulf Coast states

    Class comprehensive works in —76

    For Florida, see —759

—761   Alabama

—761 2   Gulf and Lower Coastal Plain counties

    Class here *Alabama, *Tombigbee Rivers

—761 21   Baldwin County

    Class here *Perdido River

—761 22   Mobile County

    Including *Mobile River

    Class here Mobile

—761 23   Lime Hills counties

    For specific counties, see —76124–76127

>   —761 24–761 27 Specific Lime Hills counties

    Class comprehensive works in —76123

—761 24   Washington and Clarke Counties

—761 243   Washington County

—761 245   Clarke County

—761 25   Monroe County

—761 26   Conecuh and Escambia Counties

—761 263   Conecuh County

—761 265   Escambia County

—761 27   Covington County

—761 29   Lime sink counties (Wire-grass region)

—761 292   Geneva County

—761 295   Houston County

—761 3   Southern red hills counties

—761 31   Henry County

—761 32   Barbour County

*For a specific part of this jurisdiction, region, or feature, see the part and follow instructions under —4–9

—761 33	Dale County
—761 34	Coffee County
—761 35	Pike County
—761 36	Crenshaw County
—761 37	Butler County
—761 38	Wilcox County
—761 39	Marengo and Choctaw Counties
—761 392	Marengo County
—761 395	Choctaw County
—761 4	**Black Belt counties**
—761 41	Sumter County
—761 42	Greene County
—761 43	Hale County
—761 44	Perry County
—761 45	Dallas County
—761 46	Autauga and Lowndes Counties
—761 463	Autauga County
—761 465	Lowndes County
—761 47	Montgomery County
	Class here Montgomery
—761 48	Bullock and Russell Counties
—761 483	Bullock County
—761 485	Russell County
—761 49	Macon County
—761 5	**Counties of *Piedmont**
	Class here *Tallapoosa River
—761 52	Elmore County
—761 53	Tallapoosa County
	Class here *Lake Martin
—761 55	Lee County
—761 56	Chambers County

*For a specific part of this jurisdiction, region, or feature, see the part and follow instructions under —4–9

—761 57	Randolph County
—761 58	Clay County
—761 59	Coosa County
—761 6	Coosa Valley region counties
	Class here *Coosa River
—761 61	Talladega County
—761 63	Calhoun County
—761 64	Cleburne County
—761 65	Cherokee County
—761 66	De Kalb County
—761 67	Etowah County
—761 69	Saint Clair County
—761 7	Central Plateau and Basin counties
—761 72	Blount County
—761 73	Cullman County
—761 74	Winston County
—761 76	Walker County
—761 78	Jefferson County
—761 781	Birmingham
—761 79	Shelby County
—761 8	Central pine belt counties
—761 81	Chilton County
—761 82	Bibb County
—761 84	Tuscaloosa County
—761 85	Pickens County
—761 86	Lamar County
—761 87	Fayette County
—761 89	Marion County
—761 9	Tennessee Valley counties
	Class here *Tennessee River in Alabama
—761 91	Franklin and Colbert Counties

*For a specific part of this jurisdiction, region, or feature, see the part and follow instructions under —4–9

—761 913	Franklin County
—761 915	Colbert County
—761 92	Lawrence County
—761 93	Morgan County
—761 94	Marshall County
	Class here *Guntersville Lake
—761 95	Jackson County
—761 97	Madison County
	Class here Huntsville
—761 98	Limestone County
	Class here *Wheeler Lake
—761 99	Lauderdale County
—762	Mississippi
—762 1	Southeastern counties
—762 12	Jackson County
—762 13	Harrison County
—762 14	Hancock County
—762 15	Pearl River County
—762 16	Stone and George Counties
—762 162	Stone County
—762 165	George County
—762 17	Greene and Perry Counties
—762 173	Greene County
—762 175	Perry County
—762 18	Forrest County
—762 19	Lamar County
—762 2	Southwestern counties
—762 21	Marion County
—762 22	Walthall County
—762 23	Pike County
—762 24	Amite County

*For a specific part of this jurisdiction, region, or feature, see the part and follow instructions under —4–9

—762 25	Wilkinson County
—762 26	Adams County
	Class here Natchez
—762 27	Franklin County
—762 28	Jefferson and Claiborne Counties
—762 283	Jefferson County
—762 285	Claiborne County
—762 29	Warren County
—762 4	**West central counties (Yazoo Mississippi Delta)**
	Class here *Big Black, *Yazoo Rivers
—762 41	Issaquena and Sharkey Counties
—762 412	Issaquena County
—762 414	Sharkey County
—762 42	Washington County
—762 43	Bolivar County
—762 44	Coahoma County
—762 45	Quitman and Tallahatchie Counties
—762 453	Quitman County
—762 455	Tallahatchie County
—762 46	Leflore County
—762 47	Sunflower County
—762 48	Humphreys County
—762 49	Yazoo County
—762 5	**South central counties (Piney woods region)**
	Class here *Pearl River
—762 51	Hinds County
	Class here Jackson
—762 52	Copiah County
—762 53	Lincoln and Lawrence Counties
—762 534	Lincoln County
—762 536	Lawrence County

*For a specific part of this jurisdiction, region, or feature, see the part and follow instructions under —4–9

—762 54	Jefferson Davis and Covington Counties
—762 543	Jefferson Davis County
—762 545	Covington County
—762 55	Jones County
—762 57	Wayne and Jasper Counties
—762 573	Wayne County
—762 575	Jasper County
—762 58	Smith and Simpson Counties
—762 582	Smith County
—762 585	Simpson County
—762 59	Rankin County
—762 6	**Central and east central counties (Plateau region)**
	For Northern Plateau region, see —7628
—762 62	Madison and Holmes Counties
—762 623	Madison County
—762 625	Holmes County
—762 63	Carroll and Grenada Counties
—762 633	Carroll County
—762 635	Grenada County
—762 64	Montgomery and Attala Counties
—762 642	Montgomery County
—762 644	Attala County
—762 65	Leake and Scott Counties
—762 653	Leake County
—762 655	Scott County
—762 67	Newton, Clarke, Lauderdale Counties
—762 672	Newton County
—762 673	Clarke County
—762 676	Lauderdale County
	For Meridian, see —762677
—762 677	Meridian
—762 68	Kemper and Neshoba Counties

—762 683	Kemper County
—762 685	Neshoba County
—762 69	Winston, Choctaw, Webster Counties
—762 692	Winston County
—762 694	Choctaw County
—762 697	Webster County
—762 8	Northwestern counties (Northern Plateau region)
—762 81	Calhoun County
—762 82	Yalobusha County
—762 83	Lafayette County
—762 84	Panola County
—762 85	Tate County
—762 86	Tunica County
—762 87	De Soto County
—762 88	Marshall County
—762 89	Benton County
—762 9	Northeastern counties
—762 92	Tippah and Union Counties
—762 923	Tippah County
—762 925	Union County
—762 93	Pontotoc and Lee Counties
—762 932	Pontotoc County
—762 935	Lee County
—762 94	Chickasaw and Clay Counties
—762 942	Chickasaw County
—762 945	Clay County
—762 95	Oktibbeha and Noxubee Counties
—762 953	Oktibbeha County
—762 955	Noxubee County
—762 97	Lowndes and Monroe Counties
—762 973	Lowndes County
—762 975	Monroe County

—762 98	Itawamba and Prentiss Counties
—762 982	Itawamba County
—762 985	Prentiss County
—762 99	Alcorn and Tishomingo Counties
—762 993	Alcorn County
—762 995	Tishomingo County
—763	Louisiana
—763 1	Eastern parishes
—763 11	Washington Parish
—763 12	Saint Tammany Parish
—763 13	Tangipahoa Parish
—763 14	Livingston Parish
—763 15	Saint Helena Parish
—763 16	East Feliciana Parish
—763 17	West Feliciana Parish
—763 18	East Baton Rouge Parish
	Class here Baton Rouge
—763 19	Ascension Parish
—763 3	Southeastern parishes (Mississippi Delta)
—763 31	Saint James Parish
—763 32	Saint John the Baptist Parish
	Including *Lake Maurepas
—763 33	Saint Charles Parish
—763 34	*Lake Pontchartrain
—763 35	Orleans Parish (New Orleans)
—763 36	Saint Bernard Parish
—763 37	Plaquemines Parish
—763 38	Jefferson Parish
—763 39	Lafourche Parish
—763 4	South central parishes
—763 41	Terrebonne Parish

*For a specific part of this jurisdiction, region, or feature, see the part and follow instructions under —4–9

—763 42	Saint Mary Parish
—763 43	Assumption Parish
—763 44	Iberville Parish
—763 45	West Baton Rouge and Pointe Coupee Parishes
—763 452	West Baton Rouge Parish
—763 454	Pointe Coupee Parish
—763 46	Saint Landry Parish
—763 47	Lafayette Parish
—763 48	Saint Martin Parish
—763 49	Iberia Parish

—763 5   **Southwestern parishes**

—763 51	Vermilion Parish
—763 52	Cameron Parish

Including Calcasieu, *Sabine Lakes

—763 54	Calcasieu Parish
—763 55	Jefferson Davis Parish
—763 56	Acadia Parish
—763 57	Evangeline Parish
—763 58	Allen Parish
—763 59	Beauregard Parish

—763 6   **West central parishes**

Class here *Red River in Louisiana

—763 61	Vernon Parish
—763 62	Sabine Parish

Class here *Toledo Bend Reservoir

—763 63	De Soto Parish
—763 64	Red River Parish
—763 65	Natchitoches Parish
—763 66	Winn Parish
—763 67	Grant Parish
—763 69	Rapides Parish

*For a specific part of this jurisdiction, region, or feature, see the part and follow instructions under —4–9

—763 7	East central parishes
	Class here *Ouachita River
—763 71	Avoyelles Parish
—763 73	Concordia Parish
—763 74	Catahoula Parish
—763 75	La Salle Parish
—763 76	Caldwell Parish
—763 77	Franklin Parish
—763 79	Tensas Parish
—763 8	Northeastern parishes
—763 81	Madison Parish
—763 82	East Carroll Parish
—763 83	West Carroll Parish
—763 84	Morehouse Parish
—763 86	Richland Parish
—763 87	Ouachita Parish
—763 89	Union Parish
—763 9	Northwestern parishes
—763 91	Lincoln Parish
—763 92	Jackson Parish
—763 93	Bienville Parish
—763 94	Claiborne Parish
—763 96	Webster Parish
—763 97	Bossier Parish
—763 99	Caddo Parish
	Including *Caddo Lake
	Class here Shreveport
—764	Texas
	Class here *Brazos, *Colorado Rivers
—764 1	Coastal plains

> For East Texas timber belt and blackland prairie, see —7642; for Rio Grande Plain, see —7644

*For a specific part of this jurisdiction, region, or feature, see the part and follow instructions under —4–9

—764 11	Nueces and neighboring counties
	Class here *Nueces River
—764 113	Nueces County
	Class here Corpus Christi
—764 115	San Patricio County
—764 117	Bee County
—764 119	Refugio County
—764 12	Calhoun and neighboring counties
	Class here *Guadalupe, *San Antonio rivers
—764 121	Calhoun County
—764 122	Aransas County
—764 123	Goliad County
—764 125	Victoria County
—764 127	Jackson County
—764 13	Matagorda and neighboring counties
—764 132	Matagorda County
—764 133	Wharton County
—764 135	Fort Bend County
—764 137	Brazoria County
—764 139	Galveston County
—764 14	Harris and neighboring counties
	Class here *East Texas; *Sabine, *Trinity rivers
—764 141	Harris County
—764 141 1	Houston
—764 143	Chambers County
—764 145	Jefferson County
—764 147	Orange County
—764 15	Montgomery and neighboring counties
	Class here *Neches River
—764 153	Montgomery County
—764 155	Liberty County

---

*For a specific part of this jurisdiction, region, or feature, see the part and follow instructions under —4–9

—764 157	Hardin County
—764 159	Jasper County
—764 16	Newton and neighboring counties
—764 162	Newton County
—764 163	Tyler County
—764 165	Polk County
—764 167	San Jacinto County
—764 169	Walker County
—764 17	Trinity and neighboring counties
—764 172	Trinity County
—764 173	Angelina County
—764 175	San Augustine County
—764 177	Sabine County
—764 179	Shelby County
—764 18	Nacogdoches and neighboring counties
—764 182	Nacogdoches County
—764 183	Cherokee County
—764 185	Rusk County
—764 187	Panola County
—764 189	Gregg County
—764 19	Harrison and neighboring counties
—764 192	Harrison County
—764 193	Marion County
—764 195	Cass County
—764 197	Bowie County

—764 2　　East Texas timber belt and blackland prairie

For Austin-San Antonio region, see —7643

—764 21	Red River and neighboring counties
—764 212	Red River County
—764 213	Franklin County
—764 215	Titus County
—764 217	Morris County

—764 219	Camp County
—764 22	Upshur and neighboring counties
—764 222	Upshur County
—764 223	Wood County
—764 225	Smith County
—764 227	Henderson County
—764 229	Anderson County
—764 23	Freestone and neighboring counties
—764 232	Freestone County
—764 233	Leon County
—764 235	Houston County
—764 237	Madison County
—764 239	Robertson County
—764 24	Burleson and neighboring counties
—764 241	Burleson County
—764 242	Brazos County
—764 243	Grimes County
—764 245	Washington County
—764 247	Lee County
—764 249	Waller County
—764 25	Fayette and neighboring counties
—764 251	Fayette County
—764 252	Austin County
—764 253	Colorado County
—764 255	Lavaca County
—764 257	Gonzales County
—764 259	De Witt County
—764 26	Lamar and Fannin Counties
	Class here *blackland prairie
—764 263	Lamar County
—764 265	Fannin County

*For a specific part of this jurisdiction, region, or feature, see the part and follow instructions under —4–9

—764 27	Hunt and neighboring counties
—764 272	Hunt County
—764 273	Delta County
—764 274	Hopkins County
—764 275	Rains County
—764 276	Van Zandt County
—764 277	Kaufman County
—764 278	Rockwall County
—764 28	Dallas and neighboring counties
—764 281	Dallas and Ellis Counties
—764 281 1	Dallas County

                                           For Dallas, see —7642812

—764 281 2	Dallas

                                  Class here Dallas-Fort Worth metropolitan area

                                      For Fort Worth, see —7645315

—764 281 5	Ellis County
—764 282	Navarro County
—764 283	Hill County
—764 284	McLennan County
—764 285	Limestone County
—764 286	Falls County
—764 287	Bell County
—764 288	Milam County
—764 289	Williamson County
—764 3	Austin-San Antonio region

                                  For Comal County, see —764887; for Hays County, see —764888

—764 31	Travis County

                                  Class here Austin

—764 32	Bastrop County
—764 33	Caldwell County
—764 34	Guadalupe County
—764 35	Bexar County

—764 351	San Antonio
—764 4	**Rio Grande Plain (Lower Rio Grande Valley)**
	Class here *Rio Grande
—764 42	Medina County
—764 43	Uvalde and neighboring counties
—764 432	Uvalde County
—764 433	Kinney County
—764 435	Maverick County
—764 437	Zavala County
—764 44	Frio and neighboring counties
—764 442	Frio County
—764 443	Atascosa County
—764 444	Karnes County
—764 445	Wilson County
—764 447	Live Oak County
—764 45	McMullen and neighboring counties
—764 452	McMullen County
—764 453	La Salle County
—764 455	Dimmit County
—764 46	Webb and neighboring counties
—764 462	Webb County
—764 463	Duval County
—764 465	Jim Wells County
—764 47	Kleberg and neighboring counties
	Class here *Padre Island
—764 472	Kleberg County
—764 473	Kenedy County
—764 475	Brooks County
—764 48	Jim Hogg and neighboring counties
—764 482	Jim Hogg County
—764 483	Zapata County

*For a specific part of this jurisdiction, region, or feature, see the part and follow instructions under —4–9

—764 485	Starr County
—764 49	Hidalgo and neighboring counties
—764 492	Hidalgo County
—764 493	Willacy County
—764 495	Cameron County
—764 5	North central plains

> For Burnet-Llano region, see —7646; for northwestern lowland counties, see —7647

| —764 51 | Mills and neighboring counties |

Class here *Grand Prairie

—764 512	Mills County
—764 513	Lampasas County
—764 515	Coryell County
—764 518	Bosque County
—764 52	Somervell and neighboring counties
—764 521	Somervell County
—764 522	Hood County
—764 524	Johnson County
—764 53	Tarrant and neighboring counties
—764 531	Tarrant County
—764 531 5	Fort Worth

Class comprehensive works on Dallas-Fort Worth metropolitan area in —7642812

—764 532	Wise County
—764 533	Cooke County
—764 54	Montague and neighboring counties
—764 541	Montague County
—764 542	Clay County
—764 543	Archer County
—764 544	Jack County
—764 545	Young County
—764 546	Stephens County

*For a specific part of this jurisdiction, region, or feature, see the part and follow instructions under —4–9

—764 547	Eastland County
—764 548	Brown County
—764 549	Hamilton County
—764 55	**Erath and neighboring counties**
—764 551	Erath County
—764 552	Palo Pinto County
—764 553	Parker County
—764 554	Comanche County
—764 555	Denton County
—764 556	Collin County
—764 557	Grayson County
—764 6	**Burnet-Llano region**
—764 62	Llano County
—764 63	Burnet County
—764 64	Blanco County
—764 65	Gillespie County
—764 66	Mason County
—764 67	McCulloch County
—764 68	San Saba County
—764 7	**Northwestern lowland counties**
—764 71	Concho County
—764 72	Tom Green and neighboring counties
—764 721	Tom Green County
—764 723	Coke County
—764 724	Runnels County
—764 725	Coleman County
—764 726	Callahan County
—764 727	Taylor County
—764 728	Nolan County
—764 729	Mitchell County
—764 73	Scurry and neighboring counties
—764 731	Scurry County

—764 732	Fisher County
—764 733	Jones County
—764 734	Shackelford County
—764 735	Throckmorton County
—764 736	Haskell County
—764 737	Stonewall County
—764 738	Kent County
—764 74	Dickens and neighboring counties
—764 741	Dickens County
—764 742	King County
—764 743	Knox County
—764 744	Baylor County
—764 745	Wichita County
—764 746	Wilbarger County
—764 747	Hardeman County
—764 748	Foard County
—764 75	Cottle and neighboring counties
—764 751	Cottle County
—764 752	Motley County
—764 753	Hall County
—764 754	Childress County
—764 8	Great Plains
	Class here *Llano Estacado
—764 81	Northern Panhandle counties
—764 812	Dallam County
—764 813	Sherman County
—764 814	Hansford County
—764 815	Ochiltree County
—764 816	Lipscomb County
—764 817	Hemphill County
—764 818	Roberts County

*For a specific part of this jurisdiction, region, or feature, see the part and follow instructions under —4–9

—764 82	Middle Panhandle counties
—764 821	Hutchinson County
—764 822	Moore County
—764 823	Hartley County
—764 824	Oldham County
—764 825	Potter County
—764 826	Carson County
—764 827	Gray County
—764 828	Wheeler County
—764 83	Southern Panhandle counties
—764 831	Collingsworth County
—764 832	Donley County
—764 833	Armstrong County
—764 834	Randall County
—764 835	Deaf Smith County
—764 836	Parmer County
—764 837	Castro County
—764 838	Swisher County
—764 839	Briscoe County
—764 84	Floyd and neighboring counties
—764 841	Floyd County
—764 842	Hale County
—764 843	Lamb County
—764 844	Bailey County
—764 845	Cochran County
—764 846	Hockley County
—764 847	Lubbock County
—764 848	Crosby County
—764 849	Yoakum County
—764 85	Lynn and neighboring counties
—764 851	Lynn County
—764 852	Garza County

—764 853	Borden County
—764 854	Dawson County
—764 855	Gaines County
—764 856	Andrews County
—764 857	Martin County
—764 858	Howard County
—764 859	Terry County
—764 86	Midland and neighboring counties
—764 861	Midland County
—764 862	Ector County
—764 863	Upton County
—764 87	Counties of *Edwards Plateau
—764 871	Sterling County
—764 872	Glasscock County
—764 873	Reagan County
—764 874	Irion County
—764 875	Crockett County
—764 876	Schleicher County
—764 877	Menard County
—764 878	Kimble County
—764 879	Sutton County
—764 88	Val Verde and neighboring counties
—764 881	Val Verde County
—764 882	Edwards County
—764 883	Real County
—764 884	Kerr County
—764 885	Bandera County
—764 886	Kendall County
—764 887	Comal County
—764 888	Hays County
—764 9	Western mountain and basin region
	Class here *Pecos River

*For a specific part of this jurisdiction, region, or feature, see the part and follow instructions under —4–9

—764 91	Pecos Basin counties
—764 912	Loving County
—764 913	Winkler County
—764 914	Ward County
—764 915	Crane County
—764 92	Counties of Stockton Plateau
—764 922	Terrell County
—764 923	Pecos County
—764 924	Reeves County
—764 93	Counties of Big Bend Region
—764 932	Brewster County

Including Big Bend National Park

—764 933	Presidio County
—764 934	Jeff Davis County
—764 94	Culberson County

Including Guadalupe Mountains National Park

For Guadalupe Mountains National Park in Hudspeth County, see —76495

—764 95	Hudspeth County
—764 96	El Paso County

Class here El Paso; *upper Rio Grande of Texas

—766	Oklahoma

Class here *Canadian River

—766 1	Northwestern counties

Class here former *Oklahoma Territory; *North Canadian River

—766 13	Panhandle counties

For Beaver County, see —76614

—766 132	Cimarron County
—766 135	Texas County
—766 14	Beaver County
—766 15	Harper and Ellis Counties
—766 153	Harper County

---

*For a specific part of this jurisdiction, region, or feature, see the part and follow instructions under —4–9

—766 155	Ellis County
—766 16	Roger Mills County
—766 17	Custer County
—766 18	Dewey County
—766 19	Woodward County
—766 2	North central counties
—766 21	Woods County
—766 22	Alfalfa County
—766 23	Grant County
—766 24	Kay County
—766 25	Osage County
—766 26	Pawnee County
—766 27	Noble County
—766 28	Garfield County
—766 29	Major County
—766 3	Central counties
—766 31	Blaine County
—766 32	Kingfisher County
—766 33	Logan County
—766 34	Payne County
—766 35	Lincoln County
—766 36	Pottawatomie County
—766 37	Cleveland County
—766 38	Oklahoma County
	Class here Oklahoma City
—766 39	Canadian County
—766 4	Southwestern counties
—766 41	Caddo County
—766 42	Washita County
—766 43	Beckham County
—766 44	Greer and Harmon Counties
—766 443	Greer County

—766 445	Harmon County
—766 45	Jackson County
—766 46	Tillman County
—766 47	Kiowa County
—766 48	Comanche County
—766 49	Cotton County
—766 5	South central counties

Class here former *Indian Territory; *Arbuckle Mountains; *Washita River

—766 52	Jefferson County
—766 53	Stephens County
—766 54	Grady County
—766 55	McClain County
—766 56	Garvin County
—766 57	Murray County

Including Platt National Park

—766 58	Carter County
—766 59	Love County
—766 6	Southeastern counties

Class here *Ouachita Mountains; *Red River

—766 61	Marshall County

Class here *Lake Texoma

—766 62	Bryan County
—766 63	Choctaw County
—766 64	McCurtain County
—766 65	Pushmataha County
—766 66	Atoka County
—766 67	Coal County
—766 68	Johnston County
—766 69	Pontotoc County
—766 7	Southeast central counties
—766 71	Seminole County

*For a specific part of this jurisdiction, region, or feature, see the part and follow instructions under —4–9

—766 72	Hughes County
—766 73	Okfuskee County
—766 74	McIntosh County
—766 75	Pittsburg County
—766 76	Latimer County
—766 77	Haskell County
—766 79	Le Flore County
—766 8	Northeast central counties

Class here *Ozark Plateau in Oklahoma; *Boston Mountains in Oklahoma; *Arkansas River in Oklahoma

—766 81	Sequoyah County
—766 82	Muskogee County
—766 83	Okmulgee County
—766 84	Creek County
—766 86	Tulsa County

Class here Tulsa

—766 87	Wagoner County

Class here *Fort Gibson Reservoir

—766 88	Cherokee County
—766 89	Adair County
—766 9	Northeastern counties
—766 91	Delaware County
—766 93	Mayes County
—766 94	Rogers County
—766 96	Washington County
—766 97	Nowata County
—766 98	Craig County
—766 99	Ottawa County
—767	Arkansas
—767 1	Northwestern counties

Class here *Ozark Mountains, *Ozark Plateau

—767 13	Benton County

---

*For a specific part of this jurisdiction, region, or feature, see the part and follow instructions under —4–9

—767 14	Washington County
—767 15	Madison County
—767 16	Newton County
—767 17	Carroll County
—767 18	Boone County
—767 19	Marion and Searcy Counties
—767 193	Marion County
	Class here *Bull Shoals Lake
—767 195	Searcy County
—767 2	North central counties
	Class here *White River
—767 21	Baxter County
—767 22	Fulton County
—767 23	Sharp County
—767 24	Randolph County
—767 25	Lawrence County
—767 26	Independence County
—767 27	Izard County
—767 28	Stone and Cleburne Counties
—767 283	Stone County
—767 285	Cleburne County
—767 29	Van Buren County
—767 3	Northwest central counties
	Class here *Arkansas River
—767 31	Conway County
—767 32	Pope County
—767 33	Johnson County
—767 34	Franklin County
—767 35	Crawford County
—767 36	Sebastian County
—767 37	Logan County

*For a specific part of this jurisdiction, region, or feature, see the part and follow instructions under —4–9

—767 38	Yell County
—767 39	Perry County
—767 4	**Southwest central counties**
	Class here *Ouachita Mountains in Arkansas
—767 41	Garland County
	Including Hot Springs National Park
—767 42	Hot Spring County
—767 43	Montgomery County
—767 44	Scott County
—767 45	Polk County
—767 47	Sevier County
—767 48	Howard and Pike Counties
—767 483	Howard County
—767 485	Pike County
—767 49	Clark County
—767 5	**Southwestern counties**
—767 52	Nevada County
—767 54	Hempstead County
—767 55	Little River County
—767 56	Miller County
—767 57	Lafayette County
—767 59	Columbia County
—767 6	**South central counties**
—767 61	Union County
—767 63	Bradley County
—767 64	Calhoun County
—767 66	Ouachita County
—767 67	Dallas County
—767 69	Cleveland County
—767 7	**Central counties**
—767 71	Grant County

*For a specific part of this jurisdiction, region, or feature, see the part and follow instructions under —4–9

—767 72	Saline County
—767 73	Pulaski County
	Class here Little Rock
—767 74	Faulkner County
—767 76	White County
—767 77	Prairie County
—767 78	Lonoke County
—767 79	Jefferson County
—767 8	Southeastern counties
	Class here *Mississippi River in Arkansas
—767 82	Lincoln and Drew Counties
—767 823	Lincoln County
—767 825	Drew County
—767 83	Ashley County
—767 84	Chicot County
—767 85	Desha County
—767 86	Arkansas County
—767 87	Monroe County
—767 88	Phillips County
—767 89	Lee County
—767 9	Northeastern counties
—767 91	Saint Francis County
—767 92	Woodruff County
—767 93	Cross County
—767 94	Crittenden County
—767 95	Mississippi County
—767 96	Poinsett County
—767 97	Jackson County
—767 98	Craighead County
—767 99	Greene and Clay Counties
—767 993	Greene County

*For a specific part of this jurisdiction, region, or feature, see the part and follow instructions under —4–9

—767 995	Clay County
—768	Tennessee
	Class here *Tennessee River and Valley
—768 1	Mississippi Valley counties
—768 12	Lake County
	Including *Reelfoot Lake
—768 13	Obion County
—768 15	Dyer County
—768 16	Lauderdale County
—768 17	Tipton County
—768 19	Shelby County
	Class here Memphis
—768 2	West Tennessee Plain counties
—768 21	Fayette County
—768 22	Haywood and Crockett Counties
—768 223	Haywood County
—768 225	Crockett County
—768 23	Gibson County
—768 24	Weakley County
—768 25	Carroll County
—768 26	Henderson and Chester Counties
—768 263	Henderson County
—768 265	Chester County
—768 27	Madison County
—768 28	Hardeman County
—768 29	McNairy County
—768 3	Western Tennessee River Valley counties
—768 31	Hardin County
—768 32	Decatur County
—768 33	Benton County
—768 34	Henry County

*For a specific part of this jurisdiction, region, or feature, see the part and follow instructions under —4–9

—768 35	Stewart County
—768 36	Houston County
—768 37	Humphreys County
—768 38	Perry County
—768 39	Wayne County
—768 4	**West Highland Rim counties**

Class here comprehensive works on Highland Rim counties

For east Highland Rim counties, see —7686

—768 42	Lawrence County
—768 43	Lewis and Hickman Counties
—768 432	Lewis County
—768 434	Hickman County

Class here *Duck River

—768 44	Dickson County
—768 45	Montgomery County
—768 46	Cheatham and Robertson Counties
—768 462	Cheatham County
—768 464	Robertson County
—768 47	Sumner County
—768 48	Trousdale and Macon Counties
—768 482	Trousdale County
—768 484	Macon County
—768 49	Clay County

Class here *Dale Hollow Lake

—768 5	**Central Basin counties**

Class here *Cumberland River

—768 51	Jackson County
—768 52	Smith County
—768 53	De Kalb and Cannon Counties
—768 532	De Kalb County

Class here *Center Hill Lake

---

*For a specific part of this jurisdiction, region, or feature, see the part and follow instructions under —4–9

—768 535	Cannon County
—768 54	Wilson County
—768 55	Davidson County
	Class here Nashville
—768 56	Williamson County
—768 57	Rutherford County
—768 58	Bedford and Marshall Counties
—768 583	Bedford County
—768 585	Marshall County
—768 59	Maury County
—768 6	**East Highland Rim counties**
—768 61	Giles County
—768 62	Lincoln and Moore Counties
—768 624	Lincoln County
—768 627	Moore County
—768 63	Franklin County
—768 64	Coffee County
—768 65	Warren and Van Buren Counties
—768 653	Warren County
—768 657	Van Buren County
—768 66	White County
—768 67	Putnam County
—768 68	Overton and Pickett Counties
—768 684	Overton County
—768 687	Pickett County
—768 69	Fentress County
—768 7	**Counties of *Cumberland Plateau**
—768 71	Scott County
—768 72	Campbell County
—768 73	Anderson County
	Class here *Clinch River

*For a specific part of this jurisdiction, region, or feature, see the part and follow instructions under —4–9

—768 74	Morgan County
—768 75	Cumberland County
—768 76	Bledsoe County
—768 77	Sequatchie County
	Class here *Sequatchie River
—768 78	Grundy County
—768 79	Marion County
—768 8	Southeastern counties
—768 82	Hamilton County
	Including *Lookout Mountain
	Class here Chattanooga; *Chickamauga Lake
—768 83	Rhea and Meigs Counties
—768 834	Rhea County
—768 836	Meigs County
—768 84	Roane County
—768 85	Knox County
	Including *Fort Loudoun Lake
	Class here Knoxville
—768 86	Loudon and McMinn Counties
—768 863	Loudon County
—768 865	McMinn County
—768 87	Bradley and Polk Counties
—768 873	Bradley County
—768 875	Polk County
—768 88	Monroe and Blount Counties
—768 883	Monroe County
—768 885	Blount County
—768 89	*Great Smoky Mountains area
	Class here *Great Smoky Mountains National Park
—768 893	Sevier County
—768 895	Cocke County
	Class here *French Broad River

*For a specific part of this jurisdiction, region, or feature, see the part and follow instructions under —4–9

—768 9	Northeastern counties
—768 91	Greene County
—768 92	Hamblen and Jefferson Counties
—768 923	Hamblen County
—768 924	Jefferson County
—768 93	Grainger and Union Counties
—768 932	Grainger County
—768 935	Union County
	Class here *Norris Lake
—768 94	Claiborne and Hancock Counties
—768 944	Claiborne County
	Class here *Cumberland Mountains in Tennessee
—768 946	Hancock County
—768 95	Hawkins County
—768 96	Sullivan County
—768 97	Washington County
—768 98	Unicoi and Carter Counties
—768 982	Unicoi County
—768 984	Carter County
—768 99	Johnson County
—769	Kentucky
—769 1	Southern mountain region counties
	Including *Cumberland Plateau in Kentucky
	Class here *Cumberland Mountains
—769 12	Bell and Knox Counties
—769 123	Bell County
—769 125	Knox County
—769 13	Whitley and McCreary Counties
—769 132	Whitley County
—769 135	McCreary County
—769 14	Laurel and Clay Counties

*For a specific part of this jurisdiction, region, or feature, see the part and follow instructions under —4–9

—769 143	Laurel County
—769 145	Clay County
—769 15	Leslie and Harlan Counties
—769 152	Leslie County
—769 154	Harlan County
—769 16	Letcher and Knott Counties
—769 163	Letcher County
—769 165	Knott County
—769 17	Perry and Owsley Counties
—769 173	Perry County
—769 176	Owsley County
—769 18	Jackson and Lee Counties
—769 183	Jackson County
—769 185	Lee County
—769 19	Breathitt County
—769 2	Northern mountain region counties
	Class here *Big Sandy River and *Tug Fork in Kentucky
—769 21	Wolfe and Magoffin Counties
—769 213	Wolfe County
—769 215	Magoffin County
—769 22	Floyd County
—769 23	Pike County
—769 24	Martin and Johnson Counties
—769 243	Martin County
—769 245	Johnson County
—769 25	Morgan and Elliott Counties
—769 253	Morgan County
—769 255	Elliott County
—769 26	Lawrence County
—769 27	Boyd County
—769 28	Carter County

*For a specific part of this jurisdiction, region, or feature, see the part and follow instructions under —4–9

—769 29	Greenup and Lewis Counties
—769 293	Greenup County
—769 295	Lewis County
—769 3	**Northern Bluegrass counties**
	Class here *Kentucky River
—769 32	Mason and Bracken Counties
—769 323	Mason County
—769 325	Bracken County
—769 33	Pendleton County
—769 34	Campbell County
—769 35	Kenton County
—769 36	Boone and Gallatin Counties
—769 363	Boone County
—769 365	Gallatin County
—769 37	Carroll and Trimble Counties
—769 373	Carroll County
—769 375	Trimble County
—769 38	Oldham and Henry Counties
—769 383	Oldham County
—769 385	Henry County
—769 39	Owen and Grant Counties
—769 393	Owen County
—769 395	Grant County
—769 4	**Southern Bluegrass counties**
—769 41	Harrison, Robertson, Nicholas Counties
—769 413	Harrison County
—769 415	Robertson County
—769 417	Nicholas County
—769 42	Bourbon and Scott Counties
—769 423	Bourbon County
—769 425	Scott County

*For a specific part of this jurisdiction, region, or feature, see the part and follow instructions under —4–9

—769 43	Franklin and Shelby Counties
—769 432	Franklin County
	Including Frankfort
—769 435	Shelby County
—769 44	Jefferson County
	Class here Louisville
—769 45	Bullitt and Spencer Counties
—769 453	Bullitt County
—769 455	Spencer County
—769 46	Anderson and Woodford Counties
—769 463	Anderson County
—769 465	Woodford County
—769 47	Fayette County
	Class here Lexington
—769 48	Jessamine and Mercer Counties
—769 483	Jessamine County
—769 485	Mercer County
—769 49	Washington and Nelson Counties
—769 493	Washington County
—769 495	Nelson County
—769 5	The Knobs counties
—769 51	Marion County
—769 52	Boyle and Garrard Counties
—769 523	Boyle County
—769 525	Garrard County
—769 53	Madison County
—769 54	Clark County
—769 55	Montgomery and Bath Counties
—769 553	Montgomery County
—769 555	Bath County
—769 56	Fleming County
—769 57	Rowan County

—769 58	Menifee and Powell Counties
—769 583	Menifee County
—769 585	Powell County
—769 59	Estill County
—769 6	Eastern Pennyroyal counties

Class here *Highland Rim in Kentucky, comprehensive works on Pennyroyal counties

For western Pennyroyal counties, see —7697

—769 62	Rockcastle and Lincoln Counties
—769 623	Rockcastle County
—769 625	Lincoln County
—769 63	Pulaski County

Class here *Lake Cumberland

—769 64	Wayne County
—769 65	Clinton and Russell Counties
—769 653	Clinton County
—769 655	Russell County
—769 66	Casey County
—769 67	Taylor and Adair Counties
—769 673	Taylor County
—769 675	Adair County
—769 68	Cumberland and Monroe Counties
—769 683	Cumberland County
—769 685	Monroe County
—769 69	Metcalfe and Green Counties
—769 693	Metcalfe County
—769 695	Green County
—769 7	Western Pennyroyal counties
—769 71	Larue and Hart Counties
—769 713	Larue County
—769 715	Hart County
—769 72	Barren County

*For a specific part of this jurisdiction, region, or feature, see the part and follow instructions under —4–9

—769 73	Allen and Simpson Counties
—769 732	Allen County
—769 735	Simpson County
—769 74	Warren County
—769 75	Edmonson and Butler Counties and environs
—769 752	Edmonson County
—769 754	*Mammoth Cave National Park
—769 755	Butler County
—769 76	Logan County
—769 77	Todd County
—769 78	Christian County
—769 79	Trigg County
	Class here *Land Between the Lakes; *Lake Barkley
—769 8	Western Basin counties
	Class here *Green River
—769 81	Lyon and Caldwell Counties
—769 813	Lyon County
—769 815	Caldwell County
—769 82	Hopkins and McLean Counties
—769 823	Hopkins County
—769 826	McLean County
—769 83	Muhlenberg and Ohio Counties
—769 832	Muhlenberg County
—769 835	Ohio County
—769 84	Grayson and Hardin Counties
—769 842	Grayson County
—769 845	Hardin County
—769 85	Meade and Breckinridge Counties
—769 852	Meade County
—769 854	Breckinridge County
—769 86	Hancock and Daviess Counties

*For a specific part of this jurisdiction, region, or feature, see the part and follow instructions under —4–9

—769 862	Hancock County
—769 864	Daviess County
	Class here Owensboro
—769 87	Henderson County
—769 88	Webster and Union Counties
—769 883	Webster County
—769 885	Union County
—769 89	Crittenden and Livingston Counties
—769 893	Crittenden County
—769 895	Livingston County
	Class here *Kentucky Lake
—769 9	Counties west of Tennessee River
—769 91	Marshall County
—769 92	Calloway County
—769 93	Graves County
—769 95	McCracken County
—769 96	Ballard County
—769 97	Carlisle County
—769 98	Hickman County
—769 99	Fulton County
—77	**North central United States** **Lake states**

Class here *Middle West; *Mississippi River and Valley, *Ohio River and Valley; *Great Lakes

SUMMARY

—771	**Ohio**
—772	**Indiana**
—773	**Illinois**
—774	**Michigan**
—775	**Wisconsin**
—776	**Minnesota**
—777	**Iowa**
—778	**Missouri**

*For a specific part of this jurisdiction, region, or feature, see the part and follow instructions under —4–9

>	**—771–776 Lake states**
	Class comprehensive works in —77
	For New York, see —747; for Pennsylvania, see —748
—771	**Ohio**
—771 1	**Northwestern counties**
	Class here *Maumee River
—771 11	Williams and Fulton Counties
—771 113	Williams County
—771 115	Fulton County
—771 12	Lucas County
	For Toledo, see —77113
—771 13	Toledo
—771 14	Defiance County
—771 15	Henry County
—771 16	Wood County
—771 17	Paulding County
—771 18	Putnam County
—771 19	Hancock County
—771 2	**North central counties**
	Class here *Lake Erie
—771 21	Ottawa and Sandusky Counties
—771 212	Ottawa County
—771 214	Sandusky County
	Class here *Sandusky Bay
—771 22	Erie County
—771 23	Lorain County
—771 24	Seneca County
—771 25	Huron County
—771 26	Wyandot County
—771 27	Crawford County

*For a specific part of this jurisdiction, region, or feature, see the part and follow instructions under —4–9

—771 28	Richland County
—771 29	Ashland County
—771 3	Northeastern counties
—771 31	Cuyahoga County
	Class here *Cuyahoga River
	For Cleveland, see —77132
—771 32	Cleveland
—771 33	Lake and Geauga Counties
—771 334	Lake County
—771 336	Geauga County
—771 34	Ashtabula County
—771 35	Medina County
—771 36	Summit County
	Class here Akron
—771 37	Portage County
—771 38	Trumbull County
—771 39	Mahoning County
	Class here Youngstown; *Mahoning River
—771 4	West central counties
—771 41	Van Wert and Mercer Counties
—771 413	Van Wert County
—771 415	Mercer County
	Class here *Grand Lake (Lake Saint Marys)
—771 42	Allen County
—771 43	Auglaize County
—771 44	Hardin County
—771 45	Shelby County
—771 46	Logan and Champaign Counties
—771 463	Logan County
—771 465	Champaign County
—771 47	Darke County

*For a specific part of this jurisdiction, region, or feature, see the part and follow instructions under —4–9

—771 48	Miami County
—771 49	Clark County
—771 5	**Central counties**
	Class here *Scioto River
—771 51	Marion and Morrow Counties
—771 514	Marion County
—771 516	Morrow County
—771 52	Knox County
—771 53	Union and Delaware Counties
—771 532	Union County
—771 535	Delaware County
—771 54	Licking County
—771 55	Madison County
—771 56	Franklin County
	For Columbus, see —77157
—771 57	Columbus
—771 58	Fairfield County
—771 59	Perry County
—771 6	**East central counties**
—771 61	Wayne County
—771 62	Stark County
—771 63	Columbiana County
—771 64	Holmes County
—771 65	Coshocton County
—771 66	Tuscarawas County
—771 67	Carroll County
—771 68	Harrison County
—771 69	Jefferson County
—771 7	**Southwestern counties**
	Class here *Miami River
—771 71	Preble County

*For a specific part of this jurisdiction, region, or feature, see the part and follow instructions under —4–9

—771 72	Montgomery County
	For Dayton, see —77173
—771 73	Dayton
—771 74	Greene County
—771 75	Butler County
—771 76	Warren and Clinton Counties
—771 763	Warren County
—771 765	Clinton County
—771 77	Hamilton County
	For Cincinnati, see —77178
—771 78	Cincinnati
—771 79	Clermont and Brown Counties
—771 794	Clermont County
—771 796	Brown County
—771 8	South central counties
—771 81	Fayette and Pickaway Counties
—771 813	Fayette County
—771 815	Pickaway County
—771 82	Ross County
—771 83	Hocking and Vinton Counties
—771 835	Hocking County
—771 837	Vinton County
—771 84	Highland and Pike Counties
—771 845	Highland County
—771 847	Pike County
—771 85	Jackson County
—771 86	Adams County
—771 87	Scioto County
—771 88	Lawrence County
—771 89	Gallia County
—771 9	Southeastern counties
—771 91	Muskingum County
	Class here *Muskingum River

*For a specific part of this jurisdiction, region, or feature, see the part and follow instructions under —4–9

—771 92	Guernsey County
—771 93	Belmont County
—771 94	Morgan County
—771 95	Noble County
—771 96	Monroe County
—771 97	Athens County
	Class here *Hocking River
—771 98	Washington County
—771 99	Meigs County
—772	**Indiana**
—772 1	Southeastern counties
—772 11	Dearborn County
—772 12	Ohio and Switzerland Counties
—772 123	Ohio County
—772 125	Switzerland County
—772 13	Jefferson County
—772 14	Ripley County
—772 15	Franklin County
—772 16	Decatur County
—772 17	Jennings County
—772 18	Scott and Clark Counties
—772 183	Scott County
—772 185	Clark County
—772 19	Floyd County
—772 2	South central counties
—772 21	Harrison County
—772 22	Washington County
—772 23	Jackson County
—772 24	Bartholomew County
—772 25	Brown and Monroe Counties
—772 253	Brown County

*For a specific part of this jurisdiction, region, or feature, see the part and follow instructions under —4–9

—772 255	Monroe County
—772 26	Lawrence County
—772 27	Orange County
—772 28	Crawford County
—772 29	Perry County
—772 3	Southwestern counties
	Class here *White River
—772 31	Spencer County
—772 32	Warrick County
—772 33	Vanderburgh County
—772 34	Posey County
—772 35	Gibson County
—772 36	Pike County
—772 37	Dubois County
—772 38	Martin and Daviess Counties
—772 382	Martin County
—772 385	Daviess County
—772 39	Knox County
—772 4	West central counties
	Class here *Wabash River
—772 41	Sullivan County
—772 42	Greene County
—772 43	Owen County
—772 44	Clay County
—772 45	Vigo County
—772 46	Vermillion and Parke Counties
—772 462	Vermillion County
—772 465	Parke County
—772 47	Fountain County
—772 48	Montgomery County
—772 49	Putnam County

*For a specific part of this jurisdiction, region, or feature, see the part and follow instructions under —4–9

—772 5	Central counties
—772 51	Morgan and Johnson Counties
—772 513	Morgan County
—772 515	Johnson County
—772 52	Marion County
	Class here Indianapolis
—772 53	Hendricks County
—772 54	Boone County
—772 55	Clinton and Tipton Counties
—772 553	Clinton County
—772 555	Tipton County
—772 56	Hamilton County
—772 57	Madison County
—772 58	Hancock County
—772 59	Shelby County
—772 6	East central counties
—772 61	Rush County
—772 62	Fayette and Union Counties
—772 623	Fayette County
—772 625	Union County
—772 63	Wayne County
—772 64	Henry County
—772 65	Delaware County
	Including Muncie
—772 66	Randolph County
—772 67	Jay County
—772 68	Blackford County
—772 69	Grant County
—772 7	Northeastern counties
—772 71	Huntington County
—772 72	Wells County
—772 73	Adams County

—772 74	Allen County
	Class here Fort Wayne
—772 75	Whitley County
—772 76	Noble County
—772 77	De Kalb County
—772 78	Steuben County
—772 79	Lagrange County
—772 8	North central counties
—772 81	Elkhart County
—772 82	Kosciusko County
—772 83	Wabash County
—772 84	Miami County
—772 85	Howard County
—772 86	Cass County
—772 87	Fulton County
—772 88	Marshall County
—772 89	Saint Joseph County
	Class here South Bend
—772 9	Northwestern counties
—772 91	La Porte County
—772 92	Starke and Pulaski Counties
—772 923	Starke County
—772 925	Pulaski County
—772 93	White County
—772 94	Carroll County
—772 95	Tippecanoe County
—772 96	Warren County
—772 97	Benton, Newton, Jasper Counties
—772 972	Benton County
—772 974	Newton County
—772 977	Jasper County
—772 98	Porter County

—772 99	Lake County
	Including Gary
—773	Illinois
—773 1	Cook County
—773 11	Chicago
—773 2	Northeastern counties
	Class here *Des Plaines River
	For Cook County, see —7731
—773 21	Lake County
—773 22	McHenry County
—773 23	Kane County
—773 24	Du Page County
—773 25	Will County
—773 26	Kendall and Grundy Counties
—773 263	Kendall County
—773 265	Grundy County
—773 27	La Salle County
—773 28	De Kalb County
—773 29	Boone County
—773 3	Northwestern counties
	Class here *Rock River
—773 31	Winnebago County
—773 32	Ogle County
—773 33	Stephenson County
—773 34	Jo Daviess and Carroll Counties
—773 343	Jo Daviess County
—773 345	Carroll County
—773 35	Whiteside County
—773 36	Lee County
—773 37	Bureau and Putnam Counties
—773 372	Bureau County

*For a specific part of this jurisdiction, region, or feature, see the part and follow instructions under —4–9

—773 375	Putnam County
—773 38	Henry County
—773 39	Rock Island and Mercer Counties
—773 393	Rock Island County

           Class comprehensive works on Davenport-Rock Island-Moline tri-city area in —77769

—773 395	Mercer County
—773 4	West central counties
—773 41	Henderson and Warren Counties
—773 413	Henderson County
—773 415	Warren County
—773 42	McDonough County
—773 43	Hancock County
—773 44	Adams County
—773 45	Pike and Scott Counties
—773 453	Pike County
—773 455	Scott County
—773 46	Morgan and Cass Counties
—773 463	Morgan County
—773 465	Cass County
—773 47	Brown and Schuyler Counties
—773 473	Brown County
—773 475	Schuyler County
—773 48	Fulton County
—773 49	Knox County
—773 5	Central counties

           Class here *Illinois River

—773 51	Stark and Marshall Counties
—773 513	Stark County
—773 515	Marshall County
—773 52	Peoria County
—773 53	Woodford County

*For a specific part of this jurisdiction, region, or feature, see the part and follow instructions under —4–9

—773 54	Tazewell County
—773 55	Mason and Menard Counties
	Class here *Sangamon River
—773 553	Mason County
—773 555	Menard County
—773 56	Sangamon County
	Including Springfield
—773 57	Logan County
—773 58	Macon and De Witt Counties
—773 582	Macon County
—773 585	De Witt County
—773 59	McLean County
—773 6	East central counties
—773 61	Livingston County
—773 62	Ford County
—773 63	Kankakee County
—773 64	Iroquois County
—773 65	Vermilion County
—773 66	Champaign County
—773 67	Piatt and Moultrie Counties
—773 673	Piatt County
—773 675	Moultrie County
—773 68	Douglas County
—773 69	Edgar County
—773 7	Southeastern counties
—773 71	Clark County
—773 72	Coles County
—773 73	Cumberland County
—773 74	Jasper County
—773 75	Crawford County
—773 76	Lawrence County

*For a specific part of this jurisdiction, region, or feature, see the part and follow instructions under —4–9

—773 77	Richland County
—773 78	Wabash County
—773 79	Counties south of Decatur
—773 791	Edwards County
—773 792	Wayne County
—773 793	Jefferson County
—773 794	Marion County
—773 795	Clay County
—773 796	Effingham County
—773 797	Fayettè County
—773 798	Shelby County
—773 8	Southwestern counties
—773 81	Christian County
—773 82	Montgomery County
—773 83	Macoupin County
—773 84	Greene County
—773 85	Calhoun and Jersey Counties
—773 853	Calhoun County
—773 855	Jersey County
—773 86	Madison County
—773 87	Bond and Clinton Counties
—773 873	Bond County
—773 875	Clinton County
—773 88	Washington County
—773 89	Saint Clair County
—773 9	Southern counties
—773 91	Monroe County
—773 92	Randolph County
—773 93	Perry County
—773 94	Franklin County
—773 95	Hamilton County
—773 96	White County

—773 97	Gallatin County
—773 98	Hardin County
—773 99	Southernmost counties
—773 991	Pope County
—773 992	Saline County
—773 993	Williamson County
—773 994	Jackson County
—773 995	Union County
—773 996	Johnson County
—773 997	Massac County
—773 998	Pulaski County
—773 999	Alexander County
—774	Michigan

Class here Lakes *Huron, *Michigan

>	—774 1–774 8 Lower Peninsula

Class comprehensive works in —774

—774 1	Southwestern counties of Lower Peninsula
—774 11	Berrien County
—774 12	Cass County
—774 13	Van Buren County
—774 14	Allegan County
—774 15	Ottawa County

Class here *Grand River

—774 16	Barry County
—774 17	Kalamazoo County
—774 19	Saint Joseph County
—774 2	South central counties of Lower Peninsula
—774 21	Branch County
—774 22	Calhoun County
—774 23	Eaton County

*For a specific part of this jurisdiction, region, or feature, see the part and follow instructions under —4–9

—774 24	Clinton County
—774 25	Shiawassee County
—774 26	Ingham County
	For Lansing and East Lansing, see —77427
—774 27	Lansing and East Lansing
—774 28	Jackson County
—774 29	Hillsdale County
—774 3	**Southeastern counties of Lower Peninsula**
—774 31	Lenawee County
—774 32	Monroe County
—774 33	Wayne County
	Including Dearborn; *Detroit River
	For Detroit, see —77434
—774 34	Detroit
—774 35	Washtenaw County
	Including Ann Arbor
—774 36	Livingston County
—774 37	Genesee County
	Including Flint
—774 38	Oakland County
—774 39	Macomb County
	Including *Lake Saint Clair
—774 4	**Southeast central counties of Lower Peninsula**
—774 41	Saint Clair County
	Including *Saint Clair River
—774 42	Lapeer County
—774 43	Sanilac County
—774 44	Huron County
—774 45	Tuscola County
—774 46	Saginaw County
—774 47	Bay County
	Class here *Saginaw River; *Saginaw Bay

*For a specific part of this jurisdiction, region, or feature, see the part and follow instructions under —4–9

—774 48	Midland County
—774 49	Gratiot County
—774 5	Southwest central counties of Lower Peninsula
—774 51	Isabella County
—774 52	Mecosta County
—774 53	Montcalm County
—774 54	Ionia County
—774 55	Kent County

For Grand Rapids, see —77456

—774 56	Grand Rapids
—774 57	Muskegon County
—774 58	Newaygo County
—774 59	Oceana County
—774 6	Northwest central counties of Lower Peninsula
—774 61	Mason County
—774 62	Manistee County
—774 63	Benzie and Leelanau Counties
—774 632	Benzie County
—774 635	Leelanau County
—774 64	Grand Traverse County

Class here *Grand Traverse Bay

—774 65	Kalkaska County
—774 66	Missaukee County
—774 67	Wexford County
—774 68	Lake County
—774 69	Osceola County
—774 7	Northeast central counties of Lower Peninsula

Class here *Au Sable River

—774 71	Clare County
—774 72	Gladwin County
—774 73	Arenac County

*For a specific part of this jurisdiction, region, or feature, see the part and follow instructions under —4–9

—774 74	Iosco County
—774 75	Ogemaw County
—774 76	Roscommon County
—774 77	Crawford County
—774 78	Oscoda County
—774 79	Alcona County
—774 8	**Northern counties of Lower Peninsula**
—774 81	Alpena County
—774 82	Presque Isle County
—774 83	Montmorency County
—774 84	Otsego County
—774 85	Antrim County
—774 86	Charlevoix County
—774 87	Cheboygan County
—774 88	Emmet County
—774 9	**Upper Peninsula**
	Class here *Lake Superior
—774 91	Chippewa County
	Including *Saint Marys River; *Whitefish Bay
—774 92	Mackinac and Luce Counties
—774 923	Mackinac County
	Including *Straits of Mackinac
—774 925	Luce County
—774 93	Alger and Schoolcraft Counties
—774 932	Alger County
—774 935	Schoolcraft County
—774 94	Delta County
—774 95	Menominee and Dickinson Counties
—774 953	Menominee County
—774 955	Dickinson County
—774 96	Marquette County

*For a specific part of this jurisdiction, region, or feature, see the part and follow instructions under —4–9

—774 97	Baraga and Iron Counties
—774 973	Baraga County
—774 975	Iron County
—774 98	Gogebic and Ontonagon Counties
—774 983	Gogebic County
—774 985	Ontonagon County
—774 99	Houghton and Keweenaw Counties
	Class here Keweenaw Peninsula
—774 993	Houghton County
—774 995	Keweenaw County
	For Isle Royale, see —774997
—774 997	Isle Royale (Isle Royale National Park)
—775	Wisconsin
	Class here *Wisconsin River
—775 1	Northwestern counties
	Class here *Saint Croix River
—775 11	Douglas County
	Including Superior
	Class comprehensive works on Duluth and Superior in —776771
—775 13	Bayfield County
—775 14	Burnett County
—775 15	Washburn County
—775 16	Sawyer County
—775 17	Polk County
—775 18	Barron County
—775 19	Rusk County
—775 2	North central counties
—775 21	Ashland County
—775 22	Iron County
—775 23	Vilas County
—775 24	Price County

*For a specific part of this jurisdiction, region, or feature, see the part and follow instructions under —4–9

—775 25	Oneida County
—775 26	Taylor County
—775 27	Lincoln County
—775 28	Clark County
—775 29	Marathon County
—775 3	Northeastern counties
—775 31	Forest County
—775 32	Florence County
—775 33	Marinette County
—775 35	Langlade and Menominee Counties
—775 354	Langlade County
—775 356	Menominee County
—775 36	Shawano County
—775 37	Oconto County
—775 38	Waupaca County
—775 39	Outagamie County
—775 4	West central counties
	Class here *Chippewa River
—775 41	Saint Croix County
—775 42	Pierce County
—775 43	Dunn County
—775 44	Chippewa County
—775 45	Eau Claire County
—775 47	Pepin County
—775 48	Buffalo County
—775 49	Trempealeau County
—775 5	Central counties
—775 51	Jackson County
—775 52	Wood County
—775 53	Portage County
—775 54	Monroe County

*For a specific part of this jurisdiction, region, or feature, see the part and follow instructions under —4–9

—775 55	Juneau County
—775 56	Adams County
—775 57	Waushara County
—775 58	Marquette County
—775 59	Green Lake County
—775 6	**East central counties**
	Class here *Fox River
—775 61	Brown County
—775 62	Kewaunee County
—775 63	Door County
	Class here *Green Bay
—775 64	Winnebago County
	Class here *Lake Winnebago
—775 66	Calumet County
—775 67	Manitowoc County
—775 68	Fond du Lac County
—775 69	Sheboygan County
—775 7	**Southwestern counties**
—775 71	La Crosse County
—775 73	Vernon County
—775 74	Crawford County
—775 75	Richland County
—775 76	Sauk County
—775 77	Grant County
—775 78	Iowa County
—775 79	Lafayette County
—775 8	**South central counties**
—775 81	Columbia County
—775 82	Dodge County
—775 83	Dane County
	Class here Madison

*For a specific part of this jurisdiction, region, or feature, see the part and follow instructions under —4–9

—775 85	Jefferson County
—775 86	Green County
—775 87	Rock County
—775 89	Walworth County
—775 9	Southeastern counties
—775 91	Washington County
—775 92	Ozaukee County
—775 93	Waukesha County
—775 94	Milwaukee County
	For Milwaukee, see —77595
—775 95	Milwaukee
—775 96	Racine County
—775 98	Kenosha County
—776	Minnesota
—776 1	Southeastern counties
—776 11	Houston County
—776 12	Winona County
—776 13	Wabasha County
—776 14	Goodhue County
—776 15	Dodge and Olmsted Counties
—776 153	Dodge County
—776 155	Olmsted County
—776 16	Fillmore County
—776 17	Mower County
—776 18	Freeborn County
—776 19	Steele and Waseca Counties
—776 193	Steele County
—776 195	Waseca County
—776 2	Southwestern counties
—776 21	Blue Earth County
—776 22	Faribault County
—776 23	Martin and Jackson Counties

—776 232	Martin County
—776 235	Jackson County
—776 24	Nobles County
—776 25	Rock County
—776 26	Pipestone County
—776 27	Murray County
—776 28	Cottonwood County
—776 29	Watonwan County
—776 3	Southwest central counties
	Class here *Minnesota River
—776 31	Brown County
—776 32	Nicollet County
—776 33	Sibley County
—776 34	Renville County
—776 35	Redwood County
—776 36	Lyon and Lincoln Counties
—776 363	Lyon County
—776 365	Lincoln County
—776 37	Yellow Medicine County
—776 38	Lac qui Parle County
—776 39	Chippewa County
—776 4	West central counties
—776 41	Swift County
—776 42	Stevens County
—776 43	Big Stone and Traverse Counties
—776 432	Big Stone County
—776 435	Traverse County
—776 44	Grant County
—776 45	Douglas County
—776 46	Pope County
—776 47	Stearns County

*For a specific part of this jurisdiction, region, or feature, see the part and follow instructions under —4–9

—776 48	Kandiyohi County
—776 49	Meeker County
—776 5	Southeast central counties
—776 51	Wright County
—776 52	McLeod County
—776 53	Carver County
—776 54	Scott County
—776 55	Le Sueur and Rice Counties
—776 553	Le Sueur County
—776 555	Rice County
—776 56	Dakota County
—776 57	Hennepin County
—776 579	Minneapolis

Class here Twin Cities

For Saint Paul, see —776581

—776 58	Ramsey County
—776 581	Saint Paul

Class comprehensive works on Twin Cities in —776579

—776 59	Washington County
—776 6	East central counties
—776 61	Chisago County
—776 62	Pine County
—776 63	Kanabec County
—776 64	Isanti County
—776 65	Anoka County
—776 66	Sherburne County
—776 67	Benton County
—776 68	Mille Lacs County
—776 69	Morrison County
—776 7	Northeastern counties
—776 71	Crow Wing County
—776 72	Aitkin County

—776 73	Carlton County
—776 75	Cook County
—776 76	Lake County
—776 77	Saint Louis County

Including Voyageurs National Park; *Mesabi Range

For Voyageurs National Park in Koochiching County, see —77679

—776 771	Duluth

Class here comprehensive works on Duluth and Superior, Wisconsin

For Superior, see —77511

—776 78	Itasca County
—776 79	Koochiching County

Including *Rainy River; *Rainy Lake

—776 8	North central counties
—776 81	Lake of the Woods County

Class here *Lake of the Woods

—776 82	Beltrami County
—776 83	Clearwater County
—776 84	Becker County
—776 85	Hubbard County
—776 86	Cass County
—776 87	Wadena County
—776 88	Todd County
—776 89	Otter Tail County
—776 9	Northwestern counties

Class here *Red River of the North in Minnesota

—776 91	Wilkin County
—776 92	Clay County
—776 93	Norman County
—776 94	Mahnomen County
—776 95	Polk County

*For a specific part of this jurisdiction, region, or feature, see the part and follow instructions under —4–9

—776 96	Red Lake and Pennington Counties
—776 963	Red Lake County
—776 965	Pennington County
—776 97	Marshall County
—776 98	Roseau County
—776 99	Kittson County
—777	Iowa
	Class here *Des Moines River
—777 1	Northwestern counties
	Including *Big Sioux River in Iowa
—777 11	Lyon and Osceola Counties
—777 114	Lyon County
—777 116	Osceola County
—777 12	Dickinson and Emmet Counties
—777 123	Dickinson County
—777 125	Emmet County
—777 13	Sioux County
—777 14	O'Brien County
—777 15	Clay and Palo Alto Counties
—777 153	Clay County
—777 155	Palo Alto County
—777 16	Plymouth County
—777 17	Cherokee County
—777 18	Buena Vista County
—777 19	Pocahontas County
—777 2	North central counties
—777 21	Kossuth County
—777 22	Winnebago County
—777 23	Worth and Mitchell Counties
—777 232	Worth County
—777 234	Mitchell County

*For a specific part of this jurisdiction, region, or feature, see the part and follow instructions under —4–9

—777 24	Hancock County
—777 25	Cerro Gordo County
—777 26	Floyd County
—777 27	Humboldt and Wright Counties
—777 272	Humboldt County
—777 274	Wright County
—777 28	Franklin County
—777 29	Butler County
—777 3	Northeastern counties
—777 31	Howard and Chickasaw Counties
—777 312	Howard County
—777 315	Chickasaw County
—777 32	Winneshiek County
—777 33	Allamakee County
—777 34	Bremer County
—777 35	Fayette County
—777 36	Clayton County
—777 37	Black Hawk County
—777 38	Buchanan and Delaware Counties
—777 382	Buchanan County
—777 385	Delaware County
—777 39	Dubuque County
—777 4	West central counties
—777 41	Woodbury County
	Including Sioux City
—777 42	Ida and Sac Counties
—777 422	Ida County
—777 424	Sac County
—777 43	Calhoun County
—777 44	Monona County
—777 45	Crawford County
—777 46	Carroll and Greene Counties

—777 465	Carroll County
—777 466	Greene County
—777 47	Harrison County
—777 48	Shelby and Audubon Counties
—777 484	Shelby County
—777 486	Audubon County
—777 49	Guthrie County
—777 5	Central counties
—777 51	Webster County
—777 52	Hamilton County
—777 53	Hardin and Grundy Counties
—777 535	Hardin County
—777 537	Grundy County
—777 54	Boone and Story Counties
—777 544	Boone County
—777 546	Story County
—777 55	Marshall County
—777 56	Tama County
—777 57	Dallas County
—777 58	Polk County
	Class here Des Moines
—777 59	Jasper and Poweshiek Counties
—777 594	Jasper County
—777 596	Poweshiek County
—777 6	East central counties
	Class here *Iowa River
—777 61	Benton County
—777 62	Linn County
—777 63	Jones County
—777 64	Jackson County
—777 65	Iowa and Johnson Counties

*For a specific part of this jurisdiction, region, or feature, see the part and follow instructions under —4–9

—777 653	Iowa County
—777 655	Johnson County
—777 66	Cedar County
—777 67	Clinton County
—777 68	Muscatine County
—777 69	Scott County

Class here Davenport-Rock Island-Moline tri-city area

For Rock Island County, Illinois, see —773393

—777 7	Southwestern counties
—777 71	Pottawattamie County
—777 72	Cass County
—777 73	Adair County
—777 74	Mills County
—777 75	Montgomery County
—777 76	Adams County
—777 77	Fremont County
—777 78	Page County
—777 79	Taylor County
—777 8	South central counties
—777 81	Madison County
—777 82	Warren County
—777 83	Marion County
—777 84	Mahaska County
—777 85	Union and Clarke Counties
—777 853	Union County
—777 856	Clarke County
—777 86	Lucas and Monroe Counties
—777 863	Lucas County
—777 865	Monroe County
—777 87	Ringgold and Decatur Counties
—777 873	Ringgold County
—777 875	Decatur County

—777 88	Wayne County
—777 89	Appanoose County
—777 9	Southeastern counties
—777 91	Keokuk County
—777 92	Washington and Louisa Counties
—777 923	Washington County
—777 926	Louisa County
—777 93	Wapello County
—777 94	Jefferson County
—777 95	Henry County
—777 96	Des Moines County
—777 97	Davis County
—777 98	Van Buren County
—777 99	Lee County
—778	Missouri
	Class here *Missouri River in Missouri
—778 1	Northwestern counties
—778 11	Atchison and Holt Counties
—778 113	Atchison County
—778 115	Holt County
—778 12	Nodaway and Andrew Counties
—778 124	Nodaway County
—778 126	Andrew County
—778 13	Buchanan and Platte Counties
—778 132	Buchanan County
—778 135	Platte County
—778 14	Worth and Gentry Counties
—778 143	Worth County
—778 145	Gentry County
—778 15	De Kalb and Clinton Counties
—778 153	De Kalb County

*For a specific part of this jurisdiction, region, or feature, see the part and follow instructions under —4–9

—778 155	Clinton County
—778 16	Clay County
—778 17	Harrison County
—778 18	Daviess and Caldwell Counties
—778 183	Daviess County
—778 185	Caldwell County
—778 19	Ray County
—778 2	North central counties
	Class here *Chariton River
—778 21	Mercer and Grundy Counties
—778 213	Mercer County
—778 215	Grundy County
—778 22	Livingston and Carroll Counties
—778 223	Livingston County
—778 225	Carroll County
—778 23	Putnam and Sullivan Counties
—778 232	Putnam County
—778 235	Sullivan County
—778 24	Linn County
—778 25	Chariton County
—778 26	Schuyler and Adair Counties
—778 262	Schuyler County
—778 264	Adair County
—778 27	Macon County
—778 28	Randolph and Howard Counties
—778 283	Randolph County
—778 285	Howard County
—778 29	Boone County
—778 3	Northeastern counties
—778 31	Scotland and Knox Counties
—778 312	Scotland County

*For a specific part of this jurisdiction, region, or feature, see the part and follow instructions under —4–9

—778 315	Knox County
—778 32	Shelby and Monroe Counties
—778 323	Shelby County
—778 325	Monroe County
—778 33	Audrain and Callaway Counties
—778 332	Audrain County
—778 335	Callaway County
—778 34	Clark and Lewis Counties
—778 343	Clark County
—778 345	Lewis County
—778 35	Marion and Ralls Counties
—778 353	Marion County
—778 355	Ralls County
—778 36	Pike County
—778 37	Lincoln County
—778 38	Montgomery and Warren Counties
—778 382	Montgomery County
—778 386	Warren County
—778 39	Saint Charles County
—778 4	West central counties
—778 41	Jackson County
—778 411	Kansas City

Class here Greater Kansas City

For Wyandotte County, Kansas, see —78139

—778 42	Cass County
—778 43	Bates County
—778 44	Vernon County
—778 45	Lafayette and Johnson Counties
—778 453	Lafayette County
—778 455	Johnson County
—778 46	Henry and Saint Clair Counties
—778 462	Henry County

—778 466	Saint Clair County
—778 47	Saline County
—778 48	Pettis County
—778 49	Benton and Hickory Counties
—778 493	Benton County
	Class here *Lake of the Ozarks
—778 496	Hickory County
—778 5	Central counties
—778 51	Cooper County
—778 52	Moniteau County
—778 53	Morgan County
—778 54	Camden County
—778 55	Cole County
	Including Jefferson City
—778 56	Miller County
—778 57	Pulaski County
—778 58	Osage County
—778 59	Maries and Phelps Counties
—778 592	Maries County
—778 594	Phelps County
—778 6	East central counties
—778 61	Gasconade County
—778 62	Crawford County
—778 63	Franklin County
—778 64	Washington County
—778 65	Saint Louis County
—778 66	Independent city of Saint Louis
—778 67	Jefferson County
—778 68	Saint Francois County
—778 69	Sainte Genevieve and Perry Counties
—778 692	Sainte Genevieve County

*For a specific part of this jurisdiction, region, or feature, see the part and follow instructions under —4–9

—778 694	Perry County
—778 7	Southwestern counties
—778 71	Barton County
—778 72	Jasper County
—778 73	Newton and McDonald Counties
—778 732	Newton County
—778 736	McDonald County
—778 74	Cedar and Dade Counties
—778 743	Cedar County
—778 745	Dade County
—778 75	Lawrence County
—778 76	Barry County
—778 77	Polk County
—778 78	Greene County
—778 79	Christian, Stone, Taney Counties
—778 792	Christian County
—778 794	Stone County
—778 797	Taney County
—778 8	South central counties
	Class here *Ozark Plateau in Missouri
—778 81	Dallas and Laclede Counties
—778 813	Dallas County
—778 815	Laclede County
—778 82	Webster and Wright Counties
—778 823	Webster County
—778 825	Wright County
—778 83	Douglas and Ozark Counties
—778 832	Douglas County
—778 835	Ozark County
—778 84	Texas County
—778 85	Howell County

*For a specific part of this jurisdiction, region, or feature, see the part and follow instructions under —4–9

—778 86	Dent County
—778 87	Shannon and Oregon Counties
—778 873	Shannon County
—778 875	Oregon County
—778 88	Iron and Reynolds Counties
—778 883	Iron County
—778 885	Reynolds County
—778 89	Carter and Ripley Counties
—778 892	Carter County
—778 894	Ripley County
—778 9	Southeastern counties
—778 91	Madison County
—778 92	Wayne County
—778 93	Butler County
—778 94	Bollinger County
—778 95	Stoddard County
—778 96	Cape Girardeau County
—778 97	Scott County
—778 98	Mississippi and New Madrid Counties
—778 983	Mississippi County
—778 985	New Madrid County
—778 99	Dunklin and Pemiscot Counties
—778 993	Dunklin County
—778 996	Pemiscot County
—78	**Western United States**

Class here the West; *Great Plains; *Rocky Mountains; *Missouri River

For Great Basin and Pacific Slope region, see —79

*For a specific part of this jurisdiction, region, or feature, see the part and follow instructions under —4–9

SUMMARY

—781   Kansas

Class here *Arkansas River in Kansas

—781 1   Northwestern counties

—781 11   Cheyenne and Sherman Counties

—781 112   Cheyenne County

—781 115   Sherman County

—781 12   Wallace and Rawlins Counties

—781 123   Wallace County

—781 125   Rawlins County

—781 13   Thomas and Logan Counties

—781 132   Thomas County

—781 135   Logan County

—781 14   Decatur and Sheridan Counties

—781 143   Decatur County

—781 145   Sheridan County

—781 15   Gove and Norton Counties

—781 152   Gove County

—781 155   Norton County

—781 16   Graham and Trego Counties

—781 163   Graham County

—781 165   Trego County

—781 17   Phillips County

—781 18   Rooks County

—781 19   Ellis County

*For a specific part of this jurisdiction, region, or feature, see the part and follow instructions under —4–9

—781 2	North central counties
	Class here *Republican, *Solomon Rivers
—781 21	Smith and Osborne Counties
—781 213	Smith County
—781 215	Osborne County
—781 22	Jewell County
—781 23	Mitchell County
—781 24	Republic County
—781 25	Cloud County
—781 26	Ottawa County
—781 27	Washington and Clay Counties
—781 273	Washington County
—781 275	Clay County
—781 28	Riley County
—781 29	Geary County
—781 3	Northeastern counties
	Class here *Kansas (Kaw) River
—781 31	Marshall County
—781 32	Pottawatomie County
—781 33	Nemaha and Jackson Counties
—781 332	Nemaha County
—781 335	Jackson County
—781 34	Brown County
—781 35	Doniphan County
—781 36	Atchison County
—781 37	Jefferson County
—781 38	Leavenworth County
—781 39	Wyandotte County
	Class here Kansas City
	Class comprehensive works on Greater Kansas City in —778411
—781 4	West central counties

*For a specific part of this jurisdiction, region, or feature, see the part and follow instructions under —4–9

—781 41	Greeley and Hamilton Counties
—781 413	Greeley County
—781 415	Hamilton County
—781 42	Wichita and Kearny Counties
—781 423	Wichita County
—781 425	Kearny County
—781 43	Scott County
—781 44	Finney County
—781 45	Lane County
—781 46	Ness County
—781 47	Hodgeman County
—781 48	Rush County
—781 49	Pawnee County
—781 5	Central counties
—781 51	Russell County
—781 52	Barton County
—781 53	Lincoln and Ellsworth Counties
—781 532	Lincoln County
—781 535	Ellsworth County
—781 54	Rice and Saline Counties
—781 543	Rice County
—781 545	Saline County
—781 55	McPherson County
—781 56	Dickinson County
—781 57	Marion County
—781 58	Morris County
—781 59	Chase County
—781 6	East central counties
—781 61	Wabaunsee County
—781 62	Lyon County
—781 63	Shawnee County
	Class here Topeka

—781 64	Osage and Coffey Counties
—781 643	Osage County
—781 645	Coffey County
—781 65	Douglas County
—781 66	Franklin County
—781 67	Anderson and Johnson Counties
—781 672	Anderson County
—781 675	Johnson County
—781 68	Miami County
—781 69	Linn County
—781 7	Southwestern counties
—781 71	Stanton and Morton Counties
—781 712	Stanton County
—781 715	Morton County
—781 72	Grant and Stevens Counties
—781 723	Grant County
—781 725	Stevens County
—781 73	Haskell and Seward Counties
—781 732	Haskell County
—781 735	Seward County
—781 74	Gray County
—781 75	Meade County
—781 76	Ford County
—781 77	Clark County
—781 78	Edwards and Kiowa Counties
—781 782	Edwards County
—781 785	Kiowa County
—781 79	Comanche County
—781 8	South central counties
—781 81	Stafford and Pratt Counties
—781 813	Stafford County
—781 815	Pratt County

—781 82	Barber County
—781 83	Reno County
—781 84	Kingman and Harper Counties
—781 843	Kingman County
—781 845	Harper County
—781 85	Harvey County
—781 86	Sedgwick County
	Class here Wichita
—781 87	Sumner County
—781 88	Butler County
—781 89	Cowley County
—781 9	Southeastern counties
—781 91	Greenwood, Elk, Chautauqua Counties
—781 913	Greenwood County
—781 915	Elk County
—781 918	Chautauqua County
—781 92	Woodson and Wilson Counties
—781 923	Woodson County
—781 925	Wilson County
—781 93	Montgomery County
—781 94	Allen County
—781 95	Neosho County
—781 96	Labette County
—781 97	Bourbon County
—781 98	Crawford County
—781 99	Cherokee County
—782	Nebraska
	Class here *Platte River
—782 2	Missouri River lowland counties
—782 22	Dixon, Dakota, Thurston Counties
—782 223	Dixon County

*For a specific part of this jurisdiction, region, or feature, see the part and follow instructions under —4–9

—782 224	Dakota County
—782 227	Thurston County
—782 23	Cuming and Dodge Counties
—782 232	Cuming County
—782 235	Dodge County
—782 24	Burt and Washington Counties
—782 243	Burt County
—782 245	Washington County
—782 25	Douglas and Sarpy Counties
—782 254	Douglas County
	Class here Omaha
—782 256	Sarpy County
—782 27	Cass and neighboring counties
—782 272	Cass County
—782 273	Otoe County
—782 276	Johnson County
—782 278	Nemaha County
—782 28	Richardson, Pawnee, Gage Counties
—782 282	Richardson County
—782 284	Pawnee County
—782 286	Gage County
—782 29	Lancaster and Saunders Counties
—782 293	Lancaster County
	Class here Lincoln
—782 296	Saunders County
—782 3	South central counties
—782 32	Butler, Seward, Saline Counties
—782 322	Butler County
—782 324	Seward County
—782 327	Saline County
—782 33	Jefferson and Thayer Counties
—782 332	Jefferson County

—782 335	Thayer County
—782 34	Fillmore and York Counties
—782 342	Fillmore County
—782 345	York County
—782 35	Polk, Hamilton, Clay Counties
—782 352	Polk County
—782 354	Hamilton County
—782 357	Clay County
—782 37	Nuckolls, Webster, Franklin Counties
	Class here *Republican River in Nebraska
—782 372	Nuckolls County
—782 374	Webster County
—782 377	Franklin County
—782 38	Harlan, Furnas, Gosper Counties
—782 382	Harlan County
—782 384	Furnas County
—782 387	Gosper County
—782 39	Phelps, Kearney, Adams Counties
—782 392	Phelps County
—782 394	Kearney County
—782 397	Adams County
—782 4	Central counties
—782 41	Hall County
—782 42	Merrick and Nance Counties
—782 423	Merrick County
—782 425	Nance County
—782 43	Howard County
—782 44	Sherman County
—782 45	Buffalo County
—782 46	Dawson County
—782 47	Custer County

*For a specific part of this jurisdiction, region, or feature, see the part and follow instructions under —4–9

—782 48	Valley County
—782 49	Greeley County
—782 5	Northeast central counties
—782 51	Boone County
—782 52	Platte County
—782 53	Colfax and Stanton Counties
—782 532	Colfax County
—782 535	Stanton County
—782 54	Madison County
—782 55	Antelope County
—782 56	Pierce County
—782 57	Wayne County
—782 58	Cedar County
—782 59	Knox County
—782 7	North central counties
	Class here *Niobrara River
—782 72	Boyd and Keya Paha Counties
—782 723	Boyd County
—782 725	Keya Paha County
—782 73	Cherry and Brown Counties
—782 732	Cherry County
—782 736	Brown County
—782 74	Rock and Holt Counties
—782 743	Rock County
—782 745	Holt County
—782 76	Wheeler, Garfield, Loup Counties
—782 762	Wheeler County
—782 764	Garfield County
—782 767	Loup County
—782 77	Blaine, Thomas, Hooker Counties
—782 772	Blaine County

*For a specific part of this jurisdiction, region, or feature, see the part and follow instructions under —4–9

—782 774	Thomas County
—782 777	Hooker County
—782 78	Grant and Arthur Counties
—782 783	Grant County
—782 785	Arthur County
—782 79	McPherson and Logan Counties
—782 793	McPherson County
—782 795	Logan County
—782 8	Southwestern counties
—782 82	Lincoln County
—782 83	Hayes and Frontier Counties
—782 832	Hayes County
—782 835	Frontier County
—782 84	Red Willow and Hitchcock Counties
—782 843	Red Willow County
—782 845	Hitchcock County
—782 86	Dundy County
—782 87	Chase County
—782 88	Perkins County
—782 89	Keith County
—782 9	Northwestern counties (Panhandle)
—782 91	Deuel and Garden Counties
—782 913	Deuel County
—782 915	Garden County
—782 92	Sheridan County
—782 93	Dawes County
—782 94	Box Butte County
—782 95	Morrill County
—782 96	Cheyenne County
—782 97	Kimball and Banner Counties
—782 973	Kimball County
—782 975	Banner County

—782 98	Scotts Bluff County
—782 99	Sioux County
—783	South Dakota
—783 1	Northeastern counties
—783 12	Roberts County
—783 13	Marshall County
—783 14	Day and Brown Counties
—783 142	Day County
—783 144	Brown County
—783 15	Edmunds County
—783 16	McPherson County
—783 17	Campbell County
—783 18	Walworth County
—783 19	Potter County
—783 2	East central counties
—783 21	Faulk and Spink Counties
—783 213	Faulk County
—783 217	Spink County
—783 22	Clark County
—783 23	Codington County
—783 24	Grant County
—783 25	Deuel County
—783 26	Hamlin County
—783 27	Brookings, Kingsbury, Beadle Counties
—783 272	Brookings County
—783 273	Kingsbury County
—783 274	Beadle County
—783 28	Hand, Hyde, Sully Counties
—783 282	Hand County
—783 283	Hyde County
—783 284	Sully County
—783 29	Hughes County
	Including Pierre

—783 3	Southeastern counties
	Class here *Missouri River in South Dakota, *James River
—783 31	Buffalo County
—783 32	Jerauld County
—783 33	Sanborn County
—783 34	Miner County
—783 35	Lake County
—783 36	Moody County
—783 37	Minnehaha and neighboring counties
—783 371	Minnehaha County
	Including Sioux Falls
—783 372	McCook County
—783 373	Hanson County
—783 374	Davison County
—783 375	Aurora County
—783 38	Brule and neighboring counties
	Class here *Lake Francis Case
—783 381	Brule County
—783 382	Charles Mix County
—783 383	Douglas County
—783 384	Hutchinson County
—783 385	Turner County
—783 39	Lincoln and neighboring counties
	Class here *Big Sioux River
—783 391	Lincoln County
—783 392	Union County
—783 393	Clay County
—783 394	Yankton County
—783 395	Bon Homme County
—783 4	Northwestern counties
—783 42	Harding County

*For a specific part of this jurisdiction, region, or feature, see the part and follow instructions under —4–9

—783 43	Butte County
—783 44	Meade County
—783 45	Perkins County
—783 5	Central counties
	Class here *Lake Oahe
—783 52	Corson County
—783 53	Ziebach County
—783 54	Dewey County
—783 55	Stanley County
—783 56	Haakon County
—783 57	Jackson and Jones Counties
—783 572	Jackson County
—783 577	Jones County
—783 58	Lyman County
—783 59	Gregory County
—783 6	South central counties
—783 61	Tripp County
—783 62	Todd County
—783 63	Mellette County
—783 64	Washabaugh County
—783 65	Bennett County
—783 66	Shannon County
—783 9	Southwestern counties
	Class here *Black Hills
—783 91	Lawrence County
—783 93	Pennington County
	Including Badlands National Park
	For Badlands National Park in Jackson County, see —783572; for Badlands National Park in Shannon County, see —78366
—783 95	Custer County
	Including Wind Cave National Park
—783 97	Fall River County

*For a specific part of this jurisdiction, region, or feature, see the part and follow instructions under —4–9

—784	North Dakota
—784 1	Red River Valley counties
	Class here *Red River of the North
—784 12	Richland County
—784 13	Cass County
	Including Fargo
—784 14	Traill County
—784 16	Grand Forks County
—784 18	Walsh County
—784 19	Pembina County
—784 3	Sheyenne River Valley and adjacent counties
	Class here *Sheyenne River
—784 31	Sargent and Ransom Counties
—784 314	Sargent County
—784 315	Ransom County
—784 32	Barnes County
—784 33	Steele County
—784 34	Griggs County
—784 35	Nelson County
—784 36	Ramsey County
—784 37	Cavalier County
—784 38	Towner County
—784 39	Benson County
—784 5	James River Valley and adjacent counties
	Class here *James River in North Dakota
—784 51	Eddy and Foster Counties
—784 512	Eddy County
—784 516	Foster County
—784 52	Stutsman County
—784 53	La Moure County
—784 54	Dickey County

*For a specific part of this jurisdiction, region, or feature, see the part and follow instructions under —4–9

—784 55	McIntosh County
—784 56	Logan County
—784 57	Kidder County
—784 58	Wells County
—784 59	Pierce and Rolette Counties
—784 591	Pierce County
—784 592	Rolette County
—784 6	**Souris River Valley counties**
	Class here *Souris River
—784 61	Bottineau County
—784 62	McHenry County
—784 63	Ward County
—784 64	Renville County
—784 7	**Counties north and east of Missouri River**
	Class here *Missouri River in North Dakota
—784 71	Divide County
—784 72	Burke County
—784 73	Williams County
—784 74	Mountrail County
—784 75	McLean County
	Class here *Lake Sakakawea (Garrison Reservoir)
—784 76	Sheridan County
—784 77	Burleigh County
	Including Bismarck
—784 78	Emmons County
—784 8	**Counties south and west of Missouri River**
	For Badlands counties, see —7849
—784 81	McKenzie County
—784 82	Dunn County
—784 83	Mercer County
—784 84	Oliver and Stark Counties

*For a specific part of this jurisdiction, region, or feature, see the part and follow instructions under —4–9

—784 843	Oliver County
—784 844	Stark County
—784 85	Morton County
—784 86	Hettinger County
—784 87	Grant County
—784 88	Sioux County
—784 89	Adams County
—784 9	Badlands counties
—784 92	Bowman County
—784 93	Slope County
—784 94	Billings County
—784 95	Golden Valley County

\>   —786–789   Rocky Mountains states

Class comprehensive works in —78

For Idaho, see —796

—786	Montana

Class here *Missouri River in Montana

—786 1	North central counties

Class here *Great Plains in Montana; *Milk River

—786 12	Toole County
—786 13	Liberty County
—786 14	Hill County
—786 15	Blaine County
—786 16	Phillips County
—786 17	Valley County

Class here *Fort Peck Lake

—786 2	Northeastern and central plains counties
—786 21	Daniels and Sheridan Counties
—786 213	Daniels County
—786 218	Sheridan County

*For a specific part of this jurisdiction, region, or feature, see the part and follow instructions under —4–9

—786 22	Roosevelt County
—786 23	Richland County
—786 24	Dawson County
—786 25	Prairie County
—786 26	McCone County
—786 27	Garfield County
—786 28	Petroleum County
—786 29	Fergus and Chouteau Counties
—786 292	Fergus County
—786 293	Chouteau County

—786 3   **Southeastern counties**

Class here *Yellowstone River

—786 31	Golden Valley, Musselshell, Treasure Counties
—786 311	Golden Valley County
—786 312	Musselshell County
—786 313	Treasure County
—786 32	Rosebud County
—786 33	Custer County
—786 34	Wibaux County
—786 35	Fallon County
—786 36	Carter County
—786 37	Powder River County
—786 38	Big Horn County
—786 39	Yellowstone County

—786 5   **Northwest central counties**

Class here *Rocky Mountains in Montana

—786 52   Glacier County

Including *Glacier National Park, *Waterton-Glacier International Peace Park

—786 53	Pondera County
—786 55	Teton County

—786 6   **Southwestern and central mountain counties**

*For a specific part of this jurisdiction, region, or feature, see the part and follow instructions under —4–9

—786 61	Cascade, Meagher, Lewis and Clark Counties
—786 611	Cascade County
—786 612	Meagher County
—786 615	Lewis and Clark County
	Including Helena
—786 62	Judith Basin County
—786 63	Wheatland County
—786 64	Sweet Grass County
—786 65	Stillwater and Carbon Counties
—786 651	Stillwater County
—786 652	Carbon County
—786 66	Park and neighboring counties
—786 661	Park County
—786 662	Gallatin County
—786 663	Madison County
—786 664	Broadwater County
—786 67	Jefferson County
—786 68	Silver Bow County
	Including Butte
—786 69	Beaverhead County
—786 8	Northwestern counties
	Class here *Bitterroot Range
—786 81	Lincoln County
—786 82	Flathead County
—786 83	Lake and Sanders Counties
—786 832	Lake County
	Class here *Flathead Lake
—786 833	Sanders County
—786 84	Mineral County
—786 85	Missoula County
—786 86	Powell County

*For a specific part of this jurisdiction, region, or feature, see the part and follow instructions under —4–9

—786 87	Deer Lodge County
—786 88	Granite County
—786 89	Ravalli County
—787	Wyoming
—787 1	Eastern counties
	Class here *Great Plains in Wyoming
—787 12	Campbell County
—787 13	Crook County
—787 14	Weston County
—787 15	Niobrara County
—787 16	Converse County
	Class here *North Platte River
—787 17	Platte County
—787 18	Goshen County
—787 19	Laramie County
	Including Cheyenne
—787 2	*Rocky Mountains in Wyoming
—787 3	Counties of *Big Horn Mountains
—787 32	Sheridan County
—787 33	Big Horn County
—787 34	Washakie County
—787 35	Johnson County
—787 4	Counties of *Absaroka Range
—787 42	Park County
—787 43	Hot Springs County
	Including *Owl Creek Mountains
—787 5	Yellowstone National Park and Teton County
—787 52	*Yellowstone National Park
—787 55	Teton County
	Including Grand Teton National Park; *Teton Range
	Class here *Snake River in Wyoming

---

*For a specific part of this jurisdiction, region, or feature, see the part and follow instructions under —4–9

—787 6	Counties of *Wind River Range
—787 63	Fremont County
—787 65	Sublette County
—787 8	Southwestern counties
—787 82	Lincoln County
—787 84	Uinta County
—787 85	Sweetwater County
	Including *Green River in Wyoming
—787 86	Carbon County
	Class here *Medicine Bow Range
—787 9	Counties of *Laramie Mountains
—787 93	Natrona County
—787 95	Albany County
—788	Colorado
	Class here *Rocky Mountains in Colorado
—788 1	Northern counties of *Colorado Plateau
—788 12	Moffat County
	Class here Dinosaur National Monument
	For Dinosaur National Monument in Uintah County, Utah, see —79221
—788 14	Routt County
—788 15	Rio Blanco County
—788 16	Garfield County
—788 17	Mesa County
	Class here *Colorado River in Colorado
—788 18	Delta County
—788 19	Montrose County
—788 2	Southern counties of Colorado Plateau
—788 22	Ouray County
—788 23	San Miguel County
—788 25	San Juan County

*For a specific part of this jurisdiction, region, or feature, see the part and follow instructions under —4–9

—788 26	Dolores County
—788 27	Montezuma County
	Including Mesa Verde National Park
—788 29	La Plata County
—788 3	Southern counties of Rocky Mountains
	Class here *San Juan Mountains; *San Luis Valley; *Rio Grande in Colorado
—788 32	Archuleta County
—788 33	Conejos County
—788 35	Costilla County
—788 36	Alamosa County
—788 37	Rio Grande County
—788 38	Mineral County
—788 39	Hinsdale County
—788 4	West central counties of Rocky Mountains
—788 41	Gunnison County
—788 43	Pitkin County
—788 44	Eagle County
—788 45	Summit County
—788 46	Lake County
—788 47	Chaffee County
—788 49	Saguache County
	Including Great Sand Dunes National Monument; *Sangre de Cristo Mountains
	For Great Sand Dunes National Monument in Alamosa County, see —78836
—788 5	East central counties of Rocky Mountains
—788 51	Huerfano County
—788 52	Custer County
—788 53	Fremont County
—788 55	Pueblo County
—788 56	El Paso County
	Class here Colorado Springs

*For a specific part of this jurisdiction, region, or feature, see the part and follow instructions under —4–9

—788 58	Teller County
—788 59	Park County
—788 6	**Northern counties of Rocky Mountains**
	Class here *Front Range
—788 61	Clear Creek County
—788 62	Gilpin County
—788 63	Boulder County
—788 65	Grand County
—788 66	Jackson County
	Class here *Park Range
—788 68	Larimer County
—788 69	*Rocky Mountain National Park
—788 7	**Northern counties of Great Plains**
	Class here *Great Plains in Colorado; *South Platte River
—788 72	Weld County
—788 74	Morgan County
—788 75	Logan County
—788 76	Sedgwick County
—788 77	Phillips County
—788 78	Yuma County
—788 79	Washington County
—788 8	**Central counties of Great Plains**
—788 81	Adams County
—788 82	Arapahoe County
—788 83	Denver County (Denver)
—788 84	Jefferson County
—788 86	Douglas County
—788 87	Elbert County
—788 89	Lincoln County
—788 9	**Southern counties of Great Plains**
	Class here *Arkansas River in Colorado

*For a specific part of this jurisdiction, region, or feature, see the part and follow instructions under —4–9

—788 91	Kit Carson County
—788 92	Cheyenne County
—788 93	Kiowa County
—788 94	Crowley County
—788 95	Otero County
—788 96	Las Animas County
—788 97	Bent County
—788 98	Prowers County
—788 99	Baca County
—789	New Mexico
—789 2	Northeastern counties
	Class here *Great Plains in New Mexico
—789 22	Colfax County
—789 23	Union County
—789 24	Harding County
—789 25	Guadalupe County
—789 26	Quay County
—789 27	Curry County
—789 3	Roosevelt and Lea Counties
	Class here *Llano Estacado in New Mexico
—789 32	Roosevelt County
—789 33	Lea County
—789 4	Pecos Valley counties
	Class here *Pecos River in New Mexico
—789 42	Eddy County
	Including Carlsbad Caverns National Park
—789 43	Chaves County
—789 44	De Baca County
—789 5	Counties of *Rocky Mountains
—789 52	Rio Arriba County
—789 53	Taos County

*For a specific part of this jurisdiction, region, or feature, see the part and follow instructions under —4–9

—789 54	Mora County
—789 55	San Miguel County
—789 56	Santa Fe County
	Class here Santa Fe
—789 57	Sandoval County
—789 58	Los Alamos County
—789 6	**Basin and Range region counties**
	Class here *Rio Grande in New Mexico
—789 61	Bernalillo County
	Class here Albuquerque
—789 62	Socorro County
	Including *Elephant Butte Reservoir
—789 63	Torrance County
—789 64	Lincoln County
—789 65	Otero County
	Including White Sands National Monument; *Sacramento Mountains
	For White Sands National Monument in Doña Ana County, see —78966
—789 66	Doña Ana County
—789 67	Sierra County
	Class here *San Andres Mountains
—789 68	Luna County
—789 69	Grant and Hidalgo Counties
—789 692	Grant County
—789 693	Hidalgo County
	Class here *Peloncillo Mountains
—789 8	**Northwestern counties**
—789 82	San Juan County
—789 83	McKinley County
—789 9	**West central counties**
—789 91	Cibola County
—789 92	Valencia County

*For a specific part of this jurisdiction, region, or feature, see the part and follow instructions under —4–9

—789 93	Catron County

—79   **Great Basin and Pacific Slope region of United States**   **Pacific Coast states**

Class here new Southwest

SUMMARY

—791	Arizona
—792	Utah
—793	Nevada
—794	California
—795	Oregon
—796	Idaho
—797	Washington
—798	Alaska

—791	Arizona

—791 3	Colorado Plateau region

Class here *Colorado River

—791 32	*Grand Canyon National Park

—791 33	Coconino County

Class here *Painted Desert; *Little Colorado River

—791 35	Navajo County

—791 37	Apache County

Including Petrified Forest National Park

For Petrified Forest National Park in Navajo County, see —79135

—791 5	Mountain region
—791 51	Greenlee County
—791 53	Cochise County
—791 54	Graham County
—791 55	Gila County
—791 57	Yavapai County
—791 59	Mohave County

—791 7	Plains region

Class here *Gila River

—791 71	Yuma County

---

*For a specific part of this jurisdiction, region, or feature, see the part and follow instructions under —4–9

—791 72	La Paz County
—791 73	Maricopa County
	Class here Phoenix
—791 75	Pinal County
—791 77	Pima County
—791 776	Tucson
—791 79	Santa Cruz County
—792	Utah
—792 1	Wyoming Basin region
—792 12	Cache County
—792 13	Rich County
—792 14	Summit County
	Including *Uinta Mountains
—792 15	Daggett County
—792 2	Rocky Mountains region
	Class here *Wasatch Range
—792 21	Uintah County
—792 22	Duchesne County
—792 23	Wasatch County
—792 24	Utah County
—792 25	Salt Lake County
—792 258	Salt Lake City
—792 26	Morgan County
—792 27	Davis County
—792 28	Weber County
—792 4	Great Basin region
—792 42	Box Elder County
	Class here *Great Salt Lake
—792 43	Tooele County
	Class here *Great Salt Lake Desert
—792 44	Juab County

*For a specific part of this jurisdiction, region, or feature, see the part and follow instructions under —4–9

—792 45	Millard County
—792 46	Beaver County
—792 47	Iron County
—792 48	Washington County

Class here Zion National Park

For Zion National Park in Iron County, see —79247; for Zion National Park in Kane County, see —79251

—792 5	Colorado Plateau region

Class here *Colorado River in Utah, *Green River

—792 51	Kane County
—792 52	Garfield County

Including Bryce Canyon National Park

For Bryce Canyon National Park in Kane County, see —79251

—792 53	Piute County
—792 54	Wayne County

Including *Capitol Reef National Park

—792 55	Sevier County
—792 56	Sanpete and Carbon Counties
—792 563	Sanpete County
—792 566	Carbon County
—792 57	Emery County
—792 58	Grand County

Including Arches National Park

—792 59	San Juan County

Including Canyonlands National Park; *Glen Canyon National Recreation Area; *San Juan River; *Lake Powell

Class here *Four Corners Region

For Canyonlands National Park in Wayne County, see —79254

—793	Nevada
—793 1	Eastern region
—793 12	*Lake Mead National Recreation Area
—793 13	Clark County

*For a specific part of this jurisdiction, region, or feature, see the part and follow instructions under —4–9

—793 135	Las Vegas
—793 14	Lincoln County
—793 15	White Pine County
	Including Great Basin National Park
—793 16	Elko County
	Class here *Humboldt River
—793 3	Central region
—793 32	Eureka County
—793 33	Lander County
—793 34	Nye County
—793 35	Esmeralda County
—793 5	Western region
—793 51	Mineral County
—793 52	Churchill County
—793 53	Pershing County
—793 54	Humboldt County
	Including *Black Rock Desert
—793 55	Washoe County
	Including Reno
—793 56	Storey County
	Including Virginia City
—793 57	Carson City
	Including *Lake Tahoe in Nevada
—793 58	Lyon County
—793 59	Douglas County
—794	California
—794 1	Northwestern counties
	Class here *Coast Ranges in California
—794 11	Del Norte County
—794 12	Humboldt County
	Including Redwood National Park
	For Redwood National Park in Del Norte County, see —79411

*For a specific part of this jurisdiction, region, or feature, see the part and follow instructions under —4–9

—794 14	Trinity County
—794 15	Mendocino County
—794 17	Lake County
—794 18	Sonoma County
—794 19	Napa County
—794 2	Northeastern counties

Class here *Cascade Range in California

—794 21	Siskiyou County

Including Lava Beds National Monument

Class here *Klamath Mountains in California

For Lava Beds National Monument in Modoc County, see —79423

—794 23	Modoc County
—794 24	Shasta County

Including *Lassen Volcanic National Park

—794 26	Lassen County
—794 27	Tehama County
—794 29	Plumas County
—794 3	North central counties
—794 31	Glenn County
—794 32	Butte County
—794 33	Colusa County
—794 34	Sutter County
—794 35	Yuba County
—794 36	Sierra County
—794 37	Nevada County
—794 38	Placer County

Including *Lake Tahoe

—794 4	East central counties

Class here *Sierra Nevada

—794 41	El Dorado County
—794 42	Amador County

*For a specific part of this jurisdiction, region, or feature, see the part and follow instructions under —4–9

—794 43	Alpine County
—794 44	Calaveras County
—794 45	Tuolumne County
—794 46	Mariposa County
—794 47	*Yosemite National Park
—794 48	Mono County
—794 5	**Central counties**

Class here *Central Valley (Great Valley); *Sacramento River

—794 51	Yolo County
—794 52	Solano County
—794 53	Sacramento County

For Sacramento, see —79454

—794 54	Sacramento
—794 55	San Joaquin County
—794 57	Stanislaus County
—794 58	Merced County
—794 6	**West central counties**

Class here *San Francisco Bay Area

See also —16432 for San Francisco Bay

—794 61	San Francisco County (San Francisco)
—794 62	Marin County
—794 63	Contra Costa County
—794 65	Alameda County

For Oakland, see —79466; for Berkeley, see —79467

—794 66	Oakland
—794 67	Berkeley
—794 69	San Mateo County
—794 7	**Southern Coast Range counties**
—794 71	Santa Cruz County
—794 73	Santa Clara County

For San Jose, see —79474

---

*For a specific part of this jurisdiction, region, or feature, see the part and follow instructions under —4–9

—794 74	San Jose
—794 75	San Benito County
—794 76	Monterey County

        Class here *Salinas River

           See also —16432 for Monterey Bay

—794 78	San Luis Obispo County

        Class here *Santa Lucia Range

—794 8	**South central counties**

        Class here *San Joaquin River

—794 81	Madera County
—794 82	Fresno County

        Including Kings Canyon National Park

           For Fresno, see —79483; for Kings Canyon National Park in Tulare County, see —79486

—794 83	Fresno
—794 85	Kings County
—794 86	Tulare County

        Including Sequoia National Park; *Mount Whitney

—794 87	Inyo County

        Class here *Death Valley National Park

—794 88	Kern County
—794 9	**Southern counties (Southern California)**
—794 91	Santa Barbara County

        Including Channel Islands National Park; *Santa Barbara Islands

           For Anacapa Island, see —79492

—794 92	Ventura County
—794 93	Los Angeles County

        Including Pasadena; *San Gabriel Mountains

           For Los Angeles, see —79494

—794 94	Los Angeles

*For a specific part of this jurisdiction, region, or feature, see the part and follow instructions under —4–9

—794 95	San Bernardino County
	Including *San Bernardino Mountains
	Class here *Mojave Desert
—794 96	Orange County
	Including *Santa Ana Mountains
—794 97	Riverside County
	Including Joshua Tree National Park

> *For Joshua Tree National Park in San Bernardino County, see —79495*

—794 98	San Diego County
—794 985	San Diego
—794 99	Imperial County
	Including *Salton Sea
	Class here *Imperial Valley; *Colorado Desert
—795	Oregon

Class here Pacific Northwest; *Cascade and *Coast Ranges

> *For British Columbia, see —711; for Idaho, see —796; for Washington, see —797*

—795 2	Southwestern counties
	Class here *Klamath Mountains
—795 21	Curry County
	Class here *Rogue River
—795 23	Coos County
—795 25	Josephine County
—795 27	Jackson County
—795 29	Douglas County
	Class here Umpqua River
—795 3	West central counties
	Class here *Willamette River
—795 31	Lane County
—795 33	Lincoln County
—795 34	Benton County

*For a specific part of this jurisdiction, region, or feature, see the part and follow instructions under —4–9

—795 35	Linn County
—795 37	Marion County
	Including Salem
—795 38	Polk County
—795 39	Yamhill County
—795 4	Northwestern counties
	Class here *Columbia River in Oregon
—795 41	Clackamas County
—795 43	Washington County
—795 44	Tillamook County
—795 46	Clatsop County
—795 47	Columbia County
—795 49	Multnomah County
	Class here Portland
—795 6	North central counties
—795 61	Hood River County
	Including *Mount Hood
—795 62	Wasco County
	Class here *Deschutes River
—795 64	Sherman County
—795 65	Gilliam County
—795 67	Morrow County
—795 69	Umatilla County
—795 7	Northeastern counties
	Class here *Blue Mountains; *Snake River in Oregon
—795 71	Union County
—795 73	Wallowa County
	Including *Wallowa Mountains
—795 75	Baker County
—795 78	Grant County
—795 8	Central counties

*For a specific part of this jurisdiction, region, or feature, see the part and follow instructions under —4–9

—795 81	Wheeler County
—795 83	Crook County
—795 85	Jefferson County
—795 87	Deschutes County
—795 9	Southeastern counties
—795 91	Klamath County
—795 915	Crater Lake National Park
—795 93	Lake County
—795 95	Harney County
—795 97	Malheur County
—796	Idaho
—796 1	*Southern Idaho
	Class here *Snake River
—796 2	Southwestern counties
—796 21	Owyhee County
—796 23	Canyon County
—796 24	Payette County
—796 25	Washington County
—796 26	Adams County
—796 27	Gem County
—796 28	Ada County
	Including Boise
—796 29	Elmore County
	Including *Sawtooth Range
	Class comprehensive works on Sawtooth Mountains in —79672
—796 3	South central counties
—796 31	Camas County
—796 32	Blaine County
—796 33	Minidoka County
—796 34	Lincoln County
—796 35	Jerome County

*For a specific part of this jurisdiction, region, or feature, see the part and follow instructions under —4–9

—796 36	Gooding County
—796 37	Twin Falls County
—796 39	Cassia County
—796 4	Southeastern counties
—796 41	Oneida County
—796 42	Franklin County
—796 44	Bear Lake County

Including *Wasatch Range in Idaho

—796 45	Caribou County
—796 47	Bannock County
—796 49	Power County
—796 5	Northeastern counties of southern Idaho
—796 51	Bingham County
—796 53	Bonneville County
—796 54	Teton County
—796 55	Madison County
—796 56	Fremont County
—796 57	Clark County
—796 58	Jefferson County
—796 59	Butte County

Including Craters of the Moon National Monument

For Craters of the Moon National Monument in Blaine County, see —79632

—796 6	*Central Idaho

Class here *Bitterroot Range in Idaho

—796 7	South central counties

Class here *Salmon River Mountains

—796 72	Custer County

Including *Sawtooth Mountains

See also —79629 for Sawtooth Range

—796 74	Boise County
—796 76	Valley County

*For a specific part of this jurisdiction, region, or feature, see the part and follow instructions under —4–9

—796 78	Lemhi County
—796 8	North central counties
—796 82	Idaho County
	Class here *Salmon River
—796 84	Lewis County
—796 85	Nez Perce County
	Including *Clearwater River
—796 86	Latah County
—796 88	Clearwater County
—796 9	Northern Idaho
—796 91	Shoshone County
	Including *Coeur d'Alene Mountains
—796 93	Benewah County
—796 94	Kootenai County
—796 96	Bonner County
—796 98	Boundary County
—797	Washington
	Class here *Columbia River
—797 2	Northeastern counties
—797 21	Pend Oreille County
—797 23	Stevens County
	Including *Franklin D. Roosevelt Lake
—797 25	Ferry County
—797 28	Okanogan County
—797 3	East central counties
—797 31	Douglas County
—797 32	Grant County
—797 33	Franklin County
—797 34	Adams County
—797 35	Lincoln County
—797 37	Spokane County
	Class here Spokane

*For a specific part of this jurisdiction, region, or feature, see the part and follow instructions under —4–9

—797 39	Whitman County
	Class here *Palouse River
—797 4	**Southeastern counties**
	Class here *Snake River in Washington
—797 42	Asotin County
—797 44	Garfield County
—797 46	Columbia County
	Including *Blue Mountains in Washington
—797 48	Walla Walla County
—797 5	**Central counties**
	Class here *Cascade Range in Washington
—797 51	Benton County
—797 53	Klickitat County
—797 55	Yakima County
	Class here *Yakima River
—797 57	Kittitas County
—797 59	Chelan County
—797 7	**Puget Sound counties**
	See also —16432 for Puget Sound
—797 71	Snohomish County
—797 72	Skagit County
—797 73	Whatcom County
	Including North Cascades National Park
	For North Cascades National Park in Chelan County, see —79759; for North Cascades National Park in Skagit County, see —79772
—797 74	San Juan County
—797 75	Island County
—797 76	Kitsap County
—797 77	King County
—797 772	Seattle
—797 78	Pierce County

*For a specific part of this jurisdiction, region, or feature, see the part and follow instructions under —4–9

—797 782	Mount Rainier National Park
	For Mount Rainier National Park in Lewis County, see —79782
—797 788	Tacoma
—797 79	Thurston County
	Including Olympia
—797 8	Southwest central counties
—797 82	Lewis County
	Class here *Cowlitz River
—797 84	Skamania County
—797 86	Clark County
—797 88	Cowlitz County
—797 9	Coastal counties
	Class here *Coast Ranges in Washington
—797 91	Wahkiakum County
—797 92	Pacific County
—797 94	*Olympic Peninsula
	Class here *Olympic Mountains
—797 95	Grays Harbor County
—797 97	Mason County
—797 98	Jefferson County
	Class here Olympic National Park
	For Olympic National Park in Mason County, see —79797; for Olympic National Park in Clallam County, see —79799
—797 99	Clallam County
	See also —16432 for Strait of Juan de Fuca
—798	Alaska
—798 2	Southeastern region (Panhandle)
	Including Haines, Ketchikan Gateway Boroughs; Juneau, Sitka; Glacier Bay National Park and Preserve, Misty Fjords National Monument

---

*For a specific part of this jurisdiction, region, or feature, see the part and follow instructions under —4–9

—798 3   South central region

> Pacific Coast area from Icy Bay to Cape Douglas, inland to crest of Alaska and Aleutian Ranges

> Including Kenai Peninsula, Matanuska-Susitna Boroughs; Denali National Park and Preserve, Kenai Fjords National Park, Wrangell-Saint Elias National Park and Preserve; Kenai Peninsula; *Alaska Range

>> *For Wrangell-Saint Elias National Park in southeastern region, see —7982*

>> *See also —16434 for Gulf of Alaska, Cook Inlet*

—798 35   Greater Anchorage Area Borough

—798 4   Southwestern region

> Area from Cape Douglas to Stuart Island

> Including Bristol Bay, Kodiak Island Boroughs; Katmai National Park and Preserve; Aleutian, Kodiak Islands; *Kuskokwim River

>> *See also —16434 for Bristol Bay*

—798 6   Central region

> Area from the crest of Alaska Range to North Slope Borough

> Including Fairbanks North Star, Yukon-Koyokuk Boroughs; Gates of the Arctic National Park and Preserve, Kobuk Valley National Park, Lake Clark National Park and Preserve; Seward Peninsula

> Class here *Yukon River

>> *For Gates of the Arctic National Park and Preserve in North Slope Borough, see —7987*

>> *See also —16434 for Norton Sound*

—798 7   North Slope Borough

> Including Brooks Range

—8   South America

> Class here Latin America, Spanish America, the *Andes

>> *For Middle America, see —72*

---

*For a specific part of this jurisdiction, region, or feature, see the part and follow instructions under —4–9

SUMMARY

—81	Brazil
—82	Argentina
—83	Chile
—84	Bolivia
—85	Peru
—86	Colombia and Ecuador
—87	Venezuela
—88	Guiana
—89	Paraguay and Uruguay

—81　　**Brazil**

—811　　　Northern region

　　　　　Class here *Amazon River

—811 1　　Rondônia state [*formerly* —8175]

—811 2　　Acre state

—811 3　　Amazonas state

—811 4　　Roraima state

—811 5　　Pará state

—811 6　　Amapá state

—811 7　　Tocantins state [*formerly* —8173]

—812　　　Maranhão and Piauí states

—812 1　　Maranhão state

—812 2　　Piauí state

—813　　　Northeastern region

　　　　　For Maranhão and Piauí states, see —812; for Sergipe and Bahia states, see —814

—813 1　　Ceará state

—813 2　　Rio Grande do Norte state

—813 3　　Paraíba state

—813 4　　Pernambuco state

　　　　　Including Fernando de Noronha archipelago [*formerly* —8136]

—813 5　　Alagoas state

—[813 6]　Fernando de Noronha archipelago

　　　　　Relocated to —8134

*For a specific part of this jurisdiction, region, or feature, see the part and follow instructions under —4–9

—814	Sergipe and Bahia states
—814 1	Sergipe state
—814 2	Bahia state

        Class here *São Francisco River

—815	Southeastern region

        For São Paulo state, see —8161

—815 1	Minas Gerais state
—815 2	Espírito Santo state
—815 3	Rio de Janeiro state

        Including former Guanabara

        Class here Rio de Janeiro

—816	São Paulo state and Southern region

        Class here *Paraná River in Brazil

—816 1	São Paulo state

        Class here São Paulo

>	—816 2–816 5 Southern region

        Class comprehensive works in —816

—816 2	Paraná state
—816 4	Santa Catarina state
—816 5	Rio Grande do Sul state
—817	West central region
—817 1	Mato Grosso do Sul state
—817 2	Mato Grosso state
—817 3	Goiás state

        Tocantins state, formerly part of Goiás state, relocated to —8117

—817 4	Federal District

        Including Brasília

—[817 5]	Rondônia state

        Relocated to —8111

---

*For a specific part of this jurisdiction, region, or feature, see the part and follow instructions under —4–9

—82	**Argentina**
—821	South central region
—821 1	Capital Federal
	Including Buenos Aires
—821 2	Buenos Aires province
	See also —16368 for Bahía Blanca Estuary, Río de la Plata
—821 3	La Pampa province
—822	Mesopotamian provinces
	Class here *Paraná, *Uruguay Rivers
—822 1	Entre Ríos
—822 2	Corrientes
—822 3	Misiones
—822 4	Santa Fe
—823	Northeastern provinces
—823 4	Chaco
—823 5	Formosa
—824	Northwestern provinces
—824 1	Jujuy
—824 2	Salta
—824 3	Tucumán
—824 5	Catamarca
—824 6	La Rioja
—825	North central provinces
—825 2	Santiago del Estero
—825 4	Córdoba
—826	Central Highland provinces
—826 2	San Luis
—826 3	San Juan
—826 4	Mendoza

*For a specific part of this jurisdiction, region, or feature, see the part and follow instructions under —4–9

—827   Patagonian region

Class here comprehensive works on Patagonia

For Patagonian region in Chile, see —83644

—827 2   Neuquén province

—827 3   Río Negro province

See also —16368 for Gulf of San Matias

—827 4   Chubut province

See also —16368 for Gulf of San Jorge

—827 5   Santa Cruz province

See also —16368 for Bahía Grande, Gulf of San Jorge

—827 6   Tierra del Fuego archipelago

Class here comprehensive works on Tierra del Fuego island

Class south Atlantic Ocean islands claimed by Argentina in —9711

For Tierra del Fuego province of Chile, see —83646

—83   Chile

—831   Tarapacá, Antofagasta, Atacama regions

—831 2   Tarapacá region

—831 23   Arica province

—831 27   Iquique province

—831 3   Antofagasta region

—831 32   Tocopilla province

—831 35   El Loa province

—831 38   Antofagasta province

—831 4   Atacama region

—831 42   Chañaral province

—831 45   Copiapó province

—831 48   Huasco province

—832   Comquimbo and Valparaíso regions

—832 3   Coquimbo region

—832 32   Elqui province

—832 35   Limarí province

—832 38   Choapa province

—832 4	Valparaíso region
	Former name: Aconcagua region
	Class here former Aconcagua province
	For Quillota, Valparaíso, San Antonio provinces, see —8325; for Easter Island, see —9618
—832 42	Los Andes province
—832 45	San Felipe province
—832 48	Petorca province
—832 5	Quillota, Valparaíso, San Antonio provinces
	Class here former Valparaíso province
	Class comprehensive works on Valparaíso region in —8324
—832 52	Quillota province
—832 55	Valparaíso province
—832 58	San Antonio province
—833	Central regions
—833 1	Metropolitana region
	Former name: Santiago province
—833 15	Santiago
—833 2	Cachapoal province
	Class here Libertador General Bernardo O'Higgins region, former O'Higgins province
	For Colchagua province, see —8333
—833 3	Colchagua province
—833 4	Curicó province
—833 5	Talca province
	Class here Maule region
	For Curicó province, see —8334; for Linares province, see —8337
—833 7	Linares province
—833 8	Ñuble province
—833 9	Concepción province
—834	Bíobío and Araucanía regions

—834 1   Bíobío (Bío-Bío) region

> *For Ñuble province, see —8338; for Concepción province, see —8339; for Arauco province, see —8342; for Bío-Bío province, see —8343*

—834 2   Arauco province

—834 3   Bío-Bío province

—834 5   Malleco province

—834 6   Cautín province

        Class here Araucanía region

> *For Malleco province, see —8345*

—835   Los Lagos region

—835 2   Valdivia province

—835 3   Osorno province

—835 4   Llanquihue province

—835 6   Chiloé province

—836   Aisén del General Carlos Ibáñez del Campo and Magallanes y Antártica Chilena regions

—836 2   Aisén del General Carlos Ibáñez del Campo region

—836 22   Aisén province

—836 25   General Carrera province

—836 28   Capitán Prat province

—836 4   Magallanes y Antártica Chilena region

—836 42   Ultima Esperanza province

—836 44   Magallanes province

> *See also —1674 for Strait of Magellan*

—836 46   Tierra del Fuego province

        Class comprehensive works on Tierra del Fuego archipelago in —8276

—836 48   Antártica Chilena province

—84   **Bolivia**

—841   Mountain region departments

—841 2   La Paz

        Class here La Paz, *Lake Titicaca

---

*For a specific part of this jurisdiction, region, or feature, see the part and follow instructions under —4–9

—841 3	Oruro
—841 4	Potosí
—842	Valley region departments
—842 3	Cochabamba
—842 4	Chuquisaca
	Including Sucre
—842 5	Tarija
—843	Santa Cruz department
	Class here plains region
—844	Amazon region departments
—844 2	El Beni (Beni)
—844 3	Pando
—85	**Peru**
—851	Northern departments
—851 2	Tumbes
—851 3	Piura
—851 4	Lambayeque
—851 5	Cajamarca
—851 6	La Libertad
—852	Central departments
—852 1	Ancash
—852 2	Huánuco
—852 3	Pasco
—852 4	Junín
—852 5	Lima
	Class here Lima
—852 6	Callao
—852 7	Ica
—852 8	Huancavelica
—852 9	Ayacucho and Apurímac
—852 92	Ayacucho

—852 94	Apurímac
—853	Southern departments
—853 2	Arequipa
—853 4	Moquegua
—853 5	Tacna
—853 6	Puno
	Including Lake Titicaca in Peru
—853 7	Cuzco
—854	Eastern departments
—854 2	Madre de Dios
—854 3	Ucayali
	Loreto, formerly part of Ucayali, relocated to —8544
—854 4	Loreto [*formerly* —8543]
	Class here *Amazon River in Peru
—854 5	San Martín
—854 6	Amazonas
—86	**Colombia and Ecuador**
—861	Colombia
—861 1	Caribbean Coast region
—861 12	Córdoba
—861 13	Sucre
—861 14	Bolívar
—861 15	Atlántico
—861 16	Magdalena
—861 17	La Guajira
—861 2	Northeastern region and Pacific Coast
—861 23	César
—861 24	Norte de Santander
—861 25	Santander
—861 26	Antioquia

*For a specific part of this jurisdiction, region, or feature, see the part and follow instructions under —4–9

—861 27	Chocó
—861 3	North central region

For Casanare, Cundinamarca, Bogotá, see —8614

—861 32	Risaralda
—861 34	Quindío
—861 35	Caldas
—861 36	Tolima
—861 37	Boyacá
—861 38	Arauca
—861 39	Vichada
—861 4	Casanare, Cundinamarca, Bogotá
—861 43	Casanare
—861 46	Cundinamarca
—861 48	Bogotá
—861 5	South central region
—861 52	Valle del Cauca
—861 53	Cauca
—861 54	Huila
—861 56	Meta
—861 6	Southern region

For Amazonas, see —8617

—861 62	Nariño
—861 63	Putumayo
—861 64	Caquetá
—861 65	Vaupés
	Guaviare, formerly part of Vaupés, relocated to —86166
—861 66	Guaviare [*formerly* —86165]
—861 67	Guainía
—861 7	Amazonas
—861 8	San Andrés y Providencia
	Islands in Caribbean Sea
—866	Ecuador

—866 1	Sierra Region

For southern provinces of Sierra Region, see —8662

—866 11	Carchi
—866 12	Imbabura
—866 13	Pichincha

Including Quito

—866 14	Cotopaxi
—866 15	Tungurahua
—866 16	Bolívar
—866 17	Chimborazo
—866 2	Southern provinces of Sierra Region
—866 23	Cañar
—866 24	Azuay
—866 25	Loja
—866 3	Coasta Region
—866 31	El Oro
—866 32	Guayas

See also —1641 for Gulf of Guayaquil

—866 33	Los Ríos
—866 34	Manabí
—866 35	Esmeraldas
—866 4	Eastern Region
—866 41	Sucumbíos and Napo provinces (Former Napo province)
—866 412	Sucumbíos
—866 416	Napo
—866 42	Pastaza
—866 43	Morona-Santiago
—866 44	Zamora-Chinchipe
—866 5	Galapagos Islands (Colón)
—87	**Venezuela**

Class here *Orinoco River

---

*For a specific part of this jurisdiction, region, or feature, see the part and follow instructions under —4–9

—871	Southwestern states
—871 2	Táchira
—871 3	Mérida
—871 4	Trujillo
—872	Northwestern states
—872 3	Zulia

             Class here *Lake Maracaibo

—872 4	Falcón

             See also —16365 for Gulf of Venezuela

—872 5	Lara
—872 6	Yaracuy
—873	North central states

             Including Federal Dependencies

             For Distrito Federal, see —877

—873 2	Carabobo
—873 4	Aragua
—873 5	Miranda
—874	Central states
—874 2	Apure
—874 3	Barinas
—874 5	Portuguesa
—874 6	Cojedes
—874 7	Guárico
—875	Northeastern states
—875 2	Anzoátegui
—875 3	Sucre

             See also —16366 for Gulf of Paria

—875 4	Nueva Esparta
—875 6	Monagas
—876	Southeastern region

*For a specific part of this jurisdiction, region, or feature, see the part and follow instructions under —4–9

—876 2	Delta Amacuro territory
—876 3	Bolívar state
—876 4	Amazonas territory
—877	Distrito Federal
	Including Caracas
—88	**Guiana**
—881	Guyana
	Former name: British Guiana
—881 1	North West district
—881 2	Essequibo district
—881 3	Essequibo Islands district
—881 4	West Demerara district
—881 5	East Demerara district
	Including Georgetown
—881 6	West Berbice district
—881 7	East Berbice district
—881 8	Rupununi
—881 9	Mazaruni-Potaro district
—882	French Guiana (Guyane)
	Overseas department of France
	Including Cayenne and Saint-Laurent du Maroni arrondissements
	Class here Inini
—883	Surinam (Suriname)
	Former name: Dutch Guiana
—883 1	Nickerie district
—883 2	Coronie district
—883 3	Saramacca district
—883 4	Para district
—883 5	Paramaribo district
	Class here Paramaribo
—883 6	Suriname district

—883 7	Commewijne district
—883 8	Marowijne district
—883 9	Brokopondo district
—89	**Paraguay and Uruguay**
—892	Paraguay

Class here Paraguay River

—892 1	Oriental region
—892 12	South departments
—892 121	Capital District

Including Asunción

—892 122	Central
—892 123	Paraguarí
—892 124	Ñeembucú
—892 125	Misiones
—892 126	Itapúa
—892 127	Caazapá
—892 128	Guairá
—892 13	North departments
—892 132	Alto Paraná
—892 133	Canendiyú
—892 134	Caaguazú
—892 135	Cordillera
—892 136	San Pedro
—892 137	Amambay
—892 138	Concepción
—892 2	Occidental region

Class here *Chaco Boreal

—892 23	Presidente Hayes
—892 24	Boquerón
—892 25	Nueva Asunción
—892 26	Chaco

*For a specific part of this jurisdiction, region, or feature, see the part and follow instructions under —4–9

—892 27	Alto Paraguay
—895	Uruguay
	Class here *Uruguay River in Uruguay
—895 1	Coastal departments
	See also —16368 for Río de la Plata
—895 11	Colonia
—895 12	San José
—895 13	Montevideo
	Class here Montevideo
—895 14	Canelones
—895 15	Maldonado
—895 16	Rocha
—895 2	Central departments
—895 21	Lavalleja
—895 22	Treinta y Tres
—895 23	Cerro Largo
—895 24	Durazno
—895 25	Florida
—895 26	Flores
—895 27	Soriano
—895 28	Río Negro
—895 3	Northern departments
—895 31	Paysandú
—895 32	Tacuarembó
—895 34	Rivera
—895 35	Salto
—895 36	Artigas

—9 **Other parts of world and extraterrestrial worlds   Pacific Ocean islands**

---

*For a specific part of this jurisdiction, region, or feature, see the part and follow instructions under —4–9

SUMMARY

—93	New Zealand
—94	Australia
—95	Melanesia New Guinea
—96	Other parts of Pacific Ocean Polynesia
—97	Atlantic Ocean islands
—98	Arctic islands and Antarctica
—99	Extraterrestrial worlds

> ## —93–96 *Pacific Ocean islands

Class comprehensive works in —9

—93   New Zealand

See Manual at T2—93

SUMMARY

—931	North Island
—932	Auckland Region
—933	Waikato Region
—934	Bay of Plenty, Gisborne, Hawke's Bay, Taranaki Regions
—935	Manawatu-Wanganui Region
—936	Wellington Region
—937	South Island
—938	Canterbury Region
—939	Otago and Southland Regions and outlying islands

—931   *North Island

Use of this number for comprehensive works on specific islands discontinued; class in —93

—[931 1]   Outlying islands

Relocated to —9399

—931 2   Former *Auckland Province

Use of this number for North Island discontinued; class in —931

—[931 22]   Former Auckland Province

Number discontinued; class in —9312

—[931 23]   Former Taranaki Province

Relocated to —9348

—[931 25]   Former Hawkes Bay Province

Relocated to —9346

*For a specific part of this jurisdiction, region, or feature, see the part and follow instructions under —4–9

—[931 27]	Former Wellington Province
	Relocated to —936

>	—931 3–931 8 Northland Region

Class comprehensive works in —9313

—931 3	Far North District

Class here Northland Region

For Whangarei District, see —9316; for Kaipara District, see —9318

—[931 5]	South Island
	Relocated to —937
—[931 575]	Stewart Island
	Relocated to —9396
—931 6	Whangarei District
—931 8	Kaipara District
—932	Auckland Region
—932 1	Rodney District

Including Kawau Island

—932 2	North Shore City

Class here Takapuna

—932 3	Waitakere City
—932 4	Auckland City

Including Little Barrier, Great Barrier, Waiheke Islands

Class here Auckland

—932 5	Manukau City
—932 6	Papakura District
—932 7	Franklin District in Auckland Region
—933	Waikato Region
—933 1	Franklin District

For Franklin District in Auckland Region, see —9327

—933 2	Thames Coromandel and Hauraki districts

—933 23   Thames Coromandel District

                    Class here Coromandel Peninsula

—933 27   Hauraki District

—933 3   Waikato District

—933 4   Hamilton City

                    Class here Hamilton

—933 5   Matamata Piako and Waipa districts

—933 53   Matamata Piako District

—933 57   Waipa District

—933 6   South Waikato District, and Rotorua District in Waikato Region

—933 63   South Waikato District

—933 67   Rotorua District in Waikato Region

—933 7   Otorohanga District

—933 8   Waitomo District

                    For Waitomo District in Manawatu-Wanganui Region, see —93517

—933 9   Taupo District

                  Including Lake Taupo

                    For Taupo District in Bay of Plenty Region, see —93424; for Taupo District in Hawke's Bay Region, see —93463; for Taupo District in Manawatu-Wanganui Region, see —93513

—934   Bay of Plenty, Gisborne, Hawke's Bay, Taranaki Regions

—934 2   Bay of Plenty Region

—934 21   Tauranga District

—934 22   Western Bay of Plenty District

—934 23   Rotorua District

                    For Rotorua District in Waikato Region, see —93367

—934 24   Taupo District in Bay of Plenty Region

—934 25   Whakatane District

                  Including Urewera National Park

                    For Urewera National Park in Wairoa District, see —93462

—934 26   Kawerau District

                  Class here Kawerau

—934 28   Opotiki District

—934 4	Gisborne Region (Gisborne District)
—934 6	Hawke's Bay Region

Class here former *Hawkes Bay Province [*formerly* —93125]

—934 62	Wairoa District
—934 63	Taupo District in Hawke's Bay Region
—934 64	Rangitikei District in Hawke's Bay Region
—934 65	Hastings District
—934 67	Napier City
—934 69	Central Hawke's Bay District
—934 8	Taranaki Region

Class here former *Taranaki Province [*formerly* —93123]

—934 82	New Plymouth District

Including Egmont National Park

For Egmont National Park in Stratford District, see —93485; for Egmont National Park in South Taranaki District, see —93488

—934 85	Stratford District

For Stratford District in Manawatu-Wanganui Region, see —9353

—934 88	South Taranaki District
—935	Manawatu-Wanganui Region

For Taupo District, see —9339

—935 1	Taupo and Waitomo districts in Manawatu-Wanganui Region
—935 13	Taupo District in Manawatu-Wanganui Region
—935 17	Waitomo District in Manawatu-Wanganui Region
—935 2	Ruapehu District

Including Tongariro National Park, Whanganui National Park

For Tongariro National Park in Taupo District, see —9339; for Whanganui National Park in Wanganui District, see —9354

—935 3	Stratford District in Manawatu-Wanganui Region
—935 4	Wanganui District
—935 5	Rangitikei District

For Rangitikei District in Hawke's Bay Region, see —93464

*For a specific part of this jurisdiction, region, or feature, see the part and follow instructions under —4–9

—935 6   Manawatu District

—935 7   Tararua District

> *For Tararua District in Wellington Region, see —9369*

—935 8   Palmerston North City

> Class here Palmerston North

—935 9   Horowhenua District

—936   Wellington Region

> Class here former Wellington Province [*formerly* —93127]
>
> *For Manawatu-Wanganui Region, see —935*

—936 1   Kapiti Coast District

—936 2   Porirua City

—936 3   Wellington City

> Class here Wellington

—936 4   Lower Hutt City

—936 5   Upper Hutt City

\>   —936 6–936 9   Wairarapa

> Class comprehensive works in —9366

—936 6   South Wairarapa District

> Class here Wairarapa
>
> *For Carterton District, see —9367; for Masterton District, see —9368; for Tararua District in Wellington Region, see —9369*

—936 7   Carterton District

—936 8   Masterton District

—936 9   Tararua District in Wellington Region

—937   South Island [*formerly* —9315]

> *For Canterbury Region, see —938; for Otago and Southland Regions, see —939*

\>   —937 1–937 4   West Coast Region

> Class comprehensive works in —9371

—937 1   Westland District

Including Mount Aspiring National Park, Westland National Park

Class here West Coast Region, former Westland Province; *Southern Alps

> *For Grey District, see —9372; for Buller District, see —9373; for Tasman District in West Coast Region, see —9374; for Mount Aspiring National Part in Queenstown-Lakes District, see —9395; for Mount Aspiring National Park in Southland District, see —9396*

—937 2   Grey District

—937 3   Buller District

Including Paparoa National Park

> *For Paparoa National Park in Grey District, see —9372*

—937 4   Tasman District in West Coast Region

Including Nelson Lakes National Park

>   —937 5–937 9   Nelson-Marlborough Region

Class comprehensive works in —9375

—937 5   Marlborough District

Class here Nelson-Marlborough Region, former *Marlborough Province, former *Nelson Province

> *For Nelson City, see —9376; for Tasman District, see —9377; for Kaikoura District, see —9378; for Hurunui District in Nelson-Marlborough Region, see —9379*

—937 6   Nelson City

—937 7   Tasman District

Including Abel Tasman National Park

> *For Tasman District in West Coast Region, see —9374*

—937 8   Kaikoura District

—937 9   Hurunui District in Nelson-Marlborough Region

—938   Canterbury Region

Class here former Canterbury Province

---

*For a specific part of this jurisdiction, region, or feature, see the part and follow instructions under —4–9

—938 1   Hurunui District

                           Including Arthur's Pass National Park

                             For Arthur's Pass National Park in Grey District, see —9372; for Arthur's Pass National Park in Selwyn District, see —9385; for Hurunui District in Nelson-Marlborough Region, see —9379

—938 2   Waimakariri District

—938 3   Christchurch City

                             Class here Christchurch

—938 4   Banks Peninsula District

                             Class here Banks Peninsula

—938 5   Selwyn District

—938 6   Ashburton District

—938 7   Timaru District

—938 8   MacKenzie District

                             Including Mount Cook National Park; Lake Pukaki

                             For Mount Cook National Park in Westland District, see —9371

—938 9   Waimate District, and Waitaki District in Canterbury Region

—938 93   Waimate District

—938 97   Waitaki District in Canterbury Region

                             Including Lake Ohau

—939   Otago and Southland Regions and outlying islands

                             Class here former Otago Province

>   —939 1–939 5   Otago Region

                             Class comprehensive works in —9391

—939 1   Waitaki District

                             Class here Otago Region

                             For Waitaki District in Canterbury Region, see —93897; for Dunedin City, see —9392; for Clutha District, see —9393; for Central Otago District, see —9394; for Queenstown-Lakes District, see —9395

—939 2   Dunedin City

—939 3   Clutha District

—939 4   Central Otago District

—939 5   Queenstown-Lakes District

                 Including Lakes Hawea, Wakatipu, Wanaka

>   —939 6–939 8   Southland Region

            Class comprehensive works in —9396

—939 6   Southland District

                 Including Stewart Island [*formerly* —931575]; Fiordland National Park; Lakes Manapouri, Te Anau

                 Class here Southland Region

                     For Gore District, see —9397; for Invercargill District, see —9398

—939 7   Gore District

—939 8   Invercargill District

—939 9   Outlying islands [*formerly* —9311]

                 Including Chatham Islands, Kermadec Islands, Subantarctic Islands (Antipodes, Auckland, Bounty, Campbell, Snares, Traps Islands)

—94   **Australia**

            Class here *Great Dividing Range

SUMMARY

—941	Western Australia	
—942	Central Australia	
—943	Queensland	
—944	New South Wales	
—945	Victoria	
—946	Tasmania	
—947	Australian Capital Territory	
—948	Outlying islands	

—941   Western Australia

—941 1   Perth metropolitan district

            Including Fremantle

—941 2   Southwestern district

            Including Albany, Bunbury, Collie, Geraldton, Katanning, Manjimup, Narrogin, Northam; Kalbarri, Nelson and Hay, Nornalup, Stirling Range National Parks; Darling, Stirling Ranges; Blackwood, Swan Rivers

               For Perth metropolitan district, see —9411

---

*For a specific part of this jurisdiction, region, or feature, see the part and follow instructions under —4–9

—941 3   Northwestern district

Including Port Hedland; Barrow Island, Bernier and Dorre Islands, Cape Range National Parks; Gascoyne River

—941 4   Kimberley district

Including Broome, Wyndham; Ord River

—941 5   North central district

Class here Gibson, Great Sandy, *Great Victoria Deserts

—941 6   South central district

Including Coolgardie, Kalgoorlie

—941 7   Southern district

Including Esperance, Norseman; Cape Le Grand, Esperance National Parks

—942   Central Australia

—942 3   South Australia

—942 31   Adelaide metropolitan district

—942 32   Central district

Including Angaston, Clare, Gawler, Murray Bridge, Port Pirie, Salisbury, Victor Harbour; Chaunceys Line Reserve National Park; Mount Lofty Ranges

For Adelaide metropolitan district, see —94231

—942 33   Eastern district

Including Barmera, Berri, Loxton, Renmark

—942 34   Southern district

Including Mount Gambier; Canunda National Park

—942 35   West central district

Including Flinders Chase National Park; Yorke Peninsula; Kangaroo Island

—942 36   North central district

Including Quorn

—942 37   Northern district

Class here *Flinders Ranges; *Coopers Creek

—942 38   Western district

Including Port Augusta, Port Lincoln, Whyalla; Lincoln National Park; Eyre Peninsula; Lakes Eyre, Gairdner

*For a specific part of this jurisdiction, region, or feature, see the part and follow instructions under —4–9

—942 9	Northern Territory

Class here northern Australia

For Western Australia, see —941; for Queensland, see —943

—942 91	Southern district

Including Alice Springs; Ormiston Gorge, Palm Valley, Uluru (Ayers Rock)-Mount Olga National Parks; Davenport Range; Ayers Rock

—942 95	Northern district

Including Darwin, Katherine, Tennant Creek; Cobourg Peninsula, Katherine Gorge National Parks; Arnhem Land; Groote Eylandt; Daly, Roper Rivers

—943	Queensland

Class here *Great Barrier Reef

—943 1	Brisbane metropolitan district
—943 2	Southeastern district

Including Bundaberg, Gympie, Ipswich, Kingaroy, Maryborough, Southport, Surfers Paradise; Bunya Mountains, Cooloola, Lamington, Mount Barney National Parks; Fraser Island

Class here *Brisbane River

For Brisbane metropolitan district, see —9431

—943 3	Downs district

Including Dalby, Millmerran, Oakey, Stanthorpe, Toowoomba; Granite Belt National Park; Darling Downs

—943 4	Southwestern district

Including Charleville, Mitchell

—943 5	Central district

Including Barcaldine, Blackall, Clermont, Gladstone, Longreach, Monto, Rockhampton, Yeppoon; Carnarvon, Dipperu, Isla Gorge, Robinson Gorge, Salvator Rosa National Parks; Fitzroy River

—943 6	Northeastern district

Including Atherton, Bowen, Cairns, Charters Towers, Ingham, Innisfail, Mackay, Mareeba, Townsville; Bellenden Ker, Conway Range, Eungella, Hinchinbrook Island, Mount Elliott, Mount Spec, Whitsunday Island, Windsor Tableland National Parks; Whitsunday Islands; Burdekin River

---

*For a specific part of this jurisdiction, region, or feature, see the part and follow instructions under —4–9

—943 7 Northwestern district

Including Mount Isa; Simpson Desert National Park

See also —16475 for Gulf of Carpentaria

—943 8 Peninsula and Torres Strait Islands

Including Cape York Peninsula

—944 New South Wales

Class here *Australian Alps; *Murray River

—944 1 Sydney metropolitan district

Including Parramatta, Penrith; Ku-ring-gai Chase National Park

—944 2 Lower north coast district

Including Cessnock, Forster, Gloucester, Gosford, Maitland, Muswellbrook, Newcastle, Port Macquarie, Singleton, Taree; Brisbane Waters National Park; Hawkesbury, Hunter Rivers

—944 3 Upper north coast district

Including Ballina, Casino, Coffs Harbour, Grafton, Kempsey, Kyogle, Lismore, Murwillumbah; Gibraltar Range National Park; Richmond River

Class here *Macleay Rivers

—944 4 North central district

Including Armidale, Coonabarabran, Glen Innes, Inverell, Tamworth, Tenterfield; Mount Kaputar, New England National Parks

Class here *Gwydir River

—944 5 Central district

Including Bathurst, Cowra, Dubbo, Forbes, Gilgandra, Katoomba, Lithgow, Mudgee, Orange, Wellington; Blue Mountains National Park; *Blue Mountains

—944 6 Upper south coast district

Including Camden, Campbelltown, Port Kembla, Wollongong; Morton, Royal National Parks; Nepean River

—944 7 Southeastern district

Including Batemans Bay, Bega, Bombala, Eden, Goulburn, Moruya, Narooma, Nowra, Queanbeyan, Yass; Kosciusko, Shoalhaven National Parks; Shoalhaven River

Class here *Snowy Mountains

Class Australian Capital Territory in —947

*For a specific part of this jurisdiction, region, or feature, see the part and follow instructions under —4–9

—944 8   Southern district

> Including Albury, Cootamundra, Corowa, Griffith, Junee, Leeton, Wagga Wagga; Cocoparra National Park; Wakool River

> Class here Murrumbidgee River

—944 9   Western district

> Including Bourke, Broken Hill, Cobar, Nyngan, Walgett, Warren; Menindee Lake

> Class here *Lachlan River

—945   Victoria

—945 1   Melbourne metropolitan district

—945 2   Central district

> Including Geelong, Healesville, Mornington, Queenscliff, Sorrento, Sunbury, Torquay, Werribee; Kinglake National Park; French, Phillip Islands

> Class here Yarra River

> *For Melbourne metropolitan district, see —9451*

—945 3   North central district

> Including Castlemaine, Creswick, Daylesford, Heathcote, Maldon, Maryborough, Woodend

—945 4   Northern district

> Including Bendigo, Echuca, Inglewood, Kyabram, Nathalia, Rushworth, Shepparton

> Class here *Goulburn River

—945 5   Northeastern district

> Including Beechworth, Benalla, Corryong, Euroa, Rutherglen, Wangaratta, Wodonga; Mount Buffalo National Park

> Class here *Ovens Rivers

—945 6   Gippsland district

> Including Bairnsdale, Lakes Entrance, Moe, Morwell, Traralgon, Warragul; Mallacoota Inlet, Wilsons Promontory National Parks

—945 7   Western district

> Including Ararat, Ballarat, Colac, Hamilton, Port Fairy, Portland, Warrnambool

—945 8   Wimmera district

> Including Horsham, Stawell

---

*For a specific part of this jurisdiction, region, or feature, see the part and follow instructions under —4–9

—945 9   Mallee district

> Including Merbein, Mildura, Swan Hill; Hattah Lakes, Wyperfeld National Parks; *Wimmera River

—946   Tasmania

—946 1   Hobart metropolitan district

—946 2   Southern district

> Including Kingston, New Norfolk, Port Cygnet; Hartz Mountains, Lake Pedder, Mount Field National Parks; Bruny Island

> *For Hobart metropolitan district, see —9461*

—946 3   Central district

> Including Deloraine, Oatlands; Cradle Mountain-Lake Saint Clair National Park; Cradle Mountain; Great Lake; Lake Saint Clair

—946 4   Eastern district

> Including Port Arthur, Scottsdale; Ben Lomond, Freycinet, Maria Island National Parks; Tasman Peninsula

—946 5   Northwestern district

> Including Beaconsfield, Burnie, Devonport, Launceston, Smithton, Stanley, Wynyard

> Class here *Tamar River

—946 6   Western district

> Including Queenstown; Frenchmans Cap National Park

—946 7   Bass Strait Islands

> Including Furneaux Islands

—947   Australian Capital Territory

—947 1   Canberra

—948   Outlying islands

> Including Christmas Islands

> *For Cocos Islands, see —699*

—948 1   Lord Howe Island

—948 2   Norfolk Island

—95   **Melanesia   New Guinea**

> Class here Oceania

> Class Polynesia, Micronesia in —96

---

*For a specific part of this jurisdiction, region, or feature, see the part and follow instructions under —4–9

>   —951–957   New Guinea

        Class comprehensive works in —95

—951   Irian Jaya

        Former names: Irian Barat, Netherlands New Guinea, West Irian, West New Guinea

—953   Papua New Guinea   New Guinea region

        Class here former German New Guinea, former territory of New Guinea

           For Papuan region, see —954; for Highlands region, see —956; for Momase region, see —957; for Bismarck Archipelago, see —958; for North Solomons Province, see —9592

—954   Papuan region

—954 1   Milne Bay Province

        Including D'Entrecasteaux Islands, Murua (Woodlark) Island, Trobriand Islands

—954 2   Northern (Oro) Province

—954 5   National Capital District

        Class here Port Moresby

—954 6   Central Province

        Including Bereina

—954 7   Gulf Province

        Class here *Purari River

—954 9   Western (Fly River) Province

—956   Highlands region

        Class here *Bismarck Range

—956 1   Southern Highlands Province

—956 3   Enga Province

—956 5   Western Highlands Province

        Class here Jimi River

—956 7   Simbu (Chimbu) Province

—956 9   Eastern Highlands Province

        Including Goroka

---

*For a specific part of this jurisdiction, region, or feature, see the part and follow instructions under —4–9

—957   Momase (Northern coastal) region

—957 1   Morobe Province

Including Lae; Siassi Islands; Markham River

—957 3   Madang Province

—957 5   East Sepik Province

Class here *Sepik, *Yuat Rivers

—957 7   West Sepik (Sandaun) Province

—958   Bismarck Archipelago

Part of Papua New Guinea

—958 1   Manus Province

Including Admiralty Islands

—958 3   New Ireland Province

Including Kavieng

—958 5   East New Britain Province

Including Rabau

Class here comprehensive works on New Britain

For West New Britain Province, see —9587

—958 7   West New Britain Province

—959   Other parts of Melanesia

—959 2   North Solomons Province

Part of Papua New Guinea

Including Bougainville, Buka islands

—959 3   Solomon Islands

Independent nation

Former name: British Solomon Islands

—959 31   Western Province

—959 33   Guadalcanal Province

—959 35   Central Province

Class here former Central Islands and Santa Isabel Province

Isabel Province relocated to —95936

—959 36   Isabel Province [*formerly* —95935]

*For a specific part of this jurisdiction, region, or feature, see the part and follow instructions under —4–9

—959 37	Malaita Province
—959 38	Makira and Ulawa Province [*formerly* —95939]
—959 39	Temotu Province
	Class here former Makula and Temotu Province
	Makira and Ulawa Province relocated to —95938
—959 5	Vanuatu
	Former name: New Hebrides
—959 7	New Caledonia
	Including Loyalty Islands
—96	**Other parts of Pacific Ocean Polynesia**
—961	Southwest central Pacific Ocean islands, and isolated islands of southeast Pacific Ocean
—961 1	Fiji
—961 2	Tonga (Friendly Islands)
—961 3	American Samoa
	Class here comprehensive works on Samoa
	For Western Samoa, see —9614
—961 4	Western Samoa
—961 5	Tokelau (Union) Islands
—961 6	Wallis and Futuna Islands
—961 8	Isolated islands of southeast Pacific Ocean
	Including Easter, Oeno, Pitcairn
—962	South central Pacific Ocean islands
	Class here French Polynesia
	For Marquesas Islands, see —9631; *for Tuamotu Islands, see* —9632
—962 1	Society Islands
—962 11	Tahiti
—962 2	Gambier and Tubuai (Austral) Islands
—962 3	Cook Islands
	For Manihiki Atoll, see —9624
—962 4	Manihiki Atoll
	Part of Cook Islands

—962 6   Niue

—963   Southeast central Pacific Ocean islands

       For isolated islands of southeast Pacific Ocean, see —9618

—963 1   Marquesas Islands

       Part of French Polynesia

—963 2   Tuamotu Islands (Low Archipelago)

       Part of French Polynesia

       For Gambier Islands, see —9622

—964   Line Islands (Equatorial Islands)

       Including Kiritimati (Christmas)

       For Palmyra, see —9699

—965   *West central Pacific Ocean islands (Micronesia)   *Trust Territory of the Pacific Islands

       Including Wake Island

—966   Federated States of Micronesia and Republic of Palau

       Including Truk Islands

       Class here Caroline Islands

—967   Mariana Islands

       Including Guam, Saipan, Tinian

       Class here Commonwealth of the Northern Mariana Islands

—968   Islands of eastern Micronesia

—968 1   Kiribati

       Including Gilbert Islands

       For Line Islands, see —964

—968 2   Tuvalu

       Class here Ellice Islands

—968 3   Marshall Islands

       Including Bikini, Enewetak, Kwajalein Atolls

—968 5   Nauru (Pleasant Island)

—969   North central Pacific Ocean islands   Hawaii

---

*For a specific part of this jurisdiction, region, or feature, see the part and follow instructions under —4–9

> —969 1–969 4 Hawaii

State of the United States of America

Class comprehensive works in —969

—969 1   Hawaii County (Hawaii Island)

—969 2   Maui County

—969 21   Maui Island

—969 22   Kahoolawe Island

—969 23   Lanai Island

—969 24   Molokai Island

Including Kalawao County

—969 3   Honolulu County (Oahu Island)

—969 31   Honolulu

—969 4   Kauai County

—969 41   Kauai Island

—969 42   Niihau Island

—969 9   Outlying islands

Including Howland, Johnston, Midway, Palmyra Islands

—97   ***Atlantic Ocean islands**

—971   Falkland Islands, South Georgia and South Sandwich Islands, Bouvet Island

—971 1   Falkland Islands (Islas Malvinas)

South Georgia and South Sandwich Islands relocated to —9712; South Orkney Islands, South Shetland Islands, comprehensive works on British Antarctic Territory relocated to —989

—971 2   South Georgia and South Sandwich Islands [*formerly* —9711]

Class here South Georgia Island, South Sandwich Islands

—971 3   Bouvet Island

—973   Saint Helena and dependencies

Including Ascension Island; Tristan da Cunha Islands

—98   **Arctic islands and Antarctica**

---

*For a specific part of this jurisdiction, region, or feature, see the part and follow instructions under —4–9

> —981–988 *Arctic islands

  Class comprehensive works in —98

—981   Svalbard

  Including Spitsbergen Island

—982   Greenland

—983   Jan Mayen Island

—985   Franz Josef Land

  Part of Arkhangel´sk province of Russia

—986   Novaya Zemlya

  Part of Arkhangel´sk province of Russia

—987   Severnaya Zemlya

  Part of Krasnoyarsk territory of Russia

—988   New Siberian Islands

  Part of Yakutia republic of Russia

—989   Antarctica

  Including South Orkney Islands, South Shetland Islands, comprehensive
  works on British Antarctic Territory [*formerly* —9711]; Dronning Maud
  (Queen Maud), Ellsworth, Enderby Lands; South Pole

—99   Extraterrestrial worlds

  Worlds other than Earth

  Class space in —19

  See Manual at T2—99 vs. T2—19

> —991–994 Solar system

  Class comprehensive works in —99

—991   Earth's moon

—992   Planets of solar system and their satellites

—992 1   Mercury

—992 2   Venus

—992 3   Mars

*For a specific part of this jurisdiction, region, or feature, see the part and follow instructions
  under —4–9

—992 4	Asteroids (Planetoids)
—992 5	Jupiter
—992 6	Saturn
—992 7	Uranus
—992 8	Neptune
—992 9	Pluto and transplutonian planets
—993	Meteoroids and comets
—994	Sun

Table 3. Subdivisions for the Arts, for Individual Literatures, for Specific Literary Forms

Notation from Table 3 is never used alone, but may be used as required by add notes under subdivisions of individual literatures or with base numbers for individual literatures identified by * under 810–890. It is never used for individual literatures that lack instructions to add from Table 3; the number for works of or about such literatures ends with the language notation, e.g., Navaho poetry 897.2

Notation from Table 3 may also be used where instructed in 700.4, 791.4, 808–809

Table 3 is divided into three subtables:

Table 3–A for description, critical appraisal, biography, single or collected works of an individual author

Table 3–B for description, critical appraisal, biography, collected works of two or more authors; also for rhetoric in specific literary forms

Table 3–C for additional elements used in number building within Table 3–B and as instructed in 700.4, 791.4, 808–809

Turn to Table 3–A or 3–B for full instructions on building numbers for individual literatures, to 808–809 for other uses of Table 3–B and 3–C for literature, to 700.4 for uses of Table 3–C for the arts, to 791.4 for uses of Table 3–C for motion pictures, radio, television

See Manual at Table 3

Table 3–A. Subdivisions for Works by or about Individual Authors

Procedures for building numbers for individual authors:

1.   Look in the schedule 810–890 to find the base number for the language. The base number may be identified in an add note, e.g., at 820.1–828 ("add to base number 82") or another note, e.g., at 896 ("896.392 Swahili"); otherwise, it is the number given for the literature, e.g., Dutch-language literature 839.31. If there is a specific literary form, go to step 2; if not, go to the instructions under —8 in Table 3–A

2.   In Table 3–A find the correct subdivision for the literary form, e.g., poetry — 1. Add this to the base number, e.g., Swahili poetry 896.3921, Dutch poetry 839.311. If the literary form appears as a subdivision of —8 Miscellaneous writings, go to the instructions under —8 in Table 3–A; otherwise, go to step 3

3.   Turn back to the appropriate number in the schedule 810–890 to see whether there is an applicable period table. If there is one, go to step 4; if not, complete the class number by inserting a point between the third and fourth digits, e.g., drama in English by a 20th-century New Zealand author 822, Khmer (Cambodian) poetry by a 20th-century author 895.9321

> (Option: Where two or more countries share the same language, either [1] use initial letters to distinguish the separate countries, or [2] use the special number designated for literatures of those countries that are not preferred. Either option makes feasible the use of period tables for affiliated literatures, e.g., drama in English by a 20th-century New Zealand author NZ822.2 or 828.993322. Full instructions appear under 810.1–818, 819, 820.1–828, 828.99, 840.1–848, 848.99, 860.1–868, 868.99, 869, 869.899. If the option is used, go to step 4)

4.   Select the appropriate period number. Add this number to the number already derived; always insert a point after the third digit. The class number is complete (except for William Shakespeare), since standard subdivisions are never added for individual authors, e.g., Spenser's *Faerie Queene* 821.3 (821 English poetry + 3 Elizabethan period)

See Manual at Table 3–A; also at 800: Literary criticism

> ## —1–8 Specific forms

Unless other instructions are given, observe the following table of preference for works combining two or more literary forms, e.g., drama written in verse —2 (*not* —1):

Drama	—2
Poetry	—1
Class epigrams in verse in —8	
Fiction	—3
Essays	—4
Speeches	—5
Letters	—6
Miscellaneous writings	—8

A single work of humor or satire, or a collection of humor or satire by an individual author in one form is classed with the form, e.g., satirical fiction —3. Humor or satire without identifiable form is classed according to the instructions at —8, plus notation 07 from the table under —81–89 if there is an applicable period table. A collection of humor or satire by an individual author in more than one form is classed according to the instructions at —8, plus notation 09 from the add table under —81–89 if there is an applicable period table

Class comprehensive works (description, critical appraisal, biography, or collected works that cover two or more forms of literature by an individual author) with the form with which the author is chiefly identified, e.g., a biography that discusses the poetry and fiction of a mid-19th-century American writer known primarily as a novelist 813.3; or, if the author is not chiefly identified with any one form, class comprehensive works as instructed at —8, plus notation 09 from the table under —81–89 if there is an applicable period table, e.g., the collected poetry and fiction of a mid-19th-century American writer not chiefly identified with any one form 818.309

See Manual at Table 3–A

(Option: Class description, critical appraisal, biography, single and collected works of all individual authors regardless of form in —8)

—1   Poetry

Class epigrams in verse in —8

See Manual at T3A—2, T3B—2 vs. T3A—1, T3B—102

—11–19   Poetry of specific periods

Add to —1 notation from the period table for the specific literature in 810–890, e.g., earliest period —11; do not add standard subdivisions. If there is no applicable period table, add nothing to —1, e.g., poetry in English by an Australian author of the earliest period 821 (*not* 821.1)

(Option: Use notation from the period table for an affiliated literature with either option given after step 3 at beginning of Table 3–A, e.g., poetry in English by an Australian author of the earliest period A821.1 or 828.993411)

—2   Drama

Class here closet drama, drama written in poetry

See Manual at T3A—2, T3B—2 vs. T3A—1, T3B—102

—21–29   Specific periods

Add to —2 notation from the period table for the specific literature in 810–890, e.g., earliest period —21; do not add standard subdivisions. If there is no applicable period table, add nothing to —2, e.g., drama in English by a New Zealand author of the earliest period 822 (*not* 822.1)

(Option: Use notation from the period table for an affiliated literature with either option given after step 3 at beginning of Table 3–A, e.g., drama in English by a New Zealand author of the earliest period NZ822.1 or 828.993321)

—3   Fiction

Class here novels, novelettes, short stories

Class graphic novels (cartoon or comic strip novels) in 741.5

—31–39   Specific periods

Add to —3 notation from the period table for the specific literature in 810–890, e.g., earliest period —31; do not add standard subdivisions. If there is no applicable period table, do not add anything to —3, e.g., fiction in French by a Canadian author of the colonial period 843 (*not* 843.3)

(Option: Use notation from the period table for an affiliated literature with either option given after step 3 at beginning of Table 3–A, e.g., fiction in French by a Canadian author of the colonial period C843.3 or 848.99233)

—4   Essays

—41–49   Specific periods

Add to —4 notation from the period table for the specific literature in 810–890, e.g., earliest period —41; do not add standard subdivisions. If there is no applicable period table, do not add anything to —4, e.g., essays in Spanish by a 19th-century Mexican author 864 (*not* 864.2)

(Option: Use notation from the period table for an affiliated literature with either option given after step 3 at beginning of Table 3–A, e.g., essays in Spanish by a 19th-century Mexican author M864.2 or 868.992142)

—5   Speeches

—51–59   Specific periods

Add to —5 notation from the period table for the specific literature in 810–890, e.g., earliest period —51; do not add standard subdivisions. If there is no applicable period table, add nothing to —5, e.g., speeches in Spanish by a 19th-century Chilean author 865 (*not* 865.2)

(Option: Use notation from the period table for an affiliated literature with either option given after step 3 at beginning of Table 3–A, e.g., speeches in Spanish by a 19th-century Chilean author Ch865.2 or 868.993352)

—6   Letters

See Manual at T3A—6 and T3B—6

—61–69   Specific periods

Add to —6 notation from the period table for the specific literature in 810–890, e.g., earliest period —61; do not add standard subdivisions. If there is no applicable period table, add nothing to —6, e.g., letters in Portuguese by a 20th-century Brazilian author 869.6 (*not* 869.64)

> (Option: Use notation from the period table for an affiliated literature with either option given after step 3 at beginning of Table 3–A, e.g., letters in Portuguese by a 20th-century Brazilian author B869.64 or 869.899264)

—8   Miscellaneous writings

Procedures for building numbers:

1.   To the base number add notation 8, e.g., miscellaneous writings in English 828. Go to step 2

2.   Turn back to the appropriate number in the schedule 810–890 to see whether there is an applicable period table. If there is one, go to step 3; if not, complete the class number by inserting a point between the third and fourth digits, e.g., miscellaneous writings in English by a 20th century New Zealand author 828, miscellaneous writings in Khmer (Cambodian) by a 20th century writer 895.9328

> (Option: Where two or more countries share the same language, either [1] use initial letters to distinguish the separate countries, or [2] use the special number designated for literatures of those countries that are not preferred. Either option makes feasible the use of period tables for affiliated literatures, e.g., miscellaneous writings in English by a 20th-century New Zealand author NZ828.2 or 828.993382. Full instructions appear under 810.1–818, 819, 820.1–828, 828.99, 840.1–848, 848.99, 860.1–868, 868.99, 869, 869.899. If the option is used, go to step 3)

3.   Select the appropriate period number, e.g., the Victorian period in the English literature of Great Britain 8. Then follow the instructions under —81–89

(Option: Class here description, critical appraisal, biography, single and collected works of all individual authors regardless of form; prefer —1–8)

—81–89 **Specific periods**

Add to —8 notation from the period table for the specific literature in 810–890, e.g., earliest period —81; then add further as follows, but in no case add standard subdivisions:

02   Anecdotes, epigrams, graffiti, jokes, quotations
       Including riddles that are jokes
       Class riddles as folk literature, interdisciplinary works on riddles in 398.6
         See Manual at T1—0207 vs. T3B—7, T3A—8 + 02, T3B—802, T3B—8 + 02, T3A—8 + 07, T3B—807, T3B—8 + 07; also at T3A—8 + 02, T3B—802, T3B—8 + 02 vs. 398.6, 793.735

03   Diaries, journals, notebooks, reminiscences
         See Manual at T3A—8 + 03 and T3B—803, T3B—8 + 03

07   Works without identifiable literary form
       Class here experimental and nonformalized works
       Class experimental works with an identifiable literary form with the form, e.g., experimental novels —3
         See Manual at T1—0207 vs. T3B—7, T3A—8 + 02, T3B—802, T3B—8 + 02, T3A—8 + 07, T3B—807, T3B—8 + 07

08   Prose literature
       Collections or discussions of works in more than one prose form
       Class here collections and criticism of selected prose works of an individual author that do not include the author's main literary form, e.g., a collection of the prose works of an English Victorian poet 828.808, a collection of the stories and plays of an English essayist of the romantic period 828.708
       Never class here comprehensive collections or criticisms of an author's work; class them in the author's main literary number, either with the predominant literary form or in 09 for individual authors not limited to or chiefly identifiable with one specific form
       Class prose without identifiable literary form in 07. Class a specific form of prose literature with the form, e.g., essays —4

09   Individual authors not limited to or chiefly identifiable with one specific form
       Class here description, critical appraisal, biography, collected works

If there is no applicable period table, add nothing to —8, e.g., prose literature in English by an Indian author of the later 20th century 828 (*not* 828.308)
(Option: Use notation from the period table for an affiliated literature with either option given after step 2 in the instructions under —8, e.g., prose literature in English by an Indian author of the later 20th century In828.308 or 828.99358308)

Table 3–B. Subdivisions for Works by or about More than One Author

Table 3–B is followed and supplemented by Table 3–C, which provides additional elements for building numbers within Table 3–B

Procedures for building numbers for works by or about more than one author, limited to literatures of specific languages:

1.   Look in the schedule 810–890 to find the base number for the language. The base number may be identified in an add note, e.g., at 820.1–828 ("add to base number 82") or another note, e.g., at 896 ("896.392 Swahili"); otherwise, it is the number given for the literature, e.g., Dutch-language literature 839.31. If there is a specific literary form, go to step 2; if not, go to step 8

2.   In Table 3–B find the subdivision for the literary form, e.g., poetry — 1. Add this to the base number, e.g., English poetry 821, Dutch poetry 839.311. If the literary form appears as a subdivision of — 8 Miscellaneous writings, go to the instructions under — 8 in Table 3–B. If the work deals with poetry, drama, fiction, or speech of specific media, scopes, kinds for which there is special notation in Table 3–B (e.g., — 1042 sonnets), go to step 3. For other works that deal with or fall within a limited time span (fewer than three literary periods—unless a single century spans three literary periods, then a single century), go to step 4. For other works not limited by time period, go to step 7

3.   Use the notation in Table 3–B for the kind of poetry, drama, fiction, or speech, e.g., sonnets in English literature 821.042. Insert a point after the third digit. Check whether the specific form is (1) the sole kind in a heading identified by * or (2) is named in a subdivisions-are-added note as a kind for which subdivisions may be added or (3) appears in a class-here note under a heading identified by *. If none of these conditions holds, the number is complete, e.g., collections of English-language clerihews 821.07. If one of the three conditions does hold, follow the instructions in the table under — 102–108 in Table 3–B. Following these instructions will involve using Table 3–C for literature of specific periods, literature displaying specific features or emphasizing specific subjects, and literature for and by specific kinds of persons, e.g., collections of English sonnets 821.04208, collections of English sonnets about love 821.042083543

(continued)

Table 3–B. Subdivisions for Works by or about More than One Author (continued)

4.   Turn back to the appropriate number in the schedule 810–890 to see whether there is an applicable period table. If there is one, go to step 5; if not, complete the class number by inserting a point between the third and fourth digits, e.g., 20th-century drama in English by New Zealand authors 822, Khmer (Cambodian) poetry by 20th-century authors 895.9321

> (Option: Where two or more countries share the same language, either [1] use initial letters to distinguish the separate countries, or [2] use the special number designated for literatures of those countries that are not preferred. Either option makes feasible the use of period tables for affiliated literatures, e.g., 20th-century drama in English by New Zealand authors NZ822.2 or 828.993322. Full instructions appear under 810.1–818, 819, 820.1–828, 828.99, 840.1–848, 848.99, 860.1–868, 868.99, 869, 869.899. If the option is used, go to step 5)

5.   Select the appropriate period number. Add this number to the number already derived, e.g., English poetry of the Elizabethan period 821.3; always insert a point after the third digit. Go to step 6

6.   Under the number for the literary form in Table 3–B, go to the subdivisions for specific periods, e.g., under —1 for poetry go to —11–19. Follow the instructions given there, which will lead to use of the table under —1–8. For literature displaying specific features, literature emphasizing subjects, and literature for and by specific kinds of persons, the instructions at —1–8 will lead to use of Table 3–C, e.g., critical appraisal of idealism in English Elizabethan poetry 821.30913

7.   If the work is not limited by time period, go to the first subdivisions under the particular form in Table 3–B, e.g., under —1 for poetry go to —1001–1009. Follow the instructions given there, which will lead to use of the table under —1–8. For literature displaying specific features, literature emphasizing subjects, and literature for and by specific kinds of persons, the instructions at —1–8 will lead to use of Table 3–C, e.g., collections of English poetry about war 821.0080358, collections of English poetry by rural authors 821.008091734

8.   If the work is not limited to a specific literary form, consult —01–09 in Table 3–B. Follow the instructions at the number selected, making use of Table 3–C when specified, e.g., collections of English literature in many forms about holidays 820.80334. Use period notation 08001–08009 and —09001–09009 only if there is an applicable period table

> (Option: Where two or more countries share the same language, either [1] use initial letters to distinguish the separate countries, or [2] use the special number designated for literatures of those countries that are not preferred. Either option makes feasible the use of period tables for affiliated literatures, e.g., collections of 20th-century Australian writings in English A820.8003 or 828.993408003. Full instructions appear under 810.1–818, 819, 820.1–828, 828.99, 840.1–848, 848.99, 869, 869.899)

(continued)

Table 3–B. Subdivisions for Works by or about More than One Author (continued)

The procedures described above require the use of schedule 810–890, Table 3–B, and Table 3–C in varying order. Sometimes also other tables are used. Example:

82	English (810–890)
1	poetry (Table 3–B)
914	of later 20th century (810–890)
080	collections (Table 3–B)
32	about places (Table 3–C)
4253	Lincolnshire (Table 2)

Thus, collections of contemporary English-language poetry about Lincolnshire 821.914080324253

Note that literary form —8 Miscellaneous writings is arranged first by period and then by specific miscellaneous forms

Instructions in the use of notation from Table 3–B for rhetoric in specific literary forms, collections of literary texts from more than two literatures, and history, description, critical appraisal of more than two literatures are found in 808–809

See Manual at Table 3–B; also at 800

SUMMARY

—01–09	[Standard subdivisions; collections; history, description, critical appraisal]
—1	Poetry
—2	Drama
—3	Fiction
—4	Essays
—5	Speeches
—6	Letters
—7	Humor and satire
—8	Miscellaneous writings

—01–07   **Standard subdivisions**

Standard subdivisions are used for general works consisting equally of literary texts and history, description, critical appraisal, e.g., a serial consisting equally of literary texts and history, description, critical appraisal of a variety of literature in English 820.5. Works limited to specific topics found in Table 3–C are classed in —08, plus notation from Table 3–C

Class collections of literary texts in —08; class history, description, critical appraisal in —09

—08   **Collections of literary texts in more than one form**

Class history, description, critical appraisal of a specific literature in —09

See Manual at T3B—08 and T3B—09: Preference order

—080 001–080 99   Standard subdivisions; specific periods; literature displaying specific features, or emphasizing subjects, or for and by specific kinds of persons

> Add to —080 notation 001–99 from Table 3–C, e.g., collections of literary texts about holidays —080334

> Works consisting equally of literary texts and history, description, critical appraisal of a specific literature are classed here if limited to specific topics found in Table 3–C, e.g., texts and criticism of English-language literary works about war 820.80358

—09   **History, description, critical appraisal of works in more than one form**

> Class here collected biography

> *See Manual at T3B—08 and T3B—09: Preference order*

—090 001–090 008   Standard subdivisions

—090 009   Historical and geographic treatment

· —[090 009 01–090 009 05]   Historical periods

> Do not use; class in —09001–09009

—090 01–090 09   Literature from specific periods

> Add to —0900 notation from the period table for the specific literature, e.g., earliest period —09001. If there is no applicable period table, this provision for indicating period cannot be used, e.g., history of literature in Spanish by Chilean authors of early 20th century 860.9 (*not* 860.9001), history of early Cornish literature 891.6709
> (Option: Use notation from the period table for an affiliated literature, e.g., history of literature in Spanish by Chilean authors of early 20th century Ch860.90042 or 868.9933090042. Full instructions appear under 810.1–818, 819, 820.1–828, 828.99, 840.1–848, 848.99, 860.1–868, 868.99, 869, and 869.899)

> *See Manual at T3B—091–099 vs. T3B—09001–09009*

—091–099   Literature displaying specific features or emphasizing subjects, and for and by specific kinds of persons

> Add to —09 notation 1–9 from Table 3–C, e.g., history and description of literature on Faust —09351

> *See Manual at T3B—091–099 vs. T3B—09001–09009*

> ## —1–8 Specific forms

Unless other instructions are given, observe the following table of preference for works combining two or more literary forms, e.g., poetic drama —2 (*not* —1):

Drama	—2
Poetry	—1
Class epigrams in verse in —8	
Fiction	—3
Essays	—4
Speeches	—5
Letters	—6
Miscellaneous writings	—8
Humor and satire	—7

When told to add as instructed under —1–8, add as follows:

1–7   Standard subdivisions

> Standard subdivisions are used for general works consisting equally of literary texts and history, description, critical appraisal, e.g., a serial consisting equally of literary texts and history, description, critical appraisal of poetry in English 821.005. Works limited to specific topics found in Table 3–C are classed in 801–809
>
> Class collections of literary texts in 8; class history, description, critical appraisal in 9

8   Collections of literary texts

> General works consisting equally of literary texts and history, description, critical appraisal are classed in 1–7, in the number for the specific form, or the specific form plus literary period. Works limited to specific topics found in Table 3–C are classed in 801–809

8001–8007   Standard subdivisions

[8008]   History and description with respect to kinds of persons
>   Do not use; class in 808–809

[8009]   Historical, geographic, persons treatment
>   Do not use; class in 9

801–809   Collections displaying specific features or emphasizing specific subjects, for and by specific kinds of persons

> Add to 80 notation 1–9 from Table 3–C, e.g., collections dealing with places 8032
>
> Works consisting equally of literary texts and history, description, critical appraisal are classed here if limited to specific topics found in Table 3–C

9   History, description, critical appraisal

> Class here collected biography
>
> Follow the instructions under 8 for works consisting equally of literary texts and history, description, critical appraisal

901–907   Standard subdivisions

(continued)

> ## —1–8 Specific forms (continued)

[908]	History and description with respect to kinds of persons Do not use; class in 98–99
[909]	Historical, geographic, persons treatment Do not use for historical and persons treatment; class in 9. Do not use for geographic treatment; class in 99
91–99	History, description, critical appraisal of texts displaying specific features or emphasizing specific subjects, for and by specific kinds of persons Add to 9 notation 1–9 from Table 3–C, e.g., critical appraisal of works by children 99282

Class comprehensive works on two or more forms in the base number for the individual literature, plus notation 01–09 from Table 3–B if applicable, adding 0 when required to make a three-figure number, e.g., comprehensive works on English poetry and fiction 820; however, class comprehensive works on prose literature in —808

—1   Poetry

See Manual at T3B—1: Preference order

—100 1–100 9   Standard subdivisions; collections; history, description, critical appraisal

Add to —100 as instructed under —1–8, e.g., collections of poetry dealing with places —1008032

> —102–108 Specific kinds of poetry

Limited to the kinds provided for below

Except for modifications shown under specific entries, add to each subdivision identified by * as follows:

01–07   Standard subdivisions
Standard subdivisions are used for general works consisting equally of literary texts and history, description, critical appraisal, e.g., a serial consisting equally of literary texts and history, description, critical appraisal of narrative poetry in English — 10305. Works limited to specific topics found in Table 3–C are classed in 08, plus notation from Table 3–C
Class collections of literary texts in 08; class history, description, critical appraisal in 09

08   Collections of literary texts
Add to 08 notation 001–99 from Table 3–C, e.g., collections dealing with places 0832, collections of English sonnets of the Elizabethan period 821.0420803
Works consisting equally of literary texts and history, description, critical appraisal of the form in a specific kind are classed here if limited to specific topics found in Table 3–C, e.g., texts and criticism of narrative poems about war — 10308358

09   History, description, critical appraisal
Class here collected biography
Add to 09 notation 001–99 from Table 3–C, e.g., critical appraisal of works by children 099282, critical appraisal of 20th century French lyric poetry 841.0409091
Follow the instructions under 08 for works consisting equally of literary texts and history, description, critical appraisal

Class epigrams in verse in —8; class comprehensive works in —1

See Manual at T3B—102–108, T3B—205, T3B—308 vs. T3C—1, T3C—3

—102   *Dramatic poetry

Including dramatic monologues

See also —2 for poetic plays

See Manual at T3A—2, T3B—2 vs. T3A—1, T3B—102

—103   *Narrative poetry

Including fabliaux

For ballads, see —1044

—103 2   *Epic poetry

—103 3   *Medieval metrical romances

See also —3 for prose versions of medieval romances

*Add as instructed under —102–108

—104   *Lyric and balladic poetry

                  Including concrete poetry

                  Class here poetry of minnesingers and troubadours

                  Subdivisions are added for lyric and balladic poetry together, for lyric
                  poetry alone

                  Class dramatic lyric poems in —102

—104 1   *Haiku

—104 2   *Sonnets

—104 3   *Odes

—104 4   *Ballads

—105   *Didactic poetry

—107   *Humorous and satirical poetry

                  Including clerihews

                  Subdivisions are added for either or both topics in heading

                  Class humor and satire in two or more literary forms, including both verse
                  and prose, in —7

—107 5   *Limericks

—108   *Ephemeral and light verse

                  Including greeting card verse

                  Subdivisions are added for either or both topics in heading

                  Class humorous poetry in —107

—11–19   Poetry of specific periods

                  Add to —1 notation from the period table for the specific literature in 810–890,
                  e.g., earliest period —11; then add 0 and to the result add further as instructed
                  under —1–8, e.g., collections from the earliest period dealing with places
                  —1108032

                  If there is no applicable period table, add nothing to —1, e.g., collections of
                  poetry in English by Australian authors of the earliest period 821 (*not* 821.108)
                  (Option: Use notation from the period table for an affiliated literature, e.g.,
                  collections of poetry in English by Australian authors of the earliest period
                  A821.108 or 828.99341108. Full instructions appear under 810.1–818, 819,
                  820.1–828, 828.99, 840.1–848, 848.99, 860.1–868, 868.99, 869, 869.899)

                  Class specific kinds of poetry from specific periods in —102–108

*Add as instructed under —102–108

—2   Drama

> Class here closet drama, drama written in poetry
>
> *See Manual at T3B—2: Preference order; also at T3A—2, T3B—2 vs. T3A—1, T3B—102*

—200 1–200 9   Standard subdivisions; collections; history, description, critical appraisal

> Add to —200 as instructed under —1–8, e.g., collections of drama dealing with places —2008032

> **—202–205**   Drama of specific media, scopes, kinds
>
> Add to each subdivision identified by * as instructed under —102–108, e.g., collections of comedies dealing with places —205230832
>
> Class comprehensive works in —2

> **—202–203**   Drama for mass media
>
> Class comprehensive works in —2

—202   Drama for radio and television

—202 2   *Drama for radio

—202 5   *Drama for television

—203   *Drama for motion pictures

—204   Drama of restricted scope

> Class drama of restricted scope for mass media in —202–203

—204 1   *One-act plays

> Including interludes, sketches

—204 5   *Monologues

—205   Specific kinds of drama

> Limited to the kinds provided for below
>
> Including masques
>
> Class specific kinds of drama for mass media in —202–203; class specific kinds of drama of restricted scope in —204
>
> *See Manual at T3B—102–108, T3B—205, T3B—308 vs. T3C—1, T3C—3*

—205 1   *Serious drama

> Class here Nō plays

---

*Add as instructed under —102–108

—205 12	*Tragedy
	Class tragicomedy in —20523
—205 14	*Historical drama
—205 16	*Religious and morality plays
	Not limited to medieval plays
	Class here miracle, mystery, passion plays
	Subdivisions are added for either or both topics in heading
—205 2	*Comedy and melodrama
—205 23	*Comedy
	Including tragicomedy
	Class humor and satire in two or more literary forms, including both verse and prose, in —7
—205 232	*Farce
—205 27	*Melodrama
	Including modern detective and mystery (suspense) drama
—205 7	*Variety drama
	Use of this number for miscellaneous drama discontinued; class in —2

—21–29   **Drama of specific periods**

Add to —2 notation from the period table for the specific literature in 810–890, e.g., earliest period —21; then add 0 and to the result add further as instructed under —1–8, e.g., critical appraisal of drama of earliest period —2109

Observe restrictions on use of period notation given at —11–19

Class drama of specific media, scopes, kinds from specific periods in —202–205

—3   **Fiction**

Class here novelettes and novels

Class graphic novels (cartoon or comic strip novels) in 741.5

See Manual at T3B—3: Preference order

—300 1–300 9	Standard subdivisions; collections; history, description, critical appraisal
	Add to —300 as instructed under —1–8, e.g., collections of fiction dealing with places —3008032

---

*Add as instructed under —102–108

>   —301–308   Fiction of specific scopes and kinds

          Add to each subdivision identified by * as instructed under —102–108, e.g., collections of short stories dealing with places —3010832

          Class comprehensive works in —3

—301   *Short stories

          Class short stories of specific kinds in —308

—308   Specific kinds of fiction

          Limited to the kinds provided for below

          Unless other instructions are given, observe the following table of preference, e.g., historical adventure fiction —3081 (*not* —3087):

Historical and period fiction	—3081
Adventure fiction	—3087
Love and romance	—3085
Psychological, realistic, sociological fiction	—3083

          See Manual at T3B—102–108, T3B—205, T3B—308 vs. T3C—1, T3C—3

—308 1   *Historical and period fiction

          Subdivisions are added for either or both topics in heading

—308 3   *Psychological, realistic, sociological fiction

          Subdivisions are added for any or all topics in heading

—308 5   *Love and romance

          Modern romantic fiction

          Subdivisions are added for either or both topics in heading

          Class medieval prose romances in —3

          See Manual at T3B—308729 vs. T3B—3085

—308 7   *Adventure fiction

          Unless other instructions are given, observe the following table of preference, e.g., Gothic horror fiction —308729 (*not* —308738):

Science fiction	—308762
Gothic fiction	—308729
Western fiction	—30874
Detective, mystery, suspense, spy fiction (*except* —308729)	—30872
Ghost fiction	—308733
Horror fiction	—308738
Fantasy fiction	—308766

---

*Add as instructed under —102–108

—308 72	*Detective, mystery, suspense, spy, Gothic fiction

> Subdivisions are added for a combination of two or more topics in heading, for detective fiction alone, for mystery fiction alone, for suspense fiction alone, for spy fiction alone

—308 729	*Gothic fiction

> Class modern romantic fiction in which the supernatural has little or no role in —3085
>
> *See Manual at T3B—308729 vs. T3B—3085*

—308 73	*Ghost and horror fiction
—308 733	*Ghost fiction
—308 738	*Horror fiction
—308 74	*Western fiction
—308 76	*Science and fantasy fiction
—308 762	*Science fiction
—308 766	*Fantasy fiction
—31–39	**Fiction of specific periods**

> Add to —3 notation from the period table for the specific literature in 810–890, e.g., earliest period —31; then add 0 and to the result add further as instructed under —1–8, e.g., critical appraisal of fiction of earliest period —3109
>
> Observe restrictions on use of period notation given at —11–19
>
> Class specific scopes and kinds from specific periods in —301–308

—4   Essays

—400 1–400 9	Standard subdivisions; collections; history, description, critical appraisal

> Add to —400 as instructed under —1–8, e.g., collections of essays dealing with places —4008032

—41–49   Essays of specific periods

> Add to —4 notation from the period table for the specific literature in 810–890, e.g., earliest period —41; then add 0 and to the result add further as instructed under —1–8, e.g., critical appraisal of essays of the earliest period —4109
>
> Observe restrictions on use of period notation given at —11–19

—5   Speeches

—500 1–500 9	Standard subdivisions; collections; history, description, critical appraisal

> Add to —500 as instructed under —1–8, e.g., collections of speeches dealing with places —5008032

*Add as instructed under —102–108

>   —501–506   Specific kinds of speeches

Limited to the kinds provided for below

Add to each subdivision identified by * as instructed under —102–108, e.g., collections of recitations dealing with places —5040832

Class comprehensive works in —5

—501   *Public speeches (Oratory)

Including after-dinner, platform, radio speeches; speeches and toasts for special occasions

For debates and public discussions, see —503

—503   *Debates and public discussions

Subdivisions are added for either or both topics in heading

—504   *Recitations

—505   *Texts for choral speaking

—506   *Conversations

—51–59   **Speeches of specific periods**

Add to —5 notation from the period table for the specific literature in 810–890, e.g., earliest period —51; then add 0 and to the result add further as instructed under —1–8, e.g., critical appraisal of speeches of the earliest period —5109

Observe restrictions on use of period notation given at —11–19

Class specific kinds from specific periods in —501–506

—6   Letters

See Manual at T3A—6 and T3B—6

—600 1–600 9   Standard subdivisions; collections; history, description, critical appraisal

Add to —600 as instructed under —1–8, e.g., collections of letters dealing with places —6008032

—61–69   **Letters of specific periods**

Add to —6 notation from the period table for the specific literature in 810–890, e.g., earliest period —61; then add 0 and to the result add further as instructed under —1–8, e.g., critical appraisal of letters of the earliest period —6109

Observe restrictions on use of period notation given at —11–19

*Add as instructed under —102–108

—7   Humor and satire

Limited to collections and criticism of works in two or more literary forms including both verse and prose

Class here parody

See also —808 for humor and satire in two or more prose forms

See Manual at T1—0207 vs. T3B—7, T3A—8 + 02, T3B—802, T3B—8 + 02, T3A—8 + 07, T3B—807, T3B—8 + 07; also at T3B—7 vs. T3C—17

(Option: Give precedence to humor and satire over all other literary forms)

—700 1–700 9   Standard subdivisions; collections; history, description, critical appraisal

> Add to —700 as instructed under —1–8, e.g., collections of humor and satire dealing with places —7008032

—71–79   **Humor and satire of specific periods**

Add to —7 notation from the period table for the specific literature in 810–890, e.g., earliest period —71; then add 0 and to the result add further as instructed under —1–8, e.g., critical appraisal of humor and satire of the earliest period —7109

Observe restrictions on use of period notation given at —11–19

—8   Miscellaneous writings

Procedures for building numbers:

1.   To the base number for the literature add notation 8, e.g., miscellaneous writings in English 828. If the work covers a limited time span (fewer than three literary periods--unless a single century spans three periods, then a single century), go to step 2; if not, go to step 4

2.   Turn back to the appropriate number in the schedule 810–890 to see whether there is an applicable period table. If there is one, go to step 3; if not, go to step 4
(Option: Where two or more countries share the same language, either [1] use initial letters to distinguish the separate countries, or [2] use the special number designated for literatures of those countries that are not preferred. This option makes feasible the use of period tables for affiliated literatures, e.g., miscellaneous writings in English by 20th-century New Zealand authors NZ828.2 or 828.993382. Full instructions appear under 810.1–818, 819, 820.1–828, 828.99, 840.1–848, 848.99, 860.1–868, 868.99, 869, 869.899. If the option is used, go to step 3)

3.   Select the appropriate period number, e.g., the Victorian period in the English literature of Great Britain 8. Then follow the instructions under —81–89

4.   If the work does not cover a limited time period, or if there is no applicable period table, consider whether the work is limited to one of the forms of miscellaneous writing listed in —802–808. If it is limited to one of those forms, go to step 5; if not, complete the class number by inserting a point between the third and fourth digits, e.g., miscellaneous writings in Russian from many time periods 891.78, miscellaneous writings in English by 20th-century New Zealand authors 828, miscellaneous writings in Khmer (Cambodian) by 20th-century authors 895.9328

5.   Class the work in the appropriate number from the span —802–808, then complete the number by inserting a point between the third and fourth digits, e.g., prose literature in Russian from many time periods 891.7808, prose literature in English by 20th-century New Zealand authors 828.08, prose literature in Khmer (Cambodian) by 20th-century authors 895.932808

See Manual at Table 3–B: Number building

—800 1–800 9   Standard subdivisions; collections; history, description, critical appraisal

Add to —800 as instructed under —1–8, e.g., critical appraisal of miscellaneous writings from more than one period —8009

\>   —802–808 Specific kinds of miscellaneous writings

Limited to kinds provided for below

Class in each number without further subdivision history, description, critical appraisal, biography, collections of works of authors from more than one period

Class comprehensive works in —8

—802   Anecdotes, epigrams, graffiti, jokes, quotations

Including riddles that are jokes

Class humor and satire in two or more literary forms, including both verse and prose, in —7; class riddles as folk literature, interdisciplinary works on riddles in 398.6

See Manual at T1—0207 vs. T3B—7, T3A—8 + 02, T3B—802, T3B—8 + 02, T3A—8 + 07, T3B—807, T3B—8 + 07; also at T3A—8 + 02, T3B—802, T3B—8 + 02 vs. 398.6, 793.735

—803   Diaries, journals, notebooks, reminiscences

Class interdisciplinary collections of diaries in 900. Class diaries, journals, notebooks, reminiscences of nonliterary authors with the appropriate subject, e.g., diary of an astronomer 520.92

See Manual at T3A—8 + 03 and T3B—803, T3B—8 + 03

—807   Works without identifiable literary form

Class here experimental and nonformalized works

Class experimental works with an identifiable literary form with the form, e.g., experimental novels —3

See Manual at T1—0207 vs. T3B—7, T3A—8 + 02, T3B—802, T3B—8 + 02, T3A—8 + 07, T3B—807, T3B—8 + 07

—808   Prose literature

Collections and discussions of works in more than one literary form

Class prose without identifiable literary form in —807. Class a specific form of prose literature with the form, e.g., essays —4

—81–89   Miscellaneous writings of specific periods

Add to —8 notation from the period table for the specific literature in 810–890, e.g., earliest period —81; then add further as follows:

001–009   Standard subdivisions; collections; history, description, critical appraisal

Add to 00 as instructed under —1–8, e.g., collections 008

02   Anecdotes, epigrams, graffiti, jokes, quotations

Including riddles that are jokes

Class humor and satire in two or more literary forms, including both verse and prose, in —7; class riddles as folk literature, interdisciplinary works on riddles in 398.6

See Manual at T1—0207 vs. T3B—7, T3A—8 + 02, T3B—802, T3B—8 + 02, T3A—8 + 07, T3B—807, T3B—8 + 07; also at T3A—8 + 02, T3B—802, T3B—8 + 02 vs. 398.6, 793.735

(continued)

—81–89   **Miscellaneous writings of specific periods (continued)**

0201–0209   Standard subdivisions; collections; history, description, critical appraisal
> Add to 020 as instructed under —1–8, e.g., collections 0208

03   Diaries, journals, notebooks, reminiscences
> *See Manual at T3A—8 + 03 and T3B—803, T3B—8 + 03*

0301–0309   Standard subdivisions; collections; history, description, critical appraisal
> Add to 030 as instructed under —1–8, e.g., collections 0308

07   Works without identifiable literary form
> Class here experimental and nonformalized works
> Class experimental works with an identifiable literary form with the form, e.g., experimental novels —3
> *See Manual at T1—0207 vs. T3B—7, T3A—8 + 02, T3B—802, T3B—8 + 02, T3A—8 + 07, T3B—807, T3B—8 + 07*

0701–0709   Standard subdivisions; collections; history, description, critical appraisal
> Add to 070 as instructed under —1–8, e.g., collections of stream of consciousness writings 0708025

08   Prose literature
> Collections and discussions of works in more than one literary form
> Class prose without identifiable literary form in 07. Class a specific form of prose literature with the form, e.g., essays —4

0801–0809   Standard subdivisions; collections; history, description, critical appraisal
> Add to 080 as instructed under —1–8, e.g., collections 0808

If there is no applicable period table, class anecdotes, epigrams, graffiti, jokes, quotations from specific periods in —802; class diaries, journals, notebooks, reminiscences from specific periods in —803; class works without identifiable literary form from specific periods in —807; class prose literature from specific periods in —808, e.g., collections of 20th-century Albanian prose literature 891.991808, collections of prose literature in English by Australian authors of the early 20th century 828.08 (*not* 828.20808)
> (Option: Use the notation from the period table for an affiliated literature for either option given after step 2 under —8 in Table 3–B, e.g., prose literature in English by Australian authors of early 20th century A828.20808 or 828.9934820808)

Table 3–C. Notation to Be Added Where Instructed in Table 3–B, 700.4, 791.4, 808–809

See Manual at Table 3–B: Preference order

SUMMARY

—001–009	**Standard subdivisions**
—01–09	**Specific periods**
—1	**Arts and literature displaying specific qualities of style, mood, viewpoint**
—2	**Literature displaying specific elements**
—3	**Arts and literature dealing with specific themes and subjects**
—4	**Literature emphasizing subjects**
—8	**Literature for and by persons of racial, ethnic, national groups**
—9	**Literature for and by other specific kinds of persons**

—001–008   Standard subdivisions

—009   Historical and geographic treatment

—009 01–009 05   Historical periods

> Do not use for literature of a specific language; class in —01–09

—01–09   Specific periods

> Add to —0 notation from the period table for the specific literature, e.g., earliest period —01

—1   Arts and literature displaying specific qualities of style, mood, viewpoint

> Do not use if redundant, e.g., horror (—164) in horror fiction (—308738 in Table 3–B)
>
> Class literature displaying specific elements and specific qualities in —2; class arts and literature dealing with specific themes and subjects and displaying specific qualities in —3
>
> *See Manual at T3B—102–108, T3B—205, T3B—308 vs. T3C—1, T3C—3*

—11   Nontraditional viewpoints

> Including impressionism
>
> Class here avant-garde, experimental approaches in the arts
>
> *For a specific type of avant-garde or experimental approach not provided for here, see the type, e.g., experimental literary works without identifiable literary form —807 in Table 3–B*

428

—112	Modernism
—113	Postmodernism
—114	Futurism
—115	Expressionism
—116	Dadaism and surrealism
—116 2	Dadaism
—116 3	Surrealism

—12   **Realism and naturalism**

Including determinism

—13   **Idealism**

—14   **Classicism and romanticism**

Class pastoral arts and literature in —321734

—142	Classicism
—145	Romanticism

Including primitivism

—15   **Symbolism, allegory, fantasy, myth**

Standard subdivisions are added for any or all topics in heading

Including the grotesque, science fiction in the arts

Class symbolism, allegory, fantasy, myth associated with a specific style or viewpoint with the style or viewpoint, e.g., surrealism —1163

For science fiction as a type of fiction, see —308762 in Table 3–B

See Manual at T3C—37 vs. T3C—15

—16   **Tragedy and horror**

—162   Tragedy

For tragedy as a kind of drama, see —20512 in Table 3–B

—164   Horror

For horror fiction, see —308738 in Table 3–B

—17   **Comedy**

Class humor and satire in two or more literary forms in —7 in Table 3–B

For comedy as a kind of drama, see —20523 in Table 3–B

See Manual at T3B—7 vs. T3C—17

—18   **Irony**

—2   Literature displaying specific elements

Class literature dealing with specific themes and subjects and displaying specific elements in —3

—22   Description

> Including setting

—23   Narrative

—24   Plot

—25   Stream of consciousness

—26   Dialogue

—27   Characters

> Including the "double" (Doppelgänger) in literature

—3   Arts and literature dealing with specific themes and subjects

Do not use if redundant, e.g., historical themes (—358) in historical fiction (—3081 in Table 3–B)

See Manual at T3B—102–108, T3B—205, T3B—308 vs. T3C—1, T3C—3

—32   Places

> Class here landscapes, civilization of places

> Add to —32 notation 1–9 from Table 2, e.g., the sea —32162, pastoral themes —321734, the American West —3278, California —32794

> Class western fiction as a type of fiction in —30874 in Table 3–B; class historical and political themes, historical events in specific places in —358

> *For supernatural, mythological, legendary places, see —372*

—33   Times

> Including seasons; parts of day, e.g., dawn

> Class time as a philosophic concept in —384

—334   Holidays

> Including religious holidays, e.g., Christmas

—35   **Humanity**

Including the human form

Class here human existence, works dealing with contemporary viewpoints

Unless other instructions are given, observe the following table of preference, e.g., artistic themes associated with artists —357 (*not* —3527):

Specific persons	—351
Historical and political themes	—358
Life cycle	—354
Social themes	—355
Artistic and literary themes	—357
Scientific and technical themes	—356
Human qualities and activities	—353
Specific kinds of persons	—352

—351   Specific persons

Real, fictional, legendary, mythological persons

Including Count Dracula, Don Juan, Faust, Joan of Arc, Job, Julius Caesar, King Arthur, Odysseus, Pierrot

—352   Specific kinds of persons

Including heroes

Add to —352 notation 03–99 from Table 7, e.g., women —352042

See also —375 for paranatural beings of human and semihuman form, —8–9 for literature for and by specific kinds of persons

See Manual at T3C—353–358 vs. T3C—352

>   —353–358 Specific human, social, scientific, technical, artistic, literary, historical, political themes

Class comprehensive works in —35

See Manual at T3C—353–358 vs. T3C—352

—353   Human characteristics and activities

Biological, moral, psychological aspects

Including alienation, chivalry, dreams, fear, friendship, happiness, heroism, justice, melancholy, mental illness, personal beauty, pride, sexual orientation, snobbishness, success

—353 8   Sex

Class here erotica, sexuality

Class sexual orientation in —353

—354   Life cycle

Including birth, youth, aging

—354 3	Love and marriage
—354 8	Death
—355	Social themes

Including commerce, costume, crime, dancing, dwellings, economics, education, environment, exile, food, law, sports, travel, violence, work

Class here everyday life

—356	Scientific and technical themes

Including flight, medicine, ships

Class science fiction in literature in —308762 in Table 3–B; class science fiction in the arts in —15

For physical and natural phenomena, see —36

—357	Artistic and literary themes

Including architecture, books, music, painting

—358	Historical and political themes

Including nationalism, peace, war

Class here historical events in specific places

—36   Physical and natural phenomena

Including fire, weather

Class landscapes in —32; class times (e.g., seasons, times of day) in —33

—362	Animals

Add to base number —362 the numbers following 59 in 592–599, e.g., cats —3629752

Class supernatural, mythological, legendary animals in —374

—364	Plants

Class here gardens

Class supernatural, mythological, legendary plants in —37

—37   The supernatural, mythological, legendary

Standard subdivisions are added for any or all topics in heading

Including spiritualism, magic, witchcraft

Class here monsters

Class specific legendary and mythological persons in —351; class specific kinds of legendary and mythological persons in —352; class religious mythology in —3829113

See Manual at T3C—37 vs. T3C—15

—372   Places

> Including Atlantis, utopia
>
> Class religious treatment of places associated with life after death in —3829123

—374   Animals

> Including dragons, werewolves

—375   Paranatural beings of human and semihuman form

> Including centaurs, fairies, ghosts, vampires
>
> Class gods, goddesses, other objects of worship and veneration in —382
>
> > *For ghost fiction as a kind of fiction, see —308733 in Table 3–B; for specific paranatural beings of human and semihuman form, see —351; for werewolves, see —374*

—38   **Philosophic and abstract themes**

—382   Religious themes

> Add to base number —382 the numbers following 2 in 210–290, e.g., Buddhism —382943; however, for religious holidays, see —334; for specific persons connected with religion, see —351; for kinds of persons associated with religion, see —3522
>
> > *See also —42 for religious works not basically belletristic but discussed as literature*

—384   Philosophic themes

> Including existentialism, humanism, nihilism, self, time, transcendentalism
>
> Class times (e.g., seasons, times of day) in —33; class human moral qualities and activities in —353

—4   Literature emphasizing subjects

> Works not basically belletristic discussed as literature, where the real interest is in the literary quality of the text rather than the subject of the text
>
> Add to —4 notation 001–999, e.g., religious works as literature —42, biography as literature —492
>
> Class literary examination of a text in order to reach conclusions about its meaning, structure, authorship, date, where the real interest is in the subject of the text with the text, e.g., literary criticism of Bible 220.66

> ## —8–9 Literature for and by specific kinds of persons

Do not use if redundant, e.g., collections of English-language poetry for and by the English 821.008 (*not* 821.0080821)

Unless other instructions are given, observe the following table of preference, e.g., literature for or by Roman Catholic girls —92827 (*not* —9222 or —9287):

Persons of specific age groups	—9282–9285
Persons of specific sexes	—9286–9287
Persons occupied with geography, history, related disciplines	—929
Persons of specific occupational and miscellaneous characteristics	—9204–9279
Persons of racial, ethnic, national groups	—8
Persons resident in specific continents, countries, localities	—93–99
Persons resident in specific regions	—91

Class literature displaying specific features for and by specific kinds of persons in —1–3; class comprehensive works in the appropriate number in Table 3–B

—8 Literature for and by persons of racial, ethnic, national groups

Add to —8 notation 03–99 from Table 5, e.g., literature by Africans and persons of African descent —896, literature by Africans and persons of African descent in Brazil —896081

Literature for and by persons of racial, ethnic, national groups in continents, countries, localities where the groups predominate relocated to —93–99

See Manual at T3C—93–99, T3C—9174 vs. T3C—8

—9 Literature for and by other specific kinds of persons

—91 Literature for and by persons resident in specific regions

Not limited by continent, country, locality

Add to —91 the numbers following —1 in notation 11–19 from Table 2, e.g., literature by rural authors —91734

Class literature for and by persons of racial, ethnic, national groups in —8; class literature for and by persons resident in specific continents, countries, localities in —93–99

See Manual at T3C—93–99, T3C—9174 vs. T3C—8

—92 Literature for and by persons of specific classes

—920 4–927 9   Persons of specific occupational and miscellaneous characteristics

> Add to —92 notation 04–79 from Table 7, e.g., literature by painters —9275; however, for persons of specific age groups and sexes, see —928
>
> *For persons occupied with geography, history, related disciplines, see —929*

—928   Persons of specific age groups and sexes

\>   —928 2–928 5 Age groups

Class comprehensive works in —928

—928 2   Children

—928 26   Boys

—928 27   Girls

—928 3   Young people twelve to twenty

—928 36   Males twelve to twenty

—928 37   Females twelve to twenty

—928 5   Persons in late adulthood

\>   —928 6–928 7 Sexes

Class comprehensive works in —928

—928 6   Men

—928 7   Women

—929   Persons occupied with geography, history, related disciplines

> Add to —929 the numbers following —9 in notation 91–99 from Table 7, e.g., literature by archaeologists —9293

—93–99   **Literature for and by persons resident in specific continents, countries, localities**

Class here literature for and by persons of racial, ethnic, national groups in continents, countries, localities where the groups predominate [*formerly* —8]

Add to —9 notation 3–9 from Table 2, e.g., literature (other than in Japanese language) by residents of Japan —952, a collection of Japanese-language literature by residents of Hokkaidō 895.60809524, a collection of English literature by residents of Australia 820.80994

Class literature for and by persons of racial, ethnic, national groups not dominant in their continents, countries, localities in —8; class literature for and by persons in specific regions not limited by continent, country, locality in —91

See Manual at T3C—93–99; also at T3C—93–99, T3C—9174 vs. T3C—8

(Option: Do not use for literatures of specific countries if the literatures are separately identified in accordance with options given under 810, 819, 820, 828.99, 840.1–848, 848.99, 860.1–868, 868.99, 869, 869.899)

Table 4. Subdivisions of Individual Languages and Language Families

The following notation is never used alone, but may be used as required by add notes under subdivisions of specific languages or language families, or with the base numbers for individual languages identified by * as explained under 420–490, e.g., Norwegian (base number 439.82) phonology (— 15 in this table): 439.8215. A point is inserted following the third digit of any number thus constructed that is longer than three digits. Notation from Table 1 is added to the notation in Table 4 when appropriate, e.g., —509 history of grammar, 439.82509 history of Norwegian grammar

See Manual at 410; also at 411–418 and T4—1–8

SUMMARY

—01–09	Standard subdivisions
—1	Writing systems, phonology, phonetics of the standard form of the language
—2	Etymology of the standard form of the language
—3	Dictionaries of the standard form of the language
—5	Grammar of the standard form of the language
—7	Historical and geographic variations, modern nongeographic variations
—8	Standard usage of the language (Prescriptive linguistics) Applied linguistics

—01   **Philosophy and theory**

> Class schools and theories of linguistics in —018

—014   Language and communication

> Class here lexicology, terminology

> *For dictionaries, see —3; for lexicography, see —3028; for discursive works on terminology intended to teach vocabulary, see —81. For terminology of a specific subject or discipline, see the subject or discipline, plus notation 014 from Table 1, e.g., terminology of accounting 657.014*

> *See Manual at T4—3 vs. T4—81*

—014 1   Discourse analysis

> Class here content analysis, semiotics

> Class discourse analysis of a specific subject with the subject, plus notation 014 from Table 1, e.g., discourse analysis of science 501.4

> *For semantics, see —0143*

—[014 2]	Etymology

Do not use; class in —2

—014 3	Semantics

For history of word meanings, see —2

See Manual at 401.43 vs. 306.44, 401.9, 412, 415

—[014 8]	Abbreviations and symbols

Do not use for abbreviations and symbols as part of writing systems; class in —11. Do not use for dictionaries of abbreviations and symbols; class in —31

—018	Schools and theories of linguistics

Including functionalism, structural linguistics

For works on schools and theories of linguistics that stress syntax, or syntax and phonology, see —5

—02	**Miscellany**

—03	**Encyclopedias and concordances**

Do not use for dictionaries of standard form of language; class in —3. Do not use for dictionaries of historical and geographic variations, of modern nongeographic variations in the language; class in —7

—04	**Special topics**

—042	Bilingualism

Class here multilingualism

Add to —042 notation 2–9 from Table 6 for the language that is not dominant in the area in which the linguistic interaction occurs, e.g., works dealing with the dominant language and English —04221

See also 306.446 for sociology of bilingualism and multilingualism

—05–08	**Standard subdivisions**

See Manual at 407.1, T1—071 vs. 401.93, 410.71, 418.0071, T4—80071

—09	**Historical, geographic, persons treatment**

Do not use for works that stress distinctive characteristics of historical and geographic variations from the standard form of the language; class in —7

> ## —1–5   Description and analysis of the standard form of the language

Class writing systems, phonology, etymology, dictionaries, grammar of historical and geographic variations, of modern nongeographic variations of the language in —7; class standard usage, prescriptive and applied linguistics in —8; class comprehensive works in the base number for the language (adding 0 when required to make a three-figure number), e.g., comprehensive works on phonology, etymology, dictionaries, grammar of standard French 440

See Manual at T4—1–5 and T4—8 vs. T4—7

—1   Writing systems, phonology, phonetics of the standard form of the language

—11   Writing systems

Including alphabets, ideographs, syllabaries; braille; abbreviations, acronyms, capitalization, punctuation, transliteration

Class here paleography in the narrow sense of study of ancient and medieval handwriting

Class dictionaries of abbreviations and acronyms in —31; class paleography in the broad sense of all aspects of early writings in the base number for the language (adding 0 when required to make a three-digit number), e.g., Latin paleography 470; class paleography (in both broad and narrow senses) of historical and geographic variations, of modern nongeographic variations of the language in —7, e.g., paleography of postclassical Latin 477; class manual alphabets regardless of language in 419

For spelling, see —152

—15   Phonology, phonetics, spelling

Standard subdivisions are added for phonology, phonetics, spelling together; for phonology and phonetics together; for phonology alone

Class comprehensive works on phonology and morphology, on phonology and syntax, or on all three in —5

For suprasegmental features, see —16

See also —3 for dictionaries

—152   Spelling (Orthography) and pronunciation

Class here description and analysis of the nature, history, and function of spelling and pronunciation

Class specialized spelling and pronouncing dictionaries in —31; class training in standard spelling and pronunciation in —81; class finger spelling in 419; class speech training for public speaking, debating, conversation in 808.5; class comprehensive works on writing systems in —11

—158	Phonetics
—16	**Suprasegmental features**

Phonology and phonetics of vocal effects extending over more than one sound segment

Including juncture (pauses), pitch, stress

Class here intonation

See Manual at 808.1 vs. 414.6

—2 Etymology of the standard form of the language

—24 **Foreign elements**

Add to —24 notation 1–9 from Table 6, e.g., French words in the language —2441, French words in English 422.441

—3 Dictionaries of the standard form of the language

See Manual at T4—3 vs. T4—81

—302 8 Techniques, procedures, apparatus, equipment, materials

Class here lexicography

—31 **Specialized dictionaries**

Including dictionaries of abbreviations, acronyms, antonyms, clichés, eponyms, homonyms, idioms, paronyms, puns, synonyms; crossword-puzzle, picture, reverse dictionaries; speller-dividers

Spellers relocated to —81

Class etymological dictionaries in —203; class bilingual specialized dictionaries in —32–39

—32–39 **Bilingual dictionaries**

Add to —3 notation 2–9 from Table 6, e.g., dictionaries of the language and English —321, dictionary of French and English 443.21

A bilingual dictionary with entry words in only one language is classed with that language, e.g., an English-French dictionary 423.41. A bilingual dictionary with entry words in both languages is classed with the language in which it will be more useful; for example, most libraries in English-speaking regions will find English-French, French-English dictionaries most useful classed with French in 443.21, Chinese-French, French-Chinese dictionaries with Chinese in 495.1341. If classification with either language is equally useful, give priority to the language coming later in 420–490, e.g., French-German, German-French dictionaries 443.31

See Manual at T4—32–39

—5   Grammar of the standard form of the language

Descriptive study of morphology and syntax

Including case, categorial, dependency, generative, relational grammar

Class here grammatical relations; parts of speech; comprehensive works on phonology and morphology, on phonology and syntax, or on all three

Class derivational etymology in —2

> *For phonology, see —15; for prescriptive grammar, including inflectional schemata designed for use as aids in learning languages, see —8*

—7   Historical and geographic variations, modern nongeographic variations

Including slang

Class here early forms; dialects, pidgins, creoles

Subdivisions of —7 are given under some individual languages in 420–490

Use notation 7 only for works that stress differences among the forms of a language

Topics classed in —1–5 and —8 when applied to standard forms of the language are classed here when applied to historical and geographic variations, to modern nongeographic variations, e.g., the distinctive grammatical characteristics of a particular dialect

> *See Manual at T4—7; also at T4—1–5 and T4—8 vs. T4—7*

—8   Standard usage of the language (Prescriptive linguistics)   Applied linguistics

General, formal, informal usage

Class here works for persons learning a second language, works for native speakers who are learning the acceptable patterns of their own language

Class purely descriptive linguistics in —1–5; class prescriptive and applied linguistics applied to historical and geographic variations, to modern nongeographic variations of the language in —7

> *For dictionaries, see —3; for rhetoric, see 808.04*

> *See Manual at T4—1–5 and T4—8 vs. T4—7; also at 410*

—800 1–800 9   Standard subdivisions

> *See Manual at 407.1, T1—071 vs. 401.93, 410.71, 418.0071, T4—80071*

—802 Translation to and from other languages

Class here interpretation

Use the base number for the language being translated into

Add to —802 notation 2–9 from Table 6 for the language being translated from, e.g., translating from Chinese —802951, translating from Chinese into English 428.02951

—81 **Words**

Meaning, pronunciation, spelling

Including spellers [*formerly also* —31]

Class formal presentation of vocabulary in —82; class audio-lingual presentation of vocabulary in —83

See also —152 for nonprescriptive treatment of spelling and pronunciation, —3 for dictionaries, 783.043 for pronunciation for singing

See Manual at T4—3 vs. T4—81

—82 **Structural approach to expression**

Formal (traditional) presentation of grammar, vocabulary, reading selections

Class here verb tables and inflectional schemata designed for use as aids in learning a language

For words, see —81; for reading, see —84

—824 Structural approach to expression for those whose native language is different

Add to —824 notation 2–9 from Table 6, e.g., the language for Spanish-speaking people —82461, English for Spanish-speaking people 428.2461

—83 **Audio-lingual approach to expression**

Informal presentation through practice in correct usage

Class here the "hear-speak" school of learning a language

For pronunciation, see —81

—834 Audio-lingual approach to expression for those whose native language is different

Class here bilingual phrase books

Add to —834 notation 2–9 from Table 6, e.g., the language for Spanish-speaking people —83461, English for Spanish-speaking people 428.3461

—84 **Reading**

For readers, see —86

—840 19	Psychological principles

> Class psychology of reading in 418.4019 unless there is emphasis on the specific language being read

—842	Remedial reading

> Correcting faulty habits and increasing the proficiency of poor readers

—843	Developmental reading

> Including reading power and efficiency of good readers

—843 2	Rapid reading (Speed reading)
—86	**Readers**

> Graded selections with emphasis on structure and vocabulary as needed

> Including readers compiled for training college students in reading comprehension

> Class here texts intended primarily for practice in reading a language

> (Option: Class elementary readers in 372.4122)

—862	Readers for new literates

> Class here remedial readers

> *See Manual at T4—862*

—864	Readers for those whose native language is different

> Add to —864 notation 2–9 from Table 6, e.g., readers for Spanish-speaking people —86461, English readers for Spanish-speaking people 428.6461

> *See Manual at T1—014 vs. T4—864*

Table 5. Racial, Ethnic, National Groups

The following numbers are never used alone, but may be used as required (either directly when so noted or through the interposition of notation 089 from Table 1) with any number from the schedules, e.g., ethnopsychology (155.84) of the Japanese (—956 in this table): 155.84956; ceramic arts (738) of Jews (—924 in this table): 738.089924. They may also be used when so noted with numbers from other tables, e.g., notation 174 from Table 2

Except where instructed otherwise, and unless it is redundant, add 0 to the number from this table and to the result add notation 1 or 3–9 from Table 2 for area in which a group is or was located, e.g., Germans in Brazil —31081, but Germans in Germany —31; Jews in Germany or Jews from Germany —924043. If notation from Table 2 is not added, use 00 for standard subdivisions; see below for complete instructions on using standard subdivisions

Notation from Table 2 may be added if the number in Table 5 is limited to speakers of only one language even if the group discussed does not approximate the whole of the group specified by the Table 5 number, e.g., Bavarians in Brazil —31081, but Amhara in United States —928 (*not* —928073 because Amharic is not the only language spoken by Ethiopians and Eritreans included in —928)

Notation from Table 2 may be added for either present or past specific location of the group discussed if only one specific location is relevant, e.g., sociology of Jews from many different countries now in United States 305.8924073, contributions to music around the world of Jews who previously lived in Poland 780.899240438

If both present and past specific locations of the group discussed are relevant, then notation from Table 2 is added only for present location of the group, e.g., Jews from Germany in the United States —924073 (*not* —924043). An exception occurs when the present location of the group is defined by the class number to which racial, ethnic, national group notation is added, e.g., Jews in United States history 973.04924. The area notation added to Table 5 numbers is then available to show the past location of the group, e.g., Jews from Germany in United States history 973.04924043, Jews from Germany in United States higher education 378.73089924043

Standard subdivisions may be added to Table 5 notation when that notation is added directly to the base number, e.g., periodicals about sociology of Irish Americans 305.8916207305. However, standard subdivisions are not added to Table 5 notation when that notation is used through interposition of notation 089 from Table 1, e.g., an exhibition of ceramic arts of Russian Jews 738.089924047 (*not* 738.089924047074)

(continued)

Table 5. Racial, Ethnic, National Groups (continued)

When Table 5 notation is not followed by 0 plus notation from Table 2, use 00 for standard subdivisions, e.g., periodicals about sociology of Japanese 305.8956005, biography of an Irish American in New York City 974.7100491620092. When Table 5 notation is followed by 0 plus notation from Table 2, however, use 0 for standard subdivisions, e.g., periodicals about sociology of Japanese Americans 305.895607305. (For the purpose of this rule, notation 96073 African Americans is treated as Table 5 notation, e.g., periodicals on sociology of African Americans 305.896073005, periodicals on sociology of African Americans in Ohio 305.896073077105.)

Except where instructed otherwise, give preference first to ethnic group, second to nationality, last to basic races, e.g., United States citizens of Serbian descent —91822073 (*not* — 13), United States citizens of the Caucasian race — 13 (*not* —034073). In this table "ethnic group" most often means a group with linguistic ties, but it can also mean a group with cultural or racial ties. The numbers for basic races are used only for works treating races as extremely broad categories. Thus notation 036 Negro race is used for works treating Black peoples of African and Asian or Oceanian origin as belonging to the same race, but — 96 is used for Black peoples of African origin

Except where instructed otherwise, when choosing between two ethnic groups, give preference to the group for which the notation is different from that for the nationality of the people, e.g., a work treating equally Hispanic and native American heritage of bilingual Spanish-Guaraní mestizos of Paraguay —983820892 (*not* —68892)

Except where instructed otherwise, when choosing between two national groups, give preference to the former or ancestral national group, e.g., people from the former Soviet Union who became United States citizens —917073 (*not* — 13)

See Manual at Table 5

SUMMARY

—03–04	[Basic races, mixtures of basic races]
—1	North Americans
—2	British, English, Anglo-Saxons
—3	Nordic (Germanic) people
—4	Modern Latin peoples
—5	Italians, Romanians, related groups
—6	Spanish and Portuguese
—7	Other Italic peoples
—8	Greeks and related groups
—9	Other racial, ethnic, national groups

—03   **Basic races**

Limited to the three basic races listed below

Class races considered as narrower categories than basic races with the appropriate ethnic groups, e.g., Australoid race with the Australian native peoples —9915

> *See also —994 for Polynesian race, —995 for Melanesian and Micronesian races*

—034   Caucasian race

Class here comprehensive works on Indo-European peoples

> *For a specific Indo-European people, see the people in —1–91, e.g., French —41*

> *See also —9996 for peoples who speak, or whose ancestors spoke, Caucasian languages*

—035   Mongoloid race

Use of this number is limited to works that discuss East Asians and American native peoples as belonging to one race

Class Asian Mongoloid races in —95; class comprehensive works on North and South American native races in —97

—036   Negro race

Use of this number is limited to works that discuss Black peoples of African and Asian or Oceanian origin as belonging to the same race

Class African Negro races in —96; class Aeta, Andamanese, Semang peoples in —9911

> *See also —9915 for Australoid race*

—04   **Mixtures of basic races**

Limited to works that emphasize mixture of basic races

Class works about racially mixed people that do not emphasize mixture of basic races with the ethnic or national groups stressed in the works or with the groups with which the people are most closely identified, e.g., works about Métis that emphasize their North American native roots —97 (*not* —042)

—042   Caucasians and Mongoloids

—043   Mongoloids and Negroes

—044   Negroes and Caucasians

—046   Caucasians, Mongoloids, Negroes

>   **—1–9   Specific racial, ethnic, national groups**

By origin or situation

Class comprehensive works in 001–999 without adding notation from Table 5

See Manual at Table 5

(Option: To give local emphasis and a shorter number to a specific group, place it first by use of a letter or other symbol, e.g., Arabs —A [preceding —1]. Another option is given at —1)

—1   North Americans

For Spanish Americans, see —68; for North Americans of Celtic (Irish, Scots, Manx, Welsh, Cornish) origin, see —916; for North American native peoples, see —97

See Manual at T5—1

(Option: To give local emphasis and a shorter number to a specific group, e.g., Sinhalese, class it in this number; in that case class North Americans in —2. Another option is given at —1–9)

—11   Canadians

For Canadians not of British or French origin, see the racial or ethnic group of origin, e.g., Canadians of German origin —31071, Inuit —9712071

—112   Canadians of British origin

See Manual at T5—112, T5—114 vs. T5—2, T5—41

—114   Canadians of French origin

See Manual at T5—112, T5—114 vs. T5—2, T5—41

—13   People of United States ("Americans")

Class here United States citizens of British origin, people of United States as a national group

For United States citizens of other origins, see the racial or ethnic group of origin, e.g., German Americans —31073, African Americans —96073

See Manual at T5—13 vs. T5—2073, T5—21073

—2   British, English, Anglo-Saxons

Subdivisions are added for British, English, Anglo-Saxons together; for British as an ethnic group; for English as an ethnic group

For North Americans of British origin, see —1; for Anglo-Indians (Indian citizens of British origin), see —91411; for people of Celtic (Irish, Scots, Manx, Welsh, Cornish) origin, see —916

See Manual at Table 5; also at T5—112, T5—114 vs. T5—2, T5—41; also at T5—13 vs. T5—2073, T5—21073; also at T5—201–209 vs. T5—2101–2109

—21   **People of British Isles**

Class here United Kingdom citizens of British origin, United Kingdom citizens as a national group

For United Kingdom citizens of other origins, see the racial or ethnic group of origin, e.g., United Kingdom citizens of Indian origin —91411041

See Manual at T5—13 vs. T5—2073, T5—21073; also at T5—201–209 vs. T5—2101–2109

—23   **New Zealanders**

Class here New Zealanders of British origin, New Zealanders as a national group

For New Zealanders of other origins, see the racial or ethnic group of origin, e.g., New Zealanders of Irish origin —9162093, Maori —99442

—24   **Australians**

Class here Australians of British origin, Australians as a national group

For Australians of other origins, see the racial or ethnic group of origin, e.g., Australians of Italian origin —51094, Australian native peoples —9915

—28   **South Africans of British origin**

Class South Africans as a national group in —968

See also —2106891 for Zimbabweans of British origin

—3   **Nordic (Germanic) people**

For English, Anglo-Saxons, see —2

—31   **Germans**

—35   **Swiss**

Class here Swiss Germans, comprehensive works on people of Switzerland

For Swiss citizens of other ethnic groups, see the ethnic group, e.g., French-speaking Swiss —410494, Romansh-speaking Swiss —5, Italian-speaking Swiss —510494

—36   **Austrians**

—39   **Other Germanic peoples**

Including Goths, Vandals

—392   Friesians

—393   Netherlandish peoples

—393 1   Dutch

—393 2   Flemings (Flemish)

> Class here comprehensive works on Belgians
>
> *For Walloons, see —42*

—393 6   Afrikaners

> Class South Africans as a national group in —968

—395   Scandinavians

> *For specific Scandinavian groups, see —396–398*
>
> *See also —94541 for Finns, —9455 for Sami*

—396   West Scandinavians

—396 1   Icelanders

—396 9   Faeroese

—397   Swedes

—398   Danes and Norwegians

—398 1   Danes

—398 2   Norwegians

—4   Modern Latin peoples

> *For Italians, Romanians, related groups, see —5; for Spanish and Portuguese, see —6*

—41   French

> Class Canadians of French origin in —114
>
> *For Corsicans, see —58; for Basques, see —9992*
>
> *See Manual at T5—112, T5—114 vs. T5—2, T5—41*

—42   Walloons

—49   Catalans

—5   Italians, Romanians, related groups

> Including Rhaetians

—51   Italians

—56   Sardinians

—57   Dalmatians

—58   Corsicans

—59   Romanians

—6   Spanish and Portuguese

—61   People of Spain (Spaniards)

For Catalans, see —49; for Basques, see —9992

—68   Spanish Americans

Class here comprehensive works on Latin Americans

For Latin American peoples not provided for here, see the people, e.g., Brazilians —698

See also —9141 for people of Guyana and Suriname as national groups, —96972 for Central American and Caribbean national groups of majority African origin, e.g., —9697282 for Belizeans, —9697294 for Haitians

—687–688   National groups

Citizens of independent and partly independent jurisdictions having a Spanish-speaking majority or Spanish as an official language

Add to base number —68 notation 7–8 from Table 2, e.g., Puerto-Ricans —687295, Chileans —6883; then add further as instructed at beginning of Table 5, e.g., Chileans in United States —6883073; however, for comprehensive works on Spanish Americans in jurisdictions where they are a minority, see —6804–6809, e.g., Spanish Americans in United States —68073

—69   Portuguese-speaking peoples

—691   People of Portugal

—698   Brazilians

Class here Brazilians of Portuguese origin, Brazilians as a national group

For Brazilian citizens of other origins, see the racial or ethnic group of origin, e.g., Brazilians of Italian origin —51081, Brazilians of African origin —96081

—7   Other Italic peoples

For Etruscans, see —9994

—71   Ancient Romans

—79   Osco-Umbrians

—8   Greeks and related groups

Subdivisions are added for Greeks and related groups together, for Greeks as an ethnic group alone

For Macedonians, see —91819

—81   **Ancient Greeks**

> Class here comprehensive works on ancient Greeks and Romans
>
> *For ancient Romans, see —71*

—89   **Modern Greeks and related groups**

—893   Greek nationals

—895   Cypriots

> Class here comprehensive works on people of Cyprus
>
> *For Turkish Cypriots, see —943505693*

—9   Other racial, ethnic, national groups

SUMMARY

—91	**Other Indo-European peoples**
—92	**Semites**
—93	**North Africans**
—94	**Peoples of North and West Asian origin or situation; Dravidians**
—95	**East and Southeast Asian peoples; Mundas**
—96	**Africans and people of African descent**
—97	**North American native peoples**
—98	**South American native peoples**
—99	**Aeta, Andamanese, Semang; Papuans; Australian native peoples; Malayo-Polynesian and related peoples; miscellaneous peoples**

—91   **Other Indo-European peoples**

SUMMARY

—914	**South Asians**
—915	**Iranians**
—916	**Celts**
—917	**East Slavs**
—918	**Slavs**
—919	**Balts and other Indo-European peoples**

—914   South Asians

> Class here Indic peoples (peoples who speak, or whose ancestors spoke, Indic languages), Indo-Aryans
>
> *For Dravidians and Scytho-Dravidians, see —948; for South Asians who speak, or whose ancestors spoke, languages closely related to East and Southeast Asian languages, see —95*
>
> *See also notation 08621 in Table 1 for Brahmans as an elite social group, —2945 in Table 7 for Brahmans as a religious group*
>
> *See Manual at T5—948 vs. T5—914*

—914 1	National groups

Citizens of independent and partly independent jurisdictions of South Asia and of largely South Asian origin

Including Guyanese, Maldivians, Mauritians, Surinamers

For nationals of specific ethnolinguistic groups, see —9142–9149; for Nepalese national group, see —91495; for Trinidadians of South Asian origin, see —96972983; for Fijians of South Asian origin, see —995

See Manual at T5—9141

—914 11	Indians

Including Anglo-Indians (Indian citizens of British origin), post-1975 Sikkimese

Class comprehensive works on Sikkimese in —91417

—914 12	Pakistanis and people of Bangladesh
—914 122	Pakistanis
—914 126	People of Bangladesh
—914 13	Sri Lankans (Ceylonese)

For Sinhalese as an ethnic group, see —9148; for Tamil as an ethnic group, see —94811

—914 17	Sikkimese

For post-1975 Sikkimese, see —91411

—914 18	Bhutanese

Class Bhutia as an ethnic group in —954

—914 2	Punjabis
—914 3	Hindis
—914 4	Bengali

For Bengali of Bangladesh, see —914126

—914 5	Assamese, Bihari, Oriya
—914 7	Gujar, Gujarati; Bhil; people who speak, or whose ancestors spoke, Rajasthani
—914 8	Sinhalese
—914 9	Other Indic peoples

Including Nuri

—914 95   Nepali

         Class here Nepali as an ethnic group, comprehensive works on people of Nepal

         For citizens of Nepal belonging to other ethnic groups, see the ethnic group, e.g., Bihari —9145, Chepang and Newar —95

—914 96   Pahari

—914 97   Romany people

—914 99   Dardic peoples

         Including Kashmiris, Kohistanis

         Use of this number for Nuri discontinued; class in —9149

         Class Romany people in —91497

—915   Peoples who speak, or whose ancestors spoke, Iranian languages

         Including Kushans, Scythians

—915 5   Persians

         Class here Persians as an ethnic group, comprehensive works on people of Iran

         For citizens of Iran belonging to other ethnic groups, see the ethnic group, e.g., Azerbaijani —94361055

—915 7   Tajik [*formerly —9159*]

         Including Galcha

—915 9   Other Iranian peoples

         Including Ossets, Pamiri

         Tajik relocated to —9157

—915 93   Afghans (Pashtun)

         Class here Afghans as an ethnic group, comprehensive works on people of Afghanistan

         For citizens of Afghanistan belonging to other ethnic groups, see the ethnic group, e.g., Tajik —91570581

—915 97   Kurds

—915 98   Baluchi

—916   Celts

         Including Gauls

—916 2   Irish

—916 3   Scots

—916 4	Manx
—916 6	Welsh (Cymry)
—916 7	Cornish
—916 8	Bretons
—917	East Slavs

Class here people of former Soviet Union, of Commonwealth of Independent States

Class comprehensive works on Slavs in —918

> *For a specific ethnic group of former Soviet Union or Commonwealth of Independent States, see the group, e.g., Uzbek —94325*

—917 1	Russians
—917 14	Cossacks
—917 9	Ukrainians, Ruthenians, Belarusians
—917 91	Ukrainians and Ruthenians

Subdivisions are added for Ukrainians and Ruthenians together, for Ukrainians alone

> *See also —215 in Table 7 for Ruthenians as a religious group*

—917 99	Belarusians
—918	Slavs

> *For East Slavs, see —917*

—918 1	Bulgarians and Macedonians

Class here comprehensive works on South Slavs

> *For Serbs, Montenegrins, Croats, Bosnian Muslims, see —9182; for Slovenes, see —9184*

—918 11	Bulgarians
—918 19	Macedonians
—918 2	Serbs, Montenegrins, Croats, Bosnian Muslims

Class here Yugoslavs; peoples who speak, or whose ancestors spoke, Serbo-Croatian

Class comprehensive works on South Slavs in —9181

> *For citizens of former Yugoslavia of other ethnic groups, see the ethnic group, e.g., Macedonians —918190497, Slovenes —91840497, Albanians —919910497*

> *See also notation 2971 from Table 7 for Muslims as a religious group*

—918 22   Serbs and Montenegrins

> Subdivisions are added for Serbs and Montenegrins together, for Serbs alone

—918 23   Croats

—918 4   Slovenes

—918 5   West Slavs   Poles

> Including Kashubs

> *For Cossacks, see —91714; for Moravians and Czechs, see —9186; for Slovaks, see —9187; for Wends, see —9188*

—918 6   Moravians [*formerly* —9187] and Czechs

> Class here Czechoslovaks

> Subdivisions are added for either or both topics in heading

> *For Slovaks, see —9187*

> *See also —246 in Table 7 for Moravians as a religious group*

—918 7   Slovaks

> Moravians relocated to —9186

—918 8   Wends (Lusatians, Sorbs)

—919   Balts and other Indo-European peoples

> Subdivisions are added for Balts and other Indo-European peoples together, for Balts alone

—919 2   Lithuanians

—919 3   Latvians (Letts)

—919 9   Albanians, Armenians, Hittites

—919 91   Albanians

—919 92   Armenians

—92   **Semites**

—921   Akkadians, Amorites, Assyrians, Babylonians

> Use of this number for Chaldeans discontinued; class in —92

—922   Aramaeans

—924   Hebrews, Israelis, Jews

> Class here Beta Israel

> Subdivisions are added for any or all topics in heading

> *See also notation 296 in Table 7 for Jews as a religious group*

—926	Canaanites and Phoenicians

For Amorites, see —921

—927	Arabs and Maltese

Subdivisions are added for Arabs and Maltese together, for Arabs alone

—927 2	Bedouins

See also —933 for Berbers and Tuareg

—927 4	Palestinian Arabs
—927 5–927 6	National groups of Arabs

Citizens of independent or partly independent jurisdictions having an Arab or Arabic-speaking majority or Arabic as the official language

Add to base number —927 notation 5–6 from Table 2, e.g., Iraqis —927567, Sudanese —927624; then add further as instructed at beginning of Table 5, e.g., Sudanese in Ethiopia —927624063; however, for comprehensive works on Arabs as a minority group in a country of Asia or Africa where Arabic is not the official language, see —92705–92706, e.g., Arabs in Iran —927055; for Mauritanians as a national group, see —9661

—[927 7]	Maltese

Relocated to —9279

—927 9	Maltese [*formerly* —9277]
—928	Ethiopians and Eritreans

Including Amhara, Gurage, Harari, Tigre, Tigrinya; comprehensive works on people of Eritrea

Class here comprehensive works on people of Ethiopia

For Beta Israel, see —924; for Cushitic peoples of Ethiopia and Eritrea, see —935

—929	Mahri and Socotrans

Class here South Arabic peoples

—93	**North Africans**

Class here peoples who speak, or whose ancestors spoke, non-Semitic Afro-Asiatic languages

For Arabs, see —927; for Ethiopians and Eritreans, see —928

—931	Ancient Egyptians
—932	Copts

See also notation 215 in Table 7 for Copts as members of the Coptic Church

—933   Berbers and Tuareg

—935   Cushitic and Omotic peoples

        Including Oromo, Somali

        Class Beta Israel in —924; class Djiboutians as a national group in —96771; class Somali as a national group in —96773

—937   Hausa

        Class the people of Niger as a national group in —96626

—94   **Peoples of North and West Asian origin or situation; Dravidians**

        For Indo-European peoples of these regions, see —91; for Semites, see —92

—941   Tungusic peoples

        Including Evenki, Nanai

—942   Mongols

—943   Turkic peoples

        Add to base number —943 the numbers following —943 in notation 9431–9438 from Table 6, e.g., Turks —9435, Uzbek —94325; then add further as instructed at beginning of Table 5, e.g., Turks in Germany —9435043; however, for Chuvashes, see —9456

        Class Cossacks in —91714

        See Manual at T5—9435

—944   Samoyed

—945   Finno-Ugrians

—945 1   Ugrians

        Including Ostyaks, Vogul

—945 11   Hungarians

—945 3   Permiaks, Votyak, Komi (Zyrian)

—945 4   Finnic peoples

        Including Karelians, Livonians, Veps

        For Permiaks, Votyak, Komi, see —9453; for Sami, see —9455; for Cheremis, Chuvashes, Mordvin, see —9456

—945 41   Finns

—945 45   Estonians

—945 5   Sami

—945 6   Cheremis (Mari), Chuvashes, Mordvin

—946	Paleo-Asiatic (Paleosiberian) peoples

Including Ainu

—948	Dravidians and Scytho-Dravidians

Including Maratha (Mahratta), Sindhi

Subdivisions are added for Dravidians and Scytho-Dravidians together, for Dravidians alone

> *See also —914 for speakers of Indic languages who are not Scytho-Dravidians, —915 for Scythians*
>
> *See Manual at T5—948 vs. T5—914*

—948 1	South Dravidians

Including Toda

Class here peoples who speak, or whose ancestors spoke, South Dravidian languages

—948 11	Tamil
—948 12	Malayalis
—948 14	Kanarese
—948 2	Central Dravidians

Including Gond, Kandh

Class here peoples who speak, or whose ancestors spoke, central Dravidian languages

—948 27	Telugu
—948 3	North Dravidians Brahui

Including Kurukh

Class here peoples who speak, or whose ancestors spoke, North Dravidian languages

—95	**East and Southeast Asian peoples; Mundas**

Including Chepang, Karen, Newar

Class here Asian Mongoloid races; South Asian peoples who speak, or whose ancestors spoke, languages closely related to East and Southeast Asian languages; comprehensive works on Asian peoples

> *For a specific Asian people not provided for here, see the people, e.g., Persians —9155, Aeta and Andamanese —9911, Malays —9928*

—951	Chinese
—954	Tibetans

Class here Bhutia as an ethnic group

> *See also —91418 for Bhutanese as a national group*

—956	Japanese

Including Ryukyuans

For Ainu, see —946

—957	Koreans
—958	Burmese
—959	Miscellaneous southeast Asian peoples; Mundas

Limited to peoples provided for below

—959 1	Tai peoples

Class here peoples who speak, or whose ancestors spoke, Tai languages

—959 11	Thai (Siamese)
—959 19	Other Tai peoples
—959 191	Lao
—959 2	Viet-Muong peoples Vietnamese

Class here peoples who speak, or whose ancestors spoke, Viet-Muong languages

Class comprehensive works on Montagnards of Vietnam in —9593

—959 3	Mon-Khmer peoples Khmer (Cambodians)

Including comprehensive works on Montagnards of Vietnam

Class here peoples who speak, or whose ancestors spoke, Mon-Khmer languages

Class Montagnards of a specific ethnic group with the ethnic group, e.g., Rhade —9922

For Semang, see —9911

—959 4	Miao (Hmong) and Yao peoples

Class here peoples who speak, or whose ancestors spoke, Miao-Yao languages

—959 42	Miao (Hmong) people
—959 5	Mundas
—96	**Africans and people of African descent**

Class here African Negro races, African pygmies

For Arabs, see —927; for Ethiopians and Eritreans, see —928; for North Africans, see —93

—960 73   African Americans (United States Blacks)

> Unless it is redundant, add 0* to —96073 and to the result add notation 1–9 from Table 2 for area, e.g., African Americans in England —96073042, African Americans in New York —960730747, but African Americans in United States —96073

> *See Manual at T5—96073*

—961   Khoikhoi and San

—963   Peoples who speak, or whose ancestors spoke, Niger-Congo languages

> Including peoples who speak, or whose ancestors spoke, Ijoid languages, Kordofanian languages; Dogon

> Add to base number —963 the numbers following —963 in notation 9632–9639 from Table 6, e.g., Zulu —963986; then add further as instructed at beginning of Table 5, e.g., Zulu in Malawi —96398606897

—965   Peoples who speak, or whose ancestors spoke, Nilo-Saharan languages

> Including Nilotic peoples, Nubians, Luo, Songhai

> Class here peoples who speak or whose ancestors spoke Chari-Nile (Macrosudanic) languages

—966–968   National groups in Africa

> Citizens of independent and partly independent jurisdictions

> Add to base number —9 notation 66–68 from Table 2, e.g., South Africans —968, Namibians —96881; then add further as instructed at beginning of Table 5, e.g., South Africans in the United Kingdom —968041

> Class nationals of specific ethnolinguistic groups in —961–965, e.g., South African Zulu —963986068

>> *For South Africans of British origin, see —28; for Afrikaners, see —3936*

>> *See also —9276 for national groups of African Arabs, e.g., modern Egyptians —92762, Sudanese —927624; —928 for Ethiopians and Eritreans as national groups; —931 for ancient Egyptians as a national group*

—969   Other national groups of largely African descent

> Citizens of independent and partly independent jurisdictions

> Add to base number —969 notation 4–9 from Table 2, e.g., Haitians —9697294, Virgin Islanders —96972972; then add further as instructed at beginning of Table 5, e.g., Haitians in the United States —9697294073

> Class nationals of specific ethnolinguistic groups in —961–965; class minority groups of African descent in —9604–9609, plus notation from Table 2 as instructed at beginning of Table 5 to show where the groups are located, e.g., persons of African descent in Canada —96071

---

*Add 00 for standard subdivisions; see instructions at beginning of Table 5

—97   **North American native peoples**

Including Tarascans

Class here North American native races; people who speak, or whose ancestors spoke, North American native languages; comprehensive works on North and South American native peoples, on North and South American native races

Add to base number —97 the numbers following —97 in notation 971–979 from Table 6, e.g., Inuit —9712; then add further as instructed at beginning of Table 5, e.g., Inuit in Canada —9712071

Comprehensive works on Woodland Indians are classed in —97. Specific groups of Woodland Indians are classed according to the language that they speak or their ancestors spoke, e.g., Iroquois Indians —9755

Comprehensive works on Plains Indians are classed in —97078. Specific groups of Plains Indians are classed according to the language that they speak or their ancestors spoke, e.g., Cheyenne Indians —973

Comprehensive works on Pueblo Indians are classed in —974. Specific groups of Pueblo Indians are classed according to the language that they speak or their ancestors spoke, e.g., Hopi —9745

Class national groups of modern Central America where Spanish is an official language in —68728 even if the majority of their population is of North American native origin, e.g., Guatemalans as a national group —687281

For South American native peoples and races, see —98

—98   **South American native peoples**

Including peoples who speak, or whose ancestors spoke, Araucanian, Cahuapanan, Mataco-Guaicuru, Tacanan, Uru-Chipaya, Witotoan, Yanomam languages; Hixkaryana, Warao, Yaruro

Class here South American native races; peoples who speak, or whose ancestors spoke, South American native languages

Add to base number —98 the numbers following —98 in notation 982–984 from Table 6, e.g., Quechua —98323; then add further as instructed at beginning of Table 5, e.g., Quechua in Bolivia —98323084

Class national groups of modern South America where Spanish is an official language in —688 even if the majority of their population is of South American native origin, e.g., Peruvians as a national group —6885

—99   **Aeta, Andamanese, Semang; Papuans; Australian native peoples; Malayo-Polynesian and related peoples; miscellaneous peoples**

—991   Aeta, Andamanese, Semang; Papuans; Australian native peoples

—991 1   Aeta, Andamanese, Semang

—991 2   Papuans

Class here peoples who speak, or whose ancestors spoke, Papuan
languages; Papua New Guineans as a national group

Class peoples of New Guinea who speak, or whose ancestors spoke,
Austronesian languages in —995

For Andamanese, see —9911

—991 5   Australian native peoples

Including Tasmanian native peoples

Class here comprehensive works on Australoid race

*For peoples of Australia who speak, or whose ancestors spoke,
Papuan languages, see —9912. For a specific people regarded as
belonging to Australoid race, see the people, e.g., Papuans of New
Guinea —9912*

—992   Peoples who speak, or whose ancestors spoke, Malayo-Polynesian
languages

Class here comprehensive works on peoples who speak, or whose ancestors
spoke, Austronesian languages

*For Malagasy, see —993; for Polynesians, see —994; for Melanesians
and Micronesians, see —995*

—992 1   Filipinos

Class here people of the Philippines

*For Aeta, see —9911. For Philippine citizens of non-Filipino ethnic
groups, see the ethnic group, e.g., Philippine citizens of Chinese
origin —9510599*

—992 2   Peoples who speak, or whose ancestors spoke, Indonesian and
Chamic languages

Including Jarai, Rhade

Class here people of Indonesia

Class comprehensive works on Montagnards of Vietnam in —9593

*For Formosan native peoples, see —9925; for peoples who speak, or
whose ancestors spoke, Malay (Bahasa Malaysia), and Malaysians
as a national group, see —9928*

—992 5   Formosan native peoples

Including Ami, Atayal, Bunun, Paiwan, Thao, Yami

Class here peoples who speak, or whose ancestors spoke, Taiwan
(Formosan) languages

*See also —951 for peoples who speak, or whose ancestors spoke,
Taiwanese dialect of Chinese*

—992 8   Malays

> Class here people who speak, or whose ancestors spoke, Malay (Bahasa Malaysia); people of Malaysia

—993   Malagasy

—994   Polynesians

> Class here Polynesian race; peoples who speak, or whose ancestors spoke, Polynesian languages; national groups of Polynesia

> Add to base number —994 the numbers following —994 in notation 9942–9948 from Table 6, e.g., Tahitians —99444; then add further as instructed at beginning of Table 5, e.g., Tahitians in New Zealand —99444093

> *For Fijians, see —995*

—995   Melanesians and Micronesians

> Including Melanesian race; peoples who speak, or whose ancestors spoke, Austronesian languages of Melanesia; national groups of Melanesia; Fijians

> *For Papua New Guineans as a national group and peoples who speak, or whose ancestors spoke, Papuan languages, see —9912; for peoples of Polynesian descent, see —994*

—995 2   Micronesian peoples

> Class here Micronesian race; peoples who speak, or whose ancestors spoke, Austronesian languages of Micronesia; national groups of Micronesia

—999   Miscellaneous peoples

> Limited to peoples provided for below

—999 2   Basques

—999 3   Elamites

—999 4   Etruscans

—999 5   Sumerians

—999 6   Georgians, Ingush, Chechen, Circassians, related peoples

> Class here peoples who speak, or whose ancestors spoke, Caucasian (Caucasic) languages

> Add to base number —9996 the numbers following —9996 in notation 99962–99969 from Table 6, e.g., Georgians —99969; then add further as instructed at beginning of Table 5, e.g., Georgians in Canada —99969071

Table 6. Languages

The following notation is never used alone, but may be used with those numbers from the schedules and other tables to which the classifier is instructed to add notation from Table 6, e.g., translations of the Bible (220.5) into Dutch (—3931 in this table): 220.53931; regions (notation 175 from Table 2) where Spanish language (—61 in this table) predominates: Table 2 notation 17561. When adding to a number from the schedules, always insert a point between the third and fourth digits of the complete number

Unless there is specific provision for the old or middle form of a modern language, class these forms with the modern language, e.g., Old High German —31, but Old English —29

Unless there is specific provision for a dialect of a language, class the dialect with the language, e.g., American English dialects —21, but Swiss-German dialect —35

Unless there is a specific provision for a pidgin or creole, class it with the source language from which more of its vocabulary comes than from its other source language(s), e.g., Crioulo language —69, but Papiamento —68

The numbers in this table do not necessarily correspond exactly to the numbers used for individual languages in 420–490 and in 810–890. For example, although the base number for English in 420–490 is 42, the number for English in Table 6 is —21, not —2

(Option A: To give local emphasis and a shorter number to a specific language, place it first by use of a letter or other symbol, e.g., Arabic language —A [preceding —1]. Option B is described at —1)

SUMMARY

—1	**Indo-European languages**
—2	**English and Old English (Anglo-Saxon)**
—3	**Germanic (Teutonic) languages**
—4	**Romance languages**
—5	**Italian, Sardinian, Dalmatian, Romanian, Rhaeto-Romanic**
—6	**Spanish and Portuguese**
—7	**Italic languages**
—8	**Hellenic languages**
—9	**Other languages**

—1   **Indo-European languages**

Including Nostratic hypothesis

For specific Indo-European languages, see —2–91

(Option B: To give local emphasis and a shorter number to a specific language, e.g., Ukrainian, class it in this number, and class Indo-European languages in —91. Option A is described in the introduction to Table 6)

>   **—2–91   Specific Indo-European languages**

Class comprehensive works in —1

—2   **English and Old English (Anglo-Saxon)**

—21   **English**

Including dialects

Class Old English in —29

—217   **English-based pidgins and creoles**

Including Bislama, Krio, Sea Islands Creole (Gullah), Tok Pisin

—219   Middle English, 1100–1500

—29   **Old English (Anglo-Saxon)**

See also —219 for Middle English

—3   **Germanic (Teutonic) languages**

For English and Old English (Anglo-Saxon), see —2

—31   **German**

Class here comprehensive works on dialects of German

For specific dialects of German, see —32–38

See also —394 for Old Low German

>   **—32–38   German dialects**

Class comprehensive works in —31

For Low German (Plattdeutsch), see —394

—32   **Franconian dialect**

—33   **Swabian dialect**

—34   **Alsatian dialect**

—35   **Swiss-German dialect**

—[37]   **Yiddish (Judeo-German)**

       Relocated to —391

—38   **Pennsylvania Dutch (Pennsylvania German)**

—39   **Other Germanic languages**

—391   Yiddish [*formerly* —37]

       Use of this number for comprehensive works on Old Low Germanic languages discontinued; class in —39

       Old Frisian relocated to —392; Old Low Franconian relocated to —3931; Old Low German, Old Saxon relocated to —394

>   —392–394   Low Germanic languages

       Class here West Germanic languages

       Class comprehensive works in —39

—392   Frisian

       Including Old Frisian [*formerly* —391]

—393   Netherlandish languages

—393 1   Dutch

       Including Old Low Franconian [*formerly* —391]

       Class here Flemish

—393 6   Afrikaans

—394   Low German (Plattdeutsch)

       Including Old Low German, Old Saxon [*both formerly* —391]

—395   Scandinavian (North Germanic) languages

       For specific Scandinavian languages, see —396–398

>   —396–398   Specific Scandinavian languages

       Class comprehensive works in —395

—396   West Scandinavian languages

—396 1   Old Norse (Old Icelandic)

—396 9   Modern West Scandinavian languages

—396 91   Icelandic

       See also —*39699 for Faeroese*

—396 99   Faeroese

>   —397–398   East Scandinavian languages

           Class comprehensive works in —395

—397   Swedish

—398   Danish and Norwegian

—398 1   Danish

           Class Dano-Norwegian in —3982

—398 2   Norwegian (Bokmål, Riksmål)

           Class here Dano-Norwegian, comprehensive works on Norwegian

           For New Norse, see —3983

—398 3   Norwegian (New Norse, Nynorsk, Landsmål)

           Class comprehensive works on Norwegian in —3982

—399   East Germanic languages

           Including Burgundian, Gothic, Vandalic

—4   Romance languages

           Class comprehensive works on Italic languages in —7

           For Italian, Romanian, Rhaeto-Romanic, see —5; for Spanish and Portuguese, see —6

—41   French

           Langue d'oc relocated to —491

           Class Franco-Provençal, Provençal in —49

—417   French-based pidgins and creoles

—49   Provençal, Franco-Provençal, Catalan

—491   Provençal

           Class here Langue d'oc [*formerly* —41], Occitan

           Class Franco-Provençal in —49

—499   Catalan

—5   Italian, Sardinian, Dalmatian, Romanian, Rhaeto-Romanic

           Class comprehensive works on Romance languages in —4; class comprehensive works on Italic languages in —7

—51   Italian

—56	**Sardinian**
—57	**Dalmatian**
	Class here Vegliote dialect
—59	**Romanian and Rhaeto-Romanic**
—591	Romanian
—599	Rhaeto-Romance languages
	Including Friulian, Ladin, Romansh

—6   Spanish and Portuguese

Class comprehensive works on Romance languages in —4

—61	**Spanish**
	Including Spanish-based pidgins and creoles
	For Judeo-Spanish (Ladino), see —67; for Papiamento, see —68
—67	**Judeo-Spanish (Ladino)**
—68	**Papiamento**
—69	**Portuguese**
	Including Galician (Gallegan); Portuguese-based pidgins and creoles, e.g., Crioulo
	For Papiamento, see —68

—7   Italic languages

For Romance languages, see —4

—71	**Latin**
	Class comprehensive works on Latin and Greek in —8
—79	**Other Italic languages**
—794	Latinian languages other than Latin
	Including Faliscan, Lanuvian, Praenestian, Venetic
—797	Sabellian languages
	Including Aequian, Marrucinian, Marsian, Paelignian, Sabine, Vestinian, Volscian
—799	Osco-Umbrian languages
	Including Oscan, Umbrian

—8   Hellenic languages

Class here comprehensive works on classical (Greek and Latin) languages

For Latin, see —71

—81   Classical Greek

—87   Preclassical and postclassical Greek

Including the language of Minoan Linear B; Biblical Greek, Koine (Hellenistic Greek); Byzantine Greek

See also —926 for Minoan Linear A

—89   Modern Greek

Including Demotic, Katharevusa

—9   Other languages

Including language of Indus script

SUMMARY

—91	**East Indo-European and Celtic languages**
—92	**Afro-Asiatic (Hamito-Semitic) languages Semitic languages**
—93	**Non-Semitic Afro-Asiatic languages**
—94	**Altaic, Uralic, Hyperborean, Dravidian languages**
—95	**Languages of East and Southeast Asia Sino-Tibetan languages**
—96	**African languages**
—97	**North American native languages**
—98	**South American native languages**
—99	**Non-Austronesian languages of Oceania, Austronesian languages, miscellaneous languages**

—91   East Indo-European and Celtic languages

SUMMARY

—911	**Indo-Iranian languages**
—912	**Sanskrit**
—913	**Middle Indic languages**
—914	**Modern Indic languages**
—915	**Iranian languages**
—916	**Celtic languages**
—917	**East Slavic languages**
—918	**Slavic (Slavonic) languages**
—919	**Baltic and other Indo-European languages**

—911   Indo-Iranian languages

For Indo-Aryan (Indic) languages, see —912–914; for Iranian languages, see —915

\>   —912–914   Indo-Aryan (Indic) languages

Class comprehensive works in —911

—912	Sanskrit
—912 9	Vedic (Old Indic)
—913	Middle Indic languages

Class here comprehensive works on Prakrit languages

For modern Prakrit languages, see —914

—913 7	Pali
—914	Modern Indic languages

Class here modern Prakrit languages

Class comprehensive works on Prakrit languages in —913

—914 1	Sindhi and Lahnda
—914 11	Sindhi
—914 19	Lahnda
—914 2	Panjabi
—914 3	Western Hindi languages
—914 31	Standard Hindi
—914 39	Urdu
—914 4	Bengali

Class here comprehensive works on Bengali and Assamese

For Assamese, see —91451

—914 5	Assamese, Bihari, Oriya
—914 51	Assamese
—914 54	Bihari

Including Bhojpuri, Magahi, Maithili

—914 56	Oriya
—914 6	Marathi

Including Konkani

—914 7	Gujarati, Bhili, Rajasthani
—914 71	Gujarati
—914 79	Rajasthani

Including Jaipuri, Marwari

—914 8	Sinhalese-Maldivian languages	Sinhalese

Including Divehi (Maldivian)

—914 9	Other Indo-Aryan (Indic) languages

Including Awadhi, Bagheli, Chattisgarhi, Eastern Hindi, Nuristani (Kafiri), Pahari

See also —948 for Dravidian languages, —954 for Tibeto-Burman languages, —9595 for Munda languages

—914 95	Nepali
—914 97	Romany [*formerly* —91499]
—914 99	Dardic (Pisacha) languages

Including Kashmiri, Khowar, Kohistani, Shina

Use of this number for Nuristani (Kafiri) discontinued; class in —9149

Romany relocated to —91497

—915	Iranian languages
—915 1	Old Persian

Class here ancient West Iranian languages

See also —9152 for Avestan language

—915 2	Avestan

Class here ancient East Iranian languages

—915 3	Middle Iranian languages

Including Khotanese (Saka), Pahlavi (Middle Persian), Sogdian

—915 5	Modern Persian (Farsi)

Dari relocated to —9156

Class Tajik in —9157

—915 6	Dari [*formerly* —9155]
—915 7	Tajik [*formerly* —9159]
—915 9	Other modern Iranian languages

Including Pamir languages; Ossetic

Tajik relocated to —9157

—915 93	Pashto (Afghan)

Use of this number for Pamir languages discontinued; class in —9159

—915 97	Kurdish languages Kurdish (Kurmanji)

Including Kurdi

—915 98	Baluchi
—916	Celtic languages
	Including Gaulish
—916 2	Irish Gaelic
—916 3	Scottish Gaelic
—916 4	Manx
—916 6	Welsh (Cymric)
—916 7	Cornish
—916 8	Breton
—917	East Slavic languages
	Class comprehensive works on Slavic (Slavonic) languages in —918
—917 1	Russian
—917 9	Ukrainian and Belarusian
—917 91	Ukrainian
—917 99	Belarusian
—918	Slavic (Slavonic) languages
	Including Common Slavic
	Class here comprehensive works on Balto-Slavic languages
	For East Slavic languages, see —917; for Baltic languages, see —919
—918 1	South Slavic languages
	For Serbo-Croatian, see —9182; for Slovenian, see —9184
—918 11	Bulgarian
—918 17	Old Bulgarian (Church Slavic)
—918 19	Macedonian
—918 2	Serbo-Croatian
	Including Dalmatian language (Slavic)
—918 4	Slovenian
—918 5	West Slavic languages
	Including Kashubian
	For Czech, see —9186; for Slovak, see —9187; for Wendish, see —9188; for Polabian, see —9189
—918 51	Polish

—918 6   Czech

> Including Moravian dialects [*formerly* —9187]

—918 7   Slovak

> Moravian dialects relocated to —9186

—918 8   Wendish (Lusatian, Sorbian)

—918 9   Polabian

—919   Baltic and other Indo-European languages

>   —919 1–919 3   Baltic languages

> Class comprehensive works in —919

—919 1   Old Prussian

—919 2   Lithuanian

—919 3   Latvian (Lettish)

—919 9   Other Indo-European languages

—919 91   Albanian

—919 92   Armenian

—919 93   Illyrian and Thraco-Phrygian languages

> Including Illyrian, Ligurian, Messapian, Phrygian, Thracian

—919 94   Tocharian

—919 98   Anatolian languages   Hittite

> Including Luwian, Lycian, Lydian, Palaic

> *See also* —*999 for Hurrian languages*

—92   **Afro-Asiatic (Hamito-Semitic) languages   Semitic languages**

> *For non-Semitic Afro-Asiatic languages, see* —*93*

—921   East Semitic languages   Akkadian (Assyro-Babylonian)

> Including Assyrian, Babylonian

> *For Eblaite, see* —*926*

> *See also* —*9995 for Sumerian*

>   —922–929   West Semitic languages

> Class comprehensive works in —92

—922	Aramaic languages

> *For Eastern Aramaic languages, see —923*

—922 9	Western Aramaic languages

> Including Biblical Aramaic (Chaldee) and Samaritan

—923	Eastern Aramaic languages Syriac
—924	Hebrew
—926	Canaanite languages

> Including Ammonite, Eblaite, Moabite, Phoenician, language of Minoan Linear A
>
> Class here comprehensive works on Canaanitic languages
>
> > *For Hebrew, see —924*
> >
> > *See also —87 for Minoan Linear B*
> >
> > *See Manual at T6—926: Minoan Linear A*

—926 7	Ugaritic
—927	Arabic

> Including Judeo-Arabic
>
> Class here classical Arabic
>
> > *See also —929 for South Arabian languages*

—927 9	Maltese
—928	Ethiopian languages

> Including Gurage, Harari
>
> Class here comprehensive works on South Semitic languages
>
> > *For South Arabian languages, see —929*

—928 1	Ge'ez
—928 2	Tigré
—928 3	Tigrinya
—928 7	Amharic

> Use of this number for Argobba discontinued; class in —928

—929	South Arabian languages

> Including Mahri, Sokotri
>
> Class comprehensive works on South Semitic languages in —928
>
> > *See also —927 for Arabic*

—93	**Non-Semitic Afro-Asiatic languages**
—931	Egyptian

Including Demotic Egyptian

For Coptic, see —932

—932	Coptic
—933	Berber languages

Including Rif, Siwa

—933 3	Tamazight
—933 4	Kabyle
—933 8	Tamashek
—935	Cushitic and Omotic languages

Standard subdivisions are added for Cushitic and Omotic languages together, for Cushitic languages alone

Including Afar, Beja

—935 4	Somali
—935 5	Oromo
—935 9	Omotic languages
—937	Chadic languages

Including Angas

—937 2	Hausa
—94	**Altaic, Uralic, Hyperborean, Dravidian languages**

>	—941–943 Altaic languages

Class comprehensive works in —94

For Ainu, see —946; for Japanese, see —956; for Korean, see —957

—941	Tungusic languages

Including Even (Lamut), Evenki (Tungus), Manchu, Nanai (Goldi)

—942	Mongolian languages

Including Buriat, Kalmyk

—942 3	Mongolian Khalkha Mongolian
—943	Turkic languages
—943 1	Old Turkic and Chuvash

—943 15	Chuvash

> —943 2–943 8   Common Turkic languages

Class comprehensive works in —943

—943 2	Eastern Turkic languages

> *For Northeast Turkic languages, see —9433; for Southern Turkic languages, see —9436*

—943 23	Uighur
—943 25	Uzbek
—943 3	Northern Turkic languages

Including Tuva-Altai languages

Class here Northeast Turkic languages

Class Old Turkic in —9431

> *For Eastern Turkic languages, see —9432*

—943 32	Yakut languages Yakut

Including Dolgan

—943 4	Central Turkic languages

Including Kara-Kalpak, Nogai

—943 45	Kazakh
—943 47	Kirghiz
—943 5	Turkish (Osmanli)

Class here Ottoman Turkish

—943 6	Southern Turkic languages

Including Gagauz, Khalaj, Salar

Class here Southwest Turkic languages

> *For Turkish, see —9435; for Western Turkic languages, see —9438*

—943 61	Azerbaijani
—943 64	Turkmen

Including Chagatai

—943 8   Western Turkic languages

Including Bashkir, Karachay-Balkar, Karaim

Class here Northwest Turkic languages

For Northern Turkic languages, see —9433; for Kara-Kalpak, Nogai, see —9434; for Kazakh, see —94345; for Kirghiz, see —94347

—943 87   Tatar

Class here comprehensive works on Tatar languages

For Crimean Tatar, see —94388

—943 88   Crimean Tatar

>   —944–945   Uralic languages

Class comprehensive works in —945

—944   Samoyedic languages

Including Nganasan, Ostyak Samoyed, Yenisei Samoyed (Enets), Yurak Samoyed (Nenets)

See also —9451 for Ostyak (Khanty), —946 for Yenisei Ostyak (Ket)

—945   Finno-Ugric languages

Class here comprehensive works on Uralic languages, on Uralic and Yukaghir languages

For Samoyedic languages, see —944; for Yukaghir languages, see —946

—945 1   Ugric languages

Including Ostyak (Khanty), Vogul

See also —944 for Ostyak Samoyed, —946 for Yenisei Ostyak (Ket)

—945 11   Hungarian (Magyar)

—945 3   Permic languages

Including Votyak (Udmurt), Zyrian (Komi)

—945 4   Finnic languages

Including Karelian, Livonian, Veps

For Permian languages, see —9453; for Sami, see —9455; for Middle Volga languages, see —9456

—945 41   Finnish (Suomi)

—945 45   Estonian

—945 5   Sami

—945 6   Middle Volga languages

> Including Mari, Mordvin

—946   Hyperborean (Paleosiberian) languages

> Including Chukchi-Kamchatkan (Luorawetlin), Yukaghir families; Ainu, Nivkh (Gilyak), Ket (Yenisei-Ostyak)
>
> Class comprehensive works on the Uralic and Yukaghir languages in —945
>
> *See also —944 for Ostyak Samoyed, Yenisei Samoyed (Enets), —9451 for Ostyak, —9714 for Yupik languages, —9719 for Aleut language*

—948   Dravidian languages

—948 1   South Dravidian languages

> Including Kota, Toda
>
> Class here Dravida group

—948 11   Tamil

—948 12   Malayalam

—948 14   Kannada (Kanarese)

—948 2   Central Dravidian languages

—948 23   Gondi

—948 24   Khond (Kandh)

—948 27   Telugu

—948 3   North Dravidian languages   Brahui

> Including Kurukh (Oraon), Malto

—95   **Languages of East and Southeast Asia**   **Sino-Tibetan languages**

> Including Karen
>
> Here are classed South Asian languages closely related to the languages of East and Southeast Asia
>
> *For Austronesian languages of East and Southeast Asia, see —992*

—951   Chinese

—951 1   Mandarin (Putonghua)

> Class here Beijing dialect [*formerly* —9517]

—951 7   Chinese dialects

> Including Hakka, Mǐn, Wú, Xiāng, Yuè (Cantonese) dialects
>
> Beijing dialect relocated to —9511

—954   Tibeto-Burman languages

                           Including Baric, Bodish, Loloish languages

                           Class Karen in —95

                           For Burmese, see —958

—954 1   Tibetan

—954 9   Eastern Himalayan languages

                           Including Chepang, Limbu, Magari, Sunwar; Newari

                           Class here Kiranti languages

                           Use of this number for Himalayan languages other than Kiranti languages and Newari discontinued; class in —954

                           See also —91495 for Nepali

—956   Japanese

—957   Korean

—958   Burmese

—959   Miscellaneous languages of Southeast Asia; Munda languages

                           Limited to the languages provided for below

                           Class Austroasiatic languages in —9593

                           For Austronesian languages, see —992

—959 1   Tai languages

—959 11   Thai (Siamese)

—959 19   Other Tai languages

                           Including Shan

                           For Viet-Muong languages, see —9592

—959 191   Lao

—959 2   Viet-Muong languages

                           Former heading: Annam-Muong languages

—959 22   Vietnamese

—959 3   Austroasiatic languages   Mon-Khmer languages

                           Including Semang, Senoic languages; Khasi, Mon, Sedang, Srê

                           For Viet-Muong languages, see —9592; for Munda languages, see —9595

—959 32   Khmer (Cambodian)

—959 5   Munda languages

             Including Gadaba, Ho, Mundari, Santali

—959 7   Hmong-Mien (Miao-Yao) languages

—959 72   Hmong (Miao)

—96   **African languages**

             Class Afrikaans in —3936; class Malagasy in —993. Class an African creole having a non-African primary source language with the source language, e.g., Krio —217

             For Ethiopian languages, see —928; for non-Semitic Afro-Asiatic languages, see —93

SUMMARY

—961	**Khoisan languages**	
—963	**Niger-Congo languages**	
—965	**Nilo-Saharan languages**	

—961   Khoisan languages

             Including Khoikhoi, San

—963   Niger-Congo languages

             Including Ijoid, Kordofanian languages; Dogon

SUMMARY

—963 2	**West Atlantic languages**	
—963 3	**Igboid, Defoid, Edoid, Idomoid, Nupoid, Oko, Ukaan-Akpes languages; Kwa languages; Kru languages**	
—963 4	**Mande languages**	
—963 5	**Gur (Voltaic) languages**	
—963 6	**Benue-Congo and Adamawa-Ubangi languages**	
—963 9	**Bantu languages**	

—963 2   West Atlantic languages

—963 21   Senegal group

             Including Serer

             For Fulani, see —96322

—963 214   Wolof

—963 22   Fulani (Fulah)

—963 3   Igboid, Defoid, Edoid, Idomoid, Nupoid, Oko, Ukaan-Akpes
                languages; Kwa languages; Kru languages

                Igboid, Defoid, Edoid, Idomoid, Nupoid, Oko, Ukaan-Akpes languages,
                formerly considered Kwa languages, are now considered Benue-Congo
                languages

                Class comprehensive works on Benue-Congo languages in —9636

—963 32   Ibo (Igbo)

—963 33   Yoruba group   Yoruba

—963 37   Kwa languages

                Including Adangme

                For Volta-Comoe group, see —96338

—963 374   Ewe group   Ewe

—963 378   Gã

—963 38   Volta-Comoe group

—963 385   Central Volta-Comoe (Tano) subgroup   Akan

                Including Anyi, Baoulé

                Class here Fante, Twi

—963 4   Mande languages

—963 45   Mandekan languages

—963 452   Bambara

—963 48   Mende-Bandi group   Mende

—963 5   Gur (Voltaic) languages

                Including Dagomba, Moré, Senufo

                Class Dogon in —963

—963 6   Benue-Congo and Adamawa-Ubangi languages

                Former heading: Benue-Niger languages

                Standard subdivisions are added for Benue-Congo and
                Adamawa-Ubangi languages together, for Benue-Congo languages alone

                Including Bamileke

                Class here Bantoid languages

                *For Igboid, Defoid, Edoid, Idomoid, Nupoid, Oko, Ukaan-Akpes
                languages, see —9633; for Bantu languages, see —9639*

—963 61   Adamawa-Ubangi languages

                Including Gbaya, Zande

—963 616	Sango
—963 64	Cross River languages
	Including Ibibio
—963 642	Efik
—963 9	Bantu languages
	Bantu proper (Narrow Bantu)
	Including Kari group

With the exception of zone J, groups and zones of Bantu languages are based on Malcolm Guthrie's *Comparative Bantu; an Introduction to the Comparative Linguistics and Prehistory of the Bantu Languages, 1967–1971*

> *See also —9636 for Bantoid languages other than Bantu proper*

> *See Manual at T6—9639*

—963 91	Central Bantu languages Central eastern Bantu languages

Including Bena-Kinga, Gogo, Pogolo, Shambala, Zigula-Zaramo groups (from Guthrie's zone G); Bisa-Lamba, Fipa-Mambwe, Lenje-Tonga, Nyakyusa-Konde, Nyika-Safwa groups (from Guthrie's zone M); Manda, Senga-Sena, Tumbuka groups (from Guthrie's zone N)

> *For Swahili group, see —96392; for central western Bantu languages, see —96393*

—963 915	Bemba group Bemba
—963 918	Nyanja group Nyanja
	Class here Chichewa (Chewa)
—963 92	Swahili group Swahili
—963 93	Central western Bantu languages

Including Kimbala, Kiyaka groups (from Guthrie's zone H); Kaonde, Luba, Lunda, Nkoya, Pende, Songe groups (Guthrie's zone L)

—963 931	Kikongo group Kongo
—963 932	Kimbundu (Mbundu) group Kimbundu (Mbundu)
	Limited to Guthrie's zone H
—963 94	Northern Bantu languages Northeastern Bantu languages

Including Bembe-Kabwari, Bira-Huku, Konjo, Lega-Kalanga, Mbole-Ena groups (from Guthrie's zone D); Ilamba-Irangi, Sukuma-Nyamwezi, Tongwe groups (Guthrie's zone F)

Class here comprehensive works on zone J

> *For north northeastern Bantu languages, see —96395; for northwestern Bantu languages, see —96396*

—963 946	Rwanda-Rundi group
—963 946 1	Rwanda (Kinyarwanda)
—963 946 5	Rundi
—963 95	North northeastern Bantu languages

Including Chaga (Shaka), Haya-Jita, Masaba-Luhya, Nyika-Taita, Ragoli-Kuria (Gusii) groups (from Guthrie's zone E)

—963 953	Kikuyu-Kamba group

For Kikuyu, see —963954

—963 954	Kikuyu
—963 956	Nyoro-Ganda group

Including Chiga, Nyankore

For Ganda (Luganda), see —963957

—963 957	Ganda (Luganda)
—963 96	Northwestern Bantu languages

Including Bafia, Basa, Bube-Benga, Kaka, Lundu-Balong, Maka-Njem, Sanaga, Yaunde-Fang groups (Guthrie's zone A); Kele, Mbete, Myene, Njabi, Shira-Punu, Teke, Tende-Yanzi, Tsogo groups (Guthrie's zone B); Kuba, Mboshi, Mongo-Nkundu, Ngombe, Ngundi, Soko-Kele, Tetela groups (from Guthrie's zone C)

—963 962	Duala group Duala
—963 968	Bangi-Ntumba group
—963 968 6	Losengo cluster Lingala
—963 97	Southern Bantu languages Southeastern Bantu languages

Including Makua, Matumbi, Yao groups (Guthrie's zone P); Chopi, Venda groups (from Guthrie's zone S)

For Nguni group, see —96398; for southwestern Bantu languages, Lozi, see —96399

—963 975	Shona group Shona
—963 977	Sotho-Tswana group

Including Ndebele (South Africa) [*formerly* —96398]

—963 977 1	Northern Sotho

Class comprehensive works on northern and southern Sotho in —963977

—963 977 2	Southern Sotho
—963 977 5	Tswana

—963 978	Tswa-Ronga group	Tsonga

—963 98   Nguni group

         Including Ndebele (Zimbabwe)

         Ndebele (South Africa) relocated to —963977

—963 985   Xhosa

         Class Fanakalo in —963986

—963 986   Zulu

         Including Fanakalo

—963 987   Swazi (siSwati)

—963 99   Southwestern Bantu languages

         Including Chokwe-Luchazi, Lozi, Luyana, Subiya groups (Guthrie's zone K); Herero, Ndonga, Umbundu, Yeye groups (Guthrie's zone R)

—965   Nilo-Saharan languages

         Including Nilotic, Nubian languages; Luo, Songhai

         Class here Chari-Nile (Macrosudanic) languages

—97   **North American native languages**

         Including Tarascan

         Class here comprehensive works on North and South American native languages

         For South American native languages, see —98

—971   Inuit (Inuktitut), Yupik, Aleut languages

—971 2   Inuit (Inuktitut) languages

         Including Inupiaq, Kalâtdlisut (Greenlandic)

         Class comprehensive works on Inuit and Yupik languages in —971

—971 24   Eastern Canadian Inuktitut

—971 4   Yupik languages

         Including Siberian Yupik languages; Yuit

—971 9   Aleut

—972   Na-Dene languages

         Including Apache, Navajo; Chipewyan; Haida, Tlingit

         Class here the Athapascan-Eyak family

—973   Macro-Algonkian languages

         Including Cree, Delaware, Ojibway; Muskogean languages

—974 Penutian, Mixe-Zoquean, Mayan, Uto-Aztecan, Kiowa-Tanoan languages

—974 1 Penutian, Mixe-Zoquean, Mayan languages

Standard subdivisions are added for Penutian, Mayan, Mixe-Zoquean languages together, for Penutian languages alone

Including Chinook, Tsimshian

Class Muskogean languages in —973; class Yukian languages in —975; class Zuni in —979; class Araucanian, Uru-Chipaya languages in —98

—974 15 Mayan languages

Including Cakchikel, Kekchí, Quiché, Tzeltal, Tzotzil

—974 152 Yucatecan languages   Maya

Including Itzá, Lacandón, Mopán

Class here Yucatec Maya

—974 5 Uto-Aztecan languages

Including Cahuilla, Hopi, Paiute, Tohono O'Odham (Papago), Ute

—974 52 Aztecan languages

Class here Nahuatl (Aztec)

—974 9 Kiowa-Tanoan languages

—975 Siouan, Iroquian, Hokan, Yukian languages

Class Caddoan, Keresan languages in —979

—975 2 Siouan languages

Including Crow, Dakota

Class Yuchian languages in —979

—975 5 Iroquoian languages

Including Cherokee, Huron, Mohawk

—975 7 Hokan languages

Including Pomo, Yuman languages

—976 Otomanguean languages

Including Mangue, Mixtec, Otomí, Popoloca, Zapotec

—978 Chibchan languages of North America, Misumalpan languages

Including Guaymi; Miskito, Sumo

Class comprehensive works on Chibchan languages in —982

—979   Other North American languages

>   Including Caddoan languages, Keresan languages, Arawakan languages of
>   Central America and West Indies, Salishan languages, Wakashan
>   languages, Yuchian languages; Cuitlatec, Zuni

>   Class Yukian languages in —975; class comprehensive works on Arawakan
>   languages in —9839

—98   South American native languages

>   Including Araucanian, Cahuapanan, Mataco-Guaicuru, Tacanan, Uru-Chipaya,
>   Witotoan, Yanomam languages; Hixkaryana, Warao, Yaruro

—982   Chibchan and Paezan languages

>   Class Yanomam languages, Warao in —98

>   *For Chibchan languages of North America, see —978*

—983   Quechuan (Kechuan), Aymaran, Tucanoan, Tupí, Arawakan languages

>   Former heading: Andean-Equatorial languages

>   Use of this number for Yaruro discontinued; class in —98

—983 2   Quechuan (Kechuan) and Aymaran languages

>   Former heading: Andean languages

—983 23   Quechuan (Kechuan) languages   Quechua (Kechua)

>   Aymaran languages relocated to —98324

—983 24   Aymaran languages [*formerly* —98323]   Aymara

—983 5   Tucanoan languages

>   Including Tucano

—983 7   Jivaroan languages

>   Class Yaruro in —98

>   *For Jivaro proper, see —98372*

—983 72   Jivaro proper   Shuar

>   Including Huambisa

—983 8   Tupí languages

>   Including Munduruku, Sirionó; Oyampi

—983 82   Narrow Tupí group   Guaraní

—983 829   Tupí (Nhengatu)

—983 9   Arawakan languages

>   Class Arawakan languages of Central America and West Indies in —979

—984 Carib, Macro-Gê, Nambiquaran, Panoan languages

Class Hixkaryana, Mataco-Guaicuru, Tacanan, Witotoan languages in —98

—99 **Non-Austronesian languages of Oceania, Austronesian languages, miscellaneous languages**

—991 Non-Austronesian languages of Oceania

—991 2 Papuan languages

Non-Austronesian languages of New Guinea and related languages spoken nearby

Including Sepik-Ramu, Trans New Guinea languages

See also —995 for Austronesian languages of New Guinea

—991 5 Australian and Tasmanian languages

Standard subdivisions are added for Australian and Tasmanian languages together, for Australian languages alone

Aboriginal languages of Australia and Tasmania, and related languages of adjacent islands

Class Papuan languages spoken in Australia in —9912

—992 Austronesian languages   Malayo-Polynesian languages

Including Taiwan (Formosan) languages

Class here Malay languages

For Malagasy, see —993; for Polynesian languages, see —994; for Austronesian languages of Melanesia and Micronesia, see —995

—992 1 Philippine languages

—992 11 Tagalog (Filipino)

—992 2 Indonesian and Chamic languages

Standard subdivisions are added for Indonesian and Chamic languages together, for Indonesian languages alone

Including Borneo languages; Balinese, Madurese, Sundanese

For Malay (Bahasa Malaysia), see —9928

—992 21 Indonesian (Bahasa Indonesia)

Class comprehensive works on Indonesian (Bahasa Indonesia) and Malay (Bahasa Malaysia) in —9928

—992 22 Javanese

—992 8   Malay (Bahasa Malaysia)

           Including Melayu Asli (Proto-Malay) languages; Jakun

           Class here comprehensive works on Malay (Bahasa Malaysia) and Indonesian (Bahasa Indonesia)

           Class Semang, Senoic languages in —9593

           For Indonesian (Bahasa Indonesia), see —99221

—993   Malagasy

—994   Polynesian languages

           Including Rapanui

           Class here comprehensive works on Oceanic (Eastern Austronesian) languages

           For Austronesian languages of Melanesia and Micronesia, see —995

—994 2   Marquesic languages   Hawaiian

           Including Marquesan

—994 4   Tahitic languages

           Including Rarotongan

—994 42   Maori

—994 44   Tahitian

—994 6   Samoic Outlier languages

           Including Nukuoro, Rennellese, Tuvalu

—994 62   Samoan

—994 8   Tongic languages

           Including Niuean, Tonga

—995   Austronesian languages of Melanesia and Micronesia

           Including Fijian

           Class Polynesian languages of Melanesia and Micronesia and comprehensive works on Oceanic (Eastern Austronesian) languages in —994

           See also —9912 for Non-Austronesian languages of Melanesia

—995 2   Austronesian languages of Micronesia

—999   Miscellaneous languages

           Limited to Hurrian languages and the languages provided for below

—999 2   Basque

—999 3   Elamite

—999 4   Etruscan

—999 5   Sumerian

                     See also —926 for Eblaite language

—999 6   Caucasian (Caucasic) languages

\>   —999 62–999 64   North Caucasian languages

         Class comprehensive works in —9996

—999 62   Abkhazo-Adyghian (Northwest Caucasian) languages

                 Including Abazin, Ubykh

—999 623   Abkhaz

—999 624   Circassian languages

                 Including Kabardian

                 For Adyghe, see —999625

—999 625   Adyghe

—999 64   Nakho-Daghestan (Northeast Caucasian) languages

                 Including Avar-Andi-Dido group; Avaric, Dargwa, Lak, Lezghian, Tabasaran

                 Class here Daghestan languages

—999 641   Nakh languages

                 Including Chechen, Ingush

                 Class here north central Caucasian languages

—999 68   Kartvelian (South Caucasian) languages

                 Including Laz, Svan

                 For Georgian, see —99969

—999 69   Georgian

—999 9   Artificial languages

                 Including Afrihili

—999 92   Esperanto

—999 93   Interlingua

Table 7. Groups of Persons

The following notation is never used alone, but may be used as required with any appropriate number from the schedules, e.g., collections from more than one literature (808.8992) by Lutherans (notation 241 from this table): 808.8992241. The notation may also be used when so noted with numbers from other tables, e.g., chemistry (540) for (notation 024 from Table 1) dentists (notation 6176 from this table): 540.246176. Do not add from this table if the resultant concept is redundant, e.g., dentistry for dentists, Lutheran doctrine among Lutherans

SUMMARY

—01–09	[Persons by various nonoccupational characteristics; generalists, novices]
—1	Persons occupied with philosophy, parapsychology and occultism, psychology
—2	Persons occupied with or adherent to religion
—3	Persons occupied with social sciences and socioeconomic activities
—4	Persons occupied with languages, linguistics, lexicography
—5	Persons occupied with natural sciences and mathematics
—6	Persons occupied with applied sciences (Technologists)
—7	Persons occupied with the arts Persons occupied with fine and decorative arts
—8	Persons occupied with creative writing and speaking
—9	Persons occupied with geography, history, related disciplines and activities

—01   Individual persons

Class specific kinds of individuals in —03–99

—02   Groups of persons

Class groups of specific kinds of persons in —03–99

>   —03–08   Persons by various nonoccupational characteristics

Unless other instructions are given, class a subject with aspects in two or more subdivisions of Table 7 in the number coming last, e.g., gifted upper middle-class Jewish male young adults —0829 (*not* —0622, —0562, —041, or —03924)

Class comprehensive works in 001–999, without adding notation from Table 7

—03   Persons by racial, ethnic, national background

Class here comprehensive works on members of nondominant racial, ethnic, national groups [*formerly* —0693]

Add to base number —03 notation 03–99 from Table 5, e.g., North American persons —031

490

—04 **Persons by sex and kinship characteristics**

\> —041–042 Persons by sex

Class comprehensive works in —04

—041 Males

—042 Females

\> —043–046 Persons by kinship characteristics

Class comprehensive works in —04

—043 Direct ancestors and their surrogates

—043 1 Parents

Class here adoptive and foster parents; stepparents

—043 2 Grandparents

Direct forebears other than parents

—044 Direct descendants and their counterparts

—044 1 Sons and daughters

Class here adopted and foster children; stepchildren

—044 2 Grandchildren

Direct descendants other than first generation

—045 Siblings

Brothers and sisters by blood, adoption, foster care, remarriage of parents

—046 Collateral kinsmen

Uncles, aunts, nephews, nieces, cousins

—05 **Persons by age**

—054 Young people

Class here children

—054 2 Infants

Children from birth to age two

—054 3 Children three to five

Class here preschool children

—054 4   Children six to eleven

           Class here school children

             For children over eleven, see —055

—055   Young people twelve to twenty

           Variant names: adolescents, teenagers, young adults, youth

           Comprehensive works on young adults relocated to —0562

           Class youth twenty-one and over in —0562

—056   Adults

           Class adult males in —041; class adult females in —042

—056 2   Young adults

           Aged twenty-one and above

           Class here comprehensive works on young adults [*formerly* —055]

             For young adults under twenty-one, see —055

—056 4   Persons in middle adulthood

—056 5   Persons in late adulthood

—06   **Persons by miscellaneous social characteristics**

           Not provided for elsewhere

           Add to base number —06 the numbers following —086 in notation 0862–0869 from Table 1, e.g., criminals —06927; however, comprehensive works on members of nondominant racial, ethnic, national groups relocated from —0693 to —03; comprehensive works on members of nondominant religious groups relocated from —0693 to —2; for members of specific nondominant racial, ethnic, national groups, see —03; for members of specific nondominant religious groups, see —2

—08   **Persons by physical and mental characteristics**

—081   Persons by physical characteristics

—081 2   Healthy persons

—081 4   Persons with illnesses

—081 6   Persons with physical disabilities

—081 61   Persons with blindness and visual impairments

            Standard subdivisions are added for either or both topics in heading

            Class here blind-deaf persons

—081 62   Persons with hearing impairments

            Class here deaf persons

            Class blind-deaf persons in —08161

—081 64	Persons with speech disorders
—081 66	Persons with mobility impairments
—082	Persons by mental characteristics
—082 2	Healthy persons
—082 4	Persons with mental illnesses and disabilities
—082 6	Persons with mental retardation
—082 9	Gifted persons

                 Including geniuses

> **—09–99   Persons by various occupational characteristics**

         Class comprehensive works in 001–999, without adding from Table 7

—09   Generalists and novices

         Generalists: persons occupied with several or many subjects and activities, or with specific subjects and activities of a general nature, as study, profession, vocation, hobby

         Standard subdivisions are added for generalists and novices together, for generalists alone

—090 01–090 09	Standard subdivisions
—090 1	Academicians, researchers, scholars

             Standard subdivisions are added for any or all topics in heading

             Class persons occupied with education in —37

—090 3	Persons occupied with systems

             For persons occupied with systems engineering, see —62

—090 4	Persons occupied with computer science

             Class here persons occupied with data processing

             For persons occupied with computer engineering, see —6213

—090 9	Amateurs and novices

             Standard subdivisions are added for either or both topics in heading

             Including collectors

—091	Persons occupied with bibliography
—092	Persons occupied with library and information science

             Standard subdivisions are added for either or both topics in heading

             For persons occupied with bibliography, see —091

—093 Encyclopedists

> Class persons occupied with lexicography in —4

—096 Persons occupied with museology

—097 Persons occupied with publishing and journalism

> **—1–9 Specialists**

Persons occupied with specific disciplines, subjects, activities as study, profession, vocation, hobby, affiliation

The numbers from —1 through —9 have been developed from a reduction and an adaptation of the numbers from the whole classification; however, the mnemonic matches are by no means perfect, and the table should not be used without consultation, e.g., judges —343, *not* —347

Class persons occupied with specific subjects or activities of a general nature in —09; class comprehensive works in 001–999, without adding notation from Table 7

—1 Persons occupied with philosophy, parapsychology and occultism, psychology

—11 Philosophy

—13 Parapsychology and occultism

> Standard subdivisions are added for either or both topics in heading

—15 Psychology

—2 Persons occupied with or adherent to religion

Class here comprehensive works on members of nondominant religious groups [*formerly* —0693]; founders, central and local administrative heads, clergy, missionaries, members of religious congregations and orders, saints

—204 Persons occupied with or adherent to Christianity and to denominations and sects of Christian church

> *For persons occupied with or adherent to a specific denomination or sect of Christian church, see the denomination or sect in —21–28, e.g., persons occupied with Roman Catholic Church —22*

—204 4 Persons occupied with or adherent to Protestantism and to denominations and sects of Protestant churches

---

> **—21–28 Persons occupied with or adherent to Christianity and to denominations and sects of Christian church**

Class comprehensive works in —204

—21   **Persons occupied with early church and Eastern churches**

—211   Apostolic Church

         Including church fathers

—215   Eastern churches

         For Eastern Orthodox churches, see —219

—219   Eastern Orthodox churches

—22   **Persons occupied with Roman Catholic Church**

         Class modern Catholic schismatics in —248

—23   **Persons occupied with Anglican churches**

—24   **Persons occupied with Protestant churches of Continental origin and related bodies**

         For Baptist churches, see —261; for Church of the New Jerusalem, see —284; for Mennonite churches, see —287

—241   Lutheran churches

—242   Calvinistic and Reformed churches of European origin

         Standard subdivisions are added for either or both topics in heading

         Class here comprehensive works on Calvinistic churches, on Reformed churches

         For Huguenot churches, see —245; for Presbyterian churches, see —251; for Reformed churches centered in America, see —257

—243   Hussite and Anabaptist churches

—244   Albigensian, Catharist, Waldensian churches

—245   Huguenot churches

—246   Moravian churches

         For Hussite churches, see —243

—248   Modern schisms in Roman Catholic Church

—249   Arminian and Remonstrant churches

—25   **Persons occupied with Presbyterian churches, Reformed churches centered in America, Congregational churches, Puritanism**

—251   Presbyterian churches

—257   Reformed churches centered in America

—258   Congregationalism

—26   **Persons occupied with Baptist, Disciples of Christ, Adventist churches**

—261	Baptist churches
—266	Disciples of Christ
—267	Adventist churches

—27   **Persons occupied with Methodist churches, churches related to Methodism**

> Standard subdivisions are added for persons occupied with Methodist churches, churches related to Methodism together; for persons occupied with Methodist churches alone
>
> Including persons occupied with Church of the Nazarene, Salvation Army

—28   **Persons occupied with other denominations and sects**

—281	Unitarian and Universalist churches
—283	Latter-Day Saints (Mormons)
—284	Church of the New Jerusalem (Swedenborgianism)
—285	Church of Christ, Scientist (Christian Science)
—286	Society of Friends (Quakers)
—287	Mennonite churches
—288	Shakers
—289	Denominations and sects not provided for elsewhere

> Including Jehovah's Witnesses; Pentecostal churches

—29   **Persons occupied with other religions; with agnosticism, atheism, deism**

—291	Agnosticism, atheism, deism

> Theosophy relocated to —2999

—292	Classical (Greek and Roman) religion
—293	Germanic religion
—294	Religions of Indic origin
—294 3	Buddhism
—294 4	Jainism
—294 5	Hinduism

> Class here Brahmanism

—294 6	Sikhism
—295	Zoroastrianism (Mazdaism, Parseeism)

—296	Judaism
—297	Islam, Babism, Bahai Faith

           Class Sikhism in —2946

—297 1	Islam

           For Black Muslim movement, see —2977

—297 7	Black Muslim movement
—297 8	Babism
—297 9	Bahai faith
—299	Other religions
—299 1	Druidism
—299 5	Religions of East and Southeast Asian origin
—299 51	Religions of Chinese origin
—299 512	Confucianism
—299 514	Taoism
—299 56	Shintoism
—299 6	Religions originating among Black Africans and people of Black African descent
—299 7	Religions of North American native origin
—299 8	Religions of South American native origin
—299 9	Religions of other origin

           Not provided for elsewhere

           Including theosophy [*formerly* —291]

—3   Persons occupied with social sciences and socioeconomic activities

SUMMARY

—300 1–300 9	Standard subdivisions
—309	Persons occupied with sociology and anthropology
—31	Persons occupied with statistics
—32	Persons occupied with political science and politics
—33	Persons occupied with economics and related activities
—34	Persons occupied with law
—35	Persons occupied with public administration and military science
—36	Persons occupied with welfare and public protection
—37	Persons occupied with education
—38	Persons occupied with commerce, communications, transportation
—39	Persons occupied with customs, etiquette, folklore

—300 1–300 9	Standard subdivisions
—309	Persons occupied with sociology and anthropology

       Standard subdivisions are added for either or both topics in heading

       Including educational sociologists [*formerly* —37], ethnologists, ethnographers, social anthropologists, social ecologists

       Class comprehensive works on ecologists in —577

            For criminal anthropology, see —364; for physical anthropology, see —599

—31   **Persons occupied with statistics**

       Class comprehensive works on statisticians in —51

—32   **Persons occupied with political science and politics**

       For persons occupied with law, see —34; for persons occupied with public administration, see —35

—321	Political scientists and theorists

       Standard subdivisions are added for either or both topics in heading

—323	Civil rights workers
—328	Legislators
—329	Politicians

       Other than legislators, public administrators, judges, legal officers

       See also —351 for heads of state and central governments

—33   **Persons occupied with economics and related activities**

—331	Labor-oriented persons
—331 7	Workers

       See also —0623 for working class

—331 8	Labor leaders
—332	Bankers and financiers

       Standard subdivisions are added for either or both topics in heading

—333	Conservationists and landowners
—335	Socialists, communists, anarchists
—338	Entrepreneurs
—339	Economists

—34   **Persons occupied with law**

—341 Persons occupied with international organizations

—342 Supreme court justices

—343 Judges

> *For supreme court justices, see —342*

—344 Lawyers

—349 Local and auxiliary legal officers

> Including coroners, justices of the peace, notaries
>
> *See also —3632 for police*

—35 Persons occupied with public administration and military science

> Standard subdivisions are added for persons occupied with public administration and military science together, for persons occupied with public administration alone

—351 Heads of governments and their deputies

> Standard subdivisions are added for either or both topics in heading
>
> Class here heads of local governments [*formerly* —354]; dictators, governors, monarchs, premiers, presidents, prime ministers

—[351 1–351 8] Specific kinds of heads of governments

> Numbers discontinued; class in —351

—352 Other government personnel

> *See also —355 for military personnel*

—352 1 Cabinet members and councillors of state

> Standard subdivisions are added for either or both topics in heading

—352 2 Envoys

> Class here ambassadors, diplomats
>
> *For delegates to international organizations, see —341*

—[352 3] Administrators and commissioners

> Number discontinued; class in —352

—352 7 Civil service personnel

> Class here local government workers [*formerly* —354]
>
> Class civil service personnel occupied with a specific discipline, subject, activity with the discipline, subject, activity, e.g., economists —339

—[354] Local government personnel

> Heads of local governments relocated to —351; local government workers relocated to —3527

—355   Military personnel

> Class here land forces personnel

>> *For air and space forces personnel, see —358; for naval personnel, see —359*

—358   Air and space forces personnel

—359   Naval personnel

—36   **Persons occupied with welfare and public protection**

> Standard subdivisions are added for persons occupied with welfare and public protection together, for persons occupied with welfare alone

> Class socially disadvantaged persons in —0694

—361   Humanitarianism, philanthropy, social reform

—362   Social work

—363   Public protection and utilities

—363 2   Police

—363 3   Fire fighting

—363 6   Public utilities

—364   Crime and delinquency

> Standard subdivisions are added for crime and delinquency together, for crime alone

> Including criminologists

>> *For juvenile delinquents, predelinquents, see —06923; for criminals and other offenders, see —06927; for law, see —34; for public protection, see —363*

—365   Administration of penal and related institutions

> Standard subdivisions are added for administration of penal and related institutions together, for administration of penal institutions alone

> Class here prison administration

—366   Persons occupied with or belonging to associations

>> *For persons occupied with or belonging to general clubs, see —367; for persons occupied with or belonging to hereditary, military, patriotic, young people's societies; racial, ethnic, service clubs, see —369*

—366 1   Freemasonry

—366 2   Knights of Pythias

—366 3   Independent Order of Odd Fellows and International Association of Rebekah Assemblies

—366 5	Benevolent and Protective Order of Elks
—367	Persons occupied with or belonging to general clubs
	Including persons occupied with or belonging to social and study clubs
—368	Insurance
—369	Persons occupied with or belonging to hereditary, military, patriotic, young people's societies; racial, ethnic, service clubs
—369 2	Hereditary, military, patriotic societies
—369 4	Young people's societies
	Including Scouts
—369 5	Service clubs
	Including Lions International, Rotary International

—37   Persons occupied with education

Educational sociologists relocated to —309

>	—371–375 Specific educational activities
	Class specific educational institutions in —379; class comprehensive works in —37
—371	School and college administration
	Standard subdivisions are added for either or both topics in heading
—372	Teaching
—375	Students
—379	Specific educational institutions
	Including administrators, teachers, students, alumni

—38   Persons occupied with commerce, communications, transportation

	Including traders
—381	Internal commerce (Domestic trade)
—382	International commerce (Foreign trade)
—383	Postal communication
—384	Communication Telecommunication
	For postal communication, see —383
—385	Railroad transportation
—386	Inland waterway and ferry transportation

—387	Water, air, space transportation
	For inland waterway and ferry transportation, see —386
—387 5	Ocean (Marine) transportation
—387 7	Air transportation
—387 8	Space transportation
—388	Transportation Ground transportation
	For railroad transportation, see —385; for water, air, space transportation, see —387

—39   **Persons occupied with customs, etiquette, folklore**

—4 Persons occupied with languages, linguistics, lexicography

Standard subdivisions are added for any or all topics in heading

—5 Persons occupied with natural sciences and mathematics

Standard subdivisions are added for persons occupied with natural sciences and mathematics together, for persons occupied with natural sciences alone

Class here scientists

—51   **Persons occupied with mathematics**

Including comprehensive works on statisticians

For statisticians as collectors of statistics, see —31

—52   **Persons occupied with astronomy and allied sciences**

—521   Astronomy

—526   Geodesy, map making, surveying

—527   Celestial navigation

—529   Chronology

—53   **Persons occupied with physics**

—539   Nuclear physics

—54   **Persons occupied with chemistry and allied sciences**

—541   Chemistry

—548   Crystallography

—549   Mineralogy

—55   **Persons occupied with earth sciences**

Including oceanography

—551	Meteorology and climatology
—552	Petrology
—553	Geology

> Use of this number for oceanography discontinued; class in —55

—56 **Persons occupied with paleontology**

—57 **Persons occupied with life sciences**

> Class here persons occupied with biology

> *For persons occupied with paleontology, see —56; for persons occupied with botany, see —58; for persons occupied with zoology, see —59*

—[572–573] Physical ethnology and anthropology

> Relocated to —599

—[574] Biology

> Use of this number for comprehensive works on biology discontinued; class in —57

> Ecology relocated to —577, microbiology to —579

—577 Ecology [*formerly* —574]

> *For social ecology, see —309*

—579 Microbiology [*formerly* —574], fungi and algae [*both formerly* —58]

> Including bacteriology [*formerly* —589], protozoology [*formerly* —593]

—58 **Persons occupied with botany**

> Persons occupied with fungi and algae relocated to —579

—[589] Bacteriology

> Relocated to —579

—59 **Persons occupied with zoology**

—[593] Protozoology

> Relocated to —579

—595 Helminthology and entomology

—597 Ichthyology and herpetology

—598 Ornithology

—599 Physical ethnology [*formerly* —572], physical anthropology [*formerly* —573], mammalogy

> Standard subdivisions are added for mammalogy, physical ethnology and anthropology together; for mammalogy alone

—6 Persons occupied with applied sciences (Technologists)

SUMMARY

—604	**Persons occupied with technical drawing**	
—61	**Persons occupied with medical sciences**	**Persons occupied with medicine**
—62	**Persons occupied with engineering and allied operations**	
—63	**Persons occupied with agriculture and related technologies**	
—64	**Persons occupied with home economics and family living**	
—65	**Persons occupied with managerial services**	
—66	**Persons occupied with chemical engineering and related technologies**	
—67	**Persons occupied with manufacturing**	
—68	**Persons occupied with manufacture of products for specific uses**	
—69	**Persons occupied with buildings**	

—604   Persons occupied with technical drawing

—61   **Persons occupied with medical sciences   Persons occupied with medicine**

Class here physicians

—613   Nursing and promotion of health

Standard subdivisions are added for nursing and promotion of health together, for nursing alone

—614   Public preventive medicine

—615   Pharmacology, pharmacy, therapeutics, toxicology

Class therapeutics of specific diseases or group of diseases in —616–618

—616   Specific medical specialities

For surgery and related topics, see —617; for gynecology, obstetrics, pediatrics, geriatrics, see —618

—617   Surgery and related topics

Including anesthesiology

—617 1   Surgery

—617 6   Dentistry

—617 7   Ophthalmology

—617 8   Otology and audiology

—618   Gynecology, obstetrics, pediatrics, geriatrics

—618 1   Gynecology and obstetrics

Standard subdivisions are added for either or both topics in heading

—618 9   Pediatrics

—62   **Persons occupied with engineering and allied operations**

> Standard subdivisions are added for persons occupied with engineering and allied operations together, for persons occupied with engineering alone
>
> Including persons occupied with systems engineering
>
> Class here persons occupied with manufacturing of products of various branches of engineering
>
> Class comprehensive works on persons occupied with systems in —0903; class comprehensive works on persons occupied with manufacturing in —67
>
> *For persons occupied with chemical engineering, see —66*

—620 01–620 09   Standard subdivisions

—620 1   Engineering mechanics and materials

—620 2   Acoustical engineering

—620 8   Biotechnology

—621   Applied physics

> Including cryogenic, hydraulic-power, mechanical, pneumatic, steam, tool engineering

—621 3   Electrical, electronic, magnetic, communications, computer engineering

—621 4   Heat engineering and prime movers

> Including solar engineering
>
> Class hydraulic-power and steam engineering in —621

—621 48   Nuclear engineering

—622   Mining and related operations

> Standard subdivisions are added for mining and related operations together, for mining alone
>
> Including prospecting

—623   Military and nautical engineering

—623 1   Military engineering

—623 8   Nautical engineering and seamanship

> Standard subdivisions are added for nautical engineering and seamanship together, for nautical engineering alone

—624   Civil engineering

> Including bridge, structural, tunnel engineering
>
> *For a specific kind of civil engineering not provided for here, see the kind, e.g., construction of buildings —69*

—625   Engineering of railroads and roads

—627   Hydraulic engineering

—628   Sanitary and municipal engineering   Environmental protection engineering

—629   Other branches of engineering

         Including navigation

—629 1   Aerospace and aeronautical engineering and operation

         Standard subdivisions are added for any or all topics in heading

         Including air controllers, aircraft engineers, pilots

         For astronautical engineering and operation, see —6294

—629 2   Motor land vehicle engineering and operation

         Standard subdivisions are added for either or both topics in heading

         See also —7967 for motor vehicle racing

—629 4   Astronautical engineering and operation

         Standard subdivisions are added for either or both topics in heading

         Including astronauts, cosmonauts

—629 8   Automatic control engineering

—63   **Persons occupied with agriculture and related technologies**

         Standard subdivisions are added for persons occupied with agriculture and related technologies together, for persons occupied with agriculture alone

—[631]   Farming

         Number discontinued; class in —63

—633   Field and plantation crop farming

—634   Fruit growing and forestry

—635   Horticulture and gardening

         Standard subdivisions are added for either or both topics in heading

—636   Animal husbandry

         Including veterinary sciences

         Class here stock raising

         Class raising dairy cattle in —637; class culture of nondomesticated animals in —639

—637   Dairying

—638	Insect culture
—639	Hunting, fishing, conservation, related technologies

> *For sports hunting and fishing, see —799*

—639 1	Hunting and trapping

> Standard subdivisions are added for either or both topics in heading

—639 2	Fishing, whaling, sealing
—639 3	Culture of cold-blooded vertebrates Culture of fish
—639 9	Conservation
—64	**Persons occupied with home economics and family living**

> Standard subdivisions are added for persons occupied with home economics and family living together, for persons occupied with home economics alone

> Class here persons occupied with domestic arts and sciences

—641	Cooks and nutritionists
—642	Caterers and restaurateurs

> Standard subdivisions are added for either or both topics in heading

—646	Seamstresses, cosmetologists, related occupational personnel
—646 4	Seamstresses and tailors

> Standard subdivisions are added for either or both topics in heading

—646 5	Hatters

> Class here milliners

—646 7	Cosmetologists, hairdressers, barbers
—647	Hotelkeepers and motelkeepers

> Standard subdivisions are added for either or both topics in heading

—648	Launderers
—649	Homemakers
—65	**Persons occupied with managerial services**
—651	Office services

> Including bookkeepers, clerks, file clerks, office managers, secretaries, typists

—657	Accounting

> *For bookkeepers, see —651*

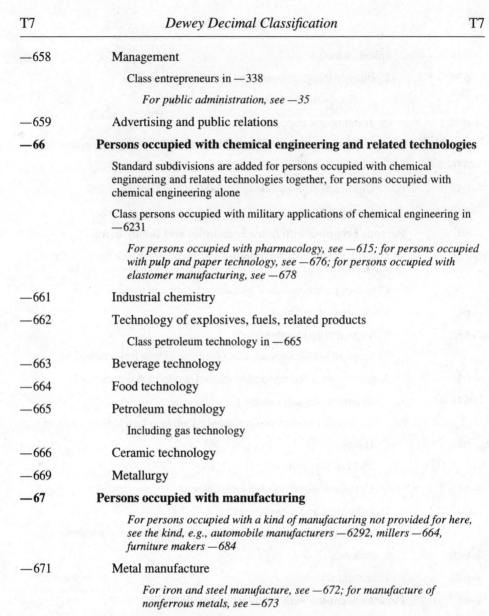

—658   Management

Class entrepreneurs in —338

For public administration, see —35

—659   Advertising and public relations

—66   **Persons occupied with chemical engineering and related technologies**

Standard subdivisions are added for persons occupied with chemical engineering and related technologies together, for persons occupied with chemical engineering alone

Class persons occupied with military applications of chemical engineering in —6231

For persons occupied with pharmacology, see —615; for persons occupied with pulp and paper technology, see —676; for persons occupied with elastomer manufacturing, see —678

—661   Industrial chemistry

—662   Technology of explosives, fuels, related products

Class petroleum technology in —665

—663   Beverage technology

—664   Food technology

—665   Petroleum technology

Including gas technology

—666   Ceramic technology

—669   Metallurgy

—67   **Persons occupied with manufacturing**

For persons occupied with a kind of manufacturing not provided for here, see the kind, e.g., automobile manufacturers —6292, millers —664, furniture makers —684

—671   Metal manufacture

For iron and steel manufacture, see —672; for manufacture of nonferrous metals, see —673

—672   Iron and steel manufacture

—673   Manufacture of nonferrous metals

—674   Lumbering and manufacture of wooden products

Class furniture manufacture in —684

—675   Leather and fur industries

        Including furriers, tanners

        Class leather goods in —685

—676   Pulp and paper technology

—677   Textiles

        Class manufacture of clothing in —687

—678   Elastomer manufacture

        Including rubber manufacture

—679   Manufacture of other products of specific kinds of materials

—679 7   Tobacco

—68   **Persons occupied with manufacture of products for specific uses**

        Not provided for elsewhere

        Class here persons occupied with handicrafts

        Class persons occupied with manufacture of products based on specific branches of engineering in —62

          For persons occupied with artistic handicraft work, see —745

—681   Manufacture of precision instruments and other devices

          See also —6213 for manufacture of electronic computers

—681 1   Clockmaking and watchmaking

—681 4   Optical work

—681 8   Manufacture of musical instruments

—682   Blacksmithing

—683   Hardware and household appliances

        Including gunsmithing, locksmithing

—684   Furniture manufacture

—685   Manufacture of leather goods and their substitutes

        Standard subdivisions are added for either or both topics in heading

          See also —675 for fur goods

—685 1   Saddlery and harness making

        Standard subdivisions are added for either or both topics in heading

—685 3   Shoemaking and shoe repairing

        Standard subdivisions are added for either or both topics in heading

—685 4   Glove and mitten making

> Standard subdivisions are added for either or both topics in heading

—686   Printing and related activities

—686 2   Printing

> Including typesetting

—686 3   Bookbinding

—686 4   Photocopying (Photoduplication)

—687   Manufacture of clothing

> *For seamstresses and tailors, see —6464; for hatters, see —6465; for shoemaking, see —6853; for glove and mitten making, see —6854*

—688   Manufacture of accessories for personal grooming, costume jewelry, models and miniatures, recreational equipment, smokers' supplies, toys

—69   **Persons occupied with buildings**

> Construction work and related occupations

—693   Construction work

> Including bricklaying, masonry, plastering
>
> *For carpentry, see —694*

—694   Carpentry

—695   Roofing

—696   Plumbing and pipe fitting

—697   Heating, ventilating, air conditioning

—698   Painting, glazing, paperhanging

—7   **Persons occupied with the arts   Persons occupied with fine and decorative arts**

> *For persons occupied with creative writing and speaking, see —8*

SUMMARY

—71	**Persons occupied with civic and landscape art**
—72	**Persons occupied with architecture**
—73	**Persons occupied with sculpture and other plastic arts**
—731	Sculpture
—736	Glyptics
—737	Numismatics
—738	Ceramic arts
—739	Art metalwork
—74	**Persons occupied with drawing and decorative arts**
	Including illustration
—741	Commercial art
—743	Drawing
—745	Handicrafts
	Class textile handicrafts in —746; class glass in —748
—746	Textile arts
	Class here textile handicrafts
—747	Interior decoration
—748	Glass
—749	Furniture design
—75	**Persons occupied with painting**
—76	**Persons occupied with graphic arts**
	Including engraving, printmaking
	For persons occupied with a specific graphic art not provided for here, see the art, e.g., painting —75
—77	**Persons occupied with photography**
—78	**Persons occupied with music**
—781	General principles
	Including music theory
—781 6	Traditions of music
	Including folk music, jazz, rock
—781 7	Sacred music

—782   Vocal music

         Including dramatic music, opera

         Class stage presentation of dramatic music and opera in —7925

—784   Instrumental ensembles and their music

         Standard subdivisions are added for either or both topics in heading

         For chamber music, see —785

—785   Chamber music

—786   Keyboard, mechanical, electrophonic, percussion instruments and their music

—787   String instruments and their music

         Standard subdivisions are added for either or both topics in heading

—788   Wind instruments and their music

         Standard subdivisions are added for either or both topics in heading

—79   **Persons occupied with performing arts and recreation**

         For persons occupied with music, see —78

—791   Public performances

         For stage presentations, see —792; for magic, see —7938

         See also —78 for musical performances, —793–799 for sport and game performances

—791 3   Circus performance

—791 4   Motion picture, radio, television

—791 5   Puppetry

—792   Stage presentations

         Class here theater

         For motion picture, radio, television, see —7914

—[792 1]   Drama

         Number discontinued; class in —792

—792 5   Opera

         Class here persons occupied with stage presentations of dramatic music

         Class singers in —782

         For musical plays, see —7926; for variety shows, see —7927

—792 6   Musical plays

—792 7	Variety shows
—792 8	Ballet and modern dance

        Standard subdivisions are added for either or both topics in heading

        Class here comprehensive works on dancing

          For social, folk, national dancing, see —7933

—793	Indoor games and amusements

        Class games of chance in —795

          For indoor games of skill, see —794

—793 3	Social, folk, national dancing
—793 8	Magic
—794	Indoor games of skill

        Class games combining skill and chance in —795

—794 1	Chess
—794 6	Bowling
—794 7	Billiards and pool

        Standard subdivisions are added for either or both topics in heading

—794 8	Electronic games Computer games
—795	Games of chance

        Including card playing

        Class here gambling

—796	Athletics and outdoor sports and games

        Standard subdivisions are added for any or all topics in heading

        Class here coaching

          For aquatic and air sports, see —797; for equestrian sports and animal racing, see —798; for fishing, hunting, shooting, see —799

—796 3	Ball games
—796 32	Basketball and volleyball
—796 33	Football, rugby, soccer
—796 34	Badminton, lacrosse, rackets, squash, table tennis, tennis
—796 35	Baseball, cricket, croquet, field hockey, golf, polo
—796 4	Weight lifting, track and field, gymnastics
—796 5	Hiking, mountaineering, spelunking

—796 6	Cycling
—796 7	Motor vehicle racing
—796 8	Combat sports

> Including boxing, fencing, wrestling

—796 9	Ice and snow sports
—797	Aquatic and air sports

> Standard subdivisions are added for aquatic and air sports together, for aquatic sports alone

—797 1	Boating
—797 2	Swimming and diving
—797 3	Surfing and water skiing
—797 5	Air sports

> Including skydiving, stunt flying

—798	Equestrian sports and animal racing

> Standard subdivisions are added for equestrian sports and animal racing together, for equestrian sports alone

—799	Fishing, hunting, shooting
—799 1	Fishing
—799 2	Hunting
—799 3	Trapshooting, skeet and target shooting, archery

—8 Persons occupied with creative writing and speaking

> Standard subdivisions are added for persons occupied with creative writing and speaking together, for persons occupied with creative writing alone

—81	**Poetry**
—82	**Drama**
—83	**Fiction**
—84	**Essays**
—85	**Debate, oratory, conversation**
—86	**Letter writing**
—87	**Satire and humor**

> Standard subdivisions are added for either or both topics in heading

—9 **Persons occupied with geography, history, related disciplines and activities**

—91 **Geography and travel**

Including exploration

—92 **Biography**

—93 **Archaeology**

—97 **History**

—99 **Genealogy**

Relocations and Reductions

The following two lists show all the relocations and reductions since Edition 20, with the exception of relocations and reductions within several major revisions. Separate comparative and equivalence tables are provided to show relocations and reductions within the following table and schedules: T2 — 47 Eastern Europe ' Russia, 350–354 Public administration, 370 Education, and 560–590 Life sciences.

The column headed *Edition 20* indicates in numerical order each number in that edition from which a topic or group of topics has been shifted; the column headed *Edition 21* indicates each corresponding number in the present edition to which those topics or groups of topics have been shifted. If two or more topics have been shifted from one number to two or more numbers, each separate shift is shown.

Numbers in the *Edition 20* column printed in square brackets are no longer in use; those not printed in brackets have lost part of their meaning through relocation or reduction, but still retain some of their original meaning.

Relocations

In a relocation one or more topics are shifted to a number differing from the old in respects other than length. If the relocation is partial, the original number remains valid; but if it is total, the original number is no longer used. Relocations are described and explained in the Introduction.

Relocations that have appeared previously in *Dewey Decimal Classification Additions, Notes and Decisions (DC&)* volume 5 are indicated by * next to the Edition 20 number. Relocations that eliminate dual provision for the same topic or topics are indicated by † next to the Edition 20 number.

For example, in Table 2 some of the topics that were in T2 — 1641 in Edition 20 have been relocated to T2 — 72875 in Edition 21; all of the topics in T2 — 4977 have been relocated to T2 — 499. All the topics in 200.14 have been relocated to 210.14 to eliminate dual provision.

"Scattered" means that a topic has been relocated to so many numbers throughout 000–999 that it is not feasible to name them all. If the scattering is within a limited range, the range is given. For example, at 346.033 the topic has been relocated only to numbers within 342–347.

An indented number is an element of an add table. The number or span under which it is indented shows the location of the add table or the add instruction related to an add table. For example, the [06] and 65 under 292–299 indicates that the [06] and 65 are elements of the add table at 292–299.

For details of the specific relocated topics the classifier should consult the appropriate entries in the tables and schedules.

Edition 20	Edition 21	Edition 20	Edition 21
[T1 — 02403–02408]†	T1 — 08	T2 — 71344	T2 — 71345
T1 — 0288	T1 — 091	[T2 — 71348]	T2 — 71347
	028	[T2 — 71351]	T2 — 71338
T1 — 0288	T1 — 093–099	[T2 — 71355]	T2 — 71356
	028	[T2 — 71368]	T2 — 71367
T1 — 071†	T1 — 019	[T2 — 71374]	T2 — 71373
T1 — 0722–0724	T1 — 0727	[T2 — 71376]	T2 — 71375
T1 — 0835	T1 — 0842	[T2 — 71377]	T2 — 71375
T1 — 08692	T1 — 086942	[T2 — 71386]	T2 — 71385
T1 — 08693	T1 — 0882	T2 — 729374	T2 — 729377
T1 — 08693	T1 — 089	T2 — 729384	T2 — 729381
T1 — 09	T1 — 0212	T2 — 72943	T2 — 729442
T1 — 09	T1 — 024	T2 — 72945	T2 — 729442
T1 — 0922	T1 — 0923	[T2 — 8136]*	T2 — 8134
T2 — 1641	T2 — 72875	T2 — 8173*	T2 — 8117
T2 — 482*	T2 — 4831	[T2 — 8175]*	T2 — 8111
T2 — 482*	T2 — 4832	T2 — 8543	T2 — 8544
T2 — 4823*	T2 — 4821	T2 — 86165	T2 — 86166
T2 — 4845*	T2 — 4843	[T2 — 9311]*	T2 — 9399
T2 — 4845*	T2 — 4844	[T2 — 93123]*	T2 — 9348
T2 — 4845*	T2 — 4846	[T2 — 93125]*	T2 — 9346
T2 — 48913	T2 — 48914	[T2 — 93127]*	T2 — 936
T2 — 4956*	T2 — 4957	[T2 — 9315]*	T2 — 937
[T2 — 4977]	T2 — 499	[T2 — 931575]*	T2 — 9396
T2 — 499*	T2 — 49515	T2 — 95935	T2 — 95936
T2 — 499*	T2 — 4954	T2 — 95939	T2 — 95938
T2 — 499*	T2 — 4957	T2 — 9711	T2 — 9712
T2 — 499*	T2 — 4958	T2 — 9711	T2 — 989
T2 — 4998*	T2 — 4959	T3C — 8*	T3C — 93–99
T2 — 5127*	T2 — 5129	T4 — 31*†	T4 — 81
T2 — 5525	T2 — 5527	T5 — 9159	T5 — 9157
[T2 — 5645]*	T2 — 5693	T5 — 9187	T5 — 9186
T2 — 56954	T2 — 56959	[T5 — 9277]	T5 — 9279
T2 — 56956	T2 — 56957	[T6 — 37]	T6 — 391
T2 — 56958	T2 — 56959	T6 — 391	T6 — 392
T2 — 66925*	T2 — 66926	T6 — 391	T6 — 3931
T2 — 66944*	T2 — 66943	T6 — 391	T6 — 394
T2 — 66946*	T2 — 66945	T6 — 41	T6 — 491
T2 — 66948*	T2 — 66949	T6 — 91499	T6 — 91497
T2 — 66954*	T2 — 66956	T6 — 9155	T6 — 9156
T2 — 66957*	T2 — 66956	T6 — 9159	T6 — 9157
T2 — 66962*	T2 — 66963	T6 — 9187	T6 — 9186
T2 — 66973*	T2 — 66976	T6 — 9517	T6 — 9511
T2 — 66978*	T2 — 66977	T6 — 96398	T6 — 963977
T2 — 66985*	T2 — 66987	T6 — 98323	T6 — 98324
T2 — 66988*	T2 — 66989	T7 — 055	T7 — 0562
T2 — 71137*	T2 — 71133	T7 — 0693	T7 — 03
[T2 — 71335]	T2 — 71334	T7 — 0693	T7 — 2
[T2 — 71337]	T2 — 71336	T7 — 291	T7 — 2999

*Previously published
†Eliminates dual provision

Edition 20	Edition 21	Edition 20	Edition 21
[T7 — 354]	T7 — 351	[236.6]	236.4
[T7 — 354]	T7 — 3527	[236.7]	236.4
T7 — 37	T7 — 309	[239.001–.009]	239.01–.09
[T7 — 572–573]	T7 — 599	[239.5]	239.7
[T7 — 574]	T7 — 577	[239.6]	239.7
[T7 — 574]	T7 — 579	[239.8]	239.7
T7 — 58	T7 — 579	239.9	239.7
[T7 — 589]	T7 — 579	242.2	242.6
[T7 — 593]	T7 — 579	242.3	242.6
[001.4222]	001.433	242.37	242.36
[004.32]	005.434	[245]	264.23
[004.54]	005.435	248.06	267
004.6*†	384	248.29†	234.132
005.136	005.2	[248.463]	263.041
005.44	005.434–.436	252.67	252.63
[005.748]	005.741	[259.8]	253.7
006.42	006.32	[263.4]	263.3
006.6	006.7	263.97	263.93
027.8*	027.7	264.036†	264.032
155.5	155.65	[267.33]†	267.306
158.9	299.936	[267.53]†	267.506
160	121.68	270.82	280.042
175	179.3	[271.05]	271.791
200	230	289.9*	287.99
200.1	210	[291.01]	210
[200.12]†	291.14	[291.011]†	200.11
[200.14]†	210.14	[291.013]†	200.13
[200.6]†	291.65	[291.014]†	210.14
[200.68]†	291.6	[291.015]†	200.15
[201]	230.01	[291.019]†	200.19
[202–203]	230.002–.003	[291.02–.03]†	200.2–.3
[204.5]	230	[291.05]†	200.5
[205]	230.005	[291.06]†	291.65
[206]	260	[291.07–.09]†	200.7–.9
[207]	230.007	291.446	291.351
[207.1]	230.071	[291.62]	291.61
[207.4–.9]	230.07114–.07119	291.63	291.61
[208]	270.08	[291.64]	291.61
[209]	270	292–299	292–299
[210.11]†	200.11	[06]	65
[210.12]†	291.14	[292.006]	292.65
[210.13]†	200.13	[294.306]†	294.365
[210.15]†	200.15	[294.506]†	294.565
[210.19]†	200.19	[296.06]†	296.67
[215.6]	215.7	296.09014	296.09013
[216]	214	296.09015	296.09014
[221.042]	223	[296.17]	296.18
229.5	229.6	[296.385]	296.36
[234.12]	234.13	[296.3872]	296.39

*Previously published
†Eliminates dual provision

Edition 20	Edition 21	Edition 20	Edition 21
[296.3875]	296.37	[321.804209969]*†	324.6309969
[296.3877]	296.382	[323.422]	Scattered within 340
[296.387835]	296.74	323.46	330
[296.38785]	296.383	323.46	331.011
[296.38787]	296.3827	324.3094–.3099	324.24–.29
296.41	296.45		014
[296.42]	296.47	324.5094–.5099	324.24–.29
296.43–.44	296.453–.454		015
296.72	296.45	324.52094–.52099	324.24–.29
296.8	296.09		0152
[296.8346]	296.8341	324.54094–.54099	324.24–.29
[297.06]†	297.65		0154
297.1–.3	297.4	324.56094–.56099	324.24–.29
297.14	340.59		0156
[297.197]	297.26–.28	324.63*†	328.3347
[297.1978358]	297.577	[325.31]	353.15
297.24	297.61	327.3–.9	326.11–.17
[297.32–.33]	297.39	[328.30601]	328.0601
[297.35093–.35099]	297.353–.359	[331.111]†	331.1109
297.38	297.35	[332.67255]	332.67208
297.38†	297.36	333.952	333.956
297.4	297.57	333.959	333.954
297.43	297.3	334.0919	334.0601
297.446	297.35	337*†	338.91
297.446	297.435	338.09	338.06
[297.447]	297.446	339.3	339.01
[297.447]	297.45	[340.0917]	349.1
[297.448]	297.57	[340.52094–.52099]†	340.524–.529
297.5–.7	297.4	340.59†	297.14
297.5	297.31	341.026	341.66026
[297.51]	297.34	341.22–.24†	352.6211
[297.52]	297.3822	[341.22068]†	352.112
297.53†	297.362	341.223†	352.112
[297.55]	297.352	[341.2324]†	352.113
297.65	297.61	341.233†	352.113
299.512*	181.112	341.759	341.751153
[299.65]	299.64	342–347	342–347
302.23	Scattered	[0917]	Scattered within
305.235	305.242		342–347
305.7	305.8	[342.00917]	342.1
[306.738]	306.848	342.02–.09	342.1
307.2†	304.6	342.0413	342.0412
321*†	324	342.062	342.0664
[321.14]	321.00902	342.0853	344.078
[321.14]	321.0093	[343.00917]	343.1
[321.4]	321.8	343.01–.09	343.1
[321.80420973]*†	324.630973	[344.00917]	344.1
[321.80420974–	324.630974–.630979	344.01–.09	344.1
.80420979]*†		344.02	343.05242

*Previously published
†Eliminates dual provision

Edition 20	Edition 21	Edition 20	Edition 21
344.04634	344.04633	[359.8068]†	359.621
344.04634	344.046336	359.82	327.1743
344.05†	344.047	359.82	359.07
344.0542	344.099	[359.8201–.8209]	359.801–.809
344.0769†	344.0791	[361.323]	361.06
[345.00917]	345.1	[362.796]	362.7083
345.01–.08	345.1	[362.796]	362.7089
[346.00917]	346.1	[362.797]	362.7089
346.01–.09	346.1	[362.799]†	362.708691
346.033	Scattered within	[362.799]†	362.7091732
	342–347	[362.799]†	362.7091734
[346.0332]	344.0411	362.8682†	371.223
346.04	346.0166	362.8682	378.32
346.0432†	346.042	[363.98]	363.92
[347.00917]	347.1	[364.14001–.14009]	364.1401–.1409
347.01–.09	347.1	[366.17]†	366.108351
347.017*	362.58	366.18†	366.1082
[348.00917]	348.1	366.18†	366.108352
348.02–.05	348.1	368.81†	368.094
[351.0034]	324	[370.156]†	T1 —019
[351.0036]	324	[370.19]	306.43
351.7223	328.378	371.104	306.432
351.74	363.2068	[371.3078]*	027.7
351.993	342.068	[371.3078]*	027.8
[355.0072]	355.07	[371.6234]	Scattered
355.03	327.174	[371.624]	796.068
[355.43001–.43009]	355.4301–.4309	[371.629]	727
[355.58]	355.52	[371.77]	363.119371
[355.6211]	355.6212	[371.774]	363.379
[355.63]	355.685	[371.7752]	363.1257
[355.67]	355.12068	[371.7754]	363.147
355.8	355.621	[371.84]	T1 —06
[355.8068]†	355.621	[371.854]	T1 —06
355.82	327.174	371.89†	790.2088375
355.82	355.07	371.89*	796.042
[355.8201–.8205]	355.801–.805	371.9127†	419
[355.8206]	355.806	371.9127†	419.071
[355.82068]	355.621	[373.192–.198]	T1 —0712
[355.8207]	355.807	374.012†	323.60715
[355.8208–.8209]	355.808–.809	[375.008]	T1 —071
356–359	356–359	[375.01–.03]	Scattered within
8	6		010–039
[8068]†	6	[375.04]	Scattered within
356.11	356.16		001–006
[356.18]	356.11	[375.05–.99]	Scattered within
357.2†	357.185		050–999
[358.40072]	358.407	[376]	371.822
[359.0072]	359.07	[377]	371.07
359.8	359.621	378.103	306.432

*Previously published
†Eliminates dual provision

Edition 20	Edition 21	Edition 20	Edition 21
[378.1992–.1998]	T1 —0711	532.052	532.0595
379.11	353.824	532.0595	532.597
379.158	353.88284	532.51	532.595
[382.1044]	338.52	532.595	532.597
[382.173]	332.042	533.21†	533.295
[382.174]	332.042	535.4†	774.0153
384.55065	384.554	[536.4001–.4009]	536.401–.409
389.15	389.109	[536.53]	536.50287
[392.9]†	390.0846	538.72†	538.79
[394.2682]*	394.265	538.78	538.727
[394.26828]*	394.266	541.223	547.1223
[394.268296]*	394.267	541.2252	547.12252
[394.2683]*	394.261–.264	[541.2253]	547.59044242
[394.2684]*	394.261–.264	[541.244–.246]	541.224
[398.042]*†	398.09	[542.5]	542.4
398.2093–.2099	398.2093–.2099	[546.44001–.44009]	546.4401–.4409
01*	001	547.225	547.7704593
02*	002	[551.5252]	551.52509
05*	005	[551.542]	551.5409
07*	007	[551.564]	551.563
398.21–.27*	398.2093–.2099	[551.5712]	551.57109
398.22*	398.21	[551.5747]	551.5787
398.22*	398.27	552.2	551.23
401.51†	410.151	552.58†	552.4
402.85†	410.285	553.22	553.87
[437.947]	439.1	553.29	553.879
439.1	439.2	[572]	599.97
439.1	439.31	[572.8]	599.98
439.1	439.4	[573]	599.9
447.8†	449	[573.3]	569.9
491.499	491.497	[574.5]	591.5
491.55	491.56	[575.10724]	660.65
491.59	491.57	[575.5]	591.562
491.87	491.867	[576.163]	664.001579
492.77	492.79	[578]	580.282
512.942†	515.38	[578]	590.282
514.223†	514.3	[579]	580.75
515†	514.74	[579]	580.752
515.223	515.93	[579]	590.75
515.223	515.94	[579]	590.752
515.7†	515.9	[589]	579
523.1125	523.1126	[589.9]	579.3
523.80212	523.80216	598	636.5
[523.843]	523.841	599	636
[530.16]	530.801	[612.014487]	612.014486
530.43†	530.444	[612.01579]†	611.01816
[530.8021]†	530.81	[613.3]	613.2
[531.31]	531.55	[616.00724]*†	619
531.62†	530.11	[616.0793]	616.0798

*Previously published
†Eliminates dual provision

Edition 20	Edition 21	Edition 20	Edition 21
616.0795	616.0797–.0799	[634.81]	634.881
616.39808†	616.8526	634.9562†	634.9565
616.85227	616.8584	635.65	633.3
616.85227	616.85841	635.94	635.9153
616.8552†	616.8553	635.955	635.9525
[616.89022]	616.8900835	635.965	635.9678
[617.3]	616.7	635.9672	635.9528
[617.3]	617.47	[635.969]	635.9152
[617.3]	617.5	636.0079†	636.0811
[617.307]	617.9	636.01	636.0845
[617.719009]	617.71909	[636.08551]	636.086
[617.95001–.95009]	617.9501–.9509	[636.08552]	636.0862
[618.22]	618.2075	[636.08554]	636.086
618.3101–.3109	618.31001–.31009	[636.087]	636.0855
[621.31932]	621.31933	[636.0881]	636.082
622.8	622.20289	636.08844†	636.97
622.8	Scattered within	636.0886†	636.0888
	622.22–.29	636.0888	636.0811
[623.819]	623.810287	636.11–.17	636.109
[624.1042]	624.0299	636.12	636.175
[624.1042]	624.10299	636.14	636.15
624.28	624.20288	[636.41]	636.4088
[625.17]	625.100288	636.61	636.69
625.21–.26†	625.19	[636.823]	636.822
[625.7042]	625.70289	636.825	636.824
[627.136]	627.130288	[636.91]	636.92
[627.136]	627.1370288	[636.91]	636.929
[627.136]	627.1380288	[637.125]	637.1240284
[627.705]	627.700288	[637.22]†	637.20287
627.81	627.80284	[637.32]†	637.30287
628.24	628.20288	[638.142]	638.140284
628.25	628.23	[638.3]	638.5
[629.042]	629.040289	639.1	799.2
629.1345	Scattered within	[639.123]†	639.12833
	629.1332–.1333	[639.124]†	639.12841
629.1346	Scattered within	[639.376]	639.378
	629.1332–.1333	[639.377]	639.3782
[629.445]	629.442	[639.4811]	639.46
[629.4501]	919.904	639.5	639.6
[629.455]	919.9204	[639.542–.544]	639.56–.58
[629.8318]	629.830288	[641.1]†	613.2
631.53	631.52	641.2	613.2
[631.877]	631.875	641.566†	641.568
632.19	632.3	641.6*	641.552
632.2	632.3	646.308351	646.32
[632.631]	632.3	646.308352	646.34
[633.001–.009]	633.01–.09	646.4008351	646.402
[633.374]†	633.32	646.4008352	646.404
[633.374]†	633.366	649.58	372.4

*Previously published
†Eliminates dual provision

Edition 20	Edition 21	Edition 20	Edition 21
649.68	371.042	0289	0288
649.68	371.30281	[042]†	087
651.028	651.29	[043]†	0846
[651.2001–.2009]	651.201–.209	[043]†	0877
[651.74001–.74009]	651.7401–.7409	723.3†	720.9460902
[658.3041]†	658.30089	731.028	731.4
[658.3042]†	658.30081	731.4	731.028
[658.3042]†	658.30082	731.48	731.0289
[658.3042]†	658.30083	738.14	738.028
[658.3042]†	658.30084	738.18	738.0289
658.3045†	658.30087	739.14	739.028
658.31245	658.312408	[739.16]	739.0288
[658.8348]	658.83408	[739.16]	739.0289
[659.292]	200	739.224	739.22028
[659.2935]	352.748	[739.226]	739.220288
[659.29355]†	355.342	[739.226]	739.220289
660.28448	668.92	739.274	739.27028
[664.096]	664.00286	[739.276]	739.270288
664.11	664.1028	[739.276]	739.270289
664.11	664.10284	741.2	741.028
664.119	664.10286	[741.218]	741.0288
[664.369]	664.368	[741.219]	741.0288
664.7209	664.7200286	[741.219]	741.0289
664.725	664.724	745.10289	745.10288
[665.78]	665.70286	746	746
[667.36]	667.30286	[0488]	0288
667.9	Scattered	746.3*	746
677.028	677.0028		0433
[677.029]	677.00286	746.92*	746
677.112–.117	677.11028		0432
677.212–.217	677.21028	746.94–.98*	746
677.312–.317	677.31028		0434–0438
677.3912–.3917	677.391028	748.50289	748.50288
681.4†	681.25	749.10289	749.10288
[681.416]	681.25	751.4	750.28
685.38	681.761	[751.67]	750.289
697.0028†	697.07	[758.6]†	758.96
697.50028†	697.507	759.7	759.9584–.9587
[697.934]	697.933	[769.18]	769.0288
[698.10282]	698.10284	771	770.28
702.89	702.88	790.133	796.156
711.1	711.028	792.8	792.78
712*	715	[795.438]	793.85
712.3	712.028	[796.019]*	796.08
720.289	720.288	796.21*	796.22
[720.42]	720.87	796.3322	796.332028
[720.43]	720.846	796.51	796.58
[720.43]	720.877	796.8155*†	613.7148
721–729	721–729	[799.242]	799.246

*Previously published
†Eliminates dual provision

Edition 20	Edition 21	Edition 20	Edition 21
[799.243]	799.24833	[973.315]	973.308
[799.24841]	799.244	973.38	973.3092
[799.24861]	799.246	973.528	973.52092
[799.24865]	799.2465	973.628	973.62092
[801.951]	808.1	[973.715]	973.708
[801.952]	808.2	973.898	973.89092
[801.953]	808.3	[981.013]	981.031
[801.954]	808.4	[981.02]	981.032
[801.955]	808.5	981.062	981.063
[801.956]	808.6	981.063	981.064
[801.957]	808.7		
808.8†	810–890		
809†	810–890		
[839.09]	839.1		
839.1	839.2		
839.1	839.31		
839.1	839.4		
891.499	891.497		
891.55	891.56		
891.59	891.57		
891.62	891.62		
2	3		
4	3		
891.87	891.86		
929.1072*	929.1028		
[929.82]	929.6		
[929.82]	929.9		
[940.315]	940.308		
[940.5315]	940.5308		
940.5475094–.5475099†	940.54754–.54759		
[949.30001–.30009]	949.3001–.3009		
949.503*	949.502		
949.506*	949.507		
949.506*	949.5072		
[949.77]	949.9		
949.9*	949.58		
949.98*	949.59		
[951.0001–.0009]	951.001–.009		
952.031	951.035		
[956.45]*	956.93		
959.5503	959.5504		
959.5505	959.5504		
959.70431	959.704308		
959.70438	959.7043092		
[964.0001–.0009]	964.001–.009		
968.001–.008	968.0001–.0008		
968.009	968.0009		
968.0481	968.04808		
968.0488	968.048092		

*Previously published
†Eliminates dual provision

Reductions

A reduction is the result of shifting one or more topics to a number shorter than the old but otherwise not differing from it. If all topics in a given number are thus shifted, the number is no longer valid. Reductions are described and explained in the Introduction.

In addition, several numbers have been dropped because their content in Edition 20 was meaningless within the context of Edition 21.

Reductions that have appeared previously in *Dewey Decimal Classification Additions, Notes and Decisions* volume 5 are indicated by * next to the Edition 20 number.

"Main number" means that the provision for the topic within a table has been discontinued to the numbers to which the table number would previously have been added.

For example in Table 7, T7 —[3523] has been discontinued and all of its contents moved up to the broader number T7 — 352, while only some of the topics in T7 — 553 have been moved up to T7 — 55. At 629.455, the contents of the table numbers 02–05 have been discontinued from the table to the numbers to which the table number would previously have been added.

An indented number is an element of an add table. The number or span under which it is indented shows the location of the add table. For example, [0487] and 048 under 746 indicate that [0487] and 048 are elements of the add table at 746.

For details of the specific reduced topics the classifier should consult the appropriate entries in the tables and schedules.

Edition 20	Edition 21	Edition 20	Edition 21
T1 —0212	T1 —021	[267.34–.35]	267.3
[T1 —07152–07154]	T1 —0715	[267.51–.52]	267.5
[T2 —1723]	T2 —172	[267.54–.55]	267.5
T2 —931*	T2 —93	[267.613]	267.61
T2 —9312*	T2 —931	[268.61–.62]	268.6
[T2 —93122]*	T2 —9312	[268.68]	268.6
T3B —2057	T3B —2	[269.4]	269
T5 —91499	T5 —9149	[291.448]	291.44
T5 —921	T5 —92	[296.387]	296.38
T6 —391	T6 —39	[296.61092]	296.61
T6 —91499	T6 —9149	[296.673–.675]	296.67
T6 —91593	T6 —9159	296.74	296.7
T6 —9287	T6 —928	[297.12264–.12266]	297.1226
T6 —9549	T6 —954	297.12268	297.1226
T6 —983	T6 —98	[297.13]	297.1
[T7 —3511–3518]	T7 —351	[297.19]	Without meaning
[T7 —3523]	T7 —352	[297.291]	297.29
T7 —553	T7 —55	[297.295]	297.29
[T7 —574]	T7 —57	[297.297]	297.29
[T7 —631]	T7 —63	[297.42]	297.4
[T7 —7921]	T7 —792	[297.448]	297.44
[001.4224–.4225]	001.422	[297.61092]	297.61
[004.32]	004.3	[303.42–.43]	303.4
004.33	004	306.1*	306
[004.54]	004.5	306.4*	306
[133.3239]	133.323	[321.12]	321.1
[152.1828]	152.182	[323.422]	323.42
[155.4562]	155.456	[325.31]	325.3
[155.45675]	155.4567	328.3	328
158.5	158	328.304	328.3
[175.1–.9]	175	[328.3042]	328.304
[180.938]	180	[328.361]	328.36
[204]	Without meaning	328.378	328.37
[215.1]	215	[341.7519]	341.751
[215.24–.25]	215	342.075	342.07
[215.4–.5]	215	343.0775	343.077
[215.72–.74]	215.7	355.82	355.8
[215.8–.9]	215	[357.58]	357.5
[232.915–.916]	232.91	359.82	359.8
[232.924–.926]	232.92	362.7083	362
[241.32]	241.3	[362.79]	362.7
[241.57]	241.5	[382.174]	382.17
[242.721]	242.72	388.3222	388.322
[242.723–.726]	242.72	[394.268]*	394.26
[253.73]	253.7	[394.2683]*	394.26
264.032	264.03	[394.2684]*	394.26
[264.037]	264.03	[398.04]*	398
[264.5–.6]	264	398.21*	398.2
[267.31–.32]	267.3	439.1	439

*Previously published

Edition 20	Edition 21	Edition 20	Edition 21
491.499	491.49	[551.5633]	551.563
491.593	491.59	[551.5714–.5717]	551.571
492.877	492.8	[551.5747]	551.574
495.17	495.1	[551.578461]	551.57846
495.49	495.4	[551.578465–.578466]	551.57846
[502.822]	502.82	[612.01454–.01457]	612.0145
[502.824]	502.82	[612.01543–.01547]	612.0154
[512.53]	512.5	[616.85834]	616.8583
[513.122–.123]	513.12	[616.99524]	616.995
[513.132–.133]	513.13	[618.326001–.32609]	618.326
[513.142–.143]	513.14	[620.1899]	620.189
516.13	516	[621.166]	621.16
[516.363]	516.36	[621.38486–.38488]	621.3848
[519.26]	519.2	[621.38862–.38864]	621.3886
[522.684]	522.68	[623.262–.263]	623.26
[523.111]	520	[624.104]	624.1
[526.92]	526.9	624.28	624.2
[527.5]	527	[625.704]	625.7
[530.1332–.1334]	530.133	[627.132]	627.13
[530.81021]	530.81	[627.134]	627.13
[531.162]	531.16	[627.33]	627.3
[532.04]	532	[627.85]	627.8
533.295	Without meaning	[628.1667]	628.166
[534.32]	534.3	[628.16742]	628.1674
[535.322]	534.32	[628.16746]	628.1674
[535.523–.524]	535.52	[628.1675–.1676]	628.167
[536.31–.34]	536.3	[628.16823]	628.1682
[536.445]	536.44	[628.4404]	628.44
[536.45]	536.4	[628.963]	628.96
[537.123–.125]	537.12	628.964	628.96
[537.14]	537.1	[628.967]	628.96
[537.2442]	537.24	[628.9697]	628.969
[537.533]	537.53	[629.13457]	629.1345
[537.61]	537.6	[629.259]	629.25
538.744	538.74	[629.4542–.4545]	629.454
[539.761]	539.76	629.455	629.455
[541.243]	541.24	[02–05]	Main number
[544.953]	544.95	[630.2018]	630
[545.42–.43]	545.4	[632.58]	632.5
[545.813]	545.81	632.952	632.95
[548.843–.845]	548.84	[634.9741–.9749]	634.974
[549.113]	549.11	635.94	635.9
[549.119]	549.11	[635.942]	635.9
[551.115]	551.11	[635.944]	635.94
[551.119]	551.11	[635.946–.948]	635.9
[551.383]	551.38	[636.08241–.08243]	636.0824
551.436	551.43	[636.161]	636.16
[551.5152–.5153]	551.515	636.825	636.82
551.5276	551.527	636.826	636.82
[551.557]	551.55	637.14	637.1

Edition 20	Edition 21
637.54	637.5
[637.541]	637.5
[637.543–.548]	637.54
[637.59]	637.5
[638.11]	638.1
[639.122]	639.12
639.311	639.31
639.344	639.34
[639.4811]	639.4
639.54	639.5
[639.541]	639.54
[639.73]	639.7
[639.752–.758]	639.75
639.979	639.9
[641.309]	641.3
[641.583]	641.58
646.21*	646.2
[646.7242]	646.724
[646.7245]	646.724
[648.56]	648.5
[649.1562]	649.156
[649.15675]	649.1567
658.3254	658.325
658.542	658.54
[664.092]	664.09
[664.369]	664.36
664.725	664.72
[669.1419]	669.141
671.529	671.52
[673.29]	673
[673.71]	673.7
[673.725]	673.72
[673.75]	673.7
[673.79]	673.7
[698.10288]	698.1
746	746
[0487]	048
[751.67]	751.6
[778.554]	778.55
[796.0191]*	796
839.1	839
891.499	891.49
891.593	891.59
895.49	895.4
[899.99301–.9938]	899.993
930–990	930–990
[00992]*	0099
[981.012]	981.01

*Previously published

Comparative Tables

The following lists, each arranged alphabetically by topic, show changes in notation from Edition 20 to Edition 21 for a substantial number of topics in the following revisions: T2 —47 Eastern Europe   Russia, 350–354 Public administration, 370 Education, and 560–590 Life sciences. The tables are not substitutes for complete indexes to the revised schedules.

For each topic, usually only the comprehensive number is given. If part of the topic has been relocated or discontinued elsewhere, the subtopic and its numbers are also given. For example:

Topic	Edition 20	Edition 21
Collective bargaining	351.832	354.73
personnel management	351.174, 352.005174	352.68

This indicates that in 350 Public administration the comprehensive works number for collective bargaining has been changed from 351.832 to 354.73, and the number for collective bargaining as part of personnel management has been changed from both 351.174 and 352.005174 to 352.68.

In some cases, only comprehensive works on a subject are relocated or discontinued; specific subtopics or aspects may remain where they were. For example:

Topic	Edition 20	Edition 21
Student violence	371.58	371.782

In this case, student violence as a disciplinary problem remains in 371.58.

The abbreviation *T1* in these lists means Table 1 Standard Subdivisions, and *T2* means Table 2 Geographic Areas, Historical Periods, Persons.

Eastern Europe   Russia

Topic	Edition 20	Edition 21
Armenia	T2 —4792	T2 —4756
Azerbaijan	T2 —4791	T2 —4754
Baltic Sea area of Russia	T2 —474	T2 —4721
Baltic States	T2 —474	T2 —479
Belarus	T2 —4765	T2 —478
Carpathian Mountains	T2 —47718	T2 —4779
Caspian Sea	T2 —479	T2 —475
Caucasus	T2 —479	T2 —475
Crimea province	T2 —47717	T2 —4771
Don River	T2 —4777	T2 —4749
Donets Basin	T2 —47716	T2 —4774
Eastern area of European Russia	T2 —478	T2 —474
Estonia	T2 —4741	T2 —4798
Georgia	T2 —4795	T2 —4758
Gor'ki province	T2 —4781	T2 —4741
Kiev province	T2 —47714	T2 —4777
Kirov province	T2 —4781	T2 —4742

Topic	Edition 20	Edition 21
Latvia	T2 —4743	T2 —4796
Leningrad province	T2 —47453	T2 —4721
Lithuania	T2 —475	T2 —4793
Moldova	T2 —4775	T2 —476
Moscow province	T2 —47312	T2 —4731
Nizhnegorod province	T2 —4781	T2 —4741
Northern area of European Russia	T2 —472	T2 —471
Odessa province	T2 —47717	T2 —4772
Saint Petersburg	T2 —47453	T2 —4721
Tatarstan republic	T2 —4783	T2 —4745
Ukraine	T2 —4771	T2 —477
Ural Mountains region	T2 —4787	T2 —4743
Volga River	T2 —478	T2 —474
Western area of Russia	T2 —476	T2 —472

Public administration

Only the numbers for the topic as part of the administration of central governments (the 351 number) and as part of local governments (the 352 number) are given in the Edition 20 column. Only the comprehensive works number for the topic is given in the Edition 21 column. How these numbers correspond to related numbers in both Editions 20 and 21 is discussed at the beginning of both equivalence tables for public administration.

Topic	Edition 20	Edition 21
Abdication of monarchs	351.0036	324
Abuse of power	351.991, 352.002	353.46
Accidents	351.783, 352.3	353.9
Accountability in public administration	351.9, 352.002	352.35
Administrative agencies	351, 352.008	352.29
Administrative reports	351.0006, 352.0006	351.05
Advisory bodies	351.0093, 352.009	352.743
Agricultural industries	351.8233	354.5
Air pollution	351.82324, 352.942324	354.3735
Air transportation	351.8777	354.79
Animal husbandry	351.82336	354.56
Animal resources	351.82328	354.349
Aquatic biological resources	351.82328	354.57
Archives	351.7146, 352.1646	352.744
Arts	351.854, 352.9454	353.77
Automobiles	351.87834, 352.91834	354.765
Banks and banking	351.8252	354.86
Bilingual programs	351.85	353.7
Biological resources	351.82328	354.349
Birth certificates	351.816, 352.9416	353.59
Birth control	351.815, 352.9415	353.59
Broadcasting	351.874	354.75
Budgets	351.72252, 352.1252	352.48
Building industry	351.8242, 352.94242	354.64
Building management	351.7133, 352.1633	352.56
Bureaucracy	351.001, 352	352.63
Bus transportation	351.878322, 352.918322	354.7653
urban	351.87841322, 352.91841322	354.769
Cabinets	351.004	352.24
Celebrations	351.859, 352.9459	353.77
Cemeteries	351.86, 352.72	353.6
Censorship	351.75, 352.935	353.37
Census	351.819	352.75
Centralization	351.0073, 352.000473	352.283
Charters	351.8, 352.8	352.84
Chief executives	351.003, 352.008	352.23
Children	351.847, 352.9447	353.536
Cities	352.00724	352.16
City planning	351.82326, 352.96	354.353
Civil defense	351.755, 352.9355	353.95
Civil rights	351.811, 352.9411	353.48

Topic	Edition 20	Edition 21
Civil rights violations	351.996, 352.002	353.46
Civil service	351.6, 352.0056	352.63
Civil service examinations	351.3, 352.0053	351.076
Civil service pensions	351.5, 352.0055	353.549
Claims against government	351.91, 352.002	352.885
Collective bargaining	351.832	354.97
personnel management	351.174, 352.005174	352.68
Commerce	351.826, 352.9426	354.73
Commissions	351.009, 352.009	352.25
Commodity brokers	351.826	354.88
Commodity exchanges	351.826	354.88
Communicable diseases	351.841, 352.9441	353.63
Communication in management	351.7142, 352.1642	352.384
Communications	351.874	354.75
Compensation	351.835	354.98
personnel management	351.1232, 352.0051232	352.67
Computer communication	351.8743	354.75
Conditions of employment	351.835, 352.9435	354.98
personnel management	351.16, 352.00516	352.67
Conflict of interest	351.995, 352.002	353.46
Conservation of natural		
resources	351.8232, 352.94232	354.334
Consultants	351.00722, 352.0004722	352.373
Construction industry	351.8242, 352.94242	354.64
Consumer protection	351.820423, 352.942	352.746
Contracting	351.711, 352.161	352.53
Contracts (Labor agreements)	351.174, 352.005174	352.68
Control	351.0091, 352.0092	352.8
executive management	351.0075, 352.000475	352.35
Copyright	351.824	352.749
Corrections	351.849, 352.9449	353.39
Corruption in government	351.994, 352.002	353.46
Counties	352.0073	352.15
Credit institutions	351.825	354.86
Crime prevention		
criminology	351.8492, 352.94492	353.39
police services	351.75, 352.935	353.36
Culture	351.85, 352.945	353.7
Customs (Tariff)	351.7246	352.448
Death certificates	351.816, 352.9416	353.59
Debt management	351.72, 352.1	352.45
Decentralization	351.0073, 352.000473	352.283
Decision making	351.00725, 352.0004725	352.33
Disabled persons	351.844, 352.9444	353.539
Disadvantaged workers	351.836, 352.9436	354.908
Disasters	351.754, 352.9354	353.95
Discipline	351.147, 352.005147	352.66
Disease control	351.776, 352.4	353.628
Domestic commerce	351.826, 352.9426	354.73
Drug traffic	351.765, 352.9365	353.37
Drugs (Pharmaceuticals)		
product safety	351.7784, 352.4	353.998

Topic	Edition 20	Edition 21
Economic development	351.82, 352.942	354.27
Economics	351.82, 352.942	354
Education	351.851, 352.9451	353.8
Education of employees	351.15, 352.00515	352.66
Efficiency	351.147, 352.005147	352.375
Electric power	351.8722, 352.9122	354.49
Embassies	351.892	353.13
Employee organizations	351.173, 352.005173	352.68
Employer-employee relationships		
personnel management	351.17, 352.00517	352.68
Employment security	351.834	354.98
Energy conservation	351.8232, 352.94232	354.43
Environmental protection	351.82321	354.328
Equal employment opportunity	351.833, 352.9433	354.908
personnel management	351.104, 352.005104	352.608
Equipment management	351.7134, 352.1634	352.55
Ethnic groups		
government programs	351.814, 352.9414	353.5339
social welfare	351.8484, 352.94484	353.5339
Excise tax	351.72471, 352.135	352.44
Executive branch of government	351, 352	351
Executive departments	351, 352.008	351
Executive management	351.007, 352.00047	352.3
Executive messages	351.0035, 352.008	352.238
Executives	351.0074, 352.000474	352.39
Fact finding	351.0093, 352.009	352.743
Families	351.8482, 352.94482	353.5331
Federal administration	351	351
Fees	351.726, 352.14	352.44
Finance departments	351.72, 352.1	352.4
Financial institutions	351.825	354.8
Financial management	351.72, 352.1	352.4
Fire safety	351.782, 352.3	353.979
Flood control	351.82329	354.3627
Food		
product safety	351.7782, 352.4	353.997
Foreign aid	351.89	353.13273
Foreign relations	351.89	353.13
Foreign trade	351.827	354.74
Forestry	351.82338	354.55
Freight services	351.875	354.764
Fuel resources	351.82327	354.4
Gambling		
public control	351.76, 352.936	353.37
Gas supply	351.8723, 352.9123	354.4628
Gift tax	351.72476	352.44
Governing boards	351.009, 352.009	352.25
Government contracts	351.711, 352.161	352.53
Government corporations	351.0092, 352.009	352.266
Government liability	351.91, 352.002	352.885
Government procurement	351.712, 352.162	352.53
Government securities	351.72, 352.1	352.45

Topic	Edition 20	Edition 21
Government-sponsored insurance	351.8256	353.54
Government workers biography	351.00092, 352.00092	351.092
Governors	351.00313	352.23213
Grants-in-aid	351.72	352.73
Grievances (Labor)	351.176, 352.005176	352.68
Grievances against government	351.91, 352.002	352.885
Ground transportation	351.878, 352.918	354.76
Grounds management	351.7132. 352.1632	352.57
Gun control	351.75, 352.935	353.36
Handicapped persons	351.844, 352.9444	353.539
Hazardous materials	351.783, 352.3	353.993
Hazardous wastes	351.772, 352.63	353.994
Health services	351.841, 352.9441	353.6
personnel management	351.16, 352.00516	352.67
Historic preservation	351.859, 352.9459	353.77
Home departments	351.03	353.3
Hours of work	351.163, 352.005163	352.67
Housing	351.865, 352.75	353.55
Humanities	351.854, 352.9454	353.77
Impeachment	351.993, 352.002	342.068
chief executives	351.0036, 352.008	342.068
Inaugural addresses	351.00354, 352.008	352.2386
Income tax	351.7244, 352.135	352.44
Independent agencies	351.009, 352.009	352.264
Industrial development	351.82, 352.942	354.27
Industrial relations	351.832	354.9
Industry	351.82, 352.942	354
Information management	351.00722, 352.0004722	352.38
Information services	351.819, 352.9419	352.74
Inheritance tax	351.72476	352.44
Inland waterway transportation	351.876	354.78
Inspection external control	351.0091, 352.0092	352.83
internal control	351.0076, 352.000476	352.35
Insurance	351.8255	354.85
Intergovernmental administration	351.09	353.33
Intergovernmental fiscal relations	351.725	352.73
International debt	351.72	352.45
Interprovincial relations	351.091	352.133
Interstate relations	351.091	352.133
Inventory	351.713042, 352.163042	352.54
Investments	351.8258	354.88
Job classification	351.103, 352.005103	352.64
Job security	351.834	354.98
Justice	351.88	353.4
Kings	351.00312	352.23
Labor	351.83, 352.943	354.9
Labor unions	351.832	354.97
personnel management	351.173, 352.005173	352.68
Laboring classes	351.8485, 352.94485	354.9

Topic	Edition 20	Edition 21
Land management (Plant management)	351.7132, 352.1632	352.57
Land resources	351.82326, 352.942326	354.34
Land subdivision	351.82326, 352.962	354.34
Law enforcement	351.74, 352.2	353.36
Leadership	351.0074, 352.000474	352.39
Leadership role of chief executives	351.00323, 352.008	352.236
Leaves of absence	351.164, 352.005164	352.67
Lending institutions	351.825	354.86
Libraries	351.852, 352.9452	352.744
Licensing	351.8, 352.8	352.84
Liquor traffic	351.761, 352.9361	353.37
Local government	352	352.14
Lottery income	351.726, 352.14	352.44
Management by objectives	351.0078, 352.000478	352.36
Management consultants	351.00722, 352.0004722	352.373
Manufacturing industries	351.8242, 352.94242	354.66
Marine biological resources	351.82328	354.57
Marine resources	351.82325	354.369
Materials management	351.7134, 352.1634	352.55
Mayors	352.008	352.23216
Mediation	351.832	354.97
personnel management	351.174, 352.005174	352.68
Mental health services	351.842, 352.9442	353.64
Merit system (Civil service)	351.6, 352.0056	352.63
Mineral resources	351.82327	354.39
Minority groups		
government programs	351.814, 352.9414	353.53
social welfare	351.8484, 352.94484	353.53
Misconduct in office	351.9, 352.002	353.46
Modernization	351.0073, 352.000473	352.367
Money	351.822	354.84
Morale	351.147, 352.005147	352.66
Morality	351.76, 352.936	353.37
Mortgages	351.825	354.86
Motivation	351.147, 352.005147	352.66
Museums	351.853, 352.9453	352.76
National debt	351.72	352.45
National-local relations	351.093	353.334
National-state relations	351.092	353.333
Natural resources	351.8232, 352.94232	354.3
Natural sciences	351.855	352.745
Naturalization	351.817	353.484
Noise control	351.772, 352.6	354.338
Nontax revenues	351.726, 352.14	352.44
Occupational licensing	351.8243046, 352.94243	354.9284
Ocean transportation	351.8775	354.78
Office workers	351.1, 352.0051	352.63
Oil (Petroleum)	351.82327	354.45
Older persons	351.846, 352.9446	353.537
Ombudsmen	351.91, 352.002	352.88

Topic	Edition 20	Edition 21
Organization (Management)	351.0073, 352.000473	352.2
Oversight	351.0075, 352.000475	352.35
Parking facilities	351.878474, 352.918474	354.765
Parks	351.82326	354.34
natural resources	351.82326	354.34
recreation	351.8632, 352.732	353.78
Passenger services	351.875, 352.915	354.763
Passports	351.898	353.13
Patents	351.824	352.749
Payroll administration	351.125, 352.005125	352.47
Pensions	351.835	353.54
Personnel management	351.1, 352.0051	352.6
Pest control	351.772, 352.6	354.339
Petroleum	351.82327	354.45
Physical fitness	351.773, 352.4	353.6274
Pipeline transportation	351.878	354.764
Plant resources	351.82328	354.349
Police services	351.74	353.36
local	352.2	363.2068
Policy making	351.0072, 352.000472	352.34
Pollution	351.82323, 352.942323	354.335
Population control	351.815	353.59
Ports	351.8771	354.78
Postal service	351.873	354.759
Poverty	351.845, 352.9445	353.5332
Preferential hiring	351.13243, 352.00513243	352.6508
Presidents	351.00313	352.23
Preventive medicine	351.77, 352.4	353.628
Price control	351.820424	352.85
Primary industries	351.823, 352.9423	354.3
Prime ministers	351.00313	352.23
Prison administration	351.8495, 352.94495	353.39
Procurement	351.712, 352.162	352.53
Product safety	351.778, 352.4	353.99
Production controls (Economic		
programs)	351.82, 352.942	354.28
Professions	351.8243, 352.94243	354.93
Project management	351.007, 352.00047	352.365
Property management	351.713, 352.163	352.5
Property tax	351.7242, 352.1352·	352.44
Prostitution	351.76, 352.936	353.37
Provinces (Central governments)	351	352.14
Provinces (Local governments)	352.0073	352.15
Public administrators		
biography	351.00092, 352.00092	351.092
Public buildings		
building management	351.7133, 352.1633	352.56
public works	351.862, 352.5	352.77
Public contracts	351.711, 352.161	352.53
Public finance	351.72, 352.1	352.4
Public health	351.841, 352.9441	353.6
Public order	351.75, 352.935	353.3

Topic	Edition 20	Edition 21
Public records	351.714, 352.164	352.387
Public relations	351.819, 352.9419	352.748
Public safety	351.75, 352.935	353.9
Public utilities	351.87, 352.91	354.728
Public works	351.86, 352.7	352.77
Radio	351.8745	354.75
Railroad transportation	351.875	354.767
Rationing	351.829, 352.942	352.86
Real property tax	351.7242, 352.1352	352.44
Recreation	351.858, 352.9458	353.78
Recruiting personnel	351.131, 352.005131	352.65
Reduction in force	351.184, 352.005184	352.69
Refugees	351.848, 352.9448	353.5338
Regulatory agencies	351.0091, 352.0092	352.8
Reorganization	351.0073, 352.000473	352.2
Research	351.819, 352.9419	352.74
Research and development	351.82, 352.942	354.27
noneconomic fields	351.819, 352.9419	352.7
Retirement	351.182, 352.005182	352.69
Revenue	351.726, 352.14	352.44
Revenue sharing	351.725	352.73
Road transportation	351.87831, 352.91831	354.77
Rural government	352.00722	352.17
Safety	351.78, 352.3	353.9
Sales tax	351.7247, 352.135	352.44
Sanitation	351.772, 352.6	353.93
Sciences	351.855	352.745
Secondary industries	351.824, 352.9424	354.6
Separation from service	351.18, 352.00518	352.69
Service industries	351.8243, 352.94243	354.68
Small business	351.82048, 352.942	354.2799
Social security	351.84	353.5
government-sponsored insurance	351.8256	353.54
Social welfare	351.84, 352.944	353.5
Soil conservation	351.82326, 352.942326	354.3434
Space transportation	351.8778	354.79
Special districts	351.009, 352.009	352.19
Sports	351.858, 352.9458	353.78
Standards	351.821, 352.9421	352.83
State-local relations	351.093	353.334
States	351	352.13
Strategic planning	351.0072, 352.000472	352.34
Substance abuse		
personnel management	351.16, 352.00516	352.67
social welfare	351.8429, 352.94429	353.64
Subsurface resources	351.82327	354.39
Supervision	351.102, 352.005102	352.66
Supply management	351.7135, 352.1635	352.55
Surveys	351.819, 352.9419	352.75
Systems analysis	351.0073, 352.000473	352.33
Taxes	351.724, 352.13	352.44

Topic	Edition 20	Edition 21
Technology	351.856	352.745
Technology assessment	351.856	354.27
Telecommunication	351.874	354.75
Television	351.87455	354.75
Tenure	351.834	354.98
Title (Property)	351.8, 352.8	354.34
Trademarks	351.824	352.749
Traffic control	351.87831, 352.91831	354.7728
Training	351.15, 352.00515	352.669
Transportation	351.875, 352.915	354.76
Transportation safety	351.87500289, 352.91500289	353.98
Unemployment insurance	351.84	353.54
Unmarried mothers	351.848, 352.9448	353.5331
Urban development	351.818, 352.9418	354.2793
Urban transportation	351.8784, 352.9184	354.769
User fees	351.726, 352.14	352.44
Veterans	351.812	353.538
Veterans' preference	351.13243, 352.00513243	352.6508697
Victims of crime	351.8488, 352.94488	353.5337
Victims of oppression	351.848	353.5338
Visas	351.898	353.13
Voluntary service groups	351.896	352.78
Waste control	351.772, 352.63	353.93
Water resources	351.82325	354.36
Water transportation	351.877	354.78
Weather bureaus	351.85551163	354.37
Weights and measures	351.821, 352.9421	352.83
Welfare services	351.84, 352.944	353.5
Women		
government programs	351.813, 352.9413	353.535
social welfare	351.848, 352.9448	353.535
Women workers	351.837, 352.9437	354.9082
Work environment		
personnel management	351.161, 352.005161	352.67
Work teams	351.14, 352.00514	352.66
Worker security	351.834	354.98
Workers' compensation insurance	351.8256	353.69
Young people	351.847, 352.9447	353.536
Zoning	351.82326, 352.961	354.333

Education

The 370 Education schedule has been extensively revised. Many topics have been relocated or given longer or shorter numbers; however, most topics have the same number in both editions. For example, the number for elementary education of reading comprehension has been relocated from 372.41 to 372.47, the number for reading readiness has been shortened from 372.4142 to 372.414, but the number for remedial reading has remained the same at 372.43.

A substantial number of topics whose numbers have changed are listed below. Many relocations that simply regularize standard subdivisions, discontinue a topic to a shorter number, or relocate a standard subdivision to a preexisting regular schedule number to eliminate dual provision are given only in the 370 Education equivalence tables. For example, the relocation of 372.0287 Testing and measurement to 372.126 is shown in the equivalence tables, not in this comparative table.

Topic	Edition 20	Edition 21
Accountability in public education	379.154	379.158
Accreditation of schools	371.204	379.158
higher education government commissions	379.158	353.88284
Achievement tests use of specific tests	371.264	371.262
Admissions and related topics higher education	378.105	378.161
Adult education specific agencies	374.29	374.94–.99
specific kinds of agencies	374.29	374.8
specific schools	374.84–.89	374.94–.99
Advanced placement higher education	378.105	378.1664
Affirmative action	370.19342	379.26
Auto-instructional methods	371.3944	371.3943
Bilingual education	371.97	370.1175
Busing (School desegregation)	370.19342	379.263
Citizenship programs	374.012	323.60715
Coeducation	376	371.822
College level examinations	378.168	378.1662
College year	378.14	378.163
Community centers for adult education	374.28	374.8
Community-school relations	370.1931	371.19
Comparative education	370.195	370.9
Compensatory education	371.967	370.111
Computers elementary education	372.35	372.34
Correspondence schools adult education specific schools	374.44–.49	374.4094–.4099

Topic	Edition 20	Edition 21
Credits		
higher education	378.168	378.1618
Curricula		
specific educational objectives	375.008	370.11
specific subject objectives	375.008	T1 —071
specific subjects	375.01–.9	T1 —071
Dance		
elementary education	372.66	372.868
Deans of students	378.112	378.194
Desegregation	370.19342	379.263
Drama in education	371.332	371.399
elementary level	372.1332	372.66
Education for effective use of		
leisure	370.116	370.119
Education for individual		
fulfillment	370.116	370.119
Education for international		
understanding	370.115	370.116
Education of teachers	371.10071	370.71
Education of women	376	371.822
Education, research, related		
activities in teaching	371.10207	370.7
Educational buildings	371.62	371.6
noninstructional facilities	371.625	Scattered
Educational equalization	370.1934	379.26
Educational exchanges	370.196	370.116
Educational games	371.397	371.337
Educational sociology	370.19	306.43
Educational technology	371.3078	371.33
Educational toys	371.3078	371.337
Educational vouchers	379.13	379.111
Equal educational opportunity	370.1934	379.26
Evening schools		
higher education	378.1544	378.158
Exchange of students	370.1962	370.1162
Exchange of teachers	370.1963	370.1163
Experimental secondary schools	373.042	373.214
Extension education		
higher education	378.1554	378.175
Financial management		
agencies supporting public		
education	379.1	353.824
colleges and universities	378.02	378.106
public school systems	379.11	371.206
Fire safety	371.774	363.377
Foreign students	371.829	371.82691
Fundamental education	370.194	370.111
Grants for international study		
higher education	378.35	378.33
Greek-letter societies		
specific fields	371.854	T1 —06

Topic	Edition 20	Edition 21
Guidance counselors		
personnel management	371.2022	371.40683
higher education	378.112	378.1940683
Home and school associations	370.19312	371.19206
Home schools and schooling	649.68	371.042
In-service training of teachers	371.146	370.715
Individualized reading instruction		
elementary education	372.4147	372.417
Industry-school relations	371.19316	371.195
Instructional facilities		
specific subjects	371.6234	Scattered
Instructional materials	371.209	371.33
elementary reading	372.4028	372.412
Instructional materials centers	371.3078	027.7
Intercultural education	370.196	370.117
Intercultural educational aid	370.1965	379.11
international	370.1965	379.129
Internal organization of schools	371.208	371.207
International intercultural		
educational aid	370.1965	379.129
Intramural sports	371.89	796.042
Leadership of schools	371.207	371.2011
higher education	378.107	378.111
Leisure education	370.116	370.119
Manual alphabet instruction	371.9127	419.071
Mass media in adult education	374.27	374.26
Middle management of schools	371.207	371.2011
higher education	378.107	378.111
Monitorial system of instruction	371.59	371.39
Multicultural education	370.19341	370.117
National support of secondary		
education	379.1212	379.1213
Nongraded grouping	371.254	371.255
Open plan schools	371.208	371.256
Parent-teacher associations	370.9312	371.19206
Part-word methods (Reading)		
elementary education	372.4145	372.465
Personalized reading instruction		
elementary education	372.4147	372.417
Phonetic methods (Reading)		
elementary education	372.4145	372.465
Phonetics		
elementary reading	372.622	372.465
Physical education facilities	371.624	796.068
Physical health of students	371.712	371.71
Practice teaching	370.733	370.71
Prayer in public schools	377.14	379.28
Private education		
secondary level		
public support	379.322	379.323
Psychology of learning		
specific subjects	370.156	T1—019

Topic	Edition 20	Edition 21
Psychology of teaching	371.102019	370.15
Public education	371.01	370
aims and objectives	379.201	370
Public entertainment activities		
of students	371.89	790.2088375
Reading comprehension		
elementary education	372.41	372.47
Religion in public schools	377.1	379.28
Religious schools	377	371.07
Research in education	370.78	370.72
School accountability	379.154	379.158
School accreditation	371.204	379.158
higher education		
government commissions	379.158	353.88284
School administrators		
personnel management		
public control	379.157	371.2011
School and society		
(Interdisciplinary works)	370.193	306.432
School attendance		
administration	371.24	371.294
social aspects	370.19341	371.294
School buildings	371.62	371.6
noninstructional facilities	371.625	Scattered
School desegregation	370.19342	379.263
School discipline		
higher education	378.18	378.195
School evaluation	379.154	379.158
School materials	371.209	371.67
School psychologists		
personnel management	371.2022	371.7130683
School safety programs	371.77	363.119371
athletic safety	371.7754	363.147
fire safety	371.774	363.377
street crossing guards	371.7752	363.1257
School social workers		
personnel management	371.2022	371.46
School standards	371.204	379.158
higher education		
government commissions	379.158	353.88284
School year		
higher education	378.14	378.163
Sight methods (Reading)		
elementary education	372.4144	372.462
Sign language instruction	371.9127	419.071
Sixth-form colleges	373.238	378.1543
Sociology of education	370.19	306.43
Storytelling		
elementary education	372.642	372.677
Student clubs	371.89	371.83
Student organizations		
specific fields	371.84	T1 — 06

Topic	Edition 20	Edition 21
Student participation in administration		
higher education	378.107	378.1959
Student violence	371.58	371.782
Students distinguished by ethnic origin	371.97	371.829
Students distinguished by social class	371.96	371.826
Study techniques for parents	649.68	371.30281
Supervisors	371.2013	371.203
Tape recorders in instruction	371.3333	371.3332
Teacher-parent relations	371.103	371.192
Teacher training	371.122	370.71
Teachers		
personnel management		
public control	379.157	371.1
Teachers and society (Inter-disciplinary works)	371.104	306.432
Teachers' centers	370.72	370.715
Teachers' colleges	370.73	370.711
Teachers' conferences	370.72	370.715
Teaching materials	371.209	371.33
elementary reading	372.4028	372.412
Tenure of teachers	371.14	371.104
higher education	378.122	378.121
Top management of schools	371.207	371.2011
higher education	378.107	378.111
Tuition in public schools	379.13	371.206
Undergraduate departments and schools	378.1552	378.1542
University extension	378.1554	378.1735
Vandalism	371.58	371.782
Veterans' education benefits	362.8682	371.223
higher education	362.8682	378.32
Vocational education		
public control	379.1552	370.113
secondary level	373.0113	373.246
Whole-word methods (Reading)		
elementary education	372.4144	372.462
Women in education	376	370.82
Workshops for teachers	370.72	370.715

Life sciences

One of the major revisions in Edition 21 is 560–590 Life sciences. Of these schedules, 570 Life sciences   Biology and 583 Magnoliopsida (Dicotyledons) are completely revised; 560 Paleontology, the rest of 580 Plants, and 590 Animals are extensively revised. Life sciences topics are given in the following five lists:

(1) General topics in biology

Topics such as physiology and ecology that are found in 570–578, 579.1, 581–582, and 591. (Many topics that were located in 581 and 591 in Edition 20, e.g., physiology of plants and animals, are located in 571–575 in Edition 21.) General topics that are or were found among the names of specific kinds of organisms in the taxonomic spans, e.g., bones and mycology are also included in this list. Relocated geological periods, however, are found in the Paleontology list below.

(2) Microorganisms, fungi, algae

Names of specific kinds of organisms that were located in 576, 589, and 593.1 in Edition 20 and are located in 579 in Edition 21.

(3) Plants

Names of specific kinds of plants located in 583–588 in both Edition 20 and 21.

(4) Animals

Names of specific kinds of animals located in 592–599 in both Edition 20 and 21.

(5) Paleontology

Names of specific kinds of organisms represented in the fossil record located in 561–569 in both Edition 20 and 21, and geological periods relocated within 560.17.

General topics in biology

Topic	Edition 20	Edition 21
Abdomen	591.1042	573.997
Acclimatization	574.542	578.42
Adaptation	574.5	578.4
animals	591.5	591.4
plants	581.5	581.4
Aging	574.372	571.878
animals	591.372	571.8781
plants	581.372	571.8782
Alkaloids	574.19242	572.549
Alternation of generations	574.163	571.884
Anabolism	574.133	572.45
Anaerobic respiration	574.128	572.478
Anatomy	574.4	571.3
animals	591.4	571.31
plants	581.4	571.32
Animal behavior	591.51	591.5
Animals	591	590
Anthropology	573	599.9
Antibodies	591.293	571.967
Aquatic animals	591.92	591.76
Aquatic biology	574.92	578.76
Aquatic ecology	574.5263	577.6
Aquatic plants	581.92	581.76
Arctic ecology	574.52621	577.0911
Arctic plants	581.9091	580.911
Arid land ecology	574.52652	577.54
Asexual reproduction	574.162	571.89
Autoimmunity	574.29	571.973
Bacterial diseases	574.2322	571.993
Bark		
anatomy	582.047	575.45233
descriptive botany	582.047	581.47
Beneficial animals	591.61	591.63
Beneficial organisms	574.61	578.63
Beneficial plants	581.61	581.63
Berries	582.1304166	581.464
anatomy	582.130446	575.6733
descriptive botany	582.130446	581.464
physiology	582.1304166	575.67
Biochemical genetics	574.873224	572.8
Biochemistry	574.192	572
animals	591.192	572.1
plants	581.192	572.2
Bioclimatology	574.5222	577.22
animals	591.5222	591.722
plants	581.5222	581.722
Bioelectricity	574.19127	572.437
Bioenergetics	574.19121	572.43
Biogenesis	577	576.83
Biogeochemistry	574.5222	577.14

Topic	Edition 20	Edition 21
Biogeography	574.9	578.09
Biological rhythms	574.1882	571.77
animals	591.1882	571.771
plants	581.1882	571.772
Biological specimens		
preservation	579	570.752
Biologists	574.092	570.92
Biology	574	570
Bioluminescence	574.19125	572.4358
Biomechanics	574.191	571.43
animals	591.1852	571.431
plants	581.191	571.432
Biophysics	574.191	571.4
animals	591.191	571.41
plants	581.191	571.42
Biosociology	574.524	577.8
Biosynthesis	574.1929	572.45
Blood-forming system	591.14	573.155
Blood vessels	591.116	573.18
Body temperature	591.1912	571.76
Bones	596.01852	573.76
Botanical gardens	580.744	580.73
Botanists	581.092	580.92
Botany	581	580
Carbohydrates	574.19248	572.56
biosynthesis	574.19294	572.5645
metabolism	574.133	572.564
Cardiovascular system	591.11	573.1
anatomy	591.41	573.133
Cell biology	574.87	571.6
animals	591.87	571.61
plants	581.87	571.62
Cell differentiation	574.87612	571.835
Cell-mediated immunity	574.29	571.966
Chemical senses	591.1826	573.877
Chromosomes	574.87322	572.87
Chronobiology	574.1882	571.77
Circulation (Biology)	574.11	573.1
animals	591.11	573.1
plants	581.11	575.7
Communicable diseases	591.23	571.98
Community ecology	574.5247	577.82
animals	591.5247	591.782
plants	581.5247	581.782
Connective tissues	591.1852	571.56
anatomy	591.47	571.5633
Coral reef biology	574.91	578.7789
Cryobiology	574.19167	571.4645
Cytochemistry	574.876042	572
Cytogenetics	574.87322	572.8
Cytology	574.87	571.6
Cytopathology	574.8765	571.936

Topic	Edition 20	Edition 21
Darwinism	575.0162	576.82
Death	574.2	571.939
cell death	574.8765	571.936
Deformities	574.22	571.976
Degeneration	574.2	571.935
animals	591.2	571.9351
plants	581.2	571.9352
Deoxyribonucleic acid	574.873282	572.86
Desert ecology	574.52652	577.54
Developmental biology	574.3	571.8
animals	591.3	571.81
cells	574.8761	571.84
plants	581.3	571.82
Digestion	574.132	573.3
animals	591.132	573.3
plants	581.132	572.42
Digestive system	591.132	573.3
anatomy	574.43	573.333
Diseases	574.2	571.9
animals	591.2	571.91
plants	581.2	571.92
DNA	574.873282	572.86
Ears	591.1825	573.89
anatomy	591.48	573.8933
Eating	591.132	591.53
physiology	591.132	573.35
Ecology	574.5	577
animals	591.5	591.7
plants	581.5	581.7
Economic biology	574.6	578.6
Eggs	591.166	591.468
physiology	591.166	575.68
Electricity		
biophysics	574.1917	571.47
Electrophysiology	574.19127	572.437
Embryology	574.33	571.86
animals	591.33	571.861
plants	581.33	571.862
Endangered animals	591.529	591.68
Endangered plants	581.529	581.68
Endangered species	574.529	578.68
Endocrine system	591.142	573.4
anatomy	591.44	573.433
Environmental diseases	574.24	571.95
animals	591.24	571.951
plants	581.24	571.952
Enzymes	574.1925	572.7
animals	591.1925	572.71
plants	581.1925	572.72

Comparative Tables

Topic	Edition 20	Edition 21
Epidermis	574.1	573.5
anatomy	574.47	573.533
animals	591.1858	573.5
anatomy	591.47	573.533
plant anatomy	581.47	575.45133
Estuarine ecology	574.526365	577.786
Ethnology	572	599.97
Evolution	575	576.8
humans	573.2	599.938
Excretion	574.14	573.49
animals	591.149	573.49
plants	581.14	575.79
Experimental biology	574.0724	570.724
Experimental botany	581.0724	580.724
Experimental zoology	591.0724	590.724
Extinct animals		
recently extinct	591.529	591.68
Extinct plants		
recently extinct	581.529	581.68
Extinction	575.7	576.84
Extraterrestrial life	577	576.83
Eyes	591.1823	573.88
anatomy	591.48	573.8833
Fats	574.19247	572.57
Female genital system	591.166	573.66
Flowers	582.1304166	582.13
anatomy	582.1304463	575.633
descriptive botany	582.1304463	582.13
physiology	582.1304166	575.6
Flying	591.1852	573.798
Food chains	574.53	577.16
Food microbiology	576.163	664.001579
Forest ecology	574.52642	577.3
Freshwater biology	574.929	578.76
Freshwater ecology	574.52632	577.6
Fruit	582.1304166	581.464
anatomy	582.0464	575.6733
descriptive botany	582.0464	581.464
flowering plants	582.130446	581.464
physiology	582.1304166	575.67
Fungus diseases	574.2326	571.995
Gene pools	575.15	576.58
Genes	574.87322	572.86
animals	591.87322	572.861
plants	581.87322	572.862
Genetic engineering	575.10724	660.65
Genetic transcription	574.873223	572.8845
Genetic translation	574.873223	572.645
Genetics	575.1	576.5
animals	591.15	591.35
humans	573.21	599.935
plants	581.15	581.35

Topic	Edition 20	Edition 21
Genital system	591.166	573.6
anatomy	591.46	573.633
Germ cells	574.32	571.845
Germination	581.334	571.862
Glacier ecology	574.52621	577.586
Glands	591.14	571.79
Grassland ecology	574.52643	577.4
Growth	574.31	571.8
animals	591.31	571.81
cells	574.8761	571.849
plants	581.31	571.82
Harmful organisms	574.65	578.65
Heat (Biophysics)	574.19162	571.467
Herbariums	580.742	580.74
Heredity	575.1	576.5
animals	591.15	591.35
plants	581.15	581.35
Hibernation	591.543	591.565
High-temperature biology	574.19162	571.467
Histochemistry	574.8212	572
Histogenesis	574.17	571.835
animals	591.17	571.8351
plants	581.17	571.8352
Histology	574.824	571.5
Histopathology	574.828	571.9
Histophysiology	574.821	571.5
Homeostasis	574.188	571.75
Human evolution	573.2	599.938
Human genetics	573.21	599.935
Human races	572	599.97
Immunity	574.29	571.96
animals	591.29	571.96
Inbreeding	575.133	576.544
Ingestion	574.132	573.35
animals	591.132	573.35
Innervation	591.188	573.85
Inorganic biochemistry	574.19214	572.51
Integument	574.1	591.47
anatomy	574.47	573.533
physiology	574.1	573.5
Internal biological processes		
of specific organisms	580–590	571–575
of plants in general	581	571–575
of animals in general	591	571–573
Irritability	591.1827	573.85
Island biology	574.91	578.752
Island ecology	574.5267	577.52
Jungle ecology	574.52642	577.34
Lake ecology	574.526322	577.63

Topic	Edition 20	Edition 21
Leaves	581.10427	581.48
anatomy	581.497	575.5733
descriptive botany	581.497	581.48
physiology	581.10427	575.57
Legs	591.1042	591.479
physiology	591.1042	573.79
Life		
biological nature	577	570.1
origin	577	576.83
Life cycle	574.3	571.8
Life on other planets	574.999	576.83
Limnology	574.52632	577.6
Lipids	574.19247	572.57
biosynthesis	574.19293	572.5745
metabolism	574.133	572.574
Lipolytic enzymes	574.19253	572.757
Lipoproteins	574.192454	572.68
Locomotion	591.1852	573.79
Longevity	574.374	571.879
animals	591.374	571.8791
plants	581.374	571.8792
Low-temperature biology	574.19165	571.464
Male genital system	591.166	573.65
Marine biology	574.92	578.77
Marine ecology	574.52636	577.7
Marsh ecology	574.526325	577.68
Maturation	574.3	571.87
animals	591.3	571.871
plants	581.3	571.872
Meadow ecology	574.52643	577.46
Mechanical forces		
biophysics	574.1913	571.43
Membranes	574.875	571.64
Metabolism	574.133	572.4
animals	591.133	572.41
plants	581.133	572.42
Metamorphosis	591.334	571.876
Microbiology	576	579
Microscopy	578	570.282
of plants	578	580.282
of animals	578	590.282
Migration	591.525	591.568
Mineral biochemistry	574.19214	572.51
Molecular biology	574.88	572.8
Molecular genetics	574.87328	572.8
Moor ecology (Heath ecology)	574.5264	577.38
Morphology	574.4	571.3
animals	591.4	571.31
plants	581.4	571.32
Mountain ecology	574.5264	577.53
Movement	591.18	573.7
plants	581.18	575.97

Topic	Edition 20	Edition 21
Muscles	591.1852	573.75
anatomy	591.47	573.7533
Musculoskeletal system	591.1852	573.7
anatomy	591.47	573.733
Mutation	575.292	576.549
Mutualism	574.52482	577.852
Natural selection	575.0162	576.82
Nervous system	591.188	573.8
anatomy	591.48	573.833
Nucleic acids	574.87328	572.8
Nucleoproteins	574.87328	572.84
Nutrition		
physiology	574.13	572.4
animals	591.132	572.41
plants	581.13	572.42
Nuts	582.1304166	581.464
anatomy	582.130446	575.6733
descriptive botany	582.130446	581.464
physiology	582.1304166	575.67
Olfaction	591.1826	573.877
Organ culture	574.0724	571.538
animals	591.0724	571.5381
plants	581.0724	571.5382
Organic compounds	574.1924	572
Origin of life	577	576.83
Parasitic animals	591.5249	591.65
Parasitic diseases	574.23	571.999
Parasitic plants	581.5249	581.65
Parasitism	574.5249	577.857
animals	591.5249	591.7857
plants	581.5249	581.7857
Particle radiation		
biophysics	574.19156	571.459
Pathological anatomy	574.22	571.933
animals	591.22	571.9331
Pathology	574.2	571.9
animals	591.2	571.91
cytology	574.8765	571.936
plants	581.2	571.92
Peptides	574.192456	572.65
Photosynthesis	581.13342	572.46
Physical anthropology	573	599.9
Physical biochemistry	574.19283	572.43
Physiological balance	574.188	571.75
Physiological genetics	574.87322	572.8
Physiology	574.1	571
animals	591.1	571.1
plants	581.1	571.2
Pigments		
biochemistry	574.19218	571.59
Plant diseases	581.2	571.92
Plants	581	580

Topic	Edition 20	Edition 21
Poisonous animals	591.69	591.65
Poisonous plants	581.69	581.659
Pollen anatomy	582.0463	571.845
flowering plants	582.1304463	571.845
Pollination	582.01662	571.8642
Pollution ecology	574.5222	577.27
Polymers	574.192	572.33
Pond ecology	574.526322	577.636
Population ecology	574.5248	577.88
Population genetics	575.15	576.58
Prairie ecology	574.52643	577.44
Prehistoric humans	573.3	569.9
Pressure (Biophysics)	574.19135	571.437
Proteins	574.19245	572.6
biosynthesis	574.19296	572.645
animals	591.19296	572.6451
plants	581.13345	572.6452
metabolism	574.133	572.64
Protoplasm	574.873	571.6
Races (Ethnology)	572	599.97
Radiation (Biophysics)	575.1915	571.45
Radiobiology	575.1915	571.45
Radiogenetics	575.131	576.542
Rare animals	591.529	591.68
Rare plants	581.529	581.68
Rare species	574.529	578.68
Reef biology	574.91	578.7789
Reef ecology	574.526367	577.789
Regeneration	574.31	571.889
Regional anatomy		
animals	591.49	573.9933
plants	581.49	575.433
Regional physiology	574.1042	571.59
animals	591.1042	573.99
plants	581.1042	575.4
Reproduction	574.16	571.8
Reproductive adaptation	574.56	578.46
animals	591.56	591.46
plants	581.56	581.46
Reproductive system	574.16	573.6
anatomy	574.46	573.633
animals	591.16	573.6
anatomy	591.46	573.633
plants	581.16	575.6
anatomy	581.46	575.633
Respiration	574.12	572.47
animals	591.12	573.2
cells	574.8764	572.47
plants	581.12	572.472
Respiratory system	591.12	573.2
anatomy	591.42	573.233
Ribonucleic acid	574.873283	572.88

Topic	Edition 20	Edition 21
River ecology	574.526323	577.64
RNA	574.873283	572.88
Roots	581.10428	581.498
anatomy	581.498	575.5433
physiology	581.10428	575.54
Salt lake ecology	574.52636	577.639
Saltwater ecology	574.52636	577.7
Sap	581.113	575.75
Savanna ecology	574.52643	577.48
Seashore ecology	574.52638	577.699
Seasonal adaptation	574.543	578.43
animals	591.543	591.43
plants	581.543	581.43
Secretory organs	574.14	571.79
anatomy	574.44	571.7933
animals	591.14	571.791
anatomy	591.44	571.79331
plants	581.14	571.792
anatomy	581.44	571.79332
Seeds	582.1304166	581.467
anatomy	582.0467	575.6833
flowering plants	582.1304467	575.6833
descriptive botany	582.0467	581.467
physiology	582.1304166	575.68
Semiarid land ecology	574.52652	577.54
Sense organs	591.182	573.87
anatomy	591.48	573.8733
Sex cells	574.32	571.845
Sex differentiation	574.36	571.882
Sex hormones	574.16	571.8374
Sexes		
evolution	575.9	576.855
Sexual selection	575.5	591.562
Shore biology	574.90946	578.7699
Sight	591.1823	573.88
Skeleton	591.1852	573.76
anatomy	591.471	573.7633
specimen preparation	579.1	573.760752
Skin	591.1858	591.47
anatomy	591.47	573.533
Smell	591.1826	573.877
Social behavior	591.51	591.56
Sociobiology	574.524	577.8
Soil biology	574.90948	578.757
Soil ecology	574.526404	577.57
Space biology	574.999	571.0919
Spontaneous generation	577	576.83
Stems	581.10425	581.495
anatomy	581.495	575.433
physiology	581.10425	575.4
Steroids	574.19243	572.579
Stream ecology	574.526323	577.64

Topic	Edition 20	Edition 21
Sugars	574.192481	572.565
Swamp ecology	574.526325	577.68
Symbiosis	574.52482	577.85
Synecology	574.524	577.8
Taiga ecology	574.52642	577.37
Taste	591.1826	573.878
Teeth	591.132	591.4
physiology	591.132	573.356
Teratology	574.22	571.976
animals	591.22	571.976
Terrestrial ecology	574.5264	577
Thermobiophysics	574.1916	571.46
Tissue biology	574.82	571.5
animals	591.82	571.51
plants	581.82	571.52
Tissue culture	574.0724	571.538
animals	591.0724	571.5381
plants	581.0724	571.5382
Touch	591.1827	573.875
Trace elements	574.19214	572.515
metabolism	574.133	572.5154
plants	581.13356	572.51541
Transformation	575.2	572.9648
Translation	574.873223	572.645
Translocation	575.29	572.877
Transpiration	581.129	575.8
Transposons	575.2	572.869
Tropical ecology	574.52623	577.0913
Tundra ecology	574.52644	577.586
Urban ecology	574.5268	577.56
Urinary system	591.149	573.49
anatomy	591.44	573.4933
Variation	575.2	576.54
animals	591.158	591.35
plants	581.158	581.35
Vegetative reproduction	574.165	571.89
animals	591.165	571.891
plants	581.165	575.49
Vibrations		
biophysics	574.1914	571.443
Viral diseases	574.234	571.992
Vitamins	574.1926	571.58
Water		
biochemistry	574.19212	572.539
Wetland ecology	574.526325	577.68
Wings	591.1042	591.479
anatomy	591.49	573.79833
descriptive zoology	591.49	591.479
physiology	591.1042	573.798
Woody plants	582.15	582.16
X rays		
biophysics	574.19155	571.457

Topic	Edition 20	Edition 21
Xylem		
anatomy	581.41	575.4633
Zoologists	591.092	590.92
Zoology	591	590
Zoos	590.744	590.73

Microorganisms, fungi, algae

Topic	Edition 20	Edition 21
Algae	589.3	579.8
Algology	589.3	579.8
Animal viruses	576.6484	579.2
Ascomycetes	589.23	579.56
Bacteria	589.9	579.3
Basidiomycetes	589.22	579.59
Blue-green algae	589.46	579.39
Bread molds	589.258	579.53
Brown algae	589.45	579.88
Bunt	589.227	579.593
Ciliates	593.17	579.49
Club fungi	589.2225	579.597
Coral fungi	589.2225	579.597
Cup fungi	589.23	579.57
Deuteromycetes	589.24	579.55
Diatoms	589.481	579.85
Dinoflagellates	589.43	579.87
Downy mildew	589.252	579.546
Eubacteriales	589.95	579.3
Euglenoids	589.44	579.84
Eumycophyta	589.2	579.5
Foraminifera	593.12	579.44
Fungi	589.2	579.5
Fungi Imperfecti	589.24	579.55
Gill fungi	589.222	579.6
Golden algae	589.48	579.86
Green algae	589.47	579.83
Green bacteria	589.9	579.38
Herpesviridae	576.6484	579.2434
Kelps	589.45	579.887
Lichens	589.1	579.7
Microorganisms	576	579
Mildew	589.25	579.53
Molds	589.25	579.53
Mushrooms	589.222	579.6
Mycology	589.2	579.5
Oomycetes	589.251	579.54
Penicillium	589.23	579.5654
Phages	576.6482	579.26
Phycology	589.3	579.8
Plant viruses	576.6483	579.28
Prokaryotes	589.9	579.3

Topic	Edition 20	Edition 21
Protozoa	593.1	579.4
Puffballs	589.221	579.599
Red algae	589.41	579.89
Red tide	589.43	579.87
Rickettsias	576.62	579.327
Rusts	589.225	579.592
Saddle fungi	589.23	579.578
Salmonella	589.95	579.344
Schizophyta	589.9	579.3
Seaweeds	589.45	579.88
Slime molds	589.29	579.52
Smuts	589.227	579.593
Sporozoa	593.19	579.47
Thallophyta	589	579
Toadstools	589.222	579.6
Truffles	589.23	579.57
Viroids	576.6483	579.29
Viruses	576.64	579.2
Yeasts	589.233	579.562
Yellow-green algae	589.486	579.82
Zooflagellates	593.18	579.42

Plants

Topic	Edition 20	Edition 21
Abaca	584.21	584.39
Acacias	583.321	583.748
Acanthuses	583.81	583.95
Aconites	583.111	583.34
African violets	583.81	583.95
Agaves	584.43	584.352
Ailanthuses	583.24	583.77
Aloe (Hemp)	584.43	584.352
Aloe (Lily)	584.324	584.32
Amaranths	583.913	583.53
Amaryllis	584.25	584.34
Anemones	583.111	583.34
Arborvitaes	585.2	585.4
Arrowheads	584.721	584.72
Arrowroot	584.21	584.39
Ashes	583.74	583.87
Aspens	583.981	583.65
Asteridae	583.55	583.9
Asters	583.55	583.99
Azaleas	583.62	583.66
Baby's breaths	583.152	583.53
Balms	583.24	583.77
Balsams (Impatiens)	583.216	583.79
Bamboos	584.93	584.9
Banyan	583.962	583.45
Baobabs	583.19	583.68

Topic	Edition 20	Edition 21
Barberries	583.117	583.34
Bay rum tree	583.931	583.765
Begonias	583.46	583.627
Belladonna	583.79	583.952
Bellflowers	583.57	583.98
Bent grasses	584.93	584.9
Birches	583.976	583.48
Bladderworts	583.81	583.95
Bleeding hearts	583.122	583.35
Bluebells (Boraginaceae)	583.77	583.94
Bluebells (Campanulaceae)	583.57	583.98
Bluebells (Liliaceae)	584.324	584.32
Bluebonnet	583.322	583.74
Bluegrasses	584.93	584.9
Bog mosses	588.1	588.29
Borage	583.77	583.94
Bog myrtle (Sweet gale)	583.974	583.43
Boston ivy	583.279	583.86
Bougainvilleas	583.933	583.53
Boxwoods	583.394	583.69
Bridal wreaths	583.372	583.73
Broomrapes	583.81	583.95
Buckeyes	583.28	583.78
Buckthorns	583.279	583.86
Bulbs	584.04165	584.146
Buttercups	583.111	583.34
Cacao	583.19	583.68
Cacti	583.47	583.56
Caladiums	584.64	584.64
Camellias	583.166	583.624
Candytufts	583.123	583.64
Cannas	584.21	584.39
Capparidales	583.131	583.64
Carnations	583.152	583.53
Castor-oil plant	583.95	583.69
Catalpas	583.54	583.95
Catnip	583.87	583.96
Cattails	584.613	584.68
Century plants	584.43	584.352
Chickweeds	583.152	583.53
Chestnuts	583.976	583.46
Chokeberries	583.372	583.73
Christmas roses	583.111	583.34
Cinquefoils	583.372	583.73
Chrysanthemums	583.55	583.99
Clematises	583.111	583.34
Clovers	583.332	583.74
Coca	583.214	583.79
Cocksfoot	584.93	584.9
Cornflower	583.55	583.99
Columbines	583.111	583.34
Comfreys	583.77	583.94

Topic	Edition 20	Edition 21
Compositae	583.55	583.99
Conifers	585.2	585
Cork trees	583.972	583.77
Cosmos	583.55	583.99
Cowslip	583.672	583.675
Cottonwoods	583.981	583.65
Crab apples	583.372	583.73
Crape myrtle	583.44	583.76
Crocuses	584.24	584.38
Crown of thorns	583.95	583.69
Cycads	585.9	585.9
Cyclamens	583.672	583.675
Cymbidiums	584.15	584.4
Cypresses	585.2	585.4
Daffodils	584.25	584.34
Dahlias	583.55	583.99
Daisies	583.55	583.99
Dandelions	583.55	583.99
Dogbanes	583.72	583.93
Dogwoods	583.687	583.84
Dusty miller (Caryophyllaceae)	583.152	583.53
Ebonies	583.685	583.674
Elms	583.962	583.45
Ericales	583.62	583.66
Eucalyptus	583.42	583.766
Evening primroses	583.44	583.76
Fabales	583.332	583.74
Fagales	583.976	583.46
Ficus	583.962	583.45
Fireweeds (Onagraceae)	583.44	583.76
Fleabanes	583.55	583.99
Forget-me-nots	583.77	583.94
Four-o'clock	583.933	583.53
Foxgloves	583.81	583.95
Freesias	584.24	584.38
Fuchsias	583.44	583.76
Gardenias	583.52	583.93
Gentians	583.75	583.93
Geraniums	583.216	583.79
Gladiolus	584.24	584.38
Gloxinias	583.81	583.95
Goldenrods	583.55	583.99
Gooseberries	583.397	583.72
Gourds	583.46	583.63
Gum trees	583.687	583.766
Hawthorns	583.372	583.73
Heather	583.62	583.66
Heliotropes	583.77	583.94
Heveas	583.95	583.69
Hibiscuses	583.17	583.685
Hickories	583.973	583.49
Hollies	583.271	583.85

Topic	Edition 20	Edition 21
Hollyhocks	583.17	583.685
Honeysuckles	583.52	583.92
Hornbeams	583.976	583.48
Hornworts (Anthocerotae)	588.32	588.3
Hornworts (Ceratophyllaceae)	583.111	583.29
Hyacinths	584.324	584.32
Hydrangeas	583.397	583.72
Hyssop	583.87	583.96
Impatiens	583.216	583.79
Indian hemp	583.72	583.93
Insectivorous plants	583.121	583.75
Irises	584.24	584.38
Ironweeds (Asteraceae)	583.55	583.99
Ironwoods	583.394	583.48
Ivies	583.687	583.84
Jacob's ladders	583.76	583.94
Jade plants	583.38	583.72
Jasmines	583.74	583.87
Jewelweeds	583.216	583.79
Jimsonweed	583.79	583.952
Juglandales	583.973	583.49
Junipers	585.2	585.4
Katsura tree	583.114	583.43
Kudzu	583.322	583.74
Lamiales	583.87	583.96
Larkspurs	583.111	583.34
Lavenders	583.87	583.96
Lilacs	583.74	583.87
Lilies	584.324	584.3
Liverworts	588.33	588.3
Lobeliaceae	583.57	583.98
Locoweeds	583.111	583.74
Locusts	583.322	583.74
Loosestrifes (Lythraceae)	583.44	583.76
Magnolias	583.114	583.22
Mahoganies	583.25	583.77
Maidenhair tree	585.7	585.7
Mallows	583.17	583.685
Malvales	583.17	583.68
Mandrakes	583.79	583.952
Mangroves	583.42	583.763
Maples	583.28	583.78
Marigolds	583.55	583.99
Mayflower	583.62	583.34
Meadow beauties	583.42	583.76
Mesquite	583.321	583.748
Milkweeds	583.72	583.93
Mimosas	583.321	583.748
Mistletoes	583.94	583.88
Mock oranges	583.397	583.72
Monkshoods	583.111	583.34
Morning glories	583.79	583.94

Topic	Edition 20	Edition 21
Mulberries	583.962	583.45
Myricales	583.974	583.43
Myrtales	583.42	583.76
Narcissus	584.25	584.34
Nasturtiums (Tropaeolaceae)	583.216	583.79
Nepenthales	583.922	583.75
Nettles	583.962	583.45
Nightshades	583.79	583.952
Oaks	583.976	583.46
Oleales	583.74	583.87
Oleanders	583.72	583.93
Orchard grass	584.93	584.9
Orchids	584.15	584.4
Pansies	583.135	583.625
Partridgeberry	583.52	583.93
Passionflowers	583.456	583.626
Peonies	583.111	583.62
Periwinkles	583.72	583.93
Personales	583.81	583.95
Petunias	583.79	583.952
Phloxes	583.76	583.94
Pinks	583.152	583.53
Piperales	583.925	583.25
Pipeworts	584.81	584.87
Pitcher plants	583.121	583.75
Pitcher plants (New World)	583.121	583.36
Pitcher plants (Old World)	583.922	583.75
Plane tree	583.394	583.44
Poinsettias	583.95	583.69
Poison ivies	583.28	583.77
Poison oaks	583.28	583.77
Pokeweed	583.913	583.53
Polemoniales	583.76	583.94
Poplars	583.981	583.65
Poppies	583.122	583.35
Primroses	583.672	583.675
Privets	583.74	583.87
Queen Anne's lace	583.48	583.849
Quillworts	587.1	587.9
Ragweeds	583.55	583.99
Redbuds	583.323	583.749
Redtops	584.93	584.9
Redwoods	585.2	585.5
Rhamnales	583.279	583.86
Rhododendrons	583.62	583.66
Ribes	583.38	583.72
Rosales	583.37	583.73
Rose of Sharon	583.17	583.685
Roses	583.372	583.734
Rubber plant	583.962	583.45
Rubber tree	583.95	583.69
Rusher	584.45	584.82

Topic	Edition 20	Edition 21
Safflower	583.55	583.99
Saffron	584.24	584.38
Saint-John's-worts	583.163	583.624
Salicales	583.981	583.65
Sandalwoods	583.94	583.88
Sassafras	583.931	583.23
Saxifrages	583.38	583.72
Scotch broom	583.322	583.74
Scrophulariales	583.81	583.95
Sensitive plants	583.321	583.748
Sequoias	585.2	585.5
Serviceberries	583.372	583.73
Shamrocks	583.216	583.74
Skunk cabbages	584.64	584.64
Smoke trees (Anacardiaceae)	583.28	583.77
Snapdragons	583.81	583.95
Snowballs	583.52	583.92
Sorrel	583.917	583.57
Sourwood	583.62	583.66
Spanish moss	584.22	584.85
Spicebush (Lanraceae)	583.931	583.23
Spiderworts	584.38	584.86
Spurges (Euphorbiaceae)	583.95	583.69
Stars-of-Bethlehem	584.324	584.32
Stewartia	583.166	583.624
Sumacs	583.28	583.77
Sundews	583.121	583.75
Sunflowers	583.55	583.99
Sweet alyssum	583.123	583.64
Sweet gums	583.394	583.44
Sweet williams	583.76	583.53
Sycamores	583.394	583.44
Tamarind	583.322	583.74
Tamarisk	583.158	583.628
Teak	583.88	583.96
Tequila	584.43	584.352
Thistles	583.55	583.99
Timothy	584.93	584.9
Tobacco	583.79	583.952
Touch-me-nots	583.216	583.79
Trillium	584.325	584.32
Tulip tree	583.114	583.22
Tulips	584.324	584.32
Tung tree	583.95	583.69
Urticales	583.962	583.45
Venus's flytrap	583.121	583.75
Verbenas	583.88	583.96
Vervains	583.88	583.96
Vetches	583.332	583.74
Violets	583.135	583.625
Virginia creeper	583.279	583.86
Wandering Jews	584.38	584.86

Topic	Edition 20	Edition 21
Water chestnuts	583.44	583.765
Water lilies	583.111	583.29
Willows	583.981	583.65
Wintergreens	583.62	583.66
Wisterias	583.322	583.74
Witch hazels	583.394	583.44
Wolfbanes	583.111	583.34
Wormwoods	583.55	583.99
Wood sorrels	583.216	583.79
Yews	585.2	585.6
Yuccas	584.43	584.352
Zingiberales	584.21	584.39
Zinnias	583.55	583.99

Animals

Topic	Edition 20	Edition 21
Aardvark	599.75	599.31
Agoutis	599.3234	599.359
Albacore	597.58	597.783
Amphibians	597.6	597.8
Amphipoda	595.371	595.378
Anchovies	597.55	597.45
Angelfishes	597.58	597.72
Anglerfishes	597.53	597.62
Annelida	595.14	592.6
Antelopes	599.7358	599.64
Apoda	597.7	597.82
Apodiformes	598.899	598.76
Apterygota	595.71	595.72
Arrowworms	595.186	592.38
Arthropods	595.2	595
Articulata	593.91	593.92
Aschelminthes	595.18	592.5
Asses	599.725	599.665
Aye-ayes	599.81	599.83
Baboons	599.82	599.865
Badgers	599.74447	599.767
Baleen whales	599.51	599.5
Basses	597.58	597.73
Beaked whales	599.53	599.545
Bears	599.74446	599.78
Beavers	599.3232	599.37
Bee eaters	598.892	598.78
Bee flies	595.771	595.773
Beluga	599.53	599.542
Birds of prey	598.91	598.9
Bison	599.7358	599.643
Bivalvia	594.11	594.4
Black flies	595.771	595.772
Blackbirds	598.881	598.874

Topic	Edition 20	Edition 21
Blue whale	599.51	599.5248
Bony fishes	597.5	597
Bovines	599.7358	599.64
Brachyura	595.3842	595.386
Branchiura	595.31	595.36
Bream	597.58	597.482
Bristletails	595.713	595.723
Brush turkeys	598.612	598.64
Bryozoa	594.7	594.67
Buffalo (Bison)	599.7358	599.643
Buffaloes	599.7358	599.642
Burros	599.725	599.665
Bush babies	599.81	599.83
Bustards	598.31	598.32
Buzzards	598.916	598.94
Camels	599.736	599.6362
Canaries	598.883	598.885
Canidae	599.74442	599.77
Caribou	599.7357	599.658
Carnivores	599.74	599.7
Carp	597.52	597.483
Cartilaginous ganoids	597.44	597.42
Catbirds	598.841	598.844
Caterpillars	595.78043	595.78139
Catfishes	597.52	597.49
Cats	599.74428	599.752
Cattle	599.7358	599.6422
Cavies	599.3234	599.3592
Cheetah	599.74428	599.759
Chelicerates	595.39	595.4
Chickens	598.617	598.625
Chimpanzee	599.8844	599.885
Chinchillas	599.3234	599.3593
Chipmunks	599.3232	599.364
Cichlidae	597.58	597.74
Civets	599.74422	599.742
Clams	594.11	594.4
Clingfishes	597.53	597.62
Cockroaches	595.722	595.728
Cods	597.53	597.633
Condors	598.912	598.92
Conies (Hyraxes)	599.62	599.68
Coots	598.31	598.32
Coraciiformes	598.892	598.78
Cowbirds	598.881	598.874
Coyote	599.74442	599.7725
Crabs	595.3842	595.386
Cranes	598.31	598.32
Crawfish	595.3841	595.384
Crayfish	595.3841	595.384
Croakers	597.58	597.725
Curassows	598.614	598.64

Topic	Edition 20	Edition 21
Darters (Fish)	597.58	597.75
Decapoda (Crustaceans)	595.384	595.38
Deer	599.7357	599.65
Deer flies	595.771	595.773
Dingo	599.74442	599.772
Dogs	599.74442	599.772
Dormice	599.3233	599.3596
Dragonfishes (Pegasiformes)	597.58	597.64
Dromedary	599.736	599.6362
Drums	597.58	597.725
Duikers	599.7358	599.64
Eagles	598.916	598.942
Earthworms	595.146	592.64
Eels	597.51	597.43
Elands	599.7358	599.642
Elephant seals	599.748	599.794
Elephants	599.61	599.67
Elk (Moose)	599.7357	599.657
Elk (Wapiti)	599.7357	599.6542
Falcons	598.918	598.96
Ferrets (Black-footed)	599.74447	599.76629
Finback whales	599.51	599.5246
Finches	598.883	598.88
Flamingos	598.34	598.35
Flatfishes	597.58	597.69
Flatworms	595.12	592.4
Flounders	597.58	597.69
Flukes	595.122	592.48
Flying fishes	597.53	597.66
Flying lemurs	599.34	599.33
Foxes	599.74442	599.775
Frogfishes	597.53	597.62
Fur seals	599.746	599.7973
Galliformes	598.61	598.6
Gars	597.47	597.41
Gazelles	599.7358	599.6469
Gerbils	599.3233	599.3583
Giraffe	599.7357	599.638
Gnats	595.771	595.772
Goats	599.7358	599.648
Goldfish	597.52	597.484
Gorilla	599.8846	599.884
Great apes	599.884	599.88
Gray whale	599.51	599.522
Groundhog	599.3232	599.366
Groupers	597.58	597.736
Grouse	598.616	598.63
Gruiformes	598.31	598.32
Grunts	597.58	597.7
Guinea fowl	598.618	598.64
Guinea pigs	599.3234	599.3592
Haddocks	597.53	597.632

Topic	Edition 20	Edition 21
Hairworms	595.184	592.59
Halibuts	597.58	597.695
Hamsters	599.3233	599.356
Hares	599.322	599.328
Harriers	598.916	598.94
Hartebeests	599.7358	599.645
Hawks	598.916	598.944
Helminthology	595.1	592.3
Hermit crabs	595.3844	595.387
Herring	597.55	597.452
Hippopotamuses	599.734	599.635
Hogs	599.734	599.633
Hornbills	598.892	598.78
Horse flies	595.771	595.773
Horses	599.725	599.6655
Horseshoe crabs	595.392	595.492
Hummingbirds	598.899	598.764
Humpback whales	599.51	599.525
Hydras	593.71	593.55
Hydroids	593.71	593.55
Hydrozoa	593.71	593.55
Hyenas	599.74427	599.747
Hyraxes	599.62	599.68
Jackals	599.74442	599.772
Jellyfish	593.7	593.53
John Dories	597.58	597.64
Kangaroo mice	599.3232	599.3598
Kangaroo rats	599.3232	599.35987
King crabs	595.3844	595.387
Kingfishers	598.892	598.78
Kites	598.916	598.945
Kudus	599.7358	599.6423
Land vertebrates	597.6	596
Lantern fishes	597.55	597.61
Larks	598.812	598.825
Leeches	595.145	592.66
Lemmings	599.3233	599.3582
Lemurs	599.81	599.83
Leopards	599.74428	599.7554
Lice	595.751	595.756
Lion	599.74428	599.757
Lobsters	595.3841	595.384
Lungfishes	597.48	597.39
Mackerel	597.58	597.782
Mantises	595.725	595.727
Marlins	597.58	597.78
Marmosets	599.82	599.84
Martens	599.74447	599.7665
Martins	598.813	598.826
Meadowlarks	598.881	598.874
Medusas	593.7	593.53
Mice	599.3233	599.35

Topic	Edition 20	Edition 21
Midges	595.771	595.772
Millipedes	595.61	595.66
Minks	599.74447	599.76627
Minnows	597.52	597.482
Mockingbirds	598.841	598.844
Mongooses	599.74422	599.742
Monkeys	599.82	599.8
Monotremata	599.1	599.29
Moonfishes (Perciformes)	597.58	597.7
Moose	599.7357	599.657
Morays	597.51	597.43
Mosquitoes	595.771	595.772
Moths	595.781	595.78
Mountain lion	599.74428	599.7524
Mud puppies	597.65	597.85
Mullets	597.58	597.7
Muskrats	599.3233	599.3579
Mussels	594.11	594.4
Narwhal	599.53	599.543
Needlefishes	597.53	597.66
Nematoda	595.182	592.57
Newts	597.65	597.85
Nutria	599.3234	599.359
Ocelot	599.74428	599.752
Okapi	599.7357	599.638
Orangutan	599.8842	599.883
Orioles	598.881	598.874
Osprey	598.917	598.93
Ostriches	598.51	598.524
Otters	599.74447	599.769
Oxen	599.7358	599.6422
Oysters	594.11	594.4
Pacas	599.3234	599.359
Paddlefishes	597.44	597.42
Pandas (Giant)	599.74443	599.789
Partridges	598.617	598.623
Peafowl	598.617	598.6258
Peccaries	599.734	599.634
Penguins	598.441	598.47
Perches	597.58	597.75
Pheasants	598.617	598.625
Pigs	599.734	599.633
Pikas	599.322	599.329
Pikes	597.53	597.59
Pipefishes	597.53	597.679
Piranhas	597.52	597.48
Platyhelminthes	595.12	592.4
Platypus	599.1	599.29
Polecats (New World)	599.74447	599.768
Polecats (Old World)	599.74447	599.7662
Pollocks	597.53	597.632
Polyzoa	594.7	594.67

Topic	Edition 20	Edition 21
Porcupines	599.3234	599.3597
Portuguese man-of-war	593.71	593.55
Poultry	598.61	598.6
Prairie dogs	599.3232	599.367
Prawns	595.3843	595.388
Progoneata	595.6	595.7
Puffer fishes	597.58	597.64
Rabbits	599.322	599.32
Raccoons	599.74443	599.7632
Rails	598.31	598.32
Rats	599.3233	599.35
Reindeer	599.7357	599.658
Rhinoceroses	599.728	599.668
Ricinulei	595.41	595.455
Robber flies	595.771	595.773
Rockfishes	597.58	597.68
Rodents	599.323	599.35
Rollers	598.892	598.78
Roquals	599.51	599.524
Roundworms	595.182	592.57
Ruminants	599.735	599.63
Sable	599.74447	599.7665
Sailfishes	597.58	597.78
Salamanders	597.65	597.85
Salmon	597.55	597.56
Sand fleas	595.371	595.378
Sardines	597.55	597.45
Scallops	594.11	594.4
Sea lilies	593.91	593.92
Sea lions	599.746	599.7975
Sea slugs	594.36	594.34
Sea spiders	595.394	595.494
Seahorses	597.53	597.6798
Seals	599.745	599.79
Secretary bird	598.915	598.9
Segmented worms	595.14	592.6
Shads	597.55	597.45
Sharks	597.31	597.3
Sheep	599.7358	599.649
Shells	594.0471	594.177
Shrimps	595.3843	595.388
Siamese fighting fish	597.58	597.7
Silverfish	595.713	595.723
Sipuncula	595.17	592.35
Skippers	595.784	595.788
Skunks	599.74447	599.768
Smelts	597.55	597.5
Snappers	597.58	597.72
Soldier flies	595.771	595.773
Soles	597.58	597.69
Sparrow (Passer)	598.873	598.887
Sperm whale	599.53	599.547

Topic	Edition 20	Edition 21
Spiny anteaters	599.1	599.29
Spiny-headed worms	595.13	592.33
Spiny rats	599.3234	599.359
Springhaas	599.3232	599.359
Springtails	595.715	595.725
Squirrels	599.3232	599.36
Stick insects	595.724	595.729
Sticklebacks	597.53	597.672
Sturgeons	597.44	597.42
Suckers	597.52	597.48
Sunfishes	597.58	597.738
Swallows	598.813	598.826
Swifts	598.899	598.762
Swine	599.734	599.633
Swordfish	597.58	597.78
Tamarins	599.82	599.84
Tanagers	598.882	598.875
Tapeworms	595.121	592.46
Tapirs	599.727	599.66
Tetras	597.52	597.48
Thrips	595.731	595.758
Tiger	599.74428	599.756
Toadfishes	597.53	597.62
Topminnows	597.53	597.66
Tree shrews	599.81	599.338
Triggerfishes	597.58	597.64
Trout	597.55	597.57
Trumpeters	598.31	598.32
Tunas	597.58	597.783
Turbots	597.58	597.69
Turkeys	598.619	598.645
Tyrant flycatchers	598.811	598.823
Ungulates	599.7	599.6
Vicuña	599.736	599.6367
Vireos	598.871	598.878
Voles	599.3233	599.354
Vultures (New World)	598.912	598.92
Vultures (Old World)	598.916	598.94
Walkingsticks	595.724	595.729
Walleye	597.58	597.758
Walrus	599.747	599.799
Wapiti	599.7357	599.6542
Warthog	599.734	599.633
Water bears	595.187	592.72
Water birds	598.2924	598.176
Weasels	599.74447	599.7662
Weaverbirds	598.873	598.887
White whale	599.53	599.542
Whitings (Cods)	597.53	597.633
Wildebeests	599.7358	599.6459
Wolverine	599.74447	599.766
Wolves	599.74442	599.773

Topic	Edition 20	Edition 21
Woodchuck	599.3232	599.366
Worms	595.1	592.3
Yak	599.7358	599.6422
Zebras	599.725	599.6657
Zooplankton	592.092	592.176

Paleontology

Topic	Edition 20	Edition 21
Acanthocephala	565.1	562.33
Acanthopterygii	567.5	567.64
Actinopterygii	567.5	567
Adunata	563.91	563.92
Allotheria	569.17	569.29
Amphibians	567.6	567.8
Angiospermae	561.2	561
Annelida	565.1	562.6
Apodiformes	568.8	568.7
Architarbi	565.49	565.4
Archosauria	567.97	567.91
Arthropoda	565.2	565
Articulata	563.91	563.92
Artiodactyla	569.73	569.63
Aschelminthes	565.1	562.5
Astrapotheria	569.75	569.62
Bivalvia	564.11	564.4
Brachiopoda	564.8	564.68
Bryozoa	564.7	564.67
Camerata	563.91	563.92
Carboniferous period	560.1727	560.175
Carnivora	569.74	569.7
Chaetognatha	565.1	562.38
Chelicerata	565.39	565.4
Clupeomorpha	567.5	567.45
Condylarthra	569.75	569.62
Coniferales	561.52	561.5
Coraciiformes	568.8	568.7
Cordaitales	561.55	561.59
Creodonta	569.74	569.7
Cretaceous period	560.1766	560.177
Crossopterygii	567.4	567.39
Cupressaceae	561.52	561.54
Cystoidea	563.97	563.95
Dermoptera	569.34	569.33
Devonian period	560.1726	560.174
Dinosaurs	567.91	567.9
Dipnoi	567.4	567.39
Elopomorpha	567.5	567.43
Enteropneusta	563.993	563.99
Entoprocta	565.1	564.6
Eurypterida	565.391	565.496

Topic	Edition 20	Edition 21
Fissipedia	569.74	569.7
Foraminifera	563.12	561.994
Gneticae	561.51	561.58
Graptolitoidea	563.71	563.55
Gymnophiona	567.7	567.8
Hemichordata	563.993	563.99
Horseshoe crabs	565.392	565.492
Ice age	560.178	560.1792
Inadunata	563.91	563.92
Isoetales	561.71	561.79
Jurassic period	560.1764	560.1766
Labyrinthodontia	567.6	567.8
Lagomorpha	569.322	569.32
Lamp shells	564.8	564.68
Lepospondyli	567.6	567.8
Litopterna	569.75	569.62
Mesosauria	567.93	567.92
Mississippian period	560.1727	560.1751
Monotremata	569.12	569.29
Nemertea	565.1	562.32
Notoungulata	569.75	569.62
Onchopods	565.5	562.7
Ordovician period	560.1724	560.1731
Ornithischia	567.97	567.914
Ostiechthyes	567.5	567
Osteoglossiformes	567.5	567.47
Paracanthopterygii	567.5	567.62
Pararthropoda	565.5	562.7
Pennsylvanian period	560.1728	560.1752
Perissodactyla	569.72	569.66
Permian period	560.1729	560.1756
Petrified wood	561.21	561.16
Phoronida	565.1	562.3
Pinnipedia	569.74	569.79
Planctosphaeroidea	563.993	563.99
Platyhelminthes	565.1	562.4
Pleistocene epoch	560.178	560.1792
Podocarpaceae	561.52	561.53
Postglacial epoch	560.178	560.1793
Progoneata	565.6	565.7
Prototheria	569.12	569.29
Protozoa	563.1	561.99
Pterobranchia	564.7	563.99
Pterodactylus	567.97	567.918
Pycnogonida	565.394	565.49
Quaternary period	560.178	560.179
Radiolaria	563.14	561.995
Recent epoch	560.178	560.1793
Rodents	569.323	569.35
Ruminants	569.73	569.63
Sarcopterygii	567.4	567.39
Saurischia	567.97	567.912

Topic	Edition 20	Edition 21
Scopelomorpha	567.5	567.61
Scyphozoa	563.73	563.5
Silurian period	560.1725	560.1732
Spermatophyta	561.2	561
Stromatoporoidea	563.78	563.58
Synxiphosura	565.391	565.496
Taeniodontia	569.36	569.31
Taxales	561.52	561.56
Taxodiaceae	561.52	561.55
Teleostei	567.5	567
Tillodontia	569.35	569.31
Trees	561.21	561.16
Trilobita	565.393	565.39
Tubulidentata	569.75	569.31
Urodela	567.6	567.8
Worms	565.1	562.3
Xiphosura	565.392	565.492

Equivalence Tables

The following equivalence tables lead in each Table A from Edition 20 numbers to Edition 21 numbers, and in each Table B from Edition 21 numbers to Edition 20 numbers for T2 —47 Eastern Europe   Russia, 350–354 Public administration, 370 Education, 560 Paleontology, 570 Life sciences   Biology, 580 Plants, and 590 Animals.

In most cases, the topics in an Edition 20 number are assigned to the corresponding Edition 21 number (and vice versa). If the topics are assigned to different numbers, the topics are listed separately in the Note column. For example, in Table A for Public administration, public works and cemeteries were both classed in 351.86 in Edition 20, but in Edition 21 they are classed in 352.77 and 353.6, respectively.

Normally, subdivisions of a number are listed only when they are relocated or discontinued to different numbers from those for the main topic. For example, in Table A for public administration, three entries for 351.0073 are listed because not all of the topics are classed in subdivisions of 352.3, the Edition 21 number given opposite 351.007. On the other hand, 351.0074–.0078 are not listed because they are all classed in 352.3 and its subdivisions.

In some cases, only comprehensive works on a subject are relocated or discontinued; specific subtopics or aspects may remain where they were. In Table A for Education, for example:

Edition 20	Edition 21	Notes
371.58	371.782	Student violence

Here comprehensive works on student violence have been relocated to 371.782, but student violence as a disciplinary problem remains in 371.58.

Eastern Europe   Russia

Table A

Edition 20	Edition 21	Notes
T2 —472	T2 —471	
T2 —4723	T2 —4711	Nenets National District
T2 —4723	T2 —4713	Murmansk province
T2 —4723	T2 —4717	Arkhangel´sk province
T2 —4723	T2 —4719	Vologda province
T2 —4725	T2 —4715	
T2 —4731	T2 —4732	Yaroslavl´ province
T2 —4731	T2 —4733	Ivanovo, Kostroma, Ryazan, Vladimir provinces
T2 —4731	T2 —4734	Tula province
T2 —47312	T2 —4731	
T2 —474	T2 —479	
T2 —4741	T2 —4798	
T2 —4743	T2 —4796	
T2 —4745	T2 —4722	Novgorod province

Edition 20	Edition 21	Notes
T2 —4745	T2 —4723	Pskov province
T2 —47453	T2 —4721	Leningrad province, Saint Petersburg
T2 —4747	T2 —4724	
T2 —475	T2 —4793	
T2 —476	T2 —472	
T2 —4762	T2 —4725	Bryansk province
T2 —4762	T2 —4726	Kaluga province
T2 —4762	T2 —4727	Smolensk province
T2 —4762	T2 —4728	Tver´ (Kalinin) province
T2 —4765	T2 —478	
T2 —47652	T2 —4786	Mensk (Minsk) province
T2 —47652	T2 —4788	Hrodzen (Grodno) province
T2 —47652	T2 —4789	Brėst province
T2 —47656	T2 —4781	Homel´ (Gomel´) province
T2 —47656	T2 —4782	Mahili͡oŭ (Mogilev) province
T2 —47656	T2 —4784	Vitebsk province
T2 —4771	T2 —477	Ukraine
T2 —47714	T2 —4776	Cherkasy, Kirovohrad provinces
T2 —47714	T2 —4777	Kiev province
T2 —47714	T2 —4778	Khmel´nyts´kyy, Vinnytsa, Zhytomyr provinces
T2 —47715	T2 —4775	Kharkiv province
T2 —47715	T2 —4776	Chernihiv, Poltava, Sumy provinces
T2 —47716	T2 —4774	Donets Basin
T2 —47717	T2 —4771	Crimea province
T2 —47717	T2 —4772	Odessa province
T2 —47717	T2 —4773	Kherson, Mykolayiv (Nikolayev), Zaporizhzhya provinces
T2 —47718	T2 —4779	
T2 —4775	T2 —476	
T2 —4777	T2 —4749	
T2 —478	T2 —474	
T2 —4781	T2 —4741	Nizhnegorod province
T2 —4781	T2 —4742	Kirov province
T2 —4781	T2 —4746	Mari El, Udmurtia republics
T2 —4783	T2 —4744	Samara (Kuĭbyshev) province
T2 —4783	T2 —4745	Tatarstan republic
T2 —4783	T2 —4746	Penza, Ul´yanovsk provinces; Chuvashia, Mordvinia republics
T2 —4785	T2 —4746	Saratov province
T2 —4785	T2 —4747	Volgograd province
T2 —4785	T2 —4748	Astrakhan province, Kalmykia republic
T2 —4787	T2 —4743	
T2 —479	T2 —475	
T2 —4791	T2 —4754	
T2 —4792	T2 —4756	
T2 —4795	T2 —4758	
T2 —4797	T2 —4752	

Eastern Europe   Russia

Table B

Edition 21	*Edition 20*
T2 — 471	T2 — 472
T2 — 4711–4713	T2 — 4723
T2 — 4715	T2 — 4725
T2 — 4717–4719	T2 — 4723
T2 — 472	T2 — 476
T2 — 4721	T2 — 47453
T2 — 4722–4723	T2 — 4745
T2 — 4724	T2 — 4747
T2 — 4725–4728	T2 — 4762
T2 — 4731	T2 — 47312
T2 — 4732–4734	T2 — 4731
T2 — 474	T2 — 478
T2 — 4741–4742	T2 — 4781
T2 — 4743	T2 — 4787
T2 — 4744–4745	T2 — 4783
T2 — 4746–4748	T2 — 4785
T2 — 4749	T2 — 4777
T2 — 475	T2 — 479
T2 — 4752	T2 — 4797
T2 — 4754	T2 — 4791
T2 — 4756	T2 — 4792
T2 — 4758	T2 — 4795
T2 — 476	T2 — 4775
T2 — 477	T2 — 4771
T2 — 4771–4773	T2 — 47717
T2 — 4774	T2 — 47716
T2 — 4775–4776	T2 — 47715
T2 — 4777–4778	T2 — 47714
T2 — 4779	T2 — 47718
T2 — 478	T2 — 4765
T2 — 4781–4784	T2 — 47656
T2 — 4786–4789	T2 — 47652
T2 — 479	T2 — 474
T2 — 4793	T2 — 475
T2 — 4796	T2 — 4743
T2 — 4798	T2 — 4741

Public administration

Table A

The Edition 20 numbers listed below are limited to 351–352, 353.1–.8, and 354.1. Other numbers from 350–354 are discussed in the notes below.

The Edition 20 numbers in 350.0001–.9 correspond directly to the Edition 20 numbers in 351.0001–.9. The 350 number can easily be derived by converting the first three digits in the 351 number to 350, e.g., 351.991 converts to 350.991. The same Edition 21 number is used for either the 350 or 351 number from Edition 20.

The Edition 21 numbers that correspond to the Edition 20 numbers in 352.1–.9 can end with notation 214, 215, 216, 2167, 2169, 217, or 219, all derived from 352.14–.19 for general works on the topic, e.g., general works on abuse of power in local administration 353.46214. The Edition 21 numbers that correspond to the Edition 20 numbers in 352.1–.8 can also end with notation 09 plus the Table 2 number for the locality, e.g., abuse of power in New York City public administration 353.46097471. More detailed information on local administration is found in Manual note 351.3–.9 vs. 352.12–.19.

Usually, the Edition 20 numbers in 353–354 are built numbers consisting of four parts: the base number for specific central governments plus Table 2 notation of the specific government plus notation for the general topic plus notation for the specific topic derived from 351. These built numbers are *not* given below. They can be converted to Edition 21 numbers by doing the following: determine the 351 number from which the notation was derived, locate that number in the Edition 20 column, then take the corresponding number in the Edition 21 column and add 09 plus the Table 2 number for the specific government. For example, in Edition 20 abuse of power in California was classed in 353.979400991, base number for administration of specific states 353.9 + Table 2 notation for California 794 + notation for malfunctioning of administration 009 + notation for abuse of power 91 derived from 351.991. The Edition 21 number that corresponds to 351.991 is 353.46, to which 09 + 794 for California is added. Thus, the complete Edition 21 number is 353.4609794. Because the United States federal departments of cabinet rank were given schedule numbers in 353.1–.8 in Edition 20, these numbers are given below.

Edition 20	Edition 21	Notes
350	351	Comprehensive works on public administration
351	351	Comprehensive works on administration of central governments
351.0001–.0005	351.01–.05	
351.0006	351.05	
351.0007–.0009	351.07–.09	
351.001	352.63	
351.003	352.23	
351.0036	342.068	Impeachment of chief executives
351.004	352.24	
351.007	352.3	
351.0073	352.2	Organization
351.0073	352.33	Systems analysis
351.0073	352.367	Modernization

Edition 20	Edition 21	Notes
351.009	352.26	
351.0091	352.8	Regulatory agencies
351.0093	352.743	
351.01	353.13	
351.02	352.4	
351.03	353.3	
351.05	353.4	
351.06	355.6	
351.07–.08	352–354	Apply same comparison given below in 351.7–.8
351.09	353.33	
351.091	352.133	
351.1	352.6	
351.125	352.47	
351.2	351.025	
351.3	351.076	
351.4	352.63	
351.5	353.549	
351.6	352.63	
351.71	352.5	
351.714	352.387	
351.72	352.4	
351.722	352.48–.49	
351.7223	328.378	Enactment of budgets
351.723	352.43	
351.724	352.44	
351.725	352.73	
351.726	352.44	
351.74	363.2068	Operative management of police
351.74	353.36	Public administration of police
351.75	353.9	
351.75	353.36	Control of public gatherings and of explosives and firearms
351.75	353.37	Censorship
351.76	353.37	
351.77	353.6	
351.772	353.93	Environmental sanitation and comfort
351.772	353.6	Disposal of dead
351.778	353.99	
351.782	353.979	
351.783	353.9	
351.8	352.84	Administration of charters, licenses, certification, registration
351.811	353.48	
351.812–.814	353.53	
351.815–.816	353.59	
351.817	353.484	
351.818	354.279	
351.819	352.74	Information and research services
351.819	352.75	Census taking
351.82	354	
351.820422	354.274	

Edition 20	Edition 21	Notes
351.820423	352.746	
351.820424	352.85	
351.82043	354.28	
351.82044	354.08	
351.82048	354.2799	
351.821	352.83	
351.822	354.84	
351.8232	354.3	
351.8233	354.5	
351.8236	354.349	Hunting
351.82362	354.57	Fisheries
351.8238	354.39	
351.82388	354.45	
351.824	354.6	Secondary industries
351.824	352.749	Patents, copyrights, trademarks
351.8243046	352.84	
351.825	354.8	
351.8256	353.54	
351.826	354.73	
351.827	354.74	
351.829	352.86	
351.83	354.9	
351.84	353.5	
351.841	353.539	Services not predominately health related
351.841	353.6	Health services
351.842	353.64	
351.843	353.65	
351.844	353.539	Services not predominately health related
351.844	353.66	Health services
351.849	353.39	
351.85	353.7	
351.851	353.8	
351.852	352.744	Comprehensive works on libraries
351.852	353.73	Public libraries
351.853	352.76	
351.855	352.745	
351.8555163	354.37	
351.856	352.745	
351.859	352.744	History and archaeology
351.859	353.77	Historic preservation, monuments and shrines
351.86	352.77	Public works
351.86	353.6	Cemeteries
351.862	352.77	
351.863	353.78	
351.864	354.77	
351.865	353.55	
351.867	354.36277	
351.87	354.728	Public utilities
351.871	354.366	
351.8722	354.49	
351.8723	354.4628	

Edition 20	Edition 21	Notes
351.873	354.759	
351.874	354.75	
351.875	354.76	
351.876–.877	354.78	Water transportation
351.8777	354.79	
351.878	354.76	
351.87831	354.7728	
351.88	353.4	
351.89	353.13	
351.9	353.46	
351.91	352.885	
351.993	342.068	
352	352.14	Comprehensive works on administration of local governments
352.002	353.46	
352.003	320.85	
352.005	352.6	
352.005125	352.47	
352.0052	351.025	
352.0053	351.076	
352.0055	353.549	
352.006	320.859	
352.0072	352.16	
352.00722	352.17	
352.0073	352.15	
352.008	320.854	Forms of municipal government
352.008	352.23	Municipal executives
352.009	352.25	Commissions
352.009	352.266	Corporations
352.0092	352.264	Autonomous authorities
352.0092	352.8	Regulatory agencies
352.0093	352.19	
352.0094	352.167	
352.0095	352.143	
352.1	352.4	Financial management
352.12	352.48	
352.13–.14	352.44	
352.16	352.5	
352.17	352.43	
352.2	363.2068	
352.3	363.37068	Fire protection
352.3	353.9	Accident prevention
352.4	353.6	
352.5	354.6	
352.6	353.93	
352.61	354.366	
352.7	352.77	
352.72	353.6	
352.73	363.68068	
352.75	353.55	
352.8	352.84	
352.91	354.728	Public utilities

Edition 20	Edition 21	Notes
352.911	354.366	
352.9122	354.49	
352.9123	354.4628	
352.915	354.76	
352.916–.917	354.78	
352.918	354.76	
352.91831	354.7728	
352.92	354.64	
352.935	353.9	Public safety
352.935	353.36	Control of public gatherings and control of explosives and firearms
352.935	353.37	Censorship, control of information
352.936	353.37	
352.9411	353.48	
352.9412–.9414	353.53	
352.9415–.9416	353.59	
352.9417	353.484	
352.9418	354.279	
352.9419	352.74	Information and research services
352.9419	352.75	Census taking
352.942	354	
352.9421	352.83	
352.94232	354.3	
352.94233	354.5	
352.94236	354.349	Hunting
352.942362	354.57	Fisheries
352.94238	354.39	
352.942388	354.45	
352.9424	354.6	
352.9426	354.73	
352.943	354.9	
352.944	353.5	
352.9441	353.6	Health services
352.9441	353.539	Services to persons with physical illnesses
352.9442	353.64	
352.9443	353.65	
352.9444	353.539	Services to persons with physical disabilities
352.9449	353.39	
352.945	353.7	
352.9451	353.8	
352.9452	352.744	Comprehensive works on libraries
352.9452	353.73	Public libraries
352.9453	352.76	
352.9455	352.745	
352.94555163	354.37	
352.9456	352.745	
352.9459	352.744	History and archaeology
352.9459	353.77	Historic preservation, monuments and shrines
352.96	354.333	
352.98	353.4	

Edition 20	*Edition 21*	*Notes*
353	351.73	Comprehensive works on administration of United States federal government
353.1	353.130973	
353.2	352.40973	
353.3	354.30973	
353.4	354.7530973	
353.5	353.40973	
353.6	355.60973	
353.63	358.4160973	
353.7	359.60973	
353.81	354.50973	
353.82	354.730973	
353.83	354.90973	
353.842	353.60973	
353.844	353.80973	
353.85	353.550973	
353.86	354.760973	
353.87	354.40973	
353.88	353.5380973	
353.9	352.130973	Comprehensive works on administration of specific states of United States
354.1	352.11	Comprehensive works on international administration
354.1	352.112	Comprehensive works on League of Nations
354.103	352.113	Comprehensive works on United Nations
354.3–.9	351.3–.9	Comprehensive works on specific central governments other than those of United States

Public administration

Table B
When there are two numbers in the Edition 20 column, the Edition 21 number also represents the second number plus 09, 214, 215, 216, 2167, 2169, 217, or 219.

Use the following table to select the appropriate Edition 20 number. The first number is the Edition 21 number, the second the Edition 20 number. The X represents the digits that vary from one number to another. (When the X is in the third position in the number, the decimal point is omitted since the number of digits is variable.)

35X–351.X
The topic as a part of the administration of central government as a whole, e.g., abuse of power in central governments 353.46–351.991

35X–352.X
The topic is a part of the administration of local governments in general or of a specific local government, and is listed in an including note, e.g., abuse of power in local governments 353.46–352.002

35X–350.X
Comprehensive works on the topic are part of the administration of governments, e.g., abuse of power in governments 353.46–350.991
The 350 number from Edition 20 is derived by converting the first three digits in the 351 number to 350

35X09–353.X or 354.X
The topic is a part of the administration of a specific central government, e.g., abuse of power in California 353.4609794–353.979400991
The 353 and 354 numbers from Edition 20 are derived by following the various add instructions in 353 and 354. For subdivisions of these two numbers, the 351 number in the second column is the ultimate source of the final digits of the full number. For example, in Edition 20 abuse of power in California was classed in 353.979400991, administration of specific states 353.9 + California 794 (add instruction at 353.97–.99) + malfunctioning of administration 009 + abuse of power 91 from 351.991 (add instruction at 009 in the add table under 353.97–.99)

35X09–352.X09
The topic is a part of the administration of a specific local government and is not listed in an including note, e.g., malfunctioning of the Los Angeles administration 353.460979494–352.0020979494

35X214–352.X

The topic is a part of the administration of local governments in general and is not listed in an Including note, e.g., malfunctioning in local governments 353.46214–352.002

This guideline also applies when the 214 is replaced by 215, 216, 2167, 2169, 217, or 219 for specific kinds of local administration

Edition 21	Edition 20	Notes
342.068	351.0036	Impeachment of head of state
342.068	351.993	Impeachment
351	350	
351.025	351.2	
351.05	351.0005	Serial publications
351.05	351.0006	Serial administrative reports
351.076	351.3, 352.0053	
351.3–.9	354.3–.9	Central administrations other than United States
351.3–.9	352.03–.09	Administration of specific local governments
351.73	353	United States federal administration
351.74–.79	353.974–.979	Administration of specific states of United States
351.9969	353.9969	State administration of Hawaii
352.11	354.1	
352.13	351	Comprehensive works
352.1309	353–354	States and provinces of specific countries
352.14	352	
352.15	352.0073	
352.16	352.0072	
352.167	352.0094	
352.17	352.00722	
352.19	352.0093	
352.2	351.0073, 352.000473	
352.23	351.003, 352.008	
352.24	351.004, 352.008	
352.25–.26	351.009, 352.009	
352.3	351.007, 352.00047	
352.387	351.714, 352.164	
352.4	351.72, 352.1	
352.4	351.02	Treasury departments and ministries
352.48–.49	351.722, 352.12	
352.5	351.713, 352.16	
352.6	351.1, 351.0051	
352.63	351.6, 352.0056	Civil service system
352.63	351.001, 352	Bureaucracy
352.63	351.1, 352.0051	Government service
352.63	351.4, 352.0054	Interdisciplinary works on government workers
352.7	351, 352	
352.73	351.725, 352.1	
352.74	351.819, 352.9419	
352.743	351.0093, 352.009	

Edition 21	Edition 20	Notes
352.744	351.852, 352.9452	Libraries
352.744	351.859, 352.9459	Historical research
352.745	351.855, 352.9455	Natural science
352.745	351.856, 352.9456	Technology
352.746	351.820423, 352.942	
352.749	351.824, 352.9424	
352.75	351.819, 352.9419	
352.76	351.85, 352.945	
352.77	351.86, 352.5	
352.78	351.84, 352.944	
352.8	351.0091, 352.0092	Regulatory agencies
352.83	351.821, 352.9421	
352.84	351.8, 352.84	
352.85	351.820424, 352.942	
352.86	351.829, 352.942	
352.88	351.009, 352.009	Use of watch-dog and oversight agencies
352.88	351.91, 352.002	Interdisciplinary works on ombudsmen
353.1	351.89	
353.13	351.01	Departments and ministries of foreign affairs
353.3	351.03	Home departments and ministries, European style interior ministries
353.33	351.09	
353.36	351.74, 352.2	Police services
353.36	351.75, 352.935	Control of crowds, explosives, guns
353.37	351.76, 352.936	Regulating persons conduct
353.37	351.75, 352.935	Censorship
353.39	351.849, 352.9449	
353.4	351.88, 352.98	Administration of justice
353.4	351.05	Departments of justice
353.46	351.9, 352.002	
353.48	351.811, 352.9411	
353.484	351.817, 352.9417	
353.5	351.84, 352.944	
353.53	351.812–.814, 352.9412–.9414	Programs for specific groups
353.53	351.84, 352.944	Equal opportunity programs
353.54	351.8256, 352.94256	Government sponsored insurance
353.549	351.5, 352.0055	
353.55	351.865, 352.75	
353.59	351.815, 352.9415	Birth control
353.59	351.816, 352.9416	Birth and death certificates
353.6	351.841, 352.9441	Comprehensive works on administration of public health
353.6	351.77, 352.6	Safeguarding public health
353.64	351.842, 352.9442	
353.65	351.843, 352.9443	
353.66	351.844, 352.9444	
353.69	351.8256	
353.7	351.85, 352.945	
353.78	351.858, 352.9458	Recreation
353.78	351.863, 352.73	Parks and recreational facilities

Edition 21	Edition 20	Notes
353.8	351.851, 352.9451	
353.9	351.75, 352.935	
353.93	351.772, 352.6	
353.979	351.782	
353.99	351.778, 352.4	
354	351.82, 352.942	
354.08	351.82044, 352.942	
354.274	351.820422, 352.942	
354.279	351.818, 352.9418	
354.2799	351.82048, 352.942	
354.28	351.82043, 352.942	
354.3	351.823, 352.9423	
354.333	351.82326, 352.961	Zoning
354.36277	351.867, 352.7	
354.366	351.871, 352.61	
354.367	351.871, 352.921	
354.37	351.8555163	
354.39	351.82327, 352.942327	Mineral resources
354.39	351.8238, 352.94238	Mining
354.4	351.8232, 352.94232	
354.45	351.82388, 352.942388	
354.46	351.82388, 352.942388	Natural resource
354.46	351.8723, 352.9123	Public utility
354.49	351.8722, 352.9122	
354.5	351.8233, 352.94233	
354.57	351.8236, 352.94236	
354.6	351.824, 352.9424	
354.64	351.8242, 352.92	Regulation of construction
354.64	351.8242, 352.94242	Comprehensive works on construction
354.728	351.87, 352.91	Control of public utilities
354.73	351.826, 352.9426	
354.74	351.827, 352.9426	
354.75	351.874, 352.914	
354.759	351.873, 352.913	
354.76	351.875, 352.915	Transportation
354.76	351.878, 352.918	Ground transportation
354.765	351.8783, 352.9183	
354.767	351.875, 352.915	
354.769	351.8784 352.9184	
354.77	351.878, 352.918	Road transportation
354.77	351.864, 352.74	Highways and related public works
354.78	351.877, 352.917	Water transportation
354.78	351.876, 352.916	Inland water transportation
354.79	351.8777, 352.9177	Air transportation
354.79	351.8778, 352.9178	Space transportation
354.8	351.825	
354.84	351.822	
354.9	351.83, 352.943	
354.908	351.836–.838, 352.9236–.9238	

Education

Table A

Edition 20	Edition 21	Notes
370.11	370	Basic education
370.11	370.13	Value of education
370.115	370.116	Education for international understanding
370.116	370.119	
370.156	T1 — 19	
370.19	306.43	Sociology of education
370.1931	371.19	
370.1934	379.26	Educational equalization
370.19341	370.117	Multicultural education
370.19341	371.294	School attendance
370.19342	379.26	Affirmative action
370.194	370.111	
370.195	370.9	
370.196	370.116	Educational exchanges
370.196	370.117	Intercultural education
370.1965	379.11	Intercultural educational aid
370.1965	379.129	International intercultural educational aid
370.28	371.67	Apparatus, equipment, materials
370.288	371.68	
370.712	374.00711	Teachers in adult education
370.7122	372.0711	
370.7123	373.0711	
370.7124	378.00711	
370.72	370.715	
370.73	370.711	
370.7326	374.00711	Institutions for higher education in adult education
370.73262	372.0711	
370.73263	373.0711	
370.73264	378.00711	
370.733	370.71	
370.76	371.200711	
370.77	370.79	Competitions, awards, financial support
370.775	370.75	
370.776	370.76	
370.777	370.77	
370.778	370.78	
370.78	370.72	
371.0028	370.28	Auxiliary techniques and procedures
371.0028	371.67	Apparatus, equipment, materials
371.00288	371.68	
371.01	370	Public education
371.1–.8	379	Public policy issues in schools and their activities
371.10071	370.71	
371.102019	370.15	
371.10207	370.7	

Edition 20	Edition 21	Notes
371.103	371.192	Comprehensive works on teacher-parent relations
371.104	306.43	Interdisciplinary works on teachers and society
371.122	370.71	
371.123	371.12	
371.14	371.104	Tenure
371.146	370.715	In-service training
371.146	371.1	Staff handbooks
371.20028	370.28	Auxiliary techniques and materials
371.20028	371.67	Apparatus, equipment, materials
371.200288	371.68	
371.2013	371.203	
371.2022	371.40683	Guidance counselors
371.2022	371.46	School social workers
371.2022	371.7130683	School psychologists
371.204	379.158	
371.207	371.2011	Leadership, top and middle management
371.208	371.207	Internal organization
371.208	371.256	Open-plan schools
371.209	371.67	
371.218	371.21	Comprehensive works on articulation
371.24	371.294	School attendance
371.2421–.2424	371.242	
371.254	371.255	Nongraded grouping
371.262013	371.26013	
371.264	371.262	Use of specific achievement tests
371.2721–.2722	371.272	
371.29	371.2	Other topics
371.3028	371.3	Basic techniques not enumerated
371.302812–.302814	371.30281	
371.30282	371.3	
371.3078	371.33	Use of apparatus, equipment, materials in study and teaching
371.3078	027.7	Interdisciplinary works on instructional materials centers
371.3078	027.8	Interdisciplinary works on school resource centers
371.331	371.3068	
371.332	371.3	Teaching methods
371.332	371.399	Use of drama
371.3333	371.3332	
371.33582–.33589	371.3358	
371.3944	371.3943	Auto-instructional methods
371.39442	371.3944	
371.4042	371.4068	
371.4044	371.4	
371.58	371.5	Comprehensive works on discipline problems
371.58	371.782	Comprehensive works on student violence, vandalism
371.59	371.39	Monitorial system of education

Edition 20	Edition 21	Notes
371.62	371.6	Comprehensive works on school buildings
371.623	371.621	Instructional spaces other than laboratories
371.6232	371.623	
371.6234	Scattered	
371.624	796.068	
371.71	371.7	School social services
371.712	371.71	Physical health of students
371.77	363.119371	
371.774	363.377	
371.7752	363.1257	
371.7754	363.147	
371.81	371.8	Student attitudes
371.84	T1 — 06	
371.854	T1 — 06	
371.89	371.8	Comprehensive works on student activities
371.89	371.83	Student clubs
371.89	790.2088375	Public entertainment activities of students
371.89	796.042	Intramural sports
371.9	371.9	
028	5	Apparatus, equipment, materials
0288	5	
0682	5	
3	028	Auxiliary techniques and procedures
371.9042	371.9068	
371.9043	371.9028	Auxiliary techniques and materials
371.9043	371.9045	Maintenance and repair
371.91	371.9	Comprehensive works on students with disabilities
371.912028	371.9125	Apparatus, equipment, materials
371.9120288	371.9125	
371.9122	371.912068	
371.9123	371.912028	Auxiliary techniques and procedures
371.916	371.91	General works on students with brain damage
371.9280028	371.92805	Apparatus, equipment, materials
371.92800288	371.92805	
371.92802	371.9280068	Management
371.92803	371.9280028	Auxiliary techniques and procedures
371.9282–.9284	371.928	
371.95028	371.955	Apparatus, equipment, materials
371.950288	371.955	
371.950682	371.955	
371.96	371.826	
371.967	370.111	Compensatory education
371.967	371.9308694	Socially disadvantaged delinquent and problem students
371.97	371.829	Students distinguished by ethnic origin
371.97	370.1175	Bilingual education
372–374	379	Public policy issues of specific levels of education
372.011	372.013	Value of elementary education
372.028	372.167	Apparatus, equipment, materials

Edition 20	Edition 21	Notes
372.0287	372.126	
372.0288	372.168	
372.101–.103	372.01–.03	
372.104	372	
372.1042	372	Comprehensive works on kinds of schools
372.105–.108	372.05–.08	
372.1332	372.66	
372.192–.198	372.011	Curricula (Specific educational objectives)
372.192–.198	372.3–.8	Curricula (Specific subject objectives)
372.35	372.34	Computers
372.4028	372.412	Teaching materials
372.40287	372.48	
372.4142	372.414	
372.4144	372.462	
372.4145	372.465	
372.4147	372.417	
372.642	372.677	
372.66	372.868	Dance
373.011	373.013	Value of secondary education
373.0113	373.246	
373.028	373.167	Apparatus, equipment, materials
373.0287	373.126	
373.0288	373.168	
373.04	373	Special topics
373.042	373.214	
373.101–.09	373.01–.09	
373.192–.198	373.011	Curricula (Specific educational objectives)
373.192–.198	T1 —0712	Curricula (Specific subject objectives)
373.201–.209	373.01–.09	Standard subdivisions
373.2068	373.12	
373.22	373.213–.214	Private and public community and alternative schools
373.222	373.24–.26	Private schools (other than modern academic schools) identified by type of curriculum
373.238	378.1543	Comprehensive works on sixth form colleges
374.0028	374.167	Apparatus, equipment, materials
374.00287	374.126	
374.000288	374.168	
374.0068	374.12	
374.00682	374.16	
374.012	323.60715	Citizenship programs
374.101–.109	374.01–.09	
374.1068	374.12	
374.27	374.26	
374.28	374.8	
374.29	374	Comprehensive works on agencies
374.29	374.8	Specific kinds of agencies
374.29	374.94–.99	Specific agencies
374.44–.49	374.4094–.4099	
374.8	374	Comprehensive works on schools

Edition 20	Edition 21	Notes
374.801–.808	374.001–.008	
374.8068	378.12	
374.809	374.9	
374.84–.89	374.94–.99	
375.008	370.11	Curricula (Specific educational objectives)
375.008	T1 —071	Curricula (Specific subject objectives)
375.009	375.00091–.00099	
375.01–.9	T1 —071	
376	371.822	Education of women
376	370.82	Women in education
376.6	374.1822	Adult education of women
376.63	373.182352	Secondary education of women
376.63	373.082	Women in secondary education
376.65	378.19822	Higher education of women
376.65	378.0082	Women in higher education
377	371.07	Religious schools
377.1	379.28	
378	379	Public policy issues in higher education
378.0028	378.1967	Apparatus, equipment, materials
378.00287	378.166	
378.00288	378.1968	
378.01	378.0013	Value of higher education
378.02	378.106	
378.04–.05	378.03	Private and public alternative schools
378.1001–.1009	378.01–.09	
378.105	378.161	Admissions and related topics
378.105	378.1664	Advanced placement
378.107	378.111	Leadership, top and middle management
378.107	378.1959	Student participation in management
378.111	378.11	Comprehensive works on academic staff
378.112	378.194	Guidance counselors, deans of men and women
378.12071	378.0071	
378.122	378.121	Tenure
378.12507	378.007	
378.14	378.163	
378.1544	378.158	
378.155	378	Comprehensive works on universities
378.1552	378.1542	
378.1553	378.155	
378.1554	378.175	
378.168	378.1618	Credits
378.168	378.1662	College-level examinations
378.18	378.195	
378.1992–.1998	378.01	Curricula (Specific educational objectives)
378.1992–.1998	T1 —0711	Curricula (Specific subject objectives)
378.24	378.2	Comprehensive works on earned degrees
378.3	378.0079	Financial support of education and research in higher education
378.35	378.33	
379.1	379	Comprehensive works on support and control

Edition 20	*Edition 21*	*Notes*
379.11	353.824	Financial management of agencies supporting public education
379.11	371.206	Financial management of public school systems
379.1212	379.1213	National support of secondary education
379.13	371.206	Tuition in public schools
379.13	379.111	Educational vouchers
379.154	379.15	Policy and planning
379.154	379.158	School accountability and evaluation
379.1552	370.113	
379.157	371.1	Public control of specific actions: teachers
379.157	371.2011	Public control of specific actions: administrators
379.158	353.88284	Government commissions on standards and accreditation in higher education
379.2	379	Comprehensive works on policy issues in public education
379.201	370	Aims and objectives of public education
379.201	370.13	Value of public education
379.201	379	Effect of political process on public education
379.322	379.323	Public support of private secondary education

Education

Table B

Edition 21	*Edition 20*	*Notes*
370	371.01	Public education
370	370.11	Basic education
370	379.201	Aims and objectives of public education
370.11	375.008	Curricula: specific educational objectives
370.111	370.194	Fundamental education
370.111	371.967	Compensatory education
370.113	379.1552	Public control
370.116	370.115	Education for international understanding
370.116	370.196	Educational exchanges
370.117	370.19341	Multicultural education
370.117	370.196	Intercultural education
370.1175	371.97	
370.119	370.116	
370.13	370.11	Value of education
370.13	379.201	Value of public education
370.15	371.102019	Psychology of teaching
370.28	371.0028	Auxiliary techniques and procedures of schools
370.28	371.20028	Auxiliary techniques and procedures of school administration
370.7	371.10207	Education, research, related topics of teaching

Edition 21	Edition 20	Notes
370.71	370.733	Practice teaching
370.71	371.10071	Education of teachers
370.71	371.122	Training teachers
370.711	370.73	Institutions of higher education
370.715	370.72	Centers, workshops, conferences
370.715	371.146	In-service training of teachers
370.72	370.78	
370.75–.78	370.775–.778	
370.79	370.77	
370.82	376	
370.9	370.195	Comparative education
371.042	649.68	
371.07	377	
371.1	371.146	Staff handbooks
371.1	379.157	Public control of specific actions
371.104	371.14	Tenure
371.12	371.123	Participation in professional activities
371.19	370.1931	
371.192	371.103	Teacher-parent relations
371.200711	370.76	Professional education
371.2011	371.207	Leadership, top and middle management
371.2011	379.157	Public control of specific actions
371.203	371.2013	School supervisors
371.206	379.11	Financial management of public school systems
371.206	379.13	Tuition in public schools
371.207	371.208	Internal organization
371.21	371.218	Articulation
371.242	371.2421–.2424	Specific kinds of periods, class schedules
371.255	371.254	
371.256	371.208	Open plan schools
371.26013	371.262013	Value of standardized tests
371.262	371.264	Use of specific achievement tests
371.294	370.19341	School attendance: administration
371.294	371.24	School attendance: social factors
371.3	371.3028	Basic techniques
371.3	371.30282	Classroom techniques
371.3	371.332	Teaching methods
371.30281	371.302812–.302814	Techniques for students and teachers
371.30281	649.68	Techniques for parents
371.33	371.3078	
371.33068	371.331	
371.3332	371.3333	Tape recorder and recordings
371.3358	371.33582–.33589	Specific aspects
371.39	371.59	Monitorial system of education
371.3943	371.3944	Auto-instruction methods
371.3944	371.39442	
371.399	371.332	
371.4	371.4044	Guidance methods
371.4068	371.4042	
371.40683	371.2022	Personnel management of guidance counselors

Edition 21	Edition 20	Notes
371.46	371.2022	Personnel management of school social workers
371.5	371.58	Discipline problems
371.6	371.62	Buildings
371.621	371.623	Instructional spaces other than laboratories
371.623	371.6232	
371.67	370.28	Apparatus, equipment, materials of education
371.67	371.0028	Apparatus, equipment, materials of schools
371.67	371.20028	Apparatus, equipment, materials of school administration
371.67	371.209	Materials
371.68	370.288	Maintenance and repair in education
371.68	371.00288	Maintenance and repair of schools
371.68	371.200288	Maintenance and repair of school administration
371.7	371.71	School social services
371.71	371.712	Physical health of students
371.7130683	371.2022	Personnel management of school psychologists
371.782	371.58	Student violence, vandalism
371.8	371.81	Student attitudes
371.8	371.89	Student activities
371.822	376	Education of women
371.826	371.96	Students distinguished by social class
371.829	371.97	Students distinguished by ethnic origin
371.9	371.9	
028	3	Auxiliary techniques and procedures
5	028	Apparatus, equipment, materials
5	0288	Maintenance and repair
5	0682	Plant management
371.9	371.91	Students with disabilities
371.9028	371.9043	Auxiliary techniques and procedures
371.9068	371.9042	
371.91	371.916	Students with brain damage
371.912028	371.9123	Auxiliary techniques and procedures
371.912068	371.9122	
371.9125	371.912028	Apparatus, equipment, materials
371.9125	371.9120288	Maintenance and repair
371.928	371.9282–.9284	Specific levels of retardation
371.9280028	371.92803	Auxiliary techniques and procedures
371.9280068	371.92802	
371.92805	371.9280028	Apparatus, equipment, materials
371.92805	371.92800288	Maintenance and repair
371.9308694	371.967	
371.95028	371.956	Auxiliary equipment and materials
371.955	371.95028	Apparatus, equipment, materials
371.955	371.950288	Maintenance and repair
371.955	371.950682	Plant management
372	372.1042	Kinds of schools
372.01–.03	372.101–.103	Standard subdivisions for organization and management

Edition 21	Edition 20	Notes
372.011	372.192–.199	Curricula: Specific educational objectives
372.013	372.011	
372.05–.08	372.105–.108	Standard subdivisions for organization and management
372.0711	370.7122	Professional education
372.0711	370.73262	Schools and courses
372.126	372.0287	Testing and measurement
372.167	372.028	
372.168	372.0288	Maintenance and repair
372.3–.8	372.192–.198	Curricula: specific subject objectives
372.34	372.35	
372.412	372.4028	
372.414	372.4142	
372.417	372.4147	
372.462	372.4144	
372.465	372.4145	
372.48	372.40287	Testing and measurement
372.677	372.642	
372.868	372.66	
373.01–.09	373.101–.109	Standard subdivisions for organization and management
373.01–.09	373.201–.209	Standard subdivisions for types and levels
373.011	373.192–.198	Curricula: specific subject objectives
373.013	373.011	
373.0711	370.7123	Professional education
373.0711	370.73263	Schools and courses
373.082	373.63	
373.126	373.0287	Testing and measurement
373.167	373.028	
373.168	373.0288	Maintenance and repair
373.182352	376.63	Secondary education of women
373.213–.214	373.22	Private and public community and alternative schools
373.214	373.042	Experimental schools
373.24–.26	373.222	Private schools (other than modern academic schools) identified by type of curriculum
373.246	373.0113	Vocational education
374	374.29	Agencies
374	374.8	Schools
374.001–.008	374.101–.108	Standard subdivisions for general topics
374.001–.008	374.801–.808	Standard subdivisions for schools
374.00711	370.712	Professional education
374.00711	370.7326	Schools and courses
374.12	374.0068	
374.126	374.00287	Testing and measurement
374.16	374.00682	Plant management
374.167	374.0028	
374.168	374.00288	Maintenance and repair
374.1822	376.6	Adult education of women
374.26	374.27	Use of mass media
374.4094–.4099	374.44–.49	

Edition 21	Edition 20	Notes
374.8	374.28	Community centers
374.8	374.29	Specific kinds of agencies
374.9	374.809	Historical, geographic, persons treatment of schools
374.94–.99	374.29	Specific agencies
374.94–.99	374.84–.89	Specific schools
375.00091–.00099	375.009	
378	378.155	Universities
378.001–.009	378.101–.109	Standard subdivisions for organization and management
378.0013	378.01	
378.007	378.12507	Education, research, related topics in teaching
378.0071	378.12071	Education of faculty
378.00711	370.7124	Professional education
378.00711	370.73264	Schools and courses
378.0079	378.3	Financial support of education and research in higher education
378.0082	376.65	
378.01	378.1992–.1998	Curricula: specific educational objectives
378.03	378.04–.05	Private and public alternative schools
378.106	378.02	
378.11	378.111	Academic staff
378.111	378.107	Leadership, top and middle management
378.121	378.122	Tenure
378.1542	378.1552	Undergraduate departments
378.1543	373.238	Sixth-form colleges
378.155	378.1553	
378.158	378.1544	
378.161	378.105	
378.1618	378.168	Credits
378.163	378.14	
378.166	378.00287	Testing and measurement
378.1662	378.168	College level examinations
378.1664	378.105	Advanced placement
378.175	378.1554	Extension departments
378.194	378.112	Guidance counselors, deans of men and women
378.195	378.18	
378.1959	378.107	
378.1967	378.0028	
378.1968	378.00288	Maintenance and repair
378.19822	376.65	Higher education of women
378.2	378.24	Comprehensive works on earned degrees
378.32	362.8682	
378.33	378.35	Grants for student exchanges
379	371.1–.8	Public policy issues in schools and their activities
379	372–374	Public policy issues of specific levels of education
379	378	Public policy issues of higher education
379	379.1	Support and control

Edition 21	*Edition 20*	*Notes*
379	379.2	Policy issues in public education
379	379.201	Effect of political process on public education
379.11	370.1965	Intercultural educational aid
379.111	379.13	
379.1213	379.1212	
379.129	370.1965	International intercultural educational aid
379.15	379.154	Policy and planning
379.158	371.204	School standards and accreditation
379.158	379.154	School accountability, evaluation
379.26	370.1934	Educational equalization
379.28	377.1	
379.323	379.322	

Paleontology

Table A

Edition 20	Edition 21	Notes
560.1724	560.1731	
560.1725	560.1732	
560.1726	560.174	
560.1727	560.175	Carboniferous period
560.1727	560.1751	Mississippian period
560.1728	560.1752	
560.1729	560.1756	
560.1766	560.177	
560.178	560.179	Quaternary period
560.909–.92	560.45	
561.0914–.0919	561.1	
561.1909–.192	561.1	
561.19091–.19093	561.1911–.1913	
561.2	561	
561.21	561.16	
561.51	561.58	
561.52	561.5	Coniferales
561.52	561.53–.55	Specific Coniferales other than Pinaceae
561.52	561.56	Taxales
561.55	561.59	
561.71	561.79	
563.1	561.99	
563.71	563.55	
563.73	563.5	
563.78	563.58	
563.91	563.92	
563.97	563.95	
563.992	562.76	
563.993	563.99	
564.11	564.4	
564.19	564.27	
564.35	564.37	Pteropoda
564.36	564.34	Notaspidea
564.55	564.5	
564.7	564.67	
564.8	564.68	
565.1	562.3–.6	Worms and related animals
565.1	562.72	Tardigrada
565.2	565	
565.31	565.36	
565.34	565.36	Arguloida
565.36	565.37	
565.38	565.375	Mysidacae
565.38	565.376	Cumacea
565.38	565.3796	Hoplocarida
565.39	565.4	Chelicerata
565.393	565.39	
565.49	565.4	

Edition 20	Edition 21	Notes
565.5	562.7	
565.61–.64	565.6	
565.71	565.72	
565.72	565.739	Dermaptera
565.73	565.758	Thysanoptera
565.74	565.76	Strepsiptera
567.4	567.39	Sarcopterygii
567.5	567	Actinopterygii, Leptolepidimorpha, Osteichthyes, Teleostei
567.5	567.43	Elopomorpha
567.5	567.45	Clupeomorpha
567.5	567.47	Osteoglossomorpha
567.5	567.48	Cypriniformes
567.5	567.49	Siluriformes
567.5	567.61	Scopelomorpha
567.5	567.62	Paracanthopterygii
567.5	567.63	Gadiformes
567.5	567.64	Acanthopterygii
567.5	567.66	Atheriniformes
567.5	567.67	Gasterosteiformes
567.5	567.68	Scorpaeniformes
567.5	567.69	Pleuronectiformes
567.5	567.7	Perciformes
567.6–.7	567.8	
567.91	567.9	Dinosaurs
567.97	567.9	Archosauria
567.97	567.91	Specific Archosauria
568.8	568.7	Apodiformes, Coraciiformes
569.1	569.29	
569.3	569	
569.322	569.32	
569.323	569.35	Rodentia
569.323	569.36	Sciuridae
569.323	569.37	Castoridae
569.34	569.33	
569.35–.36	569.31	
569.7	569.6	Ungulates
569.72	569.66	
569.73	569.63	Artiodactyla
569.73	569.64	Bovidae
569.73	569.65	Cervidae
569.74	569.7	Carnivores, Credonia, Fissipedia
569.74	569.75	Felidae (Cat family)
569.74	569.76	Canoidae (Dog superfamily)
569.74	569.77	Canidae (Dog family)
569.74	569.78	Ursidae
569.74	569.79	Pinnipedia
569.75	569.62	

Paleontology

Table B

Edition 21	Edition 20	Notes
560.1731	560.1724	
560.1732	560.1725	
560.174	560.1726	
560.175	560.1727	
560.1751	560.1727	
560.1752	560.1728	
560.1756	560.1729	
560.177	560.1766	
560.179	560.178	
560.45	560.909–.92	Areas in general other than polar, temperate, tropical areas
561	561.2	
561.1	561.0914–.0919	Paleobotany in areas in general other than polar, temperate, tropical areas
561.1	561.1909–.192	Fossil plants in areas in general other than polar, temperate, tropical areas
561.16	561.21	
561.19091–.19093	561.1911–.1913	
561.5	561.52	Coniferales
561.53–.56	561.52	
561.58	561.51	
561.59	561.55	Cordaitales
561.79	561.71	Isoetales
561.99	563.1	
562.3–.6	565.1	
562.7	565.6	
562.72	565.1	
562.74	565.6	
562.76	563.992	
563.5	563.73	Scyphozoa
563.55	563.71	
563.58	563.78	
563.92	563.91	Crinozoa
563.95	563.97	Cystoidea
563.99	563.993	
564.27	564.19	
564.34	564.36	
564.37	564.35	
564.4	564.11	
564.5	564.55	Vampyromorpha
564.67	564.7	
564.68	564.8	
565	565.2	
565.36	565.31	Branchiura, Cephalocarida, Mystacocarida
565.36	565.34	Arguloida
565.37	565.36	
565.375–.376	565.38	
565.3796	565.38	

Edition 21	*Edition 20*	*Notes*
565.39	565.393	
565.4	565.39	Chelicerata
565.4	565.49	Architarbi
565.61–.64	565.6	
565.72	565.71	
565.739	565.72	
565.758	565.73	
565.76	565.74	
567	567.5	Actinopterygii, Leptolepis, Osteichthyes, Teleostei
567.39	567.4	
567.43–.49	567.5	
567.6–.7	567.5	
567.8	567.6	Amphibia
567.8	567.7	Gymnophiona
567.9	567.91	Dinosaurs
567.9	567.97	Archosauria
567.91	567.97	Specific Archosauria
568.7	568.8	Apodiformes, Coraciiformes
569	569.3	Unguiculata
569.29	569.1	
569.31	569.35	Tillodontia
569.31	569.36	Taeniodontia
569.31	569.75	Tubulidentata
569.32	569.322	
569.33	569.34	
569.35–.37	569.323	
569.6	569.7	Ungulates
569.62	569.75	Astrapotheria, Condylarthra, Litopterna, Notoungulata
569.63–.65	569.73	
569.66	569.72	
569.7	569.74	Creodonta
569.75–.79	569.74	
569.9	573.3	Homo (Prehistoric humans)

Life sciences

The listings below are generally limited to relocations and discontinuations affecting entries printed in Edition 20. It is not feasible in these tables to show the full scope of the reversal of preference between organism and process that took place between Editions 20 and 21 for internal biological processes. For example, the relocation of internal biological processes in mammals from 599.01–.08 to 571–573 is shown because the first entry appears in Edition 20, but similar relocations for individual mammals are not given. For a full explanation of the scope of the change in preference, see the Manual at 560–590.

Life sciences

Table A

Edition 20	Edition 21	Notes
572	599.97	
572.8	599.98	
572.9	599.909	
573	599.9	
573.3	569.9	
574	570	Biology
574	578	Natural history of organisms
574.1	571	Physiology
574.1	573.5	Integument
574.1042	571.59	
574.11	573.1	
574.12	572.47	
574.13	572.4	
574.132	572.35	Ingestion
574.14	571.79	Secretion
574.14	573.49	Excretion
574.16	571.8	
574.17	571.835	
574.18	573.7	
574.188	571.8	
574.191	571.4	
574.1912	572.43	
574.19125	573.95	Bioluminescent organs
574.19127	573.97	Electric organs
574.192	572	
574.1921	572.5	
574.1924	572.5	
574.19245	572.6	
574.1925	572.7	
574.1926	572.58	
574.1927	571.74	
574.19282	572.33	
574.19283	572.43	
574.19285	572.36	
574.1929	572.45	

Edition 20	Edition 21	Notes
574.2	571.9	
574.3	571.8	
574.4	571.3	Anatomy
574.41–.47	573	Anatomy of specific organs
574.5	577	Ecology
574.5	591.5	Behavior
574.5222	577.2	
574.524	577.8	
574.5263	577.6	
574.52636	577.7	
574.52642	577.3	
574.52643	577.4	
574.529	578.68	
574.53	591.53	Predation
574.542	578.42	
574.543	578.43	
574.56	578.46	
574.57	578.47	
574.6	578.6	
574.82	571.5	
574.8212	572	
574.828	571.9	
574.87	571.6	
574.87322	572.8	Cytogenetics, physiological genetics
574.873223	572.645	Translation
574.87328	572.8	
574.876042	572	
574.87612	571.835	
574.8762	571.844	
574.8764	572.47	Cell respiration
574.8765	571.936	
574.88	572.8	
574.9	578.09	
574.909–.92	578.7	
574.999	571.0919	
575	576.8	Evolution
575.1	576.5	
575.10724	660.65	Genetic engineering
575.2	576.54	Variation
575.2	572.8	Molecular mechanisms producing variation
575.5	591.562	
576	579	
576.11	571–572	
576.13	571.829	Development and maturation
576.163	664.001579	
576.62	579.327	
576.64	579.2	
577	570.1	Nature of life
577	576.83	Origin of life, conditions needed for life
578	570.282	Microscopy in biology
578	580.282	Microscopy in botany
578	590.282	Microscopy in zoology

Edition 20	*Edition 21*	*Notes*
579	570.75	Collecting and preserving biological specimens
579	580.75	Collecting and preserving botanical specimens
579	590.75	Collecting and preserving zoological specimens

Life sciences

Table B

Edition 21	*Edition 20*	*Notes*
570	574	Biology
570.1	577	Nature of life
570.282	578	
570.75	579	Collecting and preserving biological specimens
571–575	581	Internal processes of plants
571–573	591	Internal processes of animals
571–572	576.11	Internal processes of microorganisms
571	574.1	
571.0919	574.999	Space biology
571.3	574.4	
571.4	574.191	
571.5	574.82	Tissue biology
571.59	574.1042	Regional physiology
571.6	574.87	
571.7	574.188	Biological control
571.74	574.1927	Hormones
571.79	574.14	
571.8	574.16	Reproduction
571.8	574.3	Development and growth
571.835	574.17	Histogenesis
571.835	574.87612	Cell differentiation
571.8429	576.13	Development and maturation
571.844	574.8762	
571.9	574.2	Diseases
571.9	574.828	Histopathology
571.936	574.8765	
572	574.192	Biochemistry
572	574.8212	Histochemistry
572	574.876042	Cytochemistry
572.33	574.19282	
572.36	574.19285	
572.4	574.13	
572.43	574.1912	Energy phenomena in organisms
572.43	574.19283	Physical biochemistry
572.47	574.12	Respiration
572.47	574.8764	Cell respiration
572.5	574.1921–.1924	
572.58	574.1926	

Edition 21	Edition 20	Notes
572.6	574.19245	
572.645	574.873223	Genetic translation\
572.7	574.1925	
572.8	574.87322	Cytogenetics, physiological genetics
572.8	574.87328	Nucleic acids
572.8	574.88	Molecular biology
573	574.41–.47	Anatomy of specific organs
573.1	574.11	Circulation
573.1	591.11	Circulation in animals
573.2	591.12	
573.3	591.13	
573.35	574.132	Ingestion
573.4	591.142	Endocrine system
573.49	574.14	Excretion
573.49	591.149	Excretion in animals
573.5	574.1	Integument
573.5	591.1858	Integument in animals
573.6	591.16	
573.7	574.18	Movement
573.7	591.1852	Musculoskeletal system
573.8	591.188	Nervous system
573.87	591.182	
573.92	591.1	
573.95	591.19125	
573.97	591.19127	
573.99	591.1042	Regional physiology
575	581.1–.4	Parts of plants in general
575	582.01–.04	Parts of seed plants
575	582.1301–.1304	Parts of flowering plants
575.4	581.10425	
575.433	581.495	
575.48	581.31	Growth
575.54	581.10428	
575.5433	581.498	
575.57	581.10427	
575.5733	581.497	
575.6	582.130166	
575.633	582.130446	
575.7	581.11	Circulation
575.79	581.14	
575.8	581.129	
575.97	581.18	
575.98	581.18	
575.99	583.12104132	
576.5	575.1	
576.54	575.2	
576.8	575	
577	574.5	
577.2	574.5222	
577.3	574.52642	
577.4	574.52643	
577.5	574.526	

Edition 21	Edition 20	Notes
577.6	574.5263	
577.7	574.52636	
577.8	574.524	
578	574	
578.09	574.9	
578.42	574.542	
578.43	574.543	
578.46	574.56	
578.47	574.57	
578.6	574.6	Economic biology
578.68	574.529	
578.7	574.909–.92	
579	576	Microbiology
579	589	Thallobionta
579.2	576.64	
579.3	589.9	
579.327	576.62	Rickettsias
579.4	593.1	
579.5	589.2	
579.52	589.29	Myxomycotina
579.52	593.115	Mycetozoa
579.53	589.25	
579.54	589.251–.256	
579.55	589.24	
579.56	589.23	
579.57	589.23	
579.59	589.22	
579.6	589.222	
579.7	589.1	
579.8	589.3	
579.82–.89	589.4	
579.84	593.18	Euglenida
579.87	593.18	Dinoflagellida

Plants

Table A

Edition 20	Edition 21	Notes
580.742	580.74	
580.744	580.73	
581	580	
581.1–.8	571–575	Internal biological processes
581.1–.4	575	Specific parts and physiological systems
581.10425	575.4	
581.10427	575.57	
581.10428	575.54	
581.129	575.8	
581.13342	575.46	
581.15	581.35	
581.31	575.48	Growing points and layers
581.41	575.45233	Phloem
581.41	575.4633	Xylem
581.41	575.48833	Cambium
581.495	575.433	Anatomy of stems
581.497	575.5733	Anatomy of leaves
581.497	581.48	Adaptation of leaves
581.498	575.5433	Anatomy of roots
581.5	581.7	
581.529	581.68	
581.542	581.42	
581.543	581.43	
581.56	581.46	
581.57	581.47	
581.61	581.63	
581.64	581.636	
581.67	581.657	
581.69	581.659	
581.909–.92	581.7	
583.111	583.34	Ranales
583.111	583.29	Nymphaeles
583.111	583.3	Nelumbo
583.111	583.62	Paeoniaceae
583.112	583.62	
583.114	583.22	Magnoliales
583.114	583.23	Lactoridaceae
583.114	583.29	Cercidiphyllaceae
583.114	583.3	Illiciales
583.114	583.43	Trochodendraceae
583.115	583.22	
583.117	583.34	
583.121	583.75	Droseraceae, carnivorous plants
583.121	583.36	Sarraceniaceae
583.122	583.35	
583.123	583.64	
583.124	583.64	
583.131	583.64	

Edition 20	Edition 21	Notes
583.135	583.625	
583.138	583.625	Bixales
583.138	583.22	Canellaceae
583.138	583.94	Hoplestigmataceae
583.141	583.72	Pittosporaceae
583.141	583.79	Vivianiaceae
583.141	583.82	Tremandraceae
583.143	583.82	
583.152	583.53	Caryophyllales
583.152	583.624	Elatinaceae
583.158	583.628	
583.163	583.624	Guttiferales
583.163	583.72	Eucryphiaceae
583.166	583.624	Theales
583.166	583.66	Actinidiaceae
583.167	583.624	Ochnales
583.167	583.68	Sarcolaenaceae, Sphaerosepalaceae
583.17	583.68	
583.19	583.68	Tiliales
583.19	583.625	Peridiscaceae
583.19	583.79	Dirachmaceae
583.2	583.7	
583.21	583.79	
583.214	583.68	Huaceae
583.24	583.77	Rutales
583.24	583.79	Averrhoaceae (Oxalidaceae)
583.25	583.77	
583.26	583.88	
583.271	583.85	Celastrales
583.271	583.64	Koeberliniaceae, Pentadiplandraceae
583.271	583.66	Cyrillaceae, Empetraceae
583.271	583.69	Pandaceae
583.271	583.77	Cneoraceae
583.271	583.88	Cardiopteridaceae, Erythropalaceae
583.279	583.86	Rhamnales
583.279	583.82	Elaeagnales
583.28	583.78	Sapindales
583.28	583.53	Didiereaceae
583.28	583.77	Anacardiaceae, Podoaceae
583.28	583.82	Connarales
583.29	583.77	
583.32	583.74	
583.37	583.73	Rosales
583.37	583.69	Dichapetalaceae
583.374	583.23	
583.38	583.72	Saxifragales
583.38	583.92	Adoxaceae
583.38	583.98	Donatiaceae
583.394	583.44	Hamamelidales
583.394	583.43	Eucommiales
583.394	583.625	Stachyuraceae
583.394	583.69	Buxaceae, Daphniphyllaceae

Edition 20	Edition 21	Notes
583.394	583.72	Bruniaceae
583.397	583.72	Cunoniales
583.397	583.78	Greyiaceae
583.42	583.76	
583.44	583.76	Lythrales
583.44	583.72	Crypteroniaceae
583.44	583.82	Haloragales
583.44	583.96	Callitrichaceae
583.453	583.94	Loasales
583.453	583.626	Turneraceae
583.456	583.626	
583.46	583.63	Cucurbitales
583.46	583.626	Caricaceae
583.46	583.627	Begoniales
583.47	583.56	
583.48	583.849	
583.52	583.93	Rubiales
583.52	583.92	Caprifoliaceae
583.53	583.92	Valerianales (Dipsacales)
583.53	583.9	Calycerales
583.54	583.95	
583.55	583.99	
583.57	583.98	
583.58	583.98	
583.62	583.66	Ericales
583.62	583.67	Diapensiaceae
583.62	583.94	Lennoaceae
583.672	583.675	Primulales
583.672	583.5	Plumbaginales
583.677	583.675	
583.685	583.674	
583.686	583.674	
583.687	583.84	
583.74	583.93	Loganiales
583.74	583.87	Oleales
583.74	583.95	Buddlejaceae
583.75	583.93	
583.76	583.94	
583.77	583.94	
583.79	583.94	Convolvulaceae
583.79	583.95	Nolanaceae
583.79	583.952	Solanaceae
583.81	583.95	
583.87	583.96	Lamiales
583.87	583.95	Globulariaceae, Myoporaceae
583.88	583.96	
583.89	583.95	
583.913	583.53	Chenopodiales
583.913	583.5	Cynocrambales
583.917	583.57	
583.921	583.82	
583.922	583.26	Aristolochiales

Edition 20	*Edition 21*	*Notes*
583.922	583.2	Rafflesiales
583.922	583.75	Nepenthaceae
583.925	583.25	Piperales
583.925	583.23	Chloranthaceae
583.925	583.625	Lacistemataceae
583.931	583.23	Laurales
583.931	583.22	Myristicaceae
583.932	583.89	
583.933	583.53	Nyctaginaceae
583.933	583.67	Thymelaeaceae
583.933	583.76	Penaeaceae
583.933	583.85	Geissolomataceae
583.94	583.88	Santalales
583.94	583.66	Grubbiaceae
583.95	583.69	
583.961	583.43	
583.962	583.45	Urticales
583.962	583.43	Barbeyaceae
583.962	583.625	Scyphostegiaceae
583.972	583.43	
583.973	583.49	Juglandaceae
583.973	583.69	Picrodendraceae
583.973	583.77	Julianaceae
583.974	583.43	
583.975	583.43	
583.976	583.46	Fagales
583.976	583.48	Betulaceae
583.981	583.65	
583.982	583.84	
584.13	584.38	
584.15	584.4	
584.21	584.39	
584.22	584.85	
584.24	584.38	
584.25	584.34	
584.27	584.357	
584.29	584.35	Haemodorales
584.29	584.4	Apostasioideae
584.32	584.3	Liliales
584.32	584.35	Pontederiaceae, Tecophilaeaceae
584.32	584.355	Ruscaceae
584.323	584.356	
584.324	584.32	Liliaceae
584.324	584.33	Alliaceae
584.324	584.355	Asparagaceae
584.325	584.32	
584.36	584.86	
584.38	584.86	
584.42	584.353	Alstroemeriaceae
584.42	584.35	Petermanniaceae, Philesiaceae
584.43	584.352	Agavaceae
584.43	584.35	Xanthorrhoeaceae

Edition 20	Edition 21	Notes
584.45	584.82	Juncales
584.45	584.8	Restionales
584.61	584.68	Typhales
584.611	584.66	
584.71	584.37	
584.721	584.72	Alismales
584.721	584.74	Scheuchzeriaceae
584.722	584.74	
584.73	584.72	Butomaceae
584.742	584.74	Ruppiaceae
584.743	584.74	
584.744	584.74	
584.81	584.87	
584.93	584.9	
585.1	585.8	
585.2	585	Coniferales
585.2	585.3	Araucariaceae, Cephalotaxaceae, Podocarpaceae
585.2	585.4	Cupressaceae
585.2	585.5	Taxodiaceae
585.2	585.6	Taxales
586.001–.009	586.01–.09	
586.01–.08	571–575	Internal biological processes
586.01–.06	586.1	General and external biology
586.0909–.092	586.17	
587.1	587.9	
587.31	587.3	
588.1	588.29	
588.31	588.3	
588.33	588.3	
589	579	Thallobionta
589	571–572	Internal biological processes
589.1	579.7	
589.2	579.5	
589.22	579.59	
589.222	579.6	Agaricales, mushrooms
589.23	579.56	Ascomycetes
589.23	579.57	Discomycetes
589.24	579.55	
589.25	579.53	
589.251–.256	579.54	
589.29	579.52	
589.3	579.8	
589.31–.38	571–572	Internal biological processes
589.4	579.82–.89	
589.46	579.3	
589.9	579.3	
589.901–.908	571–572	Internal biological processes

Plants

Table B

Edition 21	Edition 20	Notes
580.282	578	
580.73	580.744	
580.74	580.742	Herbariums
580.75	579	Botanical specimens
581.35	581.15	
581.42	581.542	
581.43	581.543	
581.46	581.56	
581.47	581.57	
581.48	581.497	
581.63	581.61	
581.636	581.64	
581.657	581.67	
581.659	581.69	
581.68	581.529	
581.7	581.5	Ecology
581.7	581.909–.92	Plants of areas in general
583.2	583.922	Rafflesiales
583.22	583.114	Magnoliales
583.22	583.115	Annonales
583.22	583.138	Canellaceae
583.22	583.931	Myristicaceae
583.23	583.931	Laurales
583.23	583.114	Lactoridaceae
583.23	583.373	Calycanthaceae
583.23	583.925	Chloranthaceae
583.25	583.925	
583.26	583.922	
583.29	583.111	
583.3	583.111	Nelumbo (Nelumbonales)
583.3	583.114	Illiciales
583.34	583.111	Ranunculales (Ranales)
583.34	583.117	Berberidales
583.35	583.122	
583.36	583.121	
583.43	583.114	Cercidiphyllales, Trochodendrales
583.43	583.394	Eucommiales, Tetracentraceae
583.43	583.961	Balanopsidales
583.43	583.962	Barbeyales
583.43	583.972	Leitneriales
583.43	583.974	Myricales
583.43	583.975	Casuarinales
583.44	583.394	
583.45	583.962	
583.46	583.976	
583.48	583.976	
583.49	583.973	
583.5	583.672	Plumbaginales

Edition 21	Edition 20	Notes
583.5	583.913	Cynocrambales
583.53	583.152	Caryophyllales
583.53	583.913	Chenopodiales
583.53	583.28	Didiereaceae
583.53	583.933	Nyctaginaceae
583.56	583.47	
583.57	583.917	
583.62	583.111	Paeoniales
583.62	583.112	Dilleiales
583.624	583.166	Teales
583.624	583.152	Elatinaceae
583.624	583.163	Guttiferales
583.624	583.167	Ochnales
583.625	583.135	Violales
583.625	583.138	Bixales
583.625	583.19	Peridiscaceae
583.625	583.394	Stachyuraceae
583.625	583.925	Lacistemataceae
583.625	583.962	Scyphostegiaceae
583.626	583.456	Passiflorales
583.626	583.453	Turneraceae
583.626	583.46	Caricaceae
583.627	583.46	
583.628	583.158	
583.63	583.46	
583.64	583.131	Capparales
583.64	583.123	Cruciales
583.64	583.124	Resecaceae
583.64	583.271	Koeberliniaceae, Pentadiplandraceae
583.65	583.981	
583.66	583.62	Ericales
583.66	583.166	Actinidiaceae
583.66	583.271	Cyrillaceae, Empetraceae
583.66	583.94	Grubbiaceae
583.67	583.62	Diapensiales
583.67	583.933	Thymelaeales
583.674	583.685	Ebenales
583.674	583.686	Styracales
583.675	583.672	Primulales
583.675	583.677	Myrsinales
583.68	583.17	Malvales
583.68	583.19	Tiliales
583.68	583.167	Sarcolaenaceae, Sphaerosepalaceae
583.68	583.214	Huaceae
583.68	583.279	Elaeocarpaceae
583.69	583.95	Euphorbiales
583.69	583.271	Pandaceae
583.69	583.37	Dichapetalaceae
583.69	583.394	Buxaceae, Daphniphyllaceae
583.69	583.973	Picrodendraceae
583.72	583.38	Saxifragales
583.72	583.397	Cunoniales

Edition 21	Edition 20	Notes
583.72	583.141	Pittosporales
583.72	583.163	Eucryphiaceae
583.72	583.394	Bruniaceae
583.73	583.37	
583.74	583.32	
583.75	583.121	Droseraceae, carnivorous plants
583.75	583.922	Nepenthaceae
583.76	583.42	Myrtales
583.76	583.44	Lythracales
583.76	583.933	Penaeaceae
583.77	583.24	Rutales
583.77	583.25	Meliales
583.77	583.271	Cneoraceae
583.77	583.28	Anacardiaceae, Podoaceae
583.77	583.29	Coriariales
583.77	583.973	Julianaceae
583.78	583.28	Sapindales
583.78	583.397	Greyiaceae
583.79	583.21	Geraniales, Malpighiales
583.79	583.141	Vivianiaceae
583.79	583.19	Dirachmaceae
583.82	583.141	Tremandraceae
583.82	583.143	Polygalales
583.82	583.279	Elaeagnales
583.82	583.28	Connarales
583.82	583.44	Haloragales
583.82	583.921	Podostemales
583.84	583.687	Cornales (Araliales)
583.84	583.982	Garryaceae
583.849	583.48	
583.85	583.271	Celastrales
583.85	583.933	Geissolomataceae
583.86	583.279	
583.87	583.74	
583.88	583.94	Santalales
583.88	583.26	Olacales
583.88	583.271	Cardiopteridaceae, Erythropalaceae
583.89	583.932	
583.9	583.53	Calycerales
583.92	583.53	Dipsacales (Valerianales)
583.92	583.38	Adoxaceae
583.92	583.52	Caprifoliaceae
583.93	583.75	Gentianales
583.93	583.72	Apocynales
583.93	583.52	Rubiales
583.93	583.74	Loganiales
583.94	583.76	Polemoniales
583.94	583.77	Boraginales
583.94	583.138	Hoplestigmataceae
583.94	583.453	Loasales
583.94	583.62	Lennoaceae
583.94	583.79	Convolvulaceae

Edition 21	Edition 20	Notes
583.95	583.81	Scrophulariales (Personales)
583.95	583.54	Bignoniales
583.95	583.74	Buddlejaceae
583.95	583.79	Nolanaceae
583.95	583.87	Myoporaceae (Globulariaceae)
583.95	583.89	Plantaginales
583.952	583.79	
583.96	583.87	Lamiales
583.96	583.88	Verbenales
583.98	583.57	Campanulales
583.98	583.38	Donatiaceae
583.98	583.58	Goodeniales
583.99	583.55	
584.3	584.32	Liliales
584.32	584.324	Liliaceae
584.32	584.325	Trilliaceae
584.33	584.324	
584.34	584.25	
584.35	584.32	Families of Liliales other than Liliaceae, Alliaceae, Amaryllidaceae
584.35	584.29	Philydraceae, Taccaceae
584.35	584.42	Petermanniaceae, Philesiaceae
584.35	584.43	Xanthorrhoeaceae
584.352	584.43	
584.353	584.42	
584.354	584.29	
584.355	584.324	Asparagaceae
584.355	584.32	Ruscaceae
584.356	584.323	
584.357	584.27	
584.37	584.71	
584.38	584.24	Iridales
584.38	584.13	Burmanniales
584.39	584.21	
584.4	584.14	Orchidales
584.4	584.29	Apostasioideae
584.66	584.611	
584.68	584.61	
584.72	584.721	Alismales
584.72	584.73	Butomaceae
584.74	584.722	Najadales
584.74	584.721	Scheuchzeriaceae
584.74	584.742	Ruppiaceae, Potamogetonales
584.74	584.743	Aponogetonales
584.74	584.744	Juncaginales
584.8	584.45	Restionales
584.82	584.45	
584.85	584.22	
584.86	584.38	Commelinales
584.86	584.36	Xyridaceae
584.87	584.81	
584.9	584.93	Pooideae

Edition 21	*Edition 20*	*Notes*
585	585.2	Coniferales
585.3–.6	585.2	
585.8	585.1	
586.01–.09	586.001–.009	
586.1	586.01–.06	
586.17	586.0909–.092	Cryptogamia of areas in general
587.3	587.31	Polypodiales (Filicales)
587.9	587.1	Isoetales
588.29	588.1	
588.3	588.32	Anthocerotidae
588.3	588.33	Hepatidae

Animals

Table A

Edition 20	Edition 21	Notes
590.742	590.74	
590.744	590.73	
591.1–.8	571–573	Internal biological processes
591.1	573.92	Physiology of communication
591.1042	573.99	
591.11–.18	573	Physiology of specific systems
591.133	572.4	
591.15	591.35	
591.17	571.8351	
591.182	573.87	
591.1852	573.7	
591.1858	573.5	
591.188	571.71	Biological control
591.188	573.8	Nervous system
591.191	571.41	
591.1912	572.43	
591.19125	573.95	Bioluminescent organs
591.19127	573.97	Electric organs
591.2	571.91	
591.3	571.81	
591.4	571.31	
591.471	591.477	Exoskeletons
591.5	591.7	
591.51	591.5	
591.529	591.68	
591.53	591.54	Herbivorous feeding
591.542	591.42	
591.543	591.43	
591.56	591.46	Physical reproductive adaptations
591.57	591.47	
591.61	591.63	
591.69	591.65	
591.909–.92	591.7	
592–599	592–599	Add table
04	1	
0914–0919	17	
593.1	579.4	
593.115	579.52	
593.18	579.84	Euglenida
593.18	579.87	Dinoflagellida
593.71	593.55	
593.73	593.53	
593.91	593.92	
593.992	592.76	
593.993	593.99	
594.001–.009	594.01–.09	
594.01–.08	571–573	Internal biological processes
594.01–.06	594.1	General and external biological phenomena

Edition 20	Edition 21	Notes
594.0909–.092	594.17	
594.11	594.4	
594.19	594.27	
594.35	594.37	Pteropoda
594.36	594.34	Notaspidea
594.7	594.67	Bryozoa
594.73	593.99	
594.8	594.68	
595.1	592.3	
595.12	592.4	
595.124	592.32	
595.13	592.33	
595.14	592.6	
595.17	592.3	
595.18	592.5	Aschelminthes
595.186	592.38	
595.187	592.72	
595.188	594.66	
595.2	595	
595.31	595.36	
595.34	595.36	Arguloida
595.36	595.3792	
595.371	595.378	
595.381	595.376	
595.382	595.3796	
595.383	595.375	
595.384	595.38	
595.3841	595.384	
595.3842	595.386	
595.3843	595.388	
595.3844	595.387	
595.385	595.389	
595.39	595.4	
595.41	595.455	
595.5	592.7	
595.6	595.7	Progoneata
595.61	595.66	
595.7001–.7009	595.701–.709	
595.701–.708	571–573	Internal biological processes
595.701–.706	595.71	General and external biological phenomena
595.70909–.7092	595.717	
595.71	595.72	
595.721	595.739	
595.722	595.728	
595.724	595.729	
595.725	595.727	
595.731	595.758	
595.742	595.747	
595.746	595.76	
595.751	595.756	
595.7514	595.757	
595.7641	595.763	

Edition 20	Edition 21	Notes
595.7643	595.769	
595.7646	595.763	
595.7647	595.769	
595.767	595.769	
595.771	595.772	Nematocera
595.771	595.773	Brachycera
595.781	595.78	
595.784	595.788	
596.001–.009	596.01–.09	
596.01–.08	571–573	Internal biological processes
596.01–.06	596.1	General and external biological phenomena
596.0909–.092	596.17	
597.001–.009	597.01–.09	
597.01–.08	571–573	Internal biological processes
597.01–.06	597.1	General and external biological phenomena
597.092	597.177	
597.0929	597.176	
597.31	597.3	Sharks
597.31	597.33–.36	Specific sharks
597.44	597.42	
597.46	597.39	
597.47	597.41	
597.48	597.39	
597.5	597	Actinopterygii, Osteichthyes, Teleostei
597.51	597.43	
597.52	597.48	Ostariophysi, Cypriniformes
597.52	597.49	Siluriformes
597.53	597.59	Esocidae
597.53	597.62	Paracanthopterygii
597.53	597.63	Gadiformes
597.53	597.66	Atheriniformes
597.53	597.67	Gasterosteiformes
597.55	597.45	Clupeomorpha
597.55	597.47	Osteoglossomorpha
597.55	597.5	Protacanthopterygii, Salmoniformes
597.55	597.56	Salmon
597.55	597.57	Trout
597.58	597.64	Acanthopterygii
597.58	597.68	Scorpaeniformes
597.58	597.69	Pleuronectiformes
597.58	597.7	Perciformes
597.6	597.8	Amphibia
597.6	596	Land vertebrates, Tetrapoda
597.6	597.9	Herpetology
597.7	597.82	
597.83–.85	597.86	
598.042	598.168	
598.21–.28	571–573	Internal biological processes
598.21–.26	598.1	General and external biological phenomena
598.29	598.09	
598.291	598.17	
598.2922	598	

Edition 20	*Edition 21*	*Notes*
598.2924	598.176	
598.31	598.32	
598.34	598.35	Phoenicopteriformes
598.441	598.47	
598.51	598.524	
598.61	598.6	
598.612–.614	598.64	
598.616	598.63	
598.617	598.62	
598.618	598.64	
598.619	598.645	
598.811	598.823	
598.812	598.825	
598.813	598.826	
598.822–.823	598.82	
598.841	598.844	
598.871	598.878	
598.873	598.887	
598.881	598.874	
598.882	598.875	
598.892	598.78	
598.899	598.76	
598.91	598.9	
598.912	598.92	
598.915	598.9	
598.916	598.94	
598.917	598.93	
598.918	598.96	
599.001–.009	599.01–.09	
599.01–.08	571–573	Internal biological processes
599.01–.06	599.1	General and external biological phenomena
599.0909–.092	599.17	
599.1	599.29	
599.3	599	
599.322	599.32	
599.323	599.35	
599.34	599.33	
599.51	599.5	Mysticeti
599.51	599.52	Specific Mysticeti
599.53	599.5	Odontoceti
599.53	599.54	Specific Odontoceti other than dolphins and porpoises
599.61	599.67	
599.62	599.68	
599.7	599.6	Ungulates
599.72	599.66	
599.73	599.63	
599.7357	599.638	Giraffoidea
599.7357	599.65	Cervoidea
599.7358	599.64	
599.74	599.7	
599.744	599.7	

Edition 20	Edition 21	Notes
599.7442	599.74	
599.74422	599.742	
599.74426–.74427	599.743	
599.74428	599.75	
599.7444	599.76	
599.74442	599.77	
599.74446	599.78	
599.745–.748	599.79	
599.75	599.31	
599.81	599.83	Prosimii
599.81	599.33	Scandentia
599.82	599.84	Callithricidae
599.82	599.85	Cebidae
599.82	599.86	Cercopithecidae
599.884	599.88	Great apes
599.8842	599.883	
599.8844	599.885	
599.8846	599.884	

Animals

Table B

Edition 21	Edition 20	Notes
590.282	578	
590.73	590.744	
590.74	590.742	Museums
590.75	579	Zoological specimens
591.35	591.15	
591.42	591.542	
591.43	591.543	
591.46	591.56	
591.47	591.57	Protective adaptations
591.477	591.471	Exoskeletons
591.5	574.5	Behavior
591.5	591.51	Behavior of animals
591.54	591.53	
591.63	591.61	
591.65	591.69	Poisonous animals
591.68	591.529	
591.7	591.5	Ecology
591.7	591.909–.092	Animals of areas in general
592–599	592–599	Add table
1	04	
17	0914–0919	Animals of areas in general
592.01–.09	592.001–.009	
592.1	592.01–.06	
592.17	592.0909–.092	Invertebrates of areas in general
592.3	595.1	Worms
592.3	595.17	Echiurida, Phoronida, Priapulida
592.32	595.124	

Edition 21	Edition 20	Notes
592.33	595.13	
592.35	595.17	
592.38	595.186	
592.4	595.12	
592.5	595.18	
592.6	595.14	
592.7	595.5	
592.72	595.187	
592.74	595.5	
592.76	593.992	
593.53	593.73	
593.55	593.71	
593.92	593.91	
593.99	593.993	Hemichordata
593.99	594.73	Pterobranchia
594.01–.09	594.001–.009	
594.1	594.01–.06	
594.17	594.0909–.092	Animals of areas in general
594.27	594.19	
594.34	594.37	Notaspidea
594.37	594.35	Pteropoda
594.4	594.11	
594.66	595.188	
594.67	594.7	
594.68	594.8	
595	595.2	
595.36	595.31	Branchiura, Cephalocarida, Mystacocarida
595.36	595.34	Arguloida
595.375	595.383	
595.376	595.381	
595.378	595.371	
595.3792	595.36	
595.3796	595.382	
595.38	595.384	
595.384	595.3841	
595.386	595.3842	
595.387	595.3844	
595.388	595.3843	
595.389	595.385	
595.4	595.39	Chelicerata
595.455	595.41	
595.492	595.392	
595.494	595.394	
595.66	595.61	
595.7	595.6	Progoneata
595.701–.709	595.7001–.7009	
595.71	595.701–.706	
595.717	595.70909–.7092	Insects of areas in general
595.72	595.71	
595.727	595.725	
595.728	595.722	
595.729	595.724	

Edition 21	Edition 20	Notes
595.739	595.721	
595.747	595.742	Megaloptera
595.756	595.751	Lice
595.756	595.7512	Anoplura
595.757	595.7514	
595.758	595.731	
595.76	595.746	Strepsiptera
595.763	595.7641	Hydrophiloidea
595.763	595.7646	Dascilloidea, Histeroidea
595.769	595.7643	Cucjoidea
595.769	595.7647	Tenebrionidae
595.769	595.767	Meloidea, Mordellidae
595.772–.773	595.771	
595.78	595.781	Moths
595.788	595.784	
595.79	595.798	Scolioidea
596	597.6	Land vertebrates
596.01–.09	596.001–.009	
596.1	596.01–.06	
596.17	596.0909–.092	Vertebrates of areas in general
597	597.5	Actinopterygii, Osteichthyes, Teleostei
597.01–.09	597.001–.009	
597.1	597.01–.06	
597.176	597.0929	
597.177	597.092	
597.3	597.31	Selachii, sharks
597.33–.34	597.31	
597.36	597.31	
597.39	597.48	Sarcopterygii
597.39	597.46	Crossopterygii
597.41	597.47	Semionotiformes
597.42	597.44	Chondrostei
597.43	597.51	
597.45–.47	597.55	
597.48–.49	597.52	
597.5	597.55	
597.56–.57	597.55	
597.59	597.53	
597.61	597.55	
597.62–.63	597.53	
597.64	597.58	
597.66–.67	597.53	
597.68–.69	597.58	
597.7	597.58	
597.8	597.6	Amphibia
597.82	597.7	
597.86	597.83	Leiopelmatidae
597.86	597.84	Discoglossoidea, Pipoidea
597.86	597.85	Pelobatoidea
597.9	597.6	Herpetology
598	598.2922	Land birds
598.09	598.29	Geographic treatment of birds

Edition 21	Edition 20	Notes
598.1	598.21–.28	
598.168	598.042	
598.17	598.291	
598.176	598.2924	Water birds
598.32	598.31	
598.35	598.34	
598.47	598.441	
598.524	598.51	
598.6	598.61	Galli, Galliformes
598.62	598.617	
598.63	598.616	
598.64	598.612	Megapodiidae
598.64	598.614	Cracidae
598.64	598.618	Numididae
598.645	598.619	
598.76	598.899	
598.78	598.892	
598.82	598.822	Sittidae
598.82	598.823	Certhiiae
598.823	598.811	
598.825	598.812	
598.826	598.813	
598.844	598.841	
598.874	598.881	
598.875	598.882	Thraupidae
598.878	598.871	Vireonidae
598.887	598.873	
598.9	598.91	Falconiformes, birds of prey, raptors
598.9	598.915	Sagittariidae
598.92	598.912	
598.93	598.917	
598.94	598.916	
598.96	598.918	
599	599.3	Unguiculata
599.01–.09	599.001–.009	
599.1	599.01–.06	
599.17	599.0909–.092	Mammals of areas in general
599.29	599.1	
599.31	599.75	Tubulidentata
599.32	599.322	
599.33	599.34	Dermoptera
599.338	599.81	
599.35	599.323	
599.36–.37	599.3232	
599.5	599.51	Mysticeti
599.5	599.53	Odontoceti
599.52	599.51	
599.54	599.53	
599.6	599.7	Ungulates
599.63	599.73	
599.64	599.7358	
599.65	599.7357	

Edition 21	Edition 20	Notes
599.66	599.72	
599.67	599.61	
599.68	599.62	
599.7	599.74	Carnivora
599.7	599.744	Fissipedia
599.74	599.7442	
599.75	599.74428	
599.76	599.7444	
599.77	599.74442	
599.78	599.74446	
599.79	599.745	Pinnipedia
599.79	599.748	Phocidae
599.797	599.746	
599.799	599.747	
599.83	599.81	
599.84–.86	599.82	
599.88	599.884	Great apes
599.883	599.8842	
599.884	599.8846	
599.885	599.8844	

Reused Numbers

A reused number is a number with a total change in meaning from one edition to another. The list of reused numbers shows all Edition 20 numbers immediately reused in Edition 21 with the exception of reused numbers within the following completely revised table and schedules: T2 —47 Eastern Europe   Russia, 350–354 Public administration, 570 Life sciences, 583 Magnoliopsida (Dicotyledons).

T2 —4823	588.1	598.441
T2 —499	590.744	598.51
T2 —4998	591.41	598.81
T6 —391	591.42	598.823
370.116	591.43	598.841
370.712	591.54	598.871
370.72	592.01–.08	598.881
370.76	592.091	599.01–.08
370.78	592.092	599.091
378.168	593.91	599.092
398.2093–.2099	594.01–.08	599.1
01	594.091	599.51
02	594.092	599.61
05	594.1	599.75
07	595.1	599.81
439.1	595.31	839.1
560.91	595.36	949.9
560.92	595.371	949.98
561.191	595.381	
561.55	595.41	
565.36	595.61	
565.49	595.701–.708	
567.6	595.7091	
567.7	595.7092	
569.35	595.71	
569.36	595.721	
569.75	595.731	
580.744	595.751	
581.41	595.771	
581.42	596.01–.08	
581.43	596.091	
584.1	596.092	
584.38	597.01–.08	
584.4	597.091	
584.61	597.092	
584.71	597.47	
584.81	597.48	
585.1	597.51	
586.01–.08	597.6	
586.091	597.7	
586.092	597.85	
587.1	598.31	

The 21st edition of the Dewey Decimal Classification was designed by Lisa Hanifan of Albany, New York. Edition 21 was generated from an online database. Database design, technical support, and programming for this edition were provided by John Finni and Kurt Lanza from Inforonics, Inc. of Littleton, Massachusetts. Composition was done in Times Roman and Helvetica under the supervision of Inforonics, Inc. and Word Management, Inc. of Albany, New York. The book was printed and bound by Hamilton Printing Company of Rensselaer, New York.